PRAISE FOR
THE LEDGER AND THE CHAIN

"Antebellum America was simultaneously a robust market-place of strivers and a landscape of horror for the millions who were enslaved. In this groundbreaking work, Joshua Rothman reveals the intimate connection between the two. His study of the under-examined slave trade shows how it was integral to the rise of interstate commerce, the flow of credit, and the establishment of new transportation routes. He also underscores its systematic cruelty, in which men gloried in rape and casually sold children from parents yet stood as respected members of the community. *The Ledger and the Chain* is detailed, incisive, and devastating."

—T. J. STILES, Pulitzer Prize–winning author
of *The First Tycoon* and *Custer's Trials*

"The story of the international slave trade is well known to many. Much less known are the workings of the domestic slave trade in the United States that sent scores of enslaved African Americans from the Upper South to the cotton and sugar fields in the Deep South. With exhaustive research and piercing insight, Joshua Rothman's *The Ledger and the Chain* brings that history alive through the stories of three men who sat at the nexus between Southern cotton producers and Northern financial institutions. As the tragic legacies of these men are still with us, this book should be read by all who are interested in our current racial predicament."

—ANNETTE GORDON-REED, coauthor
of *Most Blessed of the Patriarchs*

"We are sometimes told that the quintessential American story is the tale of the small business that makes it big. If that's the case, there's no more American story than *The Ledger and the Chain*, Joshua Rothman's brilliant new history of the slave-trading entrepreneurs Isaac Franklin, John Armfield, and Rice Ballard."

—EDWARD E. BAPTIST, author of
The Half Has Never Been Told

"Joshua Rothman carefully and empirically builds from a forensic accounting of the lives and practices of those Frederick Douglass termed the 'man-drovers' and others called the 'soul drivers' to a social autopsy of the whole of American slavery in the nineteenth century. Essential."

—WALTER JOHNSON, author of *The Broken Heart of America*

THE
LEDGER
AND THE
CHAIN

ALSO BY JOSHUA D. ROTHMAN

Flush Times and Fever Dreams:
A Story of Capitalism and Slavery in the Age of Jackson

Notorious in the Neighborhood: Sex and Families
across the Color Line in Virginia, 1787–1861

THE LEDGER AND THE CHAIN

How Domestic Slave Traders Shaped America

Joshua D. Rothman

BASIC BOOKS

NEW YORK

Basic Books
Hachette Book Group
1290 Avenue of the Americas, New York, NY 10104
www.basicbooks.com

Printed in the United States of America
First Edition: April 2021

Published by Basic Books, an imprint of Perseus Books, LLC, a subsidiary of
Hachette Book Group, Inc. The Basic Books name and logo is a trademark of
the Hachette Book Group.

The Hachette Speakers Bureau provides a wide range of authors for speaking
events. To find out more, go to www.hachettespeakersbureau.com or call
(866) 376-6591.

The publisher is not responsible for websites (or their content) that are not
owned by the publisher.

Print book interior design by Linda Mark.

Library of Congress Cataloging-in-Publication Data
Names: Rothman, Joshua D., author.
Title: The ledger and the chain : how domestic slave traders shaped America /
 Joshua D. Rothman.
Other titles: How domestic slave traders shaped America
Description: First Edition. | New York : Basic Books, 2021. | Includes
 bibliographical references and index.
Identifiers: LCCN 2020038845 | ISBN 9781541616615 (hardcover) |
 ISBN 9781541616592 (ebook)
Subjects: LCSH: Franklin and Armfield (Firm)—History | Slave trade—
 United States—History—19th century. | Slave traders—Mississippi—Natchez—
 History—19th century. | Slave traders—Virginia—Alexandria—History—
 19th century. | Slaves—United States—Social conditions—19th century. |
 Slavery—Economic aspects—United States. | Franklin, Isaac, 1789–1846. |
 Armfield, John, 1797–1871. | Ballard, Rice C. (Rice Carter), 1800–1860.
Classification: LCC E442 .R68 2021 | DDC 306.3/620973—dc23
LC record available at https://lccn.loc.gov/2020038845

ISBNs: 978-1-5416-1661-5 (hardcover), 978-1-5416-1659-2 (ebook)

LSC-C

Printing 1, 2021

For My Children

"You know what is a swine-drover? I will show you a man-drover. They inhabit all our Southern States. They perambulate the country, and crowd the highways of the nation, with droves of human stock. You will see one of these human flesh-jobbers, armed with pistol, whip and bowie-knife, driving a company of a hundred men, women, and children, from the Potomac to the slave market at New Orleans."

> —Frederick Douglass, "What to the Slave Is the
> Fourth of July?"

"To see the wives and husbands part,
The children scream, they grieve my heart;
We are sold to Louisiana,
Come and go along with me.
Go and sound the jubilee, &c."

> —"The Poor Slave's Own Song"

"But who, sir, makes the trader? Who is most to blame?"

> —Harriet Beecher Stowe, *Uncle Tom's Cabin*

CONTENTS

	INTRODUCTION	1
ONE	ORIGINS, 1789–1815	9
TWO	CHOICES, 1815–1827	53
THREE	ASSOCIATES, 1827–1830	97
FOUR	CURRENCIES, 1830–1833	149
FIVE	DISSOLUTIONS, 1833–1837	203
SIX	REPUTATIONS, 1837–1846	257
SEVEN	LEGACIES, 1846–1871	309
EPILOGUE	THE LEDGER AND THE CHAIN	357
	ACKNOWLEDGMENTS	367
	ABBREVIATIONS IN NOTES	375
	NOTES	379
	INDEX	467

The map includes the following labels:

MN, WI, MI, Canada, NY, VT, NH, ME, MA, Boston, Providence, New York City, PA, CT, RI, NJ, SEE BELOW, DE, MD, VA, Cincinnati, OH, IN, IL, Louisville, St. Louis, Mississippi, MO, Ohio, KY, Gallatin, Cumberland, New, James, 1, Nashville, 2, TN, 3, 4, NC, Memphis, Sewanee, AR, Beersheba Springs, MS, AL, SC, GA, Vicksburg, Natchez, Mobile, TX, Red, Angola, LA, 5, Houston, Balize, New Orleans, FL, NORTH, Atlantic Ocean

1 Spotsylvania County, VA
2 Sumner County, TN
3 Surry County, NC
4 Guilford County, NC
5 West Feliciana Parish, LA

Gulf of Mexico

250 MILES
250 KILOMETERS

ABACO ISLANDS
BAHAMAS

PA, Baltimore, Annapolis, Philadelphia, MD, NJ, Frederick, P, Atlantic Ocean, Washington City, Alexandria, Warrenton, DE, Easton, Port Tobacco, MD, VA, Fredericksburg, R, C, Richmond, J, Norfolk, NC

C   Chesapeake Bay
J   James River
P   Potomac River
R   Rappahannock River

100 MILES
100 KILOMETERS

BLACKMER MAPS

The slave-trading world of Isaac Franklin, John Armfield, and Rice Ballard.

INTRODUCTION

THE BODIES WERE PILING UP AND ISAAC FRANKLIN KNEW HE had to get rid of them. It was bad enough that every enslaved person who succumbed to cholera was a total loss to the company. If word spread in and around the river port of Natchez, Mississippi, that people in Franklin's pen were dying, customers might not even buy the healthy ones. John Armfield and Rice Ballard kept shipping Franklin slaves from Virginia, but in December 1832, Franklin told his partners that in the preceding two weeks alone, disease had claimed the lives of more than fifteen of the captives they had sent. The death toll included half a dozen children, and Franklin had seven or eight others on hand who were vomiting, cramping, and experiencing uncontrollable diarrhea, their sunken eyes and cold, dry, inelastic skin telltale signs that they too might die.[1]

A man concerned about the dignity of the enslaved might have arranged for proper burials. Isaac Franklin was not that man. Dead slaves brought no profit and threatened future gains. They were useless. So Franklin and an assistant waited till nightfall, tossed the

1

corpses in a ravine by the bayou adjacent to the company showroom, shoveled a little dirt on top, and walked away. "The way we send out dead Negroes at night and keep dark is a sin to Crocket," Franklin told Ballard, using an ironic bit of slang suggesting he saw some comedy in the whole situation. Black suffering and death were built into the business of the slave trade, after all. One could not be sentimental about it.[2]

When winter turned to spring, light rain partially uncovered a teenage girl, a woman, and an infant, barely concealed beneath the soil. Further investigation unearthed still more decomposing bodies, a scene so grisly that a second set of jurors finished the coroner's inquest after the first set was too revolted to complete the task. The dead were all wearing clothing identifying them as Franklin's property, and his disposal scheme came undone. For a long while, the fact that slave traders operated in Natchez had unsettled some people, who thought it reflected poorly on the morals of the city and endangered public health and white lives. The discovery that Franklin had been dumping diseased human remains made the opinion nearly general. Horrified and outraged, white residents of Natchez circulated petitions, packed a public meeting at the courthouse, and clamored for action when the board of selectmen convened in emergency session. In April 1833, surrounded by an "unusually large" crowd and amid "loud and continuous applause," the board banned slave traders from displaying slaves for sale within city limits.[3]

Some of Franklin's fellow traders hurried to dissociate themselves from the scandal. They accounted for enslaved people they had brought to Natchez and for "the number they had sold or that had died," and they assured a local magistrate "that the negroes who had died, had not been thrown into the ravine by them." They cosigned a letter communicating "a proper respect for the feelings of the citizens," and they told city newspaper editors that they were appalled by what Franklin had done. They wanted no part of the mob's fury, and if they could undercut a competitor and curry favor with potential customers as they cleared their own names, all the better.[4]

Franklin himself was annoyed but undeterred. The cholera epidemic would pass. Franklin's banks would keep his credit lines open, Armfield and Ballard would keep providing him enslaved people to sell, and white people exercised and indignant about the slave trade and slave traders would eventually let their interests trump their fears and purported ethics. They always did. Franklin admitted nothing. He ignored the mounting anger and claimed that "he was absent from the city at the time these bodies must have been buried," and when the slave-trading ban came down, he moved. He sold his pen and showroom in the city and set up shop about a mile to the east instead, just beyond the city line at a Y-shaped intersection of two major thoroughfares connecting Natchez to cotton lands in the Mississippi countryside. The spot was known as the Forks of the Road. There, the company led by Isaac Franklin, John Armfield, and Rice Ballard reassumed its place as the largest slave-trading business in the country.[5]

In 1808, Congress exercised its constitutional prerogative to end the legal importation of enslaved people from outside the United States. But it did not end domestic slave trading, effectively creating a federally protected internal market for human beings. Already growing by the early nineteenth century, interior commerce in the enslaved was part of a massive forced migration underpinning slavery's expansion in the six decades before the Civil War. Between 1800 and 1860, American slaveholders sent roughly one million Black people from the upper South to the lower South, moving in the span of sixty years over twice as many people as were transported in two centuries to mainland North America via the transatlantic slave trade from Africa. They were responsible for the movement of millions more within individual states. By the time they were through, the number of enslaved people in the United States had more than quadrupled, the number of slave states below the Mason-Dixon Line had nearly doubled, and slavery had crossed the Mississippi River and the Rio Grande.[6]

The extension of slavery, seen across the Atlantic world in the nineteenth century, both furthered and was nurtured by technological, economic, political, and ideological changes that ushered in the modern age. Central to the process in the United States were the appearance of the cotton gin and the steam-powered sugar mill, the introduction of steamboats and railroads, the dispossession and expulsion of southeastern Indian nations, the rise of an imperialist and racist white male democracy, and the evolution of an interconnected system of national markets. As these developments converged with the maturation of transatlantic industrial textile production and global credit systems, demand for the enslaved, particularly in cotton and sugar plantation districts of the lower South, escalated dramatically. So did their market value. By 1860, four million enslaved people in the United States were a pillar of American prosperity, cumulatively worth more than the whole country had invested in manufacturing, railroads, and banks put together.[7]

White migrants to the lower South sometimes satisfied their own demand as they moved, collectively bringing with them several hundred thousand people they already enslaved. Domestic slave traders satisfied the rest, rushing to fill the market space left by the federal prohibition on imports of slaves from overseas. Capitalizing especially on a declining tobacco economy that yielded a "surplus" of slaves in the Chesapeake states of Maryland and Virginia, traders trafficked over half a million men, women, and children across state lines, locking them in holds of brigs and schooners, securing them on flatboats and steamboats and railroad cars, and fettering them with shackles for months-long marches of a thousand miles or more.

Few slave traders were more successful, and none were more influential, than Isaac Franklin, John Armfield, and Rice Ballard.

About five years before their activities provoked uproar in Mississippi, Franklin and Armfield founded a partnership to engage in long-distance domestic slave trading. Ballard joined them a few years later, and by the mid-1830s, their company was among the most formidable businesses in the South, with unmatched preeminence in the slave trade and a geographic reach rivaling any enterprise in the United States. From Alexandria and Richmond to Natchez and New Orleans, Franklin, Armfield, and Ballard controlled the fates of thousands of enslaved people. They were creditors for hundreds of white farmers and planters, and they sat at the center of capital flows connecting southern cotton and sugar fields to northeastern merchant houses to banks in New York, Philadelphia, and London. Their America incentivized entrepreneurialism, financial risk, and racial slavery, and no one made more of the junction among those things than they did. They became some of the richest men in the country as a result.[8]

Their professional dominance came in part from their command of the intimate daily savageries of the slave trade. Franklin, Armfield, and Ballard immersed themselves without hesitation in the routine brutalities and coldhearted violence of their work. The exhilarating thrill of acting with impunity animated them, feeding a roguish swagger and bold ambitions. They knew that beatings, rapes, and family separations terrified the enslaved, affronted antislavery activists, and troubled some of their fellow white southerners. Every now and then, they told others that they were better than that and that they tried to mitigate the damage. But among themselves, they reveled in it. The trembling fear and public censure confirmed that their reputations preceded them, and the discomfort showed that theirs was a dirty job that most men lacked the audacity to do. For those audacious enough, there were no limits.

But ferocity alone was not a business plan. They succeeded because of their talents for turning people into chattel and money, for managing the logistics of exchanging those people systematically over great distances, and for leveraging their advantages as they

insinuated themselves into financial networks and outdid or sub-
sumed rivals. Franklin, Armfield, and Ballard adopted what they
considered effective strategies from predecessors, and they pushed
those strategies in new directions. They had a knack for serving customer wants, they understood the necessity of keeping careful accounts, and they built an enormous operation still nimble enough
to adjust to abrupt market shifts. They established personal ties with
bankers and commission merchants that enhanced their reputability,
their clout, and their access to credit, and they were never above paying bribes or falsifying paperwork to make things go more smoothly.
Ultimately, their sway came as much through instruments of capital
like the ledger and the bill of exchange as it did through instruments
of torture like the whip and the chain.

Slave traders like Franklin, Armfield, and Ballard were vital
gears in the machine of slavery, and they helped define the financial, political, legal, cultural, and demographic contours of a growing nation, playing crucial roles as conduits of wealth and suppliers
of enslaved people whose labor and asset values were integral to the
entire American economy. We do not really understand American
history if we do not understand the slave trade, and we do not really
understand the slave trade if we do not understand those who made
it work. Yet most of what we think we know relies on generations
of accumulated stereotypes about slave traders as outliers and low-
life social outcasts. We lean on fictions and convenient clichés that
misrepresent the past and perpetuate the notion that the atrocity of
the domestic slave trade was somehow atypical of American slavery
and marginal to the broader development of the United States. In
truth, while some considered the trade distasteful, it was conducted
neither in secret nor with much shame. Slave traders worked in open
collusion with legions of slaveholders, bankers, merchants, lawyers,
clerks, judges, sheriffs, and politicians, who all recognized their in-
dispensability, and as in most occupations, their standing, both in
society and the business world, depended on perceptions of their

integrity and reliability. Pervasive in urban and rural areas alike, the slave trade was just another part of the energetic "go-ahead" spirit suffusing American commercial life before the Civil War.[9]

It was not, however, a stagnant and unchanging part of commercial life. The stories of Franklin, Armfield, and Ballard trace the story of the domestic slave trade itself, the arcs of their lives and careers revealing the ebbs, flows, and transformations of the trade over time. Leading by example, they accelerated the trade's metamorphosis from an avocation mostly pursued on a small scale in a short-term quest for extra cash into an organized profession that could bring its practitioners staggering profits, considerable power, and widespread regard. The slave trade kept evolving even after they formally retired from it, sank their money in new endeavors, and turned their attentions toward the family lives they had postponed for the sake of gain. But the companies sitting atop the trade when Franklin, Armfield, and Ballard left the field pursued the model they had created and honed. Though no one ever quite achieved what they had, it was not for lack of trying. Their immense fortunes demonstrated what could be accomplished by those savvy enough to grasp the workings of capital, sensible enough to understand how to deploy it, and heartless enough not to care about the toll on the enslaved people who bore its brunt.

The toll was incalculable. We know someone was sold somewhere in the United States about every 3.5 minutes, and we know that a young enslaved person in the upper South faced a roughly one-in-three chance of being taken into the slave trade. Yet statistics cannot measure experience, and the experience of sale, separation, and forced migration was crueler for its constancy. The ordeals suffered by most of the people Franklin, Armfield, and Ballard trafficked come down to us only in bits and pieces. We will never hear what it was like to be the man Isaac Franklin traded for $800 in steamboat freight fees, the woman so pregnant when John Armfield loaded her on a brig to New Orleans that she gave birth on board, or the child named Mary for whom Rice Ballard paid $70 and whom he described in his purchasing records as "little girl." But the stories of some among the thousands bought and sold have made their way into the historical record, and those stories are here too. Profound narratives of struggle, defiance, work, sorrow, pain, and survival, they call out from the silence imposed by the ghoulish computations and quantifications endemic to the slave trade. They refuse a consideration of slave traders in their absence, because they are stories of those haunted by having seen up close the kind of men who sold other people's children for profit.[10]

There is something inexpressible in that. I began research on this book thinking I might come to understand how and why someone would make an occupation of slave trading. I confess it still eludes me. The observation that Franklin, Armfield, and Ballard lived in a nation that sanctioned and rewarded the market exchange of people as property is true. But it is inadequate. Millions of white Americans sustained the slave trade, yet only some decided they wanted to work at it, every day, for years on end. It is too pat, and both untrue and exculpatory, to say Franklin, Armfield, and Ballard did not see their victims as entirely human. And it is too easy to suggest they were simply monsters. There was considerable monstrosity in their business, but monsters are by definition abnormal and unnatural, creatures with limited control or understanding of the things they do. Franklin, Armfield, and Ballard chose their paths. They knew what they were doing.

But they were men untroubled by conscience. They thought little about the moral quality of their actions, and at their core was a hollow, an emptiness. They understood that Black people were human beings. They just did not care. Basic decency was something they really owed only to white people, and when it came down to it, Black people's lives did not matter all that much. Black lives were there for the taking. Their world casts its long shadow onto ours.

ONE

ORIGINS, 1789–1815

EARLY IN 1809, JOHN PEYTON AND JAMES FRANKLIN JR. bought a flatboat to take them from Sumner County, Tennessee, a day's ride northeast of Nashville, down through the Mississippi Territory, and eventually to New Orleans. Of varying sizes but typically about fifteen feet wide and fifty feet long, and often equipped with a partial roof or a small cabin, a flatboat was essentially a square-ended wooden barge, as much an open rectangular box as a boat. Cheaply constructed and reasonably steady in the water despite some ungainliness, flatboats were designed for moving freight by river current, and they were the principal means by which white farmers west of the Appalachians transported goods to large markets in the generations after the American Revolution. As Peyton and Franklin floated past mile after monotonous mile of willows and cottonwoods and canebrakes, they were one party among hundreds.[1]

But the journey carried its share of trials and dangers, the folkloric image of high-spirited, pipe-smoking, fiddle-playing, jig-dancing flatboatmen notwithstanding. Peyton and Franklin spent the better part of two months on the twelve-hundred-mile passage down the Cumberland, Ohio, and Mississippi Rivers. They slept on or near their vessel, no matter the weather. They foraged for wood and food or traded for them with the occasional settler along the marshy and forested riverbanks, and they were alert to the prospect of confrontations with members of the Choctaw and Chickasaw nations through whose land they traveled. They nudged themselves clear of riverine islands and kept watch for sandbars, snags, whirlpools, and sawyers that could wreck a flatboat in an instant or stall it for days or weeks. Peyton and Franklin were already fatigued and filthy when they arrived in the malarial swamps and miasmic lowlands of southern Mississippi and Louisiana. It was hardly surprising that both eventually fell ill.[2]

They had at least managed to conduct their business first. In Natchez, a city of about fifteen hundred people that served as the gateway to the Mississippi interior, Peyton and Franklin sold more than fifty barrels of corn, five horses, and an enslaved woman. They earned a percentage from selling lumber they had agreed to haul for a man from Nashville. They traded their flatboat for cotton, and they swapped the cotton in New Orleans for bills of exchange drawn by brothers Timothy and Archibald Terrell, the former a newspaper editor and the latter in the mercantile business. While in New Orleans, Franklin also sold a twenty-year-old enslaved woman named Nancy and her two-year-old daughter Maria to Joseph McNeil, a merchant and a director of the New Orleans branch of the Bank of the United States. All told, Franklin and Peyton took in several thousand dollars. But only some of the money was in cash or coin. If they wanted the rest, they needed to bring the bills of exchange to Providence, Rhode Island, where the Terrells had an account with Brown and Ives, a massive commercial firm with far-flung global interests whose corporate genealogy included significant involvement in the transatlantic slave trade.[3]

James Franklin thought he could get the bills to Providence, because he knew that whenever he managed to get back to Tennessee, his brothers John and Isaac would be going east. James Franklin and his brothers were not simple Tennessee farmers who happened to deal in enslaved people in the course of selling other items. They were slave traders, and they had been pursuing that trade on regular trips from the Atlantic coast to the lower Mississippi Valley and back again for several years. In 1809, Isaac was twenty years old and relatively new to the business compared with James and John, who were both more than a decade his senior. But the routine was already familiar. The Franklin brothers, Isaac later recalled, went to Maryland "for the purpose of purchasing Negroes." Then they started "to the Mississippi Ter[r]itory for the purpose of making sale of the negroes."[4]

Though it was several months before James Franklin was well enough to take to the road again, he finally returned to Tennessee during the summer and gave his brothers the bills of exchange he and John Peyton had collected. John and Isaac Franklin then left Sumner County in August or September, rode across the Cumberland Plateau, through the Great Appalachian Valley, over the mountains into southwestern Virginia, and from there on to Maryland. When they got to Baltimore, John began negotiating for slaves, and Isaac took passage on a ship to Providence, where he received a lesson in the convolutions and challenges of capital circulation in the young United States. In a bill of exchange, one party signs an order to a second party to make a payment to a third party on or after a particular date. Cashing one could be a knotty process even at its most straightforward, and Isaac Franklin's visit to the counting house of Brown and Ives would not be that. He presented the bills of exchange drawn by the Terrells to the firm's clerks, and they refused to pay. Instead, "they protested the said drafts," telling Franklin that the Terrells' account lacked adequate funds to cover them.[5]

In 1825, French cartographer Ambroise Tardieu engraved this image of a flatboat, typical of those used by farmers, slave traders, and other merchants in the early republic to bring goods and enslaved people to Louisiana and Mississippi. The Historic New Orleans Collection, Gift of Mr. Winston De Ville, 1978.218.

Isaac Franklin returned to Baltimore, only to discover that his brother John had gone to Alexandria, Virginia, a Potomac River port about six miles south of the White House, to buy more slaves. Once the brothers reunited, they headed back over the mountains. The men and women and boys and girls who composed their small coffle lurched along with them on foot for six hundred miles, bound by ropes and laden with chains to prevent escape or revolt. Several years later, traveler Henry Knight saw men like the Franklins in the upper South. There were a lot of them, Knight wrote to a friend, those "young men, who make fortunes by slave-trafficking. They purchase all they can obtain, thrust them into prison for safe-keeping, [and] drive them handcuffed through the country, like cattle."[6]

The Franklins stopped at home in Tennessee, a fully recuperated James Franklin took over the operation, and he and Isaac loaded a new flatboat with their human cargo. The Franklins then repeated the voyage James had made nearly a year earlier, and when they got back to the Mississippi Territory, slave sales were not the only thing on their minds. They found the Terrells in Natchez and demanded payment on the bills of exchange that Brown and Ives had refused to pay. But the Terrells refused too, insisting that Isaac had presented the bills in Providence before the stipulated payment date and that it was not their fault the money had yet to appear in their account. Going to Providence again was an option, but the Terrells recommended that the Franklins instead go to Louisiana. Bills of exchange were negotiable instruments, and the ones from the Terrells had originated in New Orleans with the merchant firm of Kenner and Henderson. The Terrells said they had settled their accounts with that firm, so perhaps the Franklins could convert the bills into cash at Kenner and Henderson directly.

That did not pan out either. Isaac Franklin went to New Orleans with Robert Peyton, sent by his father to represent the family's interests. But Kenner and Henderson proposed paying just a fraction of the money in cash, and the rest with new bills of exchange that might be paid somewhere closer than Providence. As Robert Peyton recalled, neither he nor Franklin felt "disposed to take up with that proposition."[7]

The trip south was not a complete bust for the Franklin brothers. They sold the enslaved people they had taken out of Maryland, including at least one to David Weeks, the son of a sugar planter in an area contested by Spain and the United States known as West Florida. But neither James Franklin nor John Peyton ever received full payment on the bills of exchange from the Terrells. Eventually, they abandoned that prospect, sold the bills in Nashville at a discount, and left collection to be someone else's problem.[8]

THE SALE THE FRANKLINS MADE TO DAVID WEEKS CAME JUST a month after Isaac Franklin's twenty-first birthday, but by then his experiences were wide-ranging. More than once, he had traveled the waters and byways of North America, from New England to the Gulf of Mexico and from the Atlantic Ocean to the Mississippi River. His voyages were practical affairs undertaken for profit, but as missionary and traveler Timothy Flint observed, such trips broadened the horizons of young white men. In Flint's estimation, passing "through different states and regions," becoming "conversant with men of different nations, languages and manners," and "viewing different forms of nature and society" yielded a concomitant "expansion of mind."[9]

Among the many things Isaac Franklin came to understand was that money and slavery fed interconnected streams of relationships in constant motion. He saw how capital tenuously linked different parts of the United States, and how it flowed through the nation and around the world. He grasped the mingling of cash and credit and debt with agricultural goods and commoditized human beings. He had seen the growing cities of Baltimore, Alexandria, Natchez, and New Orleans, their busy commercial development inseparable from their situations as emergent nodes of the domestic slave trade in the early republic.

He also learned to appreciate the physical toll and logistical hurdles involved in buying slaves in one place, delivering them to another, and selling them. One of Franklin's obituary writers would describe the process as "the arduous business of transporting the surplus products of the country to New Orleans, and bringing back the returns of that trade." Conspicuously omitted was the fact that Black people constituted "surplus products" alongside corn, hogs, horses, whiskey, and flour, and that they got left behind with nothing while Franklin and his brothers took their "returns."[10]

Isaac Franklin was aware of what he did to them. Every slave trader was. But American law allowed it, American governments protected it, the American economy demanded it, and American culture suggested that only softhearted dolts worried about it. Novelist James Kirke Paulding pinpointed how the degradation of Black personhood and the dismissal of Black emotions encouraged the slave trade in the United States. Traveling from New York through the South in 1816, Paulding overheard a trader in a Virginia tavern brag about the violence he inflicted on enslaved people and shrug off the agony of the Black families he separated. Offended by what he heard, Paulding left the tavern, only to see half a dozen slaves being forcibly marched down a road in the broiling sun, barefoot, half naked, and trailing an uncovered mule-drawn cart filled with children, all under the watchful eye of an armed white man on horseback. "There is something of the true pathetic in all this," Paulding reflected, "were these people not negroes. This spoils all; for we have got such an inveterate habit of divesting them of all the best attributes of humanity, in order to justify our oppressions, that the idea of connecting feeling or sentiment with a slave, actually makes us laugh."[11]

None of what Isaac Franklin absorbed in his youth preordained that he would dedicate his professional life to the slave trade. That was a choice he would make, and it still lay in the future as he traveled home again from Mississippi in the summer of 1810. But he had been shown that done smartly and carefully, turning Black people into cash could be a reliable way for an ambitious white man to make contacts with wealthy and powerful people and to take control of his own fortune in this new America less than thirty-five years removed from independence.

Isaac Franklin's family taught him that. Yet Franklin's was not the only path to the slave trade. As Franklin came of age, the men who would work alongside him someday were still children. Their families and backgrounds were not like his, and in the eastern plateaus and plantation regions where they grew up, American slavery and its prospects did not look the way they did on the edges of white settlement west of the Appalachians. The opportunities presented by an as yet disorganized domestic slave trade, however, were not radically different. In time, they brought Isaac Franklin, John Armfield, and Rice Ballard to the same place.

Though Isaac Franklin picked up slave trading alongside his brothers, it was his father, James Franklin Sr., who modeled some of the broader impulses the trade encompassed. Extolling violence and conquest as virtues, James Sr. demonstrated the propriety of arrogating for oneself what could be taken from others, calling it enterprise, and helping impose a new order on the American landscape. He was born in 1755 near Baltimore, and he may have spent his childhood in Somerset County, Maryland, on the peninsula between the Chesapeake Bay and the Atlantic Ocean known as the Eastern Shore. But Somerset's corn and tobacco farms yielded crops inferior to those of most of the Tidewater, and if the Franklins did indeed live there, economic struggles could explain why they left. By the early 1770s, the Franklins lived in southern Virginia along the North Carolina line or in North Carolina proper. Either would have suited a farming family searching for a decent place to settle.[12]

Struggling or not, the Franklins enslaved several people, and from a young age, James understood their value. When he left home after his father's death, he was not yet twenty years old. He headed west with no sense of exactly where he was going, and it was probably by chance that he found work with a man named James Lauderdale in Botetourt County, Virginia, where the James River begins in the Shenandoah Valley, flowing toward the Chesapeake Bay. But it was no accident that he brought with him an enslaved person. James Franklin knew that wherever he landed, that person would be the most tangible and valuable asset he had.[13]

If Franklin did not yet appreciate when he arrived in Botetourt County how contested white migration into the American interior was, he learned fast. Abutting the line created by the British government in 1763 to prevent white settlement west of the Appalachians lest it inflame tensions with Native Americans, Botetourt was also just past the edge of the Ohio River valley, where those tensions were most acute right at the moment of Franklin's arrival. In 1774, Franklin enlisted in the concurrent and mutually reinforcing causes of white civilization and Indian displacement, joining a volunteer regiment for what became known as Dunmore's War, an offensive of Virginia colonists against the Shawnee, who resented and resisted white expansion along the Ohio River.[14]

Some historians maintain that for white men in backcountry Virginia, Dunmore's War was the true beginning of full-fledged revolt against British rule that spread through most of the mainland colonies less than a year later. James Franklin fought in that war too, serving in several militia regiments between 1775 and 1778 and rising to the rank of captain. Franklin also found a moment in 1775 to marry thirteen-year-old Mary Lauderdale, the daughter of his employer, and she gave birth to John in 1777 and James Jr. in 1779. Both boys were born in the Holston River valley, in what is now northeastern Tennessee and what was then an area of indeterminate sovereignty claimed by both Virginia and North Carolina. The Cherokee had ceded the region to the British in 1770, and the Franklins joined a growing cluster of white people there in 1776. But the Holston settlement was only a way station. During the campaign to shove the Shawnee north of the Ohio River, James Franklin Sr. had seen beyond the mountains, and he had determined to cast his lot there.[15]

Franklin continued moving west, joining parties of "long hunters" nearly two hundred miles from the Holston settlement in Tennessee's Central Basin, below a ridge known as the Highland Rim, amid hills and valleys through which run creeks that empty into the undulating Cumberland River. Living in the forests for weeks or months at a time as they trapped and hunted for pelts and furs, teams of long hunters had been pressing into the trans-Appalachian West since at least the 1760s. But they were not so much hunters

as poachers and advance guards for white expansion. Walking the
woods, they encroached on land and depleted game supplies that
sustained various groups of Native Americans, looked for spots they
might wish to claim for themselves, and served as scouts for speculators and land companies.[16]

As white settlement in the Cumberland swelled in the long
hunters' wake, so did Native opposition, but that had never stopped
James Franklin before. In 1780, he helped erect a fort about fifteen
miles north of the recently founded village of Nashborough, soon
to be renamed Nashville, and he brought his wife and sons there
from the Holston settlement that spring. The fort was one of more
than half a dozen assemblages of stockaded cabins, also referred to
as stations, built by whites in the Cumberland to defend against Indian attacks and to signify their intention to stay permanently. A
few years later, Franklin helped build another fort, about ten miles
east of the first one, and it was near there, on the western branch of
a Cumberland River tributary that long hunters had named Station
Camp Creek, that he finally stopped moving. The Cumberland remained chaotic, dangerous, and wracked by warfare into the 1790s.
But the forces of military might, dodgy diplomacy, state authority,
and sheer numbers accumulated slowly and surely. The result was
white American dominance, and having played multiple roles in
advancing it, James Franklin stood to benefit.[17]

The Cumberland was part of North Carolina's western land
claims and, as the Revolutionary War formally concluded in 1783,
the state carved out Davidson County there. An enormous bowl
comprising nearly twelve thousand square miles below what would
become the southern limit of Kentucky, Davidson contained more
than five thousand white settlers, and the formation of a county
provided them with a court and a rudimentary official government.
North Carolina also began selling land in the Cumberland, and as
payment for wartime service or defending frontier outposts from
Indians, it issued preemption rights to select white men allowing

them to enter claims before public sale. In 1784, James Franklin exercised his right, claiming 640 acres along Station Camp Creek, in the shadow of an outcropping called Pilot Knob. The plot would become the nucleus of a family domain ranging for miles, eventually encompassing the farms of dozens of Franklins and their extended relations.[18]

Signs of James Franklin's intentions to stay put at Pilot Knob were manifold. In 1786, nodding to the increasingly rapid influx of white farmers, North Carolina formed Sumner County out of eastern Davidson County. James Franklin served on its first grand jury, and he would serve on nearly every grand jury for years, including when it convened in a private home in January 1789 and a young lawyer named Andrew Jackson took the oath entitling him to practice in the county. Franklin also began building a sizable brick house to hold his growing family. Cramped living in log cabins and palisaded forts amid warfare with Native Americans was no obstacle to procreation for James and Mary Franklin, who added a child with impressive regularity until nearly the end of the eighteenth century. Jane Franklin was born in 1782, followed by Margaret in 1784, Ann in 1787, Isaac in 1789, Sarah in 1791, William in 1793, and Elizabeth in 1796. Many years later, James Franklin Sr. would also have a son named Albert, born out of wedlock to a woman named Elizabeth Barnes.[19]

Stories told about the young Isaac Franklin suggest he was a clever, enterprising, and hard-working boy raised to appreciate and advance the legacy of his hardy pioneer forebears. Those who knew him longest remembered that he worked on his father's land and attended "country schools, in which the mere rudiments of education were taught." Family lore recounts that he supposedly earned his very first dollar by selling to a friend a miniature wooden ship that he had carved with a pocketknife given him by his father.[20]

These are stories in keeping with the classic American frontier genre, filled as it is with tales of plucky, untutored, independent yeomen cultivating the wilderness to support themselves and their families. But the vision such stories conjure is no less mythological for its entrenchment in the American imagination. The Sumner County of Isaac Franklin's youth was more akin to an oligarchy than to a popular democracy forged by self-sufficient small farmers. A cadre of land speculators and their agents, marshaling local authority with complementary economic power and political connections, maintained outsized influence for at least a generation. Poorer white men sometimes acquired land in early Tennessee, but it was hardly a poor man's country.[21]

Nothing, of course, made Thomas Jefferson's vaunted "empire of liberty" hollower than the institution of slavery, which white Americans brought to frontier Tennessee along with their rifles and their horses and their wagons. Enslaved people came with the long hunters, and they came with migrants who huddled in forts. White settlers deployed enslaved people to build defenses and help protect them from Native Americans, and they put them to work in their fields, their kitchens, and their incipient industries.[22]

When North Carolina ceded its western lands to the federal government in 1789 with a demand that slavery there be federally protected, Congress swiftly complied. Less familiar than the Northwest Ordinance preceding it, the Southwest Ordinance, approved in 1790, designated the area that is present-day Tennessee as the Southwest Territory and provided for its organization along nearly the same terms as its northern territorial forerunner, the principal difference being a ban on congressional action that might lead to emancipation. In 1790, roughly 32,000 whites and 3,800 slaves lived in the Southwest Territory. By 1796, the white population had more than doubled, to 67,000, while the Black population had almost tripled, to 10,500. Tennessee entered the Union that same year.[23]

The Tennessee frontier of Isaac Franklin's childhood was not a free country at all. It was, rather, on the leading edge of what one historian describes as an expansive "slave country." The first census returns from Sumner County came in 1791, when Isaac Franklin was two years old. They described a population of slightly less than 2,200 people, 1,850 of whom enslaved the other 350. Similar proportions obtained in Davidson County, which made slavery in the two places somewhat more substantial than in Tennessee as a whole. It was also more widespread. Large slaveholders might claim ownership of perhaps a dozen people, but the vast majority enslaved one or two, compelling them to cook, clean, sew, take care of white children, raise livestock, and produce tobacco, corn, and some cotton for home consumption and for sale in local and distant markets.[24]

James Franklin Sr. was like most of his neighbors in this regard. He enslaved twenty-six people by the end of the 1810s, but tax records into the mid-1790s indicate he enslaved no adult men. That hardly meant he held no one in bondage or never used slave labor, as it is impossible to believe that he, his wife, and the four children under the age of eleven they had in the late 1780s worked hundreds of acres and built the house at Pilot Knob on their own. Moreover, the exploitation of enslaved people in the region went beyond their labor, and most white men who achieved any kind of prosperity participated in that exploitation in some fashion or another.[25]

Slavery in the early Cumberland, one historian observes, "was at once more intimate and more commercial" than it was in many older parts of the country. Whites and Blacks might lean on each other for survival, work alongside one another, and even live under the same roof. But the need for flexibility and especially for capital meant whites relied on enslaved people as assets and commodities far more than they pretended to embrace them as members of imagined extended families. While weaving slavery into an economy that mixed small farming and trade, they depended on the liquidity of Black bodies to facilitate growth.[26]

White settlers in the Cumberland hired out enslaved people, leased them from neighbors, and sometimes paid debts and purchased land with slaves in lieu of cash. They offered the enslaved as lottery prizes and bonuses in real estate deals, and they gifted them to their children. They passed title to them as a form of currency, and they used them as collateral for mortgages, security for loans, and guarantees backing crop deliveries. Slaves in the Cumberland were capital in human form, a kind of property nearly interchangeable with money, and a convenient store of value that could be part of a range of transactions. They could also be bought and sold at will. Isaac Franklin would have especially picked up on that as he saw the slave trade operating in and around Sumner County.[27]

White migrants to frontier Tennessee often brought enslaved people with them, but the trade in slaves increased noticeably in the 1790s. Professional slave traders bringing large numbers of people from the east was rare, but auctions of the enslaved were not. Hundreds took place in Nashville, the only sizable town near Sumner County until the county seat of Gallatin was established in 1802. Most auctions involved the sale of a single person, almost 90 percent involved people under age thirty, and nearly half were of people younger than sixteen. As it did everywhere, the trade in early Tennessee wrenched spouses and parents and children apart. Until the nineteenth century, the word "family" did not even appear in a bill of sale in reference to the people being sold.[28]

Advertisements in Nashville newspapers promised that "CASH Will be given for Three or Four Prime Young Negroes, of good character," that "a number of very likely negroes" would be auctioned alongside "horses and other articles," and that "7 or 8 Likely Negroes" could be purchased on nine months' credit, though buyers received a discount if they paid cash. Government officials participated in the slave trade too. In 1792, for example, Tennessee's territorial governor, William Blount, used federal funds intended to provision Native Americans during a treaty negotiation to buy "young slaves from Maryland" instead. He then brought them into the Cumberland for sale.[29]

By 1800, the enslaved population of Sumner County had more than tripled from what it had been in 1791, and enslaved people made up more than a quarter of the total population, almost twice what they had been a decade earlier. In the next decade, the county's enslaved population tripled again, to more than thirty-seven hundred people. By 1810, the enslaved population of Tennessee had more than quadrupled from what it had been in the mid-1790s, and nearly eight in ten enslaved people in the state lived in Sumner, Davidson, and other Middle Tennessee counties.[30]

Forced migration to Tennessee was hardly the first forced migration for people of African descent in North America. European and American traders shipped around four hundred thousand African captives to mainland North America before 1808. White colonists bought and sold tens of thousands within and among mainland colonies before the American Revolution, and they shipped tens of thousands more along the Atlantic coast and into the Caribbean. Many individual enslaved people survived more than once the uprooting of the familiar, the heartache of loss, the stress of isolation, the darkness of a ship's hold, the fear of the unknown, the threats of intimidating men, the violence of fists and feet and whips, the humiliation of being ogled and inspected and groped, and the confusing acclimation to the new. Some did not survive at all.[31]

The terror and the upheaval never stopped because the slave trade never stopped, because slaveholders never stopped moving, because there was money to make and labor demands to meet and states countenancing it all. But each dislocation was dreadful in its own way, similar to those of the past yet unique to each person and each place. And each deserved to be fought with every tool available.[32]

In the Cumberland, enslaved people strove to overcome the solitude of small farms. They created new families and communities, and they came together at churches and taverns. They devised patronage relationships with white people, hoping they would enable choices about work or earning money or would perhaps bring about manumission. Sometimes they fled, looking to retrieve the lives they had left against their will, to move toward the promise of freedom somewhere beyond the slave country, or just to get as far away as possible.[33]

And sometimes the enslaved refused to be taken into the slave trade at all, no matter what they had to do and no matter what the possible consequences. In September 1801, a Kentucky newspaper editor received a letter "from a gentleman just arrived down the Ohio river" who wrote that outside Baltimore he had met two white men, named Rogers and Elliott. Bringing with them six enslaved people, they were headed to Wheeling, in northwestern Virginia, where they intended to pick up the Ohio River and head home to the Cumberland. Rogers invited the editor's correspondent to come along. He declined, and he considered himself lucky. He reported that Rogers and Elliott had made it as far as Gallipolis, about 175 miles past Wheeling, when "the negroes killed both the white men & threw them into the river." The enslaved reversed course, undoubtedly hoping to return home or cross into free territory in what is now Ohio. They did not get far. They were captured and thrown in a Kentucky jail, and if they were not executed, they were probably sold.[34]

Stories like that did not bother Isaac Franklin and his brothers. They had been raised by a man whose every venture had held its share of risk and danger and whose pursuit of his and his family's economic welfare ignored the concerns of those who felt its impact. They had grown up in a place where they saw the value of the enslaved accrue to white people in all sorts of ways and where the willingness of white people to pay for slave labor had increased markedly in a short period of time. The grief, the resistance, the desperation, and the rage of the enslaved, sucked into the vortex of the market and subjected to white whims, were manageable, and the Franklins thought the returns from buying and selling them well worth it.

John Franklin and James Franklin Jr. acquired farms of their own in the fall of 1802, each son purchasing 130 acres out of their father's claim. But the Franklins also understood the potential of their situation in Tennessee, at nearly the exact midpoint between the stagnant tobacco districts of the Chesapeake and the vibrant cotton and sugar districts of the lower South. They were ideally positioned to be middlemen, bringing enslaved people from places where increasing numbers of white people were coming to see them as an economic millstone to places where white people were willing to spend whatever money they could pull together to acquire them.[35]

Congressional restrictions on slave imports to the Louisiana Territory, which was acquired months after the two oldest Franklin brothers bought their farms, proved ineffective and short-lived, and the federal ban imposed several years later on imports from overseas offered the Franklins what may as well have been an invitation. By providing regulations for transporting slaves within the boundaries of the United States, the same law that prohibited American involvement in the foreign slave trade stamped the approval of the federal government on the domestic one. The timing of the earliest records documenting the involvement of a Franklin in the slave trade is no coincidence. The date was December 1808. The transatlantic slave trade was closed. The domestic trade was primed to take off. Isaac Franklin, age nineteen, acted as witness on bills of sale for two enslaved people in Natchez. He would add his signature, above a cheery flourish, to thousands more before he was through.[36]

I saac Franklin's origins in the family of a long hunter, Indian fighter, and rebel militiaman might seem especially likely for a slave trader. But John Armfield could attest that a white man's destiny was not entirely a product of ancestry or upbringing, and that the training ground for the slave trade was as vast as the nation itself. Armfield came from the North Carolina Piedmont, which cuts a swath two hundred miles wide through the center of the state, marking a plateau below the Appalachians and above the coastal plain stretching inland from the Atlantic. With mountains to the west and the fall line to the east, geology boxed in the region and limited white migration until the mid-eighteenth century, when tens of thousands of white settlers starting flooding into the area. One family story has it that John Armfield's great-grandfather was among them.

The migrants mostly came from parts of Pennsylvania and Maryland where suitable farmland had become hard to find or beyond their means. Many were Ulster-Scots Presbyterians, frequently referred to as Scots-Irish, and Germans of various religious persuasions. But John Armfield's great-grandfather, also named John Armfield, was part of a smaller yet still significant movement of English people belonging to the Society of Friends, radical dissenters from the Church of England commonly known as Quakers. In the mid-1760s, Armfield is said to have left the farm he owned and the school where he taught in Bucks County, Pennsylvania, northeast of Philadelphia, embarking on a southward migration with his wife, their five sons and their families, and around one hundred other Quakers. Traveling through the Shenandoah Valley by way of what was known as the Great Wagon Road, they eventually turned off that path and headed into even more densely forested terrain. They stopped in the central Piedmont, about forty miles south of the Virginia border and a few miles east of a small settlement founded by Quakers about a decade earlier called New Garden.[37]

In part, the name reflected the settlers' belief that they were in a spot nearly untouched by human hands. Where the Armfields and their fellow Quakers took up residence was unusual for colonial North America because it effectively had no Native American inhabitants when white people began settling it. There had once been Indians on the land, mostly in villages belonging to small tribes such as the Keyauwee and the Saura, who survived by hunting and farming. European explorers and traders encountered them periodically in the seventeenth and early eighteenth centuries, but disease brought by those passing Europeans and raids carried out by larger tribes devastated the region's indigenous population. When white colonization began in earnest, only hints of a Native presence remained.[38]

The Quaker allusion to the Edenic quality of their settlement also reflected an appreciation of the land itself. The area's rivers were too small and narrow for most boats. But the topography consisted of gently rolling hills and ridges. Streams and creeks provided good drainage, and some flowed strongly enough to power mills. Hardwood forests of chestnut, oak, and hickory offered timber in abundance. Wolves and panthers could endanger people and livestock, but fish and game, from deer and rabbit to turkey and pigeon, were plentiful, and clearing a patch of forest exposed soil ideal for corn, wheat, flax, and garden crops, enabling self-sufficiency. Author J. Hector St. John de Crèvecoeur, describing the landscape around New Garden in 1782, concluded that "no spot of earth can be more beautiful. . . . I never saw a soil that rewards men so early for their labours and disbursements."[39]

New Garden sat in what was then Orange County, one of several backcountry counties created by the colonial legislature in the 1750s to accommodate Piedmont population growth. There, the Armfields farmed and contributed to the development of a tightly knit community. Isolated from distant markets, Piedmont Quakers traded mostly with each other and built an economy blending agriculture with gristmills and sawmills, a fledgling iron industry, tanneries and taverns, and a smattering of stores selling hardware and items produced by local blacksmiths, coopers, milliners, potters, and other craftspeople.[40]

But tumultuous times were on the horizon for the Armfields and everyone else in the Piedmont. In the late 1760s and early 1770s, John Armfield's oldest son William and at least two of his grandsons signed petitions endorsing the Regulator movement,

a farmer uprising against government corruption and what supporters believed were exorbitant fees and unjust taxes. Seeing that
the remoteness of county seats from growing population centers
contributed to the unrest, the colonial legislature created several
new Piedmont counties in response, and after 1771, the Armfields
lived in Guilford County, a long rectangle contiguous with the Virginia border. But the revolt failed to achieve most of its goals, it
culminated in a punitive crackdown spearheaded by the colonial
governor, and regional internecine conflict carried over into the period of the Revolutionary War, with hostilities regularly breaking
out between those who rebelled against the Crown and those who
stayed loyal to it.[41]

William Armfield considered himself among the latter. During
the Revolution, he cast aside his pacifist Quaker heritage to join a
Loyalist military unit organized by a neighbor, and he paid a price
for that decision. Jailed after being captured in a battle near Wilm-
ington in 1776, Armfield had his property threatened with con-
fiscation at the war's conclusion, and in 1785 the Quaker meeting
to which he belonged dismissed him, perhaps for having taken up
arms in contravention of his faith. But he and his family stayed in
the Piedmont after the United States achieved independence. They
continued to live near where they had before the war, in southern
and western portions of a Guilford County that the state legislature reshaped after the Revolution into the form it has today:
practically a square, twenty-five miles wide by twenty-six miles
long, with a northern boundary about twenty-five miles from the
Virginia line.[42]

By the postwar period, there were a lot of Armfields in Guilford County. William Armfield and his wife Jane had at least eight
children, as did William's brother Isaac. Many of those children
had big families too, and by the turn of the nineteenth century,
the Armfield name could be found strewn across Guilford's legal,
financial, and judicial records. William and Jane Armfield's third

child, Nathan, was born in 1762, and while he was just old enough to have fought in the Revolution like his father, there is no evidence he did so. In the early 1790s, he married Jane Field, ten years his junior and the daughter of Mary and Jeremiah Field, who had served in the same Loyalist unit as William Armfield and was captured and imprisoned alongside him. Nathan and Jane settled on 650 acres of land on the waters of Polecat Creek, a slender tributary of the Deep River that nearly bisects the southern boundary of Guilford County. They also started a family. A girl named Mary, whom everyone called Polly, came first. Their second child, a boy named John, was born in 1797.[43]

Though ensconced in his youth along Polecat Creek amid an extensive, reasonably successful, and generally respected network of kin, John Armfield received little, if any, formal education. A contemporary remembered the area's regular schools to have been "very inferior," and Armfield's penmanship would always be atrocious, his spelling even worse, and his speech unpolished. Like many rural white Americans of his generation, he probably spent his time from the age of seven or eight working on his father's farm, raising sheep and cultivating wheat and flax. His sister Polly probably worked on the Armfield homestead as well, as did the two children Nathan and Jane Armfield had after them. The name of a second son is unrecorded. But John Armfield told people he had once had a brother, and an old story recounted by a Guilford County historian that the Armfields' other boy "severely cut his foot with an axe and died at the age of sixteen" is as likely an explanation as any for what became of him. John Armfield also had a younger sister named Elizabeth, a quick-tempered redhead who went by Betsy.[44]

As the years passed, Nathan Armfield prospered and acquired some local esteem. By the time John Armfield turned eighteen, his father had expanded his landholdings to 887 acres, was serving as a justice of the peace, and was given responsibility in that capacity for making a taxable property list for his section of Guilford County.

Admired by and established among other residents in his community, he also enslaved at least two people.[45]

In the Guilford County of John Armfield's youth, slavery was something more than a marginal institution and something less than a central one. At the outset of the nineteenth century, 905 of the 9,442 people living in Guilford were enslaved. Twenty years later, the proportions had hardly budged, with 1,611 of 14,511 Guilford residents held in bondage. Such demographics, in which slaves numbered about one of every ten people, put Guilford significantly out of step with North Carolina as a whole, where the enslaved proportion of the population jumped from 28 percent to 32 percent over the same time frame.[46]

In part, slavery in Guilford was peripheral because plantation agriculture was peripheral. Slaveholders could and did deploy slave labor to grow grain and flax. But more labor-intensive crops such as tobacco and cotton would not be important to Guilford's economy until later in the nineteenth century, and the relatively small number of people who did own slaves tended not to amass them in large numbers. Among 313 slaveholders on county tax rolls in the mid-1810s, just two paid taxes for enslaving more than ten people, none claimed to enslave more than twenty, and more than 90 percent paid taxes on five or fewer.[47]

Also significant for containing slavery's growth in Guilford was the influence of the county's Quakers. Quaker slaveholding was not unusual in the Atlantic world, and Quaker merchants in England and the North American colonies engaged extensively in the transatlantic slave trade. Still, Quakers were doctrinally dedicated to the equality of all persons before God and to a moral code abjuring violence, greed, and worldliness, which meant an undercurrent of tension and discomfort with slavery ran within Quakerism practically from its beginnings in the mid-seventeenth century. Over time, scattered but sustained efforts by some Quakers to persuade others in the Society of Friends to ameliorate the condition of enslaved people, dissociate themselves from the slave trade, and liberate those they enslaved personally gained traction and started becoming formalized in the faith.[48]

In the 1750s and 1760s, Quaker meetings in both England and America began concluding that slave trading and slaveholding were incompatible with belonging to the Society of Friends, and they sometimes censured or expelled those who continued such practices. In North Carolina, Piedmont Quakers uneasy with buying and selling slaves questioned its legitimacy in the late 1760s, and by the mid-1770s, the annual meeting that set guiding principles for North Carolina Quakers forbade slave trading under most circumstances. Moreover, it urged Quakers to "Cleanse their Hands" of slavery entirely, declared that those not moving earnestly toward emancipating their slaves ought to be dismissed from membership, and created a committee to aid Quaker slaveholders with the process of manumission.[49]

This last maneuver put Quakers in direct conflict with the new state government and placed those manumitted by Quakers in jeopardy of being reenslaved, as North Carolina law barred freeing enslaved people except when they were deemed to have provided service to the state. And not all Piedmont Quakers abandoned slaveholding. But by the time of John Armfield's birth, the moral force of Quakerism in North Carolina was decidedly against it, and Quakers soon would be at the forefront of white antislavery movements beyond the Society of Friends as well.[50]

Growing up in Guilford County, Armfield would have been well aware of Quaker antagonism toward slavery, which despite being less ubiquitous in Guilford than in other places was no less brutal. He would have known that those Quakers most confirmed in their faith found it intolerable, and he probably at least knew of Levi Coffin, who was born near New Garden in 1798. Raised in a farming family of devout Quakers, Coffin was seven years old when a coffle of slaves, "chained in couples on each side of a long chain which extended between them," passed where he sat while his father chopped wood nearby. The white rider driving the coffle lagged behind, and Coffin's father began speaking with some of the enslaved, asking one man why he and the other captives were enchained as they walked. "They have taken us away from our wives and children," the man replied, "and they chain us lest we should make our escape and go back to them." Coffin's father tried explaining slavery and its meaning to his son in ways a seven-year-old might understand, but Coffin, thinking about his own mother and sisters, could only imagine "how terribly we should feel if father were taken away from us."[51]

The more Coffin observed of slavery in Guilford County, the more convinced of its evil he became. As a teenager, he started talking with the enslaved in Guilford himself and doing what he could to aid them. He struck up conversations with those bound in coffles as they moved through the county to see if he "could render them any service," and he started feeding runaways who concealed themselves in woods near his home. He listened to their stories "of hard masters and cruel treatments" and "of the glorious hope of freedom which animated their spirits in the darkest hours, and sustained them under the sting of the lash." But ultimately, Coffin felt he could only do so much in Guilford County. After a decade of acting on behalf of the enslaved, working with a local manumission society, and briefly running a school to teach the enslaved to read, he left North Carolina. Moving first to Indiana and eventually to Ohio, Coffin devoted the next forty years of his life to the cause of abolition, assisting hundreds of fugitives in their flight from slavery and acquiring the informal nickname "President of the Underground Railroad."[52]

Levi Coffin and John Armfield were born a year apart and grew up just a few miles from each other, yet one became a champion of universal human freedom while the other became one of the most infamous slave traders in American history. Religion undeniably played a role in the divergence. Quakerism was not completely foreign to Armfield. His grandfather cared enough about his faith that he and his family were reinstated to their Quaker meeting in 1799, and John Armfield was undoubtedly exposed in his youth to conventional notions of how to lead a pious Quaker life. Still, nothing indicates that his father belonged to a Quaker meeting or any other church, and Nathan Armfield ignored his own father's creed with regard to slavery, as he held as many as seven people in bondage at one point in his life and still held three when he died in 1839.[53]

John Armfield was ill suited for Quakerism and its ideals anyway. For one thing, he seems to have had little enthusiasm for community. His sisters would marry men from local families, yet he would not find a spouse among his neighbors or anywhere else in Guilford County. Nor does it appear that he looked for one. Really, he had little interest in staying in Guilford at all, because what did interest him was money.[54]

Many years after Armfield died, some of his relatives told a historian researching his life that in his adolescence, Armfield argued with his father, left the house, and swore never to go back until he "was worth more than the old man." It is impossible to know whether the story is true, and it may not be. Armfield's sister Betsy, in fact, lamented after her father's death that John and Polly had always been Nathan Armfield's "favorite children." But John Armfield would leave home after reaching adulthood, and he only returned to Guilford County sporadically thereafter. He saw little value in the lives of his father and grandfather. He did not want to be a farmer in the North Carolina Piedmont, and he did not want to settle for moderate though entirely respectable economic standing. He had a head for business and a restive spirit, and he wanted to be rich.[55]

Throughout his life, John Armfield would sometimes affect more refinement than he possessed. He liked being associated with those from moneyed and sophisticated backgrounds, and he had something of a chip on his shoulder about where he came from.

He aimed higher than that, and while the slave trade did not stand out to him immediately as the instrument of his progress, he could not have missed its significance and potential. His father may only have held a few people in bondage, but they were his most valuable assets by far. Such was the case for nearly every slaveholder, and soon enough, Armfield would take advantage of that.

Therein lay the core difference between Levi Coffin and John Armfield. In their childhoods in Guilford County, Black misery was plainly visible all around them. But when Coffin saw the elemental humanity of Black people, his sense of empathy obligated him to do anything within his power to help the enslaved break their chains. When Armfield saw the humanity of the enslaved, he dismissed it. And as an adult he would look to exploit it.

R elative to his future business partners, Rice Ballard had the most noteworthy lineage, even though details about his early life are the most elusive. He was born in Spotsylvania County, Virginia, which comprises a bit more than four hundred square miles in the northeastern portion of the state, about ten miles west of where the Potomac River turns east toward the Chesapeake Bay. The Rappahannock River and the North Anna River form the county's northern and southern boundaries, respectively, and they too flow toward the Chesapeake Bay, as does the Mattaponi River rising to the east from the confluence of four tributaries that cut across Spotsylvania like scratches from the paw of an enormous cat.[56]

Founded in 1720 and named for colonial governor Alexander Spotswood, Spotsylvania thrived for much of the eighteenth century. Its success was driven primarily by the settlement of Fredericksburg, which was laid out in 1728 and served as county seat for nearly fifty years. Situated below the falls of the Rappahannock, by midcentury Fredericksburg had become a small inland port city bustling with wharves, warehouses, taverns, and merchant firms.

Ships came and went from dozens of places around the Atlantic world, from Canada to the Caribbean and from northwestern Europe to western Africa. The population grew so quickly that the House of Burgesses enlarged Fredericksburg's boundaries four times between the 1740s and the 1760s, at which point the city was the second most populous in Virginia.[57]

In no small measure, Fredericksburg's location accounted for its abundance. Its position on the Rappahannock made it a fine gateway to the colonial era's global economy. It was convenient to passes across the Blue Ridge Mountains, making it a facility for western trade and a provision center for white migrants. And Fredericksburg sat at the intersection of more than half a dozen roads connecting it to population hubs all along the Atlantic. Fredericksburg was a transit point for goods, people, and information, and a traveler in the late 1750s who observed that the city was "by far the most flourishing one in these parts" understated matters significantly.[58]

Fredericksburg also benefited from nearby stone quarries and ironworks. But the real economic foundation of Fredericksburg and its hinterland was the tobacco crop that made the entire Virginia colony a demographic and commercial powerhouse. In the 1730s, Fredericksburg became the official receipt and shipping site for tobacco from Spotsylvania County and surrounding areas. Within a few decades, it had a dozen warehouses that together did more business than nearly anyplace else in Virginia, and wheat and flour production supplemented regional tobacco output. Fredericksburg's population was just a couple of thousand, putting it outside the class of larger cities such as Boston, New York, Philadelphia, or Charleston. But aside from those cities, few places blossomed in colonial America as Fredericksburg did.[59]

Certainly, few places could claim connections to so many leaders of the American Revolution. The estate of Augustine Washington lay across the Rappahannock from Fredericksburg, and his son George lived there as a child. James Monroe's first law office was in Fredericksburg, Patrick Henry's uncle was rector of an Anglican church in the city, and when the committee led by Thomas Jefferson wrote the Virginia Statute for Religious Freedom, it met in Fredericksburg's Rising Sun Tavern.[60]

Nurturing the illustrious leadership class of Fredericksburg and Spotsylvania County was plantation slavery, as slave labor produced the tobacco and grain on which the region's economic clout depended, not to mention rum, coffee, cocoa, sugar, and other imported Atlantic world commodities. At the end of the Revolutionary War, half the people in Spotsylvania County were enslaved. Most white families in the county enslaved at least one person, but planters who enslaved large numbers of people were conspicuously influential. Of the county's 505 slaveholders, a full 10 percent held twenty or more people in bondage. Collectively, they enslaved nearly 40 percent of the county's Black population.[61]

Every issue of Fredericksburg's newspapers in the late eighteenth century was replete with notices for slaves who could be hired out, bought at the printer's office, acquired at a farm, or purchased at estate sales. Not a week went by without advertisements seeking information on enslaved people who ran away or announcements placed by white men offering cash or trade items in exchange for enslaved laborers. When Rice Ballard was born on June 7, 1800, more than 886,000 people lived in the state of Virginia, of whom about 346,000, or 39 percent, were enslaved. Ballard's Spotsylvania County was home to 13,000 Virginians. Slightly more than half— nearly 7,000 people—lived in bondage.[62]

Rice Ballard's forebears had lived in Spotsylvania for at least seventy-five years before he was born, and looking further back than that, on both his father's and his mother's sides, his roots in the Chesapeake were about as deep as it was possible for those of white people to be. His given name was Rice Carter Ballard. The pedigree of his father, Benjamin Ballard Jr., seems to extend in Virginia at least to the 1650s. His line may reach into Maryland before that, but there were also Ballards living in Virginia by the 1630s, and several of them played important roles in the colony's early history and politics.[63]

Rice Ballard's mother, Ann Graham Heslop, was the daughter of William Heslop and Ann Carter, whose family history remains the stuff of legend. Ann Carter's great-grandfather was Thomas Carter. The son of a London merchant, Thomas Carter migrated to eastern Virginia as a young man in the 1650s, established a mercantile business, and bought eight hundred acres of land from John Carter, a relative who had accumulated thousands of acres through political connections and who would accumulate thousands more as bonuses for importing white indentured servants and African slaves to the colony. John Carter was also the father of Robert "King" Carter, who in the early eighteenth century owned nearly three hundred thousand acres of land, enslaved more than one thousand people, acted as agent for transatlantic slave traders, and became renowned as the richest man in Virginia.[64]

Thomas Carter would not achieve the obscene affluence of Robert Carter. But he entrenched himself among the interconnected gentry families who would label themselves the First Families of Virginia, served in the Virginia House of Burgesses, and amassed a sizable fortune in land and enslaved people. Thomas Carter's son John moved west across the Rappahannock in the 1710s, and his grandson, also named John, bought land even farther west, in Spotsylvania County, in the 1740s. He settled on an estate just inside the county's eastern boundary and over the next forty years became a familiar presence in Spotsylvania public life. John Carter served as an Anglican vestryman, county sheriff, and a county court justice. He held a captain's rank during the Revolutionary War, owned plantations in Spotsylvania and adjacent counties, and by the 1780s, enslaved thirty-one people. He married twice and fathered fourteen children. His fifth child with his first wife was Ann Carter, and shortly before she married William Heslop, her sister Frances married Rice Curtis III, whose great-nephew would be his namesake.[65]

If a name alone indicates rank, then Rice Ballard inherited elite status from his mother and her ancestors. But sometimes a distinguished family name is a reminder that glory fades. The connections Ballard's progenitors had to the most celebrated and extravagantly wealthy Carters were more than a century in the past when he was born, and the socioeconomic position of the Carter line of which his mother was at the end had peaked generations before his birth. Rice Ballard's great-grandfather had been prosperous, but that John Carter had divided his resources among his many children. He left his daughter Ann some property in his will, and she and William Heslop enslaved several people on a farm of a few hundred acres. But they were not rich or eminent by early national Virginia standards. Their daughter seems to have held two women in bondage when she married Benjamin Ballard Jr. in 1798, but if she knew about being a member of the planter class at all, the knowledge came from old family stories.[66]

The family of Benjamin Ballard Jr., meanwhile, had none of those stories to tell. His grandfather, Bland Ballard, had acquired land along the Rappahannock River in the 1730s, and he spent most of his life as a small farmer. He accumulated enough wealth to give an enslaved person to his daughter Ann as a wedding gift in 1764 and to buy 143 acres of land for his son Benjamin in 1769, and at the time of his death in 1792, he enslaved five women and girls. But he sold his own land six years before he died, and those enslaved people constituted almost 90 percent of his estate, the rest consisting of some livestock and household and kitchen furniture.[67]

Benjamin Ballard Sr. achieved somewhat more substantial economic status than his father had. He and his wife, Hanah Jones, had nine children, and he farmed the land his father bought for him, along a creek that fed into a Mattaponi River tributary about ten miles southwest of Fredericksburg. In 1804, he expanded his farm, buying an adjacent 157 acres, and when he died less than ten years later he owned three horses, thirty-five sheep, twenty pigs, and ten head of cattle. He also enslaved three men, six women, and five children.[68]

The fortunes of his son, Rice Ballard's father, marked a clear step backward. Like most white children in Spotsylvania, Rice Ballard and his younger sister Emily, born in 1802, lived in a slaveholding household. But Benjamin Ballard Jr. never personally enslaved more than a few people, and it is not clear that he ever acquired his own land. Instead, Rice Ballard lived his early years on his grandfather's property. He was twelve when his grandfather died, and his family appears to have stayed where they were. His father's only significant possessions, other than the people he enslaved, were a couple of horses.[69]

The Ballards were not the only Spotsylvania County family whose material status deteriorated in the early nineteenth century. It happened to many white families, because the Revolution that had drawn on the leadership of so many from Spotsylvania also accelerated forces that sent the county into a decades-long decline. Spotsylvania saw little damage from military conflict, but war cut off the export trade in tobacco. The crop's already questionable future was made no more promising by the disruption, and uncertain tobacco profits helped feed a postwar impulse among white Virginians for migration. One county historian observes that after the Revolution, "great hordes of citizens from the Rappahannock Valley moved westward." Many white Spotsylvanians left the state altogether. In the decade after Rice Ballard's birth, the white population of Spotsylvania County actually fell by almost 5 percent, the steady outflow of people slightly outpacing natural increase and movement into Spotsylvania from elsewhere.[70]

But Spotsylvania hardly became a wasteland after the Revolution. Grain superseded tobacco as the county's essential agricultural product, and while Fredericksburg was reduced from a global port to a primarily domestic one, it still saw steady business from merchants brokering barrels of flour and bushels of wheat and corn for countryside farmers. Craftspeople, storekeepers, and professionals still prospered, and the city's location became commercially advantageous in new ways. In part, that was because road quality in the United States generally improved over time. But it was also because the Virginia capital moved from Williamsburg to Richmond in 1780, and Fredericksburg was almost exactly halfway along a stage route between Richmond and the national capital, founded in 1791 and known then as Washington City.[71]

Another buffer for Spotsylvania's economy amid postwar change was the expanding slave trade, which directed a steady stream of Black people out of the Chesapeake and into locations farther south and west. The county's situation and its history as a mercantile center made it a prime location for that business too. Ultimately, the consequences of Spotsylvania's commercial and demographic transitions reverberated most profoundly through enslaved people's lives, and they pointed toward what Rice Ballard would make of his own.

Between 1800 and 1820, Virginia accounted for over 60 percent of all slave exports across state lines, and the number of enslaved people exported out of Virginia increased nearly 85 percent from the first decade of the nineteenth century to the second. In Spotsylvania County, the enslaved population grew by about 15 percent between 1800 and 1820, but in the 1810s alone, at least fifteen hundred enslaved people were forcibly taken out of Spotsylvania, which was nearly 20 percent of all the slaves in the county.[72]

Whereas the slave trade brought enslaved people into the Middle Tennessee of Isaac Franklin's youth and passed them through the central North Carolina of John Armfield's, it took them away from Rice Ballard's northeastern Virginia. The presence of white men who planned to send Black people to places unknown became increasingly obvious in the early nineteenth century. In an agricultural economy grounded in credit, cash offered by slave traders was a major appeal to sellers, and John Stannard's promise to "GIVE CASH for a few LIKELY YOUNG NEGROES," issued in the

Fredericksburg *Virginia Herald* in 1810, was a telltale sign of a trader. The motive of John Crump, a merchant who offered cash for "Thirty or Forty Negroes, in families," was unmistakable too, as was that of Anthony Buck, a Fredericksburg merchant and auctioneer who in 1811 wanted to collect sixty slaves. Buck also offered cash, and though he advertised that "it would be desirable to have a few families," he did not need to say that he would pay to fracture them if it filled his quota.[73]

It is impossible to know whether a young Rice Ballard imagined himself someday buying and selling Black people, but he must have seen them vanishing down the roads and rivers leading out of Spotsylvania County. His father demonstrated how it was done, because in September 1814, he sold someone. The records reveal little about the transaction. They do not tell us whether Benjamin Ballard Jr. sold the man because he needed money to cover debts or preferred cash to a laborer or wanted to inflict an especially spiteful form of punishment or just because he felt like it. The sources are equally silent about the man he sold, telling us nothing about whether he had a wife or children or what he liked to do in moments when he was not forced to work or whether he had any special talents or what made him laugh. All we know is that Benjamin Ballard Jr. received $200 and that the man he sold was named George.[74]

Yet whatever Benjamin Ballard Jr. showed his son about slaves and slavery, he would not be the man to show him the way out of Spotsylvania County. One wonders how much Rice Ballard wanted his father's guidance anyway. Nothing points explicitly to conflict between them. But even as Rice Ballard became exceedingly wealthy, he seems to have provided no support to his aging father, who was nearly destitute when he died in 1852. Indeed, while Rice Ballard did spend some time in Spotsylvania as an adult, he does not appear to have visited or corresponded with his father at all. If he did, he kept none of his father's letters among the hundreds of pieces of personal mail in his papers.[75]

Rather than his father, the most significant male figure in Rice Ballard's early life, and arguably his entire life, was Samuel Alsop Jr. Born in 1776, Alsop came from a large and affluent family. His father, Samuel Alsop Sr., married four times and had eleven children, and his estate grew to comprise around one thousand acres of land and at least a dozen slaves in Spotsylvania County, in addition to some real estate holdings elsewhere. But Samuel Alsop Jr.'s financial circumstances would well outstrip his father's. He owned neither land nor slaves when Rice Ballard was born in 1800, but in the ensuing decades, Samuel Alsop Jr. became the richest man in Spotsylvania County.[76]

By the late 1810s, white people in Spotsylvania commonly referred to Alsop as Big Sam or Wealthy Sam. He owned nearly four thousand acres of land scattered across the county, held real estate in other Virginia counties and in a number of other states, paid taxes on more than two dozen horses and several carriages, and enslaved around fifty people. But Alsop had a diverse portfolio of interests. In 1811, he purchased a retail license entitling him to sell "goods of foreign growth and manufacture" at his house. Three years later, he bought a license to operate a tavern at the intersection of two roads near the center of the county. One was the road from Richmond to Fredericksburg. Alsop owned the tavern for almost thirty years, and it became such a busy location that the county courthouse was relocated to the same intersection in the late 1830s.[77]

Beyond his talents for business and trade, Alsop was an architect and builder, and he supplemented his wealth further still by designing and supervising the construction of a slew of expensive houses in and around Fredericksburg. Most were two-and-a-half-story brick mansions in the Federal style. He designed at least one for himself, several for his children and their families, and the rest for other rich people. Many of the houses had names: Fairview, Mill Brook, Oakley, Kenmore Woods, Coventry. Alsop assuredly used slave labor on every one of them.[78]

It is unclear when Alsop first noticed Rice Ballard or why he decided to take him under his wing. Alsop lived ten or fifteen miles and across the county from Ballard's father, and he probably did not often have the chance to observe Rice Ballard as a boy. But hints of how they may have become acquainted point to a connection between Alsop's family and that of Rice Ballard's maternal grandmother. In 1813, Ann Carter Heslop sold Samuel Alsop her share of some land inherited from her father. The next year, she sold her share in a different inherited tract to Thomas Hicks, who was married to Alsop's sister Lucy. At still another point in the 1810s, after the death of Rice Ballard's grandfather William Heslop, Alsop bought the Heslop homestead. Ann Carter Heslop continued living there until she died, and Samuel Alsop was among the witnesses to her will.[79]

Samuel Alsop's half brother Benjamin Alsop had a relationship with the Carters too, serving as Spotsylvania County agent for Zacarias Taliaferro and Margaret Chew Taliaferro, who was Ann Carter Heslop's half sister. On at least one occasion, that personal and business association carried over to the family of Margaret Taliaferro's half niece, Rice Ballard's mother Ann Heslop Ballard. In 1814, when Benjamin Ballard Jr. sold the enslaved man named George, Benjamin Alsop was the buyer.[80]

Whatever Samuel Alsop saw in Rice Ballard, it was something he liked and something he thought could serve his interests. Given where their association would lead, it probably involved the slave trade. Alsop was always hunting for economic prospects and for places to put his money to work, and as a tavern owner, he could not have helped but notice the uptick in commerce in enslaved people in and around Spotsylvania County.

In the early nineteenth century, people gathered at taverns not only to eat and drink but also to gamble, gossip, read the newspaper, and talk business. Many taverns had lodging facilities, and itinerant slave traders found them useful for taking the measure of a place, gathering information about white people looking for slaves

to buy or possessing some they wanted to sell. Some tavern keepers outfitted their basements as dank underground dungeons or set
aside spaces in stuffy garrets for traders to stow the enslaved as they
collected them. Particularly along well-traveled roads, many taverns
had pens where traders could keep coffles enchained for the night.
By the 1810s, Alsop would have seen growing numbers of slave
traders passing through Spotsylvania. He would have talked with
them and gotten a feel for their prospects, though a man with his
resources and discernment probably had a decent sense of the slave
market in Virginia anyway. He knew it was lively and getting livelier
all the time.[81]

If he wanted to put his own funds in the market, though, he
would need someone willing to travel, someone young, someone
who wanted the opportunity, someone he thought he could trust,
and someone with no qualms about dealing in human beings. Alsop
and his wife, Dorothea, had a son of their own, but Joseph Alsop was
born in 1805. He was too young to put on the road in the 1810s, and
Samuel Alsop may have wanted him close by rather than rummag-
ing the countryside buying and selling slaves anyway. Rice Ballard,
on the other hand, was old enough, had limited prospects at home,
and may have wanted to leave. He came from a family Samuel Alsop
knew and had done business with before, and it seems to have been a
family he admired, as being Ann Carter Heslop's landlord could not
have been lucrative, yet Alsop let her stay on her land as long as she
lived. Finally, if Rice Ballard expressed misgivings or compunction
about slave trading when Samuel Alsop raised the subject, it would
be about the last time he ever expressed them in his life. It is far
more likely that when Alsop made him a proposition, he was ready
to say yes.[82]

Isaac Franklin never mentioned exactly where he and his brother
John bought slaves on their trip to the Chesapeake in the sum-

mer of 1809. In Baltimore, they might have crowded alongside other slave traders in the cluster of taverns north and west of the harbor basin off the Patapsco River. Anyone reading the city's newspapers knew traders were there, at Henry Freeburger's or Elijah Sinners's places near the head of the Cheapside wharf, at Matthew Walker's or Eli Lilly's taverns on Howard Street, at William Fowler's place near the New Market on Lexington Street, or at John Barney's tavern on Light Street, known as the Fountain Inn. They offered to pay cash, and they wanted "10 or 12 Likely Young Negroes," "young *Negro Men*; and women," or perhaps "a few young Negroes between the ages of 8 and 20 years."[83]

Alexandria had its share of taverns as well, and traders were especially fond of the Indian Queen, on the northwest corner of King and St. Asaph Streets, six blocks west of the Potomac River docks. In addition to serving food and drink, John Hodgkin sold horses and carriages there, and he enticed customers with hired musical acts and other entertainment. In 1806, he offered to buy slaves, and slave traders started advertising that they could be found at the Indian Queen too. In 1807, William Robbins wanted to purchase twenty or thirty people; in 1810, Giles Harding sought "30 or 40 Negroes"; and in 1811, James Gentry promised to pay handsomely "for a few likely young Slaves of both sexes."[84]

The Franklins did not place newspaper advertisements in 1809, but the purchasing trip that year was not their first, and it would not be their last. Theirs were familiar faces in Baltimore and Washington City, and they came through both cities frequently enough that they had mail delivered to them there. Lingering in taverns was only one way for traders to gather enslaved people anyhow. The Franklins may have checked out local jails, where sheriffs and jailors sold unclaimed runaways to the highest bidder. They may have followed notices for public auctions of slaves forfeited for debt or being sold as part of an estate settlement. Or they may have simply roamed the countryside, letting word of mouth carry the report that they had money to spend and were looking for Black people to buy.[85]

Slave traders deployed any and all of these strategies, because even as the trade gained momentum in the late eighteenth and early nineteenth centuries, it remained a haphazard business with limitations on its growth. Particularly in South Carolina, Georgia, and Louisiana, slaveholders still partially filled their labor needs with thousands of Africans imported before the transatlantic trade ban took effect in 1808. In those places and others, white migrants also predominantly brought people they already enslaved with them as they made the southwestern cotton and sugar districts of the United States ever larger. And if they wanted more slaves, they often returned east themselves to buy them instead of buying them from slave traders.[86]

Between constraints on demands for their services and an immature American banking system that made it hard for them to fund large-scale operations, most domestic slave traders working at around the time the Franklins got into the business did so sporadically, and usually as a sideline to their primary occupations. Newspaper advertisements appeared inconsistently, even from the smattering of professionals who announced where they could be found and publicized that they wanted to buy sizable numbers of people. The preponderance were placed by men who worked alone and who came and went, purchasing a few enslaved people at a time, leaving when they spent the money they had scraped together, and selling their captives either back where they had come from or wherever they happened to find customers.[87]

Flukiness and insecurity at the sales end of things was a problem for slave traders too. The Franklins knew all about that, as they repeatedly sued customers for outstanding debts. In March 1812, for example, James Franklin Jr. sold an enslaved person to David Steele, a Kentuckian passing through Natchez with a load of flour, only to sue two years later to collect nearly $300 Steele still owed on the promissory note he had used as payment. In that instance, Franklin got his money when the court garnished the flour Steele left with a New Orleans merchant. Isaac Franklin was not so lucky when he sued William Parker a few months later for $150 owed on a slave sale, because Parker was nowhere to be found. He had either left Mississippi or died or both, and he left behind not only his liability to Isaac Franklin but also debts to others in Natchez amounting to nearly $3,000.[88]

But the size and scope of the trade as a whole was irrelevant when a slave trader darkened an enslaved person's door. Because when that happened, the world cracked into pieces. Charles Ball's world was one of those ruptured by the trade. Born on a Maryland tobacco farm in the early 1780s, Ball was only four when slave traders bought his mother and all his siblings at auction from their recently deceased enslaver's estate. A nearby planter purchased Ball separately, and Ball remembered his mother wailing while she "earnestly and imploringly beoought my master to buy her and the rest of her children." He remembered, too, her breaking down as the slave trader who bought her "gave her two or three heavy blows on the shoulders with his raw-hide," yanked Ball from her arms, and dragged her off. Ball was taken away on horseback, his mother's cries becoming "more and more indistinct" until "at length they died away in the distance." It was the last time he ever heard her voice. Fifty years later, "the horrours of that day" still triggered an overwhelming sense of panic.

Ball eventually married and had children, but in 1805 he was sold again, to a trader who denied Ball even the chance to say goodbye to his family, sneering that he "would be able to get another wife" where he was going. His neck padlocked into an iron collar and his wrists secured with heavy fetters bolted shut, Ball was chained in a line with fifty other people for a forced march of five hundred miles to South Carolina. The trip took five weeks. Ball's family came to him in dreams when he managed to sleep, and he wished for death, recalling that he would have hanged himself had he "been at liberty to get a rope."

Somehow mustering his resolve, Ball escaped slavery several times. He eventually returned to Maryland and even reunited for a short time with his children and his wife before she passed away. But as a fugitive, his situation was hopelessly precarious. He remarried, this time to a free woman of color, only to flee the slave states after he was again cast back into slavery. By the time he returned to Maryland yet again to retrieve his family, it was too late. Legal freedom had meant nothing for his second wife and their four children. White people had kidnapped them in the dead of night from their own home and sold them to slave dealers in Baltimore.

White Americans routinely pushed those they forced to shoulder slavery's burdens to the brink of what human beings could be expected to take. But there are limits to every person's strength and courage and will to survive, and Charles Ball had reached his. Once the people he loved most in the world had "passed into hopeless bondage" and were "gone forever," something inside him was irreparably broken. He left the slave states for good, and while years later he published an account of his experiences, he concealed his place of residence lest he fall victim, even in old age, to the predations of the slave trade that had taken everything from him three different times and called it justice.[89]

Some white Americans saw the slave trade for the contemptible business it was and denounced slave traders as soulless miscreants. As early as 1802, the Alexandria grand jury complained about men like the Franklin brothers, "persons coming from distant parts of the United States . . . for the purpose of purchasing slaves, where they exhibit to our view a scene of wretchedness and human degradation, disgraceful to our characters as citizens of a free government." Slave traders came to the city, collected people for sale, and drove them through the streets "loaded with chains as though they had committed some heinous offence." It ought not to be allowed, the grand jury

A coffle of enslaved people outside the federal Capitol, not long after British forces set it aflame during the War of 1812. From physician Jesse Torrey's *A Portraiture of Slavery in the United States* (Philadelphia, 1817), which provided detailed accounts of the domestic slave trade and the kidnapping and enslavement of free Black Americans.

argued. Surely "the laws of justice and humanity" protected even enslaved people. Surely civil authorities could "prevent parents being wrested from their offspring, and children from their parents, without respect to the ties of nature."[90]

In the late eighteenth and early nineteenth centuries, many legislatures in the United States did in fact pass laws circumscribing the activities of domestic slave traders. But the protests of the Alexandria grand jury were more than rhetorical, because laws geared toward containing the slave trade were so widely ignored, poorly enforced, and filled with exceptions that they cast the trade in an even harsher light, exposing even the pretenses of protecting the interests of the trafficked as a sham. Indeed, the very places that tried regulating or outlawing the trade actually presided over its fastest growth. The trade would grow even more dramatically after the War of 1812, convincing Isaac Franklin that getting out of it would be crazy, persuading John Armfield and Rice Ballard that the time was right to dive in, and directing them all toward the changes that would transform it from an irregular business to a more structured and heavily capitalized operation.[91]

But some things remained constant in the years after 1815. Among them was that slave traders were hard men who could come from almost any family, any place, and any background except perhaps that of abject poverty. And they cared about the intense sorrows of the enslaved and the scattered scorn of other white people only insofar as those things made their jobs more challenging and their profits more difficult to attain.[92]

In December 1815, a young physician named Jesse Torrey traveled south from his home in upstate New York, promoting the cause of free public libraries. Arriving in Washington City, Torrey was heading out to witness Congress meeting in session when he heard a young Black boy with a stammer proclaim, "There goes the Ge-Ge-orgy-men with a drove o'niggers chain'd together, two and two." Especially among the enslaved, the "Georgia man" was a common colloquialism for slave traders in the early nineteenth century, referring to the state where so many of them brought their merchandise for sale. Sure enough, Torrey turned and saw parading down the street "a light covered waggon, followed by a procession of men, women and children, resembling that of a funeral."[93]

He trailed behind and drew closer to the caravan, catching up to it just across from the Capitol, still in ruins from its wartime burning by the British in 1814. Torrey stared at the "mute sad faces veiled with *black* despair." He heard heavy chains clanking as those bound shuffled and struggled under their weight, and after catching his breath and regaining his wits, he asked one of the two white men driving the coffle "what part of the country they were taking all these people to." "To Georgia," the man replied, leading Torrey to wonder aloud whether there were not already enough slaves there. The driver scoffed. No, he said. "Not quite enough."

As the parade headed out of the capital toward the bridge over the Potomac and southward into Virginia, a Black hack driver, gesturing toward the scene, called out to Torrey, "See there! An't that right down *murder? Don't you call that right down murder?*" Torrey hesitated for a moment. He mumbled under his breath that he was not sure. But the driver wanted an answer. Pressed to acknowledge the man's outrage, Torrey conceded the point.[94]

TWO

CHOICES, 1815–1827

ISAAC FRANKLIN VOLUNTEERED FOR MILITARY SERVICE IN THE fall of 1813, answering the Tennessee legislature's call for troops to march on Creek strongholds in Alabama. The muster came in direct response to an August assault on Fort Mims, near Mobile, during which Red Stick Creeks hostile to American incursions murdered more than two hundred people. But white Tennesseans had been itching to take the fight to the Creeks and other Native American nations for years. Trade disputes and British impressment of American sailors helped provoke the War of 1812, but it was sensational stories about English agents conspiring with western Indians against the United States, peddled by War Hawk congressmen such as Nashville's Felix Grundy, that really roused nationalist and militaristic fervor among white people in Tennessee.[1]

Bringing a gun and a horse with him to war, Isaac Franklin joined a company from Sumner and other Middle Tennessee counties that became part of the Second Regiment of Volunteer Mounted Riflemen. Led by Colonel Newton Cannon, the regiment belonged to a brigade under the command of Brigadier General John Coffee. Coffee, in turn, answered to Major General Andrew Jackson, who oversaw the offensive against the Creeks with a force of twenty-five hundred men. Though Franklin was only twenty-four years old, he received an officer's rank of lieutenant, and in the months after his enlistment, he and his fellow soldiers fought in a series of vicious, bloody, and extremely lopsided engagements.[2]

Marching from the south-central Tennessee town of Fayette-ville, Cannon's regiment headed through northern Alabama to the site of the not quite completed Fort Strother, a small square enclosure along the Coosa River. On November 3, 1813, Franklin's company joined nearly one thousand mounted men from Coffee's brigade, and a small force of allied Indians, in an attack on the Creek town of Tallushatchee, thirteen miles from the fort. It was less a battle than a rout.

Two hundred Red Sticks protected the town. In thirty minutes, Coffee's men killed nearly all of them, and they took eighty-four women and children as prisoners. Jackson bragged that he and his soldiers had "retaliated for the destruction of Fort Mims." Legend-ary frontiersman David Crockett, himself a Tennessee volunteer, described events at Tallushatchee somewhat less gloriously. In his memoir, he recalled American soldiers setting fire to a house where forty-six Creek warriors had barricaded themselves, shooting those inside "like dogs," and then eating potatoes discovered the next day in a root cellar beneath the half-burnt corpses. The soldiers had been running short on supplies, and they were hungry, though Crockett wrote he would have preferred to leave the potatoes "if I could have helped it, for the oil of the Indians we had burned up on the day before had run down on them, and they looked like they had been stewed with fat meat." Jackson's army lost five men at Tallushatchee. Several dozen were wounded.[3]

Heading deeper into Creek territory, Jackson ordered an attack on one thousand Red Sticks who were besieging Talladega, a Creek town whose residents considered themselves allies of the United States, thirty miles southwest of Tallushatchee. This time, Jackson commanded troops himself. He had twelve hundred infantrymen and eight hundred men on horseback at his disposal, Newton Cannon's cavalry regiment among them. When the battle was over, seventeen of Jackson's men were dead and eighty-five were wounded, but his forces had killed more than three hundred Red Sticks and wounded over three hundred others.[4]

Then Jackson's push began to stall, and Isaac Franklin and his fellow soldiers began to grumble. They had marched from Tennessee with scarce provisions, across more than one hundred miles of thickly forested terrain, during an unusually cold and wet season, and they were disgruntled and demoralized despite their battlefield victories. Threats of desertion mounted, and hundreds of volunteers looked eagerly to the end of their enlistment term, which they believed was for three months.[5]

The famously irascible Jackson responded to his troops' grousing by browbeating them, shaming them, and insisting that they had enlisted for longer than they had thought. But Franklin and the members of his regiment considered their service over as of January 28, 1814. In an open letter to John Coffee, Franklin and nearly two dozen other regimental officers asserted that they and those they led had volunteered "for a short time or tour, all trusting to the laws of our state which did not compell a man to serve longer than three months." With those three months about to expire, the soldiers expected formal discharges from service, yet there were rumors that the government would not be granting them, which meant either "being compelled to serve during the war" or returning home "like *deserters.*"

Franklin and the other officers claimed there was some duplicity in that. "If any tender of longer time of service than . . . three months, has been made to the general government," they wrote, "we beg leave to say it has been without our consent or knowledge." But ultimately, they used their only real leverage, which was that Coffee, Jackson, and the government needed more men to keep the war going, and breaking faith with volunteers already in the field was not likely to bring them. "Souring the minds of the people against the government and the officers," Franklin and his fellows argued, would "prevent others from entering in the service of their country, and paralize the spirit of every citizen of Tennessee which have been heretofore so proud to boast of valor and pride."

The letter's signatories assured Coffee that plenty of new men would enlist if they were "*not deterred from a fear of being entrapped by their own government.*" The officers even wrote that some of them would volunteer again, as they still felt "the same desire now, to prosecute the war with as much vigor and spirit as we ever did." But if discharges were not forthcoming, none of that would happen, and they threatened that if they had to go back to Tennessee as deserters, Coffee's reputation would suffer too. "When we are permitted to return home & mix with our neighbors, our pride would be, to be *praised* instead of *blamed*, by these officers who so gallantly led us to battle, and obtained such splendid victories. Painful it would be, to hear them accused of forcing men to serve beyond the time engaged for."

In the end, even though the letter Isaac Franklin signed suggested he might stay on in the contest against the Creeks, he knew he was never going to do that. As the letter made clear, he could not continue serving indefinitely "without ruin to individual interest." He had things to do. There were people to sell.[6]

WHETHER OR NOT ISAAC FRANKLIN AND THE OTHER VOLUNteer Mounted Riflemen ever got their discharges, hundreds of recruits did replace them in Andrew Jackson's army, which continued its crusade against the Creeks, breaking their resistance and burning their towns en route to a triumph over British forces below New

Orleans early in 1815. That battle was a stunning finish to the war Franklin had abandoned, and while he did not see the war through, its outcome served his "individual interest" anyhow, because it meant demand for his skill set was about to soar.

Cotton was the key. The desires of white farmers and policy-makers to expand the cotton frontier had always motivated conflict with the Creeks, whose forced surrender of twenty million acres of land in the aftermath of Jackson's campaign cleared the way for the expropriation of tens of millions of additional acres of Native American territory across the lower South in the decades to come. The federal government then filled its coffers by selling the land to white migrants, who moved onto it by the thousands and turned it into cotton farms. Between 1814 and 1819 alone, American cotton production increased by 138 percent, from about 73 million pounds to almost 175 million pounds. Cotton exports grew by nearly a factor of five just from 1814 to 1815, and the crop's market price in New Orleans practically doubled between 1814 and 1817.[7]

Technological, infrastructural, informational, and financial changes aided and abetted military and bureaucratic exertions on behalf of cotton growers. In the years after 1815, textile mill owners in the United States and Europe had a seemingly unlimited appetite for cotton, and the advent of the steamboat eased its delivery onto domestic and global markets, as did an American road system that became denser and of higher quality. Growing numbers of newspapers enhanced the reliability and spread of knowledge about those markets. An expanding network of state and private banks, including the Second Bank of the United States, chartered in 1816 to hold the deposits of the federal government, widened the availability of credit and boosted the nation's money supply.[8]

Whites on the cotton frontier used loans and cash from those banks not only to buy land but also to buy enslaved laborers. Sometimes they mortgaged the people they bought to buy still more land and more people. They placed the people on the land and compelled them under the lash to grow the cotton, pack it into bales, and load it onto steamboats. Then the cotton traveled around the world and pushed ahead both the early Industrial Revolution and the further expansion of slavery. The combined enslaved population of Georgia, Alabama, Mississippi, and Louisiana, the last three of which entered the Union between 1812 and 1819, grew from just under 160,000 to more than 510,000 between 1810 and 1830, an increase of 220 percent. By 1830, one-quarter of all the enslaved people in the country lived in those four states alone.[9]

Domestic slave traders responded to and fed these changes in equal measure, and the slave trade and American capitalism settled more deeply into their mutually constituent relationship. The pace of the trade accelerated noticeably in the second and third decades of the nineteenth century, and as the cotton economy's gravity pulled slavery's center in the United States inexorably toward the south and west, the trade moved with it. The eyes of the Georgia men turned toward the Mississippi Valley.

Between 1800 and 1809, whites moved sixty-five thousand enslaved people across state lines. They brought almost 90 percent of them to Georgia, Kentucky, and Tennessee, and most brought with them people they already enslaved. In the 1810s, the scale of forced migration nearly doubled, and 62 percent of the enslaved people entrapped by it in that decade ended up in Alabama, Mississippi, Louisiana, and the expanding cotton frontier areas of central and western Georgia. In the 1820s, the number of trafficked slaves grew again by 25 percent, to more than 150,000 people. Seventy percent of them ended up in those same four places. This was a level of demand for laborers that could not be met by white farmers and planters bringing people they already enslaved, or even by farmers and planters returning east for additional purchases. This was demand that seemed bottomless, and slave traders stepped into the breach. By the 1820s, they were responsible for 60 to 70 percent of the interstate movement of enslaved people, a figure that remained largely unchanged until slavery's demise.[10]

Slave prices and cotton prices tended to correlate, and both dropped significantly in the wake of the bust known as the Panic of 1819 that ended the economic boom following the War of 1812. Through the era of the Civil War, neither slave-trader profits nor cotton prices would approach what they were in the mid-to-late 1810s. But the panic did not diminish the slave trade for long, nor did it curb the growing number of white men working as slave traders. On the contrary, in the slack years, Chesapeake farmers with mounting liabilities threw more slaves onto the market for cash offered by traders, while farmers on the cotton frontier, desperate to increase volume to compensate for falling crop prices, bought those slaves on credit at prices that still brought traders handsome returns. There was a reason that critics of the trade disdained its operators as "speculators." In the constantly churning American economy that upended Black lives and turned them into assets, slave traders wagered they could earn their margins on the process.[11]

But the slave trade did change in the 1820s. As it became a progressively competitive business with an ever-larger number of players who made it an occupation rather than a sideline, success over time required more than the partial attention of a flatboatman looking for extra money or a sometime fortune seeker loitering in a tavern. As in most businesses, success in the changing slave trade required foresight and savvy, a feel for specialized markets and capital circulation, and the ability to keep pace with and take advantage of economic, technological, and demographic shifts. More than most businesses, it required ruthlessness, indifference to human suffering, and an unusual comfort with violence.

John Armfield and Rice Ballard may not have known all that when they started stepping tentatively into the slave trade in the mid-1820s. Even the more experienced Isaac Franklin could not have anticipated everything that lay ahead as he turned away from war and back into the commerce in Black people. But as they gravitated toward each other, they would learn, sometimes by observing other men whose operations showed them what could be. Franklin, Armfield, and Ballard were not the first to see the trade's future. But they would be the ones to make it.

Once Isaac Franklin got into the slave trade, he never really got out of it, though he could have if he had wanted to. In May 1815, a little over a year after ending his military service, he gave his father $500 for 132 acres of land in Sumner County on the western fork of Station Camp Creek, north of the Cumberland River and about five miles west of Gallatin. Within a few years, he enslaved between ten and fifteen people on the property. This course might have suggested a move toward a more settled life, a planter's life built around commercial farming and capital investments in slaves rather than around trading in them. It was a move his older brothers had made years earlier.[12]

After buying their own farms, John Franklin and James Franklin Jr. spent another decade or so engaged in the long-distance trade of slaves, cotton, flour, corn, and other goods. But they gradually put mercantile efforts aside. By 1820, both were married, each had numerous children, and between them they owned nearly fifteen hundred acres of land and enslaved more than one hundred people. Isaac Franklin, meanwhile, was thirty years old and unmarried, and his Tennessee property was less a working farm than a loose, if tangible, tether to his family and birthplace. He had a house there, yet he made almost no other improvements for years, and while he spent portions of the summers in Sumner County, he lived an essentially peripatetic life as a slave trader. Of thousands of white men who worked as slave traders in nineteenth-century America, few if any explained why they entered their profession. They were not a reflective bunch, and those from modest backgrounds in particular probably considered the financial opportunities the trade offered to be explanation enough. Isaac Franklin's background, however, was not modest, and he had ample prospects right in Sumner County.[13]

Isaac Franklin chose to stay in the slave trade because he was good at it, because he liked it, and because it was a family business. Franklin's older brothers used the market in Black people to get started in the world. So had Allen Purvis, Franklin's sister Margaret's husband, who in the early nineteenth century both sold people in Natchez himself and consigned enslaved people to the Franklin brothers to sell on his behalf. Isaac Franklin was mostly an apprentice in the slave trade before the War of 1812. But after it, he would become a fixture in the trade for his extended family, mentoring younger relatives as they made some money and decided whether human merchandise was the business for them.[14]

The outline of Isaac Franklin's dealings during the years after the war is faint, but unsurprisingly, the picture that emerges is one of a man in motion. Beginning in 1817, if not earlier, Franklin received letters in Baltimore, Alexandria, Natchez, Georgetown, and Washington City, gathering business information through the federal postal system, which was as vital for the slave trade as it was for most economic pursuits in the early republic. Newspapers were no less crucial, and in May 1821, Franklin placed his first advertisement, notifying readers of the Washington *Daily National Intelligencer* that he wanted "to purchase 18 or 20 likely young negro boys and girls" and would "pay a liberal price in cash" for them. Interested parties could find him "at the bar of Joshua Tennison's hotel." Located at the corner of Fourteenth Street and Pennsylvania Avenue, Tennison's is today the site of the Willard Intercontinental Hotel, two blocks east of the White House. Biding his time at the bar, Franklin might have eyed President James Monroe.[15]

But Franklin would not be at Tennison's for long. His ad ran for three weeks, and if he gathered enslaved people quickly, he probably left town before then, as he ranged widely among the Chesapeake's hotels, taverns, courthouses, and jails. In 1822, for example, Franklin stowed enslaved people in a Rockville, Maryland, jail that was twenty miles northwest of Washington City. When his prisoners escaped, he deputized an associate who lived in Frederick, a Maryland town nearly thirty miles past Rockville, to pay the reward for their recapture. A few years later, Charles Hulet, the jailor in Frederick County, Virginia, took into his cells a twenty-year-old enslaved woman named Jane, who admitted under questioning that she had run from Isaac Franklin. Jailors commonly advertised when they apprehended a fugitive from slavery, hoping that a white person would retrieve his "property" and cover imprisonment costs. Frederick County was nearly one hundred miles west of Washington City, and when Hulet thought about where Franklin might see an advertisement for Jane, he decided to use the *Enquirer*, published in Richmond. That city was over 150 miles from Frederick County, but Hulet knew Franklin covered a lot of ground.[16]

Yet even as he roved over hundreds of miles finding people to buy, Franklin gestured toward greater fixity and toward a new model of what it meant to be a domestic slave trader. In 1819, his brother James rented a lot in Alexandria, eight blocks from the Potomac River. James had come to Alexandria on and off for years, but having since settled down in Tennessee, it is unlikely that he actively used the property. More probable is that Isaac maintained the two-acre site as a base of operations and a holding pen where he could stash enslaved people as he collected them. James, meanwhile, bore responsibility for the lease in exchange for a cut of his brother's business.[17]

The business got bigger every year. As it did, Isaac Franklin became less directly involved in every transaction and every movement of enslaved people he engineered, and he started hiring agents to buy slaves on his behalf and deliver them to him in the lower South. Contracting out parts of his operation made sense in part because it was getting too big to allow him do everything himself. But Franklin also began staying longer stretches in Mississippi, which let him realize opportunities he might otherwise miss. By the early 1820s, it is clear that Franklin was making the city of Natchez the dedicated center of his sales activities.[18]

Franklin first came to Natchez with his brothers as the city and its surroundings were evolving past the limited development they had seen for most of the eighteenth century. When the United States formally established the Mississippi Territory in 1798, Natchez became the territorial capital and the heart of the Natchez District, which would eventually be the southwestern portion of the state of Mississippi. Situated about three hundred miles above New Orleans on the eastern shore of a bend in the Mississippi River, Natchez had just over a thousand inhabitants, and they occupied a spot that for years had been an isolated river trading post and a market center for tobacco and indigo grown by countryside planters using slave labor. Most Natchez residents lived atop a two-hundred-foot high bluff overlooking the river. A steep pathway cut diagonally down to the port at the base of the bluff, where a smaller number of people lived and worked in an area known as Under-the-Hill.[19]

There were only around one hundred houses in Natchez in the late 1790s, and the city would always remain compact. But it flourished in the early nineteenth century. Natchez was formally incorporated in 1803, and on a recently expanded grid of streets atop the bluff, there gathered an array of artisans and craftspeople, doctors and lawyers, groceries and market houses, merchants and banks. Natchez had a robust municipal government and several newspapers, and it nurtured a powerful coterie of wealthy planters who came to be referred to colloquially as "nabobs." Most streets were unpaved into the 1820s, and numerous visitors in the territorial era concurred with traveler Christian Schultz, who wrote in 1808 that "the buildings in general are neat, yet I found none within the town that can be considered as elegant." Still, between 1800 and 1820, the number of structures in the city quadrupled, and long after the political capital of Mississippi moved to Jackson in 1821, Natchez was the cultural and economic capital of the state.[20]

Natchez blossomed because white farmers in the Natchez District turned to growing cotton rather than tobacco. In 1794, the Natchez District produced 36,351 pounds of cotton. Four years later, its output was more than 1.2 million pounds, an increase of more than 3,200 percent. No one would have argued with planter William Dunbar, who wrote a colleague in 1799 that cotton was "by far the most profitable crop we have ever undertaken in this country." Drawn by potential profits and by formal congressional sanction of slavery in the Mississippi Territory, the population surged. In 1800, the Mississippi Territory held a little more than 8,800 people, roughly 3,500 of whom were enslaved. Ten years later, the population was a hair above 40,000, and it included more than 17,000 enslaved people. Ten thousand people lived in Natchez's Adams County alone. Fully half of them lived in bondage, as did nearly a third of the 1,512 residents of Natchez proper.[21]

All of this made attractive prospects for the slave trade in Natchez, which predated American sovereignty over the Mississippi Territory. By the 1780s, enslaved people, many of whom had been imported directly from Africa or the Caribbean, could be bought at auction on river landings or on the city's outskirts at the end of an overland route known as the Natchez Trace. In 1782, the Spanish government, whose jurisdiction then included Natchez, declared that regional slave imports would be untaxed. The Natchez city government undid that incentive and began taxing slave sales in 1804, but even as slaves sold in the ensuing years brought healthy returns and fed city coffers, the trade was mostly the province of itinerants such as the Franklin brothers and of merchants who dealt in a range of items. When river traffic and the demands of white farmers for enslaved laborers grew during and immediately after the War of 1812, however, so did the Natchez slave market.[22]

Travelers noticed it right away. Visiting Natchez in 1818, English surgeon Henry Bradshaw Fearon cast his glance toward the river and counted twenty-five flatboats, seven keelboats, and a steamboat in port. Curious about the Black people he spotted on the vessels, he discovered "that fourteen of the flats were freighted with human beings for sale. They had been collected in the several States by slave-dealers, and shipped from Kentucky for a market. They were dressed up to the best advantage, on the same principle that jockeys do horses upon sale." New Hampshire lawyer Estwick Evans, arriving in Natchez at around the same time as Fearon, concluded that there was "no branch of trade" in the area "more brisk and profitable than that of buying and selling negroes." In Natchez, he wrote, slaves were "a subject of continual speculation," brought to market every day "together with other live stock."[23]

Evans found the spectacle horrifying. "How deplorable is the condition of our country," he wrote. "So many bullocks, so many swine, and so many human beings in our market!" He was no less repulsed by the seediness of Natchez Under-the-Hill, which he considered "one of the most wretched places in the world." Sickly, crowded, and crammed with warehouses, gambling halls, taverns, brothels, and other businesses catering to boatmen coming off weeks of river travel, Under-the-Hill was notorious for debauchery and violence. It was an interracial and mostly working-class environment, and some of its reputation was certainly attributable to elite moralizing. But for enslaved people trafficked on the Mississippi River, Under-the-Hill was a squalid introduction to a part of the country where the vultures and buzzards roosting atop the bluff and watching them disembark augured poorly.[24]

Slaves not sold right off the boat or on landings in Under-the-Hill trudged up the bluff, past a stream of mule-drawn carts, and into the city, where the streets lined with cotton bales signaled the toil that lay ahead. Once in the city proper, the enslaved might be sold at public auction in front of the Franklin Hotel on North

Second Street, at the auction house of John Henderson, or at the Market House across from city hall. Tiernan and Alexander, on Fourth Street, and J. & D. Long, on Main Street, also routinely offered "likely negroes" for sale, as did other merchant houses. But slaves might be sold nearly anywhere. As an early historian of the slave trade noted, in Natchez, "negroes were sold in almost every street."[25]

Not everything went smoothly for Isaac Franklin as he found his footing in Natchez without his older brothers. A few months after leaving Andrew Jackson's army in 1814, for example, Franklin picked a fight with Gabriel Tichenor, the cashier of the Bank of the Mississippi. Established in 1809, the bank was the first in the Mississippi Territory. For a while, it was the only one, and it was thus unwise, at the very least, for Franklin to go all over town telling anyone who would listen that Tichenor had changed the figure on a check and pocketed the difference out of Franklin's account. Franklin told some people that Tichenor was "a damned rascal." He told others he would have Tichenor "brought up before the Board of Directors" of the bank because he had "committed forgery" and "cheated" Franklin "out of fifty dollars." Tichenor sued Franklin for slander, and Franklin backed down, contending that he had not meant the things he said "maliciously, or with an intention of injuring" Tichenor "in any manner whatsoever." It was an implausible claim, but it showed Franklin was learning that a slave trader needed friendly banks and friendly bankers, and that blustering accusations was not the road to friendship.[26]

Franklin also learned that slave traders would always have some unsatisfied customers. In 1819, a planter named John Hutchins sued Franklin in Natchez for damages, claiming he had bought nine people for $6,400, with Franklin's guarantee that the slaves would be "sound." But, Hutchins insisted, Franklin had "craftily and subtilly deceived" him, as six of the enslaved were "lame, blind, consumptive, cancerous, and otherwise diseased." That made them "of no use

or value" to Hutchins, who wanted his money back. It was not uncommon for the enslaved to become debilitated on forced southern
migrations. Signs of their exhaustion and illness might not be obvious to someone who prioritized selling them over caring for their
health, and Hutchins's assertion that Franklin had intentionally de-
frauded him demonstrated the suspicion that often attached to slave
traders in some degree. Whether deceit or dereliction accounted
for the condition of the people Franklin sold, he stonewalled in the
face of Hutchins's demands, and he paid a local law firm to defend
him in court. Isaac Franklin was not one to return a lot of money
without a fight.[27]

But despite the occasional lawsuit and unnecessary argument,
Franklin came out of the 1810s poised for growth. In the spring of
1821, he started selling enslaved people in Natchez from a house and
several attached lots a couple of blocks east of the original city limits.
Located along the road leading to the nearby village of Washington,
in a suburb known as Williamsburg that had been laid out in 1812,
it was no provisional place of business like the makeshift pens some
traders rented in the city. Franklin would use the property for more
than a decade, and initially his brother William worked alongside
him. Five years Isaac's junior and twenty-seven years old when he
arranged to occupy the house and lots on the Washington road in
1821, William Franklin became the fourth son of James Franklin
Sr. to work in the slave trade.[28]

The Franklin brothers found their Natchez facility through the
financial convolutions of the slave trade itself. They initially acquired
rights to it from a merchant named Samuel W. Butler and his wife
Cynthiann, who together had a partial interest in the property from
the estate of Cynthiann's mother. It was an unusual arrangement, in
which the Butlers deeded their interest to William Franklin for five
dollars while providing that ultimately that interest was to go toward the "education and support" of their children. Property owners
generally executed deeds of trust like these to cover a debt, and it

appears the deal was related to Isaac Franklin's sale of three enslaved people to Samuel Butler months earlier.

In May 1820, Franklin sold Butler a sixteen-year-old named Mary, a six-year-old named Mariah, and a four-year-old named Harry for $1,450. But Butler only paid a little more than half the purchase price in cash, executing for the rest a note that would be due, with interest, in one year, and mortgaging Mary, Mariah, and Harry back to Franklin to secure the loan. With the note about to come due in the spring of 1821, Franklin wanted additional security, and the Butlers probably offered their interest in the Washington road property. If the Butlers paid the debt, they would retain their interest. If not, it could be sold to pay Isaac Franklin. In the meantime, William Franklin could use the property as he wished. In short, the Franklins used leverage gained from selling slaves to take possession of real estate that they then used as a commercial location for selling more slaves.[29]

Samuel Butler owned other real estate in and around Natchez, but the Franklins may have wanted rights to the place on the Washington road in particular. The road led directly to the Natchez Trace, which meant that the Franklins or any of their agents bringing enslaved people overland would go right past the location on their way into Natchez, and that travelers, migrants, and planters heading to and from the city would see the Franklins' place of business without even having to look for it. Slaves the Franklins brought by water would have to walk ten or twelve blocks through the city after coming up from the river, but space for confining a significant number of people was probably easier to come by in the suburbs. And the price could not be beat. When they set up shop on the Washington road, the Franklins were among the earliest, and perhaps the first, professional slave traders to establish a regular place of business in Natchez.[30]

William Franklin got married in Sumner County in the fall of 1821, started buying real estate in the county two years later, had his first child soon after that, and headed back to Tennessee for good. But Isaac Franklin further ensconced himself in his commercial life in Mississippi. In February 1823, he spent $200 to buy outright a partial interest in the house and lots on the Washington road that he had been using for nearly two years, and he spent another $720 for unqualified ownership of an adjacent corner lot. Now a full-fledged property owner in the city of Natchez, Franklin appeared in the Adams County tax records for 1823 as the holder of two town lots valued at $3,000.[31]

The available evidence suggests Franklin sold enslaved people mostly one or a few at a time, primarily to planters and merchants who lived in or near the city. By itself, the patronage of such wealthy customers indicated that both Franklin's business and his reputation in Natchez were thriving. More telling still was the fact that in the mid-1820s, he became a member of the city's Jackson Association. Founded to support the political ambitions of Andrew Jackson, who first ran for president in 1824, the Jackson Association had about three dozen members, most of whom were planters, lawyers, bankers, and other members of the Natchez economic and political elite. Increasingly accepted by the rich and powerful in Natchez as a businessman of good standing, Isaac Franklin eased into a reciprocally supportive and productive relationship with the gentry class of the cotton frontier.[32]

He also began working with yet another family member. Replacing William Franklin as a business associate was Smith Franklin, the oldest son of Isaac Franklin's brother John. Born in 1801, Smith Franklin had already had some financial dealings with his uncle by 1823, and in 1824, he went to Natchez to see the slave-trading operation for himself. When he got there, he sold his horse and an enslaved woman he had brought with him. And when he left, he headed to Maryland with profits from those sales and $400 in cash that Isaac Franklin put in his pocket. In Maryland, he either passed the money to agents buying slaves on his uncle's behalf, used the money himself to buy slaves to send to Natchez, or both. Whatever the case, in February 1825, Smith Franklin started advertising in the Alexandria *Phenix Gazette*. "Cash in Market," read his first ad. "Wanted to purchase 60 OR 80 NEGROES of both sexes, between the ages of 12 and 25 years, either separately or in families; for which the highest price will be given." Sellers could find him at the Indian Queen Tavern.[33]

Smith Franklin stationed himself in Alexandria for the next three years, advertising that he had cash to spend and typically announcing that he was looking for twenty-five or thirty enslaved people. His uncle periodically passed through town, stopping to check in and pick up a little extra cash, preferably banknotes from the Second Bank of the United States. Those were reliable notes that anyone would accept, and after Isaac Franklin met with his nephew, he usually took the money to Maryland, where he talked with purchasing agents and bought slaves before returning to Mississippi.[34]

By 1827, the contours of Isaac Franklin's business were becoming more defined. Using a partner stationed in Virginia and purchasing agents in Maryland, whose work he supervised and supplemented by sometimes traveling to the Chesapeake himself, Franklin moved enslaved people, in groups of a few dozen at a time and mostly overland, to Natchez. There, he made sales to merchants and cotton planters and sent those proceeds back to the Chesapeake to keep the cycle of money for human beings going. Franklin had a good feel for that process, and things were going so well that he bought another third of an acre contiguous with his sales facility on the Washington road. He was planning to bring even more enslaved people to the city, and he was going to need more space.[35]

As he built his business, Isaac Franklin established trust and connections not only with the elites who made up his customer base but also with his fellow slave traders, and there seemed to be more and more of them, every place he traveled, with each passing year. When he found one outside his immediate family with whom he wanted to join forces, the relationship they forged would be the most significant and lucrative of Franklin's life.

John Armfield never had much interest in farming, but neither did he leave his father's household intending to become a slave trader. Armfield first appears in the public record as an adult in the fall of 1817, when he was twenty years old and witnessed a land transaction as a favor to William Dickey. A near neighbor to Armfield's father, Dickey was also John Armfield's brother-in-law, having recently married his sister Polly, and he was a person of some import in Guilford County. Dickey owned more than 750 acres of land and enslaved several people. He had been a colonel in the War of 1812, he would serve briefly in the North Carolina legislature, and when he married Polly Armfield, he was county sheriff.[36]

John Armfield and William Dickey were close until Dickey's untimely death in 1824, their connection grounded in mutual admiration and familial association, and also in business. In 1819, Dickey spotted Armfield some money to open a store in Surry County, two counties west of Guilford. Armfield purchased a retail license to operate in the county, and he received permission from the county court to sell alcohol on the premises as well.[37]

If John Armfield really left Guilford County in a huff after fighting with his father, as the old family story has it, he did not go far. The store he opened was only fifty or sixty miles northwest of his father's farm, about a two-day trip on horseback. Armfield's sister Betsy married a Surry County man named Moses Swaim shortly after Armfield bought his retail license, which may explain how Armfield chose the location. But Surry County would have felt familiar anyway, because it was a lot like the place where Armfield had grown up. Roughly a thousand square miles in size and extending southward for forty miles from the Virginia border, Surry lay mostly in the Piedmont, with valleys and hills that rose into the Blue

Ridge Mountains in the western portion of the county. Like Guilford, Surry had a pre-Revolutionary history of Regulator activity, a
sizable Quaker presence, and a mixed economy grounded in grain
and tobacco with some small industry and manufacturing. Several
rivers and numerous creeks and streams ran through the county, and
a scattering of small villages had sprung up by the early nineteenth
century to take advantage of their flows.[38]

The demographics of slavery in Surry County also looked like
those of Guilford County. In 1820, 12,320 people lived in Surry.
Nearly 90 percent of them were white. Slaveholding was more concentrated in Surry than in Guilford, with twice as many men paying
taxes on more than five slaves in the late 1810s, despite a smaller
white population, and with around half a dozen men who enslaved
more than twenty people. But as in Guilford, most Surry County
slaveholders enslaved fewer than five people, and the vast majority
of white farmers enslaved no one at all.[39]

For several years, John Armfield did reasonably well for himself
in Surry County. No records of his store survive, but tax rolls valued
its merchandise in 1820 at "between two thousand and five thousand
dollars." If his was similar to stores in other North Carolina cities and
towns, Armfield carried things such as coffee, tea, tobacco, sugar,
spices, flour, kitchenware, crockery, and other grocery and household
items. If his inventory included fancier goods, Armfield might have
sold linens, silks, and perhaps some men's and women's clothing.
He probably sold rum, brandy, and other liquors, and his license to
"retail spirits at his house" almost certainly meant he ran something
like a small tavern alongside the mercantile establishment.[40]

Particularly for rural communities in the early nineteenth century, storekeepers like John Armfield provided gathering places,
brought items from distant markets, and offered goods on credit to
cash-poor farmers. The last would have been especially vital at the
time Armfield opened his store, coinciding as it did with the Panic
of 1819, which left many farmers deep in debt and scrambling to

survive financially. That some of Armfield's customers were unable to pay their bills is suggested by Armfield's coming into possession in 1820 or 1821 of three small pieces of land in Surry County, totaling between 450 and 500 acres, near a stream known as the Little Fish River. Slaves, of course, could also be used to pay debts, and Armfield may have acquired the lone enslaved person on whom he paid taxes in 1822 that way too.[41]

But collecting debts from struggling people was a delicate matter, and regardless of the service Armfield provided white farmers with his store, he was an aggressive creditor who harassed and infuriated customers in arrears. John Armfield and William Dickey repeatedly sued Surry County residents to recover debts, and they received several judgments in their favor. But Armfield's belligerence when he went to take what he was owed did not sit well with the losing parties.

In February 1821, for example, Armfield and Dickey sued Richard and William Goldin. The Goldins had served as surety for a debt of $100 assumed by their neighbor, Hosea Chaney, and Chaney's inability to pay made the Goldins responsible instead. The court ruled for Armfield and Dickey, but the collection went poorly. Armfield called on Constable Richard Wright for assistance, only to end up in an argument with the Goldins that may have escalated into a fight, as William Goldin filed a criminal complaint against Armfield and Wright for assault.[42]

The assault case was ultimately dismissed, and Armfield got what he was owed in 1822 when the Surry County sheriff foreclosed on three hundred acres of William Goldin's land. But Armfield's impatience and lack of consideration for his customers' travails could backfire altogether. Sometimes he simply pressed too hard. At around the time that he sued the Goldins, Armfield sued a small farmer named William Patterson for a debt of forty-two dollars, and he followed up on the judgment in his favor by again asking Richard Wright for help. When Patterson's son Charles saw Armfield and

Wright approaching the Patterson family home, he pushed the door closed to keep them from entering. But Wright forced his way inside, which brought him and Armfield criminal charges for trespass. This time, a jury found them guilty, and the court issued a fifty-dollar fine. Armfield appealed the case to the North Carolina Supreme Court, which upheld the verdict, and William Patterson then filed a civil suit for damages. It is not clear that Patterson ever squared his debt to Armfield, and the fine Armfield had to pay was more than he would have recovered anyway.[43]

John Armfield appears often in Surry County court records in the early 1820s. He was on other occasions on the receiving end of state charges for trespass, conspiracy, and assault, seemingly under similar circumstances, and he was found guilty of trespass again at least once. But the incident at William Patterson's farm, and the subsequent prosecution, appears to have chastened him, and even as cases in which he was involved dragged on through the courts for a few more years, he became noticeably less litigious. He made other trouble for himself nonetheless, with potentially greater consequences.[44]

Shortly after he moved to Surry County, Armfield entered into a relationship with a woman a few years his junior named Mary Taliaferro. Like Armfield's sister, she went by Polly. Her family was not especially wealthy, but her father Charles was from an old Virginia family, represented Surry County in the state legislature in the 1810s, and owned 350 acres of land and paid taxes on five enslaved people. For a young man starting out in life who was looking to make a respectable future and perhaps a family, Polly Taliaferro was a good match.[45]

But if John Armfield ever intended to marry her, he changed his mind. In the spring of 1824, Taliaferro testified that Armfield was the father of her newborn child, and the state filed charges to compel him to pay child support. Armfield put up fifty dollars recognizance, which bound him "to appear & answer for bastardy." When the case came before the Surry County Court of Pleas and Quarter Sessions that summer, however, Armfield was gone. He forfeited his recognizance money, and he could not be found when the court ordered him to pay Taliaferro for the first year's maintenance of their child. He could not be found the following year either, and Taliaferro took him to court again.[46]

In the fall of 1826, Taliaferro finally received what the court had ordered she be paid, though John Armfield did not return to Surry County to pay it. Months earlier, Armfield had given power of attorney to deal with outstanding legal controversies in the county to William Hanner. A lawyer who had married Armfield's sister Polly after William Dickey's death, Hanner settled the bastardy case on his brother-in-law's behalf. John Armfield himself, having started promisingly only to prove commercially obnoxious and personally dishonorable, as well as a deadbeat father, had by then long since worn out his welcome in Surry County. When he left, nearly two years before Hanner settled his bastardy case, he knew he had to find something else to do and somewhere else to do it.[47]

A short time after John Armfield decamped from Surry County, he met Isaac Franklin. With hindsight it must have seemed like fate, though surely it was happenstance. Armfield himself recalled that he made Franklin's acquaintance in 1824, and in the early twentieth century, a correspondent of a Nashville journalist wrote that he had always been told that Armfield "was driving a stage in Old Virginia when Isaac Franklin found him and brought him to Tennessee." The story was perhaps half true.[48]

It is easy to imagine an aimless John Armfield turning to stagecoach driving. Averse to going back to Guilford County and having effectively exiled himself from Surry County, he could scout for new ventures as he drove. He could talk with passengers about where they were from and where they were going, about what they did and the things they knew. It is no more difficult to imagine Isaac Franklin passing through Virginia, boarding Armfield's stage, striking up conversation, and, during the dull hours of bumpy and dusty travel, suggesting consideration of the slave trade. Armfield, after all, had experience managing accounts, extending credit, and collecting debts. He knew his way around a courtroom and a lawsuit, and he understood markets for merchandise. Perhaps Franklin euphemized the peculiarities of the slave trade compared with running a store, or perhaps he told Armfield bluntly what was involved when the merchandise was human. Either way, some of the basic principles were the same, and for a white man with some pluck and few ethics, there was money to be made dealing in Black people. Franklin might well have counseled Armfield to give it some thought.

But the notion that Franklin and Armfield were so taken with each other that Franklin got Armfield to drop what he was doing and go with him to Tennessee is entirely fanciful. There is no evidence suggesting that John Armfield visited Sumner County in the 1820s, nor any that he and Isaac Franklin had much of a personal or business relationship at all for several years after 1824. However well the pair may have hit it off when their paths first crossed, neither man was so impulsive as to believe in the sudden finding of a kindred spirit thanks to a chance encounter on the Virginia stage.[49]

Still, Armfield did take Franklin's advice. In 1825, he went back to Guilford County, put aside lingering friction and disagreements, and told his father he planned to go into the slave trade and needed his help. Nathan Armfield was willing to oblige. John Armfield bought a gray horse from his father for $100. To get some capital to buy slaves, he persuaded his father to borrow money on his behalf from neighbors, and he convinced his father to let him use an enslaved man who, in John Armfield's recollection, would be "a trusty boy to travel with." Nathan Armfield first offered "a boy named Tony." But John Armfield had his eye on someone else. In Tony's place, he wanted a seventeen-year-old named Walker.[50]

Nathan Armfield either did not entirely trust his son, did not trust the line of work he had decided to pursue, or both, for he refused to give or sell Walker to him outright, despite repeated entreaties.

Nathan Armfield liked Walker, and while it was a proprietary fond-ness that came in the context of Walker's enslavement, it extended far enough that he wanted to protect him from the temptations his son might have to cash in on the young man as he conducted his business.

Those temptations came. John Armfield would eventually tell his father that he had been offered $1,000 for Walker. But Nathan Armfield declined the money, and he made it clear that Walker was not for sale at any price. A neighbor remembered telling Nathan Armfield that he would have taken the deal his son proposed, but Armfield replied that "he did not intend Walker should ever serve anybody but himself." Armfield told another neighbor that "he would not give a bill of sale for Walker to any man while he lived," and he told his nephew Solomon Armfield "that no reasonable sum of money would induce him to sell Walker." So far as Nathan Arm-field was concerned, his son could borrow Walker long-term, but he could never own him and he could never sell him. Too many suspicions gnawed at Nathan Armfield about his son's judgment and character to allow it. As he observed to another nephew, William A. Armfield, Walker would always be his property, because "he had never raised a child that he thought enough of to give said boy to."[51]

Whether or not he belonged to John Armfield, Walker was by Armfield's side as he plunged into the slave trade in 1825, bringing slaves from Virginia back to North Carolina, where he either sold them or carried them still farther south. People in Guilford County often saw Walker in Armfield's "employment." A farmer named Isaac Russom remembered that Walker "frequently went with John Armfield to the north after his negroes," and others recalled that Armfield gave Walker responsibility for managing captives laid up on William Dickey's property, which Armfield used for a time while acting as executor of Dickey's estate. Joseph Newman, who saw Arm-field "at Dickeys old plaice with a drove of negroes" in 1825 or 1826, said Walker was there too, "cngaged in waiting on the negroes," while Thomas McCaulock believed Armfield appointed Walker as "a kind of offerseer." Salathiel Swaim, a relative of Betsy Armfield's husband, described Walker's role in broad terms, saying that he saw him "attending to Johns business."[52]

Walker would serve as Armfield's valet, traveling companion, and assistant in the slave trade for at least a decade after 1825. Scarce archival traces of Walker's own voice make him a mostly silent if constant presence alongside Armfield. But many slave traders had an enslaved man accompanying them as factotum and superintendent, and their stories show the ways that John Armfield placed Walker in a hopeless moral position that was a unique cruelty in its own right.

William Wells Brown recalled working for a slave trader as "the longest year" he ever lived. Born enslaved in Kentucky in 1814, Brown grew up in Missouri, and in the early 1830s, he was hired out to work for a Saint Louis trader named William Walker. Brown would eventually escape from slavery, and he became an antislavery lecturer, a novelist, and a playwright. But working for Walker so haunted him that even decades later he could not find words to convey the experience adequately. "When I learned the fact of my having been hired to a negro speculator, or a 'soul-driver' as they are generally called among slaves," Brown remembered, "no one can tell my emotions."[53]

While working for William Walker, Brown escorted three coffles of enslaved people, several dozen at a time, from Saint Louis down the Mississippi River by steamboat to Natchez, New Orleans, and other smaller cities and towns. He rode with Walker through the Missouri countryside, accumulating slaves for sale and walking them along roads worse than any he had ever seen. He tried comforting a woman whom Walker repeatedly raped, and he saw Walker snatch an infant from another woman "as you would a cat by the leg" and bestow the child upon an acquaintance because he found its crying irritating. Brown saw yet another woman, whom Walker had separated from her husband and children, leap from a steamboat and drown herself, and he helped stow the enslaved in chains below decks, noting that "it was almost impossible to keep that part of the boat clean." He followed orders to shave the beards of older enslaved men, pluck out gray hairs, and blacken what remained so Walker could disguise their ages. Brown gave fresh clothing to people Walker offered for sale, to replace the rags they were wearing by the end of their forced migration, and he saw them compelled to dance, often "when their cheeks were wet with tears," so they might "appear cheerful and happy" for prospective buyers.[54]

Brown had no choice but to do as he was told. He begged his enslaver not to make him stay with Walker, as seeing his "fellow-creatures bought and sold" left him "heart-sick," but his pleas were in vain. Walker, meanwhile, threatened repeatedly to beat Brown, and once sent him to a jailor to be whipped because he overfilled the wineglasses of Walker's customers. Impracticable though it was for Brown to alter his circumstances, the roles he played in furthering the destruction of enslaved families, the degradation of those destined for sale, and the despair so deep that death seemed a respite took a psychological toll. It was only one year, but it plagued his conscience for the rest of his life.[55]

Having to witness and participate in the slave trade's ghastliness was one harrowing element of being a trader's assistant. Being ceaselessly reminded of one's own vulnerability to the trade's vagaries was another. All enslaved people understood their susceptibility to being sold. But men in William Wells Brown's position were constantly exposed to the thinness of the line separating them from those who were living out their nightmares. Brown never really believed either his enslaver or William Walker when they assured him he would return home again, and certainly the Walker who accompanied John Armfield did not rest easy because technically he belonged to Armfield's father. If John Armfield ever relayed an offer that was just too good to pass up, Walker knew he could find himself sold in an instant.

Leeriness made dissembling and the ability to manipulate the trader one worked with into essential survival skills. William Hayden understood that. Born in Virginia in 1785, Hayden was sold away from his mother as a five-year-old and then to a series of slaveholders until 1817, when he became "the waiting man" of a Kentucky slave trader named Thomas Phillips. Known to everyone as Billy, Hayden worked alongside Phillips for more than six years, traveling with him as he gathered slaves in Kentucky and the Chesapeake and brought them by flatboat to Mississippi and southern Louisiana for sale. Hayden believed a "supernatural Power" and "spiritual guide" protected him, and he never doubted he would one day acquire his freedom. Ultimately, though, it was his own resourcefulness that got him through.

For a time, Hayden tried ingratiating himself with Phillips and learning as much as possible about his designs. On his first trip down the Mississippi River, Hayden "feigned to be asleep" while he listened to Phillips and a partner argue about whether or not to sell him. When they got to Louisiana and Phillips collected his mail, Hayden pretended to be illiterate, so he could read Phillips's correspondence covertly and stay "advised of all his proceedings." When Phillips asked Hayden if he wanted to accompany him and a colleague to Virginia, Hayden thought keeping close was the best way to stay abreast of Phillips's "intentions with regard to me," and he thrilled inside at the prospect of contacting the mother he had not seen in decades. But he only told Phillips "that his will was my pleasure," and he put on "a care-devil disposition as to what" Phillips and his colleague "did with me or mine."

This sham obsequiousness had its desired effect, as Hayden's "conduct and fidelity" earned him "the entire confidence of Phillips." He began using that confidence to his advantage, expanding the license Phillips gave him to come and go as he pleased when his duties allowed it and looking for the right moment to try to liberate himself altogether. "I knew too well," Hayden later recalled, that "my deliverance, and the means of acquiring it" was "to play false to my own conscience, and my master's interests."

Playing false to his own conscience exacted a price, though, as showing loyalty to Phillips sometimes meant betraying other enslaved people. When Hayden overheard several men whom Phillips was about to ship south contriving "to effect their freedom" by "put[ting] to death all the whites on board" a flatboat, for example, he divulged the plot. But Hayden consoled himself with the knowledge that his position meant the mutineers probably would have killed him too, and he saved the plot's ringleader from certain death by withholding his name when Phillips demanded it. On other occasions, Hayden carried out "little acts of kindness" toward Phillips's captives, and he tried to maintain a semblance of dignity and self-respect in his deeply compromised circumstances by determining "to obey the orders of none, save" Phillips, "whom I knew had paid the price for me, and claimed me as his body servant."

Hayden's refusal to respect the authority of anyone other than Thomas Phillips engendered confusion and rage among other white men. But it fed Phillips's ego to believe he was the only white man who could command Hayden's deference, and it led him to treat Hayden "with as much courtesy as a master can well find heart to exercise towards his slave." Still, their relationship never moved past mutual wariness. Phillips always suspected Hayden might run away, and Hayden always suspected Phillips would renege on a deal they had made whereby Phillips agreed not to sell Hayden and to allow him to purchase his freedom if he could come up with $600. An enslaved person could never have faith in a slave trader, and as Hayden made down payments on his own body with money he earned as a barber when he and Phillips were not traveling, he "feared Phillips had some sinister motives in view, and designed to cheat me out of my money and my freedom."

He was right. Phillips fell into debt, and he tried selling Hayden with the intention of keeping both the purchase price and the several hundred dollars Hayden had deposited with him. But Hayden had insisted that Phillips put their arrangement in writing, and he kept the receipts documenting that Phillips had his money. With the assistance of some sympathetic white people in Kentucky who saw Thomas Phillips for the conniving wretch he was, Billy Hayden became a free man in 1824.[56]

Unlike William Wells Brown and William Hayden, Walker would never take his own freedom, nor would he acquire it from anyone in the Armfield family. But the wrenching dilemmas of his life still resembled theirs. So did the imperatives to stay near to John Armfield and watch what he was doing, to give him what he wanted from a slave without surrendering self-regard, and to know that any affection or esteem Armfield professed brought with it neither security nor obligation. For Walker to have remained so close to Armfield for as long as he did could only mean he was a perceptive and careful man who never let down his guard. He also must have been an intensely lonely and isolated man who saw things that could never be unseen.[57]

B y 1826, some of the things Walker saw become evident in the public record. In March, John Armfield was in New Orleans, where he sold a twenty-two-year-old enslaved man named Perry for $400 to a cotton factor and shipping agent named Jacob Hart. Joining Armfield and Walker in the city was Armfield's brother-in-law, William Hanner, who was not only a travel companion. Hanner was also a business partner who occasionally acted as Armfield's agent on slave sales in the lower South.[58]

A week after selling Perry to Jacob Hart, Armfield, Hanner, and Walker boarded the brig *Mark*. A speedy two-masted vessel built in a Maine shipyard, the *Mark* had sailed out of Portland the previous November after delivering flour and tobacco from Richmond to several northern ports. Leaving Portland with a hold full of

New England lime quarried for use in plaster and mortar, the *Mark* made its way to Kingston, Jamaica, arriving early in February, and then it ventured for New Orleans, where it picked up passengers and a cargo of "pork, lard and cotton." The *Mark* then headed out, sailing through the Gulf of Mexico, around Florida, and up the East Coast to Baltimore, where it arrived on April 19. The passengers disembarked, the freight was delivered to a merchant named Isaac Reynolds, and the *Mark* cleared Baltimore for Boston. Like hundreds of other merchant ships, the *Mark* facilitated the commerce and travel that integrated and fused together the free and slave economies of the western Atlantic.[59]

William Hanner returned to North Carolina, John Armfield and Walker stayed in the Chesapeake, and Armfield continued his work. Seven weeks after landing in Baltimore, Armfield was in Alexandria, where he announced in the newspaper that he would give cash "to purchase THIRTY-FIVE OR FORTY LIKELY NEGROES, either separately or in families." Anyone who wanted to contact Armfield could leave a message at the post office. Alternatively, they could find him at Elias P. Legg's tavern on St. Asaph Street, adjacent to what the city tax assessor called a "Negro Prison and Lot" where traders stockpiled slaves until they were ready to move them. From Alexandria, Armfield transported the people he bought to Natchez. On the Adams County tax rolls for 1826, Armfield was recorded as a "transient merchant." He reported $3,620 in slave sales.[60]

In Alexandria's hotels and taverns, Armfield would have gotten to know Isaac Franklin's nephew, Smith. He would have encountered Isaac Franklin himself, as they now traveled the same circuits and did business in the same locations. And somewhere along the way, both Armfield and Franklin would have happened upon Rice Ballard. Around the time he turned eighteen, Ballard left his father's house and established an independent household in Spotsylvania County. The next year, in the spring of 1819, he bought a bedstead, an oven, and a whipsaw at the estate sale of an uncle. The last item was an expensive piece of equipment used by professional sawyers, and Ballard may have used it working for Samuel Alsop Jr., helping build the houses Alsop designed for the wealthy. For the next few years, Ballard appears on the Spotsylvania tax rolls, the owner of one horse but of neither land nor slaves. After 1822, however, he drops off the rolls. Instead of working in the lumber business, building houses for Sam Alsop, or doing whatever else he was doing in Spotsylvania, Rice Ballard turned to the slave trade.[61]

The earliest scrap of material preserved in Ballard's personal papers is a ten-dollar note from a Virginia bank. Dated July 1822, it is nearly six years older than anything else in the collection, and one wonders whether Ballard preserved it as a souvenir from when he started working outside Spotsylvania County, like a framed dollar bill a restaurateur might mount behind the register. But Ballard's customers wanted enslaved people, and he started acquiring them at least six months before that banknote was issued. On January 2, 1822, he advertised in Alexandria that he had "three handsome young horses, suitable for saddle or harness," and that he wanted to swap them "for young negroes." He did not clarify the exchange rate of young horses for young humans, but he also had cash to buy "50 or 60 young NEGROES" beyond what the animals brought in trade.[62]

Situating himself, as John Armfield would several years later, at a tavern run by Elias P. Legg, Ballard met another slave trader named I. S. Graves. The two briefly worked together as "GRAVES & BALLARD," advertising near the end of January that they would pay "the highest prices in cash" for "30 or 40 likely young Negroes if application is made immediately." But the partnership was short-lived. Graves was advertising on his own accord just weeks later, and Ballard had a new partner, and a bankroll for his incipient business, in Sam Alsop.[63]

Though conclusive signs that Alsop and Ballard partnered in the slave trade do not appear until the second half of the 1820s, hints of it come through sooner. Tax records tell the story. Between 1817 and 1822, the number of slaves on whom Sam Alsop paid taxes in Spotsylvania County changed relatively little, fluctuating between forty-one and forty-seven people. But in 1823, the number increased dramatically, to sixty-five people, a jump coinciding with the beginning of Rice Ballard's slave trading that hardly seems like chance. Alsop also had dozens of horses on his properties. Almost certainly, he provided Ballard with horses and cash, and Ballard exchanged them for slaves in Alexandria. Then he walked the slaves back to Spotsylvania and kept them on Alsop's land, which both provided Alsop with temporary extra laborers and saved money that might have been spent renting space in a pen or a jail. It was a practice Ballard would maintain for years.[64]

From there, Ballard and Alsop may have sold some of the enslaved at Alsop's tavern. But within a few years, Ballard, assisted by Alsop's son Joseph, was selling them in Natchez, where in January 1828 Ballard brought twenty-five men and thirteen women and where he paid taxes on $5,100 in slave sales a few months later. In fact, while Isaac Franklin, John Armfield, and Rice Ballard must have known each other before the calendar turned from 1827 to 1828, it is at that moment, in Natchez, that the three can first be located definitively in the same place at the same time.[65]

Yet they were not working together. Franklin worked with his nephew. Ballard worked with I. S. Graves and then with Sam and Joseph Alsop. Armfield sometimes worked with his brother-in-law, and for part of the winter of 1827–1828, he worked with Joseph Meek Jr. Born in Washington County, Virginia, in the Blue Ridge Mountains near the Tennessee border, Meek had been advertising in Baltimore newspapers since 1824 that he had "Cash for Negroes." He would be a slave trader until at least the mid-1830s, and so were two of his brothers. But in late 1827 and early 1828, Joseph Meek and John Armfield pooled money and effort, and they split profits on a small number of enslaved people they sold to planters and merchants in Natchez and New Orleans.[66]

By the start of 1828, then, Rice Ballard and John Armfield, like Isaac Franklin, had established slave-trade businesses in which they moved coffles of three or four dozen enslaved people at a time from export markets of the Chesapeake to import markets of the lower South. Trafficking the enslaved at least once a year, mostly over land by forced march and on the water along rivers, they operated on a larger and more continuous scale than men who wandered through a place buying a small agglomeration of slaves, appeared in a city or town to make fast money on sales, and were never seen again. Franklin in particular had a bigger and more sophisticated business, with a permanent facility in Natchez, a relative stationed in Alexandria making purchases, and relationships with banks and with political and economic elites rooted in two decades of trading.

These operations entailed managing organizational complexity and handling significant sums of money. But not even Franklin had achieved the magnitude of the largest slave dealers and merchant firms who provided cotton frontier farmers and labor lords with bound Black workers. Among the dozen or so traders who advertised in Alexandria between 1824 and 1828, Smith Franklin's usual hunt for twenty-five or thirty people at a time made him and his uncle bigger players than Robert Windsor, who wanted "to purchase a few SLAVES of both sexes," or A. W. Brandon, who was looking to buy "fifteen YOUNG NEGROES, consisting of boys and girls." So did John Armfield's search for thirty-five or forty people. But neither Franklin nor Armfield quite had the regular capacity or the cash to "pay the very highest prices for 50 or 60 Young Men and Girls, from 14 to 25 years," as Ira Bowman claimed he could. Similarly, at the sales end in Natchez, Armfield was one of thirty-three "transient merchants" who paid taxes on slave sales in 1826, but his sales figures lagged behind those of twelve other men, and the taxes Rice Ballard paid in 1827 paled in comparison to those of resident merchant traders such as Leon Chabert or Thomas Henderson.[67]

Yet Franklin, Armfield, and Ballard had wider aspirations. By 1828, they had created businesses spanning enormous distances, buying and selling enslaved people whose labor and monetary value braided disparate geographic regions into the interwoven and expanding whole of the United States. As they did, they helped foster something resembling a national market in commoditized human beings that paralleled the development of national markets in an array of other goods. But they wanted to be even bigger and more sprawling. They shared an affinity and a talent for their particular kind of American entrepreneurship, in which white men made themselves on the difference between what Black people had been exploited for in one place and what they could be exploited for in another.

What it meant to make yourself that way could be measured financially in profits, in ledger entries recording a trader's share of the capital white Americans collectively extracted from the bodies of the enslaved. But there were other ways. It could be measured in authority and command projected across cities hundreds of miles apart and the landscape in between. It could be measured in the advantage felt over other white men in tavern negotiations with cash in your pocket, and in the confidence drawn from maneuvering in the interlocking worlds of bankers and merchants and planters. And it could be measured in the unchecked ability to dominate and enforce your will on frightened men and women and children who wanted to escape your control but whose chains kept them from doing so. These were some of the things the slave trade brought the traders. For Franklin, Armfield, and Ballard, who found it all exhilarating, reaching for more was a powerful urge. And there was one man who demonstrated what more might look like and what it took to get it. His name was Austin Woolfolk.

Born in North Carolina in 1796, Austin Woolfolk moved to Tennessee as a child. He enlisted in the War of 1812 when he was only sixteen, and he showed logistical skills that would serve him well throughout his career, becoming a lieutenant and quartermaster of his battalion. Months after mustering out of the militia in 1815, Woolfolk went to Baltimore, which then housed around fifty thousand people and was the third-largest city in the United States. Stationing himself in Eli Lilly's tavern at the corner of Howard and Lombard Streets, he began advertising in city newspapers that he wished "to purchase twenty-five or thirty Negroes, of different descriptions, for which a generous price will be given in cash."[68]

Soon, Woolfolk made himself available at multiple taverns and hotels near the harbor, and he dramatically increased the number of slaves he said he wanted to buy. By the spring of 1818, Woolfolk's ads blared that he wanted one hundred or two hundred people at a time. He was in the market for as many enslaved people as sellers had to offer, and when he collected a sufficient number of captives, he marched them south to Augusta, Georgia. His uncle, John Woolfolk, had run a store selling dry goods there since at least 1810, and like John Armfield, John Woolfolk turned to dealing in humans instead.[69]

Even as Austin Woolfolk established a reputation as the man who said he would pay higher prices to buy more slaves "than any Georgiaman in Baltimore," he had ideas for a slave-trading business that would lead him beyond Baltimore and beyond Georgia. He was soon the largest and best-known slave trader in the Chesapeake, and for several years he was the leading trader in the entire country. In the second half of the 1820s alone, Woolfolk purchased between 230 and 460 enslaved people annually, and between 1819 and 1832 he sent more than 2,500 slaves out of the Chesapeake and into the lower South.[70]

Woolfolk's business soared in the 1820s because of a series of innovations he deployed more aggressively than any previous domestic slave trader ever had. Taken separately, each tactic accrued to his benefit and helped him outpace competitors. Taken in concert, they made his operation more expansive, more efficient, and more devastating for the enslaved populations he scavenged.

The first significant measure Woolfolk undertook was establishing a fixed headquarters. In the summer of 1821, a few months after Isaac Franklin settled into his Natchez facility, Woolfolk announced that "persons having business to transact" could find him "in a large white house" on Pratt Street. Several blocks off the Patapsco River basin and just past the Three Tun Tavern, the house lay near "the intersection of the Washington and Frederick roads," a little off to the right for travelers headed west out of Baltimore toward the nation's capital.[71]

Woolfolk noted that the residence had "trees in front," and a visiting antislavery editor remembered it as "a pretty house" that "presented a 'smiling aspect.'" The editor also observed that behind the house was Woolfolk's private jail, equipped with "small grated windows." For the editor, the "chains, fetters, and miserable objects of suffering" imprisoned by Woolfolk "chilled the blood with horror." For Woolfolk, the house and jail were money savers and indicators of the size and permanence of his business. They set him apart from the world of inns and barrooms where smaller traders congregated. Regular businessmen had regular offices, and Woolfolk's was on Pratt Street. He would be there for almost twenty years.[72]

Amplifying Woolfolk's market presence were advertising strategies surpassing those of every other slave trader. Most traders who used newspaper advertisements in the 1820s did so sporadically and temporarily. They placed ads in a single newspaper for a few weeks or months at a time while they were in town, let the ads lapse when they took to the road, and then, perhaps, started advertising anew if and when they returned. But Woolfolk's advertisements almost never stopped, appearing daily in several Baltimore papers for years.[73]

Eventually, Woolfolk enlarged his appeal. In the late 1820s and early 1830s, he started placing ads in newspapers in Washington City and northern Virginia, and he reached beyond the big cities, especially making sure that slaveholders on Maryland's Eastern Shore knew who he was. From Elkton, near the Delaware and Pennsylvania borders, all along the peninsula stretching south through worn-out tobacco districts surrounding Centreville, Easton, Cambridge, Princess Anne, and Snow Hill, readers saw in every issue of at least half a dozen local papers that Austin Woolfolk wanted to buy slaves.[74]

Woolfolk also used more than one medium to spread the word. Among the more vivid childhood memories of Frederick Douglass, who grew up enslaved on the Eastern Shore, were Woolfolk's men, sent "into every town and county in Maryland, announcing their arrival through the papers, and on flaming hand-bills, headed 'cash for negroes.'" Located physically in Baltimore, Austin Woolfolk took advantage of emergent cheap print technology to make it seem as though he were everywhere.[75]

Because Woolfolk could not literally be in so many places at once, he built a network of buyers who fanned out across Maryland's farms, jails, hotels, taverns, auctions, and courthouses. These were the men Douglass observed. Like most American businesses in the early nineteenth century, slave-trading ventures were commonly family ventures, and many in Woolfolk's web of associates were relatives. In March 1824, Woolfolk's younger brother Joseph B. Woolfolk started advertising that he would buy slaves in Baltimore at his brother's house and "at the bar of the Globe Hotel." By the following spring, he had relocated across the Chesapeake Bay to Easton, where he worked out of Solomon Lowe's tavern, located near the county courthouse, jail, and slave auction. Working territory sixty miles to the southeast, out of the towns of Princess Anne and Salisbury, was another Woolfolk brother, Richard T. Woolfolk, who got his start in the business world as a debt collector in Richmond in the 1810s.[76]

It was not long before even the Woolfolks operating these branch offices had more business than they could handle, and they responded by creating a more hierarchical operational structure. In the late 1820s, Joseph and Richard each hired several agents and forged agreements with smaller traders who bought slaves on their behalf. Douglass described them as "generally well dressed, and very captivating in their manners." But he knew them to be "a swarm of imps, in human shape," who taunted enslaved prisoners in county jails while examining them for potential purchase, and as "debased and villainous creatures" who gambled and drank in taverns with a purpose unrelated to conviviality. "Many a child," Douglass recalled, "has been snatched from the arms of its mother by bargains arranged in a state of brutal drunkenness." Sweeping through the Eastern Shore in a fashion one scholar compares to a logging operation, the Woolfolks and their agents and partners systematically stripped out enslaved people whose owners decided they needed money more than labor.[77]

As the purchasing end of Austin Woolfolk's business swelled, the sales end of the business changed too. Rather than marching slaves overland out of the Chesapeake, Woolfolk took advantage of Baltimore's shipping facilities, renting space on merchant vessels and sending the enslaved by boat as cargo instead. Initially, he shipped enslaved people to Savannah or Charleston, where he sold them himself or consigned them to his uncle John in Augusta, who had been joined in that city by yet another Woolfolk brother, Samuel M. Woolfolk. But in the early 1820s, Samuel and John Woolfolk left Georgia for Louisiana, and they began receiving shipments of enslaved people in New Orleans. Market prices for the enslaved stayed flat in Charleston for more than a decade after the Panic of 1819, but they started increasing again in the Mississippi Valley in the early 1820s, thanks to growing sugar profits and a rise in cotton prices. By 1826, prices for young enslaved men were 70 percent higher in New Orleans than in Charleston, and like every slave trader, Austin Woolfolk followed the money.[78]

It cost a bit more to send enslaved people from Baltimore to New Orleans by boat than to force them overland. But it was significantly faster, generally taking about four weeks to sail compared with at least eight to walk. It left fewer avenues and chances for captives to escape, and while being confined in darkness and subjected to climactic extremes belowdecks in a ship that rolled with the seas was its own form of torture for the enslaved, for traders the calculus of disease and death that could undermine profits favored shipping. Perhaps most important, a trader who shipped enslaved people off to partners who awaited their arrival and handled sales was a trader who could maximize his time working in purchasing markets. The domestic slave trade ebbed and flowed with the seasons, but it bustled in the lower South between the early fall and the late spring, which meant a flourishing slave-trade business needed a steady supply chain for most of the year. Shipping let Austin Woolfolk maintain just that.[79]

None of these considerations were secrets, and Woolfolk did not invent the idea of using transportation methods commonly associated with the transatlantic slave trade for the purposes of the domestic. But no domestic trader before him used coastal shipping so extensively. He started small, sending four people aboard the brig *Temperance* in December 1818 and relatively few for several years after that. Then, in November 1821, he shipped fifty-four people on a sloop named the *Good Hope*. He sent between five and nine shipments every year after that for the next nine years. By the time Austin Woolfolk sent his last person out of the Chesapeake and on to the Atlantic in the 1840s, he had consigned nearly seventy-five shipments of enslaved cargo.[80]

UNITED STATES' INTERNAL SLAVE TRADE.
"*Hail Columbia, Happy Land!*"

"SHALL THY FAIR BANNERS O'ER OPPRESSION WAVE?"

TO THE AMERICAN PEOPLE.

The above is a faint picture of the *detestable traffic in human flesh,* carried on by citizens of this Republic in the open face of day, and in violation of the fundamental principles of our government, the maxims and precepts of Christianity, and the eternal rules of justice and equity. LOOK AT IT, *again and again* and then say whether you will permit so disgraceful, so inhuman, and so wicked a practice to continue in our country, which has been emphatically termed THE HOME OF THE FREE.—"*Malum nascens facile opprimitur, inveteratum fit robustius.*"

Like many antislavery activists, Benjamin Lundy, editor of the *Genius of Universal Emancipation*, thought the domestic slave trade in the United States especially outrageous. This illustration, from an 1823 issue of Lundy's paper, skewered national pretenses to being a free country.

As Woolfolk placed advertisements, oversaw agents, and made shipping arrangements from his command center on Pratt Street, he became the original brand name among slave dealers and a specter who tormented the enslaved whether they ended up in his clutches or not. His visibility also made him a target of white antislavery activists, whose ire had waned somewhat after the abolition of the transatlantic slave trade but who met the ballooning domestic trade with renewed outrage. Woolfolk tried forestalling criticism. He claimed he did Chesapeake slaveholders specifically and white people generally a favor by taking away rebellious or otherwise troublesome and dangerous enslaved people. He made much of saying he provided the prisoners in his jail with decent food, and he almost always moved them from Pratt Street to ships in the harbor in the middle of the night, lest the sight of innocent people being hauled off in chains provoke hostility from compassionate white citizens.[81]

But Woolfolk could never contain the critiques entirely. Like other traders who worked terrain along the Mason-Dixon Line, Woolfolk was widely suspected, and was sometimes guilty, of either kidnapping free Black people, purchasing people as slaves who he knew were free, or dealing in "term slaves," people whose enslavers had promised them freedom only to renege as a form of punishment or simply as a way to collect a bounty from the sale. Even many white people who were not uncomfortable with slavery found such illegal practices disgraceful, and to those who were antislavery on principle, Woolfolk was nearly the devil incarnate.[82]

No one hounded Woolfolk more relentlessly than Benjamin Lundy. A New Jersey–born Quaker, Lundy founded an antislavery newspaper called the *Genius of Universal Emancipation* in Baltimore in 1821, and he routinely eviscerated Woolfolk in its pages. Referring to the slave trade as a "*Satanic* traffic" and to traders as "soul-sellers" and "soul-dealers" who practiced "negro-chaining" and "man-driving," Lundy singled out Woolfolk as "the Prince of American slave-traders" and an "unprincipled monster" whose heart was "callous to the feelings of humanity, and steeled against every impression of tenderness." Noting Woolfolk's efforts "to sustain the character of a gentleman," Lundy sarcastically suggested that he ought to run for Senate.[83]

Woolfolk seethed at Lundy's denunciations for months, and his rage eventually boiled over. In January 1827, Lundy reprinted a report that Woolfolk had mocked the execution of an enslaved man named William Bowser, who had helped engineer an uprising aboard a ship on which Woolfolk had consigned him and around thirty other people. Lundy blamed Woolfolk for Bowser's death and for the deaths of the ship's captain and a crewman killed during the revolt, and he blasted Woolfolk as a "monster in human shape," arguing that no one ought to "speak of the humanity" of such an "adamantine-hearted creature" ever again. A week after the article appeared, Woolfolk approached Lundy in the street, confirmed that he had published the article in question, removed his coat, and beat Lundy to the pavement in front of a crowd of witnesses.[84]

Tried in the City Court of Baltimore for assault and battery, Woolfolk pled guilty. But while slave states sometimes passed laws to contain the activities of slave traders, or at least to pretend to contain them, local officials were more likely to be enablers or open supporters of traders and the trade. Judges and clerks and sheriffs and jailors dealt with traders all the time. Sometimes those dealings were nakedly corrupt and involved looking the other way, perhaps in return for a bribe, when traders skirted or flouted the law. Most commonly, officials saw traders simply as businessmen who contributed to public coffers. Slave traders paid licensing, court, and filing fees that applied to their activities. They used city and county jails to hold their captives, and they bought slaves at auctions of runaways or indebted estates. More often than not, the state was the slave trader's ally.

Few were shocked, then, when at Austin Woolfolk's trial in Baltimore for beating Benjamin Lundy, the chief justice of the City Court, Nicholas Brice, declared that Lundy had had it coming. Asserting that "he had never seen a case in which the provocation for a battery was greater," Brice said that "if abusive language could ever be a justification for a battery, this was that case." Confirming his approval of Woolfolk and his line of work, Brice reminded the court that Woolfolk was "engaged in a trade sanctioned by the laws of Maryland" and that "the trade itself was beneficial to the state, as it removed a great many rogues and vagabonds who were a nuisance." In fact, Brice concluded, if not "for the strict letter of the law," he would have let Woolfolk go. Seeing as he had to do something, Brice imposed a fine of one dollar.[85]

Isaac Franklin, John Armfield, and Rice Ballard all knew Austin Woolfolk. They knew him from his advertisements for "NEGROES WANTED" in Alexandria, and they knew him from the occasions he and his uncle John had transferred captives to steamboats in New Orleans and brought them upriver to Mississippi for sale. When Austin Woolfolk appeared in rooms below the Natchez Lancasterian Academy with "60 likely young Virginia born slaves" for sale, or his uncle showed up next door to the Franklin Hotel with "120 LIKELY YOUNG NEGROES," including "a large number of *Prime Field Hands, House Servants, Cooks, Carriage Drivers, Seamstresses and Washerwomen*," they stood out. And Franklin, Armfield, and Ballard knew Austin Woolfolk by reputation, because every slave trader did.[86]

But Franklin, Armfield, and Ballard did not just know Woolfolk. They watched him. They studied his operation. They saw what worked, what did not, and what could be improved upon. They paid attention to the trouble Woolfolk sometimes made for himself, and they carefully considered what it took to avoid it. Together, they thought they could do what he did, and perhaps even do it better. And when they finally came together and created a partnership of their own, they nearly put Austin Woolfolk out of business.[87]

THREE

ASSOCIATES, 1827–1830

THE BRICK TOWNHOUSE ON THE NORTH SIDE OF DUKE STREET was a handsome one. Three stories tall with a gable roof, twin chimneys, and blinds on the windows painted a pretty shade of green, it fronted directly onto the crude pavement near the western edge of Alexandria, three-quarters of a mile from the crowded wharves and bustling warehouses clustered along the Potomac River. Robert Young thought the location a sound investment and a fine spot for his family to live when he purchased a one-acre lot and had the house constructed there in 1812. Duke Street was a busy thoroughfare. To the east, it ended at the river, and to the west it became the Little River Turnpike, a recently completed toll road that connected northern Virginia's grain and tobacco farms to the port of Alexandria and, by extension, to the Atlantic economy. With other nearby infrastructure improvements in the works, additional traffic and development in the neighborhood seemed certain.[1]

A merchant and attorney, Young had lived in Alexandria since at least the 1790s. He became a commissioner of the newly founded

Mechanics' Bank of Alexandria just as he began building the house on Duke Street, and during the War of 1812, he was appointed by President James Madison as a militia brigadier general. Yet even the most successful men cannot see the future. When Young mortgaged the property in 1817 as security for a series of promissory notes, it probably seemed a reasonable risk. Then the economy turned in the Panic of 1819, and Young's debts wiped him out. In the spring of 1820, his house and the lot it sat on were put up for auction, and in the summer of 1821, they became property of the Mechanics' Bank.[2]

After Robert Young died in 1824, the bank rented the location to a series of tenants. In May 1828, it signed a multiyear lease with John Armfield, who then placed an ad in the Alexandria *Phenix Gazette*. He had taken up residence in the house, he could be found there "at all times," and he wanted to buy slaves. Looking "to purchase one hundred and fifty likely young negroes of both sexes between the ages of 8 and 25 years," Armfield promised to pay higher prices, in cash, "than any other purchasers that are in the market, or that may hereafter come into market." He signed the ad with the name of the company he and Isaac Franklin had created a few months earlier: "FRANKLIN & ARMFIELD."[3]

Robert Young had developed the Duke Street property mostly for residential purposes. The large house, an outbuilding behind it that functioned as a kitchen, and a few smaller structures had sufficed for Young, his wife, their four children, and two enslaved women who served the household. But John Armfield had other needs. He set about converting the space into a state-of-the-art slave-trading facility.[4]

By the mid-1830s, the front door of the building rented by the Mechanics' Bank as a "commodious three story BRICK DWELL-ING HOUSE, at the upper end of Duke-street" was the access point to an establishment without parallel in the city of Alexandria or any-where else in the Chesapeake. It was impossible to miss from the street, and not only because Armfield had emblazoned the company name above the entrance. Ranging away from the house to both the east and the west, taking up most of the block between Payne and West Streets, was what an observer described as a "high white-washed wall." Made of brick and standing fifteen to twenty feet tall, the wall gave the facility "the appearance of a penitentiary." Which in a way, it was.[5]

Crossing the threshold of the house, visitors came into a "well-furnished room" with wine, brandy, and other refreshments on offer from a sideboard. The room had been Robert Young's par-lor, and John Armfield used it as an office for discussing business and negotiating with clients and customers. Behind it, a rear door opened from the house onto a short passageway. To both the left and the right of the passageway were grated iron doors, "doubly locked, and strongly secured" with "padlocks and bolts."[6]

Through the door on the left lay a rectangular yard, about the size of a tennis court. Paved with bricks and enclosed by the white-washed wall that turned the corner northward from its frontage on Duke Street, the yard sometimes held several dozen men and boys, and sometimes more than a hundred, who milled about during daylight hours. Partially covered with a roof and partially open to the air, the yard also had a water pump and, beneath the covered section, a long table where the enslaved took their meals.[7]

Through the iron door leaving the passageway from the main house to the right lay a similarly sized yard where Armfield confined enslaved women and small children. This area, too, was partially covered and contained a water pump and a dining table. And it, too, was enclosed by the brick wall, which continued around from the men's side and then ran southward down the east side of the yard before ending at a perpendicular with the wall extending from the front of the facility. The women's yard also contained outbuildings: a two-story brick kitchen where enslaved women prepared food for the facility's captives, a tailor's shop where enslaved women made clothing so the people Armfield sent out had something clean to wear when they arrived "at the market," and a small infirmary where enslaved people who fell ill could be quarantined.[8]

Toward the back of the yards was a long, low-slung, two-story building where the enslaved slept at night on a brick floor. At a casual glance, it appeared to be an unremarkable barracks. A closer inspection revealed a "strong iron grated door, which closed the entrance," matching grates on the windows, which looked "like those of ordinary prisons," and several "rings, made of round iron, about three-fourths of an inch thick, fastened in the floor about as far apart as a man's length." The building was a cage, and Armfield generally kept people inside it "chained at night." One visitor noted this was a security measure, lest the captives "overpower their masters" and attempt an escape.[9]

All the way at the rear of the main yards, a gate in the brick wall led to another large area. Enclosed with a "close board fence," this part of the compound contained a few cows and mules, a stable with several horses, some storage space, and supplies to accompany a coffle of people forced to walk overland, should Armfield decide to send them south that way.[10]

There was one other space essential to the Duke Street facility, a basement under the main house. Rumors spread around town about it. It was "a dungeon," really, an underground torture chamber "where the refractory are confined," and it was known to contain "thumb-screws, and other instruments of coercion." Nearly seventy-five years after John Armfield first rented the property, the basement was still remembered as a room "where the stubborn and unruly negroes were placed." When visitors asked about it, they were told "there was no room of the kind." But there was. It was there then, and it is there now, a brick pit directly beneath the parlor, with powerful iron grates on the few small windows. Dim even at midday, it was stiflingly hot in the summer and bone-chillingly cold in the winter. The tax assessor for the city of Alexandria knew it was there too. In his mind, in fact, the basement stood in for everything that went

Built in 1812, this townhouse in Alexandria served from 1828 to 1836 as the Virginia headquarters of Franklin and Armfield, and then as offices, holding pen, and prison for a series of other slave-trading companies. The facility is surrounded by other structures today, but before the Civil War it took up half a city block. Courtesy of the Office of Historic Alexandria, photo by Erik Patten.

on at the west end of Duke Street. In the margins of his records for 1829, he described the house and lot Armfield rented as "Franklin's black hole."[11]

JOHN ARMFIELD WAS NOT ACTUALLY IN THE HOUSE ON DUKE Street "at all times," and he was not the only white person who lived there. Tax assessors routinely noted that four or five white men lived on-site, and visitors, clients, and customers who knocked at the door expecting to see Armfield sometimes found it answered by "an assistant or clerk" instead. The slave trade was almost never simply a matter of a slaveholder selling enslaved people to a slave trader who took them somewhere else, sold them to another slaveholder, and pocketed the difference between the purchase price and the sales price. Every transaction entailed the interests and involvement of a world of actors, and the world became more far-reaching and elaborate as Armfield, Isaac Franklin, and Rice Ballard forged a partnership and built their business together. In the late 1820s and early 1830s, the embryonic national exchange in Black bodies built by the first generation of professional traders grew sturdier and more intricate, and so did the array of individuals, institutions, governments, and infrastructures that supported it.[12]

Between the 1820s and the 1830s, the number of slaves transported across state lines increased by 85 percent, reaching the point where white people forced the migration of nearly thirty thousand enslaved people, on average, from one state to another every year. Trafficking on such a scale was unprecedented in the United States, and it would never be matched again in American history. By the 1830s, the slave trade had metastasized into a series of overlapping and intersecting markets spread over hundreds of thousands of square miles. It was ubiquitous throughout the slaveholding portions of the country: along rivers and the coastline, in city streets and on country roads, in taverns and hotels, at county jails and on courthouse steps, in newspapers and on broadsheets posted to buildings and trees, in private offices and public auction houses, on docks and at ports and harbors. In truth, the incessant chatter among white people about prices, the endless reports of Black people once there and now gone, and the disquiet that the enslaved could never quite shake reminded them that wherever they were, the trade was there too.[13]

Both Carolinas had moved firmly into the ranks of exporting states in the 1820s, and in the 1830s they accounted for the interstate movement of nearly 110,000 enslaved people, more than twice as many as they had sent across state lines in the previous decade. But the enslaved population of the Chesapeake remained the most deeply shattered by the domestic trade. Over 33,000 enslaved people were trafficked out of Maryland in the 1830s. By sheer volume, the number was only a bit higher than it had been in the 1820s. But it amounted to nearly a third of Maryland's enslaved population,

and exports outpaced natural increase so substantially that the number of enslaved people in the state declined by 13 percent over the
course of the decade. The nearly 120,000 enslaved people taken out
of Virginia in the 1830s, meanwhile, marked a 55 percent increase
compared with the 1820s, accounted for one of every four enslaved
people in the state, and led to almost a 5 percent drop in the state's
enslaved population by 1840.[14]

Travelers in the 1830s reported that deteriorating agricultural
production had made selling enslaved people the most reliable
source of income for slaveholders in the Chesapeake. When illus-
trator and engraver Abraham John Mason, for example, visited the
United States from England, he observed that Virginia's "principal
traffic now consists in raising slaves for the more Southern parts,
becoming a complete slave nursery." British antislavery activist Joseph Sturge noted similarly in the early 1840s that the "sterility and
ever-encroaching desolation" of land in the Chesapeake and in North
Carolina had resulted in the slaveholding sections of the country being "divided into the 'slave-breeding,' and 'slave-consuming' States."
Indeed, Sturge concluded, "human flesh is now the great staple of
Virginia."[15]

Prominent Virginians acknowledged it too. Thomas Jefferson
Randolph, grandson and namesake of the third president, lamented
that Virginia had become "one grand menagerie, where men are
reared for the market like oxen for the shambles." But others saw an
upside. State delegate James Gholson, noting that "much of [Vir-
ginia's] wealth" came from the birth of enslaved people, believed
slaveholders had as much right to profit from the increase as "the
owner of brood mares" did to profit from "their product." Congressman Charles Fenton Mercer appreciated that Virginia derived "an
annual revenue of not less than a million and a half of dollars . . .
from the exportation" of enslaved people, as did Thomas Dew, professor of political law at the College of William & Mary, who considered the slave trade "an advantage to the state." It only made

sense for slaveholders "to encourage breeding" among the enslaved, Dew thought, because "Virginia is in fact a negro-raising state for other states."[16]

Cotton-producing regions of the country still stood out most among those "other states," and the demand for slave labor there received new stimuli in the late 1820s and early 1830s. Most significant were the Indian removal policies of Andrew Jackson, who ascended to the presidency in 1829. Within a few years of taking office, Jackson engineered the mass expulsion of Native Americans from the lower South, opening new vistas for American cotton production, which increased nearly 40 percent in the first half of the 1830s. As the number of white fortune hunters soared, slave traders came to them with stolen people to pack onto their stolen land.[17]

White people brought almost thirty thousand slaves into Louisiana during the 1830s, nearly 80 percent more than they had in the 1820s, and cotton production in the state increased 63 percent between 1826 and 1834. Sugar production increased by 150 percent as well. This was strikingly fast growth, and yet Louisiana was only the third-largest importer of slave labor in the 1830s. Bigger still was Alabama, where white people brought in over ninety-six thousand slaves, almost twice as many as they had in the 1820s. The total enslaved population of Alabama more than doubled over the course of the decade, and cotton production from 1826 to 1834 increased there by almost 90 percent.

But the twinned amplification of slavery and commodity crops in Louisiana and Alabama paled in comparison to their growth in Mississippi. In the early 1830s, federal deportation of the Choctaw and Chickasaw peoples yielded eighteen million acres of land there for white settlement, more than half the acreage of the entire state. Whites brought over one hundred thousand enslaved people into Mississippi during the 1830s, more than five times as many as they had in the previous decade, and the state's enslaved population grew almost 200 percent. The cotton crop produced by the enslaved in

Mississippi multiplied more than fourfold over the course of just eight years, and by 1834 the state stood alongside Alabama as the largest producer of cotton in the United States.[18]

Massive influxes of capital and credit followed and fanned the development of the cotton and slave-trading frontiers. States experimented with chartering new kinds and larger numbers of banks. Investors from around the country and around the globe channeled millions into land and stock and bond ventures. The Second Bank of the United States, using federal money taken in mostly from public sales of Indian land, delivered over a third of its loans to the merchants, bankers, and planters of the lower South. In Mississippi alone, the number of incorporated banks grew from one to thirteen within a few years after 1829, and banking capital in the state increased tenfold. Everything at bottom was predicated on the labor and commodity value of enslaved people. Black bodies propelled the American economy toward the future.[19]

The explosive growth of the domestic slave trade generated legal pushback, political backlash, and routine defiance. Some white residents of the lower South had concerns about public safety, moral indignation swelled from increasingly vocal and organized antislavery forces, and the enslaved resisted in every way they could. But few of those things fazed Isaac Franklin, John Armfield, and Rice Ballard. Perfectly placed to take advantage of the burgeoning prospects for slave traders, they wanted to push their position to its maximum. Doing so would take raw entrepreneurial nerve. It would also require learning how to work together and to trust each other. It would mean building an organization more complex and adaptable than anything they had known before. It would entail deepening relationships with a constellation of merchants, bankers, lawyers, ship captains, purchasing agents, provisioners, judges, clerks, government officials, and other players who facilitated the slave trade's depravities. And it all began in Alexandria, in the house on Duke Street.

Isaac Franklin and John Armfield signed "articles of co-partnership" and agreed to go into business together on February 28, 1828. Though the original document has not survived, partnership agreements became more common as the slave trade expanded, and most had similar terms and conditions. Franklin and Armfield would have contributed equally to the partnership's base capital. Given the size of the company they created, somewhere in the range of $10,000 is a reasonable estimate for the initial stakes of each man, though it could have been more. That was no small figure, corresponding to roughly half a million dollars today, and the funds would be designated for purchasing slaves and associated business expenditures, with subsequent profits from sales split evenly between the partners. Slave-trading partnerships could be formalized for any period of time, and many were fleeting. But Franklin and Armfield intended to build something durable. Their agreement was for five years.[20]

In slave-trading partnerships, one trader often assumed responsibility for purchasing enslaved people while another assumed responsibility for sales. Franklin and Armfield was no exception. Franklin would command the sales end of the operation from his Natchez facility on the Washington road, and Armfield would mostly leave traveling behind to live and make purchases full time in Alexandria. That the pair was so strategically decisive from the outset and determined to make such a long-term commitment to one another and to the trade suggests the way their relationship had evolved since they first met back in 1824. They had never worked in concert before, but over several years they had gotten to know each other through the Natchez and Alexandria slave markets. In taverns and hotels and on the road, slave traders shared information about money and prices and enslaved people. They also gossiped about other traders, and as Franklin and Armfield talked to and about each other, they discovered they had complementary temperaments, overlapping ambitions, and enough cash put aside to make engaging in a daring venture seem viable.

Moreover, they had ended their existing associations in the slave trade just weeks before creating their partnership. Whether that was a coincidence in which they both found themselves at loose ends or an intentional severing of old ties in anticipation of something new, the timing was right. John Armfield and Joseph Meek made their last joint sale of enslaved people in New Orleans on February 12, 1828, when they sold two men, Willis and Paul, to merchant and cotton broker Henry William Palfrey. Isaac Franklin's nephew and colleague, Smith Franklin, placed his final newspaper advertisement in Virginia three days after that. Palfrey paid with a promissory note that would not come due for a year, and Smith Franklin's advertisement would run into early April, but those were minor details. Isaac Franklin and John Armfield were moving forward together.[21]

Franklin and Armfield chose Alexandria as their upper South base of operations partially because it skirted direct competition with Austin Woolfolk. Woolfolk was an unavoidable presence throughout the regional markets for enslaved people, and he did have an agent in Alexandria buying slaves on his behalf. But Woolfolk shipped from Baltimore, had his headquarters there, and focused his activities in eastern Maryland, particularly along the Eastern Shore. Franklin and Armfield believed they could carve out their own analogous space in southern Maryland and northern Virginia.[22]

Both Franklin and Armfield also knew Alexandria well. John Armfield had spent time in the city going back at least two years, and Isaac Franklin had been visiting it on slave-trading ventures since the early nineteenth century, when he was working with his older brothers. In fact, the Alexandria property Franklin had once used as a slave pen, rented by his brother James in 1819, was on Duke Street, just four blocks from the house and compound John

Armfield started renting in 1828. For Franklin and Armfield alike, well-established ties to Alexandria meant personal connections in the city and an understanding that its already robust slave market was primed for further growth.[23]

Founded in 1749 as a maritime center for the tobacco trade, Alexandria was for decades among mainland North America's busiest ports. In 1790, it became part of the District of Columbia, tucked into the southern point of the ten-mile square carved out of Virginia and Maryland that formed the original district, which was much larger than it is today and which also contained the urban areas of Washington City and Georgetown. Alexandria's population more than doubled between 1790 and 1810, at which point the city housed over seven thousand people, around 20 percent of whom were enslaved. But even as the grid of city streets expanded westward from the Potomac River to accommodate population growth, Alexandria's economy started stagnating. Alexandria had about half a dozen banks, and it attracted merchants, craftspeople, and some small manufacturers. But the city's dependence on exports meant it suffered during years of poor harvests. Commercial disruptions caused by transatlantic trade conflicts and the War of 1812 hurt as well, and the Panic of 1819 sent Alexandria into a downturn that would last the better part of two decades.[24]

Still, Alexandria remained a catch basin for the products of its northern Virginia hinterland. As enslaved people themselves became a more conspicuous product and a larger segment of Virginia's export economy, the slave trade emerged as a significant component of the city's economic base, and in the early nineteenth century, Alexandria stood second only to Baltimore as the premier urban center of the upper South slave trade. Black people in Alexandria tried to fight the trade as it grew, with "a serious riot" breaking out "among the negroes" in the city in the summer of 1825, "directed against the dealers in slaves." Those involved marched in the streets. They shouted "abusive epithets . . . to all who dared to purchase slaves, either as traders or cultivators of the soil," and "peace officers" who sought to restore order were "resisted violently or beaten down." But eventually, "many of the most prominent of the mob" were arrested. Their anger could not stop the trade, and reports of their protest appeared only in newspapers outside Alexandria. In the city itself, the editor of the *Phenix Gazette* thought "the whole affair was of so contemptible and unimportant a nature" that he decided not to "trouble the public with a history of it."[25]

If Franklin and Armfield were going to make a real play for the Alexandria market, however, they had to contend first with Elias P. Legg, whose taverns served as the heart of the city's slave trade for the better part of fifteen years. Born in 1796 in Fauquier County, Virginia, Eli Legg spent his early adult life catering to the appetites of other white men. He acquired an innkeepers' license in Alexandria just after he turned eighteen, and for a few years he ran a boardinghouse, where he sometimes hosted slave traders who passed through the city, including Isaac Franklin, who met Legg in 1815. By 1816, Legg operated a tavern at the upper end of King Street. Attached to a yard "enclosed 10 feet high, with a stream of water passing through it," the facility purportedly could "accommodate in safety 300 waggons and teams." But the stables might also hold enslaved people, and traders such as Matthew Hobson, George Farley, and John Alford started advertising their presence at Legg's as they bought up "likely young Negroes."[26]

In the early 1820s, Legg parlayed servicing the Alexandria slave trade into the command of multiple taverns on King Street, managing the Bell Tavern and the Eagle Tavern simultaneously and providing for slave traders at both. In 1822, Legg became even more ambitious. He took over operations at the Indian Queen, the slave trader's haunt on the corner of King and St. Asaph Streets, where he promised customers that they would "meet with the *best* accommodations," that his "BAR [would] always be stocked with the best of liquors," and that bedding would be "of the first order."[27]

Taking over the Indian Queen during the depression of the early 1820s nearly proved Legg's undoing. In 1823, he declared bankruptcy and was briefly jailed for debt, and late in 1824, he auctioned off his possessions and declared that he was planning to "remove to the country." In the event, he took whatever money he managed to salvage, perhaps borrowed some more, and got back on his feet by using what he had learned from watching slave traders in action. In 1825, Legg started advertising that he would buy as many as sixty or seventy slaves in his own right, "either singly or in families." He also reentered the tavern business on St. Asaph Street, near the site of the Indian Queen. But he continued dealing in slaves, and in 1826, Benjamin Lundy identified him in the *Genius of Universal Emancipation* as one of "the most noted slave traders that prowl the states of Maryland and Virginia in quest of human prey."[28]

John Armfield worked out of Legg's tavern when he broke into the slave trade, and after he and Isaac Franklin created their partnership, he went to Legg's again. The very first advertisement Armfield placed for the new venture of Franklin and Armfield told customers looking for information to "enquire at Mr. Elias P. Legg's, St. Asaph street, Alexandria, D.C." But Armfield's move to Duke Street a week later was a turning point for the Alexandria slave trade, Eli Legg, and Franklin and Armfield alike.[29]

In the early 1830s, Alexandria bypassed Baltimore to become the leading upper South city for slave exports, and the role of tavern keepers like Eli Legg would go into steep decline as Franklin and Armfield wielded an increasingly powerful influence over the Alexandria trade from the compound on Duke Street. Early in 1829, Legg stopped advertising that he was buying enslaved people. He worked for Franklin and Armfield instead, admitting, when asked, that he was "to a certain extent" employed by the company. Near the end of 1832, Legg went out of business altogether, and he sold all his household and kitchen furniture to pay back rent and cover outstanding debts.[30]

Eli Legg was among the first slave traders whose business was absorbed by Franklin and Armfield, but he would not be the last, because John Armfield overwhelmed the capacity of almost any other trader to keep pace. Armfield crowed in the papers about how many slaves he wanted to buy, the prices he would pay, and the volume of cash he put in the market. He broadcast his goals and boasts in more than one newspaper, adding advertisements in the *United States Telegraph*, published in Washington City, to those he placed in the Alexandria *Phenix Gazette*. He demonstrated visibly, with an office in a stylish three-story townhouse attached to a massive private jail, that he was a reliable businessman rather than a shifty drunk in a tavern.[31]

There were only so many hours in a day and so many places one man could be, of course. Armfield could not be all at the same time in his office on Duke Street waiting for customers, out in the countryside drumming up business among slaveholders who did not come to Alexandria or take a District of Columbia newspaper, and overseeing the transport of enslaved people to Isaac Franklin in the lower South. A large slave-trading business needed a lot of manpower to conduct basic operations and extend its reach. Clerks and assistants provided some of it. Smaller traders and tavern keepers like Eli Legg provided some more.

More still came from the family of Isaac Franklin, who hired two other nephews to work for Franklin and Armfield as Smith Franklin left the business. One was James Franklin Purvis, the eldest son of Franklin's sister Margaret and her husband Allen Purvis. The other was James Rawlings Franklin, Smith Franklin's younger brother and son of Isaac Franklin's brother John. Both were twenty years old. James Purvis acted as a purchasing agent, buying enslaved people in Potomac River watershed counties north and west of Alexandria. James Rawlings Franklin bought enslaved people too, and it was also his job to deliver those purchased in the countryside to John Armfield in Alexandria. And through the spring and summer of 1828, the walled yards of "Franklin's black hole" gradually filled with Black people, all fated to be human cargo bound for the lower South.[32]

As Isaac Franklin and John Armfield were getting their partnership up and running, Rice Ballard was busy with Ballard and Alsop, the formal name of the slave-trading business he had with Samuel Alsop. In that partnership, Alsop provided financial backing and probably took half the profits, while Ballard, and to a lesser extent Alsop's son Joseph, oversaw and carried out operations. For at least three years in the late 1820s, Ballard forced enslaved people to walk, in the late fall and early winter, from Virginia to the lower South, a two-month march of at least a thousand miles. Physically and psychologically torturous for the enslaved, many of whom walked barefoot and in chains, it was arduous and nerve-racking for traders as well. Though traders went by choice and typically drove a wagon or rode horseback, the rifles and whips they carried evidenced not only their unrelenting insistence on driving the enslaved past exhaustion but also the knowledge that some of their captives would gladly kill them to escape their clutches.[33]

In the lower South, Ballard offered for sale as many as sixty-five enslaved people at a time. When he was in Natchez, he advertised in newspapers as far away as New Orleans that he was at the Franklin Hotel with "some first rate house servants for families also some good Blacksmiths and an excellent assortment of young men, women and boys." Both in Natchez and just across the Mississippi River in Louisiana, Ballard sold the enslaved for cash or promissory notes and other reliable debt instruments. He took in thousands of dollars in gross receipts, and he monitored and collected what purchasers owed Ballard and Alsop.[34]

Ballard probably used some of what he collected to travel back toward Virginia by steamboat up the Mississippi River or to sail from New Orleans coastwise along the Atlantic. When he got to the Chesapeake, he started buying slaves again. Sometimes he was in Alexandria, but he spent most of the spring and summer in Spotsylvania County. He surely worked now and then out of Sam Alsop's tavern, though enslaved people could be bought at nearly any local tavern or hotel, including the Farmers' Hotel in Fredericksburg. That was where William Hayden saw him in the summer of 1828.[35]

After procuring his freedom from slave trader Thomas Phillips, Hayden spent five years working as valet to a white man in Natchez. But Hayden never forgot the mother from whom he had been sold away as a child, and when he got word that she was seriously ill, he returned to Virginia, reversing the trajectory of the slave trade that rent apart thousands of families like his. Hayden passed by stagecoach through the neighborhood where he had been born, about twenty miles northeast of the Rappahannock River. The coach stopped in the middle of the night at the Farmers' Hotel, which belonged to a man named James Young. As Hayden stood in the hotel bar and recounted "the story of my travels and the reasons which prompted me to visit the scenes of my childhood," Young and his wife marveled aloud at the tale. Their exclamations, along with Hayden's mention of Natchez, drew the attention of some slave traders who were staying at the hotel. Among them were two whom Hayden knew personally from his years in Mississippi. One was a Kentuckian named Warren Offutt. The other was Rice Ballard.[36]

Hearing more of Hayden's story, Offutt pulled "a well filled wallet from his pocket" and insisted that Hayden "take from it as much as I myself thought it would require to consummate my wishes, and secure the freedom of my mother." Ballard chimed in too, telling Hayden not to let money "stay me in my heart felt wish to free my mother." He instructed Hayden to go to any person in Fredericksburg, buy himself a wagon, a team of horses, and anything else he needed, and to use Ballard's "name with his free consent, as an endorser of my notes."

James Young knew where Hayden's mother lived, and he urged him to leave right then, even before daybreak, to find her. Hayden did so, rousing her in the darkness for a tearful reunion that was decades in the making. Hayden also later recalled Offutt's and Ballard's offers to help as great kindnesses, and he described the slave traders as some of his "strongest friends" and people whom he "highly esteemed."

A closer reading of Hayden's recollections, however, tells a different story. Hayden did procure his mother's freedom, but he declined Offutt's money and Ballard's credit, choosing instead to cobble together his own savings with funds acquired by roadside begging while wearing "an old ragged suit" akin to a jester's costume. Composed mostly of different-colored patches, filthy with grease stains, and topped off by an old wool hat that Hayden suspected another enslaved person had cast aside because it was too befouled to keep, the outfit was undignified. But it garnered sympathy from travelers, and it kept Hayden from being indebted to Warren Offutt and Rice Ballard. He knew from personal experience that men like them could never be trusted. Even degrading oneself in front of white people was better than owing a loved one's liberty to a slave trader.[37]

William Hayden understood that Rice Ballard's gesture was not really a kindness at all. He knew Ballard was at the Farmers' Hotel looking for slaves he could turn around and sell, that the credit Ballard had accrued came from the commerce in their bodies, and that drawing on that credit would be a reminder of why Hayden stood there lamenting the fate of his family in the first place. Ballard's offer to use the profits of the slave trade to help Hayden buy his mother's freedom was not a selfless act of generosity. It was a demonstration of Ballard's power, an affirmation and assertion of his ability to do as he wished with and toward Black people. Hayden decided he would rather beg than give Ballard the satisfaction.

Only after having scrimped together every last penny to liberate his mother did Hayden draw on Ballard's credit, buying a horse and wagon in the fall of 1828 to take his mother out of Virginia for good.

At nearly the same time, fifty miles to the northeast, John Armfield roused 149 enslaved people and told them it was time to move. He sorted the men, most of the women, and the older children into pairs, and he affixed cuffs and chains to their hands and feet. He had women with infants and smaller children climb into a wagon. Then he led them all out of the compound on Duke Street and marched them in a long line down to the Potomac River. There, he turned them over to a ship captain named Henry Bell, who loaded them onto the brig he commanded, a 152-ton vessel with a ten-man crew named the *United States*.[38]

As Armfield watched the *United States* set sail down the Potomac on its way toward the Chesapeake Bay and the Atlantic Ocean, he must have been at least a little anxious. The people he had consigned on board represented months of effort, thousands of dollars, and the hope that his business venture with Isaac Franklin would be successful. It was a significantly larger group of enslaved people than he had ever accumulated at once, and arranging their shipment was a new experience for him. Moreover, he had to have confidence that when Franklin met them at their destination, he would know what he was doing, because Franklin would be undertaking something he had not tried for a long time. He was going to sell slaves in New Orleans.

Waiting for the *United States* near the wharves in New Orleans, Isaac Franklin may have paused to consider how the city had changed since he had first seen it from a flatboat deck twenty years earlier. Its core was still the dense rectangular street grid laid out by the French early in the eighteenth century. Roughly coterminous with the modern French Quarter, the city nestled along a crescent-shaped bend of the Mississippi River, about one hundred miles above its estuary, in a shallow bowl with swampland to the rear and protected from inundation only by an extensive levee system. New

Orleans still thrummed with trade that came from its situation as an exchange point between the Mississippi Valley and the Atlantic world, and its creolized population still comprised a greater diversity of peoples and cultures than anyplace else in the country. One traveler described it as "Old French, American, European from all parts, with every shade of the colored race, forming a mixture of manners, language, and complexion not to be matched." For others, only an analogy of biblical scale let them get their minds around the city's vertiginous racial, ethnic, and linguistic variety: they compared it to Babel.[39]

But the New Orleans that Franklin had first visited was a territorial administrative capital of just over seventeen thousand people. The one he saw now housed more than forty-five thousand people and was the fifth-largest city in the United States. Its residents, one in every three of whom was enslaved, had burst well beyond its original boundaries and extended themselves in suburbs carved out of low-lying former plantations along the river. Most notable were the upriver Faubourg Sainte Marie, which attracted wealthy white Americans and came to be known as the American sector, and the downriver Faubourg Marigny, which was filled with a working-class mix of French Creoles, European and Caribbean immigrants, and free people of color.[40]

Growth had only quickened the commercial and financial pulse of New Orleans. Neither the scores of commission merchant firms that serviced southern planter clients, nor the more than a dozen banks that would soon hold more collective capital than the banks of New York City, might have been noticeable at a glance. But from where Franklin stood, looking for the *United States* to come into view, the transformation of New Orleans was unmistakable nonetheless. The pestilent summer was over, and the crowds in the streets swelled, dwarfing those that Franklin remembered. The change in seasons meant river traffic was coming into full swing too, and flatboats and barges now huddled against scads of steamboats and beneath a flotilla

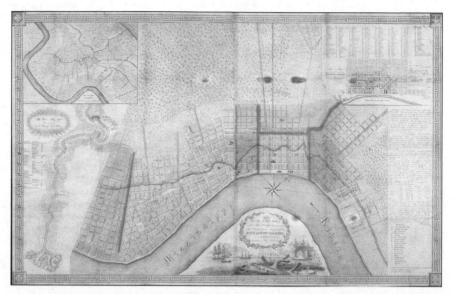

The city of New Orleans was the largest slave market in the United States, and Franklin and Armfield began selling enslaved people there in the fall of 1828. In 1829, when municipal authorities forced slave traders out of the city proper, Isaac Franklin moved his operations to locations adjacent to the city limits, in the downriver suburb of Faubourg Marigny. Bequest of Mr. Richard H. Koch at The Historic New Orleans Collection, 1971.21.

of tall ships. Arranged five or six deep for more than a mile along the levee, they made a forest of smokestacks, masts, and sails.[41]

Coming and going from the forest were beef and pork and lard, buffalo robes and bear hides and deerskins, lumber and lime, tobacco and flour and corn. But it was the cotton bales and hogsheads of sugar, stacked high on the levee, that really made the New Orleans economy hum. Cotton exports from New Orleans increased more than sevenfold in the 1820s. Pouring down the continental funnel of the Mississippi Valley to its base, they amounted by the end of the decade to more than 180 million pounds, which was more than half the cotton produced in the entire country. Nearly all of Louisiana's sugar, meanwhile, left the state through New Orleans, and the holds of more and more ships filled with it as the number of sugar plantations tripled in the second half of the 1820s.[42]

From merchant firms and banks to docks and fields, slave labor underlay everything on which New Orleans thrived. That made the city as terrifying to enslaved people brought against their will as it was enthralling to white people who came for spectacle and profit. It was also what brought Isaac Franklin from Natchez. In 1826, Louisiana legislators had passed a two-year ban on importing slaves from out of state for purpose of sale, amid concerns that long-distance traders drained the state of capital and left behind large numbers of enslaved people from places unknown. But the ban was deeply unpopular among white people in the state, as such measures everywhere usually were. On February 4, 1828, the legislature repealed the law, before the term of prohibition had even expired, and it may be no accident that Isaac Franklin and John Armfield created their partnership weeks later. Opportunities for entrepreneurs were reopening, and this race went to the swift. As the ban lifted, New Orleans again became what one newspaper called a "complete mart for the slave trade." It would be the foremost city for the exchange of enslaved people in the United States until the end of the Civil War, ultimately serving as the market for buying and selling more than 135,000 people.[43]

But before he could throw himself into that market and sell the people Armfield had sent him, Franklin had to get them into the city. On October 21, 1828, after nineteen days at sea, the *United States* arrived at the Balize, a tiny settlement that sat practically underwater, amid a reedy expanse of mud and swamp, a few miles above where the Mississippi River met the Gulf of Mexico. Described by British author Frances Trollope as "the most miserable station" she had ever seen "made the dwelling of man," the Balize was a dismal place where oceangoing ships often stopped to hire one of the boat pilots who resided there and earned a living ushering larger vessels upriver. As Henry Bell brought the *United States* around the last turn of the Mississippi the next day and finally saw New Orleans come into view, he eased as near as he could to the wharves, under the guidance of the steam towboat *Hercules*.[44]

Isaac Franklin was not the only person waiting for slaves from the *United States*. The brig held 201 captives, with the 149 sent by John Armfield sharing the misfortune of being on board with 5 people shipped by Eli Legg to a trader named James Diggs, and 47 shipped by Virginia trader William Ish to the merchant firm of Wilkins and Linton. But none of them could collect what they came for until they took care of some paperwork. In an effort to prevent smuggling, the federal law banning slave imports from overseas mandated that captains of domestic coastal slavers create a manifest listing the name, sex, age, height, and skin color of every enslaved person they carried, along with the shippers' names and places of residence. One copy of the manifest had to be deposited with the collector of the port of departure, who checked it for accuracy and certified that the captain and the shippers swore that every person listed was legally enslaved and had not come into the country after January 1, 1808. A second copy got delivered to the customs official at the port of arrival, who checked it again before permitting the enslaved to be unloaded. The bureaucracy would not be rushed.[45]

At the Customs House in Alexandria, Deputy Collector C. T. Chapman had signed off on the manifest of the *United States* and attested that he had taken the requisite depositions from John Armfield, William Ish, Eli Legg, and Henry Bell. At the Balize, a boarding officer named William B. G. Taylor looked over the manifest, made sure it had the proper signatures, and matched each enslaved person to his or her listing. Finding the lot "agreeing with description," Taylor sent the *United States* on its way. In New Orleans, Customs Inspector L. B. Willis climbed on board and performed yet another inspection of the enslaved, the third they had endured in as many weeks. Scrutinizing them closely, he proved more exacting than his Balize colleague. Willis cared about the details. After placing a small check mark by the name of every person to be sure he had seen them all, he declared the manifest "all correct or agreeing excepting that" a sixteen-year-old named Nancy, listed as "No. 120" and described as "black" on the manifest, was in his estimation "a yellow girl," and that a nine-year-old declared as "Betsey no. 144 should be Elvira."[46]

Being examined and probed was among many indignities white people routinely inflicted upon the enslaved, but those in bondage looked back. They could distinguish the gaze of someone trying to find them on a list from that of someone assessing their value in the marketplace. Taking in the noisy chaos atop the levee in New Orleans while they stumbled across the gangplank thrown from the *United States*, the people carried as freight recognized Isaac Franklin's calculating stare as he watched them disembark. Even through the haze of fatigue, they knew a slave trader when they saw one.

Appraising those who were now his merchandise, Franklin noticed their tattered clothing and enervated frames, but he liked what he saw anyway. Almost exactly the number of people John Armfield had advertised for, the vast majority were also between the ages of eight and twenty-five, as Armfield had wanted. Eighty-nine of them were boys and men, of whom forty-eight were between eighteen and twenty-five years old, and another twenty were younger teens. The sixty women and girls were on average a bit younger. Only eight of them were over twenty years old, and a little more than half were teenagers. It was a population tailored to the demands of sugarcane growers. They came to New Orleans looking for a demographically disproportionate number of physically mature boys and men they believed could withstand the notoriously dangerous and grinding labor in the cane fields, and they supplemented them with girls and women they believed maximally capable of reproduction.[47]

What and who the enslaved people on the *United States* had left behind in Maryland and Virginia is unknown and mostly unknowable. But given their stages in life, we can imagine what slave traders and their customers stole from them. Whatever simple comforts, emotional sustenance, semblance of stability, and expectations for the future could be carved out of slavery, they stole. Friends and partners and lovers, brothers and sisters and cousins, and spouses and sons and daughters, they stole.

And they stole parents. Of the 149 people Isaac Franklin collected at the levee, nearly a quarter of them, 36 in all, were under age twelve. The manifest suggests that some of the youngest, including a four-month-old named George, sailed with their mothers. But nothing indicates their fathers were there too, and more than two dozen children sailed entirely alone. Perhaps older captives helped Elizabeth and Sally, who were eight years old, or Bill and Nelson, who were nine, process what was happening to them. Though no explanation could take away their pain and their tears, they needed to remember what one historian has called their "soul value," a sense of self and self-worth independent of prices and markets. For Franklin and Armfield, however, if a boy was old enough to put in chains, he could be sold. If a girl was old enough to walk, she could be measured to meet federal customs regulations. The smallest of those measured on the *United States* was a two-year-old named Julia Ann. She was one foot eleven inches tall.[48]

Now that he had the people Armfield had sent him, Franklin made them wash away the grime and filth accumulated during weeks of travel. He stripped them until they were practically naked and checked them more meticulously. He pored over their skin and felt their muscles, made them squat and jump, and stuck his fingers in their mouths looking for signs of illness or infirmity, or for whipping scars and other marks of torture that he needed to disguise or account for in a sale. He had them change into one of the "two entire suits" of clothing Armfield sent with each person from the Alexandria compound, and he gave them enough to eat so they would at least appear hardy. He made them aware of the behavior he expected, and he delivered a warning, backed by slaps and kicks and threats, that when buyers came to look, the enslaved were to show themselves to be spry, cheerful, and obedient, and they were to claim personal histories that, regardless of their truth, promised customers whatever they wanted. It took time to make the enslaved ready to retail themselves—but not too much time, because every day that Franklin had to house and feed someone cut into his profits.[49]

Exactly where Franklin put the people from the *United States* once he led them away from the levee is unclear. There is no evidence that he owned or leased any real estate for a compound like the one he and John Armfield were setting up in Alexandria, and few slave traders had regular established locations in New Orleans in 1828. Like most of his colleagues, Franklin probably rented space in a yard, a pen, or a jail to keep the enslaved in while he worked nearby. He may have done business from a hotel, a tavern, or an establishment known as a coffee house, which is where much of the city's slave trade was conducted in the 1820s. Serving as bars, restaurants, gambling houses, pool halls, meeting spaces, auction blocks, and venues for economic transactions of all sorts, coffee houses sometimes also had lodging and stabling facilities. They were often known simply as "exchanges," reflecting the commercial nature of what went on inside, and itinerant slave traders used them to receive their mail, talk about prices of cotton and sugar and humans, locate customers, and otherwise as offices for networking and socializing.[50]

Franklin is especially likely to have spent some time at Hewlett's Exchange, which was the most important location of the day for the slave trade and arguably the most important commercial location in the city. Housed in a large stuccoed brick building at the intersection of Chartres and Saint Louis Streets, Hewlett's attracted influential planters, brokers, and merchants from the moment it opened as a coffee house in 1811. It became famous after the War of 1812 under the management of an Italian named Pierre Maspero, and after John Hewlett took it over in 1826, it grew into a spot described by one visitor as "the Soul of New Orleans," a place where "all the business and professional men of the City" congregated daily. Hewlett knew his clientele. He cultivated elite patronage, improving and upgrading the building with high ceilings, glass chandeliers, wood and marble finishings, and an enormous circular bar. Two hundred to three hundred people at a time could be served there while they drank, smoked, read the paper, and arranged their business.[51]

Nearly anything could be bought and sold at Hewlett's Exchange. But it was notorious for the auctions of enslaved people that took place every day of the week except Sunday, so much so that the cacophony and "tumultuous confusion" of a slave auction at Hewlett's became a tourist attraction, the Black sorrow on the block consumed as a holiday diversion even by those who reported finding it repellent. Legislative bans never stopped auction sales, because Toussaint Mossy, Isaac McCoy, Joseph Le Carpentier, and others in the rotating cast of auctioneers at Hewlett's mostly knocked down people who were already enslaved in Louisiana rather than those newly imported for sale from out of state. Supply met demand where white people gawked and leered amid the grandeur of Hewlett's, barraging the auctioned with intrusive questions about their bodies, their skills, their pasts. Hewlett's was where white people came if they were looking to buy slaves, and that made it the right place for a trader like Isaac Franklin to linger.[52]

Hewlett's was also proximate to the offices of many of the public functionaries known as notaries. In a civil law system, such as the one Louisiana retained from its years under French and Spanish jurisdiction, notaries act as third parties to a variety of contracts, and they are charged with drafting and keeping records of every transaction they certify. Before the Civil War, those transactions included the buying and selling of enslaved people. No slave sale could be entirely legal in Louisiana unless it was recorded in a notarial act, and nearly all of the city's dozen or so notaries could be conveniently found within a block of two of Hewlett's Exchange.[53]

But convenience only somewhat alleviated the fact that the notarial system meant the New Orleans slave trade involved still another layer of paperwork and still more people who acted as intermediaries.

On October 29, 1828, one week after the *United States* landed in New Orleans, Franklin appeared at the office of a notary named Felix DeArmas. Located on Royal Street, DeArmas's office was one block up and one block over from Hewlett's Exchange. Accompanying Franklin were two men with whom he had negotiated deals for slaves, and they wanted DeArmas to draft the contracts.[54]

It was a routine process. DeArmas asked for the names and descriptions of the enslaved people being sold and the price being paid for them. He inquired whether the sales were for cash or whether they involved a mortgage, a promissory note, or another payment plan or credit arrangement. He sent a runner to the office of Martin Duralde, recorder of mortgages, to do a title search and confirm that the people being sold were unencumbered by preexisting or outstanding mortgages or liens. Finally, DeArmas verified that Franklin stood by the standard warranty on slave sales. Unless otherwise stipulated at the time of sale, Louisiana law provided that sellers guaranteed the health and character of slaves being sold and that buyers retained a right, known as redhibition, that let them return their purchases should "defects" or "vices" become apparent. A seller who made no exceptions to the standard warranty and then refused a buyer's claims that he had knowingly sold someone with a disease or disability, a penchant for drinking, or a habit of running away could find himself dragged into court for fraud.[55]

Once DeArmas got the information he needed, he had a clerk put multiple copies of the contracts in writing, the lifeless and legalistic boilerplate belying the flesh and blood changing hands. Isaac Franklin, his customers, and Felix DeArmas signed the documents, and two clerks in the office signed as witnesses. Franklin paid a few dollars in fees for the services of DeArmas, the formal recording of the notarial acts, and the certification from the recorder of mortgages. And with that, two little girls named Celina and Maria, ages seven and eleven, became the property of ferry keeper Pierre Godefroy Bouny, who gave Isaac Franklin $500 for them.

With that, ten men, ranging from Armstead Jackson and Stephen Bladrer, age twenty-one, to Armstead Riley and Moses Hall, age thirty-four, became the property of Louise Patin. The widow of Jacques Etienne Roman, a cattle rancher and sugar planter in Saint James Parish, Patin had sent her son Zenon Roman with $6,000 to make the acquisition on her behalf.[56]

Before the year was out, Franklin would conduct forty-one different sales transactions in New Orleans, trading away the lives of 112 people. He sold roughly a quarter of those people individually. He sold others in pairs, trios, or larger groups, including one sale of 16 people at once. Felix DeArmas and another notary named William Boswell recorded most of the transactions, though Franklin also relied on the services of seven other notaries, probably in response to customer preferences. The majority of Franklin's customers, purchasers collectively of 70 people, reported their residence as being in New Orleans proper. But Franklin also sold to buyers scattered across seven different parishes in sugar-growing regions north and west of the city.[57]

In a few instances, Franklin sold slaves to free people of color, such as when he sold Eliza and Priscilla, eleven and twelve years old, to New Orleans bricklayer Myrtille Courcelle. But nearly all of Franklin's customers were white. Some were tradesmen—people like coach and harness maker Charles Bebee, goldsmith Jean Claude Mairot, and druggist Joseph Dufilho. Others were people of more significant substance and status. Franklin sold two people to John Witherspoon Smith, whose father and grandfather had both served as presidents of the College of New Jersey, known today as Princeton University, and who had himself been United States district judge for Louisiana. Franklin sold a young woman named Anna to John Ami Merle, a merchant and the Swedish and Norwegian consul in New Orleans, and he sold four young men to François Gaiennié, a wood merchant, city council member, and brigadier general in the state militia. One of Louise Patin's sons, André Roman, was speaker of the house in the state legislature. He would be elected governor in 1830.[58]

We rarely know what Franklin's customers did with the people they dispersed across southern Louisiana. Buyers of single individuals probably intended them for domestic servants or as laborers in their place of business. Many others probably put the enslaved they bought to work in the sugar industry. Few other purposes explain why sugar refiner Nathan Goodale would purchase a lot of ten boys and men, or why Christopher Colomb, an Ascension Parish plantation owner, enlisted his New Orleans commission merchant, Noel Auguste Baron, to buy six male teenagers on his behalf.[59]

Franklin mostly cared that he walked away richer from the deals, and there was no denying that. Gross sales for Franklin and Armfield in New Orleans in 1828 came to a bit more than $56,000. Revenue was split almost evenly between cash and credit, the latter extended primarily in the form of personal promissory notes that usually came due in a year or less and could often be drawn on city banks or a commission merchant's counting house. But even promissory notes needed security, and sometimes purchasers took out a "special mortgage," in which the monetary value of the slaves changing hands also guaranteed the notes. As slaveholders, creditors, and slave traders collaborated to smooth the movement of enslaved capital, they forced Black people in bondage to ground the financing of their own sales.[60]

Few of John Armfield's purchasing records have survived, making a precise tally of the company's profits impossible. But several scholars estimate that slave traders in the late 1820s and early 1830s saw returns in the range of 20 to 30 percent, which would put Franklin and Armfield's earnings for the last two months of 1828 somewhere between $11,000 and $17,000. Equivalent to $300,000 to $450,000 today, the figure does not include proceeds from slave sales the company made from ongoing operations in Natchez. Even accounting for expenses and payments to agents, clerks, assistants, and other auxiliary personnel, the money was a powerful incentive to keep going.[61]

Though focused intently on the slave trade, Isaac Franklin maintained a deep fondness for his family back in Tennessee. In notarial acts to which he was a party, he identified Sumner County as his place of residence, and he owned land there even while he lived mostly in Mississippi and Louisiana. When his father, James Franklin Sr., died in December 1828, it strengthened Isaac Franklin's desire for a connection to his birthplace, as such losses experienced at a distance often do. Left a small piece of land in his father's will, Franklin went to Sumner County in the summer of 1829 and bought another forty-two acres adjoining it and the land he already owned along the west fork of Station Camp Creek. The property was situated among the estates of many of his siblings and their families, and he imagined retiring there for good someday.[62]

Rice Ballard also thought about making a home, in due course, near where he had been born in Virginia. His relationship to his parents had long since become distant, but his bond with Samuel Alsop had grown into something familial as well as financial. In the summer of 1828, Ballard and Alsop together purchased nineteen hundred acres of land, part of a Spotsylvania County estate known as Bleakhill. They renamed the property Coventry and placed on it several dozen enslaved people and about ten horses. In time, it might be a spot where Ballard could lay claim to eminence like that his mother's ancestors had once possessed.[63]

John Armfield, by contrast, was not inclined to return to North Carolina or to think at all about what the future held for him outside the slave trade and his life in Alexandria. Planting held no interest, and the truth was that slave trading on the scale he and Isaac Franklin had begun required a single-mindedness that allowed few distractions. If he and Franklin, and Ballard, wanted to keep doing what they were doing, entertaining the idea of doing something else was more an indulgence than a serious plan. Slave trading was not merely what they did. It was too consuming to be just that. It was becoming who they were.

Ballard's dealings in Virginia and Mississippi as the 1820s ended appear mostly in snapshots: a smattering of newspaper advertisements, William Hayden's memories, a few partial inventories of enslaved people he planned to sell in the lower South, taxes paid on some sales. There is scattered evidence that Ballard sometimes operated in ways even white people considered shady. In December 1829, for example, a jailor in southwest Virginia reported he had taken into custody Thomas Brooks, who had fled from Mississippi after being sold there by Ballard despite claiming that he was "a free man." A few months later, a slaveholder named George McGehee sued Ballard in Natchez, charging that Ballard had sold and warrantied the soundness of a man named Pompey even though he was "unsound in body" and had since died. Pompey had been twenty-two years old when Ballard sold him, less than two years before. The sale was a priority. Pompey's health was not.[64]

Ballard forged useful business connections anyway. When he faced legal problems in Natchez, he could count on Peter Lapice to act as his security and on George Adams or the law firm of Buckner and Hunt to stand as his attorneys. Born in Saint-Domingue to a sugar and coffee planter, Lapice fled with his family to New Orleans as a child during the Haitian Revolution, served under Andrew Jackson during the War of 1812, and moved to Natchez to represent the New Orleans merchant firm of Laurent Millaudon, after which he became a cotton planter and merchant in his own right. George Adams had been attorney general of Mississippi, and the named partners in Buckner and Hunt came from some of the most influential families in the Natchez District. They also worked as lawyers for Isaac Franklin.[65]

Franklin and Armfield's affairs are clearer than Ballard's. Encouraged by Isaac Franklin's success in New Orleans in the final
months of 1828, John Armfield started advertising in a second
Washington City newspaper, the *Daily National Intelligencer*, and
in Alexandria he kept buying people and shipping them south. In
mid-January 1829, Franklin went back to the levee by the wharves
on the Mississippi River to receive a shipment of enslaved people
from the schooner *Lafayette*. Armfield had personally consigned
forty-six people to Franklin on the *Lafayette*, and he was eager to
send Franklin as many slaves as possible, so he arranged for the
Lafayette to carry a supplementary shipment of twenty-one more.
They were consigned by Henry Dawson, a tavern owner whose location in Lovingston, Virginia, nearly 150 miles southwest of Alexandria, speaks to Franklin and Armfield's widening geographic
reach. A little over four weeks after the *Lafayette* sailed, Armfield
sent still more people to Franklin, shipping forty boys and men and
seventeen girls and women with Captain Isaac Staples on a 138-ton
brig called the *Comet*.[66]

Business in New Orleans had proven so good so fast that Franklin needed help keeping up, especially if he was also to maintain the
company's sizable position in Mississippi. He compensated for being
stretched so thin by authorizing Natchez merchant Eli Montgomery
to act as his sometime proxy there, but his most significant personnel decision was to promote his nephew James Rawlings Franklin
from purchasing agent to his assistant sometime between the fall of
1828 and the summer of 1829. Tasked with shuttling among Natchez, New Orleans, and Alexandria, James Franklin gathered and
brought with him relevant news, kept an eye on company agents in
the field, moved enslaved people from place to place as needed, and
helped with the company books. Franklin and Armfield liked his
work, and it became obvious that Isaac Franklin had marked him
as a protégé.[67]

Between January and March 1829, Isaac Franklin sold 143 people in New Orleans, and both his reputation and his market presence were spreading. The mix of city residents to whom he sold now included a growing number of merchants, who were probably buying for countryside clients and had heard Franklin was reliable. It included institutional buyers such as the Society for the Relief of Destitute Orphan Boys, which purchased an eighteen-year-old woman named Eleanor, who the society's board of directors wanted "placed in the asylum and there employed as a seamstress." It included Felix DeArmas and his brother Octave, who were both notaries, and it included Gustave Marigny, whose father, Bernard Marigny, had developed his plantation into the Faubourg Marigny.[68]

What most notably set early-1829 sales apart from those of late 1828 was the fact that more than three-quarters of them were to buyers outside New Orleans. A few were to repeat customers, such as Louise Patin, who was so pleased with the sugar workers she had purchased that she bought twenty-five more men, women, and children from Franklin. But many were to new clients, and they came from a dozen different parishes, ranging from Saint Bernard Parish, southeast of New Orleans, all the way to Rapides Parish, which was nearly two hundred miles northwest of the city. In southern Louisiana's cane fields, work was so punishing and the disease environment was so debilitating that the enslaved died faster than they could be replaced. But Isaac Franklin would sell slaveholders as many Black laborers as they wanted.[69]

Franklin and Armfield was particularly flush by the spring of 1829, in no small part because of the fifty-seven transactions Isaac Franklin had made in New Orleans during the first three months of the year, fifty were cash sales. There was nothing especially unusual about that. Sugar and cotton harvests ended late in the calendar year, putting funds at slaveholders' disposal precisely when they were assessing their labor needs for the following season. More unusual was the sheer level of demand for slaves throughout the lower South, which had been increasing for several years. Antislavery activists consistently found the slave trade outrageous, and there were always policymakers and members of the general public who found it distasteful. But its expansiveness in the late 1820s produced new levels of unease in exactly the places Franklin and Armfield were trying to grow.[70]

In the spring of 1827, an Alexandria organization called the Benevolent Society for Ameliorating and Improving the Condition of the People of Color blasted the slave trade and "the cruelties exercised upon its wretched victims." Observing that federal law branded participation in the transatlantic trade "an act of piracy and punished [it] with death," the group wondered why the domestic trade was "sanctioned and encouraged by our laws and customs." It deplored the removal of enslaved people "from all the local attachments of early life" and their deposit "hundreds of miles from the place of their birth," the mere prospect of which drove some to suicide and caused others to die of shock and heartbreak, the "anguish of a wounded spirit." The trade was appalling, it was relentless, and it was all the more scandalous because Alexandria was in the District of Columbia, "the very fountain from which the laws of freedom and equal rights are expected to flow." The Benevolent Society implored Congress to use its authority over the District and do something. "If we are not yet prepared to strike at the root of the slave system," it concluded, "let us at least endeavor to lop off some of the branches of this evil tree, which casts so dark a shade over the prospects of our country."[71]

Pennsylvania congressman Charles Miner spent the second half of the 1820s trying to do just that, crafting resolutions and presenting petitions to abolish the slave trade and end slavery throughout the District of Columbia. In January 1829, Miner exhorted his fellow representatives to stop the men who made the District "their head quarters for carrying on the domestic slave trade." Slave traders, Miner explained, used squalid and overcrowded jails, including the public prison, to conduct their business. They funneled money covertly to federal marshals and their deputies in order to enlist their help, and they kidnapped free people of color and sold them into slavery without consequence, making precarious the circumstances of all Black people in the capital. Miner told his colleagues that their apathy allowed such "corruptions" to flourish, because traders did "not dread any expression of your displeasure. These scenes have been exhibited here by the slave dealers for nearly thirty years, under your eye, and congress has not moved to arrest their course. Your silence," Miner asserted, "gives sanction to the trade."[72]

To show "the openness with which the slave dealers proceeded," Miner read into the record slave-trader advertisements from District newspapers. He began with Franklin and Armfield, and the company's name started appearing across the country as papers and magazines reprinted Miner's speech. But the frenetic pace of the slave trade also bothered some residents of areas in the lower South where enslaved people from the District and its surroundings ended up. William Anderson, who was trafficked from Virginia to Mississippi, saw so "many slave pens" in Natchez in the late 1820s that he found it "impossible . . . to give more than a faint idea" of the trade's size in the city. Municipal authorities feared the trade was becoming unmanageable, and in the spring of 1827, they indicted twenty-three traders for ignoring a state law requiring certification that enslaved people brought into Mississippi for sale had no records of criminality in their states of origin.[73]

The crackdown had little impact, and as the fall selling season approached, one Natchez editor worried the city would be inundated by slaves imported from out of state. "We have heard it said," he wrote, "that from 1500 to 2000, will certainly be brought to this city and neighborhood." For a place with a total population of around twenty-five hundred people, such figures were shocking. The editor thought a legislative special session was in order, but the state failed to act, so the city took matters into its own hands. In the spring of

1829, the Natchez Board of Selectmen passed an ordinance "to prevent the exhibition of Negroes for sale within the limits of certain streets." Except for auctions carried out by legal officials or licensed auctioneers, it became a fineable offense "for any person or persons to keep and offer for sale any negro slave or slaves" on the bluff above the Mississippi River or in an area covering more than fifty square blocks in the heart of the city. The mayor could provide short-term exemptions to traders with fewer than ten enslaved people to sell, but the aim of the law was clear. Natchez wanted slave traders to work someplace other than the middle of town.[74]

The numbers of enslaved people being brought by slave traders seemed overwhelming in New Orleans too. The repeal of the state ban on slave imports in 1828 unleashed a torrent on the city, and the 112 enslaved people Isaac Franklin sold there were a fraction of the more than 3,000 people traders sold that year. Commerce in human beings at that level was unparalleled in the city's recent history. Domestic traders sold nearly three times as many people as in any previous year, and in 1829 they seemed likely to break even that dubious record. The editor of the *Louisiana Courier* was stunned by the numbers, writing in January that "there has been TWO THOUSAND SIX HUNDRED & SEVENTY SLAVES brought to this place since the first of Oct. last, by way of the Balize!"[75]

Weeks later, the state legislature responded with new regulations. After April 1, 1829, anyone bringing enslaved people into Louisiana for sale had to provide a certificate for each person over the age of twelve. The certificate had to contain a physical description, the names of the seller and the buyer in the enslaved person's home county, and the signatures of two white witnesses who swore that they had "known the said slave for several years" and that he or she had a "good moral character" and neither a "habit of running away" nor any criminal convictions. The certificate had to be endorsed by the clerk and the judge of the home county court, and a copy had to be deposited with a notary or parish judge in Louisiana at the time of sale. Failure to comply entailed fines and jail time, and slaves brought without certificates would be sold at public auction, with proceeds going mostly to the state. The legislature also banned the sale of any enslaved children under age ten unless their mothers accompanied them, and it enjoined the New Orleans City Council to prevent the exposure of slaves for sale "in the public and most frequented" parts of the city and to regulate conditions wherever slaves would still be allowed to be "lodged, kept, and sold."[76]

Mayor Denis Prieur had advised the city council to pass such regulations months earlier, warning in May 1828 that "the negroes imported as merchandise, into this City to be sold, are sheltered in various quarters, to the great prejudice of the neighborhood, and of the public health." With so many enslaved people crammed together in tight quarters, Prieur worried "that an epidemic could break out," and he urged the council "to order that these shelters of slaves for sale can be established only outside the body of the City." Prieur's caution had fallen on deaf ears, but the state legislature's concern led the council to make it illegal to "expose publicly, or lodge any slave or slaves introduced into the city for sale or hire, in the square of the city included within Canal, Rampart, Esplanade and Levee streets." Beginning April 15, 1829, professional slave traders would more or less be pushed outside the city of New Orleans.[77]

As the legal and political environment for the slave trade shifted, Franklin and Armfield adjusted. A few weeks after Louisiana banned sales of unaccompanied young children, for example, John Armfield changed the language of his standard newspaper advertisement. He added that he wanted to buy both "field hands" and "mechanics of every description," by which he meant blacksmiths, carpenters, and other skilled enslaved people for whom he could charge a premium. But he clarified that he was no longer interested in buying anyone less than twelve years old.[78]

Franklin and Armfield could always lie about an enslaved person's age, claim that someone obviously younger than ten was an "orphan" when purchased and thus legally sellable, or bring children to Natchez, as Mississippi had no age restrictions on slave sales. Scruples were certainly no obstacle, and Franklin and Armfield never stopped selling children. Sometimes they just gave them away, such as when Isaac Franklin presented an eleven-year-old girl named Letha as a gift in December 1829 to Louisa Chauveau, the five-year-old daughter of Louis Chauveau, a New Orleans merchant who was on the city council and managed the New Orleans Jockey Club. But playing around the edges of the law was mostly not worth the trouble. Profits on the very young were already thin.[79]

To conduct business unhindered by the broader ban on slave trading in New Orleans, meanwhile, Franklin rented a spot outside the city proper. In April 1829, he leased a house at the diagonal intersection of Esplanade Avenue and Francais Street, now known as Frenchmen Street, along with three adjacent vacant lots along Francais. Located on the downriver side of Esplanade, the house was in the Faubourg Marigny but right across the street from the city limits, making it convenient for customers. It was about a block off the levee, making it convenient for Franklin to receive shipments of enslaved people. The house had space for living quarters and an office, and the vacant lots could be converted into a slave pen by building a wall. The timing of Franklin's move conformed to city regulations, but to continue selling large numbers of people in New Orleans, establishing a facility like the one he had in Natchez and the one Armfield had in Alexandria made sense anyhow.[80]

Accommodating politics and the laws regarding the slave trade was one thing. Slowing down was quite another, and Franklin and Armfield had no intention of doing that. In Alexandria and in Congress, antislavery forces had voices but not much power. Maryland congressman John Weems responded to Charles Miner's speech about the District of Columbia slave trade with an unapologetic defense of interstate commerce in human beings, and Miner's call to action was referred to a committee whose report showed that its members cared little about either Miner's concerns or the lives of those taken in the trade. Free Black people were adequately protected by the law and jails protected the enslaved "from the inclemency of the seasons." Committee members did acknowledge that "violence may sometimes be done" to the feelings of enslaved people "in the separation of families," but they felt it ought to be "some consolation . . . to know, that their condition is more frequently bettered, and their minds happier by the exchange."[81]

In Natchez, Isaac Franklin's slave-trading facility was already beyond the boundaries imposed by the board of selectmen, and neither that regulation nor those in Louisiana were really about containing the size of the slave trade anyway. They were about allowing it to continue while protecting white people's sensibilities, anxieties, and insecurities. Certificates supposedly guaranteed that enslaved people imported by traders would not undermine slavery or endanger white lives. Forbidding sales of unaccompanied children let white people believe their cruelty had limits, and forcing traders in New Orleans to house and display slaves outside the city was a matter of delicacy as much as epidemiology. Pens holding enslaved captives were foul places, attractive to flies and lice and vermin, hazy with acrid smoke from cheap pork cooked over open flames, and reeking of sweat and urine and feces and garbage. They would be no less loathsome somewhere else, but at least the squeamish would not have to walk past them.

Franklin and Armfield carried on. In Alexandria, John Armfield tweaked company advertisements, but he still promised cash for up to "ONE HUNDRED LIKELY NEGROES" at a time, and he still packed scores of enslaved people onto coastal vessels for shipment to New Orleans. Isaac Franklin sold some of them there from the facility at Esplanade and Francais, and he sent others by steamboat to be sold in Natchez. This was a model of steady accumulation, shipment, and sale much like the company overseen by Austin Woolfolk. The seed Franklin and Armfield planted for a slave-trading colossus was sprouting.[82]

In April and May 1829, Isaac Franklin sold eighty enslaved people in New Orleans. He sold seventy-five more in November and December, by which point his operation was so large that he could manipulate the market, driving up prices by holding back some of the people he intended to sell. Gross sales in New Orleans for the calendar year came to nearly $80,000, corresponding to more than $2 million today. Sales figures from Natchez cannot be calculated, but overall profits for the company suggest they were about the same. We have a decent guess at those profits thanks to Benjamin Lundy, who was undeterred by Woolfolk's pummeling him in the street. In January 1830, working with a new editorial assistant named William Lloyd Garrison, Lundy reported in the *Genius of Universal Emancipation* that after expenses, "the celebrated firm of Franklin and Armfield realized . . . a nett profit of $33,000 for the year 1829."[83]

It was not enough. They wanted more. A lot more.

Because Franklin and Armfield complied, at least for a while, with the Louisiana certificate law, we have a rough sense of the geography the company ransacked for human merchandise. Certificates documenting the origins of 162 people the company sold in New Orleans have survived from 1829. Just over 40 percent came from Washington City, Alexandria, and half a dozen Virginia counties extending west and north of the District of Columbia into what is now the eastern panhandle of West Virginia. The rest came from four Maryland counties east and south of the District, with most coming from Prince George's and Charles Counties. Together, the locations formed a kind of unclasped necklace around Alexandria and show company agents finding Chesapeake markets where sheer purchasing power provided footholds.[84]

By the fall and winter of 1829, Franklin and Armfield were implementing changes to increase the company's profits, size, and clout further still. A critical innovation came with regard to shipping, where John Armfield thought he saw a way for the company to defray some of the seventeen dollars it cost to ship each captive from Alexandria to New Orleans. In early December, he advertised that he had chartered the *United States*, and that "persons wishing to ship" to Louisiana could apply to him directly to book space.[85]

Having coordinated multiple shipments of enslaved people since the previous fall, Armfield believed he could handle the logistics of chartering and filling an entire brig. Doing so obviously cost Franklin and Armfield more up front than paying only to transport company captives, but they would come out ahead if other shippers paid enough in fees. Armfield also understood that slave traders who shipped enslaved people wanted them delivered in a dependable and timely fashion, and that most ships could not provide predictability because they did not leave port until their holds were full. So he advertised the *United States* as a "packet brig," meaning it would sail on or very near a specific date. Armfield assured potential shippers that the *United States* would leave "about the 15th January." It sailed for New Orleans on January 17, 1830, carrying eighty-five enslaved people.[86]

Armfield consigned more than sixty of those people himself, directly to Isaac Franklin, and the revenue stream from the shipping business started small. But it was remunerative enough that Armfield chartered vessels offering packet service at least twice more in 1830, in both cases relying on ships that, like the *United States*, were familiar carriers in the coastal slave trade. In April, Armfield announced that he had space on the schooner *James Monroe*, a veteran slaver with a veteran captain named Walter Bush. In December, Armfield advertised that shippers who wanted "to avoid disappointment" ought to make "early application" for room on "the fast sailing regular packet schooner LAFAYETTE." John Armfield was becoming a specialty shipper for the domestic slave trade.[87]

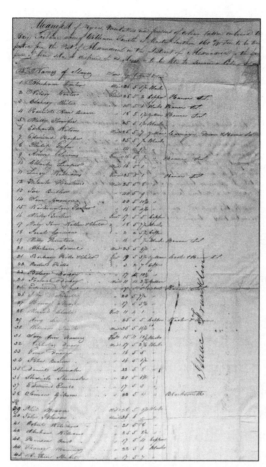

A partial manifest of a shipment of enslaved people from Alexandria to New Orleans in November 1834. Of the 101 people in this shipment, 55 were delivered directly to Isaac Franklin for sale. Argosy Collection, Albert and Shirley Small Special Collections Library, University of Virginia.

Sometimes Franklin and Armfield entrusted the captains of the ships they used with safeguarding and acting as couriers for enslaved people in transit. Captains of slavers often had experience making the coastal run to New Orleans, and it was not uncommon for them to purchase people in their own name and sell them at ports of destination for extra money. Seamen were not the most dependable sorts, which could cut different ways on a slaver. On the one hand, white crew members were infamous for inflicting violence on captives, and on the other, enslaved, free Black, and even some white sailors might be ill-disposed toward slavery and the broader economic contours of the Atlantic world. But John Armfield used vessels he considered

reliable and captains he considered responsible and able to keep sub-
ordinates in line. He counted on their desire to continue earning his
patronage.[88]

As much as self-interest, self-preservation motivated captains
and crews of coastal slavers to keep close watch on the enslaved people they carried. No one got trafficked in the slave trade willingly,
and while uprisings were more frequent on transatlantic slavers,
anger and desperation were no less widespread on domestic passages. Captives on coastal slavers were chained in holds at night, but
during the day they might not be, so captains and crews always kept
weapons on board, and vessels like the *United States* were equipped
with multiple guns. Ship personnel understood that the prospect of
revolt was real and becoming more so as the slave trade expanded in
the 1820s.[89]

John Armfield understood that too, because there had been a
rebellion on a ship he chartered just a year before he chartered it.
On November 17, 1829, the *Lafayette* was three days out from Norfolk, carrying 197 enslaved people en route to New Orleans, when
three captives, armed "with handspikes, knives, billets of wood,
&c.," grabbed Captain Benjamin Bissell and began fighting his
crew. Thirty or forty more enslaved people joined them, and the
rebels took over the crew's living quarters before being forced back
into the hold. Several were "severely wounded" in the process, and
twenty-five of them, considered "ring-leaders of the affray," were
"ring-bolted to the deck" until they got to New Orleans. Upon examination, the insurgents revealed that they had hatched their plan
in Norfolk, on another slaver from which many of them had been
transferred to the *Lafayette*, and that they had intended "to force the
crew to take them to St. Domingo or New York."[90]

The rebellion on the *Lafayette* failed, but similar plots nearly un-
folded on two other slavers out of Norfolk, and the events "produced
considerable excitement among the citizens" of New Orleans. The
editor of the *Louisiana Courier* suggested the rebellion and the plots

showed that the state legislature had erred by reopening Louisiana to the domestic slave trade, and he hoped it would reconsider and "take some effectual mode of preventing us from being overwhelmed by vicious and vagabond slaves." Shipboard resistance never made John Armfield reconsider what he was doing, but it demonstrated that captains and crews might not always adequately keep watch over company shipments, so he often sent an employee as an escort to provide more security.[91]

In 1830 alone, Armfield sent at least six different white men to accompany enslaved people from Alexandria to New Orleans. William Swann, who brought Franklin forty people on the ship *Shenandoah* in late January, was a sometime slave trader who purchased people out of a Maryland tavern. George Davis, who escorted sixty-three captives on the *United States* two weeks later, had been a carpenter before going to work for Franklin and Armfield. Thomas Coote sailed with at least sixty slaves in April on the *James Monroe*. An itinerant sawyer and weaver, Coote had also worked for a Kentucky slave trader for several years in the 1820s. Drawn from the classes of mechanics and tradesmen and from the corps of smaller slave traders who perhaps hoped to become larger ones, these couriers were some of the assistants and clerks who lived at the Duke Street facility. Bringing enslaved people to New Orleans by sea was one of their jobs, the maritime equivalent of superintending a forced march of captives across the continent.[92]

Swann, Davis, and Coote probably worked on salary. They may also have earned commissions for bringing enslaved people or their white sellers to Franklin and Armfield, and the company offered their security services on slavers to other traders. But as Franklin and Armfield vertically integrated purchasing, incarcerating, shipping, marketing, and selling enslaved people, the partners also added a new structural layer to their organization. Isaac Franklin and John Armfield had reached the point where their slave-trading business was both too big for them to coordinate and supervise alone and not nearly as big as they wanted and believed it could be. Efficient and manageable growth moving forward called for delegating some managerial and operational responsibilities so that the company partners could focus on administration, planning, and overarching strategy.[93]

The promotion of James Rawlings Franklin was the first step in this reconfiguration, and his duties grew over time. In October 1829, he arranged a shipment of seventy-five enslaved people from Alexandria, sailed with them, delivered them to his uncle, spent several weeks in New Orleans, and sold forty people from the pen on Esplanade and Francais. James Franklin Purvis started taking on larger and more important roles in the business as well. In May 1829, he too spent time in New Orleans, where he sold twenty-three people from the company facility, gaining practical experience with the notarial system and an appreciation for markets in the lower South. By late summer, Purvis was back in the Chesapeake and stationed regularly in the District of Columbia. He would stay there for more than two years, buying "likely young negroes" for Franklin and Armfield at George McCandless's tavern in Georgetown and at Washington Robey's tavern and slave pen on Ninth Street in Washington City.[94]

Isaac Franklin had worked with a series of relatives in the trade, and familiarity and the preference for keeping money within a network of kin made it unsurprising that he would install his nephews as lieutenants. But he and John Armfield were not related. They imagined their company as a modern business that could unite capital, labor, and knowledge exogenously, and they started moving more purposefully in that direction, recruiting other slave traders to work as agents in a kind of subsidiary relationship with the parent company.

Their first recruit was Jourdan Michaux Saunders. Born in 1796 in North Carolina, Saunders grew up in a wealthy slaveholding family in north-central Tennessee's Smith County. Long-distance slave traders regularly traveled with coffles through Smith County along a popular overland route that ran from northern Virginia, past Nashville, and on to Mississippi, and at around the time he turned thirty, Saunders decided he wanted to be a trader himself. In the fall of 1827, he signed articles of agreement with his brother-in-law, David Burford, to operate "in the negro speculation business" as J. M. Saunders and Company.[95]

Saunders and Burford each contributed $2,000 as initial capital, but Burford was busy with a farm, a family, and his position as the sheriff of Smith County, so Saunders conducted most company business alone. He started by canvassing for information and scouting locations in the upper South, and he decided to make Fauquier County, Virginia, his base of operations. Fauquier was located fifty miles west of Alexandria, nearly half its population was enslaved, and as in much of northeastern Virginia, its transition away from a tobacco economy left slaveholders looking to shed people they considered excess laborers. It seemed a promising spot for a slave trader, so in the spring of 1828, Saunders rented a room in Fauquier's one sizable town, the county seat of Warrenton, and got to work.[96]

His first season was a fiasco. Impatient to turn a profit, Saunders accumulated around twenty enslaved people and forced them to walk from Virginia to Louisiana in the middle of a blazing summer. He arrived in New Orleans well before slaveholders there were looking to buy slaves, and he spent months dragging his captives hundreds of miles more through the sugar parishes, selling them on credit and leaving himself holding debts that he would have to return to collect. J. M. Saunders and Company almost certainly lost money in 1828, and Saunders became pessimistic about making it in the slave trade. But he learned from his mistakes. In 1829, he started buying people later than he had in 1828, so he might be more in tune with the seasons of the trade, and he abandoned the idea of walking the enslaved overland. He decided, instead, to bring them to Alexandria and book passage on a coastal slaver.[97]

That choice changed his luck, and it altered the fates of hundreds of enslaved people in and around Fauquier County. On October 30, 1829, Saunders set sail for New Orleans on the *United States*. The 14 enslaved people for whom he had paid passage were stowed on board alongside 127 other captives, among them the 75 people James Rawlings Franklin was bringing to his uncle. Franklin got to know Saunders while they sailed together and heard about his frustrations with the trade. He probably encouraged Saunders to stop by Isaac Franklin's facility in the Faubourg Marigny if he needed advice or had trouble making sales, because four days after landing in New Orleans, Saunders sold four young men, a teenage boy, and two teenage girls to Isaac Franklin for $3,500 in cash. Franklin, in fact, invited Saunders to stay through the winter at the house on Esplanade and Francais and to keep on-site any enslaved people he wanted to sell, all of it on what Saunders considered "the cheapest terms."[98]

Perhaps Franklin asked Saunders to stay because he wanted to monitor a competitor or because he wanted companionship, or the offer may have been simply a matter of the professional courtesy in which slave traders engaged despite their usually cutthroat rivalries. But given what happened next, Franklin may have seen a man with potential. In February 1830, Franklin proposed that Saunders live in Virginia year-round and "buy throughout the season" on behalf of Franklin and Armfield. Saunders knew immediately that he would accept the offer. Franklin's "experience and acquaintance in this market gives him a decided advantage in the making of sales over allmost any other person engaged in the business," Saunders wrote to Burford, "and upon the whole I have little or no doubt of it being an excellent arrangement for me."[99]

As Saunders explained the arrangement to Burford, the companies Franklin and Armfield and J. M. Saunders and Company would each "furnish an equal amt. of capital, say eight thousand dollars. The negroes to be shipped to Isaac Franklin at N. Orleans, then and there to be disposed of, and the profits or loss to be equally divided as the case may be." It is easy to understand why Saunders said yes. With Franklin and Armfield as a financial backer, Saunders had twice as much capital at his disposal as he and Burford could muster by themselves. Saunders also spread his and Burford's personal risk, and he knew Isaac Franklin would do his best both to broker any slaves Saunders sent and to collect any debts he was owed, because Franklin's interest in sales and collections would match Saunders's.[100]

The arrangement also meant that Saunders would not have to spend months going from Virginia to Louisiana and back again. He only had to bring enslaved people to Alexandria, and John Armfield would send them from there to New Orleans, saving Saunders the physical toll of travel and time spent on shipping and sales that could be devoted to purchasing. By staying in and around Warrenton for the entire buying season, Saunders could also accumulate enslaved people in much larger numbers than he had before, and that meant larger profits than he was ever likely to see working on his own, even after splitting them with Franklin and Armfield. Finally, by working with Franklin and Armfield, Jourdan Saunders could learn about the slave trade from men at the top of the business. Only by seeing a company like Franklin and Armfield from the inside could one access the partners' insights and lessons, partake in their intelligence about markets and prices, and learn the techniques that made for success.

The arrangement was hardly all to Saunders's benefit. J. M. Saunders and Company fit nicely as Franklin and Armfield's first subsidiary, significantly extending the parent company's reach in Virginia. Fauquier County itself encompassed more than seven hundred square miles, and Saunders, either personally or through his own network of agents, sometimes purchased people from as far away as

Winchester, a Shenandoah Valley town more than fifty miles north-west of Warrenton.[101]

Isaac Franklin and John Armfield thought as well that Jourdan Saunders would make sound and productive use of the capital they were willing to commit to him. Franklin and Saunders came from the same part of Tennessee, and they probably knew people and had experiences in common. James Rawlings Franklin quickly came to consider Saunders a friend, and Isaac Franklin would never have offered Saunders a place to stay in New Orleans had he disliked his company. What mattered most, though, was that the winter Franklin spent with Saunders convinced him Saunders was good at being a slave trader.[102]

Having inspected the enslaved people Saunders brought to New Orleans and having bought half of them himself, Franklin concluded that Saunders had an eye for acquiring slaves who would appeal to customers. He also saw that Saunders had the disposition to do well in the trade. Saunders was aggressive but not reckless, decent with accounts, pitiless when it came to enslaved people, and never satisfied with what was in his pocket if he could have more. After Saunders sold the enslaved people he brought to New Orleans, he spent $7,800 of the cash he had amassed to buy sixteen more people from Franklin. He sold them all in a few weeks and then gave Franklin another $5,300 to buy ten more people "for speculation." Franklin surely pushed Saunders to assume the risks involved in the purchases, but Saunders made them pay off, confirming that he had the cool head and the drive Franklin and Armfield were looking for.[103]

J. M. Saunders and Company's first selling season working with Franklin and Armfield began in the fall of 1830. When Jourdan Saunders told David Burford in early December that he was about to send "12 No. 1 Boys & girls" to the Duke Street compound, it brought the total number of enslaved people he had sent in recent months to fifty, which was already more than twice as many people as he had ever moved before. John Armfield wanted him to keep them coming. A boat was leaving Alexandria on Christmas Day, and Armfield told Saunders the company wanted "to ship all on hand at that time." Business was brisk in New Orleans, he reported, adding, "Mr. Franklin instructs us to purchase all we can."[104]

Franklin and Armfield brought George Kephart on board at around the same time they began working with Jourdan Saunders, and on similar terms. The son of a tavern keeper from the western Maryland town of Frederick, Kephart had been selling slaves in Natchez and New Orleans since at least 1827, and he was infamous among enslaved people in and around Frederick. One man later recalled that the enslaved "trembled" when "it was reported that he was about," and not only because Kephart was especially hateful. He also worked to his particular advantage his location on the border between the slave and free states and the desire of the enslaved to cross from one to the other. Kephart was known to supplement his regular purchases by tracking and capturing runaways who fled from Maryland to Pennsylvania and then buying them cheaply from slaveholders who would rather be rid of the trouble.[105]

But the most important connection Franklin and Armfield forged as the 1830s began was with Rice Ballard, whose relationship to the parent company functioned differently than did those of Saunders, Kephart, and other agents and affiliates. While the associations Franklin and Armfield created with Saunders and Kephart entailed provisionally intertwining capital, the former had no binding interests in the operations of the latter, and either party could undo their arrangements at will. Soon after Isaac Franklin, John Armfield, and Rice Ballard started working together, however, they crafted entirely new companies whose workings remained technically separate yet contractually interlocked. Doing so helped retain clarity when it came to legal obligations and accounting. The clarity would be needed, because Ballard was to be Franklin and Armfield's man on the ground in Richmond, which was emerging as the next thriving market for Chesapeake slave exports. Other than John Armfield, Isaac Franklin, and perhaps Franklin's nephews, Rice Ballard was about to become the most significant person in the company.[106]

FOUR

CURRENCIES, 1830–1833

A PURCHASING AGENT WORKING FOR RICE BALLARD PASSED through the central Virginia town of Charlottesville and bought sixteen-year-old Martha Sweart for $350. That was between $50 and $100 more than slave traders were typically spending for young women early in 1832, but Ballard's agent believed a buyer in the lower South might pay a premium for her. He brought Sweart to Richmond and delivered her to Ballard, who imprisoned her in the city for several weeks before putting her on a steamboat that churned down the James River to Norfolk. There, Sweart and 87 other enslaved people met a coastwise vessel on its way to New Orleans, a slaver called the *Tribune* that had left Alexandria five days earlier carrying 134 captives, more than half of them consigned by John Armfield.[1]

Passage on the crowded ship was made even more perilous and difficult by a measles outbreak on board, and Sweart had still other trials ahead of her. After landing in New Orleans, she and over one hundred of her shipmates were transferred to another steamboat. It went up the Mississippi River to Natchez, where Sweart took her place in line, climbed the bluff, and stumbled through the city in chains, still wearing what she had on when she left Virginia, now reduced practically to rags. She ended up at Franklin and Armfield's compound on the Washington road, where James Rawlings Franklin awaited her. Sizing up the teenager, all of five foot two with skin described both in Rice Ballard's purchasing records and on the *Tribune* manifest as "yellow," Franklin thought Sweart a fine specimen for sale as a "fancy." The term was a euphemism that entered the lexicon of the slave trade in the 1830s to describe young women peddled to customers as sex slaves. Franklin and Armfield would market Martha Sweart as someone white men would want to rape.[2]

She was not the first. They were strewn across company records, the young, often light-skinned enslaved women and girls made available to white men as sources of pleasure, power, and profit. The commoditized fantasies of racial and sexual domination were revealed in the prices paid. Eighteen-year-old Amy Watts, like Martha Sweart, was denoted on a purchase list by Rice Ballard as "yellow." Ballard paid $500 for Watts in the fall of 1832, about 50 percent more than he paid for other women her age and more than he paid for most young enslaved men, whose prices served as the benchmark for the slave trade. Three months after shipping Watts to Natchez, Ballard consigned Elizabeth Cosby and Mary Ann Ambler for passage to the lower South. He described Cosby as "yellow," and Ambler as "brown," and while he marked down that the seventeen-year-olds were both "seamstresses," that too was often a kind of code word. No skill with the needle explained why Ballard had paid $600 apiece for Cosby and Ambler, nearly twice what other teenage women had been costing him and far more than he had been paying for young men.[3]

Ballard's expenditures could be justified by the money made speculating on the erotic desires of slaveholders. Watts, Cosby, and Ambler were sold privately in Mississippi, but in New Orleans, notarized sales of young women like them stand out. In 1830, when Isaac Franklin was getting between $350 and $450 for young women and $550 to $650 for young men, he sold nineteen-year-old Charity for $700 to Benjamin Story, a merchant, the president of the Bank of Louisiana, and resident agent of the transatlantic trading house of Alexander Brown and Company. Another customer that year, Saint James Parish slaveholder Edouard Robin de Logny, went on something of a spree. One Friday in February, he spent $600 for Mary Wheeler, a nineteen-year-old "yellow" woman, and $800 for a twenty-two-year-old "black" woman named Susan Gant. Five days later, de Logny spent another $770 to buy eighteen-year-old Phillis Carroll. De Logny paid cash for Wheeler and Gant. But Franklin sold him Carroll on credit, in the form of a promissory note payable in a year at Victor David's merchant house.[4]

In the notarial acts certifying their purchases, Story and de Logny did not made their motives explicit. Neither did George Legendre, a partner in a wholesale grocery firm and a director of the Louisiana State Bank, who bought a twenty-year-old "mulatto" named Lucinda for $760 in 1831. Nor did Lestang Prudhomme, a Natchitoches Parish slaveholder who paid the same price that year for twenty-one-year-old Fanny, also described as "mulatto." They did not have to. The women understood what was happening, and Isaac Franklin and his customers alike pushed past the mystification of high prices. Haggling over the cost was just part of the transaction, and probably the last one. First there were lascivious winks and vulgar remarks, encouragements to give those being sold a good long look, reminders of the envy they would inspire among other white men, opportunities offered to paw at a breast or run a hand up a dress, and allusions made to their histories of having been raped before.[5]

For Martha Sweart may have been raped before she got to Natchez. If she had managed to avoid being assaulted before Rice Ballard's agent purchased her, it could have occurred during the seventy-mile trek from Charlottesville to Richmond, in Ballard's jail, on board the *Tribune*, or from more than one man at more than one stage along the way. Witnesses to the slave trade testified that traders dragged girls and young women into the woods to do with them as they pleased, invited colleagues to take turns with them in wagon beds, threatened or beat them into submission in steamboat cabins, and picked them out of pens and took them to back rooms of compounds for "the basest purposes." Famously endemic to American slavery as a whole, the sexual exploitation of enslaved women was built into the working lives and business models of slave traders. John Brown, who was trafficked to New Orleans, minced no words about what he saw, writing that in the lower South, "the slave-pen is only another name for a brothel."[6]

Isaac Franklin and his nephew found the abuse gratifying. They peppered their letters with what they considered waggish remarks about it, seamlessly ranging among phallic allusions to themselves and their customers, lewd comments about women they had raped or imagined raping, and discussions of markets and logistics. In the space of a few lines, Isaac Franklin could report to Rice Ballard about sales figures and cotton prices, make banking recommendations, and detail going rates for "ordinary women" and those "of superior appearance," all before signing off with a chuckle that he "had hard work for a one eyed man." James Franklin shared his uncle's habit of mixing business communication and genital slang, telling Ballard he had made some money, but sales were sluggish, and he anticipated "tolerably tough times this spring for one eyed men." Franklin threw in a personal story too, telling Ballard of "a handsome Girl" in the Washington road compound who "to my certain knowledge has been used and that smartly by a one eyed young man about my size & age."[7]

James Franklin did not identify the "handsome Girl" by name. The suggestive assurance that he would do "the best with & for the fancy white maid & excelant cook I can" did it for him. Ballard would know whom he was talking about. Perhaps Ballard had "used" her "smartly" himself. Rape helped unite Ballard, Armfield, and the Franklins across space. The physical distance that usually separated them and that might have attenuated their interpersonal bonds was made closer through letters filled with coarse banter about enslaved women they had shared and planned to sell.[8]

They shared no one more extensively than Martha Sweart. In May 1832, James Franklin wrote to Ballard that "the <u>fair maid</u> Martha" was "still on hand" in Natchez, more than a month after her arrival. So was another young woman he hoped to sell as a "fancy," eighteen-year-old Caroline Brown, whom Franklin referred to as "our white Caroline." But business was "very slow." Franklin considered the prospect of selling either of them to be "very bad," and at some point, he returned Sweart to Ballard in Richmond. However, customer interest in sex slaves picked up again early in 1833, and Isaac Franklin started asking Ballard to send Sweart back to him. For a time, Ballard balked. He preferred to keep her for himself, and he did so for months, putting off Franklin with a pledge to deliver her to the lower South again soon.[9]

After a while, the postponements irked the elder Franklin, who thought he might "use" Sweart as his nephew had and then offer her for sale again. In early November, he wrote from Natchez, informing Ballard that "there are Great Demand for fancy maid I do believe that a Likely Girl and a Good seamstress could be sold for $1000." He had sold Allice Sparraw, a "fancy girl" Ballard had shipped earlier in the year, for $800, which was a nice return on the $375 Ballard had paid for her in Virginia. But Franklin wanted Sweart. "I was disappointed," Franklin continued, "in not finding your Charlottesville maid that you promised me."[10]

Still waiting two months later for Ballard to send Sweart, Franklin's disappointment turned to exasperation. The intensity of his desire to violate Sweart and then turn her around for a profit had made him practically priapic, and he threatened to make Ballard pay the retail price for her if he wanted to hold onto her that badly. "Your old one eyed friend," Franklin wrote, "is brought up all standing the Fancy Girl from Charlottesville will you send her out or shall I charge you $1100 for her say Quick I wanted to see her I fear the time for the 1100 Dollar prices are over and that I will not git to see the fancy maid." Ballard was taking money out of his partners' pockets. And he was being selfish, keeping several enslaved women for his own purposes in Richmond. Franklin was fed up. "I thought," he scolded Ballard, "that an old robber might be satisfyed with two or three maids."[11]

It was an especially rich jab coming from Isaac Franklin, about whom there were widespread rumors of the things he did on summer visits to his Tennessee property. But the threat to Ballard's pocketbook worked. By February 1834, Ballard had shipped Martha Sweart to the lower South for a second time. Isaac Franklin kept her for a few weeks in New Orleans before putting her on a steamboat back to Natchez, where James Franklin raped her again. Telling Ballard in March that his uncle "sent me your maid Martha," Franklin insinuated darkly about the violence he inflicted on her. "She is inclined to be compliant," he wrote.[12]

"Cuffy" was a common nineteenth-century vernacular term for Black people, and James Franklin cracked wise in an April letter to Ballard that Martha Sweart now "answers by the name of Big Cuff." Sweart, who had been circulated among Rice Ballard, Isaac Franklin, and James Franklin for over two years and had turned eighteen, was pregnant. One of the traders was responsible, and although none of them knew or cared which one, Martha Sweart herself wanted to go back to Virginia. "Martha sends her best Respects," James Franklin continued, "& says she wants to see you very much." Maybe she did. Maybe living with Ballard was preferable to being shuttled back and forth between Isaac and James Franklin, and susceptible at all times to being bought by yet another rapist. At least Virginia was home. Or maybe Franklin was suggesting that Ballard was the father of Sweart's child, his allusion to her own wishes another twisted joke at a fancy girl's expense. Maybe. Neither Ballard nor the Franklins ever wrote about her again.[13]

BEING A SLAVE TRADER FOR ANY EXTENDED PERIOD OF TIME required more than merely a willingness to hurt, degrade, and terrorize enslaved people, to ravage their lives, march them hundreds of miles, and pack them onto ships destined for some of the harshest labor regimes on the planet. It required commitment to those things, and enthusiasm for them. Isaac Franklin, James Franklin, and Rice Ballard enjoyed tormenting Martha Sweart, and as they and John Armfield reached the top of their profession in the early 1830s, the collaborative pleasure they took in inflicting pain on the enslaved helped make them successful.

The exuberant cruelty embedded in the culture of their industry and their company suffuses the surviving correspondence of the Franklins, Armfield, and Ballard. The life they chose could be taxing, all-consuming, and dangerous. But the control over Black women and men that that life provided and the financial gains reaped from making them suffer also licensed and fueled a knavish and domineering masculinity that they found rewarding. It kept them going, and it gave them a sense of entitlement and untrammeled authority that bled into their dealings with white people as well. The brutality, the hustle, the salacious gibes, and the sexual assaults made it fun to work in tandem and grow a business buying and selling enslaved people.[14]

Attitude and personal attachments cemented through violence were social currencies propelling the ascendancies of the men who composed Franklin and Armfield. But only proficiency with actual currency could really foster steady cooperation and keep the company profitable. Isaac Franklin was particularly masterful in that regard, gifted with the ability to keep track of hundreds of thousands of dollars at once. Franklin also saw that a business whose operators generally sought instant gratification and visible profits from quick cash sales could pay off more handsomely over time through connections to powerful capital networks. He understood that as the company he and John Armfield had founded grew in size and renown, its developing reputation and the volume in which it dealt could provide access to credit that would facilitate additional expansion and market influence.[15]

Franklin and Armfield was poised for such an approach when it started recruiting purchasing agents in 1830. The company's clout had swelled well beyond what it had been in 1828 and 1829. During the 1830 calendar year, the company sold 424 enslaved people in New Orleans, an increase of 42 percent from 1829 and a demonstration that John Armfield's buying and shipping strategies were seeing concrete results in Alexandria. Gross sales in New Orleans for 1830 came to nearly $225,000. Corresponding to about $6 million today, it was an increase of 185 percent from the previous year.[16]

Franklin and Armfield's sales were even more noteworthy when reckoned as an overall share of the New Orleans slave trade. The number of enslaved people imported by traders from outside Louisiana and sold in New Orleans peaked at nearly four thousand in 1829, and Franklin and Armfield accounted for less than 10 percent of those sales. In 1830, thanks in part to the documentary requirements and geographic limitations that the state and the city imposed on traders and the trade, sales in New Orleans by out-of-state dealers fell to around twenty-three hundred people. But Franklin and Armfield accounted for a bit more than 18 percent of the total, almost doubling the company's market impact.[17]

Piling advantage upon advantage, the company would become even more powerful in the years to come. Isaac Franklin supervised and conducted sales in New Orleans and Natchez, cultivated relationships with bankers and commission merchants across the United States, and sent advice, market reports, and tens of thousands of dollars in checks and other commercial paper to the Chesapeake. John

Armfield and Rice Ballard converted that money into banknotes, distributed the cash to purchasing agents, aggregated agent purchases in prisons and pens, made shipping arrangements, themselves negotiated deals for slaves, and coordinated other operational logistics. From company headquarters in Alexandria, Armfield also directed aggressive additional expansion, bringing on more agents who scoured an ever-widening range of territory in Maryland and Virginia.

At the center of it all were the bodies of the enslaved, decoupled from any individual human qualities extraneous to their prices, flattened into marketable items for sale, and transformed into pieces of paper and assets on a balance sheet. Enslaved people were a kind of currency too, and the endless financial loops into which Franklin, Armfield, and Ballard integrated them by the hundreds hemmed them in as effectively as a bolted door.

It was an undertaking as intricate as it was diabolical, and serendipity played a role in its progress. Franklin and Armfield partially owed its success to the partners' shrewdness. But like most successful entrepreneurs, they were lucky to be working in the right place at the right time. The cotton bonanza of the 1830s constituted the leading edge of an economy booming as never before in the nation's history. Cotton prices increased by 80 percent in the first half of the 1830s, and those prices, along with the easy credit and cheap money that poured into the lower South to capitalize on them, drove slave prices higher as well. They seesawed a bit early in the decade, but prices for young enslaved men in New Orleans almost doubled between 1830 and 1835, and profit margins for slave traders rose to a range of 30 to 50 percent. Though Isaac Franklin, John Armfield, and Rice Ballard might have done well in the slave trade whenever they started working together, they could not have done better than to have started precisely when they did.[18]

But fortune could turn. The slave trade's contingencies could be delicate and fickle, and political and financial currents could shift quickly and unpredictably. Franklin and Armfield's intensified dependence on credit produced incredible growth, but theirs was a precarious position to hold in what forward-looking observers suspected was a bubble economy. Even as Isaac Franklin grumbled at Rice Ballard for having not shipped Martha Sweart, he was thinking it might be time to move on.

On January 13, 1831, James Franklin wrote Jourdan Saunders from New Orleans with good news. "I am really happy I can say to you," Franklin reported, "that all of your Negroes are sold with the exception of Stephen Grant the Blacksmith and Easther the Girl that is deranged." Selling the enslaved people Saunders had sent from Virginia in the fall of 1830 had brought in almost $20,000, and Franklin estimated that they "turned out better than any of the Negroes purchased" by the other agents working with Franklin and Armfield.

Not that the other agents had poor showings. The company's whole operation was going superbly, with sales so quick and steady that the compound at Esplanade and Francais was almost empty. "We have only Eleven Negroes on hand," Franklin told Saunders, and he considered them all eminently salable, especially since he and his uncle had "succeeded in selling off our rubbish." Slave traders took up a far wider range of people than just the young, strong, healthy, and likely to reproduce their customers preferred, but feeding and housing the small and the slight and the frail was throwing good money after bad. Smart traders knew it would "not do to hold on to such stock."

The Franklins had not gotten much for the people they considered refuse, and prices for the enslaved overall had fallen a bit in recent months. But James Franklin believed that "the traders in general envy Uncle Isaac somewhat because he badly beat them this season," and he expected the company could push prices back up when the next shipment of enslaved people arrived. Heavy demand had left few slaves anywhere in the market, and so "if the Brig Comet was here which she ought to be, we think we could increase the prices a little."[19]

Franklin and Armfield had shipped people on the *Comet* before, and John Armfield considered Isaac Staples a skilled captain. But the brig was already a week late when James Franklin mentioned it in his letter. Soon he learned it would never get to New Orleans at all. The *Comet* left Alexandria on December 18, 1830, carrying 164 captives, including 125 shipped by John Armfield. Ten days out, another ship contacted the *Comet* about four hundred miles off the coast of Saint Augustine, Florida, and reported "all well," but strong winds started blowing on New Years' Eve with what Staples later described as "unabated violence." They drove the *Comet* off course, and on the night of January 3, 1831, it foundered amid "reefs and breakers" near the Abaco Islands in the Bahamian archipelago.[20]

Wreckers evacuated everyone from the *Comet* and brought them all to Nassau, the British colonial capital of the Bahamas. There Staples acquired a new vessel and began reloading ballast and supplies to continue the voyage, only to be told he could not take the enslaved with him. They were to be held pending determination of whether the landing of the *Comet* violated British law "relating to abolition of the slave trade." On January 27, Staples sailed for New Orleans on the schooner *Sarah Jane*. The captives from Alexandria stayed behind as free people, having "been released from the custody of the magistrates."[21]

The wreck of the *Comet* became a diplomatic controversy between the United States and Great Britain that would not be settled for nearly a decade. In the meantime, Franklin and Armfield needed to restore the supply chain disrupted by the liberation in the Bahamas of scores of Black people, and they faced the prospect of trying to recover the nearly $40,000 the company had spent on them. Making matters worse, Isaac Franklin was hearing rumors that the Louisiana legislature was considering new restrictions on the slave trade.[22]

Franklin reported to Rice Ballard in late February that legislators "seem determined to close every avenue to the trade," and while he was "using all my influence with the members," he liked to be prepared. If his lobbying failed and the legislature banned imports by out-of-state traders again, he mused that he might declare himself a Louisiana resident and thus become eligible to import slaves legally. Alternatively, should the legislature ban "all Agencies" of slave traders and make it so "planters if they Introduce any slaves at all must go after them in person," Ballard and Armfield could stockpile enslaved people in Virginia over the summer. They would then be ready for fall buyers, who Franklin was sure would "come on in Droves & will give nearley Louisiana prices to get them earley."[23]

Still, Franklin knew it was possible that none of his plans would work, and he was out of sorts. John Armfield had sent about one hundred enslaved people on the *Lafayette* who would replace those who had been on the *Comet*. But if legislative action forced Franklin to move everyone he held in New Orleans upriver to Mississippi, the market there would be flooded and the company would "have more . . . than can be sold to advantage." Despondent and "much depressed" about the uncertainties, Franklin wanted Ballard to know he was trying. "I have never been so much at a loss in all my trading," he wrote. "I have confidence to believe you will think I have done agreeable to my feble capasity the best for all conserned," he concluded, adding a postscript that reads as if he was talking to himself: "I have been so Trobled and bedeviled that I have almost lost the few ideas that I had."[24]

Isaac Franklin's moods often oscillated between cocksure buoyancy and mopey despair, and while his tendency to focus on things that might go wrong lent prudence to his business habits, it could lead him to exaggerate the prospect of disaster. The Louisiana legislature

A Merchant Brig and General Shipping in the Channel off Dover, unknown artist, around 1840. Sailing ships of this class, equipped with two square-rigged masts and known as brigs, were often used by Franklin and Armfield and by other American domestic slave traders for shipping enslaved people among ports along the Atlantic coast and in the Gulf of Mexico. Wikimedia Commons.

put no new constraints on the slave trade. On the contrary, it repealed the certificate law for imported slaves, a change that actually eased the trade by eliminating some of its bureaucratic hurdles. Franklin and Armfield would never retrieve the enslaved people shipped on the *Comet*. But Franklin had insured them with the Louisiana State Insurance Company and the Mississippi Marine and Fire Insurance Company of New Orleans, and Franklin and Armfield collected $37,555 on the policies, significantly diminishing the company's financial losses.[25]

Nearly everything the company did in the spring of 1831, in fact, belied the woe of Franklin's letter to Ballard. In April, the company extended its lease in New Orleans on the house and lots at Esplanade and Francais. That same month, the *Tribune* sailed from a Connecticut River shipyard. Isaac Staples, left without a helm after the wreck of the *Comet*, met the vessel when it docked in New York

City. He stayed in New York through most of the summer before departing on August 31 for Alexandria, where John Armfield would finally get a look at the brig he and Isaac Franklin had ordered. The *Tribune*, which would carry Martha Sweart on her measles-plagued journey to New Orleans, belonged to Franklin and Armfield.[26]

Franklin and Armfield was the first domestic slave-trading company in American history to purchase and operate its own slaver. It was an expensive venture. The *Tribune* cost roughly $7,000, a figure amounting to nearly $200,000 today, and owning it entailed risks and responsibilities not borne when John Armfield sent slaves on someone else's vessels, or even when he chartered a ship. But owning the *Tribune* gave Franklin and Armfield complete control over scheduling, lading, and personnel. It cut out middlemen, which both relieved the company of paying shipping fees to someone else and earned fees from other slave traders. Those fees could then be deployed to pay more for slaves, which meant Franklin and Armfield could use money it charged other traders to wrest market share from those traders. Offering shipping services to rivals also gave Franklin and Armfield a competitive advantage in the form of information, because every trader who used the *Tribune* was a trader who let John Armfield see the people he had purchased and gauge his prospects. Finally, owning the *Tribune* opened new revenue streams, enabling the company to branch beyond the one-way shipment of enslaved people and act as general commodity carriers for eastern merchants.[27]

The *Tribune* was designed and built much like many other merchant cargo vessels plying the Atlantic coast in the first half of the nineteenth century. Eighty feet long and a little over twenty-three feet wide, it had ten feet of interior height below its single deck, a carrying capacity of 161 tons, and accommodations for a small number of passengers. It was mounted with two guns and took an eight-man crew. Its hull was reddish brown from the copper sheathing and fasteners that protected it from weeds, shipworms, and saltwater corrosion, and its sails flew from a mainmast and a foremast, each jutting more than one hundred feet into the sky above the waterline. A decorative billet head adorned the bow, and a square stern provided stability and maximized space in the hold.[28]

It was only in that hold that one really noticed the features distinguishing the *Tribune* from an ordinary merchant ship. Shippers of enslaved people usually stuffed them belowdecks wherever they could fit among crates, barrels, bales, hogsheads, and other cargo containers. But Franklin and Armfield had the *Tribune* outfitted especially for human freight. "The hold is appropriated to the slaves," wrote an observer who toured the brig, "and is divided into two apartments. The after hold will carry about 80 women, and the other about 100 men." Running the length of the compartments on both sides were platforms "about 5½ or six feet deep." One a few inches off the floor and the other about halfway to the ceiling, the platforms held enslaved people while they slept at sea. Transatlantic slavers notoriously crammed Africans into spaces so tight that they might as well have crossed the ocean in coffins. The man who visited the *Tribune* noted simply that on its bare wooden planks, "the slaves lie, as close as they can stow away."[29]

John Armfield advertised the *Tribune* as a "splendid packet," and yet its acquisition was still not the most significant element of Franklin and Armfield's evolution early in 1831. On March 15, three weeks before Isaac Staples met the *Tribune* in New York, Franklin and Armfield signed a two-year agreement with "the firm of Ballard and Alsop . . . to become copartners and joint traders in the trade or business of buying and selling Negroe slaves." By its terms, each company would invest $20,000 in "capital stock" that Ballard and Alsop would draw upon to buy enslaved people "for the use and benefit of the copartnership." Ballard and Alsop would send those people to New Orleans, where Isaac Franklin would make sales and collect payments, with any and all profits divided evenly among the copartners.[30]

The agreement formalized a working relationship predating it by several months, and it entailed some asymmetry between the parties. On the one hand, the agreement pledged Ballard and Alsop to exclusivity. Their company was to buy "negroe slaves for the use and benefit of the copartnership and for no other use benefit or purpose," and neither Rice Ballard nor Samuel Alsop could deal in slaves "in any other manner than [as] members of the said copartnership." On the other hand, the arrangement was "by no means to interfere with the original firm of Franklin & Armfield nor in any way to prevent or interfere with Isaac Franklin as principal thereof from doing and attending to all the duties of the said original firm in buying and selling slaves." Franklin and Armfield could use money not staked to the copartnership to trade separately from Ballard and Alsop, but Ballard and Alsop were prohibited from doing the same.

Yet the agreement brought mutual commitments and reciprocities too. It bound Isaac Franklin, for example, to "reside in the City of New Orleans . . . from the month of November till first of May at least in each year." He normally kept that schedule anyway, but now he was contractually obligated to stick to it and work on behalf of Ballard and Alsop. The agreement also stipulated that the companies would share labor and knowledge, employing "an agent to reside with Ballard & Alsop and also one or two agents to reside with Isaac Franklin . . . to assist them in doing and performing all things necessary and pertaining to the business of the copartnership." All "necessary charges expenses and wages" of those shared agents would come out of copartnership capital stock.

The agreement laid out terms not so much for a merger as for a joint venture. It was a new endeavor, distinct from either parent company, and its operations would run through new entities. In New Orleans, Isaac Franklin would account for the disposition of enslaved people supplied by Ballard and Alsop through a company called "Franklin Ballard & Co." In Virginia, Ballard and Alsop

would maintain records of purchases and shipments of enslaved people to New Orleans through "R. C. Ballard & Co." The agreement
specified that Ballard and Alsop would base its end of the business
in Fredericksburg. But it left open the possibility of locating "at such
other place as the said copartners may here after agree on," and they
decided, practically from the outset, that Rice Ballard would work
in Richmond.[31]

A city of about sixteen thousand people, Richmond was Virginia's capital, and its location at the falls of the James River, around
one hundred miles above Norfolk, made it a natural processing and
transit point for goods passing between the Virginia interior and
the Atlantic. It had been a tobacco storage and inspection hub since
the colonial era, it sat near sizable coalfields, and along and near the
docks, in an area known as Shockoe Bottom, it was packed with
warehouses, flour mills, and tobacco factories. To a greater or lesser
degree, nearly all the city's industry and manufacturing relied on
slave labor, accounting significantly for the 40 percent of the population that was enslaved in 1830.[32]

Richmond was also the fastest growing market in the upper
South for buying and selling enslaved people, and the city's slave
trade had started to rival those of Alexandria and Baltimore. In
the eighteenth century, bartering for slaves often took place aboard
ships in the James River or across the river from Richmond in the
town of Manchester. By the post-Revolutionary period, the trade
had migrated into the capital itself. Concentrated at first at the base
of Shockoe Bottom and at the adjacent Rocketts Landing, the heart
of the trade gradually widened to take in a compact district of irregular streets and alleys a few blocks from the river, on an unpaved
and rocky slope that was dank most of the year from its proximity
to a creek.[33]

As was true everywhere, Richmond slave traders in the early
nineteenth century tended to be itinerants staying in hotels and taverns.
But as larger traders entered the field and as the trade in Richmond

specifically and Virginia generally expanded, a growing infrastructure of auction rooms, boardinghouses, and jails sprang up to sustain it. Rice Ballard came to Richmond at the cusp of this transformation. He may have worked initially at places frequented by auctioneers and other traders, such as the Bell Tavern, two blocks off the docks on the corner of Fifteenth and Main Streets, or the Eagle Hotel, downhill from the state capitol on Thirteenth and Main. He imprisoned the people he bought in private jails. Belonging to Bacon Tait, William Gaddy, and others, these were facilities like the one in which a trader had kept Henry Watson after buying him as a ten-year-old at auction in the 1820s. Nearly every trader in Richmond used private jails, Watson recalled, and each held "a great many slaves . . . waiting to be sent off as soon as their numbers increased. These jails are enclosed by a wall about sixteen feet high, and the yard-room is for the slaves to exercise in; and consists of but one room, in which all sexes and ages are huddled together in a mass."[34]

But Ballard would not pay others for their services for long. They would pay him. In January 1832, he rented his own private jail. Located on the corner of Seventeenth and H Streets, it was five blocks from the river, a few blocks east of the capitol, and adjacent to the enormous Seabrook's Tobacco Warehouse. Ballard used the jail to incarcerate enslaved people he purchased for Franklin Ballard and Company until he was ready to put them on steamboats to Norfolk, where they would meet the *Tribune* or another vessel sent from Alexandria by John Armfield and then continue to New Orleans. Ballard also rented out jail space to slaveholders and other traders looking to secure enslaved people. He charged them twenty cents per slave per day. Blankets, shoes, medical care, and other needs cost extra.[35]

While Isaac Franklin and John Armfield saw Rice Ballard's experience buying and selling enslaved people as invaluable for extending their company's reach into Richmond, it was no small matter that their alliance with Ballard and Alsop also broadened their

Chesapeake banking and credit networks. Franklin and Armfield's bank connections in and around the District of Columbia were considerable. But the copartnership with Ballard and Alsop linked them by association to Ballard and Alsop's banking ties as well. Those included accounts at the Bank of Virginia and the Farmers' Bank of Virginia, which were the most heavily capitalized banks in the state, and at the Richmond branch of the Second Bank of the United States.[36]

Establishing relationships with more banks increased the number of institutions that might provide loans on favorable terms. But it also helped ease financial transactions vital to operating effectively across long distances, because it meant more places that would be willing to give reasonable discounts on commercial paper. Isaac Franklin rarely sent money to the Chesapeake in the form of banknotes. Sending cash through the mail was chancy, and for Franklin it usually meant sending notes issued by banks in the lower South, which, like most banknotes in an era before there was a single national currency, declined markedly in value as they got farther from their point of origin. Instead, Franklin typically bought and sent checks, bills of exchange, or a similar kind of negotiable paper called acceptances that could be drawn on merchant firms, all of which were considered more stable and predictable than banknotes. Upon receipt, Franklin's partners could pass them along to the places they were payable once they came due, or they could bring them to one of their banks, which would buy them for cash for an amount less than their full value, known as a discount.[37]

Franklin's business in New Orleans, in fact, was as much about acquiring sound money as it was about selling Black people. Not infrequently, that money came from northeastern cities. In May 1831, for example, Franklin sent Ballard two bills of exchange worth a total of $8,000 that he had acquired from Samuel Hermann. A cotton broker to whom Franklin sold several enslaved people, Hermann headed a sprawling commercial empire and was one of the richest men in New Orleans. The bills Franklin sent could be drawn on Bache McEvers of New York City, and Samuel Moss and Son of Philadelphia, large merchant firms that dealt in a range of imports, including sugar, cotton, and tobacco from Louisiana. Both bills were to come due in sixty days, and Franklin told Ballard that he could forward them along "for acceptance immediately if not in absolute need of the funds." But if he needed cash for buying slaves right away, Franklin recommended that he "have them discounted and write me the Amt. of the discount."[38]

Money and credit financing the slave trade circulated this way among merchants, banks, and trading companies around the country. Ultimately it circulated internationally, as men like Samuel Hermann, Bache McEvers, and Samuel Moss entangled themselves in economic webs that wove together and promoted the development of the entire Atlantic world. The global implications of the domestic slave trade were evident even in Isaac Franklin's routine transactions. Consider the sale Franklin made to Miguel Lizardi, who bought ten women, fifteen men, and a twenty-month-old infant from Franklin in November 1830 for $13,200. Lizardi was of Spanish descent, came to New Orleans via Mexico, and was partner in several interlocking companies, including Lizardi y Hermanos, on whose behalf he made his purchase from Franklin. From offices in New Orleans, London, Paris, and Veracruz, the Lizardis oversaw interests in cotton, real estate, banks, stocks, shipping, and retailing. They were also one of the largest importers into the United States of silver specie, the hard money standard grounding the American money supply. Lizardi paid cash for the people he bought from Franklin. But the cash converged from capital streams floating the world economy, and the Black people Isaac Franklin provided became assets and labor that swelled the streams further still.[39]

Yet Isaac Franklin worried. In the first half of 1831, he sold 291 enslaved people in New Orleans. His core clientele remained city merchants and southeastern Louisiana planters, but they only bought a few dozen people more than they had in the same time frame the previous year, and gross sales figures reflected prices that had barely budged. Franklin's sales in New Orleans brought an average of $491 per person in the first half of 1830, and only a bit more than $510 per person in the first half of 1831, an increase of about 4 percent. Moreover, where sales in early 1830 had been mostly for cash, in early 1831 Franklin had to unload almost 30 percent of the people he sold on credit or for some combination of credit and banknotes.[40]

Falling sugar and cotton prices that left customers low on cash and hesitant to buy were to blame, and Franklin told Ballard the situation was "very disencouraging indeed." Certain the company would "have to work for very short profits" unless agents in Virginia brought down the prices they paid, he wanted Ballard to watch his expenditures. "Part with our money at the present prices for nothing but the wright kind," Franklin counseled. "You have been long enough in the trade to know that there is no salesman can make money if the article for sale is badley Layed in a few negroes well purchased will always make more clear money than the many badly purchased." A mantra of sorts for Franklin and Armfield, "the right kind" was a warning to everyone involved with the company to pay only appropriate prices and only for people who could be sold. As Franklin told Jourdan Saunders, "all the money is made on the purchase for if you buy unsaleable negroes it is impossible for us to make money." But "buy the wright kind and at fare prices & there is no difficulty in making money."[41]

When the spring selling season wound down in 1831, Franklin knew he had outperformed his New Orleans colleagues, many of whom became desperate in the face of stagnating sales prices and started unloading the enslaved for whatever they could get, in some cases even "for less than they absolutely cost in Virginia." But caution was the company watchword for Franklin and Armfield, and a more serious shock to the slave market would follow in short order.

This one would come less from the vagaries of agriculture than from the defiance of the enslaved.[42]

D omestic slave traders usually took stock of their commercial affairs in the summers, and at its outset the summer of 1831 promised to be no different. Sales in the lower South flagged by June to the point of insignificance, as they always did, and Isaac and James Franklin closed the compounds in New Orleans and Natchez. They headed north, where James Franklin called on company agents, books in hand, to make financial settlements from the trading year. Such an annual reckoning, Franklin reminded Jourdan Saunders in advance of his arrival, was "the best way of doing business."[43]

The Franklins also stopped in Alexandria for a visit with John Armfield that was for both business and pleasure. It let the Franklins check on the Duke Street facility, and it gave them all a chance to examine company accounts, strategize for the future, and strengthen social ties, which even the bawdiest correspondence could not fully replace. Rice Ballard stayed in Richmond, because purchases of en-slaved people in the upper South continued through the summer. But in August, James Franklin and John Armfield went to see him. It was paramount that everyone be in sync about their increasingly complex enterprise.[44]

Isaac Franklin spent most of the summer of 1831 as he usually spent summers, visiting his siblings and their families in Tennessee. There he also saw his newly enlarged plantations in operation for the first time. The previous fall, he had bought more than four hundred acres of land in Sumner County, a few miles east of the property he owned along Station Camp Creek. More than doubling Franklin's holdings in the county, the land and the seventy-seven people he enslaved on it indicated a developing vision for a future in Tennessee beyond the slave trade.[45]

As late summer approached, James Franklin left Virginia. Heading west from Ballard's Richmond jail, he had with him horses, a wagon, a small carriage known as a carryall, and "a drove of negroes" he would force to march "to the lower country" for the next trading season. He had made the trip before, always passing through Tennessee and pausing in Sumner County to see his parents, his eight brothers and sisters, and their families. He probably put the enslaved people, who had already walked six hundred miles by then, to work in his father's fields, indifferent to the way reuniting with his own relatives mocked those whom he took ever farther from theirs. Sometimes before he reassembled the coffle to continue the slog out of Tennessee, he even picked up a few more people whom members of his family wanted sold in the lower South, finding room to attach their shackles to the line and promising to return with the money they brought in the market.[46]

James and Isaac Franklin were still in Tennessee when they first heard about Nat Turner, who transformed the summer of 1831 into one unlike most others. In late August in Southampton County, near the Chesapeake Bay along Virginia's border with North Carolina, Turner led several dozen people, nearly all of whom were enslaved, as he was, in an uprising against their bondage. Over the course of two days, the rebels killed nearly sixty white people, carnage that provoked bloodthirsty reprisals from white Virginians and led the Virginia legislature to consider abolishing slavery altogether. It also prompted white residents of the lower South to imagine similar conspiracies happening among them and to wonder, once again, whether importing massive numbers of enslaved people from distant locales was really worth it.[47]

News of the rebellion did not break in Louisiana until mid-September, and while political momentum there and elsewhere in the region was gathering for a response, Isaac Franklin, John Armfield, and Rice Ballard set into motion an operation that was already much larger than anything any of them had overseen before they formed their copartnership. How much larger could be measured partially by the speed with which they collected and dispatched the enslaved from the upper South. On September 27, 1831, Isaac Staples piloted the *Tribune* from Alexandria on its maiden voyage carrying enslaved people, sailing with 139 of them to meet Isaac Franklin, who had reopened the compound at Esplanade and Francais for business. Eighteen days later, before the *Tribune* even arrived in New Orleans, Armfield shipped 114 more people on the *Lafayette*. Less than two weeks after that, still another 121 people headed Franklin's way in the hold of a schooner called the *Industry*.[48]

Nearly 400 people shipped in just over a month was stunning in terms of volume, but equally remarkable was the landscape of the upper South that Franklin, Armfield, and Ballard now covered. Of 253 enslaved people shipped on the *Tribune* and the *Lafayette*, around 40 had been purchased in Washington City, Alexandria, or Georgetown. Just over 100 others came from eight counties in Maryland, twice as many counties as Franklin and Armfield had extracted people from in 1829. The locations comprised all six counties between the District of Columbia and the Chesapeake Bay. They included Frederick County, which reflected the purchases of George Kephart. And they included Baltimore County.[49]

Franklin and Armfield had long shied away from Baltimore to avoid direct competition with Austin Woolfolk, and Armfield shipped just one person from there. But company strategy was changing. A few days before the *Lafayette* left Alexandria, James Purvis started advertising that he was no longer in the District of Columbia. He could be found, instead, in Baltimore, at Elijah Sinners's Tammany Hall Hotel on Water Street, where he wished "to purchase one hundred and fifty likely NEGROES of both sexes, from 12 to 25 years of age."[50]

The rest of the people trafficked on the *Tribune* and the *Lafayette* came from Virginia, and the enlarged reach of Franklin and Armfield was even more striking there than in Maryland. In 1829, the six Virginia counties from which Franklin and Armfield took people were almost all close to the District of Columbia, and none were more than about seventy-five miles from Alexandria. In the fall of 1831, while some of the people they shipped came from counties near the capital, Jourdan Saunders brought people to John Armfield from as far west as Shenandoah County, over one hundred miles away. Rice Ballard acquired people in Richmond and had connections with Samuel Alsop in Spotsylvania County. He also distributed thousands in cash to a host of agents and subagents. Collectively, they bought people in nine other counties, arranged in a line running east to west for over two hundred miles across the middle of the state.[51]

The origins of the enslaved people on the *Industry* are unknown. Ballard shipped more than half of them, and into the fall of 1831, Franklin sent him $4,000 or $5,000 in bills of exchange every few weeks, mostly payable at New York merchant houses. But Franklin knew the rebellion in Southampton County meant change was coming. On October 20, the New Orleans City Council announced that anyone bringing slaves into the city from outside Louisiana had to declare them and their place of origin to the mayor within twenty-four hours of arrival. Slaves known to have been involved in a "conspiracy or insurrection" or who came from a county where such an event had occurred were to be imprisoned, and rewards would be issued to anyone reporting such slaves having been imported. At the state level, meanwhile, Governor André Roman called the Louisiana legislature into special session, and Franklin told Ballard that while it was possible legislators would "fool us as they did last year," he anticipated "a prohibitory law" on the slave trade "being passed immediately."[52]

On November 19, 1831, the state of Louisiana banned the slave trade. Auctions remained legal, and with some limitations, Louisiana residents or individuals moving there could bring into the state enslaved people "as are for their own use, and are bona fide their property." But imports by nonresidents who sold slaves for a living were outlawed. Slave traders with ships at sea had a window of twelve days for those ships and their enslaved cargo to arrive, and thirty days from the law's passage to sell them and any other enslaved people they had already brought into the state. Beyond those exceptions, traders would be fined between $500 and $1,000 for each person they introduced for sale, and they would be imprisoned until the fines were paid. Contraband enslaved people would be seized, emancipated, and sent beyond the boundaries of Louisiana.[53]

Though the prospect of a slave-trading ban in Louisiana had led Isaac Franklin to worry himself into a depression earlier in the year, when it actually came, he was confident he and his colleagues could turn the situation to their advantage, telling Armfield that he saw future prospects as "very flattering." On the same day the law passed, Isaac Franklin sold all 243 enslaved people he held at the New Orleans compound to James Franklin for nearly $130,000. It was a sale in name only, designed to clarify title and ensure that the company would have the full thirty-day grace period to clear out as much of its human merchandise as possible. There was nothing dishonest about that, but Franklin had also concocted a scheme to keep selling enslaved people to Louisiana residents no matter what the state legislature said.[54]

Franklin's ploy skirted the letter of the law and obliterated its spirit. When news of the ban came down, the *Tribune* was already on its way to the lower South again, this time carrying 182 people, including 70 for consignment to Isaac Franklin. Assuming it arrived in Louisiana in the twelve-day window the ban allowed for ships at sea, the law still specified that anyone buying slaves off those ships had to remove them from the state within five days of purchase. Designed to prevent a last-minute influx of slaves, the provision would have made selling those on the *Tribune* challenging. But Armfield had mailed Franklin the *Tribune*'s invoice. The plan was for Franklin to sell people from the invoice to customers ahead of the ship's arrival and forge receipts so it would appear that the sales had been made in Virginia. Buyers could then retrieve their purchases directly from the *Tribune* and legally import those enslaved people to the state. As Armfield described it to Jourdan Saunders, Franklin would "sell the negroes at sea and lett the planters introduce themselves. We can make the Bills of Sale in this place. . . . The negroes then Become the property of the planters out of the Limits of Louisiana the negroes are shiped direct to them and of course they can swear they are for their own use for such is the fact."[55]

The scam did not come off as intended. The invoice arrived late in New Orleans, and the delay forced Franklin to send the enslaved people on board to Natchez for sale instead. But the partners remained convinced that disguising Louisiana sales with out-of-state documentation was a sound idea, and John Armfield convened Rice Ballard, Jourdan Saunders, James Purvis, and George Kephart in Alexandria for what he called "a Council of War" to coordinate their efforts and explain how it would work.[56]

Louisiana legislators had foreseen that state residents might dodge import restrictions by crossing nearby state and territorial lines to buy from traders, so the law proscribed even Louisiana slaveholders from importing people purchased in Alabama, Mississippi, Arkansas, or Florida. That meant Isaac and James Franklin could not just shift their Louisiana business from New Orleans to Natchez. Unless they made it appear that the business had been conducted in yet a third location. "We can show in Orleans," Armfield told company agents, "and pass the sales in Tennessee at Memphis." Customers could examine enslaved people shipped by the company at the docks in New Orleans, before their transfer to steamboats that would take them to Mississippi. Sales would then be conducted in Natchez, with paperwork that made it look as if they had happened in Tennessee, beyond the region proscribed by Louisiana law.[57]

Armfield reckoned the company would make a killing this way. It could keep drawing money out of New Orleans and putting it into Maryland and Virginia, even as the Louisiana law drove smaller traders from the field at the purchase end and the sales end alike. From his position at the head of the "Council of War," Armfield explained that "if we can arrange for the need full we will take a pretty Rank hold" over both a Chesapeake market with fewer competitors and falling prices and a Louisiana market that was supposedly closed altogether.[58]

Had Isaac Franklin and John Armfield been caught, it would have been neither the first nor the last time they were accused of fraud. Both faced accusations during their careers, for example, from Black people asserting that they were not slaves and that Franklin and Armfield held them illegally against their will. When asked by antislavery activists if his business "ever led to selling and buying those who were lawfully free," Armfield conceded it did but said he endeavored "all in his power to prevent such things." That would have surprised Rachel Brent, a Black woman whom a court liberated from the Alexandria compound after she claimed that Armfield had falsely imprisoned her there for nine months, during which time he "beat, bruised, and ill treated her." By that last, Brent likely meant John Armfield had raped her.[59]

Customers in the lower South sometimes complained as well, especially when they suspected that Franklin had sold them "defective" slaves. In New Orleans, Franklin refunded customers' money in part or in full at least eight times. A dozen times he exchanged an enslaved person with whom a customer found fault, and he was sued four times in redhibition cases or for failing to honor a warranty. Considering the number of enslaved people Franklin and Armfield shipped and sold, customer accusations of a swindle were few, which helped boost the company's reputation for straight dealing. Still, Franklin surely knew he sometimes sold people with chronic diseases and physical infirmities. Not selling them would have meant hundreds of dollars squandered, and anyway, taking chances with the well-being of Black people was part of the thrill of being a slave trader.[60]

So was getting over on a customer or a competitor. Franklin and his colleagues reveled in the opportunism of their business and in the pursuit of self-interest that licensed being something of a scoundrel. Moral considerations and playing by the rules held ambiguous positions for many entrepreneurial white men on American slavery's frontiers, and in the exchange of bodies for money there was sometimes neither space nor use for such things at all. Franklin and his fellows often talked of their undertaking as "the game" and of themselves and other traders as "robbers" and "pirates" who did as they wished, plundered whatever loot they could grab, and let others deal with the consequences.[61]

Chicanery did always have the potential to backfire. When Auguste Rieffel got made into a sap, for example, he nearly exposed Franklin and Armfield's plan for evading Louisiana's slave-import ban. In December 1831, James Franklin, acting on his uncle's behalf, asked Rieffel, who ran a New Orleans livery stable, to "seek out persons who should wish to purchase slaves," promising a 4 percent commission on referrals that resulted in sales. Rieffel soon introduced Franklin to Antoine Foucher Jr., who agreed to buy twenty-six enslaved people for $13,000. The legal deadline for purchasing people imported by traders had just passed, and so Franklin told Foucher "that the sale of said slaves should be made at Memphis." Rieffel then traveled to Natchez to retrieve the slaves for Foucher, only to find that Franklin had cut him out of the deal, refusing to deliver the enslaved to Rieffel or to pay his commission. Rieffel sued, telling the whole story to the Orleans Parish Court. The court subpoenaed Isaac Franklin in February 1832 to hear what he and his nephew had been up to, and he "denied generally the allegations" before hurrying back to his office. He preferred to keep such activities under wraps, and he and his partners were also facing another kind of unwelcome exposure, one far more ominous than the prospect of losing Auguste Rieffel's lawsuit.[62]

In the fall of 1831, Isaac and James Franklin had worked frantically, and with spectacular success, to sell as many enslaved people in New Orleans as they could before the slave-import ban took effect. Sales prices were only a smidge higher than they had been in the spring, caught as they were between customers knowing their time to buy slaves from traders was running short and traders knowing they had only weeks to sell all the people they had on hand. But the number of sales the Franklins made was astonishing. Between October and December 1831, they sold 361 enslaved people in New Orleans. More than twice as many as they had sold during those months in 1830, it included 240 people sold just in the thirty days between the import ban's passage and its implementation. The sales brought company totals for all of 1831 to 652 people who cumulatively sold for over $340,000, both of which were increases of more than 50 percent from the previous year.[63]

Things seemed to be going exactly as John Armfield imagined they would. "I am mutch pleased with the pasage of the Law," he wrote Jourdan Saunders in mid-December, snickering that it "plays Hell with the Land pirats," a reference to smaller traders who walked the enslaved to market and who he had heard were fleeing or avoiding New Orleans. Armfield counseled Saunders to buy "all the Likely negroes" at the lowest prices he could. "If we can prevent the planters" of the lower South "from coming to this country and Buying themselves," Armfield crowed, the Louisiana law would "Be of grate servis to us poor dealers in personages."[64]

The problem was that in the interest of selling as many enslaved people as possible, the Franklins had been overly generous in extending credit to customers so that they might make larger purchases than they would have with cash. Forty percent of all New Orleans sales in late 1831 were on credit. Buyers typically paid nothing for months or years, and sometimes the Franklins had even accepted

unendorsed promissory notes from buyers, financing the loans themselves and holding mortgages on the enslaved people they sold as
their only security. While John Armfield gloated in Alexandria and
pushed Jourdan Saunders to keep buying, the Franklins were having
trouble finding money to send to the Chesapeake and were advising
the opposite. Writing to Rice Ballard, James Franklin apologized
for a delayed remittance of funds. "We should have sent you money
sooner but we had to take all sorts of paper on every occasion," he
explained. Franklin was relieved that Ballard had slowed his purchases. In fact, he continued, "it is our particular request to stop in
toto untill further instructions."[65]

Three weeks later, early in January 1832, Isaac Franklin reversed
his nephew's directive. The Natchez branches of both the Planters'
Bank of Mississippi and the Second Bank of the United States had
"thrown a large Amt of cash into circulation and the price of cotton"
had "advanced a shade," and so now he told Ballard he projected
"considerable improvement in the price of the article in the spring
and the earley part of next fall." By "the article," he meant enslaved
people, and he instructed Ballard to start buying them again "under
easy sale" and "at reduced prices." Still, with the company holding
"upwards of two hundred thousand dollars in Bills Receivable" in
New Orleans, there was no escaping the fact that it had a systemic
cash flow issue. Franklin told Ballard that if he needed money, he
ought to "borrow from your Banks."[66]

Franklin recommended loans of sixty or ninety days, assuring
Ballard that he would be able to send money to repay them on time
and that it made more sense to take the loans than to sell company
debt on the cheap. Franklin's credit sales normally carried an annual
interest rate of 10 percent, and Ballard took bank loans at 6 percent
interest. Franklin rightly observed that it was "a saving of Interest
to borrow from the Bank instead of haveing our long paper Discounted." But projected savings depended on Franklin having money
to send Ballard, and that depended on customers paying down their

debts when they came due, hardly a foregone conclusion, considering how commonly borrowers received extensions when they asked for more time to pay what they owed. Franklin told Ballard he would be in New Orleans "to make negotiations." Unspoken were the consequences of failure.[67]

In the late 1830s, Isaac Franklin told Lewis White, a Tennessee house carpenter he hired now and then, that "there had been three times in [his] life that he had thought he had made his arrangements to retire from business." The early months of 1832 were one of those times. Franklin was forty-three years old, and a quarter of a century working as a slave trader was taking its toll. John Armfield started referring to Franklin, only eight years his senior, as "the old man." James Franklin alluded periodically to his uncle's recurrent ailments, telling Rice Ballard he had "a small tetch of those attacks as usual," and Isaac Franklin himself admitted that the traveling he did for the trade was getting to him. "I have been seeking and ranging up and Down the Mississippi," he acknowledged to Ballard, "untill I hardly know myself."[68]

Franklin had long seen his nephew as a possible successor, and after a few years of watching James Franklin grow into the business, he was giving the twenty-three-year-old larger responsibilities. James Franklin handled negotiations and notarizations on most New Orleans sales late in 1831, and on December 21, both Franklins stopped at the office of notary William Boswell, where Isaac Franklin signed a power of attorney, formally giving his nephew authority to conduct all financial affairs in his name.[69]

The most telling sign of Isaac Franklin's inclination to retire was his laying groundwork in earnest for a permanent move to Tennessee. In September 1831, he bought 918 acres of land in Sumner County, contiguous with the acres he had bought the previous year. Lying near the road connecting Gallatin to Nashville, the property took in most of the triangle formed where the east and west branches of Station Camp Creek converged and flowed into the Cumberland River. It was ideal for producing market crops and raising livestock, and Franklin set about constructing what his white neighbors considered "the finest embellished and improved place" in Tennessee. One man who lived nearby and who had seen "the improvements of the hermitage, the house of Andrew Jackson," considered those on Franklin's property to be "decidedly superior." Franklin would call the place Fairvue.[70]

At its core, Fairvue would always be a commercial farm worked by scores of men and women whom Isaac Franklin enslaved. He began developing the property with that purpose in mind, and enslaved people themselves did most of the labor. They built barns and stables, carpenter and blacksmith shops, a springhouse and a carriage house, and a gristmill and a cotton gin. They built fifteen or twenty houses, laid out like a small town, in which they would be compelled to live, along with one for the white man whom Franklin would hire as an overseer. They built a hospital where they might recover from illnesses and injuries incurred as work ground them down, and they constructed fences and walls to delimit the range of Franklin's domain. Many of the walls and buildings, including those housing the enslaved, were made of brick. Franklin envisioned his estate as one that would be like few others, a monument to its overlord and his fortune that would stand the test of time.[71]

Nothing about Fairvue spoke to its creator's ego more than the mansion where Franklin intended to live. Situated on high ground with commanding sight lines that inspired the property's name, it too was built by the enslaved and it too was made of brick. Architecturally typical of Middle Tennessee plantation houses, it stood two stories high. At identical front and rear entrances, porches projected off the center of the house on each floor. White columns supported the second-floor porch and a pediment extending from the roof, which was set between twin chimneys and covered with cedar

Fairvue, as it appeared in the 1970s. Isaac Franklin built the original house on his plantation property in Sumner County, Tennessee, in the early 1830s. He added the two-story
loggia extending off the side of the house at around the time of his marriage in 1839.
Courtesy of Tennessee State Library and Archives.

shingles and copper sheeting. The first and second floors each had
four large rooms separated by a center hall, and a few smaller rooms
were located in garret space under the roof. Kitchen, privy, and
smokehouse outbuildings stood nearby, and more lavish amenities
included a cylindrical icehouse, gardens with graveled walkways,
and a greenhouse "warmed by pipes" for flowers and shrubs. When
the house was finished, Franklin filled it with "the finest and most
costly furniture of every description." Furniture expenses alone were
at least $10,000, about as much as the house cost to build. A neigh-
boring farmer recalled that for years on end, "hardly a boat" came
up the Cumberland to Station Camp Creek without furnishings or
exotic plants destined for Fairvue.[72]

A pleasure palace surrounded by an agricultural forced labor
operation, Fairvue was a spot where Isaac Franklin could preen, en-

tertain, and enjoy the magnificence his life in the slave trade had provided, all while continuing to exploit and profit off enslaved people with a comfort and ease that that life had rarely allowed. Perhaps he might look for a bride someday and start a family with whom he could share the spoils. Until then, people noticed the "several likely mulatto girls" he held in bondage amid the resplendence.[73]

Franklin also had other reasons, aside from his age and health, for wanting to leave slave trading behind. In Louisiana, the legislature amended the terms of the state's slave-import ban about as fast as Franklin and his colleagues found a way around it. By adding Kentucky, Tennessee, and Missouri to the list of states from which slave imports were illegal and prohibiting slaveholders even from having agents import slaves on their behalf from places where it was still legal to do so, the amended law shut down the ruse that had Franklin rushing to Memphis for phony paperwork. John Armfield thought the company could still sneak enslaved people into New Orleans with spurious bills of sale that local officials in Virginia would take bribes to sign, but James Franklin recognized there were too many contortions, costs, and risks involved. Thanks to the "further restrictions relative to the introduction of slaves" in Louisiana, he told Rice Ballard, "the game is nearly blocked on us." Sales in New Orleans could not be made to work. If the company wanted to keep selling in the lower South, Franklin continued, "we shall have to do it in the Missi[ssippi] market."[74]

Yet Natchez presented challenges too. In January 1830, authorities had lifted the outright ban on traders in the core of the city, replacing it with regulations letting traders operate wherever they liked between November 15 and April 15, provided they kept enslaved people "in a back yard, and not on the public walk or street or in the immediate view thereof." But the uprising led by Nat Turner disturbed white people in Natchez no less than it did those in New Orleans, and as the biggest slave-trading company in the city, Franklin and Armfield made a ripe target for their fears. "Franklin

& Armfield are known as very extensive slave traders," warned the editor of the Natchez *Statesman and Gazette* in the fall of 1831. "The *Tribune*, is a notorious slave transport. How far is her port of destination, from Southampton? Look out for *convicted bandits*, whose sentences have been commuted."[75]

After suspending shipments of slaves for a few months while they formulated a response to the Louisiana import ban and waited for a frozen Potomac River to become navigable, John Armfield and Rice Ballard started sending captives to the lower South again in February 1832. They all ended up with James Franklin in Mississippi. But white people there were watching now, and as more slave traders leaving New Orleans moved into Natchez, residents complained to the board of selectmen that the trade was "a stigma on the good order and government" of the city and "in all probability highly dangerous to the property and health of the citizens." James Denny, a city health officer, gave their concerns substance in April, when he saw "some negroes at the Hospital belonging to Mr. Franklin" and "found two" who had been on the *Tribune* with Martha Sweart "quite sick with measles and one or two apparently convalesent from the same disease." Denny recommended "the enactment of an ordinance prohibiting any future introduction of slaves for sale within the limits of the city."[76]

It was all becoming more of a hassle than Isaac Franklin wanted to deal with anymore. The agreement he had with John Armfield, as well as the one he and Armfield had with Rice Ballard and Samuel Alsop, would terminate in 1833. He was thinking he might just leave the business and remove to Fairvue. That was how Jourdan Saunders expected things would play out, writing to his partner David Burford that his "engagement with Franklin & Co being at the will of the parties, the firm of F&A will expire in the spring of 1833."[77]

But the spring of 1833 was a year away when James Denny reported the measles cases in Natchez, and Isaac Franklin had work to do if he was to keep the bank loans and credit extensions he and his colleagues had come to depend on from crushing them. Franklin needed collections from customers to turn paper profits into actual profits, and the company needed that money to keep expanding its operation, which was becoming an imperative as well as a choice. Expansion could generate liquidity through cash sales, and while there would surely be even more bills to collect, those bills would be negotiable assets and a hedge against a stagnant or shrinking revenue stream that could put the company underwater. They also, of course, meant more potential profits over time.

In the Chesapeake, Franklin and Armfield's most significant expansion came in Baltimore, where Austin Woolfolk's grip was weakening. Woolfolk sold most of the people he trafficked in New Orleans, making the Louisiana import ban a major blow to his operation. But his reputation among Maryland slaveholders was suffering too. In March 1832, John Armfield told Rice Ballard that "we are purchasing at Baltimore" for low prices and that "Woolfolk done us a great kindness when he caused us to go into that markett." Armfield reported, with relish, that "we have gott all the jailors and some of his agents in our imploy," and he revealed plans to go to Baltimore himself "in a few days and Establish a House." With Woolfolk's "standing" having become "verry Bad" because of "the way he has Rob[b]ed the people," Armfield intended "to push the byers in that markett this year."[78]

James Purvis would run the Baltimore house. Twelve days after Armfield wrote to Ballard, Purvis signed a yearlong lease with Stephen Fell for a property along the Baltimore and Harford Turnpike that led northeast out of the city. Sitting just above the turnpike's intersection with Aisquith Street, near a Methodist church on a spot known as Gallow's Hill, the lot was less than half the size of Armfield's compound in Alexandria and had on it only a "frame dwelling house." But it could be made suitable for imprisoning the enslaved. Purvis would put up "stables out houses or other buildings." Fell agreed to enclose the property with "a strong plank fence of such height" as Purvis desired.[79]

On May 4, 1832, Purvis placed an ad in the Baltimore *Republican* announcing "THREE HUNDRED AND FIFTY *NEGROES WANTED!*" Interested sellers could visit him "at his residence," a white house "with trees in front," or they could meet with his associate John Busk, who worked on Baltimore Street, a few blocks from the Patapsco River basin. Busk ran an "intelligence and agency office," akin to a modern employment agency. He brokered free labor, slave labor, and Black bodies.[80]

Before long, Purvis made a play beyond Baltimore, advertising in Easton and Cambridge on Maryland's Eastern Shore. These were places Austin Woolfolk had for years considered his own. But they were part of the "push" Armfield mentioned to Ballard, and the push had a lethal impact on Woolfolk's business. In October 1832, Woolfolk felt compelled to advertise in newspapers across eastern Maryland "to inform the owners of Negroes in Maryland, Virginia and North Carolina, that he is not *dead* . . . but that he still lives to give them cash, and the highest prices for their Negroes."[81]

Woolfolk thought rumors of his demise had "been artfully represented by his opponents," which may have been true. But if James Purvis told people Woolfolk had died, they believed him because Purvis had buried Woolfolk in the market. Though Austin Woolfolk continued working as a slave trader for nearly another decade, he never again exercised the influence he once had. In the 1820s, Woolfolk trafficked the majority of all the enslaved people shipped from the port of Baltimore. In the 1830s, he shipped just one in five. Yet even that figure exaggerates his standing, because overall coastal shipments of enslaved people out of Baltimore fell by more than half from the 1820s to the 1830s. Franklin and Armfield had diverted much of the city's slave trade to Alexandria instead.[82]

While James Purvis was buying people to enchain and march south through Washington City and across the Potomac River to John Armfield, Rice Ballard was building up operations in Richmond. Along with Samuel Alsop, purchasing agents Andrew Grimm, James Blakey, Silas Omohundro, Nathaniel White, and Benjamin Parks helped increase the number of enslaved people Ballard accumulated from central Virginia by nearly 20 percent between 1831 and 1832. Some agents in Ballard's network had little experience in the slave trade. Omohundro, for example, ran a river ferry before going to work for Ballard at the age of twenty-four. Others, like Blakey, had familiarity with the trade stretching back years. Married and in his thirties when he started working for Ballard, Blakey had been an inn proprietor in Orange County, west of Fredericksburg, as far back as the mid-1820s.[83]

Experienced or not, most of Ballard's agents worked for commissions of five or ten dollars, plus expenses, for each person they brought to Ballard's Richmond jail. There, Ballard sat at his desk and scrawled the names of the people he imprisoned onto long lists. He recorded what he paid for them, which agent procured them, and on which vessel he shipped them south. On invoices, he pointed to their skills and talents, so that Isaac Franklin knew he should charge buyers extra for Watson Hagan, a hostler; Sarah Spencer, a cook; Amus King, a carpenter; and Davy Parker, a "house servant." Occasionally, Ballard noted that people had not survived their incarceration, jotting down that Lewis Williamson and Richard Morris were both "dead" and writing the hundreds of dollars he had spent on them off his books.[84]

It was important to maintain orderly accounts. Using double-entry bookkeeping, on one side of his ledger Ballard tracked discounts on bills he cashed, and he noted what he spent on slaves, horses, firewood, hay, bacon, flour, hats, shoes, blankets, freight, stagecoach fares, and postage. He cataloged payments to doctors and lawyers and blacksmiths and printers and midwives, and purchases of locks and handcuffs, of "Leg Irons" and a "Negro Whip." Offsetting costs and expenses on the other side of the ledger were checks, proceeds of discounted bills, cash, and the names of the enslaved and how much they sold for. He strung them together like a coffle in print, two or three people to a line, forty lines to a page: "William Fleming $540 Phillis Golden $490 Martha Gathright $450 Delphia Gaddis $400 Amos Knight $600 Moses Profit $550 Absalom Walker $600." The names and prices completed the transformation of human beings into one half of the tidy equation that made Ballard's debits and credits balance.[85]

In October 1832, John Armfield would tell the public that Franklin and Armfield was growing its business in Alexandria as well. For the first time in nearly two and a half years, Armfield would change the number of enslaved people his advertisements said he wanted to buy, increasing it from 150 to 200. A few months later, he lifted the limits altogether, promising that he would "pay cash and the highest prices for any number of Likely Negroes, of both sexes."[86]

But the strategy of expanding to restore cash flow while collecting from customers and staying ahead of bank loans did not seem to be working. On February 29, 1832, Isaac Franklin met the brig *Ajax* in New Orleans and sent forty-five people shipped by Rice Ballard up to Natchez. When they arrived, James Franklin reported them "in good health but very ragged & dirty," and as he cleaned them up and used "all exertion to get them dressed," he assured Ballard that everything would be fine. Traders with less inventory already fretted that they could not compete with Franklin and Armfield, and with John Armfield having sent even more slaves on the *Lafayette*, Franklin believed they were right. "The small fry look at me as though they were allarmed," he quipped, "& I suppose they will have some cause when F&A's lot arrives." While he waited, Franklin said he would "open my fancy stock of wool & ivory." Metonymically imagining the hair and teeth of the enslaved as trade goods, once parts of living things and now merchandise on a shelf, Franklin allowed that prices might be "reduced" from what they had been in New Orleans but predicted, "we shall sell tolerably fast."[87]

He predicted wrong. Smug as ever, James Franklin wrote in his next report to Ballard that sales were going well and that in the evenings he amused himself by raping women in the Washington road compound. He had them all to himself, as "Uncle Isaac never nocks because he is never at home at night untill 12 oclock." But he had "not sold many men yet." He was having "hard times to sustain former prices," was "doubtful that we shall succeed in doing so much longer," and had had "to take all sorts of paper in payment." Successive dispatches only brought worse news. In late April, Isaac Franklin wrote that sales were "very dull indeed," and two weeks later, James Franklin sent word that "we have not done much since my last." Sales remained "very slow," and he was "fearful that we shall have to leave some stock unsold but shall hang on as long as we can find any chance."[88]

Early in June, Isaac Franklin told Ballard that he had finally "closed the sales for the present season." Still in the compound was "one white girl," but Franklin thought he might abandon her there, because he just wanted to get out of Natchez and "leave for Tennessee." Fully disclosing what he and his nephew had been holding back, Franklin confessed that the spring of 1832 had been a debacle, with the bottom having fallen out of sales prices. The only thing that had "kept the price up" at all, he grumbled, were extensive loans to planters offered the previous fall by the Planters' Bank of Mississippi, the Bank of the State of Mississippi, and the Natchez branch of the Second Bank of the United States.

Franklin was not complaining about government and private capital bailing him out. But it was a short-term fix that had "compelled" him "to sell almost alltogether" on credit, and it portended terrible market conditions again for the fall upcoming. Most of the bank loans were on one-year terms, and planters would have to pay them out of the next season's crops. Combined with the prospect of even more small traders pouring into Natchez because they could not make sales in New Orleans, Franklin was looking at intensifying competition for a customer base without much money to spend. It was a recipe for exceedingly poor sales prices, especially for cash sales, which every trader preferred and Franklin and Armfield desperately needed. "All the land pirates will flock here next fall," Franklin concluded, "& I have no doubt the price will be verry low for any thing like cash payments."[89]

Abandoning Natchez altogether was not an option. But having determined that "if we all have to rely on the State of Mississippi it will be a Dull Business," Franklin told Ballard "the Best market will be in your place and Alexandria next fall." Presuming decent cotton and sugar crops, Franklin thought slaveholders heading north to shop would "raise the prices in your market almost to Louisiana prices." He advised "you & Armfield to sell when you can make $50 profit on each negroe clear of Expences," adding that they might also make some money on freight, by arranging for customers to ship their purchases on the *Tribune*.[90]

Armfield and Ballard did what Franklin said. They started selling enslaved people in the Chesapeake during the summer, with Armfield even clearing out the Alexandria jail when disease struck there and sending "all the negroes on hand to Richmond for sale," including some who were still sick. Armfield also had the *Tribune* spend six months on a series of wide-ranging voyages to raise revenue from freight charges. Leaving New Orleans in May, Isaac Staples captained the brig to New York, where he delivered molasses, deerskins, "bear's oil," lead, and cotton. From there, the *Tribune* sailed for Madeira and the Canary Islands before returning in September to Philadelphia filled with "wines &c. to Order," and finally making its way back to Alexandria in late October.[91]

But finding enough cash to sustain growth and stave off financial implosion remained a problem. Isaac Franklin had financiered his way into the situation. Financiering his way out was more challenging. Between January and June 1832, he managed to send Ballard $35,000, mostly drawing on New Orleans and Natchez banking connections for checks payable at the Second Bank of the United States in Philadelphia or the Phenix Bank of New York. But Franklin paid discount rates on the checks as low as half a percent, which would translate into losses when the deposit banks took their cut. Considering that Ballard had spent almost $45,000 on slaves just in the last months of 1831, Franklin was not sending nearly enough money anyway.[92]

He knew that was true, and in some measure, he blamed himself. "I have done for the Best to the Best of my abilities," he told Ballard. "If money should not arive fast enough attribute it to the want of capasity in me and not for the want of Exertions." Yet some things were beyond his control. In particular, a bill to recharter the Second Bank of the United States had gotten hung up in a congressional fight between opponents and supporters of Andrew Jackson, who considered the institution unconstitutional, untrustworthy, and a political threat. Isaac Franklin was a Jackson man, but he noted that the escalating hostility of the president and his allies toward the bank had created uncertainty in money markets and was doing Franklin no favors. By the time he left Mississippi for Tennessee, banks in Natchez and New Orleans had stopped discounting bills entirely.[93]

"Never in all my Trading [have I] found moneyed arangements so hard to make," Franklin groused, and he told Ballard the company's survival depended on him. "Franklin & Armfield is holding nearly Two hundred & fifty thousand dollars worth of Bills receivable," Franklin wrote. Most would not be collectable until at least the fall. Until then, he had no money to send. Furthermore, he added, "John Armfield writes me that he is considerably in Debt," so "you and Alsop must sustain him." Franklin wanted Ballard to sell bills of exchange to his Fredericksburg and Richmond banks, payable by

Franklin and Armfield in sixty or ninety days, in amounts sufficient to "pay Armfields debts." Armfield, in turn, was "to lay low until I can furnish funds." If things were still bad when the bills came due, Franklin continued, Ballard could have them paid by drawing on "Jas. F. Purvis Baltimore" and extend the financial shell game another sixty days.[94]

There was more than a whiff of dread in Franklin's directive, and it soon became clear to Ballard that his partners had been less than completely forthcoming about the company's financial arrangements. Under pressure and struggling to stay afloat despite the appearance of market supremacy, they began sniping at each other. As they did, newspapers reported that a global cholera epidemic had crossed the Atlantic Ocean. People were dying in New York City. Things were going to get worse for Franklin, Armfield, Ballard, and their colleagues before they got better. They would get far worse for the enslaved, whose bodies marked the traders' path back to solvency.[95]

After his annual summer tour of company agencies, James Franklin went to Richmond in July 1832 to collect eighty-five enslaved people from Rice Ballard whom he would walk to Mississippi for sale. At least several dozen people sent by John Armfield to Richmond earlier in the summer were still there too, and Franklin would take them as well. The coffle was too large for one man to conduct alone, so Franklin assembled wagons and half a dozen horses for himself and the other white men who would help guard the captives and protect the tens of thousands of dollars invested in them. The preparations gave Franklin and Ballard time to talk business and review company books, and Ballard heard and saw some things that gave him pause.[96]

For months, Isaac Franklin had been asking Ballard to keep cash flowing into the company by taking out bank loans, promising that the interest on credit sales in the lower South would compensate for the risks assumed in borrowing. But as Ballard looked over company accounts, he noticed that Franklin had been making credit sales of the enslaved people Ballard shipped on much longer terms than he had divulged. Moreover, when Franklin sent returns on the sales to R. C. Ballard and Company, it looked as if he was withholding the promised 10 percent interest and instead putting the premium toward purchasing the shabby remittances he had been passing along. The way Ballard figured it, Franklin was deploying funds that properly belonged to R. C. Ballard and Company on behalf of Franklin and Armfield, even as he was having Ballard take on more debt and extend credit that could not be collected for years.[97]

Feeling "dissatisfaction," Ballard wrote to Franklin demanding an explanation for what appeared to be a lack of transparency at best and outright deceit at worst. Franklin trod lightly in response, writing from Tennessee with apologies and flatteries even while asking Ballard to trust that he had done right by him and that his complaints were rooted in misunderstandings. Franklin conceded he had extended credit on some sales for as long as seven years in New Orleans and as long as three years in Natchez. But he had been "pressed for time" by the imposition of the Louisiana import ban, and the "discussion at the city of Washington on [the] US Bank question" had thrown money markets into chaos. If he had not sold the enslaved on the terms he did, he might not have sold them at all. Surely money collectable in the future was better than no money. Franklin implored Ballard to appreciate the situation. "You are a man," he wrote, "that I conseive is too good a judge of business to believe that any salesman could have done better."[98]

As for the interest, racing about to find reliable bills and checks to send to the Chesapeake had forced Franklin to accept terms of exchange that had eaten away at the 10 percent Ballard had been expecting. For a while, Franklin had made Ballard whole, giving his "consern credit for the full cash valuation" even at Franklin and

Armfield's expense, "believing that times would change and money matters" would improve. When they had not, Franklin had "taken the paper that no other person would discount at any rate much less 10 p[e]r[cent]."[99]

That he was "Extreamly sorry" was small consolation, but Franklin denied misappropriating funds. He kept track of every penny, "cautious of having done to the best of my feeble abilities [to] promote the Interest of RCB&Co." He told Ballard that there was "a very large amt at your credit" still on the books, and he swore that when things settled down and customers paid what they owed, R. C. Ballard and Company would come out thousands of dollars ahead of every agency with which Franklin and Armfield worked. But Ballard was welcome to collect his interest immediately and forgo full returns on the outstanding bills, to take the bills from Franklin and make collections himself, or to change the terms of how "the slaves of your part of the consern must be disposed of next season." Franklin was being disingenuous, as he knew Ballard would see that none of those options were especially good. Still, he professed, "I must have every one that does business with me satisfyed or we cannot do business at all."[100]

Delicacy was not Ballard's strong suit. But he wanted to avoid inflaming a situation that could devolve into a lawsuit if handled poorly, so he told Franklin he was content to keep things as they were. "I am very well sattisfied with the sales," he wrote, "and feel convinced that we have all the justice done us that we were intitled to." He hated to think anyone affiliated with the company had "suffered by our advantages," he did not want to ask Franklin to recalibrate his books, and he certainly did not want to deal with bills from the lower South himself. "I told you when I commenced with you," he reminded Franklin, "I did not want more Debts in that country." Mostly Ballard wanted to move forward. "I do not mean to complain on this subject any more," he wrote. "When I commenced with you it was in good faith and I know you will do what is right."

But Ballard wanted Franklin to know he was not stupid and that he resented coyness about company affairs. "You never informed us in what way you were managing our business," he snapped. Franklin had to "know any man would complain of having the funds of their concern retained and deriving no benefit from it and have to borrow money to keep the concern going." Moreover, Ballard found it galling that Franklin presumed he could afford to keep borrowing. "In that you are mistaken," Ballard observed, "for I have been in debt ever since last fall and at no time less than Eleven thousand dollars and now upwards of twenty and was at no time able to pay my debts without stoping business." Ballard believed Franklin to be a good businessman and a forthright one. But he needed Franklin to know he was no "thick headed gump" who would be taken advantage of.[101]

In their letters, Franklin and Ballard both looked ahead to the spring of 1833, "when our time expires" and they would go their separate ways. Though their anticipation partially reflected the mutual irritation provoked by their exchange, it was no wonder they were considering how their alliance would end. Heading into the fall of 1832, they were having trouble communicating. They were struggling to find enough money to keep operations running as they would like, and everyone involved in the business was in debt.[102]

Then, in late October, a convention writing a new state constitution for Mississippi included a clause in the final document banning "the introduction of slaves into this state as merchandize or for sale" as of May 1, 1833. Crafted to contain the rapid growth of Mississippi's enslaved population and in response to fears of supposedly "artful and too often unscrupulous negro trader[s]" who imported slaves "of depraved character," the provision, if enforced, would close the legal market in enslaved people brought from out of state. John Armfield, lamenting the prospect of having to move out of Natchez, observed that "the convention of Mississippi has Blocked the game."[103]

Further compounding all the predicaments was the appearance of cholera in the lower South. The same coastline, river systems, and roads that brought enslaved captives to the region also brought disease, and slave traders created almost perfect conditions for its spread. Their business depended on cramming as many Black people as possible together in squalid conditions and providing them with just enough sustenance to survive journeys that would have compromised the immune systems even of those who lived in material comfort. It was only a matter of time before the enslaved reaped what Isaac Franklin, John Armfield, Rice Ballard, and their colleagues had sown.

The first sign of the epidemic among the people they trafficked appeared in the coffle James Franklin collected in Richmond. Like most people taken into the slave trade, they were young. Sixty of the eighty-five people sent by Rice Ballard were children and teenagers, all but one was under thirty, and while Ballard sent them on a thousand-mile journey thinking they were healthy and strong, Jourdan Saunders heard that "two or three had died before they reached Tennessee." James Franklin walked everyone else to Fairvue, and when they left for Mississippi in October, Isaac Franklin noted "2 children and a boy Died at my place" and "4 or five sick" remained there. Nearly a dozen of those brought out of Richmond were already gone.[104]

After his nephew left, Isaac Franklin put his affairs in order at Fairvue, caught up with the coffle about fifty miles south of Nashville, and accompanied the procession the rest of the way to Mississippi. It arrived outside Natchez in mid-November. Ten more enslaved people, including several children, had died en route, an average of one person every three days or so. Another seven or eight were sick, and the Franklins kept everyone camped in the woods for over a week because cholera had prompted "much alarm" among whites in the city itself.[105]

The Franklins and the survivors of what had become a death march finally straggled into Natchez on November 22, 1832. James

Franklin told Rice Ballard that he was happy just to be living inside again and that he and his uncle had rented two houses in addition to the Washington road compound. They needed the space, as Isaac Franklin was heading to New Orleans to receive nearly one hundred people John Armfield had shipped on the *Tribune*, though James Franklin "entertain[ed] great fears about those shipped." As well he might. Even setting aside the hazards encountered by the enslaved freighted on a slaver during an epidemic, more than one thousand people had succumbed to cholera in New Orleans in less than a week in October. One man reported from there that people had died "faster than coffins can be made." The contagion appeared to have subsided, but Isaac Franklin was taking no chances. He planned to meet the *Tribune* "somewhere below New Orleans and take the negroes across the lake to the high lands in Mississippi" rather than have them enter the city at all.[106]

When the *Tribune* landed at the Balize, a customs officer noted that nineteen-year-old Rachel Ann Phaner and twenty-one-year-old Levenia Washington were "sick." Isaac Franklin somehow got everyone back to Natchez alive, but when Jourdan Saunders told David Burford that "we may in great measure if not altogether escape the evil" of cholera thanks to "Mr. Franklin's experience prudence and management, together with an equal portion of the favours of Divine Providence," it was wishful thinking. By early December, Franklin believed he was amid "the most trying times there ever sailed in my high seas." Captives who appeared healthy could die in a matter of hours, he was discarding their corpses under cover of darkness, and he was furious about the prices Armfield and Ballard had paid for those shipped on the *Tribune*. Given that "the cholera had driven all the purchasers out of the market" and that their business "was so hard run for money," he expected the people they bought to have been inexpensive. Instead, he discovered "the dearest invoice" he had "ever received" and a load of "little slim assed girls and boys" who "cannot be sold for a profit."[107]

Yet even as cholera amplified tensions among the partners, it had a countervailing effect of leading them to reflect on the regard they had developed for each other. Whatever residual anger Rice Ballard harbored from his summer arguments with Isaac Franklin dissipated, as he feared for his colleagues' safety. "I hope for the Best," he wrote to Franklin, urging him and James to take precautions, "guard against the disease," and remember that their own lives were always more important than those of the enslaved. "If it please God that the negroes should get it I hope you will be carefull of yourselfs," Ballard concluded. "We had better loose all and begin again than loose ourselves."

Though debts still nagged at Ballard, imagining the Franklins' peril prompted him to set his own worries aside. Continuing to sell people in Virginia might have dug him a little out of his financial hole, but he told Franklin he would "hold on" instead and ship more enslaved people to the lower South once it looked safe to do so. There was economic calculation in that, as Ballard considered the business upside of slave mortality and thought slaveholders would try to replace the "negroes lost" to cholera as quickly as they could. But Ballard also would not leave Franklin in the lurch. "I am not willing to sell and <u>let you want</u>," he wrote. "I am as poor as a dog but will try to keep a stiff upper lip until you can hit a lick for us."[108]

The slave trade made them friends, and the slave trade would see them through, together. They had encountered adversity before, and slow sales, tight money, and being surrounded by sickness and death were just challenges to be overcome. "I will not give up the shipp," Franklin told Ballard, reporting that what sales he had made after getting to Natchez had "been at fare prices," that fears of cholera seemed to be abating, and that he thought the market might turn again in their favor. "The alarm begins to subside," Franklin observed. "I am in hopes we will be able to do something soon."[109]

As the weeks went by, in fact, Franklin, Ballard, and Armfield reconsidered the decision to sever their partnership in the spring

A duplicate check for $5,000 made out to Rice Ballard, dated November 1833, drawn on the Union Bank of Louisiana and payable at the Merchants' Bank of New York. Ballard and his partners commonly used checks to move money out of the lower South and into the Chesapeake, where they could be turned into cash and used to purchase enslaved people. Union Bank Check, folder 12, Rice Carter Ballard Papers, #04850, Southern Historical Collection, Wilson Library, The University of North Carolina at Chapel Hill.

of 1833. Economic, political, and epidemiological considerations pointed toward the wisdom of winding things down, collecting outstanding bills over time, and coming out even richer men than they already were. But as cholera's worst ravages faded in the lower South, so did some of the financial strains plaguing Franklin and Armfield. When Isaac Franklin vowed to Rice Ballard that he would persevere, he also told him to look out for incoming checks "which I trust will be in time to save your credit." Franklin had gained access to a prodigious new money source, the Union Bank of Louisiana. Chartered in the spring of 1832, the Union Bank was the most heavily capitalized bank in Louisiana. Supported by a state-backed bond issue worth $7 million and by capital from the London merchant banking giant Baring Brothers, the Union Bank opened branches throughout the state, had connections to the Merchants' Bank of New York, and attracted investors across the Atlantic world.[110]

Franklin had sold two enslaved men to Union Bank president Edmond Jean Forstall, who was a partner in the Louisiana Sugar Refinery Company in addition to having banking, shipping, real estate, slaveholding, and merchant interests. But Franklin's connection to the Union Bank came less through Forstall than through Richard Booker. A former commission merchant, Booker was the cashier of the Bank of Louisiana. Like that bank's president, Benjamin Story, Booker had been a customer of Franklin's, and he agreed to act as Franklin's financial agent, brokering the sale of some of the debt Franklin held and providing liquidity by converting it into the more dependable money of the Union Bank.[111]

On December 14, 1832, Booker sent Rice Ballard a Union Bank check for $15,000, payable at the Merchants' Bank of New York, and he sent an additional $5,000 four days later. Three days after that, John Armfield sent $18,000 to William J. Roberts, the cashier of the Fredericksburg branch of the Bank of Virginia, to repay some of what Ballard had borrowed from that institution. The deposit satisfied Roberts, and he wanted more, telling Ballard he "should like to get a part of your northern checks if convenient." By the end of the year, Armfield had sent Ballard nearly another $30,000. With Ballard's finances and his capacity for buying slaves having stabilized, Armfield said nothing about the end of their partnership, indicating instead that for the moment, the company was flush. Matters were to proceed as before. "If you want money," he advised Ballard, "do not hesitate to draw."[112]

The political tides that had been rising against the company receded too. Isaac Franklin had never been overly concerned about the constitutional provision banning the slave trade in Mississippi, telling Ballard in January 1833 to keep buying people in Virginia for shipment. Franklin thought the state legislature would make "a modifycation" to the provision, but he also figured that "whether the law is repealed or not we cant loose." The mere threat of it was boosting sales among slaveholders concerned the Natchez market would close, and Ballard needed only to be careful about what he paid. "The old fellow has met with the robbers," Franklin reported, referring to the competitors he had known would come to the Natchez market, but "if you send me the wright kind of slaves at any thing like a fare price I will be sure to realise a profit." By March, Franklin's unconcern about Mississippi's prospective ban was confirmed. The legislature had adjourned, James Franklin informed Ballard, "without doing any thing with the negro law."[113]

At the same time, frustration with the restrictions imposed by the slave-import ban was mounting in Louisiana. In March 1833, the legislature there amended the ban again, repealing the portion that included Kentucky, Tennessee, and Missouri "as amongst those states and territories from whom slaves should not be introduced." Isaac Franklin told Ballard that the law mostly "remain[ed] as it was" and that the opening, though small, might mean a slight drop in sales prices. Yet it could not have been far from Franklin's mind that the adjustment might portend a broader reopening of New Orleans, and in the meantime, declining worries about cholera meant the Natchez market was humming.[114]

On January 16, 1833, John Armfield shipped eighty-three enslaved people to the lower South on the *Lafayette*, including twenty-seven men, nineteen women, and thirteen boys and girls under age fourteen to Isaac Franklin. By mid-April, Armfield would dispatch at least 250 more people in two shipments on the *Tribune*, one on the brig *Ariel*, and one on a schooner named the *Renown*. In February, Isaac Franklin told Rice Ballard he and his nephew were "selling fast." Things had slowed down by March, and James Franklin complained to Ballard of "all sorts of little pirats in market." But he still "anticipate[d] a full springs business owing I suppose to us having supplied the greater part of the purchasers."[115]

The reemergence of cholera might have suggested otherwise. It could appear suddenly and sporadically, even after an epidemic was thought to have passed. It rolled through the lower South again in the spring of 1833, making especially inopportune the macabre revelation in Natchez that Isaac Franklin had been unceremoniously throwing away the remains of the enslaved who died from it. But

James Franklin was no more perturbed than his uncle by the outcry that impelled the city's board of selectmen to push slave traders out of the city for good. He figured he ought to tell Ballard what had happened, but he did so almost as an afterthought in a letter about money. He knew Ballard would care about the latest $10,000 check from Richard Booker that was proceeds of collections made on Ballard's behalf. Less important was that the Natchez operation would have to move. "Our negroes are getting much better but they have been sickly so much," Franklin wrote. "Also the city council compels us all to leave the limits of the corporation in two days we shall have to take [to] the woods."[116]

On April 23, 1833, the day before James Franklin wrote to Ballard, Armfield placed a new advertisement in the Alexandria *Phenix Gazette*. Franklin and Armfield was "desirous to close their expense account," and Armfield was requesting "all persons having bills or accounts against them, to present the same for payment as soon as convenient." Money was flowing again, and paying off local debts in Alexandria was a nice way to clean up the books a bit as Isaac Franklin, John Armfield, and Rice Ballard considered their next moves.[117]

FIVE

DISSOLUTIONS, 1833–1837

Ethan Allen Andrews took a Potomac River steamboat from Washington City to Alexandria on a sweltering July day in 1835 to see "the establishment of Franklin and Armfield" for himself. A Connecticut lawyer, educator, and lexicographer, Andrews was also a traveling agent for the American Union for the Relief and Improvement of the Colored Race. Founded as a moderate alternative to the American Anti-Slavery Society, which stood at the forefront of abolitionism's radical turn in the 1830s, the American Union had among its goals "to collect and publish information of an authentic character respecting Slavery." Andrews was gathering material on slavery and the slave trade in Maryland, Virginia, and the nation's capital. He knew his report would be incomplete without a visit to Duke Street.[1]

By 1835, Franklin and Armfield operated what abolitionist and judge William Jay termed a "Slave-Factory," reputedly trafficking between one thousand and twelve hundred enslaved people from the Chesapeake to the lower South every year. The company was known as "the principal dealers" of slaves in the District of Columbia, and its renown among slaveholders was matched by its notoriety among slavery's opponents. Antislavery periodicals routinely republished company advertisements to show that the capital served as "a mart for slave-dealers" and a center of "the trade in blood." Black antislavery editor Philip A. Bell used a Franklin and Armfield advertisement to blast "Slave Dealers as Cannibals" who were no better than "a gang of thieves or counterfeitors," and when the American Anti-Slavery Society published a broadside illustrating the District of Columbia as the "Slave Market of America," it used company ads too. Above them appeared woodcut images, one of "a slave ship receiving her cargo of slaves" in Alexandria, and the other of a white man leading a coffle of Black people from "Franklin & Armfield's Slave Prison" toward the docks.[2]

Because he was frank about who he was and why he wanted to see company headquarters, Ethan Andrews was not sure he would be granted entry. But he was not the first abolitionist to appear at the front door. Editor and minister Joshua Leavitt had paid a call in January 1834, accompanied by Alexandria resident and antislavery activist George Drinker. British traveler Edward Abdy, who campaigned against slavery and for prison reform, was there three months after that, and a correspondent of the American Anti-Slavery Society had visited five months before Andrews. John Armfield understood how to welcome people like Andrews. Though they were not in the market for slaves, they got a sales pitch nonetheless.[3]

Armfield asked an employee, probably his clerk and assistant, Robert Windsor, to show Andrews "every part of the establishment." Windsor led Andrews from the parlor to the passageway behind the house and through the heavy iron door to the left, where Andrews saw fifty or sixty enslaved men and boys "amusing themselves with rude sports" to pass the time. Most were between the ages of eighteen and thirty, though Andrews observed several who could not have been older than ten. To give Andrews a better look, Windsor

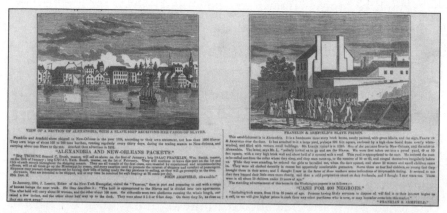

In 1836, the American Anti-Slavery Society published *Slave Market of America*, a broadside with a series of images critiquing the slave trade in the District of Columbia. Franklin and Armfield was singled out for particular scorn, with company advertisements published beneath depictions of a slaver in port at Alexandria and of "Franklin & Armfield's Slave Prison" on Duke Street. Library of Congress Rare Book and Special Collections Division.

had them all line up against the whitewashed wall surrounding their enclosure. It was surely the same protocol Windsor followed whenever a customer came to the compound, as was his spiel about the people confined there, in which he "expiated on their happy condition, when compared with that in which they had lived before they came to this place."

After ushering Andrews from the pen and bolting it shut, Windsor unlocked the door across the passageway to reveal thirty or forty enslaved women and girls. Andrews guessed that most "inmates of this apartment were of about the same ages as those who occupied the yard which I had just left," but he asked Windsor about "one mother with an infant." She was an unusual case, Windsor told him, explaining that "they did not like to purchase women with young children, as they were less saleable than others, in the market to which they sent their slaves." When Andrews inquired more generally "respecting the separation of families," Windsor assured him "that they were at great pains to prevent such separation in all cases, in which it was practicable, and to obtain, if possible, whole families."

Windsor continued the tour, showing Andrews the kitchen, the tailor shop, the barracks where the enslaved slept, and the hospital building, pointing out that "such was the health of the slaves at this time, that the building was unoccupied." Conducting Andrews out the rear of the yard, Windsor showed him "four or five tents" and "large wagons" stored there that would accompany the people he had just seen when they made their forced march to Mississippi later in the summer. Then Windsor and Andrews went back inside. John Armfield was there, and he was in good spirits, as he had "just concluded a bargain." He offered Andrews "refreshments of various kinds" in light of the "excessive heat" of the day, and Andrews took a few moments to collect himself before bidding farewell.

Reflecting on his visit, Andrews was skeptical about what Robert Windsor had shown him. Even though many of the people Andrews saw appeared "cheerful and contented," he noticed signs of a hoax. Among the enslaved women presented for his inspection, he spotted "a few who seemed to have been weeping," and among the men and boys, one "young man" in particular caught his eye. He stared at Andrews as Windsor talked, and whenever Windsor turned away, the man "shook his head." He "seemed desirous," Andrews believed, "of having me understand, that he did not feel any such happiness as was described, and that he dissented from the representation made of his condition." The man cast his glance "anxiously and fearfully," lest he be discovered objecting to Windsor's fictions, and although Andrews wrote he "would have given much to hear his tale," he recognized that the man was risking all he reasonably could. But other Black people could have told Andrews stories like those contained in the shakes of the terrified man's head.[4]

Ann, a twenty-year-old woman, could have told Andrews about how her mother had saved nearly enough to buy her out of slavery when she was seized by white men on a Richmond street in 1834, thrown into Rice Ballard's jail alongside three hundred other people, and shipped to New Orleans on the *Tribune*. Andrews had heard talk of John Armfield's reputation for "resolute efforts to prevent kidnapping." But Ann, who later acquired her freedom and made her way to Cincinnati, knew of others "kidnapped the same evening" she was, and of at least fifteen kidnapped people packed with her on the *Tribune*.[5]

Michael Shiner, a thirty-year-old enslaved man who worked at the Washington Navy Yard, could have told Andrews about his wife Phillis being "snacht" in an alley in 1833. Along with the couple's three daughters, she was sold to a "couple of gentelman Mr Franklin and mr John armfield." Armfield took no "great pains" to prevent separating the Shiner family, nor did he object to buying Phillis Shiner together with her "young children," all of whom were under age four. Whether that would have made her "less saleable than others" is unknown, as Michael Shiner, "in great distress," mustered legal and financial assistance from some white men he knew and delayed her dispatch to the lower South. After a frantic day during which he ran back and forth several times from Washington City to Alexandria, looking for more help while also making sure John Armfield still had his family, Shiner managed to get his "Wife and Childdren Clear."[6]

Most families sundered by Franklin and Armfield never saw the reunion the Shiners did. At Mount Vernon, "a very interesting lad, some 9 or 10 years old" could have told Andrews that. At around the time Andrews got his tour from Robert Windsor in the summer of 1835, white visitors encountered the boy at the Potomac River estate that had been the home of George Washington. Discovering that one of the visitors lived in Alexandria, the boy asked whether the man knew "if Mr. Armfield has got a letter yet from my father." The befuddled guests were later informed that the boy's father had been sold to Franklin and Armfield by Jane Washington, Mount Vernon's proprietor and the widow of George Washington's great-nephew. To ease the boy's anguish and "quiet the little fellow, he was told that his father would write a letter for him and send it to Mr.

Armfield's care." Now the boy asked everyone who came to Mount Vernon from Alexandria if John Armfield had his father's letter, and he was crestfallen every time he was told no letter had arrived. Perhaps when the boy got older, he would understand that Armfield had not found it "practicable" to keep his family together.[7]

Ethan Andrews struggled with what he saw and heard during his travels in the Chesapeake. He could not fathom the way white people acted as if the enslaved had no feelings worthy of consideration, nor did he understand how anyone could defend the institution of slavery in light of the slave trade's barbarism. Visiting the Duke Street compound made things no clearer. His head spinning as he left the facility, he walked back to his lodgings, "ruminating as I went, upon the countless evils, which 'man's inhumanity to man,' has occasioned in this world of sin and misery."

Andrews might have been less confused had he seen that some of the transfigurations making the slave trade acceptable to so many white Americans were right in front of him all along. But signifiers of race and class can cloud the vision, and for all his moralism and suspicions about what went on at John Armfield's place of business, Andrews found a lot to like about John Armfield. Despite Armfield's having spent "many years engaged in the traffic in human flesh," Andrews was impressed by his having "acquired great wealth," appearing "still in the prime of life," and being "a man of fine personal appearance" and "engaging and graceful manners" who treated Andrews "with great politeness." Certainly, Armfield stood in stark contrast with the man Andrews met the next day on another steamboat, whose name Andrews gave only as "N." He was a slave trader too, headed to South Carolina "with about fifty negroes," and Andrews thought him "vulgar in his manners, and mean in his personal appearance." He swore profusely, and though he made the same pretense that John Armfield and Robert Windsor had to not separating enslaved families, eventually he admitted he did so all the time, saying that "his business is to purchase, and he must take such as are in the market." Perhaps the only thing Andrews and N. shared was their respect for John Armfield, though N. had a different reason for it. He had sold seven men to Armfield days before meeting Andrews and appreciated that Armfield paid enough for N. to make "fifty dollars a head" on the deal.

On hearing that Andrews had just been at the compound in Alexandria, N. assumed he was "a planter deeply interested in the price of slaves." It was a reasonable assumption. Everyone interested in selling or buying slaves was bound to stop at Duke Street. Yet there was an irony to the attention Franklin and Armfield drew from abolitionists, the patronage they attracted from slaveholders, and the appreciation they garnered from fellow slave traders. The American slave trade in the mid-1830s was bigger business than ever, it was getting still bigger all the time, and Isaac Franklin, John Armfield, and Rice Ballard were undeniably its biggest players. But their trajectories and that of the trade were actually beginning to diverge.[8]

FEW OUTSIDE THE COMPANY WOULD HAVE GUESSED IT. ON the contrary, in the two years before Ethan Andrews's visit, Franklin and Armfield seemed to be a slave-trading juggernaut. In May 1833, Franklin, Armfield, and Ballard agreed "to continue the slave trade" on the same terms as in the agreement they had signed two years earlier. Hundreds of thousands of dollars in uncollected bills remained a serious concern. So did the ongoing unpredictability of money markets, which was exacerbated by confusion surrounding the fate of millions in federal deposits held by the Second Bank of the United States, whose recharter Andrew Jackson ultimately had vetoed in July 1832. But along with Richard Booker's ability to steer funds toward Isaac Franklin from the Union Bank of Louisiana, the renewed financial commitments accompanying the partnership extension set the company on relatively stable ground, maintained its cash flow, and underpinned additional growth.[9]

Evidence of that came the day after the partners pledged themselves anew to the business and each other, when John Armfield placed an advertisement in District of Columbia newspapers unlike any he or any other slave trader had placed before. It revived Franklin and Armfield's long-standing promises to buy "any number of *LIKELY NEGROES*" and to be at the Duke Street facility ready to pay "higher prices in Cash than any other purchaser who is now or may hereafter come into market." Setting it apart for sheer brazenness was a directory of five agencies also authorized to service "persons having likely Servants to dispose of."[10]

In Virginia, sellers could apply to R. C. Ballard and Company in Richmond or J. M. Saunders and Company in Warrenton. In Maryland, they could stop by the offices of George Kephart and Company in Frederick or James F. Purvis and Company in Baltimore, or at those of a man named Thomas M. Jones. Since at least the late 1820s, Jones had been a trader in his own right and acted as agent for several others in Mississippi. He had worked occasionally for John Armfield dating back to Armfield's partnership with Joseph Meek. Now he was to run Franklin and Armfield's agency in Easton, on the Eastern Shore.[11]

Franklin and Armfield soon enlisted three more agents and added them to the advertisement roster too. John Ware, who had bought enslaved people for the company before and worked for a time at the Alexandria compound, would run the agency in Port Tobacco, in southern Maryland's Charles County. Andrew Grimm, one of Rice Ballard's agents, received a promotion and would run his own agency in Ballard's old stomping grounds of Fredericksburg, Virginia, and a man named William Hooper would buy for Franklin and Armfield in Annapolis, the Maryland state capital. Between Ballard's operation in Richmond and the other seven agencies arranged in a circle centered on Alexandria like spoke heads on a wheel, the men who worked with the Franklin and Armfield seal of approval covered more than twenty thousand square miles of the upper South.[12]

John Armfield first placed this advertisement in the Alexandria *Phenix Gazette* in the summer of 1833, announcing that Franklin and Armfield would purchase "any number" of enslaved people. Slaveholders could make sales arrangements with Armfield in Alexandria or with one of a series of agents scattered across the Chesapeake. Courtesy American Antiquarian Society.

The company added assets to its portfolio in the summer of 1833 as well. In Richmond, Rice Ballard paid $350 to buy the jail complex he had been renting, and in Alexandria, John Armfield checked the mails for progress reports on the new brig he had ordered. Built at a cost of $7,250 at the same shipyard that made the *Tribune*, the new vessel would be that boat's twin, with nearly identical dimensions and carrying capacity. It would be called the *Uncas*, named for the seventeenth-century Mohegan sachem who had allied himself with Puritan settlers in New England and who reacquired celebrity in the 1820s thanks to a namesake character in James Fenimore Cooper's *Last of the Mohicans*. The brig arrived in New York in late September. Two weeks after that, with rumors spreading that the slave trade to Louisiana might reopen, Armfield announced in the Alexandria *Phenix Gazette* that either the *Uncas* or the *Tribune* would sail for New Orleans "every thirty days throughout the shipping season."[13]

Isaac Franklin, John Armfield, and Rice Ballard each held a one-third share of the *Tribune* and the *Uncas*, and as Franklin wrote to Ballard in August 1833 that the Franklin and Armfield name would be "always at your service" when negotiating with bankers for money, the partners' mutual dependency was obvious. So was their "friendship." Yet Franklin also meant for the upcoming trading season to be his "last effort," and the acquisition of illiquid assets pointed toward a new plan for the company. The partners would harvest and sell as many Black people as possible during the 1833–1834 season. They would satisfy as many of their liabilities as they could. Then they would turn most of the business over to Isaac Franklin's nephews and their other agents, keep some money in infrastructural components of the trade such as ships and jails, and look toward new ventures and new stages of their lives.[14]

But even that plan did not unfold as the partners anticipated. Personal setbacks and losses forced unwelcome adjustments, and politics so roiled the financial world that Franklin, Armfield, and Ballard would be nearly overwhelmed by the reliance on credit and debt that had made them successful. By the summer of 1835, they decided the time had finally come for them to start getting out of the daily traffic in human property. At the same time that the American slave trade as a whole reached its frenzied pinnacle, Franklin, Armfield, and Ballard maneuvered away from "the game." Yet they still shipped and sold hundreds of people as they withdrew, and they went out on top. Perversely charmed to the very end, they managed to put themselves in as advantageous a position as possible when cotton markets and the slave trade came crashing down in 1837 and took the economy of the entire country along with them.

S lave traders hated the late spring in the lower South. The sickliest time of year approached, the heat escalated, shipments and coffles of enslaved merchandise had ended for the season, and customers became few and far between. With most of the sales they were going to make before the summer done by mid-May, if traders had someplace else to go, they wanted to get there as soon as possible.

For Isaac and James Franklin, the spring of 1833 was worse than usual. The rented house they moved to at the Forks of the Road kept them in conformity with the new regulations against slave traders in the city. But cholera proved pesky in its resurgence. Even as John Armfield broadcast Franklin and Armfield's dominance in the Chesapeake, disease in the lower South continued to stall sales, surrounded the Franklins with gore and putridity, and took a toll on their constitutions and their moods.[15]

"If I could get clear of the cholera from among our negroes I should be happy," James Franklin reported to Rice Ballard. He was personally "not in very good health," it took "all the well negroes to attend to the sick," and alarm over the epidemic had cleared buyers from the market. And he was bored. His uncle was in New Orleans, and he was the only white person at the house. His usual "overseer," a white man named Samuel Jacobs, had succumbed to cholera, an enslaved assistant named Dorsy was sick too, and Franklin had visited the city proper just "twice in 10 days." He wondered if he would ever be able to leave Natchez. But he imagined there were marks out there still. Scribbling in haste before heading to tend to "another sick negro," he disparaged with one of his favorite expressions those who might be dumb enough to purchase slaves amid a plague. "I am in hopes," he told Ballard, "all the fools are not yet dead & some one eyed man will buy us out."[16]

Not enough fools had appeared by the time Isaac Franklin returned to Natchez early in June. "Much depressed" and "extreamly anxious to leave," he told Ballard that he was going to Fairvue whether or not he and his nephew sold the dozen or so enslaved people they had left. Feeling all of his forty-four years, Franklin "could not pretend to Describe the Distress and Suffering the Old Chief has felt" and thought he would get to Virginia for his annual summer visit with Armfield and Ballard only "if life lasts so long."

Isaac Franklin worried about money too, but despite "considerable" fatalities among the enslaved, company losses had not been nearly "as much as the other Traders in proportion to numbers." Moreover, Franklin figured that the spring's miseries would redound to the company's advantage come the fall. "A good many of the planters" had "suffered severely with the cholera," presiding in some cases over the deaths of more than half the people they held in bondage, and Franklin predicted they would look to replenish "there whole stock." He knew they would probably borrow against the lives of the enslaved people he provided, meaning the company would probably "be hard run for cash," which was not ideal. Still, Franklin and Armfield had managed to "make some money" despite all it had been through in recent months, and even though Franklin could only tell Ballard that the company would "try to do better the next season," he considered it a pretty good bet.[17]

But Franklin's usually dependable sense for the intermingling of politics, banking, and agriculture that dictated the shape and strength of markets in enslaved people eluded him this time. In September, Andrew Jackson made clear his intention to destroy the power of the Second Bank of the United States even before its charter formally expired by removing federal deposits and distributing them among politically friendly state-chartered banks instead. Partially in a fit of pique and partially in an effort to demonstrate the central bank's economic significance and perhaps procure a new charter, bank president Nicholas Biddle responded to Jackson's order by deliberately curbing credit. The bank started calling in loans, discount rates soared, capital flows stagnated, and by late fall the nation plunged toward recession. Franklin would discover that his admiration for the president could not spare him the repercussions of Jackson's brashness and financial brinksmanship.[18]

For a while, economic conditions continued to favor Franklin, Armfield, Ballard, and their associates. Near the end of September, Jourdan Saunders told David Burford he had scooped up sixty enslaved people who were "ready for market" and put them "on the road" to Alexandria. Feeling that "nothing but misfortune will prevent our making all sorts of money this year," he was "completely absorbed in business" and "purchasing almost daily."[19]

In mid-October, the *Tribune* left Alexandria on its first voyage of the new season under the command of a new captain, William Smith having replaced Isaac Staples. Sailing for New Orleans, the *Tribune* carried ninety-three enslaved people, including sixty whom Ballard had sent to Armfield for shipment. As the steamboat *Natchez* towed the *Tribune* up the Mississippi River from the Balize in early November, Isaac Franklin was waiting. "All is well," he reported back to Ballard. By then, the *Uncas* had left Alexandria too. With Captain Joseph Moore at the helm, it would arrive in New Orleans before the end of the month, delivering to Franklin at least another sixty-five people.[20]

From Natchez, James Franklin reported in late October that sales prices of young adult men averaged between $800 and $850, and of young adult women, between $575 and $600. Both were 40 to 50 percent increases from the spring, and Franklin told Ballard that he "should like to have as many negroes of the right kind as we can get." Armfield, Ballard, and the other agents could afford to do that. Between April and October, Ballard alone had received over $80,000 from Isaac Franklin, enough to buy nearly 175 enslaved people.[21]

Plans also began taking shape in October for turning Isaac Franklin's roles in Franklin and Armfield entirely over to his nephews, as he, John Armfield, James Franklin, and James Purvis became partners in "Isaac and James R. Franklin and Company." Partnership terms have not survived, but the new entity began keeping accounts with Franklin Ballard and Company and with R. C. Ballard and

Company, and Isaac Franklin later said its creation was intended to clear the path for his retirement. James Franklin "was to manage the whole business, and they were to divide the proceeds," which would "let him out from conducting the business."[22]

Things seemed to be going so famously that Ballard wanted to expand company operations even further, inquiring about adding yet another purchasing agent to the Franklin and Armfield roster. But neither Isaac nor James Franklin thought that a good idea. Isaac Franklin believed profits would be divided among too many people to make another agency worth his efforts, and James Franklin merely told Ballard it was unwise "to enlarge our present years business by making any more concerns than we have." Some money might be made and "we might all be benefited by it," but he and his uncle had all the traffic they could handle. "We have as many concerns & partners as any two men can possibly do justice by," he wrote, "& think it better to do what we do well than to do much more and badly completed."[23]

More significantly, both Franklins started noticing worrisome economic trends that dictated against heedless growth. For one thing, competition in the lower South had become fierce, as legions of slave traders looked to capitalize on a seller's market. Isaac Franklin told Ballard that traders from Kentucky were "flocking down like winters hail." James Franklin agreed. "The negroes are coming down the river very fast," he wrote, adding that the supply of enslaved people threatened to lower sales prices. He was sure they would fall unless the Louisiana legislature lifted the state import ban, and he wondered whether even that would "raise the price much." Traders anticipating the ban's repeal were already selling slaves in New Orleans "almost oppenly," and the Mississippi market remained tight anyway.[24]

Of still greater concern was news that cotton prices were declining in Europe. Isaac Franklin knew that that always translated to "a fall in slaves," and it was happening even as prices for enslaved

people in the Chesapeake were escalating and disease was returning to the lower South yet again. In mid-December, James Franklin
told Rice Ballard that he had sold around one hundred people in
the previous month and considered himself "the busiest man you
ever saw." But he had "about fifteen down the most of which are
sick with the damd cholera," and he thought ten or twelve of them
likely to die, which he was "affraid will take off all of our profits."
In addition, Ballard and Armfield were paying "high prices in Va"
that made the company into "gone suckers," and disturbances in the
money markets were becoming noticeable. Franklin was no longer
buying checks in Natchez at all, because the premium for decent
ones had become exorbitant. Customer demand for slaves remained
strong, but prices were weakening, margins were shrinking, and
nearly every sale was on credit. "As for getting cash," Franklin told
Ballard, "it is utterly out of the question."[25]

Close to midnight on Christmas Eve, 1833, Isaac Franklin
disembarked from a steamboat in New Orleans, having made yet
another trip downriver from Natchez. He spent part of Christmas Day writing to Ballard. Franklin put a more positive spin on
things than his nephew had, relaying that business had bustled at
the Forks of the Road during his most recent visit, that he had sold
more people there "than all the [other] Traders together," and that
he had managed "first rate prices and profits." He said he "would
have made for the concerns at Least $100,000" had it not been "for
this Dammed Cholera & bad luck," and he told Ballard he could
"do it any how if you can lower the price with you a little." Franklin
wanted his colleagues to "send me between you all four hundred
more slaves this season."[26]

But Franklin could not resist wallowing in how difficult the
life of selling human beings had become. "I have had a Desperate season," he moaned. "I am almost Broke down." He had no
one in New Orleans to help manage the intake of shipments from
the Chesapeake, and he also had to transport slaves to Natchez by

himself, "by which I loose a good deal of time running backwards & forwards." Franklin promised to "stand it if I can," but he acknowledged that his "health has rather failed" and he reiterated that everyone needed to prepare for his departure. "After this," he wrote, "you all must dispence with my servises its two bad to kill the old fellow after sustaining you all under so many Disadvantages." Physical decline exacerbated the melancholy that became more pronounced as Franklin saw retirement approaching. His belief that he suffered a kind of martyrdom for his labors intensified as well, and the narcissism of that could be stupefying. Complaining to Ballard about having butted heads with his nephews over money, Franklin saw nothing but his own distress, refracted through a lens of pain and suffering he could only pretend to understand because he inflicted so much of it. "I have made a slave of myself," he wrote, "for the benefit of others."[27]

Yet Franklin would stand firm, as he always did. The Louisiana legislature had finally repealed the state's slave-import ban, and while Franklin doubted "whether it will be any advantage," he was ready. "I am now busily engaged in preparing a house to keep the next shipment," he wrote, adding that he had before him the bill of lading Ballard had sent for sixty-two people consigned on the *Tribune*, which had made a quick turnaround in Alexandria after its return there in late November. Franklin planned to divide the enslaved when they arrived. Some he would send to Natchez, some he had already sold to customers sight unseen, and some he would keep at the new facility he had rented in New Orleans.[28]

He was writing from that facility, having signed a yearlong lease for it earlier in the month. The rental agreement on the property he had used before, at the intersection of Esplanade and Francais, had expired in the spring of 1833, and with slave imports then forbidden by law, Franklin had seen no point in renewing it. The spot he now intended for his showroom and stockade was bigger and grander anyway. Two blocks farther up Esplanade from the old location, it

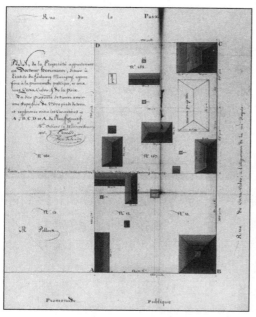

An 1815 plan of the property at the intersection of Esplanade Avenue and Casa Calvo (today known as Royal Street), in the Faubourg Marigny suburb of New Orleans. Used originally as a naval hospital and then as the home of a lawyer and his family, it served as a residence, office, and sales compound for Isaac Franklin for several years in the 1830s. The Historic New Orleans Collection, 1974.25.3.170.

was on the downtown lakeside corner of Casa Calvo Street, which is Royal Street today, and it took up most of four contiguous lots, comprising not quite two-thirds of an acre. With 120 feet of frontage on Esplanade, it ran back into the Faubourg Marigny along Casa Calvo for 230 feet, which was the length of the entire block between Esplanade and Peace Street, since renamed Kerlerec Street.[29]

Lewis Heermann, a physician commissioned as a surgeon for the United States Navy, first consolidated the lots into a single tract in 1815, and he used it as a naval hospital before selling it to a lawyer named John Francis Canonage. A suburban estate befitting a professional and his family, like the Duke Street property in Alexandria once occupied by merchant and lawyer Robert Young, the Canonage property was also optimal for becoming a slave-trading compound. Surrounded by a whitewashed brick wall about one story tall, the property had a large hip-roofed two-story dwelling house with attic space. Equipped originally with a wooden balcony and an entrance reached through a gate on Esplanade, the house had been renovated with a portico and a staircase to provide direct access from the un-paved street. Behind the house was a garden, and across the rest of the property were scattered seven or eight long, low one-story out-buildings. Lewis Heermann used many of them to house patients. Isaac Franklin would use them to imprison slaves.[30]

Others had done so before him. Sometime around 1830, John Francis Canonage sold the property to merchant and slave trader Leon Chabert. Chabert may have used the site to confine enslaved people, and in 1832 he rented it to Austin Woolfolk's uncle John Woolfolk, who certainly did. Austin Woolfolk's brother Samuel Woolfolk may have used the site too. Notwithstanding the profes-sional rivalry between the Woolfolks and Franklin and Armfield, when Isaac Franklin was in Natchez the day he was to take over the lease on the Canonage property, Samuel Woolfolk did him the favor of accepting it on his behalf.[31]

But a conspicuous location and an established reputation in the slave trade did not necessarily translate into sales. As the calendar year turned from 1833 to 1834, Franklin's suspicion that the New Orleans market might not be what it had been was borne out. The city suffered acutely from falling cotton prices and financial contrac-tion, and Franklin found no customers at all. Louisiana governor André Roman formally signed the repeal of the laws "relative to the introduction of slaves" on January 2, 1834, but Franklin soon told Ballard he had had "the stock from the Brig Tribune" on offer for two weeks and had "not sold the first negroe out of that lott."[32]

Desperate for information, Franklin lurked at Hewlett's Ex-change for a day, and he saw seventy enslaved people sold at auction. But even the highest bidders paid only what had been standard prices in Natchez months before, and they got terms of "Twelve months credit without Interest" to boot. It was a bad situation, and the weather threatened to make it worse, as freezing rain and snow im-periled the sugarcane crop. Franklin knew that if the crop were lost, some slaveholders would "have scarcely any thing for the hand[s] they have already to do." They would hardly be in the market for more. Other slaveholders might lose their plantations altogether, leading to a supply glut as they brought "there hands into market" and liquidated human assets in an attempt to salvage what they could.[33]

Franklin understood that the *Uncas* had left Alexandria just after the New Year, carrying at least fifty-five people on its second shipment of the season. But countermanding his Christmas Day request to boost supply, Franklin now advised Ballard to ease up and "purchase sparingly." With prices at a standstill, business languishing in New Orleans, and cash sales almost impossible to make anywhere at all, the company would be better off if it concentrated on collecting outstanding bills and waited for conditions to improve. Once they did, Franklin and Armfield would have enough financial cushion to sell the enslaved "on the long credit business." Using customer debt to leverage themselves out of their own, the partners could make "at the single opporation money enough to do us and not fail all our days."[34]

The advice became a directive. Hearing his uncle's dismal reports from New Orleans, James Franklin practically screamed at Ballard to stop what he was doing immediately. "For god sake," he wrote, "do not buy at any price untill the affairs of our government and everything works wright." He issued similar orders to the Chesapeake agents, and the whole company curtailed its activities dramatically for the rest of the season. John Armfield sent three more shipments from Alexandria, but where he had consigned at least fifty or sixty people at a time in the fall and early winter, he shipped twenty-five on the *Tribune* in February and twenty-nine in April. In March, he shipped just eighteen on the *Uncas*, and when Edward Abdy visited the Duke Street compound a few weeks later, he saw "but three men, and four or five women, with as many children" wandering in the yards. Armfield even pulled his advertisements from District of Columbia newspapers, stopping them entirely for almost two months. He placed one again in May, but he stripped

Looking up Esplanade Avenue, away from the Mississippi River. This photograph, taken in the 1850s, shows, on the right-hand side of the street, just across the intersection from the grocery store, the house from which Isaac Franklin did business in New Orleans between 1833 and 1836. Also visible is part of the wall designed to pen enslaved people as they awaited sale or transport to Natchez. The Historic New Orleans Collection, 1982.167.11.

out the agency names in favor of a more generic ad, which appeared only sporadically through the end of July. For a company that had trumpeted its presence all year long for half a decade, the retreat was marked.[35]

Franklin and Armfield's challenges mattered little to the enslaved people who still ended up in the company's grasp. Agnes Grimes, James Lewis, Charlotte Stuart, and Dave Tilman, teenagers packed on the *Tribune* in April 1834 with twenty-five other captives, did not care that John Armfield typically shipped more people than that, and neither did those left behind to mourn them. Adding insult to their injuries was the fact that James and Isaac Franklin would have preferred that Grimes, Lewis, and the others had never been sent to the lower South at all. In New Orleans on February 19, 1834, Isaac Franklin sold Charlotte, a seven-year-old girl he offered as an "orphan," to Helene Vascocu, the wife of a goldsmith named Jacques Vitant, for $200. More than six weeks after the repeal of the import ban, Charlotte was the first person sold from the Canonage property. Franklin would not see another customer for three weeks after that, and while he would sell 103 more enslaved people in the city by the end of May, that was just a third as many as he had sold during the same time frame when slave imports had last been legal, in 1831.[36]

Franklin sold nineteen young men to the Louisiana Board of Public Works, which intended to make them do especially deadly work clearing swamps and repairing levees. He sold nearly everyone else to buyers from cotton parishes in the northern part of the state, as slaveholders in New Orleans and Louisiana's sugar parishes had no money to spend. Franklin complained that even the cotton planters refused to pay decent prices, and nearly all of them wanted to buy on credit no matter how low the cash price. "I do not know what will become of us from the present prospects," Franklin groused. "We will be compelled to sell for a loss."[37]

James Franklin faced similar conditions in Natchez. He reported falling prices and having "to take long paper" on sales, as he could not "receive one dollar in cash for negroes." All the while, Ballard was doing his partners no favors. Ignoring Isaac Franklin's caution about purchasing, Ballard cockily insisted "he could get Lotts of money from the Banks" in Virginia and kept on paying prices for slaves that in Franklin's estimation were "never Justifyable or profitable."[38]

Moreover, Ballard was careless. Warned that smallpox outbreaks in the lower South were compounding the epidemiological dangers still posed by cholera, he had nevertheless failed to vaccinate the enslaved people he shipped. When James Franklin wrote that he "had the damd small pox to brake out in two or three plantations among negroes sold by us" and that everyone in Natchez knew the disease had "come from our negroes," he did not need to tell Ballard whose fault it was. Isaac Franklin was less oblique. As usual, the loss of enslaved lives did not bother him. Instead, he reprimanded Ballard because his sloppiness had cost the company thousands of dollars and made more bad publicity it could ill afford. "There is very little Trouble to have negroes vaxinated as fast as they come in the house," he pointed out, "and we deserve to loose for our negligence."[39]

Yet Franklin was less interested in recriminations than in the real problem at hand, which was coming up with enough money to stay solvent. Thanks to the connections he had established with banks, merchants, and other creditors in the lower South, Franklin could "get money when no other Trader can obtain a Dollar." But his connections could only help so much when all the banks in New Orleans were "doing very little," and he was struggling "to meet Bills already accepted." The fragility of a business model dependent on a steady rotation of funds out of the lower South had become obvious. Franklin would find the limits of his privileges if he could not continue fulfilling his obligations.[40]

By March, Franklin had managed to collect $130,000 in customer bills that had come due, but he was having trouble collecting over $70,000 more that was still out there. He was sitting on a pile of another $400,000 in bills not scheduled to come due for months or years, and the pile got larger with every credit sale he and his nephew made. Franklin could raise money by selling the promissory notes and other debt instruments he held, pawning them off on bill brokers he resentfully called "shavers." Discount rates approaching 20 percent made that a desperate measure, and although he liked to boast about being "almost the only man in New Orleans that has sustained their credit without being shaved," he realized he might "be compelled to put some of our paper in market."[41]

Meanwhile, several merchant houses in Natchez and New Orleans had failed during the credit crunch, leading surviving houses to hesitate on new extensions for their clients and leaving Franklin hoping that slaveholders who had drawn on bankrupt merchant houses to buy slaves would still pay what they owed. Franklin tried not to panic. He told Ballard to sell whomever he could in Virginia, even at cost or at a loss, and if he could not do that, then "in the name of God ship we can sell them for some price and Interest." But no matter what, Franklin told Ballard, "pay your debts" and "at all hazards sustain your credit." Now that "every thing that made slaves valluable had Disappeared" and "confidence [was] Lost with the whole commertial world," holding on "untill the times changes" was the only viable road ahead.[42]

As he prepared to take the company reins from his fatigued uncle in April 1834, James Franklin told Ballard that he had collected barely "one third of our notes & Bills of last year" and that if financial catastrophe were to be avoided, operations in the fall would have to be scaled back. Experience told him "our number to sell every year is too large," and he ventured that "we must all hands curtail your purchases say [by] one third." The bold growth that had seemed wise had made the company too big. "If we had ⅔ the number," Franklin suggested, "we could sell to the satisfaction of all concerned and what is better then all could hold on and sell for cash which is the business I intend to do next season."

For the moment, he was headed to meet his uncle in New Orleans, where they would look at the books together and assess the damage. Signing off sorrowfully that he was "nearly ruined" because he had sold his favorite horse, he told Ballard the company at least had enough money for him to start accumulating "a good lot for walking." He promised to get to the Chesapeake as soon as he could, intending as usual to collect enslaved people Ballard had bought and "bring [them] out by land this summer."[43]

It was a trip he would never make.

As the selling season ended in the spring of 1834, the American economy reacquired a semblance of its former equilibrium.

Under pressure from the political and business classes alike, Nicholas Biddle eased lending restrictions imposed by what remained of the Second Bank of the United States. State banks, released from Biddle's constraints and flush with federal deposits and new influxes of silver and gold, began generating loans again. Especially in the lower South, legislatures also started chartering dozens of new banks. Their bonds often backed by the states where they were chartered, and underpinned by cotton, sugar, mortgaged plantations, and enslaved people, they pumped even more capital into the system. The wheezing engine of credit roared back to life.[44]

Isaac Franklin's relief was palpable. Writing to Ballard in May 1834 with word that he was seeing cash sales at last, Franklin enclosed $9,000 in checks, payable at the Merchants' Bank of New York, and told Ballard he just needed to keep the Virginia bankers he owed at bay for a few more months. "I will be able to meet Large Amts from November to January," Franklin promised, adding that cotton prices were rising again "and should it continue slaves will sell well next fall." Moreover, he predicted Franklin and Armfield would have the Chesapeake purchasing market practically to itself because it would have money to spend while other traders would be digging themselves out from the season just ending, "hung up with paper that cannot be made available."[45]

Franklin admitted he was "much disatisfyed with the way" the company had "been compeled to do business" of late. Nonetheless, he figured, "if we do not make heavy losses in our collections we will make more money this season than we ever have." That was almost certainly true, as the company carried more than $100,000 in debt but also had over half a million dollars in outstanding bills to collect. All was in order, Franklin believed, for him to step aside. He sold the now-unused Washington road compound in Natchez, he was preparing to shut down in New Orleans for the summer, and he looked forward to getting to Tennessee.[46]

Franklin had not tied up every loose end. He still anticipated summer travels to New York for financiering and to Virginia to inspect the books with Armfield and Ballard. But he also built some vacation into his schedule, planning to visit one of the popular natural springs resorts in the Blue Ridge Mountains, where elite white southerners relaxed and escaped the summer heat. Resting and reflecting on the trading empire he had built and the plantation domain where he would retire, Franklin could ponder at his leisure how his partners and nephews would run things mostly without his help.[47]

And then James Franklin died. It is not clear what killed him. The *National Banner and Daily Advertiser*, published in Nashville, reported in late June only that "Mr. James R. Franklin, a native of Tennessee" had died in New Orleans. The sole mention of his death in the extant correspondence of his colleagues and family comes from Jourdan Saunders, who told David Burford he thought Franklin's demise "much to be lamented." Fragmentary records of Franklin's estate reveal small bequests for nieces and nephews, but they do not point to a cause of death. Disease was the likeliest culprit. It claimed many lives every summer in the lower South, even among those as young as the twenty-six-year-old Franklin. Given how often he exposed himself to any number of viral and bacterial infections in the course of doing business, it is a marvel that the justice of his contracting cholera, smallpox, or some other illness had not caught up with him sooner.[48]

Whatever the cause, James Franklin's decease forced the partners in Franklin and Armfield to reconsider their plans. Someone would have to oversee collections, fulfill company obligations, and manage sales in the lower South. James Purvis was a possible candidate, but six weeks before his cousin died, Purvis had bought a sizable lot near his jail and trading compound in Baltimore. With an expanded footprint and payments due on the property every ninety days for the next eighteen months, Purvis had commitments he could not easily drop. In any case, the limited time Purvis had spent in the lower South hardly gave him the understanding of regional markets his cousin had possessed.[49]

John Armfield had the expertise, experience, and knowledge of Franklin and Armfield's activities to assume James Franklin's position. But doing so would mean abandoning a comfortable life in Alexandria. For nearly a year, Armfield had rented Spring Bank, a twenty-five-room mansion sitting on 128 acres that belonged to George Mason VI, whose grandfather had been a delegate to the Constitutional Convention. Spring Bank was only a few miles southwest of the Duke Street facility, which was enough to give Armfield some distance from the slave trade's daily grind, and the fact that he had signed a five-year lease demonstrated he had no interest in returning to it, especially if it entailed relocating a thousand miles away. Moreover, if Armfield were to leave Virginia, someone else would have to superintend the shipping operation, and whoever that might be could never match the range and depth of Armfield's business connections.[50]

Rice Ballard had worked in the Natchez market before opening his operation in Richmond, and he knew the inner workings of Franklin and Armfield better than anyone other than the named partners themselves. Still, he had not considered becoming a slave trader in the lower South again. Richmond agreed with him. Its market in enslaved people was growing, and he owned one of the largest slave jails in the city. He had built a solid business reputation, as evidenced by his recent involvement with the city attorney Joseph Mayo, lawyer Mann Valentine, merchant traders and auctioneers Samuel Cosby and Isaac Davenport, miller R. B. Haxall, and more than fifty other political and commercial leaders in fundraising for the Unitarian Universalist Society to buy land for a church. Moreover, Richmond was near Spotsylvania County. Ballard's ties to his relatives there were not strong, but Samuel Alsop remained a mentor, business partner, and father figure, and Ballard frequently visited him and his family.[51]

Ballard was also in the process of buying enslaved people to send overland in the late summer. He had thousands of dollars laid out to subagents for purchases, and he needed to see their work through to its conclusion. But in late August, Ballard sold his jail to William Goodwin and Henry Templeman, principals in a slave-trading company who started advertising that they were "prepared to take slaves for safe-keeping" there. The partners in Franklin and Armfield had decided that Ballard would wrap up his Richmond affairs and take over company dealings in the lower South. It would take time, however, and until Ballard was ready, only one man could fill the void left by James Franklin's death. As Isaac Franklin later recalled, when his nephew "died it placed him back where he first commenced."[52]

After his summer travels, Franklin got to Fairvue on September 19, 1834. He would not be there long. Refreshed from his time at the springs, he had steeled himself for one more season in the lower South, and as he waited for the company coffle to pass his way before he left for Natchez, he was eager to prove he was still the best slave trader in the business. "When I get to market," he told Ballard, "you will see what the old fellow can do yet."[53]

The coffle would be at Fairvue soon, with John Armfield, James Purvis, and Andrew Grimm conducting it in James Franklin's stead. Heading west from Alexandria in mid-August, they turned south into the Shenandoah Valley at Winchester. From there, they paralleled the Appalachians, traveling ten to twenty miles a day, and then veered west again to cross the mountains along a portion of the Wilderness Road, tracking what is today US Route 11. From where they started, they had gone about three hundred miles by the afternoon of September 5, when they reached the New River, west of Christiansburg, Virginia. They were still there when George Featherstonhaugh saw them at dawn the next day.[54]

In the summer of 1834, British geologist George Featherstonhaugh encountered John Armfield and several colleagues in the slave trade crossing the New River in Virginia with a coffle of about three hundred enslaved people, depicted here as an illustration in Featherstonhaugh's *Excursion Through the Slave States*. Courtesy of the Library of Virginia.

Born in London, Featherstonhaugh had recently been appointed as the first US government geologist, and he was headed to the Ozark Mountains with his son on an official expedition when he happened upon Armfield and his fellows. Estimating that the "negro slave-drivers" commanded about three hundred enslaved people, Featherstonhaugh considered the scene a "singular spectacle."[55]

It was an enormous coffle, combining into a single mass all the captives Ballard, Armfield, Purvis, Grimm, and the other agents had bought during the summer. Featherstonhaugh found the logistics of moving so many people intriguing. The enslaved had spent "the preceding night in chains in the woods," and as Featherstonhaugh watched their camp get broken down and packed for the day, he noted "two hundred male slaves" already lined up to march, arranged in pairs and "manacled and chained to each other." Behind them were dozens of women and children, some huddling around fires to lift the morning chill, others sitting on logs and savoring their last moments off their feet. Because most of them would walk too, though young children and anyone injured, exhausted, or beaten into a stupor would travel in a caravan of nine wagons that also carried supplies for the journey. Standing off to the side, watching as some of the enslaved hitched horses, were Armfield, Purvis, and Grimm. "Tolerably well dressed" and wearing "broad-brimmed white hats" with "black crape round them," they were "laughing and smoking cigars."

Featherstonhaugh and his son forded the New River by ferry and paused to observe the coffle make the crossing before they moved on. It was a complicated and dangerous maneuver to traverse a flowing river two hundred yards wide. A white man on horseback led the way, probing the river for a shallow spot, and another rider tested the route, leading four horses and a wagon. The fettered men came next, bound together and each lurching under the weight of more than twenty pounds of shackles, moving as deliberately as they could lest someone slip and the current potentially sweep them all off their feet. After them came the rest of the wagons, bearing small children who held on tight and peered over the sides into the water. The women came last, borne by several flat-bottomed scows.

Absorbed as he was by the coordination involved in the coffle's movement, Featherstonhaugh thought it as "revolting a sight" as he had ever witnessed, a "disgusting and hideous" display made more so by the behavior and attire of Armfield and the white men in his company. Baffled by the black crape on their hats, which was a customary sign of mourning, Featherstonhaugh thought it might be appropriate were the "sentimental speculators" grieving "for their own callous inhuman lives." But they were not, and Featherstonhaugh "could not but be struck with the monstrous absurdity of such fellows putting on any symbol of sorrow whilst engaged in the exercise of such a horrid trade."

Featherstonhaugh went on his way without speaking to Arm-field. But he would have another chance. A week later, Feather-stonhaugh and his son booked stagecoach passage in Abingdon, a Virginia town about fifteen miles from the Tennessee border, only to discover five of the six seats inside the coach already taken. One was occupied by "a negro," the "servant of the white man opposite him," and Featherstonhaugh asked the white man "if he would let his ser-vant ride on the top of the coach and permit my son to come inside." It was a racial prerogative even white people like Featherstonhaugh, who found slavery loathsome, took for granted, and he was offended when his request was refused. "I reckon," the white passenger said, "my waiter is very well where he is."

Featherstonhaugh took the last seat inside the coach with un-disguised irritation, and during the tense but uneventful hours that followed, he could not shake the feeling that he had seen his antag-onist before. Featherstonhaugh estimated he was about forty years old. Wearing a black suit and a "huge broad-brimmed white hat" adorned with black crape, the man was tall, with black hair cut short and straight around his head in a style Featherstonhaugh associated with Methodist ministers. He sprouted "immense black whiskers," his breath reeked of onions, and while Featherstonhaugh thought his face had "one or two tolerable features," there was something "singularly sharp, and not a little piratical and repulsive" about his appearance.

Overall, Featherstonhaugh considered the man "exceedingly strange-looking," and talking with him as they rode together again the next day, he thought his speech even stranger. Combining "a far-rago of bad grammar with an affected pronunciation of his words," the man strove to sound like someone with education and polish, though Featherstonhaugh believed it obvious he had neither. Speak-ing of politics and the president with deep "solemnity of tone and manner," the man proclaimed "Gineral Jackson" to be "the most greatest and most completest idear of a man what had ever lived." He then worked himself "into such a strain of talking fine" that Feather-stonhaugh nearly started laughing, only to be "thoroughly mystified" and unable "to make out what stratum in society" the man belonged to when he bragged about having bought two barouches, which were among the most luxurious and expensive carriage models available.

Still bothered that he could not place the man, Featherston-haugh took a moment while stretching his legs and walking be-side the stagecoach to ask the driver if he knew the passenger who boasted of owning the barouches. "Why," the driver responded, "don't you know it's Armfield, the negur-driver?" Suddenly every-thing made sense—the bad manners, the subtle but unmistakable severity of expression, the ignorance betrayed by poor diction. All of it, in Featherstonhaugh's estimation, had been "formed in those dens of oppression and despair the negro prisons." Now that he re-membered where he had come across Armfield previously, Feath-erstonhaugh decided to let him "know before we parted that I had found him out."

Featherstonhaugh asked Armfield whom he was mourning that would explain the crape festooning his hat. Putting on a somber expression, Armfield said it was to honor "Marcus Layfeeyate," by whom he meant the Marquis de Lafayette, the Revolutionary War hero whose death in May 1834 prompted months of memorializa-tion in the United States. Scoffing, Featherstonhaugh replied that Lafayette "gloried in making all men free, without respect of colour; and what are you, who I understand are a negro-driver, in mourning for him for? Such men as you ought to go into mourning only when the price of black men falls." Revealing that he had seen Armfield at the New River, Featherstonhaugh said he "shouldn't be surprised if Lafayette's ghost was to set every one of your negroes free one of these nights."

Caught off-guard, Armfield fell silent, his chagrin turning to anger when his "waiter," still sitting opposite him in the coach, burst into guffaws. Featherstonhaugh never caught the waiter's name, referring to him as "the negur-driver's black man" or with the generic "Pompey." It was surely Walker, who had been Armfield's valet and assistant going on ten years. Walker had earned the boldness of laughing at Armfield's expense, but Armfield was not having it in front of someone who condescended to him as Featherstonhaugh had. "What onder arth is the matter with you, I reckon," Armfield chided. "If you think I'll stand my waiter's sniggering at me arter that fashion, I reckon you'll come to a nonplush to-night."

Having learned to read Armfield's every mood, Walker also sensed when he was about to cross the line into overfamiliarity. He assured Armfield he was "by no manner of means" laughing at him, but rather at the idea of Lafayette's emancipatory ghost. Mollified if still annoyed, Armfield got off the stagecoach shortly thereafter, at a tavern near an outpost called Bean's Station, about forty miles east of Knoxville. Saying he was feeling poorly, he told Walker to continue on and send a barouche back for him once he caught up with the coffle, which had gone ahead of them days earlier.

After Armfield departed, Walker told Featherstonhaugh that Armfield's indisposition was probably a case of heartburn. It happened all the time. Doctors in Alexandria had counseled Armfield not to gorge on the raw onions he loved, "but when he sees 'em," Walker said, "he can't stand it, and den he eats 'em, and dey makes him sick, and den he carries on jist like a house a fire; and he drinks brandy upon 'em, and dat makes him better; and den he eats ingeons agin, and so he keeps a carrying on."[56]

And Walker said more. Now that Armfield was gone, he said "a great many things that served to confirm" Featherstonhaugh's "abhorrence of this brutal land-traffic in slaves." Featherstonhaugh did not elaborate, but that night the stagecoach reached the coffle, bivouacked in the woods. Walker descended from the coach, and Featherstonhaugh asked the driver to wait. Heading with Walker to where he could see "numerous fires gleaming through the forest," Featherstonhaugh took a final look at the weary three hundred. The women warming themselves by the fires, the children sleeping in tents, and the men, enchained and passed out on the ground, still had nearly eight hundred miles ahead of them. James Purvis, Andrew Grimm, and several other white men stood guard "with whips in their hands."

George Featherstonhaugh was a snob who disdained many of the people and the material conditions he met with on his travels. Yet his encounter with John Armfield rings true. It shows Armfield's efforts to seem sophisticated as ham-fisted and limited by his rustic origins and country accent, and with a hint of self-consciousness that was of a piece with an aversion to snooty Englishmen and a veneration of Andrew Jackson's politics and pugnacious masculinity. The Armfield described by Featherstonhaugh was a braggart who did not let indigestion interfere with his appetites. Nor did he tolerate being laughed at by someone he enslaved without offering an intimation of violence, and if Walker knew Armfield too well to think his threat entirely idle, his chortles at Featherstonhaugh's jibes suggest he picked his moments for defiance anyway. He probably did so until he died, about two years later, when he fell from a steamboat and drowned in the Potomac River.[57]

Featherstonhaugh's physical description of Armfield does stand in some contrast to a portrait made several years later, in which Armfield appears clean-shaven and seated at a desk. Wearing a fashionable dark tailored coat and a low-cut white vest adorned with a watch chain, atop a matching white shirt with a high straight collar and a cravat, the Armfield in the portrait holds a quill pen in his thin-fingered right hand, resting his left on some papers on which he is tallying figures. He has paused in his task to peer out at the viewer, his dark eyes set above an aquiline nose and a slightly downturned mouth. His countenance is ambiguous. While it might be read as cold and forbidding, it lacks the malign unruliness that a face full of whiskers could impart. But Armfield still wore his cowlicked black hair in a round cut, and the trader on the road and the respectable professional in the office were, of course, the same man.

Featherstonhaugh was mistaken, however, in thinking he had humiliated Armfield by calling out his profession and his hypocrisy. Imagining that Armfield could not "digest our contempt" and had "pretended he was taken ill" to extricate himself from an awkward situation, Featherstonhaugh flattered himself and overestimated Armfield's capacity for embarrassment. Armfield had not seen Featherstonhaugh's criticism coming, but he probably considered it more obnoxious than trenchant. His failure to engage it was rooted more in a lack of interest than in a sense of shame, and while Armfield undoubtedly had had enough of Featherstonhaugh's company, he was also genuinely sick.

Armfield was only in the stagecoach to begin with because he wanted a break from driving the coffle on its overland trip, and when it got to Fairvue on September 24, 1834, he was not with it, having become feverish and unable to leave Bean's Station. Robert Windsor, administering the compound in Alexandria, would not hear from Armfield for over a month, and a distraught Isaac Franklin worried Armfield might die. Franklin had planned to accompany the coffle the rest of the way to Natchez, but he told Rice Ballard he would stay behind for at least a few days until he got word from Armfield. Leaving Fairvue without knowing his partner's fate was too much to bear. "I have a most exalted friendship for him," Franklin wrote, "and if he was to die I would have but little inducement to live." It was a rare moment of pathos, and as emotionally honest as it was, it also showed that Franklin's years in the slave trade had hampered his ability to form meaningful connections with other people. Despite being surrounded by the enslaved he trafficked and by all sorts of people in the towns and cities he worked in, he felt essentially alone. "I have no particular friendship Left," he admitted while fretting to Ballard about Armfield, "accept yourself and him."[58]

Armfield did eventually recover, Franklin caught up with the coffle, and shipping people from the Chesapeake and selling them in the lower South began once again. But Isaac Franklin was wrong in thinking that James Franklin's death had put him "back where he first commenced." He was much closer to the end than he was to the beginning.

O n October 20, 1834, the *Uncas* left Alexandria, bringing 136 enslaved people to the lower South. Captain Nathaniel Boush was at the helm, as he had been since taking command from Joseph Moore earlier in the year. Robert Windsor and Rice Ballard handled shipping arrangements during John Armfield's convalescence in Tennessee, and when the brig arrived in New Orleans, Isaac Franklin was there to claim 109 of the captives. Most of the rest had been shipped to slave traders John Hagan and Theophilus Freeman.[59]

Before leaving Virginia in August, Armfield had started advertising that the *Uncas* and the *Tribune* would "resume their regular trips" from Alexandria to New Orleans "every thirty days through-out the shipping season." And they did, the only exception being when the *Tribune*, returning to Alexandria with a load of sugar and molasses, got caught in a storm on New Years' Eve that tossed two crewmen overboard and did enough damage to keep the ship out of commission for almost two months. Between October 1834 and May 1835, the *Uncas* and the *Tribune* made seven voyages to New Orleans. Together they carried 910 enslaved people in their holds, including 202 on a single passage of the *Uncas* that was one of the largest shipments Franklin and Armfield had ever sent.[60]

Of those packed on the voyages, 561 ended up in Franklin's custody. Combined with the summer coffle and with 63 captives shipped on other vessels, Franklin and Armfield put over 900 en-slaved people into the markets of the lower South during the 1834–1835 season. With ads declaring that it would pay "CASH FOR

400 NEGROES" running again in the newspapers for the first time since the spring, the company seemed to be operating much as it had before James Franklin's death.[61]

Yet considerations had changed, as was signified most plainly by the company's near-total abandonment of sales in New Orleans itself. Isaac Franklin still worked out of the Canonage property when he was in the city. He kept enslaved people there temporarily when they disembarked from company brigs, and he lived there while he negotiated with bankers and merchants. But he recorded no sales in the last months of 1834, and he sold only three enslaved people in the city during all of 1835.[62]

The decision to withdraw from New Orleans had nothing to do with weakness in the market. Sales by slave traders in the city increased in 1835 to a level not seen since the late 1820s. Traders even started flouting the long-standing ban on exposing people for sale in the city proper, and municipal authorities chose not to enforce the prohibition until the sales season ended in the spring. Sales prices increased too. One of the three people Franklin sold in 1835, for example, was a fourteen-year-old boy named Nace, for whom Franklin's financial fixer Richard Booker paid $1,000 in cash, several hundred dollars more than Franklin had been getting even for young men of prime working age a year earlier.[63]

In part, Franklin and Armfield left the New Orleans market because they lacked the manpower to stay in it. Franklin's nephew was no longer by his side, Ballard had not yet extricated himself from Richmond, and there was only so much rushing from Mississippi to Louisiana and back again that Franklin was still willing and able to do. But the central driver of the disengagement was that Franklin, Armfield, and Ballard were starting to wind down their company, effectively by reversing the course of its expansion. Richmond and New Orleans marked the geographic limits of the company's urban growth. Pulling back from those places began its deconstruction.

That left Natchez as the primary sales venue in the lower South, and it left the Forks of the Road as the seat of Franklin's regional business activities. Franklin's spot comprised two acres on the outside of the fork where the Old Courthouse Road branched from the Washington road toward the southeast and gave the intersection its colloquial designation. Sitting off to the right as one headed away from the Mississippi River and downtown Natchez, the location was the obvious place for Franklin to move after the cholera scandal. Practically straddling the Natchez corporate line, it was as close to the city limits as he could legally operate, and it was likely to see steady traffic from travelers and cotton planters, which suited his interests.[64]

Other traders soon recognized the advantages of working at the Forks of the Road too. Isaac Franklin's predominance exerted a gravitational pull on the Natchez slave trade. Where he went, others followed, and within a few years of Franklin's relocation, the Forks of the Road was the new epicenter of the Natchez market in human beings. By the mid-1830s, at least half a dozen traders had established houses and sales compounds there, making it a commercial district known for only one kind of exchange. Some started calling it "the African Village." Benjamin Eaton and Theophilus Freeman, who signed a five-year lease in 1835 on a space about the size of Franklin's, were blunter. They advertised their Forks of the Road location as "Niggerville."[65]

The author Joseph Holt Ingraham visited the Forks of the Road in the fall of 1834, at around the time Isaac Franklin and his colleagues arrived with the coffle George Featherstonhaugh had seen in Virginia and Tennessee. Accompanying a friend who was looking to purchase Black people, Ingraham called the Forks of the Road "one of the great slave-marts of the south-west," though what he described was just "a cluster of rough wooden buildings, in the angle of two roads."[66]

Leaving their horses with an enslaved boy, Ingraham and his friend entered one of the trader compounds "through a wide gate" and went "into a narrow court-yard, partially enclosed by low buildings." Lined up in a semicircle along one side of the yard were forty enslaved men and boys, arranged in height order from tallest to shortest, while across the yard stood a line of about twenty women and girls. All of them exhibited for customers to peruse, they wore new outfits that had been shipped or carried with them from the Chesapeake and that Ingraham called "the usual uniform of slaves, when in market." The men held black fur hats, and they wore white cotton shirts under vests and short, close-fitting coats with matching pants of "coarse corduroy velvet." The women wore calico frock dresses with white aprons and capes, and most used "fancy kerchiefs" to tie their hair in a headwrap.[67]

The facility Ingraham described was not Franklin's, but had he crossed the Old Courthouse Road, he would have taken in a similar scene. Franklin or an assistant would have approached him and his friend, wishing them good morning and promising to show them "as fine a lot as ever came into market." Ingraham would have seen the enslaved presented for maximum salability, their clean and crisp outfits covering skin flayed and bruised by shackles, and the visible parts of their bodies polished to a shine belying how they came to be where they were. Ingraham would have heard customers asking captives the "usual questions," imagining they possessed such a "scrutinizing eye" that they could know in minutes whether someone was the perfect slave for their purposes.[68]

Ingraham may not have visited Franklin's sales compound, but he knew of Isaac Franklin. Observing the "extravagant prices" buyers paid for enslaved people to pick their cotton, drive their carriages, nurse their children, cook their meals, mend their clothing, tend their horses, and clean up their messes, Ingraham was unsurprised that "negro traders soon accumulate great wealth." And no trader in Natchez had accumulated what Franklin had. He was "the great southern slave-merchant," and "for the last fifteen years," Ingraham wrote, he had "supplied this country with two-thirds of the slaves brought into it," garnering "a fortune of more than a million of dollars."

If Ingraham exaggerated the scale of Franklin's influence and means, it was not by much, and he nicely summarized a career in which power and money marked achievement. Moreover, Ingraham considered Franklin's character to be as noteworthy as his business accomplishments. Though "the humane characteristics" of the slave trade depended on "the tempers and dispositions of the individuals who engage in it," Ingraham thought Franklin "a man of gentlemanly address" and not at all like "the ferocious, Captain Kidd looking fellows" that many people were "apt to imagine" when they thought of slave traders.

Ingraham did point out that Franklin was "a bachelor," and he concluded that that was probably a consequence of working in a profession some white people considered disreputable. But Franklin had never shown much interest in getting married, and he owed his bachelor status more to the time he devoted to trafficking the enslaved than to opprobrium he faced because of it. His lifestyle and his priorities allowed for little else. When he was not traveling, bargaining, or financiering, he was visiting his real estate, slaveholdings, and family in Tennessee, and even his attachments there were inseparable from his business interests, as slave trading stitched together relationships with numerous brothers, in-laws, and nephews. That intermingling of the personal and the professional became deeper still in November 1834, when John Armfield married Martha Franklin, Isaac Franklin's niece.[69]

At first glance, it was a strange match. Martha Franklin was the sixth child and third daughter of Isaac Franklin's older brother John, and the younger sister of the recently deceased James Franklin. She was nineteen years old when she married John Armfield, who was not quite twice her age. They were not especially well acquainted before their marriage and may hardly have known each

John Armfield, in a portrait probably made in the mid-1830s. Courtesy of Tennessee State Library and Archives.

other at all. In fact, if Armfield did continue on to Sumner County after recovering from the illness he had incurred while driving the coffle from Virginia, it might have been the first time he and Martha Franklin had ever met.[70]

But John Armfield's marriage to Martha Franklin was not predicated on romance, compatibility, or even familiarity. It was, rather, as transactional as most of the relationships in Armfield's adult life. The year 1834 had been difficult for Martha. She lost her older brother James and also her sister Mary and her father John. John Franklin was a wealthy and powerful man who enslaved nearly one hundred people and owned over one thousand acres of land when he died. But Martha had no experience managing an inheritance, and her widowed mother Elizabeth quickly entered a scandalous marriage to her deceased husband's overseer. Marrying her uncle's partner attached Martha to someone who was skilled in business and finance and who had her family's unconditional confidence, as John Armfield had not only worked with her brother James but also knew her oldest brother, the former slave trader Smith Franklin.[71]

Supporting the notion that John Armfield married Martha Franklin to look after her and her interests as much as he did out of affection is the fact that the union appears to have been part of a matrimonial exchange between the Franklin and Armfield families. Two months before John Armfield married Martha Franklin, another of Martha's brothers, Henry Franklin, married Jane Dickey at Armfield's rented Spring Bank estate in Virginia. Jane Dickey was Armfield's niece, the daughter of his sister Polly and her first husband, William Dickey.[72]

Armfield took no time to savor his nuptials, nor did he let them interfere with the project of shuttering Franklin and Armfield's trading operations and settling company holdings in more fixed assets. On October 5, 1834, Franklin and Armfield purchased outright the house and compound on Duke Street, along with two vacant lots comprising another acre immediately to the west, for $2,500 from the trustees of the Mechanics' Bank of Alexandria. Five months later, the company expanded its Alexandria real estate portfolio even further, buying a lot comprising nearly ten acres sitting along the road to Georgetown. In between those acquisitions, the company started telling the purchasing agents that their services were no longer needed. Their arrangements would be terminated immediately. "I learn that it is not the wish of Mr. Franklin & Ballard to continue your Branch of the consern any Longer," Armfield informed Jourdan Saunders in late December, adding unceremoniously that how and when Saunders would be paid what the company still owed him was not his problem. If Saunders wanted more information, he "had better write to Mr. Franklin on the subject."[73]

Isaac Franklin had brought Jourdan Saunders into affiliation with Franklin and Armfield, and he did right by him as it ended, ensuring he got paid and helping unload enslaved people Saunders had bought with the expectation Armfield would broker them. But that was an obligation from the past, and Franklin was looking toward a future when such obligations would be someone else's burdens. On

April 24, 1835, Franklin signed power of attorney over his New Orleans interests to the merchant firm of N & J Dick and Company,
led by Nathaniel and James Dick. The firm had operated until 1828
under the name Dicks, Booker, and Company, when the Dick brothers had partnered with Richard Booker, and among the partners in
the new firm was H. R. W. Hill, a Nashville merchant with business
interests in Louisiana who had been an associate of Franklin and his
family for several years. Prosperous and with unimpeachable status
in the overlapping worlds of banking, cotton, land, and slaves, these
were men Franklin felt he could trust absolutely.[74]

Finding merchants to act on his behalf was not only about having businessmen on the ground in New Orleans who could pay his
bills and collect his debts. It was also about securing the services of
a firm that could supply his property and broker his cotton on the
global market. Some of that cotton came from Fairvue. But when
Franklin gave power of attorney to N & J Dick, he was already
eyeing an investment opportunity for cotton production that would
make the number of bales from Fairvue look like a rounding error
on a balance sheet.[75]

On May 27, 1835, Isaac Franklin paid $150,000 for a half inter-
est in 7,767 acres of land and 205 enslaved people in West Feliciana
Parish, Louisiana. Practically flat, partially covered in dense forest,
and containing a small lake and some swamps, the land was tucked
beneath Louisiana's border with Mississippi and bounded to both the
west and the south by the Mississippi River. It sat about seventy miles
below Natchez, about two hundred above New Orleans, almost directly across from the mouth of the Red River, and just upriver from
Bayou Sara, one of the largest cotton depots and river ports in the
lower Mississippi Valley. Franklin had seen the spot for the first time
as a teenager, from the deck of a flatboat, and he had floated past it
dozens of times over the course of nearly thirty years. It was some of
the best bottomland in the state, perfect for cotton production.[76]

Two days after putting his money down, Franklin signed a five-year agreement "to become co-partners in the business of Planting" with the owner of the property, Francis Routh. The thirty-year-old Routh belonged to one of the oldest and wealthiest white families in Mississippi. His father, Job Routh, was among the first settlers of English descent in the Natchez District, moving there in the late eighteenth century and becoming a cotton baron rumored to enslave nearly five thousand people on twenty thousand acres of land. Job Routh's oldest son, Francis's brother John, came to be known as the "Cotton King." Using slave labor to produce up to four million pounds of cotton annually, by the time of the Civil War he was one of the richest men in the United States.[77]

Isaac Franklin's associations with the Routh family stretched back decades. He had sold Job Routh at least a dozen enslaved people, and he had known John Routh since they were both young men in the 1810s. Indeed, even as Franklin bemoaned his lack of genuine confidantes in the 1830s, John Routh claimed he "was on the most intimate terms of friendship" with Franklin, "had many important business transactions with him," and believed he "knew him as well as one man could know another."[78]

But if Francis Routh's accumulation of hundreds of enslaved people and of land that sprawled across more than twelve square miles showed he shared the ambitions of his father and brother, his partnership with Isaac Franklin showed he lacked their prudence. Though Routh brought some of the land into cultivation and divided it into three distinct plantations named Bellevue, Killarney, and Lochlomond, he had extended himself financially well beyond what those places could produce. He had assembled his land holdings through nearly a dozen different purchases of hundreds of acres at a time, and he repeatedly mortgaged what he had to raise money so he could buy more. By the mid-1830s, he was floundering beneath his debts, and he turned to Isaac Franklin less because he wanted help running his planting operation than because he desperately needed an infusion of capital.[79]

Franklin provided Routh with more than $106,000 in cash. He bought the rest of his interest in the property with a promissory note out of the accounts of Franklin Ballard and Company, and the terms of his partnership with Routh promised Franklin profits while demanding none of his time. Franklin's rights and authority were coequal with Routh's. But Routh was to "give his personal attention to the direction and superintendence" of the "plantation and its concerns," while Franklin could "choose to give his personal attention to the direction of said plantation" if and when he felt like it. As things turned out, Franklin wound up administering the West Feliciana property far more than he had anticipated or wanted. The imprint he left would last generations.[80]

On July 10, 1835, Isaac Franklin, John Armfield, and Rice Ballard renewed, on altered terms, their agreement to act as "copartners and joint-traders in the trade or business of buying and selling negro slaves." Franklin would reinvest and receive a full share of profits, but he would formally retire and have "no duties whatever assigned him except what he chooses voluntarily to render." Ballard would assume Franklin's responsibilities in the lower South, where he would operate under the company name Ballard Franklin and Company. Armfield would continue accumulating enslaved people in Alexandria and sending them to the lower South, though his company umbrella would change too, becoming Armfield Franklin and Company.

The renewed agreement seemed to move Franklin, Armfield, and Ballard in a direction contrary to where they had been headed, positioning them to grow their market position in the lower South and blaze an even broader and more intense trail of destruction through the enslaved population of the Chesapeake. Where their previous agreements had been for two years at a time and entailed total partner contributions of $40,000, this one was to last for five and had each partner staking $65,000 "in Bills receivable," a massive sum that would cumulatively be nearly $6 million today. The capital comprised bills that in some cases were uncollectible for years, and the agreement made it clear that after five years the partners would close the business and bring it "to a full and complete settlement." Still, until then the company would have standing access to a pool of negotiable debt useful for purchasing enormous numbers of enslaved people.[81]

Other signs suggested expansion too. Three months before the new partnership terms took effect, Armfield increased the number of enslaved people he said he wanted to buy, changing it in his advertising from four hundred to five hundred. Six weeks after that, Franklin and Ballard paid $2,000 for the Forks of the Road compound that Franklin had been renting, and they started renovating the property. And four days after signing the new agreement, Armfield announced he was doubling the frequency of his shipments. Starting on September 1 and continuing "on the 1st and 15th of each month throughout the shipping season," Armfield would send a brig to New Orleans. The *Uncas*, under the command of Nathaniel Boush, would leave first. The *Tribune* would follow two weeks later, helmed by Boush's brother Samuel. And on October 1, 1835, William Smith, formerly captain of the *Tribune*, would depart Alexandria piloting a new vessel. Its construction nearly complete at a Baltimore shipyard, the third ship Armfield commissioned, and the latest addition to the company fleet of slavers, was the brig *Isaac Franklin*.[82]

The *Isaac Franklin* had a carrying capacity of nearly 190 tons. It was about ten feet longer than the *Tribune* or the *Uncas*, and it could transport at least thirty more enslaved people than either of them, though its limits were defined less by cubic feet than by the degree of Armfield's concern for the discomfort of those he packed in its hold. The *Isaac Franklin* had a square stern, single deck, coppered hull, and twin masts. Armfield probably ordered its cargo space fitted with platforms for the enslaved like the ones on the *Tribune*, and the *Isaac Franklin* had one other very distinctive feature. Described as a "man bust head," it was a carving of the head and torso of Isaac Franklin himself, affixed to the prow. The brig was a sort of send-off from Franklin's partners and closest friends, a retirement present that was both product of and stand-in for thousands of Black people Franklin had sold from ships just like it into a world of strangers. One imagines he found the gesture touching and a point of pride.[83]

But the company that Armfield, Franklin, and Ballard operated was not going back to what it had been. For one thing, whereas the partners had built their slave-trading behemoth with an unwavering focus on the circulation of money and bodies, by the fall of 1835 their attentions were drifting elsewhere. Armfield sublet Spring Bank, bought an Alexandria town lot on Prince Street, and started building a residence there for himself and Martha. Franklin offered advice to his colleagues and still dabbled in slave trading, but mostly he found himself watching over his investment in West Feliciana Parish, and he was not happy about it. He complained that it prevented him from spending time at Fairvue, and he became increasingly aggravated with Francis Routh's incompetence, griping "frequently" to an engineer on the property "of the bad management on the place and of its getting into debt."[84]

Ballard's interests branched out as well. In the summer of 1836, he returned to Richmond and bought back the slave jail he had sold two years earlier. He also formed a "general mercantile business" in Natchez, partnering with a cousin named James Ballard Jr. and a local merchant and slave trader named Silas Lillard in the "firm of James Ballard & Co." Ballard started making forays into plantations too, investing in a place near Vicksburg, Mississippi, called Magnolia. The exact nature of the venture with Magnolia's owner, merchant Alexander McNeill, is unclear, but the 127 pairs of shoes Ballard bought in February 1836 for the people McNeill enslaved there demonstrate Ballard's stake in them and in the crop they produced.[85]

In Armfield's advertisements of increased shipments of enslaved people to New Orleans, there were hints that he was running a different kind of business than he had before. Armfield still promised his ships were "vessels of the first class, commanded by experienced and accommodating officers." All of them would still leave on time and "go up the Mississippi by steam" from the Balize, and every measure would be taken "to promote the interest of shippers and comfort of passengers." But Armfield added something else. "Servants that are intended to be shipped," he announced, "will at any time be received for safe keeping at 25 cents per day."[86]

Like every slave trader with a private jail, Armfield had surely offered the Duke Street facility before as a holding pen for customers who shipped with him. It brought in revenue, filled underused space, and offered assurance that Black people being shipped would not escape before they were sent to the lower South. Yet Armfield had never made a point of advertising the service. He started doing so because he and Ballard were cutting back on retailing, moving firmly into wholesaling and consignment, and putting the company flotilla to work mostly for other slaveholders, merchants, and traders.

The numbers of enslaved people Armfield sent to Ballard for sale still sometimes rivaled numbers from earlier in the decade. Armfield sent 52 people to Ballard Franklin and Company on the *Uncas* in December 1835, for example, and he sent 111 more on the *Isaac Franklin* four weeks after that. But such shipments were exceptional. During the 1834–1835 shipping season, Armfield sent more than 60 percent of all the enslaved people he dispatched to New Orleans on the *Uncas* and the *Tribune* directly to Isaac Franklin. After September 1835, however, just 18 percent of those Armfield sent on the *Uncas*, the *Tribune*, and the *Isaac Franklin* got delivered to Rice Ballard.[87]

The demographic profile of the people Armfield shipped changed as well. Most were still young men and women in their mid-teens to mid-twenties. Compared with previous seasons, however, the number of women sent with their small children to the lower South increased noticeably, as did the number of nuclear families sent together. Scholars observing the trend have suggested the change was about public relations, an attempt by Armfield to make his operation seem less unsavory to captious abolitionists and uneasy slaveholders. But Armfield and his partners had never given more than lip service to moral critiques before, and with Franklin in retirement and the company retailing dwindling numbers of enslaved people, there was even less reason for them to do so.[88]

The uptick in family units and in mothers with children was owed neither to humanitarian concerns nor to image management. In part, it happened because Armfield no longer had an army of agents supplying him with enslaved people, and so he sometimes bought entire lots of slaves at estate sales that limited his options to select whom he wished. In January 1836, for example, the administrators of Thomas Snowden stashed "seventy likely Negroes of different ages males and females" at the Duke Street facility so prospective buyers might "call and examine" them in advance of their sale "without reserve (to the highest bidder) in families." Armfield got the best look, and when they were auctioned at his offices, he bought most and perhaps all of them himself. A little more than two weeks later, he put 140 people on the *Isaac Franklin*. Among them were James and Matilda Thomas and their three children, Abraham and Suckey Jackson and their four children, and Judy Dorsey and her seven children. Snowden had probably enslaved all of them, and others on board too. The shipment included sixty-three children under age twelve. Four did not survive the journey.[89]

The demographics of Armfield's shipments also changed because his business was no longer about anticipating the general labor preferences of cotton and sugar planters as much as it was about filling orders. He had done that before. Late in 1831, for example, he advertised for "a family of Negroes, say from 50 to 60 in number" sought by "a resident of New Orleans . . . for his own use alone on a Cotton estate in Louisiana." But responding to merchants making bespoke requests for clients, or to individuals looking to bolster their slaveholdings in particular ways, was now the core of Armfield's operation.[90]

The demand was more powerful than ever. Beginning in the late summer of 1835 and continuing for more than a year, hardly a day passed when Armfield did not have at least one company vessel at sea. Between September 1835 and April 1836, Armfield sent the *Tribune*, the *Uncas*, and the *Isaac Franklin* to New Orleans thirteen times. On the ten voyages for which manifests and other documentation have survived, the brigs carried 1,306 enslaved people. A complete accounting would surely indicate they carried well over 1,500.[91]

In October, the enslaved shared cargo space with one hundred barrels of "pickled Potomac herrings," in March they slept alongside sixty barrels of "northern whiskey," and when the season for shipping slaves ended, Armfield made the company fleet available almost entirely for shippers of merchant goods. In late April, the *Isaac Franklin* left New Orleans for Sisal, a Mexican port on the Yucatán Peninsula, and it sailed from there for New York with 409 bales of grass and 1,911 sticks of logwood used for dyeing textiles. The *Tribune* set off from New Orleans a few days after the *Isaac Franklin*, picking up freight in Mobile and passengers in Charleston before heading up the coast to Providence. When the *Uncas* returned to Alexandria in July, it held wine, tobacco, Spanish moss used by merchants for packing, and other "sundries."[92]

Once company vessels started heading to the lower South again in the fall of 1836, initially more cargo space was devoted to agricultural products than to human beings. In late September, the *Tribune* carried just twenty-eight enslaved people to New Orleans, and when the *Isaac Franklin* followed two weeks after, it carried only thirty-three people, along with produce for seven different merchants. But Armfield had some significant trafficking of the enslaved left in him yet.[93]

On October 15, 1836, the *Uncas* left Alexandria carrying 198 people. Armfield shipped 180 of them himself, including 38 sent to Ballard. Exactly one month later, the *Isaac Franklin* set sail holding 254 enslaved people, all of them shipped by Armfield. When the brig got to New Orleans, the customs official scribbled on the manifest that "one died on the passage." He could not be bothered to indicate who it was. Eighteen different merchants, plantation owners, and slave traders claimed the 253 survivors of a voyage whose enormity shocked even those inured to the grotesqueries of the slave trade and led America's leading abolitionist paper, *The Liberator*, to refer to the shipment as "legalized piracy." It was the largest shipment of enslaved people the company created by John Armfield, Isaac Franklin, and Rice Ballard ever sent. It was also the last.[94]

When the *Tribune* returned to Alexandria on November 12, 1836, John Armfield sold it to a slave trader named William H. Williams, who worked mostly out of Washington City. Armfield sold the *Uncas* to Williams as well. But Williams retained the captains and continued advertising both brigs as "splendid New Orleans packets." One of them would still leave for the lower South on the first of every month, and Williams urged "those wishing to ship" to deliver "their servants" to him "a day or two previous to the vessels sailing." He offered jailing services too, charging shippers "25 cents per day" for each enslaved person they wanted him to lock up.[95]

William Smith landed the *Isaac Franklin* back in Alexandria on February 11, 1837. Six days later, George Kephart, Franklin and Armfield's former agent, announced in the papers that anyone wanting to send enslaved people to New Orleans on that ship could apply directly to him. He owned the *Isaac Franklin* now. He or an agent could be found "at all times" on Duke Street, "at the establishment formerly owned by Armfield, Franklin & Co.," where he would "give the highest cash price for Likely Negroes, from 10 to 25 years of age."[96]

Franklin, Armfield, and Ballard were not disbanding their company. They still owned the Forks of the Road facility, and they managed the buildings and took in rent from slave traders there. They agreed to sell the Duke Street compound to George Kephart, but the sale would not be legally completed for years. They held hundreds of thousands of dollars in customer debt that they needed to work together to collect, and they kept money in the slave trade too. In the summer of 1836, for example, Ballard Franklin and Company extended a $40,000 line of credit to Ballard's Richmond colleague, slave trader and jailor Bacon Tait, and Tait's partner Thomas Boudar, which Tait and Boudar drew on to buy enslaved people in Virginia and ship them to New Orleans.[97]

But by the fall of 1836 the partners had stopped buying enslaved people themselves, and by the spring of 1837 they were mostly out of the daily business of slave trading. Over the course of nearly nine years operating their company, they shipped enslaved people from the Chesapeake to the lower South at least sixty-eight times. They rented space on ships belonging to other people twenty-two times, chartered entire vessels nine times, and sent company-owned brigs with enslaved people on thirty-seven voyages. Manifests or other reliable accounts survive for about 80 percent of the shipments. They document 3,426 people sent directly to Isaac Franklin or Rice Ballard, 2,010 people sent by John Armfield or Robert Windsor to other merchants, slaveholders, and slave traders, and 719 people sent by other shippers on vessels the company chartered or on the *Tribune*, the *Uncas*, and the *Isaac Franklin*.[98]

The partners also organized a coffle near the end of every summer between 1829 and 1835, and perhaps in 1828 and 1836 as well. Documentation of how many enslaved people they walked overland is sparse, and the 458 people whose passage can be demonstrated is perhaps a third of the actual total. All told, evidence survives to substantiate that the partners bought, moved, and sold more than 6,600 men, women, and children. A conservative estimate accounting for missing ship manifests and coffles would place the figure somewhere in the range of 8,500 people. Including the numbers of people the partners probably dealt in before they began working together, Isaac Franklin, John Armfield, and Rice Ballard bore direct responsibility for the forced displacement and sale of well over 10,000 human beings during their careers in the slave trade. No other traders of their era came close.

Notarial records show that Isaac Franklin, his nephew James Franklin, and company agents sold 1,625 enslaved people in the city of New Orleans. They effectively sold what was probably a similar number of people to buyers who took possession of the enslaved at the levee and who would have recorded their ownership with a notary only if they chose to or when they transferred ownership to someone else. Franklin, Armfield, and Ballard dealt most of the other enslaved people they brought to the lower South in Natchez. Slaveholders throughout Mississippi and northern Louisiana kept evidence of purchases made there in their private papers. A smattering of that evidence has survived. Most of it has been lost or destroyed over time, and along with it proof of the ultimate destinies of thousands of Black people.

In a way, the partners' retreat from the slave trade came at a bad time. The federal government sold more public land in Mississippi in 1835 than it had sold in the entire country a few years earlier. Cotton production kept increasing by tens of thousands of bales annually, and average market prices between 1834 and 1836 still stayed higher than they had been in a decade. Banks in the region kept churning out banknotes and loans to capitalize on the growth, and they fueled it further. Rampant speculation and skyrocketing prices ensued for nearly everything, including and especially for enslaved people, who would bring more land into cultivation and make more cotton and justify more loans. For slave traders, there was money on the table, and nowhere was better than the lower South to place their bets.[99]

Regional prices for the enslaved had already jumped significantly in 1835–1836, and they spiked just as Franklin, Armfield, and Ballard left the trade. During the 1836–1837 season, prices averaged over $1,000, and enslaved young men routinely sold for $1,200 to $1,500 or more. In Mississippi, one man reported in the fall of 1836, "all the public highways became lined—yea literally crowded—with slaves." Traders "pitched their tents upon the brow of every hill, surrounding each town and village in the state, awaiting the call of purchasers."[100]

Given what came next, however, it might be said that the preternatural sense of timing that brought Franklin, Armfield, and Ballard together in the slave trade at precisely the right moment led them out of it at precisely the right moment too. Fixated on cotton production and convinced that expansion would continue forever, slaveholders clamoring for laborers would pay seemingly any price for them. But they only wanted to borrow against future crops, their land, and the people they already enslaved to do it. They paid for slaves with bills at 10 percent interest that would not come due for a year or two, and if merchants and bankers would give them no more credit, they "secured their debts by deeds in trust and mortgages upon nearly the whole property of the state." The same man who was stunned at the masses of enslaved people slave traders brought to Mississippi believed that by the spring of 1837, slaveholders collectively owed those traders $90 million on purchases made just since 1833, which was "two thirds of the present debt of the state."[101]

Had Franklin, Armfield, and Ballard stayed as bullish as their potential customers, they would only have been left holding a heavier bag when the scheme collapsed. By the summer of 1836, concerns among British banks that cotton demand was unsustainable and among American politicians that land speculation was raging out of control had already led to tightened credit on both sides of the Atlantic. When the bottom then fell out of cotton prices as the 1836 crop came to market, banks in Natchez began suspending specie payments and merchant firms in New Orleans began shutting their doors. In early May 1837, less than six months after John Armfield watched the *Isaac Franklin* leave Alexandria with his last consignment of enslaved people, the avalanche of failures reached New York. Credit markets throughout the country froze, and the nation entered a depression it would not recover from for years.[102]

No part of the country was more bereft in the crisis than the lower South. Bankruptcies, defaults, and sheriff's sales mushroomed. Some counties counted more lawsuits than residents, and as slaveholders panicked and enslaved people confronted the terror of being sold again because of white people and their profligacy, Isaac Franklin worried, as he always did, about money. Caught between debts he owed and debts he stood to collect, he wrote Rice Ballard from New Orleans in the spring of 1837 that he was "without money to pay Tavern Bill and pasage home." Retired or not, he and his partners stood on a precipice. Stumbling over his words on the page as he surveyed the ruin he had helped create, Franklin's anxiety was evident. "If there can be nothing done at Natchez either in the way of collections or on the Banks," he told Ballard, "we had as well surrender & give it up. I will not do it if money can be had at any sacrafice but from the present appearances I fear it will not be to be had at at all."[103]

SIX

REPUTATIONS, 1837–1846

BORN IN THE CENTRAL VIRGINIA COUNTRYSIDE WEST OF Fredericksburg, Madison Henderson recalled being no older than fifteen when Asa Brockman sold him to James Blakey in the town of Orange Court House. Henderson remained there for six weeks while Blakey accumulated more enslaved people for his "partners" in the slave trade, whose names Henderson gave as "Samuel Alsop, Mr. Ballard and James Franklin." Blakey then shackled Henderson and his other prisoners and marched them thirty miles to Alsop's plantation, where they stayed for another week before continuing to Richmond and ending up "lodged in the negro jail of Mr. Ballard." About a week after that, Ballard put Henderson and the rest of "the gang" on a steamboat to Norfolk, where they transferred to a waiting ship and sailed for New Orleans. Taking custody of them on their coastal passage was someone Henderson described as "the chief of a company of negro traders" when he told his life story to a newspaper reporter. Henderson was talking about Isaac Franklin.

Henderson claimed he became Franklin's "body servant" at sea and "remained in his service" for the next three and a half years. He procured "good and kind" treatment by giving Franklin what he wanted, and he learned that "the best means to secure his favor" was "to obey him implicitly, execute his orders literally, and watch carefully over his interests." But Henderson considered his time with Franklin utterly ruinous. He found himself apprenticed to a con man who led a crime syndicate, and that involved even more than the usual moral compromises entailed by being the enslaved assistant of a slave trader.

Henderson said he attended Franklin in carrying out "operations in selling and occasionally in buying" enslaved people that "extended to all the southern parts." He reported being with Franklin as he made sales in New Orleans, Natchez, Vicksburg, and Mobile, and accompanying Franklin as he made purchases in Baltimore, the District of Columbia, Richmond, Norfolk, and smaller Virginia towns. And Henderson remembered that under Franklin's tutelage, he became a liar and a thief. If an enslaved person seemed "unwilling to be sold," Henderson's job was "to overcome their objections" with "false tales of what my master would do for them." If a slaveholder would not part with people Franklin had his eye on, Henderson's "duty was to coax off, and harbor negroes: in other words, to aid in stealing them."

Henderson promised the enslaved that Franklin would liberate them in the free states or Canada. He told enslaved men "they would become rich and own plenty of property," and he told enslaved women they would marry "rich white men" and live "in style and splendor." They needed only to meet Henderson at an appointed place and time, and he and Franklin would take care of the rest. When the plan worked, Henderson stealthily escorted Franklin's targets to white accomplices while Franklin negotiated for legal title to the runaways. Franklin aimed for cut-rate prices in exchange for assuming the risks and costs of recapturing them. But a bill of sale could always be faked. If necessary, Franklin just had a clerk draft one.

Sometimes Franklin helped entice the enslaved himself. Henderson recalled one instance in particular when he and Franklin visited a Virginia man named Baxter who enslaved "four of the handsomest yellow girls" Henderson "ever saw." During the day, Franklin charmed Baxter's daughters by driving them around in a fancy carriage, and he professed indifference toward the slave trade, saying "he was about to quit the business." But at night, he and Henderson, "finely dressed" and "each wearing a gold watch," visited the "yellow girls." Franklin "cohabited every night with some one of them" and Henderson "with another," and Franklin convinced them "to run off" with promises to "make one of them his wife" and to bring along their mother, who was enslaved on a nearby farm.

Of course, Franklin would never free any of the people he bought or duped. Instead, once Franklin had everyone he wanted, he had "the whole drove set out for Richmond," where they joined scores of enslaved people "procured by the other partners." All of them "were lodged in Mr. Ballard's jail," Henderson recollected, "and no one saw them afterwards until we left for New Orleans."

In New Orleans, Henderson recalled, Franklin often kept company with "a negro trader by the name of Woolfolk." They spent "considerable time together at a house near the negro jail below Esplenade street" and lived "pretty high whilst there." But Franklin's primary mission in the city was "disposing of the negroes," and he introduced Henderson to that side of the business too. Franklin told Henderson of "tricks to make it profitable," taught him "how to manage" and keep "custody of large sums of money," and had him "look out for men who had money" and might be in the market for slaves. All the while, Franklin gave Henderson cash and encouraged him "to indulge with the women" being sold, though he was not to get involved with any "girl" Franklin "kept" or "interfere with him" in any way.

Henderson claimed that he traveled from the Chesapeake to the lower South and back several times during his stint as Isaac Franklin's lieutenant, and that other crimes were never far from the slave trade wherever he and Franklin went. Henderson told of helping Franklin steal thousands of dollars from a Virginia store that Franklin then burned to the ground to cover their tracks, and he even remembered running a scam in Washington City on Henry Clay. In Henderson's account, Franklin was staying at the same hotel as Clay and "professed to adore" the Kentucky Whig senator, getting along with him so famously that he finagled an invitation to dine with him "at the President's House." Henderson was solicitous of Clay too, so successfully edging aside the "free yellow man" Clay had serving him that Clay paid Franklin $1,300 to buy Henderson for himself. It was all part of the plan. A week later, Henderson fled from Clay and met up in Baltimore with Franklin, who kept Clay's money.

Eventually, Franklin decided he and Henderson "had been together long enough." With Henderson's consent, Franklin sold him aboard a Natchez-bound steamboat to Samuel G. Blanchard, who "wanted to buy a trusty servant to keep about a store." As a parting gift, Henderson claimed, Franklin gave him the $900 Blanchard paid, to do with as he wished.[1]

Isaac Franklin and his colleagues did in fact traffic Madison Henderson to the lower South. In his "purchase book," Rice Ballard recorded his agent James Blakey paying the relatively high price of $625 for "Madison Brockman," who was closer to his mid-twenties than his mid-teens when Asa Brockman sold him in the fall of 1833. Listed among twenty-four enslaved people kept by Blakey temporarily at Samuel Alsop's plantation, Henderson was then brought to Ballard's jail in Richmond. On November 4, 1833, he and dozens of other captives boarded the *Uncas* in Norfolk, joining people John Armfield had shipped from Alexandria five days earlier. In late November, Franklin claimed them all at the levee in New Orleans, marched them up Esplanade Avenue, and stashed them in the Canonage property, whose lease to John Woolfolk he was about to take over.[2]

Henderson's account of his experience with Franklin becomes hard to credit after that. Henderson spent enough time with Franklin to take the measure of his personality, temperament, and operation. He could have noticed Franklin offering those he imprisoned gestures of kindness backed with menace, and he could have heard Franklin telling enslaved people lies to ease their fears and keep them calm until he could sell them. He could have witnessed Franklin's abuse of enslaved women and his carousing with John Woolfolk, and he could have overheard Franklin complain about wanting to leave the slave-trade business. Henderson could have seen Franklin with gobs of cash, and he told at least the figurative truth often expressed by abolitionists that no matter what American law allowed, traders like Franklin and his cronies were "man-stealers."

But Franklin sold Henderson to Samuel Blanchard, a New Orleans merchant, on December 6, 1833. That was roughly two weeks after Henderson disembarked from the *Uncas*, not three and a half years after, and little of the rest of Henderson's story about Franklin can be corroborated. Henderson probably told it in part to exact some measure of vengeance against his traffickers, though he also intended it as an origin story and explanation for his life of crime, because he offered it to the reporter transcribing it as a jail cell "confession." In July 1841, Henderson and three accomplices were hanged in Saint Louis for having killed two bank clerks during a botched robbery, the last of a series of crimes Henderson claimed he committed after Franklin sold him.[3]

Still, even if Henderson did concoct much about his supposed exploits in Franklin's company, newspapers throughout the United States rarely questioned his account as they covered the trials and executions of Henderson and his confederates. And that prompted

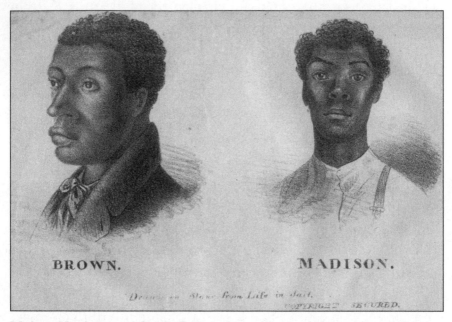

BROWN.   MADISON.

Madison Henderson and Charles Brown, who were executed along with two other men
in Saint Louis in 1841. Henderson was born into slavery in Virginia, sold in 1833 to
a purchasing agent of Rice Ballard, trafficked to New Orleans on a ship belonging to
Franklin and Armfield, and then sold by Isaac Franklin. Courtesy of Cornell University
Law Library, Trial Pamphlets Collection.

a response from Franklin and those who knew him. In the fall of
1841, the Natchez *Mississippi Free Trader* dedicated a column to "re-
futing the calumnies" directed by Henderson toward "a respectable
and worthy gentleman, well known in this vicinity."[4]

The *Mississippi Free Trader* blasted Henderson's account as a
"catch-penny concern," a "fabrication and infamous slander." It ex-
cerpted a Virginia newspaper asserting that Henderson had invented
names and places there, and it printed letters from a Nashville paper
defending Franklin. One came from H. R. W. Hill, a partner in the
New Orleans merchant firm that Franklin used, who was furious
about rumormongers spreading Henderson's claims. Hill conceded
that Henderson was bought from Asa Brockman, shipped on the
Uncas, and sold to Samuel Blanchard, but he insisted the rest was
"a *fiction*," and that he only bothered saying so for the sake of oth-

ers whose names Henderson had besmirched. In Hill's judgment, Franklin himself hardly needed the vindication, as "his character, where he is known, is an ample shield."

Hill called in reinforcements anyway. He passed along a testimonial from Henry Clay, who denied the story Henderson told about him and said that his "limited" acquaintance with Franklin left the impression of "a gentleman of honor, who inspired me with sentiments of respect." And Hill offered a communication from the retired Andrew Jackson, who wrote that Clay and Franklin "never dined at my house together during my Presidency" and that Henderson's account was "a vile slander." Moreover, Jackson knew Franklin "from his youth" and believed he had "always sustained the character of an honest and high-minded man."[5]

For Isaac Franklin to deign to respond to accusations leveled by an enslaved criminal was unusual. It might seem more remarkable still that he could muster public character endorsements from editors, merchants, and planters who also happened to be the leading figures and most famous avatars of both of the major political parties in the United States. White southerners, after all, often claimed that slave traders were reviled social outcasts. But the claim was mostly a myth.

IF THERE WAS EVER A MOMENT FOR FRANKLIN AND HIS PARTners to have been outcasts, loathed and resented by other white southerners, the depression following the economic implosion that came to be known as the Panic of 1837 was it. Politicians and slaveholders in the lower South commonly cast slave traders as scapegoats for the debts crushing them and their states in the late 1830s. Many of the excessive liabilities that produced the crisis could in fact be traced to the slave trade, and no traders were more ubiquitous creditors than Isaac Franklin, John Armfield, and Rice Ballard. Over twenty years later, memories of the grip the three had on Natchez slaveholders remained fresh in some minds. One man recalled that almost all the planters in the city, scrambling to keep their holdings intact through the crisis, pledged their land, their cotton, their slaves, and anything else they had of value as collateral for new loans. Yet they dissembled about the ultimate source of their wealth and their overextensions. "None of them," the man remembered, "told the exact amount which they owed to John Armfield, R. C. Ballard and Mr. Franklin for the negroes which gave them all their consequence."[6]

We can imagine some Natchez debtors, if pressed, contending they concealed the truth about what they owed and whom they owed it to out of embarrassment for having put themselves in thrall to people they found distasteful. It was common for white southerners to say they considered slave traders to be degenerate reprobates. Greedy, dishonest brutes, slave traders supposedly bore disproportionate responsibility for the most grievous abuses of enslaved people and for destroying their families. They exploited the financial misfortunes of white people, lured them against their better judgment into debasing and immoral forms of speculation, peddled dangerous and unsound slaves to unwitting buyers, and gave abolitionists ammunition for attacking the institution of slavery itself.[7]

At best a necessary evil, slave traders were characters whom decent white people purportedly viewed with suspicion, avoided whenever possible, and shunned outside commercial settings. Travelers heard the last bit all the time. In the spring of 1834, when Edward Abdy stayed in Warrenton, Virginia, a doctor at his hotel told him that Jourdan Saunders engaged in a business so "detested, that no respectable person in the place would speak to him." A few months later, when Joseph Ingraham asked about the standing of Isaac Franklin and his fellow slave traders in Natchez, he heard that "planters associate with them freely enough, in the way of business, but notice them no farther." Certainly, Ingraham was told, "their admission into society . . . is not recognized."[8]

Slaveholders may have been tempted to see the slave trade's shrinking scale in the wake of the Panic of 1837 as a sign that the business reputations of traders had caught up with their social reputations. The number of enslaved people forcibly moved across state lines for sale dropped by 30 to 35 percent from the 1830s to the 1840s. The number of enslaved people imported and sold in New Orleans would not reach 1836 levels for nearly a decade, and in that city and throughout the lower South, sales prices for the enslaved slipped significantly in 1837, rebounded a bit in 1838, and then declined fairly steadily for the next six years. They would not return to pre-panic levels until the mid-1850s.[9]

But more than 180,000 people were still sent on forced migrations in the 1840s. That was one of every fourteen enslaved people in the country, and they took no solace from a relative decline. For one thing, the decline was irrelevant in the face of the widespread and irreparable ruptures that slaveholders already in the lower South caused in the lives of the enslaved when they sold them to stave off debt or lost them to foreclosure during the depression. For another, the decline did not really demonstrate that white southerners had learned anything. Slave sales and slave prices fell because cotton prices fell, not because white southerners discovered fiscal responsibility. Cotton prices dropped by nearly a third from 1836 to 1837, rose by roughly the same percentage in 1838, and then nosedived in 1839, bottoming out in 1844 at 35 percent of what they had been at their peak. Cotton producers in the United States would almost never again see prices as high as those of the mid-1830s before the Civil War.[10]

Nor was the slowed pace of the slave trade in the 1840s an indication that white southerners took their pretenses of disdaining slave traders to heart, because they were mostly pretenses to begin with. To be sure, some white southerners voiced genuine ambivalence if not outright hostility toward the slave trade. Pervasive, quotidian, and unavoidably public, the trade put Black pain and sorrow on display for the world to see, and it exposed slavery's mercenary nature in a fashion that could not easily be explained away. It made slaveholders politically vulnerable, and it gave the lie to paternalistic charades about the obligations they felt toward those they kept in bondage. Displacing responsibility for slavery's degrading viciousness was a way for slaveholders to extract themselves from the transactional element of merchandizing human beings. It was a denial of the fact that at some point or another, every slaveholder would effectively be a slave trader.[11]

But rhetorical displacement did not stop slave sales, and the pariah status of slave traders was more proclaimed than enforced, more an element of proslavery propaganda than of lived reality. Close observers of slavery and the slave trade saw little evidence that traders lost social standing as a matter of course because of their profession. Abolitionist Theodore Dwight Weld traveled in the South, studied the region, and interviewed white and Black southerners. In the depths of the depression, Weld argued that while members of "the *highest class of society at the South*" liked to say "that 'Negro Brokers,' Negro Speculators, Negro Auctioneers, and Negro Breeders" were "universally despised and avoided," it was untrue. Even putting aside the question of whether elite opinion could stand in for mass opinion, Weld noted that the only slave traders white southerners ever held in contempt were either those "of limited capital, who buy up small gangs and drive their own coffles," or "the agents and pimps" of bigger traders "who are constantly scouring the breeding states to gather fresh supplies for the slave-prisons and slave-ships."[12]

Moreover, Weld suspected elite disgust with small-timers was not "because they *trade in slaves*." It was "because they are *working men*." They were itinerants like day laborers and peddlers, they tended to come from poorer backgrounds, and they were looked down upon by the wellborn as a consequence. By contrast, slave traders from the families of planters, senators, generals, judges, or ministers did not "lose caste." They were "held in repute, as honorable merchants." So were the "slave merchants, who have large establishments or factories" in major cities. These were men who had slavers sailing between American ports, advertised "in the most influential secular papers in the union," and used public prisons when their own were full. "Men of large capital," they traded in slaves "on the broadest scale" and were leading members of society. "They hold an honorable rank among the heavy capitalists and extensive merchants of our southern cities," Weld wrote, "and move in the highest social circles."[13]

Weld could have found no better examples of such "slave merchants" than Isaac Franklin, John Armfield, and Rice Ballard. As depression blanketed the country, they made for themselves lives different from those they had conducted as slave traders, but their work in the slave trade neither hindered their movements "in the highest social circles" nor prevented them from holding "an honorable rank among the heavy capitalists." If anything, having become "men of large capital" through the trade demonstrated talents that made them socially appealing to other grandees and useful allies of other businessmen during the economic downturn. No one ever expected them to disavow their old profession, disclaim old associates, or deny that they continued to earn money from their interests in the trade. Entertaining illusions about their wealth was unnecessary. As Joseph Ingraham put it, revealing his doubts about whether any stigma actually attached to dealers in Black people, "a slave trader" was "very much like other men."[14]

Slaveholders could try hiding their debts to Isaac Franklin, John Armfield, and Rice Ballard, but they could not hide forever. The partners were not forgiving sorts, and the depression was not a forgiving time. Franklin, Armfield, and Ballard were no longer selling enslaved people in the lower South, but customers collectively owed them and their company vast sums from past purchases, and leniency was a luxury they could not afford in light of their own obligations. They would pursue every possible dollar. In Natchez and New Orleans and in parishes and counties throughout Louisiana, Mississippi, Virginia, Maryland, and other states, they spent years making collections and chasing bills with any means in their power.

Sometimes the partners could be satisfied through negotiation if debtors offered enough reliable funds or bales of cotton to persuade them that more would be forthcoming and that patience would be rewarded. But cotton prices had become shaky, and even surviving merchant firms could not always pay bills when they came due. Finding banknotes acceptable for exchange at all had become challenging, and those still being taken might be discounted by 20 percent or more.[15]

Mortgaging additional land and slaves as extra security on existing loans could buy customers some time too, but if that recourse was unavailable, pleading for mercy failed, or accommodations on a debt could not be made, the result was usually a lawsuit. In 1837 and 1838, lawyers filed nearly a dozen cases on behalf of Franklin, Armfield, and Ballard in Natchez's Adams County alone. More would follow. Ultimately, the partners sued so many customers, endorsers, and merchants in so many local and district and circuit courts that locating and following them all to their conclusions would be impossible.[16]

When time expired on new mortgages or when judgments came down in favor of the partners, as they often did, debtors were out of options. Foreclosures typically ensued. The partners sometimes took those as opportunities to turn debts into assets, themselves buying land and slaves of the insolvent at public auction and then flipping the property and the people for whatever they could get in return. But sometimes, even after winning a judgment, if a debt seemed less valuable or certain, too difficult to collect, or likely to involve protracted time and expense, the partners sold it at a discount, cut their losses, and moved on.[17]

The breadth of the economic calamity sometimes meant the partners, like bankers and merchants and other creditors everywhere in the United States, became adversaries of colleagues and friends. Ballard's old associate in the trade, Warren Offutt, appealed for an extension on a debt that would "bee a destroying thing to my family" if he had to pay it on time, and Ballard got letters from James Blakey imploring him to stay a debt lawsuit that Blakey feared would land him in jail. The partners sued fellow traders Theophilus Freeman and Benjamin Eaton. They sued John Routh for a debt of nearly $75,000, and they sued Silas Lillard, Ballard's partner in the mercantile firm of James Ballard and Company. Lillard, in fact, faced multiple suits, and by 1840 he was forced to sell everything he owned in Natchez and across the Mississippi River in Louisiana. His credit never recovered.[18]

Customer debts and commercial lawsuits had always been part of the slave-trade business, and most of the initial fallout the partners experienced from the depression was a difference of magnitude from the ordinary. But unanticipated business and personal challenges piled up too. Rice Ballard's responsibilities, for example, grew well beyond those related to his partnership with Franklin and Armfield. Ballard bought all of Silas Lillard's property, acquiring multiple lots in Natchez, thousands of acres in Louisiana, and more than eighty enslaved people. The purchases were of questionable legality, designed to shield Lillard's assets from creditors and allow him to continue to live on and operate his plantations. But Ballard was the putative owner. He brokered the cotton grown on Lillard's land while he garnished some of the profits, and he would be the ultimate authority over the holdings for years.[19]

Ballard also settled the affairs of James Ballard and Company when it went under in 1839 and its named partner bankrupted. He acted as agent for Joseph Alsop's Mississippi interests, which had become significant since Alsop's years with Ballard in the slave trade in the 1820s and which involved even more collections, lawsuits, and accounts. And Ballard financially supported his sister Emily. During the depression, her improvident husband, William Freeman Read, fell "in debt very much more than what Property he has will pay," and became so "intirely deranged" that Virginia authorities locked him up, putting Ballard in the position of saving his sister and her eight children from Read's creditors.[20]

For John Armfield, company interests in the Chesapeake remained a primary concern, and he focused particularly on staying ahead of debts to the Bank of Virginia, which called in tens of thousands of dollars in loans taken out by Armfield and his partners. But family matters pulled at Armfield even more than they did Ballard. In 1838, Martha Armfield's brother Smith Franklin died, and the Armfields became guardians for John Sanderson, the adolescent son of Martha's sister Mary, who had been living with Smith Franklin since his mother's death. Then, early in 1839, Armfield's father Nathan died intestate. By law, his effects were divided among John Armfield and his sisters, and Armfield gave his share to his sister Polly. Her husband, William Hanner, had taken care of Armfield's paternity issue in Surry County in the 1820s and then had helped Armfield get started in the slave-trade business. Hanner struggled financially in the depression, and John Armfield's surrendering his claim to his father's estate was a partial return for the favors.[21]

Yet of the three partners in Franklin and Armfield, none was busier, more agitated, or more altered in his fiscal commitments by the Panic of 1837 than Isaac Franklin. He best understood the company's activities and the relationships among its various interests. He also had the longest and sturdiest ties to the bankers, merchants, and customers who would need to be alternately cajoled and browbeaten if collections were to stay ahead of liabilities. Trying to keep on top of everything put Franklin where he had been for years and did not want to be, shuttling between Natchez and New Orleans and keeping an eye on Fairvue, with the added chore of checking on the plantations he owned with Francis Routh in West Feliciana Parish.[22]

By January 1838, Franklin was already feeling overrun. "Fortune is a fickle ladi & it appears she has conspired with Fate to ruin me," he wrote Ballard from the deck of the steamboat *Paru*. Unaccustomed to circumstances that were beyond his ability to control, Franklin was unmoored, "Broken Down" in "spirits & pride." Soon he became frantic. Money was so tight in New Orleans that he worried, "we are never to have any thing more paid in this place," and he needed Ballard to make things happen in Natchez fast. "For God sake," Franklin wrote, "Hurry our collections in Mississippi." But as he signed off in distress, "Great God what will become of us," he was unsure it would be enough. By March, even the energy to panic eluded him. Franklin fell so far into despondency that he considered throwing up his hands and walking away, confessing to Ballard that he "almost came to the conclution to apandon every thing to its fate and tryal at the sacrafice of my hard Earnings."[23]

Franklin's desolation came in part from his lugubrious disposition. Wallowing in his own misery came naturally, and he was prone to cry catastrophe when anything was less than optimal. Franklin's physical condition also kept slipping. Traveling and financial pressures made him feel more decrepit all the time, and decline was certainly on his mind as he pondered abandoning his business interests. Telling Ballard he had "one Eye out" and a "sholder broke," he wondered if he should take some time "to reestablish my health." But amid the strain his lingering stake in the slave trade presented, nothing made Isaac Franklin more irritable than his venture with Francis Routh.[24]

Routh was able to force cotton production out of the people he and Franklin enslaved. In just one day in November 1837, Routh recorded that over 20,000 pounds of cotton had been picked by about ninety men and women on the Bellevue plantation. At nearly 250 pounds per person, it was almost twice the national daily average for the time. But the financial negligence that led Routh to Franklin in the first place was severe and persistent, and indifference or self-sabotage seemingly compounded Routh's ineptitude. Routh failed to pay land taxes for years, and he encumbered his half of Franklin and Routh with more than half a dozen mortgages and nearly a dozen court judgments adding up to a quarter of a million dollars in liabilities. By late 1837, John Parkinson, the sheriff of West Feliciana Parish, was seizing portions of the cotton crop. With more lawsuits pending, forfeiture was inevitable.[25]

On December 22, 1837, Parkinson confiscated thirty-six hundred acres of land and 35 enslaved people from Routh's share of the partnership holdings, and he sold it and them at public auction to satisfy a court judgment. A month later, Parkinson sold Routh's share of everything else, amounting to a half interest in several thousand acres of land, 189 enslaved people, four hundred head of cattle, several dozen oxen and horses and mules, and 240 bales of cotton. Isaac Franklin bought it all, paying $72,500 at the initial sale and $350 for the rest, though the second purchase entailed assuming the outstanding mortgages and judgments.[26]

These were significant acquisitions that Franklin made reluctantly. He had bought into the West Feliciana property expecting profits rather than responsibilities, and the entire holdings were only appraised at about $160,000, putting them significantly underwater. But among Routh's liabilities were mortgages to Franklin and to Ballard Franklin and Company worth nearly $135,000, and Franklin figured they would never be paid unless he bought Routh's share of the property, and its debts, himself. Routh's bumbling had already cost Franklin and Ballard tens of thousands of dollars. This was the only way to retrieve something from one of the few poor business decisions of Franklin's life. "If I am compelled to pay your or rather Ballard Franklin & Co. mortgage," Franklin explained to Ballard, "it will be more than the property is worth by fifty or sixty thousand but will calculate that that concern will divide the loss with me." It could have been worse. If not "for my great exertions,"

Franklin continued, "we would have been compelled to loose nearly all that we had."[27]

Ironically, Franklin, Armfield, and Ballard faced so many entanglements after the Panic of 1837 for the same reasons they had been so successful during their years working together. Their prowess in the business of slavery had given them reputations for general business acuity, and they were able to make money, sustain their credit, and gain access to capital even when no one else could. Anyone who knew them and needed assistance navigating the shoals of the depression was bound to turn to them for support and guidance.

That included, perhaps especially, anyone still engaged in the slave trade. As Franklin, Armfield, and Ballard withdrew from active trading, some of their agents and associates rushed into the market space they left behind. George Kephart was best placed to do so. Working out of the old Franklin and Armfield office and compound on Duke Street, Kephart built an operation like the one he had watched John Armfield direct. Kephart ran daily advertisements in Alexandria and Washington City newspapers that he would pay "CASH FOR NEGROES." He trafficked enslaved people on the *Isaac Franklin* and offered shipping services to other merchants and traders. He hired Robert Windsor as his bookkeeper and clerk.[28]

Kephart even fed antislavery activists the same lines Armfield had. Early in 1838, when Pennsylvania abolitionist James Miller McKim visited what had been "Franklin and Armfield's immense slave factory," the "high walls" and "bolts and bars" were still there. They penned in "50 or 60 wretched prisoners," and the "keeper" of the facility told McKim "how kind they were to the prisoners" and "how mild southern slavery was." McKim heard "how much better [was] the condition of those who were bought up in Maryland, and brought there." And of course, McKim was told "how they never separated families."[29]

McKim was having none of it. Perhaps that was because "when examined and cross questioned," his tour guide "contradict[ed] himself, and unsa[id] all he had said." Or perhaps it was because McKim had read stories like Dorcas Allen's. After the man who enslaved her died, Allen, a married mother of four, lived as a free woman in Washington City for fourteen years until August 1837, when one of the man's relatives claimed her as property. He told her she and her children would be taken to his residence in Alexandria. Instead, they ended up in the compound on Duke Street. Allen knew what would happen if they stayed there, and so on "the first night of her imprisonment," she strangled her two youngest children and "attempted to murder her other two children . . . by beating them in the face and on the head with brickbats." Arrested and held for trial, Allen said that she wanted "to prevent her children from going into slavery" and had "designed to take her own life, to save herself from bondage."[30]

To supply the shipments that enslaved people like Dorcas Allen would rather die than endure, Kephart built a network of traders like the one that had accumulated people for Franklin and Armfield. Sometimes creating actual partnerships and sometimes crafting less formal arrangements, Kephart forged connections in Baltimore with a trader named Hope Hull Slatter and maintained a relationship in the city with James Franklin Purvis. In Annapolis, he worked with Isaac Franklin Purvis, James's younger brother, their uncle's namesake and the latest in a long line of family members to become a slave trader. In Richmond, Kephart joined forces with Bacon Tait and Thomas Boudar, and he had ties to Tait and Boudar's agent and jail manager, Sidnum Grady. In Washington City, Kephart acquired people from James Birch, who had once partnered with Franklin and Armfield's agent Thomas Jones, and from Joseph Bruin, who had been a trader in Virginia and Louisiana since the early 1830s.[31]

By the early 1840s, visitors were told that Kephart confined up to four hundred people at a time at the Duke Street facility and that he shipped between fifteen hundred and two thousand enslaved people to the lower South every year. These were probably exaggerations. But Kephart and his colleagues trafficked hundreds of people at a fragile economic moment, and when they needed expert advice and the occasional financial service, they sought out Isaac Franklin, John Armfield, and Rice Ballard. They asked for their help negotiating and collecting bills, for their sense of markets in money and slaves, and for their acceptances and endorsements on notes. They wanted to know their views about spending, thoughts on potential career moves, and opinions about other traders. In return, they offered updates on discount rates and prices for the enslaved, forwarded bits of gossip, did small favors, and expressed gratitude for keeping the slave trade in motion. Bacon Tait told Ballard who was renting space in his Richmond jail, and he suggested a novel for Armfield to read. James Purvis shipped Ballard a buggy with a fancy brass-mounted harness that he had requested. Thomas Boudar sent Armfield three pet birds in a cage.[32]

Corporations and financial institutions sometimes needed slave-trading expertise during the depression too, and they knew where to go. When the directors of the West Feliciana Railroad authorized the purchase of fifty enslaved men, ten women, and ten boys to labor for the company, they asked John Armfield to help furnish them. When the Planters' Bank of Natchez wanted a trustee to administer landholdings and hundreds of slaves from clients in arrears, to "dispose of them" as would best serve "the Interest of the Institution," and to put the proceeds toward debts the bank owed the federal government, they reached out to Rice Ballard.[33]

The lawyers, judges, politicians, planters, and merchants who served as bank directors and on corporate boards trusted that Franklin, Armfield, and Ballard had the wisdom and sense to handle their affairs. That trust did not come begrudgingly. It did not come despite their involvement in the slave trade or because they had put active trading behind them. It came precisely because they had done so well at buying and selling Black people and because during hard times, they remained intact financially while so many others struggled with solvency. Discerning and dependable men, their success in the slave trade brought them more than money. It brought them esteem. The Planters' Bank of Natchez did not entrust Ballard to liquidate plantations and the human property on them just because he happened to have been a slave trader. It was also because, a few months before the request, shareholders had made Ballard a director of the bank.[34]

The regard accorded Franklin, Armfield, and Ballard ranged beyond the business world. Their social circumstances advanced too. Armfield bore a "good character" in Alexandria, and though residents considered him "a charitable man," he was not above spoiling himself. By the early 1840s, he owned most of a city block along the north side of Prince Street, between Patrick and Henry Streets. On those two acres, "acquired," in the words of an antislavery activist who saw them in 1841, "by the sale of native born Americans," Armfield built a "costly mansion" that a friendlier observer described as "the handsomest and most desirable residence in the District [of Columbia]." Two blocks west lay the Duke Street compound, and five blocks east sat St. Paul's Episcopal Church, which welcomed Martha Armfield as a member in 1837 and confirmed her in 1839. Designed in the Gothic style by famed architect Benjamin Latrobe, St. Paul's was the church of many of Alexandria's most notable white residents, including members of the Washington and Fairfax families.[35]

In Mississippi, Ballard was among the "gentlemen" serving as patrol judges for the spring races at the Natchez Jockey Club in 1838, a position that put him in company with leading and powerful white men who forged social and political alliances at horse races. The races were also a place for demonstrating wealth and authority, and both in and beyond Mississippi there were other signs that Ballard was embraced and recognized by elites. One was the fact that by 1837, correspondents began consistently addressing him as "Col. Ballard," suggesting social leadership conferred by election as a militia officer. Armfield would receive the same honor a few years later.[36]

Isaac Franklin's status had never really been in question, especially in his native Tennessee. His was among the oldest and most distinguished white families in Sumner County, and his flourishing careers as slave trader and plantation owner made him its most stunningly successful member. During the 1830s, he increased his landholdings in Sumner fivefold, until he owned nearly two thousand acres. He built one of the most extravagant mansion houses in the state, and the number of people enslaved on his property grew more than 50 percent in ten years. By 1840, Isaac Franklin enslaved 117 men, women, and children at Fairvue, making him the largest slaveholder and probably the wealthiest man in the county. Whether or not he had intended it, he was also one of largest slaveholders in West Feliciana Parish, and established figures there recognized his prominence too, choosing him as a delegate to a state Democratic convention in 1840.[37]

Only one obvious thing might have made socializing with members of the white gentry class awkward for Isaac Franklin and Rice Ballard. But the scuttlebutt was that they were looking to rectify it. "There is a rumor afloat here that Mr. Franklin & yourself each expect to be married shortly," Bacon Tait wrote Ballard from Richmond in the spring of 1839. "I know that each of you are of amorous dispositions and therefore would not be astonished to hear of your leading each a blithesome Lassie to the altar of love love love."[38]

After James Rawlings Franklin died in the summer of 1834, sexualized banter, talk of "fancy maids," and jokes about raping enslaved women disappear from the surviving correspondence of Isaac Franklin and his partners. It was as if the younger Franklin had been a kind of catalyst for their foulest remarks and making them without him hardly seemed as entertaining. But verbal restraint was not accompanied by behavioral change. So long as they dealt in the enslaved, the partners in Franklin and Armfield looked for young women to satisfy white men whose appetites for sex and power converged in the slave market. And they continued to indulge their own appetites long past that.

Sometimes the abuses left no trace in the historical record and, barring the emergence of DNA evidence like that discovered by a descendant of John Armfield and a Black woman he raped, they will probably be hidden forever, known only to the dead. But Martha Sweart knew that sometimes the abuses went on for years, that the partners might talk about them with each other, and that they kept proof in their papers of what they had done and whom they had done it to. Though Isaac Franklin and Rice Ballard had stopped laughing by the time Bacon Tait was hearing rumors of matrimony, sometimes we can still hear the unfathomable.[39]

Lucinda Jackson was the eighth person on the "Invoice of Negroes" where Ballard listed the fifty-seven people he purchased in July 1834. Ballard wrote down their names and the prices he paid for them. He identified the agents who purchased them, noted the commission the agents earned on each person they brought him, and cataloged things that might have an impact on a person's price in the market. Spencer Johnson was a "good carpenter," Easter Foster was a "good weaver," Nelly Jordan was "12 ys old." Two things stood out about Lucinda Jackson. One was that Ballard paid $575 for her, between 15 and 50 percent more than he paid for any other enslaved woman that month and more than he paid for all but three enslaved men. The other was that she was the only person on the list sold to Isaac Franklin.[40]

Most of the people on Ballard's invoice ended up in the coffle George Featherstonhaugh witnessed Armfield driving through Virginia in September 1834, and Franklin probably picked Jackson out of the lot when they arrived in Tennessee. She may have been the "girl Taken by I. Franklin Esqr." whom Ballard wrote off in his company ledger, at the discounted price of $515. Franklin would keep her at Fairvue for nearly five years.[41]

The violence of slavery ramifies through the archive, and it denies us knowledge of where Lucinda Jackson was born, who her parents were, how old she was, or what she looked like. We do know that Isaac Franklin raped her, and that she had at least one child by him. She was probably one of the "likely mulatto girls" neighbors noticed among those Franklin enslaved at Fairvue, and if what Madison Henderson reported Franklin instructing him about enslaved women bore any resemblance to the truth, Jackson and the others suffered an extended campaign of terror. Henderson remembered Franklin saying that taking sexual advantage of enslaved women was a prerogative to exercise "as much as I pleased" but also warning that getting invested emotionally could only cloud his judgment and invite vulnerability. "Upon no account" was Henderson "to take up with any one, at least not so far as to let her gain my confidence." In Henderson's telling, Franklin "appeared very anxious" about that.[42]

The question of Henderson's overall veracity notwithstanding, on this particular his account reads as credible. Franklin said similar things to Rice Ballard about Arvenia White and Susan Johnson. They were the first two entries on Ballard's "List of Purchases for the year 1832," and Ballard placed a small squiggle next to their names, indicating that he kept them in Virginia instead of shipping them to the lower South. The $237 Ballard paid for White was near the low end of the price range he paid for women that year. But he paid $425 for Johnson, significantly more than he paid for most women and more than he paid for many boys and men.[43]

Ballard probably began assaulting Johnson, and perhaps White as well, shortly after he acquired them. But before long, their relationships became complicated by the sorts of attachments Franklin disdained. At the end of his "purchase book" for the years 1832–1834, Ballard wrote, "Susan Johnson was delivered of a boy child 21 of May

1833 at 4 oclock in the morning." It was the only thing he wrote on the page, and he never recorded the day or time that any other enslaved woman gave birth. Johnson's son, though, was surely his own, and he wrote down the particulars as if doing so in the flyleaf of a family bible. White also had a child, a boy named Harvey. Whether or not he was Ballard's too, Ballard started recording expenses for White that suggest she held a special place in his Richmond household and may have helped run his jail—a pair of shoes, a large remnant of calico, grocery bills sizable enough to feed and supply dozens of people. Johnson and White came to Ballard as commodities, but he treated them differently from hundreds of others he held captive.[44]

Sometime in 1833, Ballard liberated Johnson, White, and their children, and Isaac Franklin frowned on that. "Your free family," he wrote early in 1834, "is not Like[ly] to be a profitable vestment. I do not approve of vesting funds in such stock." But he had a thought. "The old Lady and Susan could soon pay for themselves by keeping a whore house," Franklin continued. "It might be Located established at your place Alexandria or Baltimore for the Exclusive benefit of the consern and there agents." A nasty remark even by Franklin's low standards, it was an expression of contempt for Ballard, Johnson, and White all at once. White may have been as old as thirty in 1834. But Franklin's calling her "the old Lady" also mocked Ballard for acting as if White was his wife, and the notion that she and Johnson were worthy only to pimp enslaved women to slave traders was a way for Franklin to tell Ballard he was wasting money and regard on Black women who never deserved it.[45]

In this instance, Ballard did not care what Franklin thought. Arvenia White and Susan Johnson stayed with him in Richmond until he left for Natchez, and they probably accompanied him to Mississippi and remained in his household there for several years. Between them, they soon had four children. Some were Ballard's. Perhaps they all were.[46]

It is impossible to say why White and Johnson stayed with Ballard despite having their freedom. Ballard had enormous material
resources, and White and Johnson may have selected what they
thought the best of a range of bad choices for two Black women trying to survive and raise four children. But it is not unimaginable that
Ballard, White, and Johnson developed a kind of mutual affection
for each other, engaged as they were in relationships that were intimate even if they cannot be described as consensual in any modern
sense of the word. There was nothing unusual about white men ruth-
lessly exploiting those they enslaved while creating lasting, and not
necessarily less exploitative, ties to individual Black women and the
children they had with them. Slave traders may have done so more
than most. The domestic and reproductive labor of Black women
helped make their operations successful. Out of that dependence,
many traders, including some of Ballard's colleagues, developed
connections across the color line that they and the women alike
seem to have considered familial.[47]

Which is not to say there was anything redemptive about Ballard's relationships with White and Johnson. Whatever their affec-
tive contours, they were impossibly fraught and rooted ultimately
in coercion. They had no noticeable impact on Ballard's slave trading, and the presence of White, Johnson, and their children never
stopped Ballard from assaulting other enslaved women. In Richmond, there was Martha Sweart, and in October 1835, when John
Armfield shipped thirty enslaved people on the *Isaac Franklin* to
Ballard Franklin and Company, he also sent seventeen-year-old
Maria Bell, five foot one and described on the ship manifest as
"yellow," personally to Ballard. There is no reason to assume Sweart
and Bell were the only ones. Moreover, while Ballard developed
attachments to White and Johnson that Isaac Franklin might not
have allowed himself, when Ballard's plans changed, he was not so
different from Franklin after all.[48]

On July 2, 1839, John T. Edgar, pastor of the First Presbyterian Church of Nashville, married Isaac Franklin and Adelicia Hayes at Rokeby, a Federal-style mansion sitting on a thirteen-hundred-acre plantation southwest of the city. Twenty-two years old and petite, with blue eyes, an oval face, and dark brown hair worn up and fashionably parted, Hayes was a widely acknowledged beauty and one of the most desirable belles in the region. Her father, Oliver Bliss Hayes, was a Massachusetts native and a lawyer who had migrated to Tennessee and wed Sarah Hightower, the daughter of a wealthy planter and slaveholder. Hayes then moved with her to Nashville, where he purchased the Rokeby estate and garnered a fortune and a sterling public reputation through his legal practice, slaveholding, and real estate speculation, before retiring and becoming an ordained Presbyterian minister. Adelicia was the third of ten children and her parents' oldest daughter. She grew up immensely privileged, and she cared not a whit that Franklin had made most of his money in the slave trade.[49]

In some versions of the story, Adelicia Hayes and Isaac Franklin became acquainted when Hayes made her admiration for Fairvue, and her desire to meet its owner, known in Franklin's absence, kindling his interest and setting him down the path to courtship. In others, Franklin encountered Hayes at a picnic on Fairvue's grounds, offered her a tour of the house, and became entranced when Hayes sang at the piano. Taken as a whole, the stories capture the mix of personal allure, status consciousness, and material interest that brought them together.[50]

In Adelicia Hayes, Franklin saw an attractive young woman from a wealthy and prominent family. In ten years at the Nashville Female Academy, one of the finest educational institutions for girls in the South, she had learned history and geography and science, studied music and art and needlework, developed refined tastes, and cultivated a mastery of social graces. Hayes was intelligent, charming, and quick-witted. She possessed the training to man-

Isaac Franklin, in a portrait made by Tennessee artist Washington Cooper, probably in the mid-1830s. Courtesy Belmont Mansion.

age a plantation household and command those enslaved in it, and she could handle the obligations of her class with ease. Franklin adored her and appreciated her companionship, and he knew she was someone with whom he might have white children to whom he could leave a patrimony.[51]

Franklin was nearly thirty years older than Hayes, but she may have considered it a virtue that he was closer to her father's age than her own. Hayes had become familiar with heartbreak and tragedy early in life. She had been engaged before, when she was seventeen, to a young lawyer who died of typhoid fever, and four years later, her oldest brother, Richard Hightower Hayes, was murdered in a duel at the age of twenty-five. Franklin had his own health concerns, but he was well beyond the uncertainties and foolishness of youth, and he seemed secure and stable in ways that Hayes's experience had taught her men of her generation were not.[52]

Moreover, Franklin remained handsome as he entered his sixth decade. Several years before his marriage, Franklin had had his likeness made by the prolific Tennessee portraitist Washington Cooper.

It shows Franklin seated and wearing an expensive dark suit and cravat, a white shirt, and an ivory vest with the top two buttons left rakishly undone. The outfit hides neither Franklin's broad shoulders nor his rugged build. His alert, grayish brown eyes, set beneath arched brows and framed by a thatch of brown hair and long, thick sideburns, stare directly at the viewer over a straight nose, thin lips, and a clean-shaven, prominent chin. Hayes probably thought him quite dashing.

Worldly and well-traveled, Franklin could also give Hayes a life where she could have nearly anything she imagined. The significant advantages she enjoyed growing up paled in comparison to the luxury made possible by the enslavement of several hundred people on thousands of acres across multiple states. Hayes had been raised to understand the economic power and social position slaveholding conferred on white people as their due. She relished those things, and Franklin's appeal lay partially in his ability to provide more of them. Franklin's slave-trading past was not an obstacle to their marriage. Quite the opposite, it could be said instead that without that past, Hayes might never have married him at all.[53]

Still, American slavery was a regime filled with secrets and lies. There were things that Franklin thought his bride did not know and that he did not want her to find out. After their wedding, Isaac and Adelicia Franklin spent time at a resort north of Nashville, headed to New York and Philadelphia, visited John and Martha Armfield in Alexandria, and finished their honeymoon tour in the mountains of Virginia at the White Sulphur Springs. By the time they returned to Fairvue in late summer, Adelicia was pregnant, and Lucinda Jackson and the child she had by Isaac Franklin were gone. Franklin had deputized Jesse Cage, an old friend and father-in-law to several of Franklin's relatives, to get rid of them. Cage sent them to William Cotton, a Louisville slave-trading associate of Rice Ballard's who could be trusted to keep quiet. "Mr. Isaac Franklin's Girl Lucindy and child" had to vanish, Cage wrote to Cotton. Franklin had "maried a verry pretty and highly accomplishd young Girl," and "the tale must not get out on the old man." Cage knew Cotton appreciated the need for discretion. "It becomes our duty as friends," he wrote, "to assist in making all things easy."[54]

Ballard had his own secrets to bury, and he started burying them even before he got married. Ballard began looking in earnest for a wife not long after stepping away from slave trading, and he cast a wide net in his quest. He looked in Kentucky, often staying with William Cotton in Louisville and leaving such an impression in the city that a friend told him he could expect a lot of attention whenever he was there because, he said, "some of the fair ones are making strong calculation to be called Mrs. Ballard when you come." He looked in Virginia, as he passed through in the summer to check on his jail and visit with Samuel Alsop, who considered Ballard "as near as any child I have" and was "pleased to hear" his "talk of marrying."[55]

And Ballard looked in Mississippi, where his pursuit of single women often took him from Natchez upriver to the aptly named Bachelor's Bend. Located in the northwestern corner of the state and part of what would come to be known as the Mississippi Delta, a vibrant elite white social scene came into being there in the 1830s alongside massive imports of slave labor and new cotton plantations, and Ballard found the parties and the company to his liking. A merchant colleague was surprised when Ballard said he had been persuaded to dance at one gathering, though he understood why in light of "the inducements that I am well aware that <u>Bend</u> holds out to you, they are many & very tempting."[56]

But as Ballard traveled, flirted, and looked to make a match, he did not want his relationships with Arvenia White and Susan Johnson muddling his search. In the spring of 1838, he brought White, Johnson, and their four children to Cincinnati, settled them in Frances Bruster's boardinghouse, and left them there, pledging to return and saying he would send money. Cincinnati was an expanding industrial and commercial city with a large and growing free Black population. There were opportunities for White and Johnson to work and places where the children might go to school, and it was less than 150 miles up the Ohio River from Louisville, making it easy for Ballard to visit by steamboat when he was in Kentucky.[57]

But Ballard's equivocal feelings and intentions for White and Johnson were evident from the moment he left. He came back to Cincinnati now and then, but he was unresponsive for months at a time as White, whose literacy had come in handy when she helped Ballard run his household and jail, wrote him letters detailing her struggles. She earned some money by "taking in both sewing & washing," and Johnson worked occasionally as a house servant. But finding steady employment as "an entire stranger in this city" was difficult, and decent housing near where she and Johnson could get work at all was expensive. Meanwhile, Ballard had not given White nearly enough money to cover her boardinghouse bill, and she fell further behind every day.[58]

By late 1838, White had moved everyone to the cheapest house she could rent, but her son Harvey had taken ill. So had Johnson, and White could not afford wood for a fire or proper beds for her and Johnson to sleep on, even as the weather was getting colder. She apologized for her inadequacies, writing that she had planned "to of got along as to liveing without being any trouble or requesting any assistance." She tried playing on Ballard's sympathies, his sentiments, and their shared history, wondering "how I shall get through the winter with my sick child," plighting herself Ballard's "friend," and even sending "my love." In the end, though, all she could do was beg. Imploring Ballard at least to answer her letters, she hoped he would direct Calvin Fletcher, a white merchant whom

Ballard asked to keep tabs on White, Johnson, and the children, "to let me have some money if only to buy fuel."[59]

Ballard had given White, Johnson, and his and their children their freedom. But when they became inconvenient, they became disposable. On February 2, 1840, White wrote Ballard from Cincinnati with the news that she and Johnson were "almost destitute in a strange land." Work had become hard to find. Unable to pay their rent, they had been evicted and were "at no permanent place since." Someone had told White that Ballard had said "it was not your intention to assist us any more than what you had done," but she had nowhere else to turn, and she reminded Ballard of the stakes of his neglect one last time. "If you have forgotten me," she pleaded, "I hope you have not forgotten the children." Offering her love was pointless, so now she asked only "as a favor" that Ballard not "treat this letter with contempt." White signed herself "your most humble serv[an]t."[60]

Two months later, on April 9, 1840, Rice Ballard wed Louise Cabois Berthe. She was eighteen years old, more than twenty years Ballard's junior. Her father, James Berthe, had been a prominent Natchez merchant in the 1810s and 1820s, and Ballard had probably known her since her childhood. Louise, who often went by Louisa, had attended school in Louisville, and after her father's death in 1836, she went on the ball and party circuit both there and at Bachelor's Bend, where her uncle, William W. Blanton, operated a large plantation called Blantonia. She caught Ballard's eye in both places. They may have married on her uncle's property, though one man recalled that "they constructed a bateau, and with stout negroes rowed up the river to Point Chicot," in the Arkansas Territory, where a probate judge married them. After the wedding, "they returned in high glee." The bateau was "laden with all the luxuries of the season," and "the flow of champagne" at the reception "was only surpassed by the river." If Ballard ever responded to Arvenia

White's appeal, meanwhile, he did not record it. And if she ever wrote him again, he did not keep the letter in his papers.[61]

It did not seem to bother Rice Ballard that he abandoned Arvenia White and Susan Johnson in the middle of a depression, making their situation, difficult under the best of circumstances, especially dire. He found the situations of people who owed him money more unsettling. As cotton prices remained low and the economic slump in the United States grew longer and deeper with no signs of abating, debtor desperation and failure mounted.

Ballard's partners fretted too. Even life as a newlywed and an expectant father did not lift Isaac Franklin's gloom. He wrote Ballard from New Orleans in January 1840 that paltry collections in the city left him dangerously low on funds. Franklin could not cover payments on commercial notes, he owed thousands in attorney fees, and while he planned to "use all my exertions to save the credit of the concern as long as I have or can rease a Dollar," he thought Ballard and John Armfield might have to extend personal loans to the company. Franklin was sure his colleagues agreed that "the Debts of the concern should be paid before any of us should be Hording up money." If Ballard had a better idea from where he sat in Natchez, Franklin was listening. "Say who we can collect from to pay the concerns debts."[62]

The trouble was that Mississippi debts had become uniquely challenging to collect. In April 1837, Governor Charles Lynch had called the legislature into special session to address "the unexampled pecuniary embarrassment" of the state. He asked lawmakers to aid debtors and restore capital flows by, among other things, establishing an actual penalty for violating the ban on importing enslaved people for sale. Provided for by the state constitution, the ban had never been put into operation, and it was a dead letter. Lynch himself had voted against it as a delegate to the state's constitutional convention, thinking it hard to enforce and "at variance with the broad principles" of what he unironically called "our free institutions." But "the present aspect of affairs" had led him to believe a ban might "have a salutary effect in checking the immense drain of capital annually made upon us by the sale of this description of property." Legislators agreed, and they passed a law prohibiting "the business of introducing or importing Slaves into this State as merchandize or for sale." In addition to imposing a $500 fine and a prison sentence for violators, the law prospectively made "utterly void and of no effect" all contracts signed for slave sales and all debts incurred to slave traders.[63]

For a while, the law was of no consequence and was to all appearances irrelevant to Ballard and his partners, as they were no longer trading in slaves by the spring of 1837. But then some slaveholders started arguing that the law retroactively nullified every purchase from a slave trader made in Mississippi since May 1833, the constitutional implementation date for the ban, and that they did not have to pay their debts at all. It was a creative construction of a law that explicitly applied only to deals made "after the passage of this act." Yet local and state judges were sympathetic to the claim, and when Mississippi federal district court judge Samuel Gholson upheld it late in 1839 in the case of *Hickman v. Rose*, Ballard had a huge problem on his hands.[64]

Natchez papers reported, perhaps with intentional understatement, that the *Hickman* "decision must, of necessity, have an important bearing on Mississippi debts to northern negro traders, to the amount of at least *two millions of dollars*." Equivalent to more than $55 million today if accounting for inflation alone, the debt would correlate now to around $25 billion if measured relative to total national economic output. Franklin, Armfield, and Ballard held between 10 and 20 percent of that debt, and once the leanings of the courts became clear, debtors started resisting Ballard's collection pressures. Some insisted he back off "or else Judge Gholson must decide." Some just let him sue. Within months, Ballard had suits on more than $50,000 in collections tied up in courts that did not seem inclined in his favor.[65]

Reading about the *Hickman* decision in Richmond, Bacon Tait predicted that "the constitutionality of the Missi[ssippi] law" would "be made a question before the Supreme Court" and that the issues involved could ignite a political firestorm. Indeed they did. In 1835 and 1836, Robert Slaughter, a Louisiana resident, had brought slaves into Mississippi and sold them in Natchez, in exchange for promissory notes on which Moses Groves was an endorser. The purchaser eventually proved unable to pay, and Groves refused to do so in his stead, claiming that Mississippi law made the sale illegal. Lawsuits and appeals ensued, and the United States Supreme Court, led by Chief Justice Roger Taney, took up the case of *Groves v. Slaughter* in February 1841. When it did, elite women in Washington City filled the courtroom for a week straight, and senators and congressmen left their chambers to catch a glimpse of the proceedings. For the first time in American history, the Court would consider what government authority existed to regulate the domestic slave trade and which governments possessed it.[66]

One Natchez lawyer remembered that Ballard and his partners had "a deep interest in the decision of the questions of law involved in the case." Those questions related mostly to whether individual states might exercise regulatory authority over interstate commerce, a power that the Constitution seemed to grant exclusively to Congress, and whether the interstate slave trade in particular fell within the regulatory purview of anyone. In truth, Ballard and his partners were interested less in matters of slavery and federalism than in "several very large claims" they had on debtors "which involved the same legal questions." Given their enormous financial stake in the outcome of *Groves*, they were taking no chances. A month before oral arguments began, Ballard offered to help Robert Slaughter hire the best counsel money could buy. Unlike Armfield and Franklin, Ballard was a Whig, and he thought no one in the country had finer legal chops and political connections than Senator Henry Clay. Clay agreed to take the case for $5,000. Ballard contributed $4,000 of the fee himself.[67]

Robert Slaughter's legal team included not only Henry Clay but also Daniel Webster, Clay's senatorial colleague from Massachusetts and a fellow Whig Party titan. Webster, like Clay, was also one of the most recognized orators and accomplished lawyers in the country, and Walter Jones, a third lawyer working the case for Slaughter, described the pair in his presentation before the Court as "the Ajax and Achilles of the Bar." Not to be outdone, Moses Groves brought legal highfliers of his own, represented as he was by Mississippi Democratic senator Robert Walker and sitting United States Attorney General Henry Gilpin.[68]

While delivering as political spectacle, *Groves* underwhelmed as legal precedent. One justice fell ill. A second died before the decision was issued. Two others dissented from the majority, and three issued concurring opinions whose underlying reasoning varied with respect to the power of individual states to regulate the slave trade. Ultimately, the Court ruled 5–2 in favor of Robert Slaughter, on narrow grounds—namely, that Mississippi's import ban "required legislative action to bring it into complete operation" and had therefore been inoperative before the spring of 1837. Justice Smith Thompson, writing the opinion for the Court, conceded that he and the other justices in the majority had punted on the larger and more inflammatory issue of whether the import ban was "repugnant to the constitution of the United States."[69]

Nevertheless, evading questions about the constitutional legitimacy of the import ban made the *Groves* decision functionally proslavery, as the justices refused to affirm clear federal authority over commerce crossing state lines when it came to commerce in enslaved people. Moreover, *Groves* delivered Robert Slaughter, Rice Ballard, and their fellow slave traders all they really needed, which was support for the validity of their sales and the sanctity of their debts. The federal government proved a friend to the trade once again. Bacon Tait, who had been helping John Armfield with legal research and consultations in Virginia, congratulated Ballard after the decision came down. He heard that when the news arrived in Natchez, Isaac Franklin "struck up the tune of 'long time ago,'" a popular ballad, "and that Mr. Armfield and yourself joined in the chorus." Ballard's joy was understandable, as Tait felt certain that the *Groves* decision meant "the clouds which have so long darkened the horizon of your fortunes have passed away and the sunshine of prosperity is shedding its genial influence upon you."[70]

In fact, *Groves* did not magically fix the financial exigencies of Ballard and his partners. Conditions in the lower South were still dreadful. From New Orleans, Ballard's merchants kept sending letters reporting weak cotton markets, rumors of widespread bankruptcy, "general panic," and "want of confidence." In Mississippi, legislative action could not stop economic collapse. The state repudiated its debts in 1842, money from Mississippi banks was being discounted by nearly 50 percent even before then, and Ballard found that collections remained no sure thing. He put what Armfield considered "a large amount of his paper in suit" after *Groves*. But Mississippi courts often refused to be bound by it, forcing Ballard either to wait out long and expensive lawsuits and appeals he might lose or to compromise with debtors and get what he could. Following the path of least resistance netted some money, but one of Ballard's lawyers estimated that he compromised away at least $40,000. Ballard was so exasperated by the uncertainty that he tried stiffing Henry Clay on his fee, because by his lights *Groves* had not "settle[d] <u>fully</u> the question involved."[71]

Still, the partners acquired faith enough in their position to agree that the bulk of their shared dealings was behind them and that the moment had come to close their business formally. Before a

Natchez justice of the peace on November 10, 1841, Isaac Franklin, John Armfield, and Rice Ballard dissolved the partnership "trading under the name, firm, and style of Ballard, Franklin, & Co." In light of Ballard's struggles, Armfield assumed responsibility for "the unsettled business of said concern." He was authorized to pay, collect, and resolve any debts, handle all legal matters, "sell the remaining property of said firm for a fair and full price," and disburse to Franklin and Ballard "their proportion of all funds, which come to his hands," until he deemed it time to make a "final settlement." Over the next eighteen months, Armfield tied up loose company ends in Natchez and New Orleans, and by avoiding lawsuits when possible and negotiating more tactfully than Ballard had, he was able to claim in March 1843 that he had "settled nearly all the claims due to the firm . . . without much loss."[72]

The years after the Panic of 1837 appeared to bring Franklin, Armfield, and Ballard closer than ever. They saw each other more and sometimes vacationed together. They delighted together in Franklin's and Ballard's marriages and in the births of Franklin's daughter, Victoria, in March 1840 and Ballard's daughter, Ella, a year later. Ballard's teenage niece visited the Armfields nearly every week at their Alexandria home while she went to school in the city, and the Ballards were missed when they were unable to attend the marriage of one of Franklin's relatives in Tennessee. "We would have enjoyed the wedding much more if you and Mr. B had been present," Martha Armfield wrote Louisa Ballard. Hoping "we shall all meet safely in Natchez soon," she passed along that Adelicia Franklin missed them too. "Ade," she wrote, "is wanting us all to go down to the plantation" in West Feliciana Parish "and remain some weeks."[73]

Above all else, Franklin, Armfield, and Ballard had to overcome or be defeated by their shared financial travails as one. But money had created friction among them before, and shuttering Ballard Franklin and Company did not happen without incident.

When it was over, Ballard and Armfield in particular decided they were about through with one another and that, both professionally and personally, the time had come to go their separate ways.

Debts the size of Henry Turner's could make people feel like that. Late in 1835, Turner bought twenty-two enslaved men and twenty enslaved women at the Forks of the Road, paying Ballard almost $50,000 with a promissory note due in one year. Turner and Ballard agreed that the note could be renewed on request and that an annual interest rate of 10 percent would accrue until it was paid. Turner and his brother and business partner, Fielding Turner, intended the enslaved for Dulac, a plantation they operated in Terrebonne Parish, Louisiana. Southwest of New Orleans, on the Gulf of Mexico, Terrebonne was a place where enslaved people died at a rapid clip as they toiled to produce cotton and sugar, and soon Turner was back. In November 1836, he bought another twenty-four people from Ballard, again on credit, this time for just over $25,000.[74]

Terrebonne Parish was closer to New Orleans than Natchez, but the Turners also had holdings in Mississippi and they were often in Natchez visiting their sister Eliza. She lived at Monmouth, a cotton plantation adjacent to the Forks of the Road owned by her husband, John Quitman, a lawyer and militia leader who had served as a state legislator and briefly as governor. Ballard knew Quitman, and that association, along with Ballard's experience and reputation in the trade, led Henry Turner to believe Ballard's "promise to him to send first-rate hands." Always a salesman, Ballard said he "considered himself bound to send none but the best."[75]

Over the next several years, Ballard and Turner built a cordial and even friendly relationship. Ballard renewed Turner's notes without difficulty, assured Turner that he "would never distress" him for payment, and made small personal loans when Turner asked for them. But interest on Turner's debt accumulated, to the point where it amounted to more than $100,000 and was by far the largest debt outstanding to Ballard Franklin and Company. It was so large that neither Franklin nor Armfield felt comfortable with the risk to which it exposed the company, so they assigned it to Ballard for collection.[76]

As the debt ballooned, Ballard stood to profit handsomely. Then the *Hickman* decision came down, and his nerves were shaken. Wanting to have Turner's debt "arranged so as to secure him from all uneasiness," Ballard asked Turner to bolster it with a mortgage. Turner refused, so Ballard proposed that Turner "give up the original Bill of Sale." They could then "cross the Mississippi and pass a new Bill of Sale in Louisiana, which would take the matter out of the jurisdiction of the Mississippi courts." It was a dodge familiar to those who tried to bypass state slave-trading bans, and one that would let Ballard "feel safe." But Turner did not want to do that either. Sensing that Turner was hedging, perhaps with an eye toward shirking what he owed, Ballard sued in federal court in the spring of 1841 for payment on Turner's notes, along with hundreds of thousands in damages.[77]

Initially confident of victory, Ballard became unsure when he saw courts sometimes disregarding the *Groves* decision. He came to realize he might lose at trial, and while he knew he could probably recover some of what he was owed in a chancery court, which ruled on equity rather than statute, he and Turner compromised instead. In November 1842, Ballard agreed to take back the enslaved people he had sold to Turner, with Turner offering replacements for those who had died, receiving credit toward his debt for children who had been born and for "unsoundness or defects," and paying what remained in installments, with interest. In the end, Turner uprooted whoever suited his needs. He sent some people back, found people he considered interchangeable substitutions for others, and owed Ballard a debt of nearly $75,000 that he did not discharge entirely until 1857.[78]

Rice Ballard's dealings with Henry Turner probably cost him money. They definitely cost him friendships. Bacon Tait had sensed for some time that Ballard only corresponded with him when he needed something, and when Ballard asked for information "concerning certain Mississippi matters," he was fed up. Tait knew "highly valuable" things about the Turner case, but if Ballard wanted them, it was going to cost him. "I am not disposed for any thing like the paltry considerations heretofore received to say further on the subject," Tait sniffed, "much less am I disposed to impart such information gratuitously." Ballard had also invited Tait to visit him in Mississippi, but Tait considered the offer patronizing. Ballard had taken on airs over the years, and "like all other wealthy fellows," Tait wrote, "you seem to forget that poor folks like myself cannot make visits which cost money."[79]

Ballard's friendship with Turner collapsed too. Enraged at having to sue to recover his debt, Ballard bad-mouthed Turner all over Natchez. Turner was told that Ballard "used his influence every where to make people believe that I had acted in a dishonest way" and had even "formed a determination to assassinate me." After proclaiming "his intention to that effect to many gentlemen in the City Hotel," Ballard went to meet Turner and Quitman, "armed up to the teeth," saying on his return that he had held off once Quitman promised "that his claims should be satisfied" and intimating that Turner and Quitman "were afraid of him." Tempers cooled enough to work through the legal matters at play, but Turner had to be dissuaded from challenging Ballard to a duel, and he could not be moved from his belief that "the rascal ought to be severely punished."[80]

Whether or not Ballard's threats were bluster, he was stunned to discover Turner had heard about his conduct from John Armfield, who had run into Turner while traveling and related everything Ballard had been up to, even promising that "if Ballard denied" what he said, "he would publish him as a liar." When Ballard later confronted Armfield in Natchez about it, he encountered Armfield's ferocious temper. Appearing now and then in the archive, it was more than a match for Ballard's own. Armfield, in fact, was too angry to speak. He preferred to put his sentiments in writing, snarling in a letter later in the day that he would not be debating "whether I have or have not spoke disrespectfully of you." Armfield would just be "stating the facts."[81]

Part of Armfield's fury came from his sense that Ballard had "willfully misrepresented Henry Turner's contract" and "unjustly injured that man." But Armfield's problem with Ballard was really about what Armfield considered a recent pattern of deceitful and self-serving behavior. Armfield had spent a career building a personal and corporate reputation among white people for honesty and decency that, deserved or not, Ballard had been systematically undermining to preserve his own standing. "You have to some extent injured evry person with whom you have Bin connected," Armfield wrote, and while it was damaging enough that "you have entirely injured and Badly treated several persons that owed the firm and you individually," worse still was Ballard's betrayal of his own partners. "When with me and Franklin you would agree to certain measures and when Behind our Backs you would tell our debtors that you done all you could for them But that me and Franklin would Ruin evry person that we could."

Ballard was one to "make a grate parade about Honor Honesty &c." But Armfield reminded him that he knew who he really was, pointing out, for example, his sham "purchase" of Silas Lillard's property. Now Ballard wanted to know what Armfield had said about him, so Armfield would tell him. "I have stated that your conduct Has Bin that of a Infant a Liar and a Rascal." Ballard was welcome to "make another inquiry" if he had heard Armfield said anything else, but there was really nothing more to say. They were finished.[82]

The American economy finally found its bearings and achieved some genuine recovery by the mid-1840s. John Armfield's relationship with Rice Ballard did not. Neither did Isaac Franklin's. The bond between Armfield and Franklin, more ardent and older than the one either man shared with Ballard, endured and was cherished by both men. But their connections to Ballard frayed with their business ties. Drifting apart, they pursued different ends.

In October 1841, Ballard paid $35,000 for 341 acres of land east of Louisville, on the waters of Beargrass Creek, along the south side of the turnpike connecting the city to the Kentucky capital of Frankfort. It was an expensive property, and Ballard intended it less as a site of economic production than as a place to lavish his wealth. He made the dozen or so people he enslaved there grow some hemp for market, but mostly they tended horses and cows, and ministered to the wants of his wife and daughter. Ballard himself did not anticipate being around much. Stashing Louisa and Ella in Kentucky, he returned to Mississippi. He would be back in the summer. In the meantime, he had plans for his next career.[83]

Ballard's experience in selecting enslaved people for forced labor was unparalleled, and by the early 1840s, he also had considerable expertise in assessing land values, managing cotton production, and working with merchants to sell the crop on the global market. Combining those skills, he began buying real estate, boosting his personal slaveholding, and running plantations. And he found a new partner to share costs, risks, and responsibilities. Born in 1807 in Portland, Maine, Samuel Stillman Boyd graduated from Bowdoin College and studied law in Cincinnati. In the early 1830s, he moved to Mississippi and married Catherine Wilkins, the daughter of a Natchez merchant, banker, and cotton planter. Boyd started a law practice with a former Mississippi Supreme Court justice named Alexander Montgomery, bought the Arlington plantation neighboring John Quitman's Monmouth, and was already wealthy and well-connected when he met Rice Ballard in 1838 and began representing him, Isaac Franklin, and John Armfield in their many post-panic Mississippi lawsuits.[84]

In December 1842, shortly after Ballard resolved his conflict with Henry Turner, he and Boyd bought the twenty-one-hundred-acre Magnolia plantation from the estate of Alexander McNeill, along with twenty-three people McNeill had enslaved on the property. Located in Warren County, south of Vicksburg, it was a spot Ballard knew well. He had invested in the operation before McNeill's death, and Isaac Franklin had sold McNeill some of the people enslaved there.[85]

Henry Watson knew Magnolia too, and he knew it was a bad place on a landscape filled with bad places. He survived six years there after being trafficked as a child from Richmond to Natchez and purchased by McNeill, and among the innumerable horrors he remembered were the stocks McNeill had scattered across the property. Designed "for the torture of slaves," who would be locked in place and flogged hundreds of times for shortfalls in "the number of pounds of cotton" expected, for some "trivial offence," or simply for the drunken overseer's entertainment, the stocks were surely still there when Magnolia got sold. Ballard and Boyd probably left them in place, at least long enough so the dozens of additional enslaved people they brought could see them. Because Ballard and Boyd understood, as Watson did, that fear was how one got men, women, and children to pick up to ten thousand pounds of cotton daily during the harvest, from before dawn till after dark, six days a week, for months on end.[86]

In 1845, Ballard divested himself of his remaining interests in Virginia, selling his Richmond jail to James Young, the onetime keeper of the Farmers' Hotel that Ballard had frequented in Fredericksburg. Then Ballard and Boyd bought more land in Mississippi. Comprising multiple tracts straddling Warren County and its southern neighbor, Claiborne County, the land would be combined into a new property they called Karnac. For decades, Ballard had led a life practically defined by its lack of rootedness. Now he moved into the landed gentry of the lower South, turning the wealth he had extracted from Black people into more Black people and into fields that would make him richer still.[87]

John Armfield also left Virginia for good in the mid-1840s, though he had to negotiate tensions in his marriage first. Like her husband, Martha Armfield had, by her own admission, a "temper & other bad propensities" and trouble controlling them, to the point where they sometimes "frightened" her. That she and John Armfield had no children surely contributed to her anger, as did the harrowing end of one pregnancy she does seem to have had. George Henry, an enslaved boatman who worked Maryland and Virginia ports, wrote about it decades later, remembering that Martha Armfield gave birth to "twins, a girl and a boy." Their skin "as black as lamp-black," they were conjoined by "a fine link chain" of flesh that a doctor had to cut, resulting in the death of both infants. "The circumstance," Henry recalled, "was shut out from the public, so that it did not get into the papers."[88]

Henry often saw John Armfield's ships at the Alexandria wharves, and he saw the people in Armfield's coffles, "chained together" and "screaming and crying" as they marched through Washington City on their way to Duke Street. In his mind, what happened to Armfield's twins was "a judgement sent upon him from the Almighty," a punishment of seeing his own "black" children enchained and taken from him by forces beyond his control. If so, the punishment was exacting. The Armfields had been John Sanderson's guardian for several years, they had looked after Martha's younger brother, John W. Franklin, in the 1830s when he attended a Quaker school in Alexandria, and in the early 1840s they took in Smith Franklin's ten-year-old daughter, Jane. They were devoted to them all, but those children were still someone else's children. The story George Henry told had metaphorical power, but if anything like it happened at all, it left a lingering sorrow.[89]

Martha Armfield endured her heartaches while her husband traveled, and her closest relatives were in Tennessee, but the agreeable situation she and John Armfield had in Alexandria was at least some consolation. Their mansion on Prince Street, set amid flower and vegetable gardens, had fifteen large rooms "well arranged for comfort and convenience." Two ranges of outbuildings, extending away from the main house, contained matching bathing and dressing rooms, a greenhouse, and living quarters for servants and slaves. John Armfield was respected in the city and known to bear a "general character" for "nobleness," and Martha Armfield had an extensive social circle and was deeply committed to the Episcopal Church, regularly bringing her heavily annotated Bible with her to worship.[90]

So when John Armfield told his wife in the summer of 1844 that they would leave Alexandria "& not return," Martha refused, confiding to Adelicia Franklin that she would not go unless "Mr. A made some alteration that I know is necessary to my peace & happiness." Her meaning is unclear, but it was rooted in conflict at least a year in the making, and John Armfield did what she asked, as Martha wrote to Adelicia in September "that all is explained & adjusted." Whatever had happened, "Mr. A has assured me that he is sorry for the past, & I must say has done every thing to have me reconciled." Martha was ready to move, and while she knew she could be challenging, she hoped Adelicia would "check me & point out my defects." There would be ample opportunity. Martha was returning to Sumner County.[91]

It remained to be seen how much time John Armfield would spend with her. When he advertised that he was selling the Alexandria mansion, he explained it was because he found himself "compelled to spend the greater part of my time in the South." He meant he would be in Louisiana and Mississippi, and it was only in small measure because there were details of the slave-trade business still to resolve. He went to the lower South because Isaac Franklin would be there, and Franklin needed his help.[92]

Though retired from the slave trade, Franklin was incapable of really slowing down. He directed some of his energies to Fairvue,

Isaac Franklin, in a second Washington Cooper portrait made sometime around 1844. Courtesy Belmont Mansion

amplifying its already matchless opulence. He added housing for the growing number of people he enslaved on the property, and he had a new wing projected off the south side of the mansion, a long two-story brick loggia reflecting the influence of the Spanish architecture he admired in New Orleans. Outfitted with arched windows and set slightly lower than the main house, it held guest bedrooms and entertainment space for parties where Franklin was known to share his "fine stock of liquors." Franklin became an officer of the Gallatin Race Club and bought a stake in the Nashville Racecourse, and Adelicia was a proficient rider, so Franklin laid out a practice racetrack for over a dozen thoroughbreds he kept in a new training stable. He planted an orchard and embellished the gardens, and he built a playhouse for Victoria and her sister, called Adelicia after her mother, who was born in the spring of 1842.[93]

Franklin also widened his range of investments. He acquired shares in the Gallatin and Nashville Turnpike Company, and he put money into a certificate of deposit with a Nashville insurance company. He bought stock in the Commercial Bank of Manchester, Mississippi, and he purchased nearly twenty-five thousand acres of land and a half interest in another fifteen thousand or so in the Republic of Texas, which broke away from Mexico in 1836 and became the new southwestern edge of American slave and cotton imperial expansion.[94]

Franklin's West Feliciana Parish property, meanwhile, continued drawing an inordinate amount of attention. By the early 1840s, with his landholdings there having grown to more than eighty-three hundred acres, he devised plans for turning the place into a profitable venture, and maybe even a place where he would want to spend more time. First and foremost, he bought and imported to the property hundreds of enslaved people, more than doubling the number he and Francis Routh had enslaved. Soon, Franklin held nearly five hundred people in bondage in Louisiana, some of whom were to be put onto roughly thirty-three hundred undeveloped acres divided into three new plantations. Franklin called them Panola, Loango, and Angola.[95]

"Panola" was the Choctaw word for cotton, and Loango and Angola were regions in west and central Africa from which Europeans took several million people to serve as slaves in the Americas. The monikers were unusual ones for plantations, and it has become conventional wisdom that Franklin named Angola in particular as a nod to the place of origin of those he enslaved on the property. There is no evidence for the claim, and it is almost certainly untrue. None of the people Franklin enslaved had African names, and most were too young to have been born in Africa during the era of legal transatlantic traffic. The names Franklin gave his plantations were not gestures toward the people he enslaved there. They were ways of inserting himself into the global history of the industries that had made him his fortune. Franklin was gloating about the international trades in Black people and the most lucrative crop they produced, asserting a right to take the ancestral languages and words of those whose land he held and whose bodies he exploited, and claim them as his own.[96]

Angola was, however, the first of the new plantations to which Franklin began making improvements. He installed 104 enslaved people there and had them perform the grueling work of clearing a swampy cypress forest. Then he opened a woodyard with a steam-driven sawmill, and he began selling timber and lumber. Franklin built a gristmill at Angola too, and there and elsewhere he ordered an array of new machinery, upgrades, and maintenance: a ginhouse and cotton press at Lochlomond, a stable and corncrib at Killarney, extensive ditching, miles of plank fencing, half a dozen cisterns, a levee across a bayou, housing for slaves and overseers, a new barn, sheds and storehouses, an enormous signal bell forged at a Pittsburgh foundry, a corn crusher, a hospital, a cookhouse. Several hundred head of cattle, over one hundred sheep, and 650 hogs grazed and foraged the grounds. Franklin harvested and sold Spanish moss from the trees, and he considered trying to grow sugarcane. But the thousands of acres suitable for cultivation were planted mostly in cotton and corn, with foodstuffs for animals and enslaved people supplemented by grain and meat from Fairvue and by corn and pork and bacon from merchants in Nashville, New Orleans, and Cincinnati.[97]

Yet even as Franklin's efforts were personally satisfying and increased the value of his land, aggravations remained. In the fall of 1838, he had had to evict Francis Routh and his family, who refused to evacuate even after Franklin had given them slaves, farm animals, and money in exchange for their agreeing to do so. Other white squatters were people he believed "owed him ill-will enough to destroy the premises," and they were so stubborn a presence on a section of Angola Franklin called "Thieves' Harbor" that he paid them $5,000 just to get them to leave. Clearing acres for cultivation, meanwhile, was tremendously expensive, and the enslaved people forced to do it were restive. Over and over again, they ran away or were lured off by white people. They also routinely fell ill, entailing frequent visits from doctors and considerable medical bills. Sometimes they died.[98]

Franklin did like spending winters in New Orleans, where he and Adelicia stayed for weeks at a time at the St. Charles Exchange Hotel. Opened in 1837 a few blocks off the Mississippi in the American sector of the city, upriver from the French Quarter, the hotel was one of the most ornate and luxurious in the country. It was also a place where Franklin could conduct business, talk politics, observe the state of his old vocation, and see former colleagues. If they were not at the slave auctions held in the large basement-level octagonal hotel bar, they might be across the street, where there was a showroom and a large pen surrounded by a high brick wall. After the city council created regulations and a licensing system for "vendors of slaves" in 1841, enslaved people were imprisoned, displayed, sold, and auctioned there as well.[99]

But when Franklin and his family visited West Feliciana Parish, they had to stay in the house Francis Routh built at Bellevue. Made of logs and clapboard framing, it was sizable, and Franklin furnished it "with every requisite comfort or amusement." Still, it was old and unremarkable, and it did "not compare in elegance and quality with . . . the Fairvue place." Portions of the house were falling into disrepair, and Franklin often talked about letting it decay and building a "fine residence" on another site instead.[100]

For every person Franklin told of being "proud of his estate" and wanting it to be an inheritance for his children, he told another that he wished "he could sell his Louisiana property" and "wind up his business in the South, so that he could stay more at home" in Tennessee. His health was a big reason why. Anyone could see that his habitual complaints about its worsening were more than just crankiness. A second portrait made by Washington Cooper sometime around 1844 shows that Franklin's physical appearance had deteriorated in the decade or so since Cooper had first painted his likeness. Franklin had shaved his sideburns, revealing a face that was less fleshy, his chin coming to more of a point and his cheeks looking a bit hollowed out. His hair remained unruly, but it was graying around the temples and it had thinned, uncovering a slight widow's peak. The skin under Franklin's eyes sagged noticeably, and the weariness in them was unmistakable. Isaac Franklin's colleagues had called him "the old man" for decades, and he had felt like one for years. At long last, he had come to look the part.[101]

On January 24, 1844, Adelicia Franklin gave birth to a son named Julius Caesar Franklin. He died the next day after surviving for just thirteen hours. Even for a woman accustomed to loss, it was a devastating blow, and it was crushing for her husband, whose fervid desire for a male heir was evinced by the conceit of his son's name. The death also reinforced Isaac Franklin's sense that his days were better spent with his wife and children than with his Louisiana plantations. When John Armfield arrived in the lower South some months later, Franklin saw a possible lifeline, telling an employee "that he wanted to get Mr. Armfield hooked in" on the Louisiana property, "so that he might put the trouble on him."[102]

Armfield was not persuaded. But his presence heartened Franklin and somewhat eased his mind. Late in 1844, Franklin thrilled at the election of James Polk, whose presidential candidacy he had enthusiastically supported. He rejoiced too at the birth of his daughter Emma, and he celebrated the winter of 1845 as an extended family affair, with the Franklins, their three daughters, and Adelicia's younger sister Laura living together in New Orleans with the Armfields in a three-story rental house on Canal Street.[103]

While John Armfield was in the lower South, he sold the old company compound at the Forks of the Road to a slave trader named John O'Ferrall, and from a distance he finalized the sale to George Kephart of the Duke Street compound in Alexandria. Isaac Franklin went to polka lessons with his sister-in-law, managed his investments, grouched at reports of "trouble" caused by slave resistance at Fairvue, and finally got serious about designing a new house at Bellevue. If he had to keep the plantations in West Feliciana, he

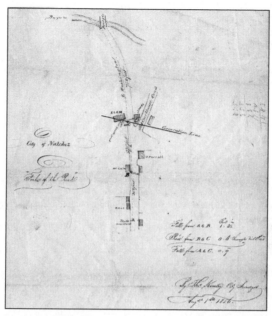

The Forks of the Road slave market in Natchez, Mississippi, as sketched by the city surveyor Thomas Kenny in 1856. In the 1830s, Isaac Franklin operated a two-acre trading facility that included the building marked "O. Ferrall" and perhaps the building beyond the marked corporation line to the right of Old Courthouse Road. Courtesy of the Archives and Records Services Division, Mississippi Department of Archives and History.

would pass winters there in the style to which he and his family were accustomed, telling the general agent on the property, James Clack, that the house would be "something very handsome" and that he would have "private tutors there for his children."[104]

The house was one thing Franklin's slaves would never build for him, no matter what he did. On April 20, 1846, as Franklin prepared to leave New Orleans and return to Tennessee for the summer, his stomach started acting up again. It was a recurring problem, and he "took some little medicine" for it. Perhaps it was the "Compound, Alterative, Anti-Dyspeptic Tonic" for which he had provided a testimonial in a Nashville newspaper, swearing it helped his "Dyspepsia and general debility of the digestive organs and liver." In a couple of days, he felt somewhat better, and he and his family took a steamboat up the Mississippi River, stopping in West Feliciana Parish for a last look at Franklin's property before heading back to Fairvue.[105]

Franklin spent some time going "round his plantations," but the pain nagged and got progressively worse. On April 25, he "took to his bed." Adelicia sent word to John Armfield, who was still in New Orleans, and to Lucas Gee, a doctor who attended the people Franklin enslaved, that they needed to come immediately. They both got to Bellevue on Monday, April 27. But they were too late. Isaac Franklin had died, in a rundown house, badly in need of repair, that probably should have been torn down altogether. He was a month short of his fifty-seventh birthday. Dr. Gee "pronounced it a case of congestion of the stomach."[106]

Armfield wrote to John Lobdell, Franklin's personal lawyer, and to Oliver Hayes to tell them the news. He ordered a winding sheet, yards of black cloth and lace, and a lead-lined mahogany coffin. He procured three barrels of whiskey to preserve the body, and on May 24, he watched as Franklin's alcohol-soaked corpse was loaded onto the steamboat *Tennessee*. Three days later, Armfield, Adelicia Franklin, her daughters, and her father arrived at the Nashville landing, accompanied by ten slaves they brought to serve them on the way. The funeral company of McCombs and Carson brought Isaac Franklin's remains by wagon from Nashville to Fairvue. A crew of enslaved people interred him there, in keeping with his wishes, on May 29, 1846.[107]

SEVEN

LEGACIES, 1846–1871

Isaac Franklin's death was national news reported by papers in nearly every state in the country and the District of Columbia. In part, that was because Franklin was enormously rich, and it was always news when a rich man died. It took a parish judge, four attorneys, and two appraisers three days of "excessive hard work" just to take an initial inventory of what Franklin owned in West Feliciana Parish, and a second inventory found additional Louisiana assets. When they were combined with his various investments and his holdings in Tennessee and Texas, Franklin's estate was valued at nearly $710,000. One obituary writer asserted the estate was "estimated considerably below its real value" and claimed Franklin actually possessed "a fortune exceeding a million of dollars." But even the legal valuation made him one of the wealthiest men in the United States. Adjusted for inflation alone, Franklin was worth around $24 million when he died. Adjusted relative to the distribution of wealth in the country at the time, Isaac Franklin died possessing the modern equivalent of more than $435 million.[1]

Over $300,000 of Franklin's estate was embodied in 636 people he enslaved. His obituaries never mentioned that, framing Franklin's life instead as that of a self-made man. In this telling, Franklin was born to sturdy "Tennessee pioneers" who started their married lives "slenderly provided with this world's wealth." Franklin's father "became entitled to" his land through military service, protecting America's frontier settlements from Indians, and Isaac Franklin spent his youth "in the usual way," working "on his father's farm." But Franklin showed "activity and intelligence" that recommended him to his older brothers for a position alongside them on flatboats, where as a teenager he undertook "momentous expedition[s]" to and from New Orleans. Filled with "perilous adventure," those voyages "laid the foundation of his fortune," not so much "by the acquisition of property" as "by gaining, that acquaintance with the world, that perseverance and steadiness of purpose, and that address and tact, in the management of business, for which he became afterwards so remarkable." It was the kind of story white Americans liked to tell about themselves.[2]

Impressing the nation's editors most of all, however, was a "munificent bequest" in Franklin's will. Franklin left some money to his brothers William and James, and to two nephews, a grandnephew, and the son of a family friend who were all named after him. He left instructions for the future of the West Feliciana plantations, and he ordered that a mausoleum be constructed at Fairvue for himself and his family. He left Fairvue itself, and the use of the people enslaved there, to Adelicia so long as she remained a widow, along with as much money as she considered "necessary for the support of herself and my children." If Adelicia remarried, Fairvue would revert back to the estate and Adelicia would receive her choice of $100,000 or an annuity of $6,000 for as long as she lived. Franklin's children were to receive two-thirds of his Louisiana properties when they reached adulthood. But the other third, along with any money the estate had left and any revenues it generated, was to be used to build "an academy or seminary" on the grounds of Fairvue. Envisioned chiefly as a place for Franklin's children, his nieces and nephews, and their descendants to receive "a substantial and good English education," he also wanted "poor children" from Sumner County and elsewhere to "be educated and supported" there, subsidized by his estate in perpetuity.[3]

The magnanimity of the endowment prompted rhapsodic public tributes describing Franklin as someone who, had he lived in classical times, would have been the subject "of the far-famed lyric poets" and "embalmed for immortality in the living pages of Thucydides, or Livy, or Tacitus." Franklin was the rare wealthy man who looked toward "nobler ends than the selfish aggrandizement of a single family." Seeing "the vast importance of the general diffusion of knowledge among the people," he refused to make "money-getting the end of his existence," having instead the "grand object in view" of doing something "for the benefit of the whole human race." A philanthropist of "truly glorious and christian benevolence" and a man whose virtues were "resplendent as a sun beam—enduring as the laws of the universe," Franklin's generosity ensured that memories of his life would be "snatched from the oblivion that so soon shrouds the name of ordinary mortals."[4]

Anyone who stopped to think about it would realize that a white Tennessean with so large a fortune could only have earned it on the backs of the enslaved, but some were stunned nonetheless when they eventually discovered who Isaac Franklin had been. At the New York *Tribune*, antislavery editor Horace Greeley wrote early in 1847 that he had not been aware when he published one of the many encomiums to Franklin that he was praising "the famous dealer in human flesh, whose name has so long been familiar throughout the country in connection with the firm of Franklin & Armfield." Now that he knew, he could not understand the eulogies he had seen. After all, he had "often been assured" that white southerners regarded slave traders "with disgust and abhorrence." Yet Franklin "amassed an immense fortune in buying and selling the bodies and souls of his fellow men" and "left the world without one expression of regret, still less of penitence, for his life of villainy." If men like him could "get to Heaven by relinquishing at death a portion of their ill-gotten wealth," then it seemed "hardly fair to exclude anybody, however corrupt or wicked, from that happy place."[5]

There was more to the story of Franklin's will than the way its public reception exposed empty white southern claims that they scorned slave traders. Franklin had actually reconsidered his plan to endow a school, and although he never formally abandoned the project, he often "expressed his intention to alter" his will, "especially in reference to the academy clause," in the year before he died. Contrary to what some saw as his altruistic resistance to entrenching generational wealth in the hands of his family, he thought he might just give everything to his wife and children after all. Moreover, William and James Franklin, named in the will as the school trustees, refused initially to "accept or execute the trust" altogether, "viewing it as rather an Utopian affair." The Tennessee legislature did incorporate the "Isaac Franklin Institute" late in 1847. But the school would never be built, and the money set aside for it would never materialize. Isaac Franklin would not be remembered as a patron of education for the poor.[6]

In some ways, the slave trade moved on without Isaac Franklin, John Armfield, and Rice Ballard. Rebounding as the broader American economy rebounded from the trough of depression, the slave-trading business by the 1850s was more robust than it had been in a generation. Slave traders and slaveholders took a quarter of a million enslaved people across state lines that decade, a 35 percent increase from the 1840s and nearly as many as in the boom years of the 1830s.

Three-quarters of the enslaved forced into the trade in the 1850s still came from Maryland, Virginia, and the Carolinas, but American slavery's movement away from the Atlantic was relentless. Slaveholders from Kentucky, which had already become a net exporter of the enslaved by 1830, sent over thirty thousand Black people out of the state in the 1850s, 65 percent more than they had in the 1830s or the 1840s. Tennessee became a net exporter of enslaved people as well, and even Georgia, which had been the destination of so many trafficked people in the early nineteenth century that it provided the sobriquet for the first generation of professional traders, started sending away more Black people than it took in.[7]

Slaveholders in Mississippi and Louisiana remained ravenous for enslaved laborers, but slavery's steady southwestward drift made Texas, which was annexed to the United States as a slave state in 1845, the new leading destination for forced migrants. Slaveholders brought nearly one hundred thousand enslaved people to Texas in the 1850s. Trafficked by land across the Louisiana border and by sea into the port of Galveston, they were more than twice as many as were imported to Mississippi and almost four times as many as were imported to Louisiana. Slave traders found bustling markets where the cotton economy had spilled across the Mississippi River into Arkansas too. The state had joined the Union in 1836, and in the 1850s, it imported nearly as many enslaved people as Mississippi, yielding a 457 percent increase in its enslaved population from 1840 to 1860. Many southern politicians and newspaper editors in the 1850s even boasted about a prospective hemispheric empire of slavery, with American markets for Black people that would extend into the Caribbean, through Mexico, and across Central and South America.[8]

Such visions were rooted partially in the arrogance wrought by slave prices, which rebounded with sales markets and began a dizzying climb. While cotton prices stabilized and then teetered between about eight and eleven cents per pound for most of the 1850s, prices for the enslaved became completely delinked from cotton and sky-rocketed upward. Such a surge in prices had happened briefly before, prior to the Panic of 1837, but the price increase in the 1850s, nearly continuous for an entire decade, was more precipitous and durable than any in American history. Sales prices in New Orleans doubled during the 1850s, reaching an average of about $1,800 for young en-slaved men. Adjusted for inflation, that was over 50 percent higher than its equivalent even at the peak of the 1830s spree. Prices rose in the upper South too, which cut into profit margins. But hundreds of ambitious white men grasped, as always, at the chance to take a cut from delivering the labor, commodity, and speculative investment values embedded in the enslaved.[9]

Slave trading also acquired a more industrial cast in the 1850s. Abolitionists had not been wrong to think of Franklin and Arm-field's Duke Street compound as a "slave factory," a facility whose proprietors made enslaved humans into products and shipped them to customers on a massive scale. But in the 1850s, traders refashioned their operations in response to modern technologies, exploiting and helping advance a stage of American capitalist de-velopment that became practically synonymous with the rest of the nineteenth century.

Traders began transporting enslaved people by railroad, often along tracks financed by slave sales and laid by the enslaved them-selves. Nearly ten thousand railroad miles were constructed across the South in the 1840s and 1850s, and for traders, trafficking people by rail was faster and cheaper than walking a coffle overland, and it minimized losses from exhaustion, hunger, injury, and death. It lessened the risk of flight or revolt from captives chained together in smoking or baggage cars, and it required no government inspection or passage through customs. The railroad shifted the geography of the trade too, as it let traders increase their presence in interior mar-kets and enabled cities and towns with already sizable markets in human beings to achieve commanding regional positions. No place demonstrated that better than Richmond, whose combination of river and rail infrastructure helped it surpass Baltimore and Alexandria to become the leading slave-export city in the upper South by the 1850s.[10]

Traders found other efficiencies and potentialities in the telegraph. They could exchange intelligence almost instantly with partners hundreds of miles away, sharing news about market conditions and prices that took days or weeks to transmit by regular mail, and avoiding the miscommunications and information gaps that had sometimes bedeviled Franklin, Armfield, and Ballard. The telegraph let traders confirm business arrangements with bankers, merchants, and customers without necessarily meeting any of them, reducing the need for travel and in-person negotiations and ironing out uncertainties about money and deals. Business conducted by telegraph never eliminated the mutual scrutiny among trader, customer, and the enslaved that was part and parcel of slave sales. But the telegraph furthered the rationalization and abstraction of the slave trade in the 1850s. Traders began systematically sorting human merchandise into discrete categories for comparison and sale, and some compiled price data into circulars, giving potential sellers and buyers alike advance notice of what markets were likely to bear.[11]

Yet even as the slave trade moved in new directions, the mark of Franklin, Armfield, and Ballard was everywhere. That was true because it was seared into the minds and memories of the people they had trafficked from the Chesapeake and scattered across the lower Mississippi Valley. It was true because so many who worked with them and for them, who shipped captives on their brigs and stashed them in their prisons, who borrowed their money and jockeyed alongside them for customers, stayed in the trade for years, creating a sort of slave-trade business diaspora rooted in their company and its personnel. It was true because Franklin, Armfield, and Ballard laid literal foundations for several prominent trading facilities and districts. Long after they sold the Alexandria headquarters on Duke Street and the Natchez compound at the Forks of the Road, the locations remained as busy as they were infamous. The New Orleans neighborhood in the Faubourg Marigny where Isaac Franklin had been the foremost proprietor of slave showrooms and pens became a neighborhood where scores of traders offered human wares. The jail Rice Ballard owned in Richmond came to sit amid one of the densest clusters of slave-trader offices, auction houses, and jails in the upper South.[12]

Slave trader business models often bore the unmistakable imprint of Franklin, Armfield, and Ballard too. Few traders after them bought their own sailing vessels or ran their own shipping companies. But strategies and tactics that Franklin, Armfield, and Ballard deployed more consistently and effectively than anyone of their time were standard for the subsequent generation's most successful slave dealers. Their influence was there in the incessant barrage of newspaper advertising, the armies of affiliates and agents who worked nearly year-round, and the partnerships that forged links across a thousand miles between the slaveries of the upper South and the lower South. It was there in companies that depended on a steady circulation of credit and cash and bodies to stay afloat, cultivated mutually beneficial relationships with merchants and bankers throughout the country, and maintained establishments in cities with big markets. The changes wrought in the slave-trade business by the technologies of the 1840s and 1850s, in fact, also led to consolidation, reinforcing the wisdom and advantage of running large operations rooted in urban centers.[13]

The company built by Isaac Franklin, John Armfield, and Rice Ballard was the fulcrum of the domestic slave trade in nineteenth-century America. The most dominant professionals of their era, and the most dominant the trade would ever see, they took a rudimentary occupation and showed what was possible in the entrepreneurial world of buying and selling Black people for profit. Building a successful business whose range sprawled across half the country was possible. Contributing with pride to the humming economic engine of a growing nation was possible. Entry to elite social and business circles, where presidents and senators vouched for your character, was possible. Vast power, and the rush that came from controlling free people's fortunes and enslaved people's fates, was possible. Wealth enough for several lifetimes was possible. For white men in a slave country, anything was possible.

In the years after Isaac Franklin's death, that was his legacy. It was the legacy of his partners as well. John Armfield and Rice Ballard distinguished themselves in new pursuits. But neither of them really left the slave trade entirely behind. Among men of their experience, there was no such thing. The slave trade might be left behind only when slavery itself fell to pieces. Arguably, it did not even happen then.

Adelicia Franklin must have wondered what she had done to deserve what her father called her "accumulated misfortunes." On the night of Friday, June 5, 1846, still reeling from the death of her husband less than six weeks before, she noticed her daughter Adelicia had a fever. Soon the child had a barking cough and a rasp in her voice. A doctor identified the symptoms as signs of croup and offered assurances that the four-year-old was in no great danger, but her condition worsened over the weekend. By Monday morning, she was having trouble swallowing and her breathing had become labored. She died at around eleven o'clock that night, leaving her mother "almost inconsolable." There was worse to come. Victoria Franklin caught the croup as well. Three days after her younger sister, she died too. She was six years old.[14]

Oliver Hayes feared that his widowed daughter would buckle under the weight of her grief and that she could not "long survive these repeated shocks." Hayes was right to worry. But Emma

Adelicia Hayes Franklin, front row, second from right, wearing mourning attire after the deaths of Isaac Franklin and two of the couple's daughters in 1846. Her father, Oliver Bliss Hayes, and younger brother, Henry, stand behind her. Seated in the front row from left to right are her sister Laura, her mother Sarah Hightower Hayes, and her sister Corinne. Courtesy of Tennessee State Library and Archives.

Franklin was a toddler who still needed a mother, and Adelicia was only twenty-nine years old and stood to become one of the richest women in the country. These were not small things to live for.[15]

Adelicia left Tennessee for the summer to clear her head and recover her strength. She returned home "much improved in health and spirits." But choices had to be made about Isaac Franklin's estate, and later in the fall she went to Louisiana, where her husband had died and his will had been probated, to figure out how to proceed with the rest of her life. John Armfield went with her. In part, he was obliged to do so, as he was Franklin's executor along with Oliver Hayes. But Armfield also took a personal interest in the disposition of Franklin's estate and the welfare of his widow and daughter. Franklin had been his closest friend in the world, and weeks after the fact, Armfield could barely convey the impact of losing him. "You may imagin yett I cannot describe my present feelings," he told Rice Ballard. It was a rare emotional aside in correspondence that had been noticeably curt since their falling out over the Henry Turner affair, and it was a brief one, because it was about all Armfield knew to say. He was stuck on his failure to get there in time for the end. "As soon as the old man was taken [sick] he sent for me," he wrote. "When I gott up I found him a corps."[16]

Impelled by duty and friendship, and advised by John Lobdell, Armfield guided his partner's widow through claiming her inheritance. In December 1846, Adelicia formally accepted the terms of her husband's will. She renounced her dower rights and her "community rights," which referred to claims she might have on assets acquired during the marriage, and she clarified her intention to take the inheritances of her daughters Victoria and Adelicia, which now devolved to her. Three months later, she and the executors settled on an annuity of $10,000 to support herself and Emma. Adjusted for inflation, it was equivalent to $339,000 per year today. Relative to the distribution of wealth in the country at the time, it brought Adelicia Franklin the modern equivalent of more than $6 million annually.[17]

There was still the matter of the school at Fairvue, the plans for which could not proceed until the properties set aside to fund it were free from financial and legal entanglements. Adelicia was entitled to use Fairvue, but she also wanted "to facilitate the opening of said academy or seminary, and to carry into effect the intentions of her said husband." Memories conjured by Fairvue were hard ones anyway, so in the spring of 1847, she bought a house in Nashville and moved there with Emma. Nine months later, she sold her Fairvue claims to William Franklin, in his capacity as trustee of the Isaac Franklin Institute, for $30,000.[18]

As he resolved the circumstances of Franklin's wife and daughter, Armfield settled the rest of Franklin's estate. He paid outstanding bills and collected unpaid debts. He deposited into estate accounts proceeds from Franklin's share of the remaining interests of Ballard Franklin and Company, and he and Oliver Hayes contracted with masons and other artisans to build a mausoleum at Fairvue. A "monumental family vault" fourteen feet high, with rubbed "solid stone" walls, it had an arched ceiling of plastered brick, a floor of inset multicolored stones, and space for at least a dozen coffins. Topped by an obelisk and decorated with an "emblematic representation," it also perhaps unthinkingly echoed elements of the business that paid for it. "Surrounded by a substantial stone fence, with a large front gate at the entrance," the vault had a window equipped with "iron grates" for ventilation and an exterior door made of wood and iron outfitted "with suitable locks."[19]

Franklin had wanted his Louisiana plantations to remain productive and expand their operations, and Armfield took care of that too. He corresponded with merchants and kept track of returns on hundreds of bales of cotton. He retained James Clack as general agent and gave him everything he needed to buy horses and mules and oxen, hire overseers and mechanics and other workmen, and build ginhouses and mills and stables. Franklin also willed the erection of "three additional negro quarters or sets or clusters of houses" and the purchase of as many as 190 more Black people, "good, young, effective and healthy slaves," to live in them. Armfield knew exactly where to go for that. Turning to Thomas Boudar, George Davis, George Kephart, and other Chesapeake colleagues from his slave-trading days, Armfield purchased Cecelia Blunt, sixteen; Mason Thomas, twenty; Mary Jane Hunter, eighteen; Samuel Davis, twenty-two; and dozens of others. Then he put them all to forced labor.[20]

Armfield was extraordinarily busy in the late 1840s. Bored when he was not working and figuring he was already selling cotton from Franklin's plantations, he took an office in New Orleans and offered his services as a cotton broker. Somehow he found time to supervise the relocation of his sister Polly and her five children too. Armfield's share of his father's estate had not been nearly enough to solve her family's financial problems, and their situation gradually became untenable after William Hanner died in 1843. So Armfield brought them all from North Carolina to Tennessee, bought them a farm in Sumner County, gave them five enslaved people to work it, and furnished it with livestock and farm equipment "of first rate quality." He made his nieces and nephews "especial objects of his bounty and care," ensured they received an education, and "indulged them in every thing." Most people thought Armfield acted toward them "in the light of a father."[21]

They were not the only ones. John and Martha Armfield also assumed formal guardianship of Jane Franklin, and they became surrogate parents to John Armfield Franklin, Adelle Franklin, and Edward Noel Franklin. Ages six, four, and three, respectively, they were Martha's niece and nephews too, born to her brother John W. Franklin and his wife, Florida Noel. John Franklin had stayed close to the Armfields after living with them in Alexandria as a teenager, his firstborn was John Armfield's namesake, and when he remarried a year after becoming a widower in 1848, he asked the Armfields to take in his children. They all went to live on a three-hundred-acre farm John Armfield bought in the spring of 1849, located on the road from Gallatin to Nashville, close to where the Hanners lived and about six miles from Fairvue. The previous owners had called the place Hard Times.[22]

By the end of 1850, John Armfield had devoted four and a half years to settling Isaac Franklin's estate. He had a slew of new commitments, and at age fifty-three, he was the head of a family with small children, as Martha had always wanted. After decades of being a junior partner, now he was the old man. On December 2, 1850, he and Oliver Hayes asked the West Feliciana Parish district court judge to make the settlement of Franklin's estate final. Armfield was ready to move on.[23]

Adelicia Franklin, it seemed, already had. It was customary for a widow to honor her husband's memory by withdrawing from society for at least a year. But when Adelicia emerged from mourning in the spring of 1847, with a slave-trading fortune complementing the charm and good looks that had enchanted Isaac Franklin, white men clamored for her attention. Joseph A. S. Acklen captured it. Born in Alabama in 1816, Acklen boasted an impressive pedigree and set of accomplishments. The grandson of John Hunt, founder of the Alabama city of Huntsville, as a teenager Acklen joined a volunteer company that aided white Americans in Texas in their revolt against Mexico. On his return, he studied to become a lawyer, and in 1840, he was appointed United States attorney for the Northern District of Alabama, a position he held for several years before volunteering again for military service. Rushing to support another imperialist venture, he fought this time in the Mexican War, as an officer, and was recognized for bravery in battle. Attractive, accomplished, and a war hero, he appealed instantly to Adelicia when they met at a Nashville ball. It was not long before their conversations turned to marriage.[24]

On May 7, 1849, Adelicia Franklin and Joseph Acklen signed what today would be called a prenuptial agreement, transferring ownership of and control over all property Adelicia brought to their union to her father, who was to use it to support her and her heirs exclusively. The couple married the next day, traveled through Europe after the wedding, and in January 1850 went to New Orleans, where Adelicia, given a choice of how to take the bequest Isaac Franklin had provided on the occasion of her remarriage, selected the lump-sum payment of $100,000. As she signed the notarial act certifying the agreement, she was noticeably pregnant, and in May she delivered a baby boy, named Joseph after his father. Both actually and symbolically, it looked like she had put Isaac Franklin in her past.[25]

And then Adelicia Acklen changed her mind about acceding to Franklin's will, responding to the petition filed by John Armfield and her father for final settlement of Franklin's estate with a lawsuit in Louisiana's Seventh Judicial District Court. She wanted to nullify everything she had previously agreed to, insisting that she was entitled to far more of the estate than she had taken. Any "attempt to despoil her of property," she argued, was "contrary to the plainest dictates of justice."[26]

Greed is the most obvious explanation for the reversal. Adelicia claimed that, at a minimum, she was due nearly $80,000 beyond what she was receiving. But it was probably more than that, and she wanted a fresh inventory and appraisal of Franklin's land, slaves, and other assets to determine the actual figure. Impatience or skepticism about the Isaac Franklin Institute may have played a role as well. Adelicia knew Franklin had "intended to make material alterations in the will, in her favor," before he died. He never did, so she let the seminary project proceed. But beyond its incorporation and the stockpiling of "a very large quantity of brick," few steps had been taken to bring it to fruition, and William Franklin had withdrawn as trustee after deciding he needed to attend to "his own family and business." The establishment of the Isaac Franklin Institute seemed an open question, and Adelicia concluded she might as well have the money that had been set aside for it if the question was not going to be answered.[27]

Whatever her motives, Adelicia contended that when Franklin died, "she was altogether inexperienced in business and ignorant of the forms and legal effects" of the documents her advisers asked her to sign. If John Lobdell, John Armfield, or her father told her she needed to sign papers "in order to carry the will into effect, and to enable her to get the benefit of the legacies therein made to her," then she did it, "without paying much attention to their contents." Vulnerable in her bereavement and believing these men "to be the friends of her deceased husband and herself," she "relied implicitly"

on their counsel and "placed the utmost confidence" in their opinions. She wanted to do as Franklin willed, "from a proper respect
to his memory." But "she never intended . . . to give away or impair
her own legal rights," and she had discovered that the advice she
received "was predicated upon an entire mistake of law."[28]

In particular, she had been told that she had to renounce her
community rights in Franklin's estate if she was to accept the terms
of the will. But that had never been true, and those rights entitled her to half of everything Franklin acquired and gained after
their marriage. And that was not all. Several months after filing her
initial lawsuit, Adelicia amended her complaint, claiming that the
endowment for the Isaac Franklin Institute was contrary to Louisiana estate law, which forbade perpetual trusts and the conditional
transfer of property from a testator to a third party, in this case the
Sumner County magistrates who were to superintend the seminary
after the deaths of the original trustees. The only fix for these errors,
Adelicia argued, was to void the agreements she had made and nullify the endowment.[29]

As a lawyer, Joseph Acklen was surely involved in bringing the
"error of facts and error of laws" to Adelicia's attention. But Adelicia was no fool. She had grown up in the home of a skilled attorney, learned a lot since Franklin's death, and made her marriage to
Acklen conditional on a prenuptial agreement so she would preserve
some authority over the land she owned and the people she enslaved.
She was entirely capable of asserting for herself that she deserved
more of the estate.[30]

The courts agreed with her. In March 1851, District Court
Judge James L. Stirling ruled that Isaac Franklin had been a resident
of Louisiana and that his property, "wherever situated, was to be gov-
erned by the law of Louisiana." Accordingly, the bequest creating the
Isaac Franklin Institute was "null and void, as being contrary to public policy and violating the spirit if not the letter" of state law. Moreover, Adelicia "was entitled to her share of the community property,"

and the notarial acts renouncing her community rights were also null and void, "the said renunciations having been made without consideration, and in error of law and facts."[31]

The Louisiana Supreme Court heard the case on appeal a year later, and Justice Pierre Adolphe Rost, writing for the majority, doubted Isaac Franklin's legal status as a Louisiana resident. Observing that Franklin had been born and raised in Tennessee, built Fairvue there, filled it with "comforts and luxuries," and asked to be buried on its grounds, Rost thought it clear that Sumner County had been Franklin's "permanent domicil" and that Adelicia accordingly could not claim community rights in Louisiana. But Rost agreed that the endowment of the Isaac Franklin Institute belonged "to a class of tenures . . . unknown to the laws of Louisiana." He ordered that the trust be "set aside and annulled" and that all "real estate, slaves and immovables" held in Louisiana by Franklin's estate be turned over to Adelicia Acklen.[32]

Though the Louisiana Supreme Court was less comprehensive in its support for Adelicia's arguments than the district court, its ruling had the same impact. John Armfield and Oliver Hayes delivered Isaac Franklin's West Feliciana properties to Adelicia Acklen, and their settlement of Franklin's Louisiana estate was accepted as final and closed. In response to yet another lawsuit, the Tennessee Supreme Court eventually ruled that the endowment of the Isaac Franklin Institute was legal in that state and that funds to underwrite it might be taken from Fairvue. But it also ruled that Fairvue's revenues first had to be used to pay Armfield and Hayes more than $40,000 for advances they had made to Franklin's estate while serving as executors. Franklin had had the legal authority to endow the Isaac Franklin Institute, but it had become financially infeasible. In the words of Tennessee Supreme Court Justice John Marshall, it would forever be only "a phantom of his brain."[33]

Armfield regretted being unable to fulfill all of Franklin's posthumous desires. But he had done his best and acted in what he believed to be good faith. It came as a relief to set down the burden of Franklin's estate once and for all, though perhaps not as much relief as Armfield felt in January 1853, when he received a tally of the very last outstanding accounts of Ballard Franklin and Company. It showed Isaac Franklin was due thousands more than Armfield and Ballard put together, prompting Armfield to tell Ballard that he thought Franklin had "the advantage of you and me" and that some corrections to the books were necessary. But they would work it out. Old grudges were behind them now. Armfield had started signing himself "your friend" in letters to Ballard again, and he would ensure the two of them got what they deserved. "You and me have suffered together," Armfield wrote, "and I want us to Be Benefited together." It was a gracious gesture, if oblivious in its consideration of "suffering." More than sixteen years after he marched to the docks in Alexandria with the last 254 enslaved people he would ever ship to New Orleans, John Armfield stared at the figures in front of him, paused for a moment, and filed the pages away.[34]

Rice Ballard would never be mistaken for someone indifferent to money. But any payouts John Armfield told him would still be coming his way from Ballard Franklin and Company were insignificant compared with the capital then already surging into his accounts. It streamed from many directions at once, as Ballard followed a pattern of wealth accumulation mirroring Isaac Franklin's.[35]

Enslaved people, real estate, and cotton provided most of Ballard's riches. In partnership with Samuel Boyd, Ballard spent the late 1840s and much of the 1850s hunting for places to supplement planting operations at Magnolia and Karnac. Sometimes Boyd passed along intelligence about distressed assets that seemed "a fair bargain." But as word spread that Ballard and Boyd were in the market, men approached them with offers—places that were "liable to seizure" and could be had cheap, others "well suited to a planter who desires to employ a large force," still others that Ballard and Boyd could not "do better than to buy" and might "conclude to purchase after [an] examination." Ballard and Boyd analyzed what the land was worth, what crops were in the ground, and what level of production might be expected over time. They assessed the value of draft animals and livestock, buildings and other improvements. They considered how many enslaved men, women, and children would be included in a potential acquisition, and whether they would want to buy more or sell some away to maximize profitability.[36]

Between 1842 and 1856, Ballard and Boyd bought at least a dozen extant planting businesses in Mississippi, Louisiana, and Arkansas. Some they held for just a few years. Others they combined into new holdings with new names. Along with Karnac and Magnolia, three acquisitions proved to be long-term ventures. Out of a purchase of 1,450 acres made in 1850 and 692 acres acquired in 1854, Ballard and Boyd made a place in Warren County, Mississippi, called Lapine. In January 1853, they bought 1,160 acres of land in Carroll Parish, in northeastern Louisiana along the Mississippi River and just below the Arkansas border, adding another 1,520 acres over the next three years and calling the place Outpost. And in December 1853, they bought at auction 2,900 acres of land in Madison Parish, below Outpost and across the Mississippi River from Vicksburg. They added another 679 acres to the property a few years later and called the place Elcho.[37]

These were enterprises that can only be called slave labor camps. The same might be said of anyplace people were kept in bondage and forced to work lest they be beaten, tortured, sold, or killed. But many slaveholders constructed an illusion of bucolic pastoralism out of the amenities they furnished for themselves, their families, and those they enslaved. At Fairvue, for instance, Isaac Franklin's expenditures on luxuries and frills disguised the exploitation that provided them and helped impart to the word "plantation" the romantic associations it still retains for too many Americans. Similarly, after

Franklin's death, Adelicia and Joseph Acklen turned their West Feliciana Parish properties into what *Southern Cultivator* magazine considered "the finest and best managed estate in the South." The Acklens built a large personal dwelling at Angola, maintained "neat frame houses" as slave quarters, and provided the enslaved with "all that is essential to health and comfort." No wonder that when British and northern visitors came to Louisiana, Adelicia proudly "show[ed] them around" and let them "see for themselves how the 'niggers' are treated," nor that the writer for *Southern Cultivator* thought that the Acklens enslaved "the happiest population I have ever seen." He saw what he wanted to see and concluded that the Acklens' benevolence explained how they got everyone to work "with the discipline of a regular trained army."[38]

Rice Ballard and Samuel Boyd never bothered with such appearances on their partnership landholdings. Ballard spent eight months of the year in the lower South. He stayed sometimes at the Mansion House Hotel in Natchez, and he often lived on the grounds of Magnolia, but he neglected to establish any "fixed place of residence," moving instead among partnership properties as he felt necessary. Boyd cycled among the properties too, but he spent much of his time in the state capital at Jackson or with his family at his plantation in Natchez. The places owned by Ballard and Boyd had no stately homes or ornamental gardens. They were not showcases for wealthy white families. The only steady white presences on them at all were managers and overseers, few of whom stayed on for more than a few years. The Ballard and Boyd partnership owned places whose sole purpose was to make Black people live and labor under the threat of violence to produce cotton until they were considered useless, deemed dispensable, or died.[39]

In 1860, Ballard and Boyd enslaved 425 people, including 118 children, across the labor camps they owned together. But census records and lists of slaves recorded by Ballard or his overseers were mirages of constancy obscuring landscapes of turmoil and movement. Ballard and Boyd shopped as steadily for human beings who might be had for a bargain as they did for land, because the environments they created at Magnolia, Karnac, Lapine, Outpost, and Elcho meant incessant churning and turnover among the enslaved.[40]

Ballard and Boyd's overseers sent reports of children who got "worms," men who suffered from "the clap" and "lock-jaw," and women whose limbs swelled so much they could not be bent. There were cases of cholera, "the bloody flux," and "the hooping caugh," of "Tiphoid newmonia" and the "chills" of yellow fever. Sometimes disease was so widespread that overseers described conditions simply as "a Good Deal of Sick." Fatalities were commonplace, and there was only one solution. As Boyd suggested to Ballard in 1850 after "two negroes died" from cholera at one of their camps, "if you chance to go to V[icks]b[ur]g and buy a couple of hands to replace them, do so."[41]

The resistance of enslaved people, especially when they ran away, also forced Ballard and Boyd to find replacement laborers. When W. H. Dixon, overseer at Magnolia, reported mass flight by at least a dozen people in 1844 and told Ballard that "the negroes declared themselves free (by action)," he was describing one instance among many. People fled from any place Ballard and Boyd tried keeping them in bondage. It was a slow but steady trickle that, in conjunction with illnesses and injuries, could leave overseers feeling beleaguered. Writing in the fall of 1853 from his position at Outpost, overseer H. Shaw was "ancious" for Ballard to arrive. "Sow much sickness and som deaths some Raning away," he wrote, "has weard me mitley."[42]

Unstable and filled with mutual recriminations, Ballard and Boyd's operations were also brutally effective. In 1852, Ballard and Boyd sent thirty-two shipments of cotton by steamboat to New Orleans from the four facilities they owned that year. The shipments, totaling 2,004 bales weighing 846,744 pounds, sold collectively for $67,406.05. After deducting freight and shipping costs, river and fire insurance, drayage and storage and weighing fees, and the standard 2.5 percent commission for their merchants, Ballard and Boyd reaped net profits of $62,214.20, or roughly $2.09 million today. Three years later, they operated six labor camps, shipped 3,280 bales of cotton weighing 1.34 million pounds, and realized profits of $94,294.35, amounting to $2.83 million in current dollars. Output and profits varied over time and depended on the weather, damage from insects and plant diseases, cotton's market price, and the ability of the men Ballard and Boyd hired to force the enslaved to work. But during the 1850s, the Black people Ballard and Boyd held in bondage picked an average of over four million pounds of seed cotton annually. Once it was cleaned, dried, ginned, pressed, and packed, it yielded more than 2,500 bales, weighing more than one million pounds, ready to be shipped every year.[43]

Ballard put some of the money from the labor camps he and Boyd operated back into the partnership for more land and more slaves. But there were profits left over, not to mention thousands still being generated by the Henry Turner settlement and Ballard's bit of trailing interest in Ballard Franklin and Company. Ballard used a portion of what came in on small acts of philanthropy. In 1848, for example, he paid the debt of the Natchez Sisters of Charity on the building they bought to establish "an asylum for poor and orphan children." It was no Isaac Franklin Institute, but the donation brought Ballard public accolades as someone whose "name will hereafter be chronicled among the great benefactors of the human race."[44]

Ballard did not share Isaac Franklin's partisan affiliation, but he shared his expansionist proslavery politics, and he put money behind those too. He supported the American annexation of Texas lest it become "a British Colony of abolitionism," and he and Boyd joined a number of white southerners and some of their northern allies in backing covert efforts to wrest Cuba from Spanish control, with a possible eye toward annexing the slaveholding island to the United States. In 1850, they purchased bonds in the "Provisional

Government of Cuba." Underwriting an illegal private paramilitary invasion, the bonds might have paid off with stolen Cuban land had the expedition not ended in the arrest and execution of its absurdly overconfident leader, a former Spanish Army officer and Cuban planter named Narciso López.[45]

But Ballard mostly looked for less delusional ways to enrich himself. He invested in banks, particularly in the Commercial Bank of Manchester, Mississippi, whose stock Isaac Franklin and John Armfield owned as well. He invested in small infrastructure projects. He bought shares in racehorses, and up the street from several large slave dealerships in downtown Louisville, he bought commercial lots and became a partner in a livery business with a brickmaker and former city councilman named Edward Crutchfield.[46]

And Ballard kept money in the slave trade, primarily through the agency of Calvin M. Rutherford. A Louisville-based trader who had also worked out of New Orleans since at least the early 1840s, Rutherford sometimes bought enslaved people upon request for Ballard and Boyd's labor camps, disposed of people they wished to discard, and scouted for people he thought they would find useful or desirable. Much of Ballard's relationship with Rutherford, however, replicated Ballard's early relationship with Samuel Alsop. Funneling money through Louisville banks and providing lines of credit on his New Orleans merchants, Ballard fronted Rutherford's slave trading and took part of the proceeds.[47]

Rutherford trafficked dozens of people at a time down the Ohio and Mississippi Rivers. He had a "slave depot" on Gravier Street in New Orleans, where he advertised that he was "constantly receiving Negroes," though he also sold people in Mobile, Baton Rouge, and Natchez, and even as far away as Shreveport and Galveston. Rutherford acquired many of the people he sold in Louisville, Lexington, and Memphis. But he brought enslaved people to the lower South from Virginia and North Carolina too, procuring some of them in partnership with a Richmond trader named Thomas McCargo, an old associate of Ballard's who had also had dealings with James Franklin Purvis and John Armfield. For six years, Rutherford fed Ballard information about markets for enslaved people. On gross sales that were the modern equivalent of several million dollars annually and brought profits of about 30 percent, he also provided Ballard with a healthy return on his stake in Rutherford's business.[48]

Even though Rice Ballard stayed involved in slave trading mostly through intermediaries, and even though he relied heavily on overseers to inform him about daily operations on the properties he owned with Samuel Boyd, his capacity for firsthand cruelty toward individual enslaved people was undiminished. No one knew that better than Virginia Boyd. Enslaved and repeatedly raped by Samuel Boyd for more than a decade, she had already given birth to two of his children by the fall of 1852, and when she became pregnant again, Samuel Boyd asked Ballard to get rid of her and the children alike. He "would not be bothered with her" any longer, and he recommended Ballard send them all to Karnac until he could arrange their disappearance, warning him to watch Virginia closely lest she escape and to "put her in the stocks" if she would "not behave."[49]

Two months later, near the end of February 1853, Ballard sent Virginia and her children to Rutherford in New Orleans. But Rutherford was afraid to sell her there, "for I know she would run off if she have a chance." In any case, her pregnancy was so far advanced that no one would take her. So Rutherford sent her and her children to Texas, shipping them in April to a colleague's Houston slave-trading compound with "special instructions" for Virginia not to be sold to anyone who would ever bring her to Louisiana or Mississippi again.[50]

Her last connections to white men on whom she had "the least shadow of claim" about to be severed, Virginia Boyd managed to get hold of pen and paper, and she gave Ballard everything she had left. Writing to him from the "Negro traders yard" in Houston, she apologized if she had "done or said any thing that had offended" him and asserted that she had "suffered enough . . . to repay all that I have ever done, to any one." She tried shaming Ballard, asking if he thought "that its treating me well to send me off among strangers to be sold," if it was not appalling "for the father of my children to sell his own offspring," and if it was really "possible that any free born American would brand his character with such stigma as that." She tried bargaining, requesting that Ballard give her a chance "to Earn the money honestly to buy" her freedom and promising to "work my finger ends off" until she had "evry dime." She tried threatening, saying she would never let "anything be exposed" about Samuel Boyd "unless I am forced from bad treatement." And she tried flattering, begging, and playing on Ballard's emotions. "I no," she wrote, "you are [an] honerable high minded man" who "would wish justice to be done to all," and who appreciated that "if I am a servent there is some thing due me better than my present situation." Pleading for Ballard to use his "influence" to call off her sale, she wanted just a bit of "mercy and pity." She was about to give birth, and Ballard had "a family of children." Surely he knew "how to simpathize with others in distress."[51]

Rice Ballard had received letters like Virginia Boyd's before. But if Boyd was aware of Ballard's history with Arvenia White and Susan Johnson, she did not say so. And if she truly thought Ballard was someone moved by compassion, she misjudged him horribly. In August 1853, Rutherford told Ballard that Boyd and one of her children had been sold. But her oldest daughter was still at the trader's yard in Houston, because Ballard had told Rutherford she was worth more sold separately.[52]

Though Virginia Boyd had no way of knowing it, appealing to Ballard as a parent with children was particularly unlikely to work, because Ballard was ambivalent about his own family. When Boyd wrote her letter, Rice and Louisa Ballard had three children, having added twins Charlotte and Ann to their household in 1847, and Ballard spared little in providing for them materially. Shortly before the twins were born, Ballard sold the farm on Beargrass Creek and moved his family into the city of Louisville proper. Between 1848 and 1854, they lived downtown on Walnut Street, and then they moved into a mansion a few blocks away, on the corner of Broadway and Brook Street, where Ballard enslaved four or five people to cater to his family's needs and make their residence function. Louisa had a piano and pleasure carriages, and Ballard paid for carpets and feather mattresses, expensive bedsteads and bureaus, china sets and bottles of perfume, and a wardrobe filled with satins and silks and linens. He shipped books, oranges, and other gifts and treats to his daughters, and when Ella was old enough, he sent her to a private school about forty miles from the city. But emotional detachment accumulated.[53]

For several years after the Ballards married, and even after Ella was born, Louisa spent extended periods with her husband and with relatives in Mississippi during the winters. The births of Charlotte and Ann, however, left Louisa feeling "pretty much tied down," and her trips became less frequent. She wrote Ballard generally affectionate letters filled with household reports and news about friends, family members, and the children, but Ballard's responses were sporadic, leading Louisa to wonder if he was sick and to ask why they had not heard from him. When Ballard did write, his letters were brief, and Louisa urged him to "write often and long letters," because she thought "it ought to be a very great pleasure to read letters and write to each other." She even gave him ideas for not being "so scarce in what you have to say," suggesting he tell her about how he spent his days. "I often feel," she wrote, "as if I should like to know what you were doing on each place."[54]

Ballard tried obliging her, and his more detailed letters filled Louisa with "a great deal of pleasure and delight" and gave her "new life." But they also fed her anxieties about his health and mood. He wrote of a leg injury from "the kick of a mule" and mentioned how busy he was, and she implored him "to take care & double care of yourself now as you have more to take charge of and more to live for." He confessed to having "very low spirits," and she fussed over "how lonely you must be after you come in the house of an evening." She said that she hoped her letters helped and that he ought to consider coming to Kentucky more often, even "if it was only for a few weeks." Writing about how the children "were growing quite fast" and observing that "they have your expression all of them more than mine," Louisa told him "how much pleasure it would afford you to have our dear little ones around you," adding, "they talk of their Papa every day and say what are you going to bring them."[55]

But Ballard never did make much time to visit his family, outside of summers. He was not there when Ann got the measles or when Ella learned to read, and he was not there when Charlotte asked again and again "if it was not time for Papa to come home." More than once, he did not get to Louisville for Christmas. The Ballards would have no more children, though Louisa was just twenty-five when the twins were born. As she slowly grasped that her life would be defined by her husband's absence, she began to unravel.[56]

In 1852, Louisa fretted that she did not have enough money, and one of her relatives, William Ellis, who checked on Ballard's family in his absence, saw signs of trouble. Louisa was falling "under the influence of persons here," he told Ballard, "that she thinks are her friends and consequently break her off from those who really are her friends." By 1854, Louisa's letters to Ballard had become irregular, and when Agatha Marshall Logan, wife of Louisville attorney Caleb Logan, received Louisa at home in 1856 after running into her in a store, she found the encounter unnerving. "She is still very handsome," Logan told a relative, "but looks unhappy, & I am afraid is not what she ought to be." A friend who had seen Louisa "gave an odd report of their conversation which lasted three hours," and Logan pitied her. Other elite women rarely visited her, "though she lives in an elegant house on Broadway," and Logan could not stop thinking of "how pretty & amiable & innocent she was once, but now changed and perhaps <u>ruined</u>."[57]

Forlorn, isolated, and increasingly angry, Louisa started drinking. William Ellis tried to help, but he threw up his hands at Louisa's resentfulness, telling Ballard that she "has used every means in her power to drive me from the House, has refused to eat at the table with me, [and] insulted my daughter grossly when she was staying with her and waiting on her in her sickness." Things had gotten so bad that Ellis "had hoped" Louisa would drink "to such an excess as to kill herself shortly which would have been a blessing to her offspring," who were "liable to be injured by the wickedness of an unnatural mother." Acknowledging the "troubles in mind" that he was sure Louisa's affliction caused Ballard, Ellis could only offer his "deepest and most heartfelt sympathy."[58]

Rice Ballard could have had Louisa and his daughters spend more time with him in the lower South, as Isaac Franklin did with his family. As Ballard approached and then passed the age at which Franklin had died, he could have turned greater responsibility for his labor camps over to employees. He could have lived more in Louisville with a wife who needed him and young children who missed him and wondered when he was coming home. He did not do any of that, because he did not want to. His wife and children would have distracted him in the lower South, and he liked his work too much to leave it to others. Louisa stopped thinking he would ever change, and the teenage Ella picked up her mother's burden, scolding and coaxing her father to do things differently. "Pa you are getting old," she wrote him in 1857 after reading a letter in which he mentioned going out in the rain for a meeting. "You ought to take more care than that of your self for if you get sick down there there would not be any person to nurse you."[59]

Among the scores of slave traders who had been colleagues or associates of Isaac Franklin, John Armfield, and Rice Ballard, James Franklin Purvis took the road least traveled. Purvis worked as a slave trader and jailor in Baltimore into the early 1840s. Offering to buy "likely young NEGROES" or imprison them "for safe-keeping," Purvis advertised that he could be found at his downtown office or at home and that sellers could also do business at the Eagle Hotel with Isaac Franklin Purvis, who moved from Annapolis to Baltimore to work alongside his older brother. But the death of the younger Purvis in June 1843, at the age of thirty, led James Purvis to rethink his life. In October, the *Christian Reflector* magazine wrote that he had "converted to Christianity under Methodist preaching, became a good man, and quit" the slave trade. Over the next thirty years, Purvis was a partner in a brick-making concern and in a general exchange and stockbroking business. He founded a bank, became president of a coal company, and treasurer of an oil company. He ran for city council as a Whig, lobbied for public schools, became a trustee of a Methodist girls' academy, and did charitable work with the Baltimore House of Refuge and the Baltimore City Association for Improving the Condition of the Poor.[60]

Purvis's path was so rare because slave traders who displayed guilt, shame, or remorse were so rare. Some of the traders associated with Franklin, Armfield, and Ballard did engage in other pursuits. Bacon Tait got elected to the Richmond City Council, joined the Richmond Fire Association, promoted railroads, and invested in real estate. George Kephart ran for Alexandria City Council, became a partner in a lumber business, and was appointed a delegate to a railroad convention and to a meeting looking to rebuild the Whig Party in Virginia. But Tait owned his slave jail in Richmond until he died, Kephart owned the Duke Street compound until the late 1850s, and many of their fellows stayed in the slave trade for most or all of the rest of their lives. Silas Omohundro, Theophilus Freeman, William Williams, Thomas Jones, and Robert Windsor were just a few who continued to make their living dealing in enslaved people, sometimes for decades. They never saw a reason or a need to stop.[61]

For men who wanted to retire from slave trading, there were obviously alternatives to the approach taken by James Purvis. One was to farm with slave labor, as Isaac Franklin and Rice Ballard did. In the 1840s, Austin Woolfolk owned thousands of acres in Tennessee and Louisiana and forced enslaved laborers to work on them, and in 1850 Woolfolk's uncle John enslaved 152 people on a plantation in western Georgia. The resources of Franklin and Armfield's former agent Jourdan Saunders were more limited, but by 1860, he was a Virginia grain farmer on 186 acres outside Warrenton, a place he called Mountain View, where he lived with his family and enslaved twelve people.[62]

Another course followed by former slave traders was to enter the hospitality industry. Ballard's former agent James Blakey regained his financial footing after the Panic of 1837, and in 1842, he leased the Franklin Hotel, on Main Street in downtown Richmond. Having been a hotel keeper before becoming a trader, he took to it again easily. A few years later, he was operating the Wall Street Hotel, on Fifteenth Street, and in 1848, he and a partner took out a multiyear lease on the Broad Street Hotel, on the corner of Ninth and Broad Streets near the state capitol and the railroad depot. Blakey managed that establishment until his death from typhoid fever in 1854, when he was lauded in the Richmond papers as a man "greatly beloved by all who knew him for his many amiable qualities and goodness of heart." After Calvin Rutherford left the slave trade, he too became a hotelier. Pooling funds with four other former traders, he opened the National Hotel in 1855, on the corner of Fourth and Main Streets in downtown Louisville.[63]

Running hotels was often not so much abandoning the slave trade as it was working adjacent to it. The National Hotel, for instance, was described "by all who have partaken of its hospitality, as being one of the finest hotels in the world" shortly after it opened. It also had auction blocks inside the building, and a large auction and commission house across the street promised to dispose "of all kinds of property." Blakey's Wall Street Hotel sat right in the middle of Richmond's slave-trading district, and the trade got conducted there alongside all sorts of other business. It went on in many slave-state city hotels, where traders negotiated deals at bars and restaurants just as they had in taverns and inns from the trade's earliest days.[64]

Slave trading and hotel keeping were also associated occupations because they both entailed satisfying the demands of wealthy white people, which made John Armfield's progression from the former to the latter entirely understandable. In the mid-1850s, Armfield came into possession of a place called Beersheba Springs. He would spend more than fifteen years as its proprietor and guiding spirit, cultivating the patronage of white elites and endeavoring to give them what they wanted, as he had for most of his adult life.

Brokering cotton in New Orleans made sense for Armfield when he had to be there dealing with Isaac Franklin's estate. Once the estate and the books of Ballard Franklin and Company were settled, however, Armfield wanted to spend more time in Tennessee with Martha and the slew of young people who depended on him. He had plenty of money. Most estimates put his wealth at between $200,000 and $500,000, though some ranged as high as a million dollars, and Armfield had large investments in stocks and other securities, including $100,000 in Virginia bonds that led newspapers to brag about the state "attracting the attention of the capitalists." Armfield also enslaved fifteen people at Hard Times. But he had never wanted to do any serious commercial farming. He was not about to start now, and there was still cash to be parked somewhere.[65]

As he closed his New Orleans brokerage, Armfield became wistful for his old business and his old partners. He cleared out his office, from which he wanted Ballard to have the "very fine desk" that had "belonged to the old firm of Ballard F. & Co." Then he went back to Sumner County, where he bought Nathan and Henrietta Bracken at an auction of 102 enslaved people sold at Fairvue to pay Franklin's estate debts in Tennessee. A married couple and living keepsakes of the most important man from Armfield's former life, the Brackens became personal servants for John and Martha Armfield.[66]

Armfield's purchase of Beersheba Springs indulged his nostalgia too. Located atop a bluff of Broad Mountain in the Cumberland Plateau, about one hundred miles southeast of Nashville, Beersheba developed as a resort in the 1830s for white southerners looking to escape summer heat and take advantage of the healing powers supposedly possessed by iron-rich chalybeate waters at the site. With a tavern, a dining hall, stables, and some guest cabins, it was the kind of place Armfield had walked past in Virginia as he forced coffles of enslaved people over the mountains, and the kind of place where he and Franklin and their wives had liked to vacation together. Late in 1854, when the owner looked to transfer the property to someone who would pay off the debts he had incurred to buy it, Armfield leaped at the opportunity.[67]

But Armfield envisioned a very different Beersheba Springs from the one he bought. In April 1855, he shut down the entire facility, announced in Tennessee newspapers that it was "undergoing a thorough repair," and spent more than two years and over $100,000 on an overhaul. He practically doubled the resort's footprint, to nearly nineteen hundred acres, and he improved and regraded the roads up the mountain. Using free and enslaved craftsmen and laborers, he erected a sawmill, a gristmill, and a brick kiln, and he tore down or moved most of the preexisting structures. In their place, he built an L-shaped two-story hotel near the springs, fronted by a long columned portico overlooking the Collins River valley to the north.

Projecting southward from the east end of the building, there was a large dining room beneath a ballroom, and additional guest rooms extended both from there and from the west end, forming a sort of quadrangle behind the main building. Distributed across the grounds, at a remove from the hotel, were twenty freestanding

The main hotel building at Beersheba Springs in 1933. After purchasing the property in the southeastern Tennessee mountains in 1854, John Armfield built the hotel and a series of private cottages. He then operated the resort, which catered mostly to wealthy southerners on summer vacations, through the era of the Civil War. Courtesy of Tennessee State Library and Archives.

cottages. One sat almost at the edge of the bluff and had belonged to a former owner of the resort, and Armfield kept it for himself. He had the rest built to the specifications of their owners, most of whom paid construction costs and a dollar a year in rent for the privilege of living "in private" and being part of the "peaceable and respectable society" Armfield hoped "to draw around" himself on the mountaintop.[68]

When Beersheba Springs reopened in June 1857, it was advertised as a spot that could not be "surpassed by any watering place in the Union." In 150 furnished guest quarters, the hotel could accommodate up to six hundred visitors at a time. They had the use of a bowling alley, horses and buggies for excursions, and could choose from "wines and liquors" for their rooms and while dining. Musicians, chefs, and enslaved servants were brought from New Orleans.

The hotel housed a post office and a barbershop, and on the premises were dry goods and tobacco stores, a bathhouse and an icehouse. Guests could play cards and billiards, go to formal balls or on a fox hunt, dance, picnic, walk or ride to behold views of the valley, and take the waters. A Memphis newspaper correspondent visiting in the summer of 1857 praised Armfield for his "spirit of liberality" and predicted Beersheba would become "the 'Saratoga of the South.'"[69]

"Many families from the South," the same writer observed, "have spent the entire season here," noting especially that "a large number of prominent citizens of the more Southern States have erected summer residences near the springs." The Beersheba cottage builders were certainly white southern elites, and most had known Armfield for years. They included John M. Bass, a lawyer and bank president who had been the mayor of Nashville and who owned plantations in Louisiana and Arkansas. Nashville doctors Thomas Harding and John Waters built cottages, as did Charles Phillips, Joseph Williams, Minor Kenner, Oliver Morgan, Charles Dahlgren, Josiah Garrett, and other planters and slaveholders from Louisiana and Mississippi.[70]

Armfield also set aside cottage lots for Episcopal Bishops Leonidas Polk of Louisiana and James Otey of Tennessee. Armfield insisted on performative elements of piety at Beersheba. Alcohol was available only at meals and in private spaces, gambling was prohibited on the property, and worship services were offered on Sundays. But evidence of Armfield's personal religiosity is scarce. The Episcopal creed appealed to him less than the social status conferred by association with the church, and his friendship with Polk in particular was rooted as much in their shared commitment to slavery as in their shared faith. Polk enslaved hundreds of people on a series of plantations in Tennessee, Louisiana, and Mississippi, and by the 1850s he, along with other influential southern clerics and laymen alike, had come to feel that a rising tide of northern abolitionism signified an "emergency that is at the door" requiring

vigorous responses from white southerners. Armfield was not usually as politically fervent as Isaac Franklin had been, but those were
sentiments he could get behind.[71]

In July 1856, Polk wrote to Episcopal bishops in nine southern states asking for help in creating a new university where young
southern white men could train for the Episcopal clergy and participate in "the advancement of learning generally," free from dangerous and destabilizing antislavery influences. As it stood, Polk
argued, "our children are expatriated or sent off to an inconvenient
distance, beyond the reach of our supervision or parental influence."
Individual dioceses could not counter such pressures on their own,
but, he continued, "what we cannot do singly, we may, with great
ease, do collectively." Meeting a few months later, the recipients of
Polk's letter unanimously supported the proposal, agreeing that the
"spread of the wildest opinions in religion and government" bespoke
its wisdom.[72]

As the bishops then turned to fundraising and finding a suitable location for the school, John Armfield wanted to help. When
hotel renovations neared completion early in 1857, Armfield suggested that the university be situated at Beersheba Springs. A few
months later, on the Fourth of July, bishops and other Episcopal
delegates gathered on Lookout Mountain, south of Chattanooga,
to commit formally to creating the university. Armfield was there,
and he signed the "Declaration of Principles" that described institutional governance and plans for a capital campaign. Armfield
soon accepted appointment as a lay member of the board of trustees,
which voted to call the school "The University of the South," and in
the summer of 1858, he hosted the board's meetings at Beersheba.[73]

Ultimately, the trustees located the university thirty miles south-
west of Beersheba on nine thousand acres of land donated by local
residents and the Sewanee Mining Company, a coal concern that
would later become the industrial behemoth known as Tennessee Coal, Iron, and Railroad. Armfield helped scout the location,

served on the committee that oversaw the property transfers, and did what he could to establish an institutional endowment. Early in 1859, he committed $25,000, payable in $1,000 annual installments, "for assisting in building & keeping in repair the buildings of the University of the South." Armfield's influence led Adelicia and Joseph Acklen to make the same pledge, and James Otey, for one, thought Armfield essential to the entire project's success. His money mattered, but his long career in the slave trade gave him an understanding of business and finance, and connections to wealthy and powerful people, that mattered even more. "The truth," Otey told Armfield, "is that we need the experience & practical knowledge of men who have been engaged in worldly pursuits in the formation & execution of many of our plans connected with the advancement of education."[74]

In August 1859, the board of trustees met again at Beersheba Springs. It agreed that everything was in order "for beginning operations and laying the cornerstone of the central building," and John Armfield was a man at peace. Wealthy, revered, and surrounded by spectacular natural beauty, he made plans to sell the Beersheba hotel to private investors, keeping his cottage on the mountain and savoring everything the slave trade had provided him. Reaching out to Rice Ballard after the board meeting, Armfield reflected on their accomplishments. He lamented only that many of their comrades were no more, admitting that it dispirited him to "think of the past" and to realize "how few of us are left. I often feal like I want to go Round and once more see all my old frends." He knew that was unrealistic, as "old age is gettinge me verry fast," but he wanted Ballard to visit him, especially since Ballard had said he was ill and Armfield believed Beersheba was restorative. "I think it probable that I added several years to my life By cominge to this place," he wrote. Promising that "this atmosphere and Chalyabutt water would Bringe you out" and that autumn was particularly "delightfull," Armfield entreated him to think it over. "Nothing would give me more pleasure than to see you once more in my House Ballard come over and Bringe your family with you."[75]

Ballard was too busy for that, and he refused to stop working even as his health worsened. His leg had never healed properly from the mule kick he had received over a decade earlier, he came down repeatedly with chills and fevers, and he suffered from hemorrhoids so painful and severe that a friend recommended surgery. His daughter Ella, who urged him to "let business alone," could not fathom his intransigence. "You have got enough for us to live on all the days of [our] lives," she wrote in the spring of 1859, telling him to "come up home" as she "would rather have a father than all the money in the world."[76]

William H. Johnson, a New Orleans merchant who was so close to Ballard that he named a child after him, agreed with Ella. "You must not forget that you are getting old now and can't stand the annoyances and exposure you could when you were younger," Johnson cautioned. "Suppose you do not make as much cotton as you would were you to stand by and see it worked what difference is it to you." Ballard was a client as well as a friend, but Johnson preferred he let up, saying, "your health and comfort are worth all the cotton that was ever grown." Even Samuel Boyd thought Ballard pushed too hard. "I am very uneasy about you," he admitted. "You have been so ailing for the last two or three years, & I think you ought to take some decided step about it." If going to doctors did not help, Boyd told him "to bundle up & travel" in the summer rather than "bother your head with business & crops."[77]

But after spending the summer of 1859 in Louisville, Ballard picked up where he left off. In November, he told Louisa he was getting sick again, but also that his "business was very much out of order" and that he would not be in Kentucky for Christmas. Just after the New Year, Ella heard that her father was "very ill," a worrisome rumor prompting her to send a telegram insisting that he "telegraph immediately" with details. In the spring of 1860, Ballard finally took Boyd's advice to travel for his health, arranging a trip to Europe with Walter Cox, who had been one of his merchants for nearly twenty years. Ballard's passport application provides the only surviving description of what he looked like. At sixty years old, he was six foot one, with a high forehead, gray eyes and hair, a short nose, an "ordinary" mouth and chin, a "rather full" face, and a "dark" complexion.[78]

Late in May, Ballard and Cox left New York on the steamship *Asia* for Liverpool, where they met with cotton merchants and brokers. In August, Ballard returned to Louisville, but the transatlantic voyage had done nothing for his health, and he was so "very feeble" that he could not even sign his own name. On August 31, he died in the mansion on the corner of Brook and Broadway. Announcing his death with "deep regret," the Louisville *Daily Democrat* described him as "an old citizen, much esteemed, and beloved by all who knew him."[79]

The New Albany *Daily Ledger*, published across the Ohio River in Indiana, described Ballard as a "well known citizen of Louisville" and a "man of immense wealth." He was assuredly that. The census taker in 1860 estimated the value of his Louisiana holdings at $550,000, with another $65,000 in Kentucky. But he conceded his figures were the "best information [he] could get," and he did not account at all for Ballard's property in Mississippi and Arkansas. A credit reporter with R. G. Dun and Company who estimated Ballard's worth that same year at "one million to one million & a half" may have been closer to the mark. Adjusting for inflation, Ballard's estate when he died probably contained the modern equivalent of roughly $31 million. Relative to the wealth distribution of the age, it held what today would be around $450 million. By the terms of Ballard's will, his family received the Louisville mansion and allowances for its upkeep and their expenses. Samuel Boyd was Ballard's executor, and he was to continue administering the partnership properties until 1868, at which point Ballard's share would be divided into four equal parts for Louisa and his daughters. Ballard also left each of them $50,000. He instructed Boyd to invest the money "in productive property, land and slaves to be preferred."[80]

Rice Ballard worked himself into the grave to make a world where he could be worth hundreds of thousands of dollars and where "land and slaves" would be eternal creators of wealth for white people. It is unlikely that many of those he held in bondage were sorry to hear he died. But it is not hard to imagine some of them a few years later wishing he was still around, if only so he could see them celebrate the collapse of everything he had built.

B y the outbreak of the Civil War, the ships Franklin and Armfield once owned were long gone. After six years as a slaver, an Atlantic world merchant ship, and even a transport for Black American emigrants to Trinidad, the *Isaac Franklin* got lost in thick fog on the way to New York in April 1841. Filled with wine and dried fruit loaded in Spain, it ran aground on Sandy Hook, New Jersey, and broke to pieces. Six months later, the *Tribune* was spotted in West Africa at the Gallinas River, a site infamous for illegal transatlantic slave trading. Nearly its entire crew had died of fever, and the brig was soon decommissioned. More than two years after that, in the spring of 1844, the *Uncas* was detained at the Gallinas River as well. Escorted back across the Atlantic by an American naval vessel, it was released to its owners despite the discovery of "grating for the hatches," the revelation that its missing cargo had been consigned to a "notorious slave dealer," and the fact that the ship was known to have traveled to and from Africa before. The evidence all favored "the presumption that the Uncas was about to engage in the slave trade," but after being cleaned and undergoing some repairs, it sailed from New Orleans in December, only to encounter a storm on its way to Havana. It was never seen again.[81]

The Alexandria slave-trading facility once occupied by Franklin and Armfield, as it appeared after its liberation by Union forces during the Civil War. Library of Congress Prints and Photographs Division.

Other components of Franklin and Armfield's business infrastructure, however, were very much intact, legal, and operational when the war began. Even though Congress banned the slave trade throughout the entire District of Columbia in 1850 and gave antislavery forces a victory they had long sought, white residents of Alexandria had voted to retrocede out of the District and back to the state of Virginia four years before. Undertaken partially to sidestep abolitionist agitation for a ban, retrocession blunted its impact and meant George Kephart could keep using the Duke Street compound as a slave-trading facility and jail. He did so, in partnership with a series of other traders, until 1858, when he sold it to John Cook and Charles Price. Kephart initially invested some money with Cook, Price, and a man named William H. Birch, but soon he withdrew, and in 1861, the painted sign on the brick facing of the Duke Street townhouse read "Price, Birch & Co., Dealers in Slaves."[82]

Northern banks, insurance companies, and cotton brokers often continued to see slave traders and the slave trade as no more problematic to work with and make money from than slavery itself. But by the 1850s, decades of abolitionist criticism of the trade began resonating with a growing number of white northerners. As more of them built their politics around opposition to slavery and slaveholders, many came to agree that the slave trade was an abomination, revealing the injustice and moral degeneracy of a system that ought to be set toward decay or destroyed entirely. In that sense, Isaac Franklin, John Armfield, and Rice Ballard furthered an industry that helped provoke its own annihilation.

Its demise began in Alexandria. On May 24, 1861, the day after white Virginians ratified the state's ordinance of secession, Union forces marched into the city and took command of the Duke Street compound, surprising a Confederate cavalry unit eating breakfast inside and finding "letters and papers . . . strewn about the floor of the office." It was evidence from a crime scene left in a hurry. Charles Price and his fellow traders had fled the facility, taking with them most of the enslaved people they confined there and leaving behind a lone older man, "chained to the middle of the floor by the leg." Union soldiers freed him, and he agreed to be their cook. But he really wanted to take up arms, insisting "he must have a musket if fighting is to be done." Photographers started selling images of the facility, abolitionists showed up to gawk and claim bricks and door bolts as trophies, and the Union Army used the compound as a military prison and hospital until the end of the war.[83]

A year after northern forces marched into Alexandria, Union Admiral David Farragut accepted the surrender of Natchez, a city whose slave trade thrived without restriction at the Forks of the Road after Mississippi repealed its questionably effective trading ban in 1846. By the late 1850s, the site John Armfield had sold to John O'Ferrall was one of three large facilities making the intersection "a great mart" of pens, brick and frame buildings, and exhibition spaces where traders offered between several hundred and several thousand enslaved people for sale at a time. But in January 1863, the last newspaper advertisements appeared for slave sales at the Forks of the Road. Union troops arrived in Natchez about six months later. When they did, officers recruited Black men to serve in the Union Army, and among the first tasks for the soldiers of Mississippi's Sixth Infantry was constructing barracks. They made them at the Forks of the Road, out of what had been Isaac Franklin's trading compound.[84]

A white Union officer reported that the order "to tear down these slave pens to obtain lumber to build" the barracks "was hailed with the wildest enthusiasm," as "many of the men composing the regiment had been sold" in the very buildings they demolished. The order came down at dusk, and soldiers who had once been "chained, gagged and whipped" worked "with a terrible earnestness" all night long. As they did, they shared stories "of the cruelty of traders, of sad partings of husband and wife, of inhuman fathers selling their own children, and a thousand other incidents," and when dawn came, "the morning sun saw the slave pens of Natchez leveled to the ground." For the rest of the war, the Forks of the Road housed a Black regiment, and thousands of other formerly enslaved people flocked to refugee camps in and around the city.[85]

As the places where he made his name and his money got dismantled, piece by piece, John Armfield sheltered at Beersheba Springs. He eagerly supported the southern cause when the Civil War began. In May 1861, even before Tennessee seceded, Armfield hosted a barbecue where men could volunteer for the Confederate Army, a gesture that led residents of Beersheba's Grundy County to bestow upon him the honorary rank of general and the local newspaper to praise him as "a whole souled, warm-hearted Southern rights man." In September, Armfield equipped Company A of the Fifth Regiment of Tennessee Volunteers, and a nephew, Albert Hanner, was elected captain. Another nephew, John Hanner, and Armfield's ward, John Armfield Franklin, enlisted to fight for the Confederacy as well.[86]

But by the summer of 1862, Armfield sensed that "the war was more like a shipwreck than anything he could compare it to," and the conflict's physical and psychological tolls mounted. Shortly after the war started, Armfield fell so ill that he was "unable to leave the house," and in the aftermath of Nashville's capture by the Union in February 1862 and Albert Hanner's death at the Battle of Shiloh six weeks later, Armfield became erratic and paranoid. He changed his will and left out the Franklin children he and Martha had raised, a decision touching off arguments with Martha so ferocious that she left Beersheba to stay with other family members in Sumner County. At around the same time, Armfield informed his longtime millwright and general agent at Beersheba, Benjamin Cagle, that he had been told that he "was in danger of being poisoned," and he asked Cagle to "get physicians and hold an inquest over" him if he were to "depart this life in a sudden or mysterious manner."[87]

Armfield also brooded about his finances. He became convinced that the "bulk of his fortune," comprising hundreds of thousands of dollars in New Orleans banks and notes on loans to wealthy southerners, was "sunk by the war beyond any reasonable hope of being reached." So Armfield enlisted Cagle to help him hide what he had left. He gave Cagle more than $100,000 worth of "stocks bank notes, gold and silver" to stick in hidey-holes and bury under stumps, and he entrusted with him, "for safe keeping," what Cagle estimated to be "half a million dollars of notes and evidences of deposits."[88]

As the calendar turned to 1863, John Armfield regained a measure of health and equanimity. Martha came back to Beersheba, and Armfield offered asylum on the mountain to wealthy Tennesseans and their families whose lives had been upended by the war. For Lucy Virginia French, a planter's wife and a writer who found sanctuary at Beersheba, the resort "assumed the role of a refuge." French remembered that she and other white women kept busy "sewing, knitting, weaving and cooking" for Confederate soldiers and that they sang "Bonnie Blue Flag" and other southern wartime anthems.[89]

The stability was short-lived. Union campaigns in 1863 unleashed chaos in the eastern Tennessee mountains, and by the spring, French saw "a continuous stream of humanity pouring through" Beersheba, "hurrying Southward into Dixie. Men, women and children—soldiers, civilians, refugees—all 'sorts and conditions' of men." Union and Confederate deserters roamed the woods, gangs of bushwhacking guerrillas threatened civilians, and nearby residents recalled that the entire area was "infested with thieves, robbers, and murderers." Armfield understood he was a likely target, as everyone knew he was a "man of large cash capital." He posted a nightly sentinel outside his cottage, stationed men inside "well armed with double-barreled shot guns and revolvers," and told Lucy French he would "not let these damned wolves run over me without some music."[90]

They ran over him anyway. Throughout the early summer of 1863, "straggling banditti" set upon Beersheba Springs every few days for food, clothing, and whatever else they could find. Then, on July 26, about fifty mounted men, "renegades from both armies," led a crowd of poor and hungry mountaineers into Beersheba and sacked the place. They rode horses through the hotel gallery, pulled down chandeliers in the dining room, and cut the cloth off the billiard tables. They set up wine bottles like pins and knocked them over with bowling balls, and they pillaged most of the cottages, grabbing armfuls of fancy dresses, taking rugs and curtains and books, and hauling away furniture.[91]

When they left, some of the people held in bondage on the mountain left too. Among them was a woman named Letha, who was enslaved by Martha Armfield. Letha's husband had run behind Union lines in 1862, and when the raiders came to Beersheba, he came with them. He freed Letha and their eight children, "and they all went off." Martha Armfield thanked a Union officer for having "afforded them an opportunity to leave," saying that many of the children were small and "of no profit to us—only a dead expense, and it is a happy riddance." There was a mask of bravado in that, but she was very much the wife of a slave trader. If there was no profit to be had or use to be made of Black people, she hardly saw the point in having them around. The contempt was mutual. Lucy French noticed that when Letha departed, she "bid no one good bye."[92]

John Armfield did not have his wife's kind of indignation left in him anymore. On July 27, the day after the raid on Beersheba Springs, Armfield swore an oath of allegiance to the United States in the nearby town of McMinnville. He spent most of the rest of the war on the mountain, and he emerged from it a diminished man in a different country.[93]

The diminishment could be seen in his accounts. Armfield was not entirely impoverished by the Civil War. But when he went to New Orleans after it ended, his fear that everything would be gone was "more than realized." Ruin was widespread, Armfield was unable "to collect from banks and individuals whose obligations he held," and he had so little liquid capital that he needed a loan to get back to Tennessee. By 1868, Armfield had used the banknotes and gold and silver Benjamin Cagle had hidden. The Grundy County census taker in 1870 recorded that Armfield had $5,000 in real estate and a personal estate valued at $30,000, much of which was in cash deposited with the Third National Bank of Nashville.[94]

The difference in the country was etched in glass. John Armfield Franklin's Civil War service ended at Appomattox, where he saw Robert E. Lee surrender to Ulysses Grant. Then he returned to Tennessee. He spent the summer of 1865 at Beersheba Springs with John and Martha Armfield, and on July 29, he scratched his signature into the front window of the Armfields' cottage, alongside the names of two other people. One was "Jeannie," probably his cousin

Jane. The other was "Sallie," the daughter of Nathan and Henrietta Bracken. After the war, the Brackens and their six children stayed at Beersheba, where they could be together in freedom and where four-year-old Sallie learned to recognize and read her name, carved in the windowpane of a house owned by the former slave trader who had bought her parents at auction.[95]

A younger John Armfield might have started over. But the John Armfield facing a new country without slavery was almost seventy years old and in chronically poor health. A rheumatic condition caused him near-constant joint and muscle pain, and he suffered repeated bouts of pneumonia. He and Martha spent the winter of 1870 in Florida in the vain hope that the climate might improve his condition. Returning to Tennessee in April 1871, he stopped in Nashville to change his will again, citing "the curtailment of my fortune by results of the war" and claiming that "certain legatees" had "not treated me with that kindness to which I think I was entitled." Armfield wanted "a sufficient, comfortable, and economical maintenance" given to his aging sister Polly. He left $1,000 to Benjamin Cagle, and he ordered whatever might be left divided among his wife and the Franklin children for whom he and Martha had "tried to act the part of parents." Then he went back up the mountain.[96]

The summer of 1871 brought Armfield "a respite from the more acute symptoms of his disease," but he fell ill again in late August. Edward Noel Franklin, who sat vigil at his bedside, reported that he had seen Armfield sick before but that this time he did not "rally" as he usually did and talked "a great deal about dying." At around midnight on September 20, 1871, John Armfield "breathed his last." Franklin anticipated many mourners. "Earth," he believed, "can illy afford to lose such a man as he was, truly one of nature's noblemen."[97]

White Tennesseans, at least, offered effusive eulogies. A public meeting in Grundy County praised Armfield as "the warm and steadfast friend of all improvements of every description" and "the

John and Martha Armfield. These photographs, probably taken in the 1860s, accompanied a remembrance of Beersheba Springs during the Civil War and tribute to John Armfield's support of the Confederacy that was published in *Confederate Veteran* magazine in 1901. Courtesy the University of Alabama Libraries Special Collections.

earnest and enthusiastic friend of the widow and orphan," as a "philanthropist" and "a benefactor" who "was a friend to virtue, an advocate of morality, and a supporter of Christianity." Armfield's obituary in a Nashville newspaper similarly considered him someone whose "whole life [had] been marked by correct dealing" and "a man of far-reaching sagacity and sound common sense." He had "unerring judgment in all matters of business" and "few equals" for benevolence, and he left behind "many friends" who grieved at "the death of one so strong in character and so resolute in good."[98]

Though the obituary writer dwelled on Armfield's efforts at Beersheba Springs, he gestured toward Armfield's "partnership with the late Isaac Franklin," observing that Armfield "accumulated a large fortune by his enterprise, energy, pluck, industry and foresight." It was quite a tribute, and its elision of the slave trade as the source of Armfield's fortune was reminiscent of the way newspapers had reported the death of Isaac Franklin. Its only mention of Black people at all presaged the sanitized and racist memory of slavery many white Americans would perpetuate for generations. Recalling a ride taken with Armfield at Beersheba, the writer claimed that "even the poor negroes looked upon him as their fastest friend, and he took delight in bearing with their many infirmities and teaching them the necessity of labor."[99]

Labor was one thing about which formerly enslaved people needed no lessons from John Armfield, who in the end had little to show for having sold so much of theirs for his own benefit. When Armfield's estate was finally settled in the late 1870s, just a bit over $22,000 was left to divide among the legatees. There was not much for Martha's support.[100]

But before he died, Armfield filed a claim with the secretary of war for funds the Union Army had confiscated from his account with the Bank of Louisiana in New Orleans. The claim was referred to the Treasury Department, which rejected it in 1868 on the grounds that it had neither the jurisdiction nor an appropriation to pay it. In 1884, however, John W. Franklin revived the claim in his capacity as his brother-in-law's executor, bringing it directly to Congress. Paeans to Armfield's integrity notwithstanding, he had lied outright in his original application, asserting that he "was an infirm old man who remained quietly at home during the war" and "gave no aid, comfort, or encouragement to the rebellion or to persons engaged therein, but throughout the war remained loyal to the Government of the United States." Franklin repeated the lie. And it worked. In January 1885, Congress authorized the secretary of the treasury to turn over $18,000 in federal funds to John W. Franklin on behalf of Martha Armfield. Equivalent to nearly half a million dollars today, it was reparation to a slave trader's widow for what was deemed unlawfully taken.[101]

THE LEDGER
AND THE CHAIN

IN JANUARY 1864, JAMES MILLER McKIM VISITED THE GALL-atin, Tennessee, headquarters of Union General Eleazer Paine. Working as a correspondent for the *National Anti-Slavery Standard*, McKim particularly wanted Paine's "account of his dealings with the freed people, and his management of certain sequestered estates." Fairvue was one of those places, and as Paine was observing that working it "on the principle of free labor" made it "yield a larger net profit than had been realized under the old system," William Franklin appeared at the door. Equipped with a sheaf of legal records, Franklin offered "whining professions of loyalty" and insisted he "ought to be in possession of the property."

McKim had been an antislavery activist for more than thirty years. He recognized John Armfield's name on some of Franklin's papers, and after Franklin confirmed that Armfield "did a very large business in negroes" with his brother, McKim saw everything "perfectly plain." William Franklin's brother was Isaac Franklin, "the chief member of the late notorious firm of Franklin and Armfield, slave-traders in Alexandria."

McKim took great satisfaction in watching William Franklin grovel. He thought slavery odious, slaveholders "liars," and southern society "*wholly corrupt.*" He had also visited the Duke Street establishment "when it was at the height of its gory prosperity." He knew what Isaac Franklin had done, and he considered him one of many "Southern pretenders to aristocracy" who "were raised to distinction by success in the domestic slave trade." None of them deserved their good names or their fortunes, and McKim relished how the Union Army "exposed the infamy of their secret places" with every advance. He was certain that when "the revolution now in progress" was complete, "the world will understand slavery as it never did before." The power of men like Isaac Franklin would be wiped from the earth.[1]

But the Union never formally confiscated Fairvue. Franklin's estate reclaimed it when the Civil War ended, and its return and the indemnification of Martha Armfield were not the only instances of federal authorities vouchsafing the ill-gotten gains of Isaac Franklin and his partners. In 1863, Union forces coming down the Mississippi River liberated the enslaved at Magnolia, Outpost, Elcho, Karnac, and Lapine. Military officials took the draft animals and the livestock. They seized and sold hundreds of cotton bales, and they confiscated the land as "abandoned," leasing it to men who would supervise the picking of cotton left in the fields and sell it, the proceeds to be split with the Treasury Department. A year later, however, Louisa Ballard successfully appealed to retake control of the land, and in 1868, she filed claims for restitution on cotton sold from Rice Ballard's properties during the war. Arguing that she had never supported the Confederacy and adducing as evidence the fact that her new husband, James H. Purdy, had been a Union Army officer, she was awarded around $40,000 by the United States Court of Claims.[2]

A Black woman stands outside what had been the Franklin and Armfield slave-trading compound in Alexandria. Taken sometime in the 1860s, the photograph also depicts what appear to be two white soldiers peering out through a grated iron door. Library of Congress Prints and Photographs Division.

Adelicia Acklen's windfall was even more spectacular, and it continued the pattern of alternating economic gains and personal losses that characterized her entire adult life. In 1853, near Nashville, she and Joseph Acklen built Belmont, an Italianate mansion and temple to their wealth with thirty rooms, a library and an art collection, gardens and greenhouses, a bowling alley, marble fountains and statues, an artificial lake, a deer park, and a zoo equipped with a bear house. Two years later, the Acklens' two-year-old twins, Laura and Corinna, died of scarlet fever, and Emma Franklin, ten years old and the last of Adelicia's children with Isaac Franklin, died of diphtheria. The Acklens had three more children between 1855 and 1859, and Joseph Acklen, who held $3 million in assets and enslaved 691 people, planned a fifty-room mansion in West Feliciana

Parish that one newspaper described as "A Palace." The outbreak of war halted construction, and Acklen died at Angola of pneumonia in 1863. But Adelicia, who had stayed in Tennessee, headed south, and she played what one federal official called "a very deep game." She got Confederate officials to exempt her from orders to burn all cotton lest it fall into enemy hands. She got Union officials to provide a gunboat escort and permission to hire wagons. Then she shipped from New Orleans more than two thousand bales of stockpiled cotton and sold it in Liverpool for nearly $1 million.[3]

Some thought Adelicia Acklen was richer after the Civil War than she had been before it. Given how much of her wealth was made up of enslaved people, that seems unlikely. But she and Martha Armfield and Louisa Ballard all obtained significant material aid and support from the United States that the people their husbands bought and sold never did. As those people crossed the boundary from a world of bondage to one of emancipation, they received no substantive recompense for their years of unpaid labor, for the physical and emotional violence they had endured, or for the trauma their families had suffered through separation. And that, in turn, meant the ledger and the chain that constrained them under slavery would manifest in new guises, persisting as dual burdens through time.[4]

In 1869, Joseph H. D. Bowmar, agent for the estates of Rice Ballard and Samuel Boyd, rented Lapine to James Gibson and his son for one year. The Gibsons were to deliver the first twenty bales of cotton they cultivated to Vicksburg, where Bowmar would sell it and keep proceeds up to $1,200. The Gibsons would get any additional proceeds on the crop, but they would have to find a way to make up the rest of the rent should sales fall short. Bowmar made the same arrangement the following year with Abraham Washington and Noris Brooks. In 1871, after a court order delivered Lapine and Elcho to Ballard's heirs and Karnac and Outpost to Boyd's, Errol Boyd, Samuel Boyd's oldest son, made similar rental agreements at Karnac with ten different men, each of whom would work a piece of land between 12.5 and 100 acres in size. Boyd repeated the arrangement in 1872 with nineteen men, and he bargained with ten other men and women to provide land, mules, and farm equipment in exchange for half the crop they raised and the cost of provisions.[5]

The Gibsons, Washington, Brooks, and the rest of the farmers were Black, and most if not all of them had probably been enslaved on the same ground they and their families continued to work in freedom. In theory, tenant farming and sharecropping arrangements like those they entered into, commonplace in the postwar era, matched Black workers without land to white landowners without workers and benefited them both in a rural South where cash and credit alike were hard to come by. In practice, the upper hand lay with landowners, who got paid first, kept definitive if not always square records of balances, and often trapped workers in cycles of debt and dependency that could tie them to the land for years. For the formerly enslaved, it was a far cry from being bought and sold as property, but it was not the same kind of freedom that most white people took as their birthright.[6]

Not that the contingencies of freedom allowed the formerly enslaved to forget how near being bought and sold could still be. In 1880, Adelicia Cheatham, her name after a third marriage, sold her Louisiana property for $100,000 to Samuel L. James, a former Confederate army officer who held a private lease from the state to operate its penitentiary. When she did, the pretense that always inhered to the term "plantation" was laid bare. The prison population in the United States was predominantly white before the Civil War, but it became predominantly Black in the postwar era. James had near-complete authority over hundreds of inmates, and into the 1890s he operated what one historian describes as "the most cynical, profit-oriented, and brutal prison regime in Louisiana history."[7]

Prisoners under the James regime, many serving lengthy sentences for the pettiest of offenses or for breaking laws designed to ensnare them, were whipped, beaten, and subjected to other forms of torture. Some slept in buildings that had housed the enslaved. James had convicts cultivate cotton and sugar, and he rented them to other landowners and to railroad companies and levee builders. James took in millions. The people at his disposal, working sunup to sundown in unrelenting heat and disease-ridden swamps, lived an average of six years in his custody. Author Douglas Blackmon refers to convict leasing and other forced labor systems of the postwar era as "slavery by another name." In at least one way they were that and then some. Widely used across the South, they delivered to private agricultural and industrial interests Black bodies that were no longer financial assets white people might consider worthy of even basic protections. Black people had become both exploitable and expendable.[8]

Dividends from the business built by Isaac Franklin, John Armfield, and Rice Ballard helped give rise to these new tyrannies, aided by the forces of capital and state power they mustered to build it. Systems of control reshaped for the modern era, they sustained overlapping and mutually reinforcing economic and racial hierarchies that continued evolving across generations. Their presence in our own day is inescapable.

In the United States today, the median white family holds ten times the wealth held by the median Black family, and the Black poverty rate is twice what it is for white Americans. Black men are six times as likely to be incarcerated as white men, Black women are twice as likely to be incarcerated as white women, and Black people make up over a third of the 2.2 million people who constitute the largest jail and prison population in the world. Protests and outrage abound, and yet Black life itself is often of no consequence when weighed against market concerns and police authority. An American history of race and capitalism that accounted fully for such structural inequalities and cultural priorities, and their broad cascade of consequences, would be neither simple nor linear. But the core of that story would describe how enslaved people were denied the capacity to keep or pass to their children the wealth they generated and how those who enslaved them took their labor and their bodies as spoils. It would explain how men profited by trafficking the enslaved to promote private gain and national growth, diffused money and credit from that traffic throughout the country so that it could be leveraged for the benefit of nearly everyone but the enslaved themselves, and accustomed Americans to think of Black people as suitable for shackles and showrooms and cells. Its hinge would be slavery and the slave trade that Franklin, Armfield, and Ballard played greater roles in shaping than anyone in American history.[9]

Tangible institutional legacies of Franklin, Armfield, and Ballard also endure. The University of the South, popularly known as Sewanee, is still in the mountains of East Tennessee. It still sits about thirty miles from Beersheba Springs, where the cottages are privately owned and the hotel serves as a retreat space and summer camp for the United Methodist Church. In Nashville, the Belmont mansion sits on the campus of Belmont University, a Baptist college that began its life inside the building as a school for women after Adelicia Cheatham's death in the late nineteenth century. In Gallatin, Isaac Franklin's Fairvue mansion stands in a subdivision of over four hundred luxury homes billed as "a premier golf and lakefront community" and called "Fairvue Plantation." In nearby Hendersonville, John Armfield's Hard Times property, now known as Spring Haven Mansion, is advertised as "a magical place to host your wedding or event."[10]

And in West Feliciana Parish in 1901, the state of Louisiana bought the land that had belonged to Isaac Franklin from the family of Samuel James and started operating a state-run penitentiary on the site. Today, the Louisiana State Penitentiary is a maximum-security prison covering eighteen thousand acres, making it the largest facility of its kind in the United States. For much of the twentieth century it was also the most violent and scandal-ridden correctional facility in the country, with conditions so hideous that in the 1950s, several dozen prisoners slashed their own Achilles tendons in a desperate plea to draw public attention to them. The prison houses Louisiana's death row, and among its predominantly Black inmate population of more than six thousand people, over half are serving life sentences. Many still work in fields and grow crops, supervised by armed guards on horseback. Befitting origins it has never escaped, and continuing to advance the inequities that created it, the Louisiana State Penitentiary is usually referred to simply as "Angola."[11]

Some of these institutions have reckoned with their pasts more thoroughly than others. Yet broader candor about Franklin, Armfield, and Ballard is rare, and reminders of their significance are in short supply on the American landscape. The memory of the domestic slave trade is like that in the United States. With progress and freedom practically a civic mantra, untethered to the realities of the past, the commerce in human beings is generally an afterthought in public spaces, lest mention of it mock the antebellum splendor it produced or the wealthy nation that rests in part on its foundation.

Finding traces of Isaac Franklin, John Armfield, and Rice Ballard is possible, if you know where to look. On Duke Street in Alexandria, the townhouse Armfield and successive slave traders used for decades as a headquarters still stands. Now known as the Freedom House, a historic marker out front denotes it as the "Franklin and Armfield Slave Office," and for more than twenty years it served as the home of the Northern Virginia Urban League, which created a small exhibit in the basement devoted to the history of the slave trade. In 2019, financial difficulties left the Urban League with no choice but to put the building up for sale, and the structure is in desperate need of repair and maintenance. But it received a lifeline from the city of Alexandria, which purchased the site and is committed to preserving the last surviving contemporaneous element of the built environment of Franklin, Armfield, and Ballard's slave-trading operation, an American door of no return for the ancestors of tens of thousands of people.[12]

What remains elsewhere are wisps and fragments. At the other end of Duke Street, a park has mostly replaced the wharves from which Armfield sent enslaved people down the Potomac River. The location of Ballard's Richmond jail is now a gas station. In New Orleans, nothing indicates that the hotel on Esplanade and Francais, now Frenchmen Street, was once a spot where Isaac Franklin sold people, and only in the last several years has the city sanctioned markers indicating sites of the slave trade at all. Among them is a small sign, set into the pavement at the corner of Esplanade and Royal, adjacent to a parking lot where once stood the rented house that Franklin used as a trading compound.

In Natchez, there is a contractor business and a vacant lot at the Forks of the Road. A few historic markers have also been there since the 1980s, and thanks to the dedication and persistence of local preservationists, historians, and activists, there is a small park nestled into the fork. A series of informational panels tells the story of forced migration to the lower South, and a rough circle of concrete studded with chain links, bolts, and shackles has been poured into the greensward as a memorial to the many thousands gone. It is a quiet space, but not as quiet as a space about ten blocks away, toward the Mississippi River, an unmarked ravine overgrown with weeds near the base of Saint Catherine Street. Passers-by would never know that on a spring day in 1833, the bodies of a teenage girl, a woman, and an infant were found there, unnamed and abandoned, ravaged with cholera, and loosely covered with dirt.[13]

ACKNOWLEDGMENTS

Nothing I say here can adequately express my gratitude to the people who made it possible for me to write this book or to the institutions that supported its creation. But I have waited a long time to try.

Archivists, librarians, and other staff at facilities across the country were unfailingly helpful as I researched this project. My thanks to everyone at the Adams County Courthouse, Natchez, Mississippi; the Albert and Shirley Small Special Collections Library at the University of Virginia; the American Antiquarian Society; the Arkansas State Archives; Baker Library Special Collections at Harvard Business School; the Beinecke Rare Book and Manuscript Library at Yale University; the Betsey B. Creekmore Special Collections and University Archives in Hodges Library at the University of Tennessee–Knoxville; the Concordia Parish Courthouse, Vidalia, Louisiana; Cornell University Libraries; the East Carroll Parish Courthouse, Lake Providence, Louisiana; the Historic Natchez Foundation; the Historic New Orleans Collection; the Houghton

Library at Harvard University; the Huntington Library; the Kentucky Department for Libraries and Archives; the Land Records Division of the Office of the Clerk of Civil District Court of Orleans Parish; the Library Company of Philadelphia; the Library of Virginia; the Local History / Special Collections Library in the Barrett Branch Public Library, Alexandria; the Louisiana and Special Collections at Earl K. Long Library, University of New Orleans; the Louisiana Research Collection at Howard-Tilton Memorial Library, Tulane University; the Louisiana State University Libraries Special Collections at Hill Memorial Library; the Madison Parish Courthouse, Tallulah, Louisiana; the Martin F. Schmidt Research Library at the Kentucky History Center; the Maryland State Archives; the Mississippi Department of Archives and History; Natchez City Hall; the New Jersey Historical Society; the New Orleans Notarial Archives Research Center; the New Orleans Public Library; the Southern Historical Collection at Wilson Special Collections Library, University of North Carolina–Chapel Hill; the State Archives of North Carolina; the Tennessee State Library and Archives; the University Archives and Special Collections Library at the University of the South; the University of Alabama Libraries; and the Virginia Historical Society (now the Virginia Museum of History and Culture).

Particular thanks go out to Mike Allard, James Amemasor, Krystal Appiah, Linda August, Barbara Batson, Walter Bowman, Trevor Brown, Christina Bryant, Ashley Cataldo, Anne Causey, Greg Crawford, Maya Davis, Jessica Dorman, Julia Downey, Jim Green, Erin Greenwald, Lance Hale, Temple Hendricks, Mandi Johnson, Gregg Kimball, Connie King, Jessica Lacher-Feldman, Tara Laver, John McClure, Mimi Miller, Melissa Murphy, Connie Phelps, Frances Pollard, Donna Ramby, Kevin Ray, Sally Reeves, Matt Reynolds, Heather Shafran, Rebecca Smith, Megan Spainhour, Jessica Strawn, Robert Ticknor, Meghan Townes, Matthew Turi, and Donnelly Walton.

I was fortunate to receive generous financial support that facilitated archival trips and time for writing from the American Council of Learned Societies; the American Philosophical Society; the Gilder-Lehrman Center for the Study of Slavery, Resistance, and Abolition at Yale University; the Historic New Orleans Collection; the Huntington Library; the Program in Early American Economy and Society at the Library Company of Philadelphia; the Virginia Historical Society (now the Virginia Museum of History and Culture); and Virginia Humanities. Thank you to everyone who sat on fellowship committees and reviewed applications, and especially to David Blight, Matthew Gibson, Lauranett Lee, Cathy Matson, Melissa McGrath, Jeanne Siler, David Spatz, and Tom Thurston. At the University of Alabama, Dean Robert Olin, Associate Dean Lisa Dorr, and Provost Kevin Whitaker made it possible for me to take a year's leave from my position as department chair to complete the manuscript. Andrew Huebner agreed in my absence to act as interim chair, a job that became far more than he anticipated when a global pandemic arrived midway through the spring semester. History Department staff members Ellen Pledger, Morta Riggs, and Marla Scott are unfailingly marvelous, and they helped me protect my schedule before Andrew's work began.

Many scholars and friends along the way offered encouragement, wrote letters of recommendation, gave feedback on book and fellowship proposals, read work in progress, commented on conference papers, invited me to give public talks, provided access to their own work and sources, helped track down bits of archival material, connected me to individuals with invaluable local knowledge, found me places to stay or let me crash in their homes on research trips, shared some glorious meals and stiff drinks, talked through thorny issues, and sometimes just listened in the moments where I needed to ramble out loud about slave traders and their miserable worlds. All of it is not even close to an exhaustive list of the gifts they gave me, and all of it is more than I can ever give back.

Thank you to Liesa Abrams, Richard Bell and the attendees of the Washington Area Early American Seminar at the University of Maryland, Leila Blackbird, Ser Seshsh Ab Heter–C. M. Boxley, Mark Brown, Karen Cox, Audrey Davis, Bill Dickinson, Max Edelson, Nicole Eramo, Richard Follett, Jeff Forret, Chip Garrett, Rebecca Goetz, Erin Greenwald, Robert Gudmestad, Jason Halbert, Louis Hyman and my fellow campers at the 2013 History of Capitalism Summer Camp, Brenda Jackson-Abernathy, Caroline Janney, Hasan Kwame Jeffries, Watson Jennison, Bruce Kaplan, Sean Kelley, Ari Kelman, Kelly Kennington, Katie Lantz and the attendees of the Early American Seminar at the University of Virginia, Susanna Lee, Jeff McClurken, Caleb McDaniel, Mimi Miller, Molly Mitchell, Brenda Mitchell-Powell, Megan Kate Nelson, Jennifer Orr, Margaret Peacock, Tanner Potts, Jon Pult, John Ratliff, Woody Register, Heather Cox Richardson, Natalie Ring, Seth Rockman, Thom Rosenblum, Calvin Schermerhorn, Rebecca Scott, Andrew and Larissa Sneathern, Rachel Stephens, Rachel Swarns, Kristin Taverna, Alan Taylor, Amy Murrell Taylor, Will Thomas, Dale Tomich, Elizabeth Varon, Kirt von Daacke, Kim Welch, Jonathan Daniel Wells, Amy Wood, and Sharon Wood.

Several people graciously offered their time and their expertise in long conversations and on personal tours of locations related to the book, and they showed and explained things to me that I could never have seen or learned otherwise. Betsy Phillips talked with me for hours on a driving tour of Fairvue and other places in Sumner County. Mark Brown let me see behind the scenes at the Belmont Mansion. Ser Seshsh Ab Heter–C. M. Boxley took me through the history of preservation efforts at the Forks of the Road and discussed the challenging and important work he has done over many years to ensure the slave trade and its legacies in Natchez are not forgotten. Sanford McGee spent an afternoon showing me Beersheba Springs, and as we carefully peeked around the grounds of the cottage that had once belonged to John and Martha Armfield, current owners Peg and Harry Williams appeared. Rather than chase away a stranger, they opened the doors and let me see as much of the inside of the place as I wished. Thanks as well to Beersheba cottage owners Garrett and Lane Adams. In Alexandria, Audrey Davis and Gretchen Bulova arranged for me to take the full measure of the house on Duke Street that once served as the headquarters of Franklin and Armfield.

While doing research one day at the Tennessee State Library and Archives, I was surfing the internet for references to Isaac Franklin, and I came upon a Facebook group for descendants of Franklin's father James. When I messaged one of the administrators, Lyn Franklin Hoyt, it was with some trepidation, but Lyn could not have been kinder or more encouraging of my research into her family's past. We talked over lunch, and she made introductions to other family members who similarly wanted to know what they could do to help. Kenneth Thomson Jr. and Terry Martin in particular have shared research materials and their vast knowledge of Franklin family history with me, and I am grateful for their generosity. I have also had the good fortune to meet numerous other Franklin descendants, as well as descendants of those raised by John and Martha Armfield. Susanna Grannis, Melanie Pflaum, Suzanne Scott, Alison Whitney, and Tom Whitney have all shared with me their experiences of learning about and trying to grapple with the legacy of their ancestors, and I have never envied them the task. I suspect this book will be a difficult one for them to read, but I want them to know how much I appreciate their contributions to it. I also owe a special thanks to Rodney Williams for sharing the story of his connection to John Armfield with me by email and for publishing it in print.

My agent, Lisa Adams, has been absolutely fantastic to work with. She is an incisive reader, a constructive sounding board, and someone who made the processes of getting the book proposal ready and shopping it to presses as painless as they could be for someone mostly unfamiliar with either. At Basic Books, Dan Gerstle first acquired and supported the project, and his successor as my editor, Brian Distelberg, pushed me to make the book better. Alex Colston, Tyiana Combs, Katie Lambright, and Melissa Veronesi helped me put some important final touches on the manuscript and made sure that I had everything in order to get it ready for production. Kathy Delfosse performed very careful copyediting, and Kate Blackmer did outstanding work in building the map.

Ed Baptist, Daina Ramey Berry, Carole Emberton, and Calvin Schermerhorn read the manuscript in its entirety and provided hugely helpful feedback. I only wish I had been able to incorporate more of their ideas.

For Rebecca, my love and appreciation are boundless. As I labored on this project, she accepted lengthy absences on research trips, two years of a "silent" alarm that still often woke her as it went off before sunrise so I could get up and write, and living with someone who is not always easy under the best of circumstances and who not infrequently had a hard time dealing with the things he found in the archives. Without ever stepping back from her own indomitable commitment to repairing the world, she took it all in and then some, not only because she is a person of immense forbearance, but also because she believed in the project and thought it important that I see it through. I owe her everything.

Over and over again while researching and writing this book, I found myself angry, disgusted, horrified, and beset with what I can only describe as grief. Yet even as I wanted to deal plainly with the men who trafficked enslaved people for profit, and with the corrupted nation that encouraged them to do it, I could never shake a sense of my inadequacy to do justice to the material. I wept over those stolen away and marveled that anyone ever survived the slave trade, and I wondered whether the emotions were really mine to feel and doubted it even made a difference when, as William Wells Brown observed, "slavery never can be represented." But those who lived through it deserve to have what happened to them told and remembered as best we can, and with the honesty denied them for generations. This book is for my children, Ben and Abigail. As they grow up, I hope they come to understand why we must make a future that tells the truth about the past.

ABBREVIATIONS
IN NOTES

COLLECTIONS, ARCHIVES, AND DOCUMENTS

ACC	Adams County Courthouse, Natchez, Mississippi
ACCR-HNF	Adams County Courthouse Records, Historic Natchez Foundation, Natchez, Mississippi
AFP	Acklen Family Papers, MS86, Louisiana Research Collection, Tulane University, New Orleans, Louisiana
APLSC	Alexandria Public Library Special Collections, Alexandria, Virginia
BJA	Family Record in Bible of Joseph A. S. Acklen, copy courtesy of Kenneth Thomson Jr., Gallatin, Tennessee
BSMN	President and Board of Selectmen Minutes, City of Natchez, Natchez City Hall, Natchez, Mississippi
DB-UTK	David Burford Papers, 1814–1864, MS1027, John C. Hodges Library Special Collections, University of Tennessee–Knoxville

DBP-UTK David Burford Papers, MS0935, John C. Hodges Library Special Collections, University of Tennessee–Knoxville

GAL Judge George W. Armstrong Library, Natchez, Mississippi

GK-NJHS Raritan Bay Union and Eagleswood Military Academy Collection, 1849–1973 (Papers of George Kephart Concerning the Slave Trade, 1832–1850), box 1, folder 2, MG285, New Jersey Historical Society, Newark, New Jersey

HNF Historic Natchez Foundation, Natchez, Mississippi

HNOC Historic New Orleans Collection, New Orleans, Louisiana

KDLA Kentucky Department for Libraries and Archives, Frankfort, Kentucky

LLMVC Louisiana and Lower Mississippi Valley Collections, Hill Memorial Library, Louisiana State University, Baton Rouge, Louisiana

LOV Library of Virginia, Richmond, Virginia

LRD-NOLA Land Records Division, Clerk of Civil District Court for the Parish of Orleans, 1340 Poydras St., Fourth Floor, New Orleans, Louisiana

MDAH Mississippi Department of Archives and History, Jackson, Mississippi

NONA New Orleans Notarial Archive, 1340 Poydras St., Suite 360, New Orleans, Louisiana

NARA National Archives and Records Administration

NOPL New Orleans Public Library, New Orleans, Louisiana

NTC Natchez Trace Collection, Dolph Briscoe Center for American History, University of Texas–Austin

QP Quitman Family Papers, Collection 616, Southern Historical Collection, Louis Round Wilson Special Collections, University of North Carolina–Chapel Hill

RCBP   Rice C. Ballard Papers, Collection 04850, South-ern Historical Collection, Louis Round Wilson Special Collections, University of North Carolina–Chapel Hill

SANC   State Archives of North Carolina, Raleigh, North Carolina

SC-UNO   Historical Archives of the Supreme Court of Lou-isiana, Earl K. Long Library, University of New Orleans, New Orleans, Louisiana

SIF   *Succession of Isaac Franklin* (n.p., 1851)

SM-NARA   Slave Manifests of Coastwise Vessels Filed at New Orleans, Louisiana, 1807–1860, National Archives and Records Administration Microfilm Publica-tion M1895, Records of the US Customs Service, Record Group 36

TSLA   Tennessee State Library and Archives, Nashville, Tennessee

USS   University Archives and Special Collections, Uni-versity of the South, Sewanee, Tennessee

UVA   Albert and Shirley Small Special Collections Li-brary, University of Virginia, Charlottesville

VHS   Virginia Historical Society, Richmond, Virginia

INDIVIDUALS/COMPANIES

BT   Bacon Tait

CMR   Calvin M. Rutherford

DB   David Burford

IF   Isaac Franklin

FBC   Franklin Ballard and Company

GK   George Kephart

JA   John Armfield

JMS   Jourdan M. Saunders

JRF   James Rawlings Franklin

LB   Louisa Ballard

RB   Rice Ballard

RCBC R. C. Ballard and Company
  RW Robert Windsor
    SB Samuel Boyd

NEWSPAPERS/JOURNALS

  AFN *Armfield Family Newsletter*
   AG Alexandria *Gazette*
 AGDA Alexandria *Gazette and Daily Advertiser*
  APG Alexandria *Phenix Gazette*
 BACDA Baltimore *American and Commercial Daily Advertiser*
 BPMA Baltimore *Patriot and Mercantile Advertiser*
  DNI Washington (DC) *Daily National Intelligencer*
  GUE *Genius of Universal Emancipation*
  JEH *Journal of Economic History*
  JER *Journal of the Early Republic*
  JSH *Journal of Southern History*
  MFT Natchez *Mississippi Free Trader*
 MJNA *Mississippi Journal and Natchez Advertiser*
 NCAJFA Natchez *Courier, and Adams, Jefferson and Franklin Advertiser*
  NCJ Natchez *Courier and Journal*
 NOCB New Orleans *Commercial Bulletin*
 NODP New Orleans *Daily Picayune*
 NOPC *New-Orleans Price-Current and Commercial Intelligencer*
  NRB Nashville *Republican Banner*
   RI *Religious Intelligencer*
 NYPC *Shipping & Commercial List, and New-York Price Current*
  THQ Tennessee Historical Quarterly
  UST *United States Telegraph*

NOTES

Unless otherwise indicated, quotations in the text can be found in the first source or sources cited in the accompanying note.

INTRODUCTION

1. IF to RCBC, December 8, 1832, folder 8, RCBP. Accounts of these incidents also appear in Robert Gudmestad, *A Troublesome Commerce: The Transformation of the Interstate Slave Trade* (Baton Rouge: Louisiana State University Press, 2003), 93–95; Calvin Schermerhorn, *The Business of Slavery and the Rise of American Capitalism, 1815–1860* (New Haven: Yale University Press, 2015), 150–151; Thom Rosenblum, "Forks of the Road Slave Market, Analysis of Historical Occupancy" (unpublished draft, July 2005), 21–36.

2. IF to RCBC, December 8, 1832, folder 8, RCBP; *NCAJFA*, April 26 and May 3, 1833; *MJNA*, April 26, 1833.

3. *MJNA*, April 26, 1833 (quotations); *NCAJFA*, April 26 and May 3, 1833; BSMN, 1832–1836, April 22 and 24, 1833; Natchez Municipal Records, Petitions—1824–1833, reel A313, GAL.

4. *MJNA*, April 26, 1833.

5. *NCAJFA*, April 26, 1833; Adams County Deed Book V, 238–240, ACC; JRF to RB, May 7, 1833, folder 11, RCBP.

6. Steven Deyle, *Carry Me Back: The Domestic Slave Trade in American Life* (New York: Oxford University Press, 2005), 4, 283–296; Michael Tadman, *Speculators and Slaves: Masters, Traders, and Slaves in the Old South* (Madison: University

of Wisconsin Press, 1989), 12; Jonathan B. Pritchett, "Quantitative Estimates of the United States Interregional Slave Trade, 1820–1860," *JEH* 61, no. 2 (June 2001): 467–475. Ira Berlin famously described the domestic slave trade as a "Second Middle Passage," succeeding the forced migration of Africans across the Atlantic. See Ira Berlin, *Generations of Captivity: A History of African-American Slaves* (Cambridge, MA: Harvard University Press, 2003), 15–18, 160–244.

7. Deyle, *Carry Me Back*, 59–60. Some scholars write of a "second slavery" as shorthand for these developments, which reversed a period in the late eighteenth and early nineteenth centuries when slavery in the Atlantic world seemed to be in retrenchment. Useful introductions to the concept of the "second slavery" include Dale Tomich, "The Second Slavery and World Capitalism: A Perspective for Historical Inquiry," *International Review of Social History* 63, no. 3 (December 2018): 477–501; Anthony E. Kaye, "The Second Slavery: Modernity in the Nineteenth-Century South and the Atlantic World," *JSH* 75, no. 3 (August 2009): 627–650.

8. Franklin, Armfield, and Ballard's operation, and the domestic slave trade generally, participated in and helped advance in the United States the inextricable creations and progressions of racism and capitalism that Cedric Robinson described as "racial capitalism." See Cedric J. Robinson, *Black Marxism: The Making of a Black Radical Tradition*, foreword by Robin D. G. Kelley (Chapel Hill: University of North Carolina Press, 2000; originally published 1983); and essays in Walter Johnson and Robin D. G. Kelley, eds., "Race, Capitalism, Justice," *Boston Review*, Forum 1 (October 2017).

9. Scott A. Sandage, *Born Losers: A History of Failure in America* (Cambridge, MA: Harvard University Press, 2005), 22–43.

10. Purchase Book, 1832–1834, folder 420, RCBP; *SIF*, 749; Manifest of the Brig *Uncas*, November 6, 1835, reel 7, SM-NARA; Deyle, *Carry Me Back*, 172; Tadman, *Speculators and Slaves*, 45; Herbert G. Gutman, *Slavery and the Numbers Game: A Critique of "Time on the Cross"* (Urbana: University of Illinois Press, 1975), 10, 124. Recent works focusing on the experiences of those trafficked in the slave trade include Edward E. Baptist, *The Half Has Never Been Told: Slavery and the Making of American Capitalism* (New York: Basic Books, 2016); Daina Ramey Berry, *The Price for Their Pound of Flesh: The Value of the Enslaved, from Womb to Grave, in the Building of a Nation* (New York: Beacon Press, 2017); Damian Alan Pargas, *Slavery and Forced Migration in the Antebellum South* (New York: Cambridge University Press, 2015).

CHAPTER ONE: ORIGINS, 1789–1815

1. John Payton Jr. v. John Franklin (1816), file 6063, Sumner County Loose Records, Lawsuits, TSLA; William C. Davis, *A Way Through the Wilderness: The Natchez Trace and the Civilization of the Southern Frontier* (New York: HarperCollins, 1995), 35–43; Michael Allen, *Western Rivermen, 1763–*

1861: Ohio and Mississippi Boatmen and the Myth of the Alligator Horse (Baton Rouge: Louisiana State University Press, 1990); Harriet Simpson Arnow, *Flowering of the Cumberland* (New York: Macmillan, 1963), 367–369; Dawson A. Phelps, "Travel on the Natchez Trace: A Study of Its Economic Aspects," *Journal of Mississippi History* 15, no. 3 (July 1953): 155–164; Richard Campanella, *Lincoln in New Orleans: The 1828–1831 Flatboat Voyages and Their Place in History* (Lafayette: University of Louisiana at Lafayette Press, 2010); Dr. John R. Bedford, "A Tour in 1807 down the Cumberland, Ohio and Mississippi Rivers from Nashville to New Orleans," *Tennessee Historical Magazine* 5, no. 1 (April 1919): 40–69.

2. Everett Dick, *The Dixie Frontier: A Social History* (New York: Alfred A. Knopf, 1948), 18–22, 109–114; William Richardson, *Journey from Boston to the Western Country and down the Ohio and Mississippi Rivers to New Orleans* (New York: Valve Pilot Corporation, 1940), 14–38; J. S. Buckingham, *The Slave States of America* (London, 1842), 1:405; F. A. Michaux, *Travels to the West of the Alleghany Mountains, in the States of Ohio, Kentucky, and Tennessea* (London, 1805), 253–255.

3. Payton v. Franklin; *Aggregate Amount of Each Description of Persons Within the United States of America; and the Territories Thereof, Agreeable to Actual Enumeration Made According to Law, in the Year 1810* (Washington, DC, 1811), 83; Emma Dicken, *Terrell Genealogy* (San Antonio: Naylor Company, n.d.), 237; John Lynd, vol. 4, Act 704, June 21, 1809, NONA; John G. Clark, *New Orleans, 1718–1812: An Economic History* (Baton Rouge, Louisiana State University Press, 1970), 336, 347; *Slavery and Justice: Report of the Brown University Steering Committee on Slavery and Justice* (Providence, RI: Brown University, 2006); Charles Rappleye, *Sons of Providence: The Brown Brothers, the Slave Trade, and the American Revolution* (New York: Simon and Schuster, 2007).

4. Payton v. Franklin; David Weeks Papers, box 1A, 1782–1818, folder 3A (1809–1812), MSS528, LLMVC; *MFT*, October 21, 1846.

5. Payton v. Franklin.

6. Arthur Singleton, Esq. [Henry C. Knight], *Letters from the South and West* (Boston, 1824), 101–102. Also see Calvin Schermerhorn, *The Business of Slavery and the Rise of American Capitalism, 1815–1860* (New Haven: Yale University Press, 2015), 10–18; Robert H. Gudmestad, "The Troubled Legacy of Isaac Franklin: The Enterprise of Slave Trading," *THQ* 61, no. 3 (Fall 2003): 195.

7. Payton v. Franklin.

8. Payton v. Franklin; David Weeks Papers, box 1A, 1782–1818, folder 3B (1810).

9. Timothy Flint, *The History and Geography of the Mississippi Valley* (Cincinnati, 1832), 1:140.

10. *NODP*, October 7, 1846.

11. James Kirke Paulding, *Letters from the South, Written During an Excursion in the Summer of 1816* (New York, 1817), 1:121–129 (quotation on 127). On white attitudes about the feelings of enslaved people they sold and separated in the

market, see Heather Andrea Williams, *Help Me to Find My People: The African American Search for Family Lost in Slavery* (Chapel Hill: University of North Carolina Press, 2012), 90–116, esp. 109–110; Phillip Davis Troutman, "Slave Trade and Sentiment in Antebellum Virginia" (PhD diss., University of Virginia, 2000), 116–195.

12. Douglas Anderson, *The Historic Blue Grass Line: A Review of the History of Davidson and Sumner Counties, Together with Sketches of Places and Events Along the Route of the Nashville-Gallatin Interurban Railway* (Nashville: Nashville-Gallatin Interurban Railway, 1913), 68–69; Wendell Holmes Stephenson, *Isaac Franklin, Slave Trader and Planter of the Old South* (Baton Rouge: Louisiana State University Press, 1938), 12; *NODP*, October 7, 1846; "Who Is James Franklin, Sumner County Settler?" *Save Captain James Franklin's Grave Site* (blog), http://savejamesfranklinsgrave.blogspot.com/p/who-is-james-franklin-sumner-county.html; *Sumner County, Tennessee, Cemetery Records,* compiled by Margaret Cummings Snider and Joan Hollis Yorgason (Owensboro, KY: McDowell Publications, 1981), 5–9; Lois Green Carr, "Diversification in the Colonial Chesapeake: Somerset County, Maryland, in Comparative Perspective," in *Colonial Chesapeake Society*, ed. Lois Green Carr, Philip D. Morgan, and Jean B. Russo (Chapel Hill: University of North Carolina Press, 1988), 342–388.

13. Anderson, *Historic Blue Grass Line*, 68; Jay Guy Cisco, *Historic Sumner County, Tennessee, with Genealogies of the Bledsoe, Cage and Douglass Families and Genealogical Notes of Other Sumner County Families* (Nashville: Folk-Keelin Printing Company, 1909), 269–271; "Who Is James Franklin, Sumner County Settler?"

14. Virgil Anson Lewis, *History of the Battle of Point Pleasant* (Charleston, WV: Tribune Printing Company, 1909), 113; Glenn F. Williams, *Dunmore's War: The Last Conflict of America's Colonial Era* (Yardley, PA: Westholme Publishing, 2017); Patrick Griffin, *American Leviathan: Empire, Nation, and Revolutionary Frontier* (New York: Hill and Wang, 2007), 97–123; Eric Hinderaker and Peter C. Mancall, *At the Edge of Empire: The Backcountry in British North America* (Baltimore: Johns Hopkins University Press, 2003), 157–160; Jack M. Sosin, "The British Indian Department and Dunmore's War," *Virginia Magazine of History and Biography* 74, no. 1 (January 1966): 34–50; Richard White, *The Middle Ground: Indians, Empires, and Republics in the Great Lakes Region, 1650–1815* (New York: Cambridge University Press, 1991), 351–365.

15. Hinderaker and Mancall, *At the Edge of Empire*, 160; Natalie Inman, "Military Families: Kinship in the American Revolution," in *Before the Volunteer State: New Thoughts on Early Tennessee, 1540–1800*, ed. Kristofer Ray (Knoxville: University of Tennessee Press, 2014), 132–135; Lewis Preston Summers, *Annals of Southwest Virginia, 1769–1800* (Abingdon, VA: L. P. Summers, 1929), 2:1391; *Veterans of the American Revolutionary War of Sumner County, Tennessee*, compiled by Alma Lackey Wilson (n.p., 1962), 19; *NODP*, October 7, 1846; Stephenson, *Isaac Franklin*, 13–14; *Sumner County, Tennessee, Cemetery Records*, 5–9; BJA; Paul

H. Bergeron, Stephen V. Ash, and Jeanette Keith, *Tennesseans and Their History* (Knoxville: University of Tennessee Press, 1999), 22–23; Thomas Perkins Abernathy, *From Frontier to Plantation in Tennessee* (Chapel Hill: University of North Carolina Press, 1932), 1–3.

16. Nashville *Rural Sun*, June 19, 1873; *History of Tennessee, from the Earliest Time to the Present* (Nashville, 1887), 797; Anderson, *Historic Blue Grass Line*, 68; Dick, *Dixie Frontier*, 4–5; Bergeron, Ash, and Keith, *Tennesseans and Their History*, 19–20; Kristofer Ray, *Middle Tennessee, 1775–1825: Progress and Popular Democracy on the Southwestern Frontier* (Knoxville: University of Tennessee Press, 2007), 3–4; Walter T. Durham, *The Great Leap Westward: A History of Sumner County, Tennessee, from Its Beginnings to 1805* (Gallatin, TN: Sumner County Public Library Board, 1969), 17–27; Cisco, *Historic Sumner County*, 8–12; Stephen Aron, *How the West Was Lost: The Transformation of Kentucky from Daniel Boone to Henry Clay* (Baltimore: Johns Hopkins University Press, 1996), 5–24.

17. *NODP*, October 7, 1846; Anderson, *Historic Blue Grass Line*, 69; *History of Tennessee*, 798–799; Malcolm J. Rohrbough, *The Trans-Appalachian Frontier: People, Societies, and Institutions, 1775–1850* (New York: Oxford University Press, 1978), 18–20, 22–81; Walter T. Durham, "Kasper Mansker, Cumberland Frontiersman," *THQ* 30, no. 2 (Summer 1971): 154–177; Abernathy, *From Frontier to Plantation*, 28–29; Cisco, *Historic Sumner County*, 18–21; *Early Times in Middle Tennessee, by John Carr, a Pioneer of the West* (Nashville, 1857), 19, 21–25; Ray, *Middle Tennessee*, 1–18; Durham, *Great Leap Westward*, 85–124; Cynthia Cumfer, *Separate Peoples, One Land: The Minds of Cherokees, Blacks, and Whites on the Tennessee Frontier* (Chapel Hill: University of North Carolina Press, 2007), 8–11, 52–75.

18. Ray, *Middle Tennessee*, 5–7; Durham, *Great Leap Westward*, 50–53; W. W. Clayton, *History of Davidson County, Tennessee, with Illustrations and Biographical Sketches of Its Prominent Men and Pioneers* (Philadelphia, 1880), 44; Anderson, *Historic Blue Grass Line*, 68; Cisco, *Historic Sumner County*, 33–34; William C. Saunders and Walter Clark, eds., *Colonial and State Records of North Carolina* (Goldsboro, NC, 1886–1905), 19:571–572, 24:629–630.

19. Sumner County Court Minutes, vol. 1 (1787–1791), 1, 3, 4, 13, 14, Sumner County Will Book 2, 175, TSLA; Durham, *Great Leap Westward*, 55–61, 148; *History of Tennessee*, 802; BJA; *Sumner County, Tennessee, Cemetery Records*, 4–46.

20. *NODP*, October 7, 1846; Kenneth C. Thomson Jr., "Isaac Franklin Was a Well-Liked Slave Trader," *Gallatin Examiner*, May 13, 1976.

21. Ray, *Middle Tennessee*, 1–18; Abernathy, *From Frontier to Plantation*, 19–32, 194–209; Arnow, *Flowering of the Cumberland*, 87–88.

22. Cumfer, *Separate Peoples, One Land*, 125–154; Bergeron, Ash, and Keith, *Tennesseans and Their History*, 30–32; Bobby L. Lovett, *The African-American History of Nashville, Tennessee, 1780–1930* (Fayetteville: University of Arkansas Press, 1999), 2–4.

23. Ray, *Middle Tennessee*, 70; Abernathy, *From Frontier to Plantation*, 112; Bergeron, Ash, and Keith, *Tennesseans and Their History*, 47–67; Cumfer, *Separate Peoples, One Land*, 11.

24. Adam Rothman, *Slave Country: American Expansion and the Origins of the Deep South* (Cambridge, MA: Harvard University Press, 2005); John Craig Hammond, "Slavery, Settlement, and Empire: The Expansion and Growth of Slavery in the Interior of the North American Continent, 1770–1820," *JER* 32, no. 2 (Summer 2012): 175–206; Bergeron, Ash, and Keith, *Tennesseans and Their History*, 60; Cumfer, *Separate Peoples, One Land*, 129–130; Durham, *Great Leap Westward*, 182–183.

25. Fourth Census of the United States, Tennessee, Sumner County, 296, microfilm reel 124, M33, NARA; Sumner County Tax Lists, 1788–1795, 1819, 1824, TSLA.

26. Anita S. Goodstein, "Black History on the Nashville Frontier, 1780–1810," *THQ* 38, no. 4 (Winter 1979): 401 (quotation); Cumfer, *Separate Peoples, One Land*, 133–135.

27. Ray, *Middle Tennessee*, 70–71; Cumfer, *Separate Peoples, One Land*, 135–136, 144–146; Goodstein, "Black History on the Nashville Frontier," 403–406.

28. Goodstein, "Black History on the Nashville Frontier," 404–405; Ray, *Middle Tennessee*, 69–71.

29. *Tennessee Gazette*, February 25, 1800 ("CASH"), August 25, 1802 ("a number," "horses"), April 6, 1803 ("7 or 8"); Hugh Williamson to John Gray Blount, November 25, 1792, in *The John Gray Blount Papers: Volume 2, 1790–1795*, ed. Alice Barnwell Keith (Raleigh: State Department of Archives and History, 1959), 218–219 ("young slaves" on 218); Ray, *Middle Tennessee*, 70.

30. Ray, *Middle Tennessee*, 69; *Return of the Whole Number of Persons Within the Several Districts of the United States* (Washington, DC, 1801), 72; *Aggregate Amount . . . in the Year 1810*, 77–78.

31. Steven Deyle, *Carry Me Back: The Domestic Slave Trade in American Life* (New York: Oxford University Press, 2005), 32, 304n48. For recent perspectives on serial displacement during forced migration from Africa to the Americas, see Alexander X. Byrd, *Captives and Voyagers: Black Migrants Across the Eighteenth-Century British Atlantic World* (Baton Rouge: Louisiana State University Press, 2008), esp. 17–56; Sowande M. Mustakeem, *Slavery at Sea: Terror, Sex, and Sickness in the Middle Passage* (Urbana: University of Illinois Press, 2016), 156–182. On transshipment of enslaved people among British North American colonies, see Gregory E. O'Malley, *Final Passages: The Intercolonial Slave Trade of British America, 1619–1807* (Chapel Hill: University of North Carolina Press, 2014).

32. On the traumas of slavery, the slave trade, and their long aftermaths, see Saidiya Hartman, *Lose Your Mother: A Journey Along the Atlantic Slave Route* (New York: Farrar, Straus, and Giroux, 2008); Christina Sharpe, *In the Wake: On Blackness and Being* (Durham, NC: Duke University Press, 2016); Kidada Williams,

They Left Great Marks on Me: African American Testimonies of Racial Violence from Emancipation to World War I (New York: NYU Press, 2012).

33. Cumfer, *Separate Peoples, One Land*, 125–154; Bill Carey, *Runaways, Coffles, and Fancy Girls: A History of Slavery in Tennessee* (Nashville: Clearbrook Press, 2018).

34. *Tennessee Gazette*, September 9, 1801.

35. Sumner County Deed Book 3, 310–311, TSLA; Michael Tadman, *Speculators and Slaves: Masters, Traders, and Slaves in the Old South* (Madison: University of Wisconsin Press, 1989), 90.

36. Rothman, *Slave Country*, 26–35; "An Act to prohibit the importation of Slaves into any port or place within the jurisdiction of the United States, from and after the first day of January, in the year of our Lord, one thousand eight hundred and eight," *United States Statutes at Large,* Ninth Congress, 2nd Sess., 426–430; David Weeks Papers, box 1A, 1782–1818, folder 3A (1809–1812).

37. There were Armfields in western North Carolina before the 1760s, and some family historians suggest John Armfield's great-grandfather was actually a man named Isaac Armfield, who received a land warrant in 1753 near where many Armfields eventually settled. See Robert W. Ramsey, *Carolina Cradle: Settlement of the Northwest Carolina Frontier, 1747–1762* (Chapel Hill: University of North Carolina Press, 1964); Parke Rouse, *The Great Wagon Road: From Philadelphia to the South* (New York: McGraw-Hill, 1973); Blackwell P. Robinson, *History of Guilford County, North Carolina*, vol. 1 (Guilford County Bicentennial Commission, 1976), 10–24; Alexander R. Stoesen, *Guilford County: A Brief History* (Raleigh: North Carolina Division of Archives and History, 1993), 2; Sallie W. Stockard, *The History of Guilford County, North Carolina* (Knoxville, TN: Gaut-Ogden Company, 1902), 148–150; Ethel Stephens Arnett, *Greensboro, North Carolina: The County Seat of Guilford* (Chapel Hill: University of North Carolina Press, 1955), 10–15; *AFN* 1, no. 3 (March 2006); 1, no. 4 (June 2006); 2, no. 4 (June 2007); Isabel Howell, "John Armfield, Slave-Trader," *THQ* 2, no. 1 (March 1943): 6.

38. Ethel Stephens Arnett, *The Saura and Keyauwee in the Land That Became Guilford, Randolph, and Rockingham* (Greensboro, NC: Media, 1975); Stoesen, *Guilford County*, 1; Ruth Y. Wetmore, *First on the Land: The North Carolina Indians* (Winston-Salem, NC: John F. Blair, 1975), 28, 53–54, 60–61.

39. J. Hector St. John de Crèvecoeur, *Letters from an American Farmer* (New York, 1904; originally published 1782), 186; Robinson, *History of Guilford County*, 1–2, 15; Stoesen, *Guilford County*, 1–2; Arnett, *Greensboro*, 1–3.

40. Robinson, *History of Guilford County*, 14–16; Arnett, *Greensboro*, 14–15; Stockard, *History of Guilford County*, 150.

41. Robinson, *History of Guilford County*, 25–37; Fred Hughes, *Guilford County, North Carolina: A Map Supplement* (Jamestown, NC: Custom House, 1988), 31–43; Marjoleine Kars, *Breaking Loose Together: The Regulator Rebellion in Pre-Revolutionary North Carolina* (Chapel Hill: University of North Carolina

Press, 2002); Arnett, *Greensboro*, 15–17; David Leroy Corbitt, *The Formation of the North Carolina Counties, 1663–1943* (Raleigh: State Department of Archives and History, 1950), xxvi; Stoesen, *Guilford County*, 3–6.

42. *AFN* 1, no. 4 (June 2006); Howell, "John Armfield, Slave-Trader," 6–7; Corbitt, *Formation of the North Carolina Counties*, 113–114.

43. *AFN* 1, no. 4 (June 2006); 2, no. 2 (December 2006); 2, no. 3 (March 2007); 3, no. 1 (September 2007); 3, no. 2 (December 2007); 3, no. 3 (March 2008); 4, no. 3 (March 2009); Testimony of Mary Hanner, Wood v. Franklin (1876), file 10769, Sumner County Loose Records, Lawsuits, TSLA; Guilford County Deed Book 6, 461, and Book 8, 113, Guilford County Will Book B, 116–117, Divorce Record of Moses and Elizabeth Swaim, Guilford County Divorces, 1820–1929, box S, SANC; Hughes, *Guilford County*, 40; Howell, "John Armfield, Slave-Trader," 7.

44. Levi Coffin, *Reminiscences of Levi Coffin, the Reputed President of the Underground Railroad* (Cincinnati, 1876), 7 ("very inferior"); Stockard, *History of Guilford County*, 153–162 ("severely cut" on 153). Also see Howell, "John Armfield, Slave-Trader," 15–16; Guilford County Inventory and Lists of Sales, vol. X-10 (1835–1842), 233–234, Deposition of John Armfield, September 23, 1848, Hanner v. Winburn, North Carolina Supreme Court Case 6574 (42 NC 142, December 1850), Guilford County Tax List for 1815, SANC; Stoesen, *Guilford County*, 13; *AFN* 2, no. 2 (December 2006); 2, no. 3 (March 2007); and 3, no. 1 (September 2007); Testimony of W. S. Munday, Wood v. Franklin; Arnett, *Greensboro*, 19, 424.

45. Guilford County Tax List for 1815, SANC.

46. *Return of the Whole Number of Persons* (Washington, DC, 1801), 56, 58; *Census for 1820* (Washington, DC, 1821), 112, 114.

47. Stoesen, *Guilford County*, 17; Guilford County Tax List for 1815, SANC.

48. Christopher Leslie Brown, *Moral Capital: Foundations of British Abolitionism* (Chapel Hill: University of North Carolina Press, 2006), 391–450; Brycchan Carey, *From Peace to Freedom: Quaker Rhetoric and the Birth of American Antislavery, 1657–1761* (New Haven: Yale University Press, 2012); Brycchan Carey and Geoffrey Plank, eds., *Quakers and Abolition* (Urbana: University of Illinois Press, 2018); David Brion Davis, *The Problem of Slavery in Western Culture* (Ithaca: Cornell University Press, 1966), 291–332; Marcus Rediker, *The Fearless Benjamin Lay: The Quaker Dwarf Who Became the First Revolutionary Abolitionist* (New York: Beacon Press, 2017); Jean R. Soderlund, *Quakers and Slavery: A Divided Spirit* (Princeton: Princeton University Press, 1985).

49. Hiram H. Hilty, *Toward Freedom for All: North Carolina Quakers and Slavery* (Richmond, IN: Friends United Press, 1984), 1–43; Marvin L. Michael Kay and Lorin Lee Cary, *Slavery in North Carolina, 1748–1775* (Chapel Hill: University of North Carolina Press, 1995), 202–203.

50. Hilty, *Toward Freedom for All*, 23–39.

51. Coffin, *Reminiscences*, 12–13.

52. Coffin, *Reminiscences*, 14, 15–17, 20.

53. Howell, "John Armfield, Slave-Trader," 5, 7; Fourth Census of the United States, North Carolina, Guilford County, 58, microfilm reel 85; Guilford County Inventory and Lists of Sales, vol. X-10 (1835–1842), 233–235.

54. Answer of Moses and Elizabeth Swaim, Hanner v. Winburn; Divorce Record of Moses and Elizabeth Swaim, Guilford County Divorces.

55. Howell, "John Armfield, Slave-Trader," 7 ("was worth more"); Answer of Moses and Elizabeth Swaim, Hanner v. Winburn ("favorite children").

56. Eva Coe Peden, *Bible and Family Records of Barren County, Kentucky, and Surrounding Areas* (Glasgow, KY: E. C. Peden, 1977), 1:145–146.

57. Barbara Pratt Willis and Paula S. Felder, *Handbook of Historic Fredericksburg, Virginia* (Fredericksburg, VA: Historic Fredericksburg Foundation, 1993), 1–4; Oscar H. Darter, *Colonial Fredericksburg and Neighborhood in Perspective* (New York: Twain Publishers, 1957), 42, 59–64, 85–93, 113; James Roger Mansfield, *A History of Early Spotsylvania* (Orange, VA: Green Publishers, 1977), 15–19, 30–31, 90–91.

58. Darter, *Colonial Fredericksburg*, 60 ("most flourishing"), 89–92; Mansfield, *Early Spotsylvania*, 131–138.

59. Darter, *Colonial Fredericksburg*, 62–63, 94, 102–107, 293–294; Silvanus Jackson Quinn, *The History of the City of Fredericksburg, Virginia* (Richmond, VA: Hermitage Press, 1908), 23–25, 43, 47–48; Mansfield, *Early Spotsylvania*, 12, 13, 31–33, 149–153; Paula S. Felder, *Forgotten Companions: The First Settlers of Spotsylvania County and Fredericksburgh Town (with Notes on Early Land Use)* (Fredericksburg, VA: Historic Publications of Fredericksburg, 1982), 6–33, 73–91; *Return of the Whole Number of Persons Within the Several Districts of the United States* (Philadelphia, 1793), 49–50.

60. Darter, *Colonial Fredericksburg*, 206–215; Willis and Felder, *Handbook of Historic Fredericksburg*, 4–5; Quinn, *History of the City of Fredericksburg*, 44, 264–265; John Tackett Goolrick, *Historic Fredericksburg: The Story of an Old Town* (Richmond, VA: Whittet & Shepperson, 1922), 23–25, 199–200.

61. "Slave Owners Spotsylvania County 1783," *Virginia Magazine of History and Biography* 4, no. 3 (January 1897): 292–299. For an overview of slavery in Spotsylvania, see Ruth Coder Fitzgerald, *A Different Story: A Black History of Fredericksburg, Stafford, and Spotsylvania, Virginia* (Fredericksburg, VA: Unicorn Books, 1979), 1–87.

62. Frederic Bancroft, *Slave-Trading in the Old South* (Baltimore: J. H. Furst, 1931), 19–21; Fitzgerald, *Different Story*, 25–31; *Return of the Whole Number of Persons* (Washington, DC, 1801), 51, 52, 55; Peden, *Bible and Family Records*, 145–146; Louisville *Daily Courier*, September 1, 1860.

63. James Branch Cabell, *The Majors and Their Marriages* (Richmond, VA: W. C. Hill Printing Company, 1915), is a decent starting point for Ballard genealogy,

but the excellent website Ballard of Virginia: A Chronicle of Descendants in the Male Line of the Colonial Families in Virginia (blog), https://ballardofvirginia .com, updates and significantly expands on Cabell's work.

64. Joseph Lyon Miller, *The Descendants of Capt. Thomas Carter of "Barford,"* *Lancaster County, Virginia* (Thomas, WV: n.p., 1912), 2–6; Martin H. Quitt and *Dictionary of Virginia Biography*, "John Carter (ca. 1613–1670)," in *Encyclopedia Virginia*, last modified December 27, 2016, www.encyclopediavirginia.org/Carter _John_ca_1613-1670; Edmund Berkeley Jr. and *Dictionary of Virginia Biography*, "Robert Carter (ca. 1664–1732)," in *Encyclopedia Virginia*, last modified November 4, 2014, www.encyclopediavirginia.org/Carter_Robert_ca_1664-1732.

65. Miller, *Descendants of Capt. Thomas Carter*, 6–7, 270–286; Mansfield, *Early Spotsylvania*, 60, 85, 224; Felder, *Forgotten Companions*, 88, 154, 234–235, 237, 238.

66. Margaret Morris Bridwell, "Notes on One of the Early Ballard Families of Kentucky, Including the Ballard Massacre," *Filson Historical Quarterly* 13, no. 1 (January 1939): 53; Spotsylvania County Deed Books K, 246–247, N, 116, 500–501, T, 326–327, U, 49–50, Spotsylvania County, Auditor of Public Accounts, Personal Property Tax Books, 1798, LOV.

67. "Bland Ballard, Sr of Spotsylvania County, Virginia (c. 1713–1791)," Ballard of Virginia, https://ballardofvirginia.com/the-children-of-thomas-ballard-of -james-city-county-virginia-william-ballard-of-york-caroline-counties-virginia -c-1668-c-17/bland-ballard-sr-of-spotsylvania-county-virginia-c-1700-1791/; Spotsylvania County Will Book E, 1130–1131, 1181–1182, LOV.

68. "Benjamin Ballard of Spotsylvania County, Virginia (c. 1725–1814)," Ballard of Virginia, https://ballardofvirginia.com/the-children-of-thomas-ballard -of-james-city-county-virginia-william-ballard-of-york-caroline-counties-virginia -c-1668-c-17/bland-ballard-sr-of-spotsylvania-county-virginia-c-1700-1791 /benjamin-ballard-of-spotsylvania-county-virginia-c-1725-1814/; Spotsylvania County Will Book H, 387–389, 413–415, 474–475, Spotsylvania County Land Tax Books, 1804, James L. Leavell and Wife et al. v. James Ballard, case 1841–055, Spotsylvania County Chancery Causes, LOV.

69. A family Bible indicates that Emily and Rice Ballard had an older brother, named G. Dudley Ballard, who was born in 1798. No other evidence firmly substantiates his existence, suggesting he died young. Benjamin Ballard Jr. did buy 190 acres of land at auction and on credit in the late 1820s, but there is no indication that he sold the property, and he did not own it when he died. He may have failed to pay the mortgage, and in any case, if he ever owned land, it was not until his son was nearly thirty years old and had left the county. See Peden, *Bible and Family Records*, 145–146; Third Census of the United States, Virginia, Spotsylvania County, 100, 104, microfilm reel 71, M252, NARA; Fourth Census of the United States, Virginia, Spotsylvania County, 63, microfilm reel 135; Fifth Census of the United States, Virginia, Spotsylvania County, 74, microfilm reel

195, M19, NARA; Spotsylvania County, Auditor of Public Accounts, Personal Property Tax Books, 1814–1816, Spotsylvania County Deed Book BB, 520–523, James L. Leavell and Wife et al. v. James Ballard, case 1841-055, Spotsylvania County Chancery Causes, LOV.

70. Darter, *Colonial Fredericksburg*, 63–64, 81–82, 113–114 ("great hordes" on 113); *Return of the Whole Number of Persons* (Washington, DC, 1801), 51; *Aggregate Amount . . . in the Year 1810*, 55a; David Hackett Fischer and James C. Kelly, *Bound Away: Virginia and the Westward Movement* (Charlottesville: University Press of Virginia, 2000), 135–201; Damian Alan Pargas, *Slavery and Forced Migration in the Antebellum South* (New York: Cambridge University Press, 2015), 25–26; Alan Kulikoff, *Tobacco and Slaves: The Development of Southern Cultures in the Chesapeake, 1680–1800* (Chapel Hill: University of North Carolina Press, 1986), 157–161; Adam Rothman, "The Domestication of the Slave Trade in the United States," in *The Chattel Principle: Internal Slave Trades in the Americas*, ed. Walter Johnson (New Haven: Yale University Press, 2004), 33–34.

71. Darter, *Colonial Fredericksburg*, 64; Willis and Felder, *Handbook of Historic Fredericksburg*, 5–6.

72. Tadman, *Speculators and Slaves*, 12; *Return of the Whole Number of Persons* (Washington, DC, 1801), 51; *Aggregate Amount . . . in the Year 1810*, 55a; *Census for 1820*, 107; "The Forced Migration of Enslaved People in the United States, 1810–1860," in *American Panorama: An Atlas of United States History*, Digital Scholarship Lab, University of Richmond, http://dsl.richmond.edu/panorama /forcedmigration.

73. Bancroft, *Slave-Trading in the Old South*, 24 (quotations); Fredericksburg *Virginia Herald*, November 13, 1804.

74. Spotsylvania County Deed Book U, 101, LOV.

75. Spotsylvania County Will Book T, 426, LOV; 1850 Federal Population Census, Free Schedule, Virginia, Spotsylvania County, 421, microfilm reel 977, M432, NARA.

76. Jerry David Alsup, *Alsop's Tables*, vol. 1 (Byhalia, MS: Alsup Press, 1986), 179–181, 216; Spotsylvania County Personal Property Tax Books, 1800, LOV.

77. Spotsylvania County Personal Property Tax Books, 1811 ("goods"), 1814, 1819, LOV; Alsup, *Alsop's Tables*, vol. 1, 217–218, 221, 224; Jerry David Alsup, *Alsop's Tables*, vol. 3, part 1 (Bloomington, IN: iUniverse, 2012), 310; Fitzgerald, *Different Story*, 23; Richmond *Whig*, December 4, 1840.

78. Alsup, *Alsop's Tables*, vol. 1, 218–224; Eileen Mead, "It's Lookin' Good at Kenmore Woods," *Free-Lance Star*, April 16, 1993.

79. Spotsylvania County Deed Books T, 326–327, U, 49–50, W, 383, DD, 378–379, Spotsylvania County Will Book M, 485, LOV; Alsup, *Alsop's Tables*, vol. 1, 221.

80. Alsup, *Alsop's Tables*, vol. 1, 181; Miller, *Descendants of Capt. Thomas Carter*, 279, 280–281; Spotsylvania County Deed Book U, 101, LOV.

81. Sharon V. Salinger, *Taverns and Drinking in Early America* (Baltimore: Johns Hopkins University Press, 2002); Sarah Hand Meacham, *Every Home a Distillery: Alcohol, Gender, and Technology in the Colonial Chesapeake* (Baltimore: Johns Hopkins University Press, 2009), 64–81; *The Life of Elisha Tyson, the Philanthropist, by a Citizen of Baltimore* (Baltimore, 1825), 9–10, 80–83; Josiah Henson, *Truth Stranger Than Fiction: Father Henson's Story of His Own Life* (Boston, 1858), 49–50; Robert H. Gudmestad, *A Troublesome Commerce: The Transformation of the Interstate Slave Trade* (Baton Rouge: Louisiana State University Press, 2003), 27; Ned Sublette and Constance Sublette, *The American Slave Coast: A History of the Slave-Breeding Industry* (Chicago: Lawrence Hill Books, 2016), 430–431; Schermerhorn, *Business of Slavery*, 40; Mansfield, *History of Early Spotsylvania*, 141–147.

82. Alsup, *Alsop's Tables*, vol. 3, part 1, 381.

83. *BACDA*, September 20, 1811, April 27, 1809, December 18, 1815; *Baltimore Directory and Register for 1814–1815* (Baltimore, 1814); Ralph Clayton, *Cash for Blood: The Baltimore to New Orleans Domestic Slave Trade* (Westminster, MD: Heritage Books, 2007), 29–34; Seth Rockman, *Scraping By: Wage Labor, Slavery, and Survival in Early Baltimore* (Baltimore: Johns Hopkins University Press, 2009), 235.

84. Alexandria *Daily Gazette*, July 16, 1810, February 25, 1811; T. Michael Miller, *Artisans and Merchants of Alexandria, Virginia, 1780–1820* (Bowie, MD: Heritage Books, 1991, 1992), 1:207–208, 225, 2:80; Tomoko Yagyu, "Slave Traders and Planters in the Expanding South: Entrepreneurial Strategies, Business Networks, and Western Migration in the Atlantic World, 1787–1859" (PhD diss., University of North Carolina–Chapel Hill, 2006), 132–133.

85. *BACDA*, November 5, 1810; *DNI*, October 10, 1810.

86. Gudmestad, *Troublesome Commerce*, 8–21, 32–33; Deyle, *Carry Me Back*, 19–20, 35–38; Tadman, *Speculators and Slaves*, 12–19.

87. Sharon Ann Murphy, *Other People's Money: How Banking Worked in the Early American Republic* (Baltimore: Johns Hopkins University Press, 2017), 38–70; Schermerhorn, *Business of Slavery*, 10–32; Yagyu, "Slave Traders and Planters in the Expanding South," 61–83.

88. Franklin v. Steele, Orleans Parish Court, Suit Records, 1814–1815, case #560, VCP290, NOPL; Isaac Franklin v. William Parker, 1814, box 28, file 44, ACCR-HNF.

89. Incidents from the life of Charles Ball described in this section can be found in Charles Ball, *Slavery in the United States: A Narrative of the Life and Adventures of Charles Ball* (Lewistown, PA, 1826), quotations on 8, 24, 49, 400.

90. Alexandria County Grand Jury Charge, January Term 1802, quoted in *APG*, June 22, 1827.

91. Rothman, "Domestication of the Slave Trade," 41–45; Lacy K. Ford, *Deliver Us from Evil: The Slavery Question in the Old South* (New York: Oxford University Press, 2009), 188–194; Tadman, *Speculators and Slaves*, 13–15; Gudmestad, *Trouble-*

some Commerce, 102–104; Deyle, *Carry Me Back*, 51–55; Lewis Cecil Gray, *History of Agriculture in the Southern United States to 1860* (Washington, DC: Carnegie Institution of Washington, 1933), 2:658–660; Winfield Hazlitt Collins, *The Domestic Slave Trade of the Southern States* (New York: Broadway Publishing Company, 1904), 109–139.

92. Steven Deyle, "Rethinking the Slave Trade: Slave Traders and the Market Revolution in the South," in *The Old South's Modern Worlds: Slavery, Region, and Nation in the Age of Progress*, ed. L. Diane Barnes, Brian Schoen, and Frank Towers (New York: Oxford University Press, 2011), 107.

93. Jesse Torrey, *A Portraiture of Domestic Slavery in the United States* (Philadelphia, 1817), 32–33; Deyle, *Carry Me Back*, 45; Edward E. Baptist, *The Half Has Never Been Told: Slavery and the Making of American Capitalism* (New York: Basic Books, 2014), 18, 21–28.

94. Torrey, *Portraiture of Domestic Slavery*, 34.

CHAPTER TWO: CHOICES, 1815–1827

1. Nashville *Whig*, January 25, 1814; Kristofer Ray, *Middle Tennessee, 1775–1825: Progress and Popular Democracy on the Southwestern Frontier* (Knoxville: University of Tennessee Press, 2007), 107–114; Paul H. Bergeron, Stephen V. Ash, and Jeanette Keith, *Tennesseans and Their History* (Knoxville: University of Tennessee Press, 1999), 82–85; Tom Kanon, "'James Madison, Felix Grundy, and the Devil': A Western War Hawk in Congress," *Filson Club History Quarterly* 75, no. 3 (Fall 2001): 433–468; Karl Davis, "'Remember Fort Mims': Reinterpreting the Origins of the Creek War," *JER* 22, no. 4 (Winter 2002): 611–636; Thomas D. Clark and John D. W. Guice, *The Old Southwest, 1795–1830: Frontiers in Conflict* (Norman: University of Oklahoma Press, 1989), 117–160; Robert V. Haynes, *The Mississippi Territory and the Southwest Frontier, 1795–1817* (Lexington: University Press of Kentucky, 2010), 283–314; Tom Kanon, *Tennesseans at War, 1812–1815: Andrew Jackson, the Creek War, and the Battle of New Orleans* (Tuscaloosa: University of Alabama Press, 2014).

2. Nashville *Whig*, January 25, 1814; *SIF*, 277–278, 287, 298; Tom Kanon, "Regimental Histories of Tennessee Units During the War of 1812," Tennessee State Library and Archives, https://sos.tn.gov/products/tsla/regimental-histories-tennessee-units-during-war-1812; Walter T. Durham, *Old Sumner: A History of Sumner County, Tennessee, from 1805 to 1861* (Gallatin, TN: Sumner County Public Library Board, 1972), 39–81.

3. Clark and Guice, *Old Southwest*, 141 ("retaliated"); David Crockett, *Narrative of the Life of David Crockett, of the State of Tennessee* (Philadelphia and Boston, 1834), 86–90 ("like dogs" on 88, "if I could have" on 90); Kanon, *Tennesseans at War*, 75–77; Gregory A. Waselkov, *A Conquering Spirit: Fort Mims and the Redstick War of 1813–1814* (Tuscaloosa: University of Alabama Press, 2006), 163–164;

Adam Rothman, *Slave Country: American Expansion and the Origins of the Deep South* (Cambridge, MA: Harvard University Press, 2005), 130.

4. Clark and Guice, *Old Southwest*, 141; Kanon, *Tennesseans at War*, 77–80; Rothman, *Slave Country*, 130.

5. Clark and Guice, *Old Southwest*, 141–144; Rothman, *Slave Country*, 130–134.

6. Nashville *Whig*, January 25, 1814.

7. Rothman, *Slave Country*, 138–139, 176–188; Lewis Cecil Gray, *History of Agriculture in the Southern United States to 1860* (Washington, DC: Carnegie Institution of Washington, 1933), 2:1026–1027; Douglass C. North, *The Economic Growth of the United States, 1790–1860* (Englewood Cliffs, NJ: Prentice-Hall, 1961), 231; Stuart Bruchey, *Cotton and the Growth of the American Economy: 1790–1860* (New York: Harcourt, Brace, and World, 1967), 14, 18, 29.

8. Edward E. Baptist, *The Half Has Never Been Told: Slavery and the Making of American Capitalism* (New York: Basic Books, 2014), 75–110. Also see Sven Beckert, *Empire of Cotton: A Global History* (New York: Vintage Books, 2014), 56–82; Walter Johnson, *River of Dark Dreams: Slavery and Empire in the Cotton Kingdom* (Cambridge, MA: Harvard University Press, 2013), 73–96; Robert H. Gudmestad, *A Troublesome Commerce: The Transformation of the Interstate Slave Trade* (Baton Rouge: Louisiana State University Press, 2003), 32–33; Robert Gudmestad, *Steamboats and the Rise of the Cotton Kingdom* (Baton Rouge: Louisiana State University Press, 2011); Thomas C. Buchanan, *Black Life on the Mississippi: Slaves, Free Blacks, and the Western Steamboat World* (Chapel Hill: University of North Carolina Press, 2004); Sharon Ann Murphy, *Other People's Money: How Banking Worked in the Early American Republic* (Baltimore: Johns Hopkins University Press, 2017), 67–70, 80–85.

9. *Aggregate Amount of Each Description of Persons Within the United States of America; and the Territories Thereof, Agreeable to Actual Enumeration Made According to Law, in the Year 1810* (Washington, DC, 1811), 1; *Abstract of the Returns of the Fifth Census, Showing the Number of Free People, the Number of Slaves, the Federal or Representative Number, and the Aggregate of Each County of Each State of the United States* (Washington, DC, 1832), 51.

10. Michael Tadman, *Speculators and Slaves: Masters, Traders, and Slaves in the Old South* (Madison: University of Wisconsin Press, 1989), 12, 22–31; Steven Deyle, *Carry Me Back: The Domestic Slave Trade in American Life* (New York: Oxford University Press, 2005), 283–289; Gudmestad, *Troublesome Commerce*, 19–20. Using somewhat different methods, Jonathan Pritchett estimates that slave traders accounted for closer to one half of the interstate migration of slaves. See Jonathan B. Pritchett, "Quantitative Estimates of the United States Interregional Slave Trade, 1820–1860," *JEH* 61, no. 2 (June 2001): 467–475.

11. Michael Tadman estimates that net profits for slave traders ranged between 60 and 80 percent during the boom years of the late 1810s but remained

substantial, around 30 percent, even after declining in the post-panic years. See Tadman, *Speculators and Slaves*, 204; Ulrich B. Phillips, *American Negro Slavery* (Baton Rouge: Louisiana State University Press, 1966; originally published 1918), chart opposite 370; Baptist, *Half*, 178–179; Gudmestad, *Troublesome Commerce*, 21; Andrew H. Browning, *The Panic of 1819: The First Great Depression* (Columbia: University of Missouri Press, 2019); Murray N. Rothbard, *The Panic of 1819: Reactions and Policies* (New York: Columbia University Press, 1962); Murphy, *Other People's Money*, 85–88.

12. Sumner County Deed Book 7, 280–281, Sumner County Tax Lists, 1818–1819, TSLA.

13. *Sumner County, Tennessee, Marriage Records, 1787–1838*, abstracted by Deane Porch (Franklin, TN: Louise G. Lynch, 1979), 15; Sumner County Deed Book 3, 310, 311, Sumner County Will Book 2, 222–223, Smith Franklin v. Zebulon Cantrel (1837), file 2543, Sumner County Loose Records, Lawsuits, Sumner County Tax Lists, 1819, 1822, TSLA; *History of Tennessee, from the Earliest Time to the Present* (Nashville, 1887), 878; Fourth Census of the United States, Tennessee, Sumner County, 296, 297, microfilm reel 124, M33, NARA; *SIF*, 278, 284, 287.

14. *Sumner County, Tennessee, Marriage Records*, 25; John Payton Jr. v. John Franklin (1816), file 6063, Sumner County Loose Records, Lawsuits, TSLA; Isaac Franklin v. William Thompson, 1814, box 26, file 54, ACCR-HNF.

15. *DNI*, May 22, 1821 (quotations), April 3, 1822; Washington, DC *Daily National Journal*, September 2, 1824; *Mississippi State Gazette*, April 15, 1820, July 10, 1824, November 12, 1825; *Georgetown Messenger*, January 4, 1817; *BPMA*, September 4, 1820; Alexandria *Herald*, August 1, 1823. On the economic and cultural significance of the early postal system, see Richard R. John, *Spreading the News: The American Postal System from Franklin to Morse* (Cambridge, MA: Harvard University Press, 1995).

16. *DNI*, April 11, 1822; Richmond *Enquirer*, September 6, 1825.

17. Alexandria City Deeds, Books I, 376–380, I-2, 170–171, LOV.

18. Isaac Franklin v. William Grissam, 1825, box 44, file 1, ACCR-HNF; *SIF*, 274.

19. D. Clayton James, *Antebellum Natchez* (Baton Rouge: Louisiana State University Press, 1968), 3–53; John Hebron Moore, *The Emergence of the Cotton Kingdom in the Old Southwest: Mississippi, 1770–1860* (Baton Rouge: Louisiana State University Press, 1988), 3–5, 73–76, 188–189; Clark and Guice, *Old Southwest*, 183–185; Haynes, *Mississippi Territory*, 2–5, 11–12.

20. Christian Schultz, *Travels on an Inland Voyage Through the States of New-York, Pennsylvania, Virginia, Ohio, Kentucky and Tennessee, and Through the Territories of Indiana, Louisiana, Mississippi, and New-Orleans* (New York, 1810), 2:133; Clark and Guice, *Old Southwest*, 185; James, *Antebellum Natchez*, 77, 83, 111–115, 136–161, 169–170; Moore, *Emergence of the Cotton Kingdom*, 188–189; Morton Rothstein, "'The Remotest Corner': Natchez on the American

Frontier," in *Natchez before 1830*, ed. Noel Polk (Jackson: University Press of Mississippi, 1989), 92–108; Haynes, *Mississippi Territory*, 203–206, 208–210; Aaron D. Anderson, *Builders of a New South: Merchants, Capital, and the Remaking of Natchez, 1865–1914* (Jackson: University Press of Mississippi, 2013), 11–39; *Census for 1820* (Washington, DC, 1821), 122; William Richardson, *Journey from Boston to the Western Country and down the Ohio and Mississippi Rivers to New Orleans* (New York: Valve Pilot Corporation, 1940), 34–35.

21. James, *Antebellum Natchez*, 51–53 ("by far" on 52); Rothman, *Slave Country*, 24–26, 45–54; Haynes, *Mississippi Territory*, 12–13, 77–78; *Return of the Whole Number of Persons Within the Several Districts of the United States* (Washington, DC, 1801), 3; *Aggregate Amount . . . in the Year 1810*, 2, 83; David J. Libby, *Slavery and Frontier Mississippi, 1720–1835* (Jackson: University of Mississippi Press, 2004), 37–59; Christian Pinnen, "Slavery and Empire: The Development of Slavery in the Natchez District, 1720–1820" (PhD diss., University of Southern Mississippi, 2012), esp. 191–275.

22. James, *Antebellum Natchez*, 45–46, 87–88; Pinnen, "Slavery and Empire," 106–114; Frederic Bancroft, *Slave-Trading in the Old South* (Baltimore: J. H. Furst, 1931), 300; Calvin Schermerhorn, *The Business of Slavery and the Rise of American Capitalism, 1815–1860* (New Haven: Yale University Press, 2015), 20–28; Gudmestad, *Troublesome Commerce*, 23–25; Thom Rosenblum, "Forks of the Road Slave Market, Analysis of Historical Occupancy" (unpublished draft, July 2005), 6–10.

23. Henry Bradshaw Fearon, *Sketches of America. A Narrative of a Journey of Five Thousand Miles Through the Eastern and Western States of America* (London, 1818), 270; Estwick Evans, *A Pedestrious Tour of Four Thousand Miles, Through the Western States and Territories, During the Winter and Spring of 1818* (Concord, NH, 1819), 213.

24. Evans, *Pedestrious Tour*, 212, 213–214 (quotations); Timothy Flint, *Recollections of the Last Ten Years, Passed in Occasional Residences and Journeyings in the Valley of the Mississippi, from Pittsburg and the Missouri to the Gulf of Mexico, and from Florida to the Spanish Frontier* (Boston, 1826), 295; J. E. Alexander, *Transatlantic Sketches, Comprising Visits to the Most Interesting Scenes in North and South America, and the West Indies* (London, 1833), 2:61–62. Also see Virginia Park Matthias, "Natchez-Under-the-Hill as It Developed Under the Influence of the Mississippi River and the Natchez Trace," *Journal of Mississippi History* 7, no. 4 (October 1945): 201–221; Timothy Ryan Buckner, "Constructing Identities on the Frontier of Slavery, Natchez, Mississippi, 1760–1860" (PhD diss., University of Texas–Austin, 2005), 98–148; James, *Antebellum Natchez*, 44, 168–169.

25. *Mississippi State Gazette*, October 7 ("likely negroes"), January 10, December 9, and December 26, 1818; Bancroft, *Slave-Trading in the Old South*, 300 ("negroes were sold").

26. Gabriel Tichenor v. Isaac Franklin, 1814, box 33, file 41, ACCR-HNF; Marvin Bentley, "The State Bank of Mississippi: Monopoly Bank on the Frontier

EISE

JOS

xxxxxxx6370

9/27/2021

Item: ï¿½0010103361613 ((book)

(1809–1830)," *Journal of Mississippi History* 40, no. 4 (November 1978): 297–318; Robert C. Weems Jr., "The Makers of the Bank of the Mississippi," *Journal of Mississippi History* 15, no. 3 (July 1953): 137–154.

27. John Hutchins v. Isaac Franklin, 1819, box 2, file 56, ACCR-HNF.

28. *Narrative of Henry Watson, a Fugitive Slave* (Boston, 1850), 10; Adams County Deed Books G, 163, L, 507–508, ACC.

29. Adams County Deed Book L, 130, 507–508, ACC.

30. Robert L. Jenkins, "African-Americans on the Natchez Trace, 1800–1865," *Southern Quarterly* 29, no. 4 (Summer 1991): 43–61.

31. *Sumner County, Tennessee, Marriage Records*, 89; Sumner County Deed Book 10, 326, Book 11, 365–367, 461–462, Book 12, 149, 221, Sumner County Tax Lists, 1824, TSLA; Adams County Deed Book M, 70, 311–312, 479–481, ACC; Adams County Tax Rolls, 1823, record group 29, Auditor of Public Accounts, MDAH.

32. Isaac Franklin v. William Grissam; Natchez *Ariel*, December 29, 1826, April 5, 1828; Natchez *Gazette*, February 4, 1826; Nashville *Whig*, April 10, 1822; Adams County Deed Books K, 491, M, 105, 418, ACC; Wendell Holmes Stephenson, *Isaac Franklin, Slave Trader and Planter of the Old South* (Baton Rouge: Louisiana State University Press, 1938), 65–66; Maximilien Doyle v. the Jackson Association, 1827, box 45, file 22, ACCR-HNF. Numerous members of the Jackson Association were leaders of the Natchez Junto, a faction of planters and merchants that one historian has called "the nearest thing to a political machine in the state" in the 1820s. See James, *Antebellum Natchez*, 113–116.

33. *APG*, February 15, 1825; Account of Isaac Franklin in Estate of John Franklin, file 357, Sumner County Loose Records, Estates, TSLA.

34. Account of Isaac Franklin in Estate of John Franklin; *APG*, May 17, 1826, May 19, 1827, February 15, 1828.

35. Adams County Deed Book U, 504–505, ACC.

36. Isabel Howell, "John Armfield, Slave-Trader," *THQ* 2, no. 1 (March 1943): 7; Guilford County Deed Book 15, 795, Guilford County Will Book B, 180–181, Answer of Moses and Elizabeth Swaim, Hanner v. Winburn, North Carolina Supreme Court case 6574 (42 NC 142, December 1850), Guilford County Tax List for 1815, SANC; Fourth Census of the United States, North Carolina, Guilford County, 75, reel 85; Sallie W. Stockard, *The History of Guilford County, North Carolina* (Knoxville, TN: Gaut-Ogden Company, 1902), 195.

37. Guilford County Will Book B, 180–181, Surry County Tax List, 1819, Surry County Minute Docket, Court of Pleas and Quarter Sessions, 1817–1820, August 11, 1819, SANC.

38. Divorce Records, Moses and Elizabeth Swaim, Guilford County Divorces, 1820–1929, box S, SANC; J. G. Hollingsworth, *History of Surry County, or Annals of Northwest North Carolina* (Greensboro, NC: W. H. Fisher, 1935); William Franklin Carter Jr. and Carrie Young Carter, *Footprints in the "Hollows,"*

or Surry County and Her People (Elkin, NC: Northwestern Regional Library, 1976), 56–67.

39. *Census for 1820*, 113; Surry County Tax List, 1819, SANC.

40. Surry County Tax List, 1820, Surry County Minute Docket, Court of Pleas and Quarter Sessions, 1817–1820, August 14, 1820, SANC. For examples of North Carolina store inventories, see Raleigh *Star*, March 19, 1819, November 17, 1819, and March 3, 1820.

41. Surry County Tax List, 1821, 1822, SANC.

42. Surry County Minute Docket, Court of Pleas and Quarter Sessions, 1820–1825, February 14, 1821, Surry County Trial and Reference Docket, Superior Court, 1822–1835, September 1821, Surry County Superior Court, State Docket, 1815–1825, September 1821, Surry County Civil Action Papers, 1821–1827 box, 1822 folder, Armfield and Dickey v. Goldin and Chaney, Surry County Superior Court Minute Docket, 1807–1823, September 7, 1821, March 8, 1822, September 7, 1822, Surry County Tax List, 1821, SANC.

43. Surry County Civil Action Papers, 1821–1827 box, 1822 folder, Armfield and Dickey v. Goldin and Chaney, Surry County Superior Court State Docket, 1815–1825, March 1821, September 1821, March 1822, September 1822, Surry County Superior Court Minute Docket, 1807–1823, September 7, 1822, Surry County Minute Docket, Court of Pleas and Quarter Sessions, 1820–1825, August 16, 1821, February 12, May 13 and 16, 1822, August 13, 1822, Surry County Trial and Reference Docket, Superior Court, 1822–1835, September 1823, September 1825, State v. Armfield, North Carolina Supreme Court 1822, case 1307, SANC.

44. Surry County Superior Court Minute Docket, 1807–1823, March 9 and September 6, 1822, SANC.

45. *Genealogies of Virginia Families, from Tyler's Quarterly Historical and Genealogical Magazine*, with an introduction by John Frederick Dorman (Baltimore: Genealogical Publishing Company, 2007), 1:509–510; Surry County Tax Lists, 1819–1821, Surry County Minute Docket, Court of Pleas and Quarter Sessions, 1820–1825, August 11, 1824, Surry County Trial and Reference Docket, Superior Court, 1822–1835, March 1825, SANC; Hollingsworth, *History of Surry County*, 277.

46. State Docket, Surry County Court of Pleas and Quarter Sessions, 1817–1824, May 1824 (quotation), August 1824, November 1824, Surry County Minute Docket, Court of Pleas and Quarter Sessions, 1820–1825, August 11, 1824, Surry County Trial and Reference Docket, Superior Court, 1822–1835, March 1825, SANC.

47. Surry County Trial and Reference Docket, Superior Court, 1822–1835, September 1825, September 1826, Surry County Superior Court Minute Docket, 1824–1849, September 7, 1825, March 8, 1826, September 6, 1826, Surry County Deed Records, Book S, 424–425, Guilford County Abstract of Marriage Bonds, William Hanner m. Polly Dickey, October 7, 1824, SANC.

48. Howell, "John Armfield, Slave-Trader," 7 (quotation); *SIF*, 337; Stephenson, *Isaac Franklin*, 23n3.

49. Howell, "John Armfield, Slave-Trader," 8n12.

50. Deposition of John Armfield ("trusty boy"), Testimony of Ebenezer Ward ("boy named Tony"), Testimony of Isaac Russom, Hanner v. Winburn; Manifest of the Brig *Mark*, March 22, 1826, reel 4, SM-NARA.

51. Testimony of Ebenezer Ward ("he did not intend"), William Ingle ("he would not give"), Solomon Armfield ("no reasonable sum"), William A. Armfield ("he had never raised"), Hanner v. Winburn.

52. Interrogatory posed to Fisher B. Taylor, testimony of Isaac Russom, Joseph Newman, Thomas McCaulock, Salathiel Swaim, Hanner v. Winburn; Guilford County Will Book B, 180–181, SANC.

53. William Wells Brown, *Narrative of William W. Brown, A Fugitive Slave* (Boston, 1847), 62, 39. Brown called the trader James Walker in his narrative, but his name was in fact William Walker. See Ezra Greenspan, *William Wells Brown: An African American Life* (New York: W. W. Norton, 2014), 61–69.

54. Brown, *Narrative of William W. Brown*, 40–52 (quotations on 49, 41, 46); Buchanan, *Black Life on the Mississippi*, 81–100. On enslaved people and suicide, see Terri L. Snyder, *The Power to Die: Slavery and Suicide in British North America* (Chicago: University of Chicago Press, 2015); Richard Bell, *We Shall Be No More: Suicide and Self-Government in the Newly United States* (Cambridge, MA: Harvard University Press, 2012), 201–246; Richard Bell, "Slave Suicide, Abolition, and the Problem of Resistance," *Slavery and Abolition* 33, no. 4 (December 2012): 525–549; Diane Miller Sommerville, *Aberration of Mind: Suicide and Suffering in the Civil War-Era South* (Chapel Hill: University of North Carolina Press, 2018), 85–119; Daina Ramey Berry, "'Broad is de Road dat Leads ter Death': Human Capital and Enslaved Mortality," in *Slavery's Capitalism: A New History of American Economic Development*, ed. Sven Beckert and Seth Rockman (Philadelphia: University of Pennsylvania Press, 2016), 149–154; Damian Alan Pargas, *Slavery and Forced Migration in the Antebellum South* (New York: Cambridge University Press, 2015), 82–83.

55. Brown, *Narrative of William W. Brown*, 42 (quotations), 52–58.

56. Incidents from the life of William Hayden described in this section can be found in William Hayden, *Narrative of William Hayden, Containing a Faithful Account of His Travels for a Number of Years, Whilst a Slave, in the South* (Cincinnati, 1846), quotations on 54, 4, 7, 55, 56, 72, 73, 77–78, 75, 74, 78, 83.

57. As Thomas Foster observes about enslaved men who worked as valets or body servants, sustained intimate contact with their enslavers "could present them with relatively better conditions and chances for labor of a different sort from exhausting agricultural labor, but it could also be emotionally suffocating and psychologically difficult." In some cases, it also left them "vulnerable to sexual violations." See Thomas A. Foster, *Rethinking Rufus: Sexual Violations of Enslaved Men* (Athens: University of Georgia Press, 2019), esp. 102–112 (quotations on 111–112).

58. Carlile Pollack, vol. 18 (January–November 1826), Act 132, March 15, 1826, William Boswell, vol. 5 (January–April 30, 1828), Act 48, January 19, 1828, NONA; Baltimore *Gazette and Daily Advertiser*, April 18, 1826; Manifest of the Brig *Mark*, March 22, 1826; Reply of W. C. Dismukes, *Wood v. Franklin* (1876), file 10769, Sumner County Loose Records, Lawsuits, TSLA.

59. Manifest of the Brig *Mark*, March 22, 1826; Portland *Eastern Argus*, November 4, 1825, May 5, 1826; Portland *Advertiser*, November 11, 1825; New York *Commercial Advertiser*, December 22, 1825; Charleston *Courier*, March 2, 1826; New York *National Advocate*, March 27, 1826; *NYPC*, November 2, 1825, April 15, 1826; Baltimore *Gazette and Daily Advertiser*, April 18, 1826 ("pork, lard"); *BACDA*, April 19, 1826; Calvin Schermerhorn, "The Coastwise Slave Trade and a Mercantile Community of Interest," in Beckert and Rockman, *Slavery's Capitalism*, 209–224; Calvin Schermerhorn, "Commodity Chains and Chained Commodities: The U.S. Coastwise Slave Trade and an Atlantic Business Network," in *New Directions in Slavery Studies: Commodification, Community, and Comparison*, ed. Jeff Forret and Christine Sears (Baton Rouge: Louisiana State University Press, 2015), 11–29.

60. *APG*, June 5, 1826; 1828 Alexandria City Land and Personal Property Tax Assessments, RG27, reel 6 (1825–1833), APLSC; Adams County Tax Rolls, 1826, MDAH; Natchez *Gazette*, November 18, 1826. William Hanner also sometimes bought slaves in Guilford County and helped sell them in Natchez as part of Armfield's business. See William Boswell, vol. 5 (January–April 30, 1828), Act 48, January 19, 1828, NONA; "Natchez Harbor Master Register of Negroes Imported for Sale, 1827–1833," 18–20 (document in private collection, copies made available to the author by Dale Tomich).

61. Spotsylvania County Will Book K, 268–269, Auditor of Public Accounts, Spotsylvania County Personal Property Tax Books, 1820–1822, LOV.

62. Alexandria *Gazette and Advertiser*, January 2, 1822; ten-dollar note in folder 338, RCBP. For other examples of traders exchanging livestock for people, see *African Observer* 1, no. 2 (May 1827): 54–55; E. A. Andrews, *Slavery and the Domestic Slave-Trade in the United States* (Boston, 1836), 49.

63. Alexandria *Gazette and Advertiser*, January 29 (quotations), February 16, and April 20, 1822.

64. "Purchase Book, 1832–1834," folder 420, RCBP; Auditor of Public Accounts, Spotsylvania County Personal Property Tax Books, 1817–1823, LOV.

65. "Natchez Harbor Master Register of Negroes Imported for Sale," 13–21, 39–42; "Auction Sales of Slaves, 1827–1830," Adams County Records, Series G, vol. 170, microfilm reel 5439, MDAH.

66. *BACDA*, January 12, 1824; "The Meeks and Their Neighbors," *Historical Society of Washington County, Va.* 2, nos. 10 and 11 (September 1973): 20–24; Joseph Meek Papers, MSS2 M4713b, VHS; Greenbury Ridgely Stringer, Conveyance Book 2, 529–530, February 12, 1828, LRD-NOLA; Hugh Gordon,

vol. 7 (January 2–May 15, 1828), Act 119, February 11, 1828, William Boswell, vol. 5 (January–April 30, 1828), Acts 48 and 106, January 19 and 31, 1828, NONA.

67. *APG*, July 7, 1825 ("to purchase a few"), December 4, 1824 ("fifteen"), May 25, 1825 ("pay the very highest prices"); Adams County Tax Rolls, 1826; "Auction Sales of Slaves, 1827–1830," MDAH.

68. Baltimore *Patriot and Evening Advertiser*, November 17, 1815. On Austin Woolfolk, see Schermerhorn, *Business of Slavery*, 33–68; Bancroft, *Slave-Trading in the Old South*, 39–44; Ned Sublette and Constance Sublette, *The American Slave Coast: A History of the Slave-Breeding Industry* (Chicago: Lawrence Hill Books, 2016), 429–438; Baptist, *Half*, 179, 183–184, 193–194; Gudmestad, *Troublesome Commerce*, 25–30, 46–47, 155–156, 163–164; Deyle, *Carry Me Back*, 98–100, 179–180; Seth Rockman, *Scraping By: Wage Labor, Slavery, and Survival in Early Baltimore* (Baltimore: Johns Hopkins University Press, 2009), 27, 235–238; Ralph Clayton, *Cash for Blood: The Baltimore to New Orleans Domestic Slave Trade* (Westminster, MD: Heritage Books, 2007), 45–81, esp. 59–81; William Calderhead, "The Role of the Professional Slave Trader in a Slave Economy: Austin Woolfolk, a Case Study," *Civil War History* 23, no. 3 (September 1977): 195–211.

69. *BPMA*, September 26, 1817, March 16 and 20, May 29, and June 6, 1818; Augusta *Chronicle*, June 30, 1810, July 26, 1811; Augusta *Herald*, July 6, 1815; Schermerhorn, *Business of Slavery*, 37; Clayton, *Cash for Blood*, 59–60.

70. *BPMA*, June 27, 1817; Calderhead, "Role of the Professional Slave Trader," 200; Clayton, *Cash for Blood*, 77, 81.

71. *BACDA*, July 4, 1821, September 4, 1823.

72. *BACDA*, September 4, 1823 (first quotation); *GUE*, November 6, 1829, 67 (remaining quotations); Schermerhorn, *Business of Slavery*, 55–56; Clayton, *Cash for Blood*, 60–61; Deyle, *Carry Me Back*, 99; Gudmestad, *Troublesome Commerce*, 27.

73. Schermerhorn, *Business of Slavery*, 35–37; Deyle, *Carry Me Back*, 99. On a short-lived effort by Baltimore newspapers to ban slave traders' advertisements, see Gudmestad, *Troublesome Commerce*, 78–80.

74. See, for example, Easton *Republican Star*, January 8, 1828; Easton *Gazette*, January 12, 1828; *Eastern Shore Whig and People's Advocate*, September 1, 1829; Elkton *Cecil Democrat*, December 22, 1832; Cambridge *Chronicle*, May 22, 1830; Centreville *Times and Publick Advertiser*, September 10, 1830; *DNI*, August 6, 1825; Alexandria *Gazette and Advertiser*, November 23, 1824. Sometimes Woolfolk placed ads in one paper with a note to editors of other papers to copy it in their own pages and send him the bill. See, for example, *Eastern Shore Whig and People's Advocate*, April 17, 1832. Also see Bancroft, *Slave-Trading in the Old South*, 28–35.

75. Frederick Douglass, *My Bondage and My Freedom* (New York, 1855), 447–448; Schermerhorn, *Business of Slavery*, 35, 39.

76. *BPMA*, March 15 (quotation) and June 12, 1824; Easton *Republican Star*, April 12, 1825; *Eastern Shore Whig and People's Advocate*, January 11, 1831;

Virginia *Argus*, April 26, 1825; Bancroft, *Slave-Trading in the Old South*, 31–34; Schermerhorn, *Business of Slavery*, 54–56; Gudmestad, *Troublesome Commerce*, 29.

77. Douglass, *My Bondage and My Freedom*, 298–300, 448; Calderhead, "Role of the Professional Slave Trader," 197–198, 209.

78. *BACDA*, October 18, 1819; Augusta *Chronicle*, September 27, 1821; Schermerhorn, *Business of Slavery*, 45; Deyle, *Carry Me Back*, 98; Phillips, *American Negro Slavery*, chart opposite 370; Laurence J. Kotlikoff, "The Structure of Slave Prices in New Orleans, 1804 to 1862," *Economic Inquiry* 17, no. 4 (October 1979): 498; Herman Freudenberger and Jonathan B. Pritchett, "The Domestic United States Slave Trade: New Evidence," *Journal of Interdisciplinary History* 21, no. 3 (Winter 1991): 457; Baptist, *Half*, 174; Richard Follett, *The Sugar Masters: Planters and Slaves in Louisiana's Cane World, 1820–1860* (Baton Rouge: Louisiana State University Press, 2005), 14–45; Gray, *History of Agriculture*, 2:1027, 1033–1034.

79. Deyle, *Carry Me Back*, 98–99; Gudmestad, *Troublesome Commerce*, 25–26; Schermerhorn, *Business of Slavery*, 43–49; Rockman, *Scraping By*, 236; Tadman, *Speculators and Slaves*, 70–71; Kotlikoff, "Structure of Slave Prices," 503; Freudenberger and Pritchett, "Domestic United States Slave Trade," 463–467, 470–474; Jennie Williams, "*Trouble the Water*: The Baltimore to New Orleans Coastwise Slave Trade, 1820–1860," *Slavery and Abolition* 41, no. 2 (June 2020): 282–283; Walter Johnson, *Soul by Soul: Life Inside the Antebellum Slave Market* (Cambridge, MA: Harvard University Press, 1999), 49.

80. Clayton, *Cash for Blood*, 78–81; Schermerhorn, *Business of Slavery*, 269n34. William Calderhead claims that in the 1820s, Woolfolk shipped "possibly 40 per cent of all slaves shipped by traders and purchasing planters by the coastwise route to the *entire* southern market." Calderhead, "Role of the Professional Slave Trader," 201. On the coastwise slave trade from Baltimore generally, see Williams, "*Trouble the Water*," 275–303. Also see Calvin Schermerhorn, "Capitalism's Captives: The Maritime United States Slave Trade, 1807–1850," *Journal of Social History* 47, no. 4 (Summer 2014): 897–921.

81. Gudmestad, *Troublesome Commerce*, 155; Calderhead, "Role of the Professional Slave Trader," 205–206; Rockman, *Scraping By*, 236; Deyle, *Carry Me Back*, 177–178; Baptist, *Half*, 183–184; *GUE*, August 26, 1826, 405; Douglass, *My Bondage and My Freedom*, 448; Andrews, *Slavery and the Domestic Slave-Trade*, 80; Alexis de Tocqueville, *Journey to America*, edited by J. P. Mayer and translated by George Lawrence (New York: Anchor Books, 1971), 159–160; Gustave de Beaumont, *Marie or Slavery in the United States: A Novel of Jacksonian America*, translated by Barbara Chapman (Stanford: Stanford University Press, 1958; originally published 1835), 45–47.

82. On kidnapping, the selling of term slaves, and their relationship to a revived antislavery movement, see Richard Bell, *Stolen: Five Free Black Boys Kidnapped into Slavery and Their Astonishing Odyssey Home* (New York: Atria Books,

2019); Max Grivno, *Gleanings of Freedom: Free and Slave Labor Along the Mason-Dixon Line, 1790–1860* (Urbana: University of Illinois Press, 2011), 1–22, 115–151; Carol Wilson, *Freedom at Risk: The Kidnapping of Free Blacks in America, 1780–1865* (Lexington: University Press of Kentucky, 1994); David Fiske, *Solomon Northup's Kindred: The Kidnapping of Free Citizens Before the Civil War* (Santa Barbara, CA: Praeger, 2016); Manisha Sinha, *The Slave's Cause: A History of Abolition* (New Haven: Yale University Press, 2016), 174–177; Winfield Hazlitt Collins, *The Domestic Slave Trade of the Southern States* (New York: Broadway Publishing Company, 1904), 84–95; Rockman, *Scraping By*, 237–239; Baptist, *Half*, 189–199; Gudmestad, *Troublesome Commerce*, 73–75, 99–100. Also see Jesse Torrey, *A Portraiture of Domestic Slavery in the United States* (Philadelphia, 1817), 45–59; *BACDA*, October 29, 1816; *GUE*, August 1821, 29, October 1821, 60, February 25, 1826, 202, February 1831, 175.

83. *GUE*, July 29, 1826, 382 ("*Satanic* traffic," "soul-dealers"), August 5, 1826, 390 ("soul-sellers," "negro-chaining," "man-driving," "sustain the character"), December 17, 1825, 126 ("Prince"), August 26, 1826, 405 ("callous," "unprincipled monster"); Schermerhorn, *Business of Slavery*, 43–44; Merton L. Dillon, *Benjamin Lundy and the Struggle for Negro Freedom* (Urbana: University of Illinois Press, 1966); Stanley Harrold, *Subversives: Antislavery Community in Washington, D.C., 1828–1865* (Baton Rouge: Louisiana State University Press, 2003), 17–23; Sinha, *The Slave's Cause*, 177–182.

84. *GUE*, January 2, 1827, 109 (quotations), January 20, 1827, 125; Eric Robert Taylor, *If We Must Die: Shipboard Insurrections in the Era of the Atlantic Slave Trade* (Baton Rouge: Louisiana State University Press, 2006), 147–150; Schermerhorn, *Business of Slavery*, 60–62; Gudmestad, *Troublesome Commerce*, 46–47.

85. *GUE*, March 31, 1827, 174 (quotations), February 24, 1827, 142.

86. Alexandria *Gazette and Advertiser*, November 23, 1824; Natchez *Statesman and Gazette*, March 14 and January 10, 1827.

87. A letter for "John Armfield" at the Augusta post office in 1827 could have been for a different man with the same name, but Armfield may have gone to Georgia to observe the Woolfolk operation firsthand. See Augusta *Chronicle*, April 4, 1827.

CHAPTER THREE: ASSOCIATES, 1827–1830

1. Janice G. Artemel, Elizabeth A. Crowell, and Jeff Parker, *The Alexandria Slave Pen: The Archaeology of Urban Captivity* (Washington, DC: Engineering Science, 1987), 1–4, 11–16, 21–23; *RI*, February 8, 1834.

2. Artemel, Crowell, and Parker, *Alexandria Slave Pen*, 21–23; T. Michael Miller, *Artisans and Merchants of Alexandria, Virginia, 1780–1820* (Bowie, MD: Heritage Books, 1991), 2:277; Alexandria *Daily Gazette*, February 18, 1812; *AGDA*, April 20, 1820; Alexandria City Deeds, Book I-2, 230, LOV.

3. *APG*, May 15, 1828 (quotations), August 9, 1826; Artemel, Crowell, and Parker, *Alexandria Slave Pen*, 24; Alexandria City Land and Personal Property Tax Assessments, 1825–1833, RG27, microfilm reel 6, APLSC; Alexandria *Gazette and Advertiser*, October 30, 1824; *SIF*, 337–338.

4. Artemel, Crowell, and Parker, *Alexandria Slave Pen*, 23, 29, 118–119; Alexandria *Herald*, April 3, 1818.

5. *APG*, August 9, 1826 (first quotation); E. A. Andrews, *Slavery and the Domestic Slave-Trade in the United States* (Boston, 1836), 135 (remaining quotations); *AG*, October 16, 1851; *RI*, February 8, 1834; Washington, DC, *National Republican*, May 28, 1861.

6. E. S. Abdy, *Journal of a Residence and Tour in the United States of North America, from April, 1833, to October, 1834* (London, 1835), 2:179 ("well-furnished," "doubly locked"); Andrews, *Slavery and the Domestic Slave-Trade*, 135–137 ("padlocks" on 137); Artemel, Crowell, and Parker, *Alexandria Slave Pen*, 29–30.

7. *RI*, February 8, 1834; Artemel, Crowell, and Parker, *Alexandria Slave Pen*, 119. Also see Abdy, *Journal of a Residence and Tour*, 179; Andrews, *Slavery and the Domestic Slave-Trade*, 137.

8. Andrews, *Slavery and the Domestic Slave-Trade*, 138–140 (quotation on 140); *RI*, February 8, 1834.

9. *RI*, February 8, 1834 ("strong iron grated," "rings"); Andrews, *Slavery and the Domestic Slave-Trade*, 140 ("like those"), 142 ("chained at night"), 143 ("overpower"); *American Anti-Slavery Almanac for 1836* (Boston, 1835), 26. In February 1834, Joshua Leavitt described the location where the enslaved slept as being belowground in something like a "cellar," while Ethan Andrews described it in July 1835 as being part of a "long building, two stories high." But both men described heavy iron doors leading to the sleeping area, and both may have described a two-story building whose first level was partially below the surface of the yard. The sleeping area's orientation is also ambiguous. Andrews described the building as being "in the rear of the yard," but whether that meant it extended across the back of the yard from east to west or ran from the back down the center of the yard from north to south is uncertain.

10. *RI*, February 8, 1834; Andrews, *Slavery and the Domestic Slave-Trade*, 140; Alexandria City Land and Personal Property Tax Assessments, 1825–1833, RG27, microfilm reel 6, APLSC.

11. Abdy, *Journal of a Residence and Tour*, 180 ("a dungeon," "where the refractory," "thumb-screws," "there was no room"); Washington, DC, *Evening Star*, October 9, 1902, 17 ("where the stubborn"); Alexandria City Land and Personal Property Tax Assessments, 1825–1833, RG27, microfilm reel 6, APLSC ("Franklin's black hole"); Washington, DC, *National Republican*, May 28, 1861; Artemel, Crowell, and Parker, *Alexandria Slave Pen*, 119. The tax assessor's reference was to the infamous "Black Hole of Calcutta," a Bengali dungeon in which dozens of British soldiers died during one night's captivity in the 1750s. Archaeological

evidence at the Duke Street site also suggests that there were two small "brick chamber[s]" outside the basement. Accessible by ladder and each equipped with a metal "grate or door," they may have allowed Armfield and his employees to take captives into and out of the basement without bringing them through the main house.

12. Andrews, *Slavery and the Domestic Slave-Trade*, 136; Alexandria City Land and Personal Property Tax Assessments, 1825–1833, 1833–1842, RG27, microfilm reels 6, 7, APLSC; Abdy, *Journal of a Residence and Tour*, 179.

13. Michael Tadman, *Speculators and Slaves: Masters, Traders, and Slaves in the Old South* (Madison: University of Wisconsin Press, 1989), 12.

14. Tadman, *Speculators and Slaves*, 12; *Abstract of the Returns of the Fifth Census, Showing the Number of Free People, the Number of Slaves, the Federal or Representative Number, and the Aggregate of Each County of Each State of the United States* (Washington, DC, 1832), 15 and 18; *Compendium of the Enumeration of the Inhabitants and Statistics of the United States* (Washington, DC, 1841), 30, 34, and 38. Maryland's enslaved population dropped slightly during the 1820s as well. For a consideration of the slave trade's impact in Maryland in the 1830s, see William Calderhead, "How Extensive Was the Border State Slave Trade? A New Look," *Civil War History* 18, no. 1 (March 1972): 42–55; Steven Deyle, *Carry Me Back: The Domestic Slave Trade in American Life* (New York: Oxford University Press, 2005), 291–293; Barbara Jeanne Fields, *Slavery and Freedom on the Middle Ground: Maryland During the Nineteenth Century* (New Haven: Yale University Press, 1985), 24–33.

15. Abraham John Mason, "Sketches of the Geography, People, and Institutions of the United States," 2:209, GEN MSS 1001, box 1, Beinecke Rare Book and Manuscript Library, Yale University, New Haven; Joseph Sturge, *A Visit to the United States in 1841* (London, 1842), 75. Also see Joseph Holt Ingraham, *The South-West, by a Yankee* (New York, 1835), 2:233–234.

16. *Slavery and the Internal Slave Trade in the United States of North America* (London, 1841), 14–16 (quotations). Especially among antislavery activists, it was a commonplace notion that slaveholders deliberately and systematically "bred" the enslaved for market in practically eugenic fashion. Historical evidence for such claims is spotty and largely anecdotal. But references to enslaved women as "breeders" were routine, and slaveholders undeniably understood the financial significance of enslaved women giving birth to as many children as possible. They encouraged and sometimes coerced reproduction among the enslaved, and they profited extensively from selling young enslaved people. The systemic link between white wealth and Black reproduction has led the authors of one book to argue that the southern economy was grounded in "the productivity of the capitalized womb." For a consideration of "slave breeding" as a matter of history and memory, see Gregory D. Smithers, *Slave Breeding: Sex, Violence, and Memory in African American History* (Gainesville: University Press of Florida, 2013). On the "capitalized

womb," see Ned Sublette and Constance Sublette, *The American Slave Coast: A History of the Slave-Breeding Industry* (Chicago: Lawrence Hill Books, 2016), esp. 21–36. Also see Tadman, *Speculators and Slaves*, 121–129; Deyle, *Carry Me Back*, 46–49; Frederic Bancroft, *Slave-Trading in the Old South* (Baltimore: J. H. Furst, 1931), 67–87; Richard Sutch, "The Breeding of Slaves for Sale and the Westward Expansion of Slavery, 1850–1860," in *Race and Slavery in the Western Hemisphere: Quantitative Studies*, ed. Stanley L. Engerman and Eugene D. Genovese (Princeton: Princeton University Press, 1975), 173–210; Robert W. Fogel and Stanley L. Engerman, "The Slave Breeding Thesis," in *Without Consent or Contract: The Rise and Fall of American Slavery (Conditions of Slave Life and the Transition to Freedom: Technical Papers, Volume 2)*, ed. Robert William Fogel and Stanley L. Engerman (New York: W. W. Norton, 1992), 455–472; Richard G. Lowe and Randolph B. Campbell, "The Slave-Breeding Hypothesis: A Demographic Comment on the 'Buying' and 'Selling' States," *JSH* 42, no. 3 (August 1976): 401–412; Amy Dru Stanley, "Slave Breeding and Free Love: An Antebellum Argument over Slavery, Capitalism, and Personhood," in *Capitalism Takes Command: The Social Transformation of Nineteenth-Century America*, ed. Gary Kornblith and Michael Zakim (Chicago: University of Chicago Press, 2012), 119–144; Daina Ramey Berry, *The Price for Their Pound of Flesh: The Value of the Enslaved, from Womb to Grave, in the Building of a Nation* (New York: Beacon Press, 2017), 10–32, 79–83; Richard Follett, *The Sugar Masters: Planters and Slaves in Louisiana's Cane World* (Baton Rouge: Louisiana State University Press, 2005), 57–61, esp. 58n16; Thelma Jennings, "'Us Colored Women Had to Go Through a Plenty': Sexual Exploitation of African-American Slave Women," *Journal of Women's History* 1, no. 3 (Winter 1990): 45–74; Richard Bell, "The Great Jugular Vein of Slavery: New Histories of the Domestic Slave Trade," *History Compass*, 11/12 (2013), 1153–1155. Thomas A. Foster importantly reminds us of the vulnerability of enslaved men to sexual abuse and forced reproduction in *Rethinking Rufus: Sexual Violations of Enslaved Men* (Athens: University of Georgia Press, 2019).

17. Mary Elizabeth Young, *Redskins, Ruffleshirts, and Rednecks: Indian Allotments in Alabama and Mississippi, 1830–1860* (Norman: University of Oklahoma Press, 1961); Thomas D. Clark and John D. W. Guice, *The Old Southwest, 1795–1830: Frontiers in Conflict* (Norman: University of Oklahoma Press, 1989), 233–253; Arthur H. DeRosier Jr., *The Removal of the Choctaw Indians* (Knoxville: University of Tennessee Press, 1970); Samuel J. Wells, "Federal Indian Policy: From Accommodation to Removal," in *The Choctaw Before Removal*, ed. Carolyn Keller Reeves (Oxford: University Press of Mississippi, 1985), 181–213; Anthony F. C. Wallace, *The Long, Bitter Trail: Andrew Jackson and the Indians* (New York: Hill and Wang, 1993); Claudio Saunt, *Unworthy Republic: The Dispossession of Native Americans and the Road to Indian Territory* (New York: W. W. Norton, 2020); Stuart Bruchey, *Cotton and the Growth of the American Economy: 1790–1860* (New York: Harcourt, Brace, and World, 1967), 18.

18. Tadman, *Speculators and Slaves,* 12; Bruchey, *Cotton and the Growth of the American Economy,* 18; Lewis Cecil Gray, *History of Agriculture in the Southern United States to 1860* (Washington, DC: Carnegie Institution of Washington, 1933), 2:1033; *Abstract of the Returns of the Fifth Census,* 36, 39–40; *Compendium of the Enumeration,* 54, 58; Edward E. Baptist, *The Half Has Never Been Told: Slavery and the Making of American Capitalism* (New York: Basic Books, 2014), 249.

19. Sharon Ann Murphy, *Other People's Money: How Banking Worked in the Early American Republic* (Baltimore: Johns Hopkins University Press, 2017), 93–95; Baptist, *Half,* 232–233, 238–239, 244–249; Stephen Campbell, *The Bank War and the Partisan Press: Newspapers, Financial Institutions, and the Post Office in Jacksonian America* (Lawrence: University Press of Kansas, 2019), 151–154; Joshua D. Rothman, *Flush Times and Fever Dreams: A Story of Capitalism and Slavery in the Age of Jackson* (Athens: University of Georgia Press, 2012), 4–8; Calvin Schermerhorn, *The Business of Slavery and the Rise of American Capitalism, 1815–1860* (New Haven: Yale University Press, 2015), 95–123; Scott Reynolds Nelson, *A Nation of Deadbeats: An Uncommon History of America's Financial Disasters* (New York: Alfred A. Knopf, 2012), 107–108.

20. *SIF,* 337–338 (quotation on 337); Wendell Holmes Stephenson, *Isaac Franklin, Slave Trader and Planter of the Old South* (Baton Rouge: Louisiana State University Press, 1938), 23; "An Agreement Between Franklin & Armfield and Ballard & Alsop," March 15, 1831, folder 421, RCBP; Robert H. Gudmestad, *A Troublesome Commerce: The Transformation of the Interstate Slave Trade* (Baton Rouge: Louisiana State University Press, 2003), 28; Hank Trent, *The Secret Life of Bacon Tait, a White Slave Trader Married to a Free Woman of Color* (Baton Rouge: Louisiana State University Press, 2017), 48–49; "Agreement Between David Burford and Jourdan M. Saunders," October 25, 1827, folder 1, DB-UTK. Throughout this book, most monetary equivalents are rooted simply in calculations of inflation over time. In some cases, I have also provided equivalents in terms of the overall size of the US economy or the distribution of wealth in the United States over time, which may provide a truer sense of the impact of Franklin, Armfield, and Ballard's slave-trading activities and of their personal power. Both discomfort and danger attend to considering the material "value" of enslaved people, of course, as doing so threatens to reaffirm some of the logic of slavery itself. Equivalents of these sorts are therefore offered here sparingly, and with the hope that they will help underscore for modern readers not only the significance of the trade to American life but also the scope of the human damage wrought by traders. All equivalents are derived from the calculator available at MeasuringWorth, www .measuringworth.com.

21. Conveyance Book 2, February 12, 1828, 529–530, LRD-NOLA; *APG,* February 15 and April 7, 1828.

22. Schermerhorn, *Business of Slavery,* 56.

23. Alexandria City Deeds, Books I, 376–380, I-2, 170–171, LOV.

24. Also detrimental to Alexandria's economy were a series of epidemics, a devastating fire in 1827, and being bypassed by emerging railroad lines that connected other places, such as Baltimore, with the Midwest. See Artemel, Crowell, and Parker, *Alexandria Slave Pen*, 12–18; Michael A. Ridgeway, "A Peculiar Business: Slave Trading in Alexandria, Virginia, 1825–1861" (MA thesis, Georgetown University, 1976), 14–17; Harold W. Hurst, *Alexandria on the Potomac: The Portrait of an Antebellum Community* (Latham, MD: University Press of America, 1991), 1–3; Tomoko Yagyu, "Slave Traders and Planters in the Expanding South: Entrepreneurial Strategies, Business Networks, and Western Migration in the Atlantic World, 1787–1859" (PhD diss., University of North Carolina–Chapel Hill, 2006), 128–131; Miller, *Artisans and Merchants of Alexandria, Virginia*, 2:xxi.

25. *Western Luminary* 2, no. 7 (August 24, 1825) ("a serious riot," "among the negroes," "directed against"): 110; Richmond *Enquirer*, July 26, 1825 ("abusive epithets," "peace officers," "resisted," "many"); *APG*, July 30, 1825 ("the whole affair," "trouble"). Also see Ridgeway, "A Peculiar Business," 18–22. Alexandria's position on the Virginia side of the Potomac River may also have boosted its position in the regional slave trade, as federal and state laws imposed some restrictions on slavery and the slave trade in Washington City and Georgetown, both of which were on the Maryland side of the Potomac River, that did not apply in Alexandria. The restrictions effectively did very little to contain the slave trade anywhere in the District, but especially in the first few decades of the nineteenth century, the confusing legal peculiarities seem to have led many District of Columbia traders to prefer working in Alexandria. On the slave trade and the law in the District of Columbia, see Robert H. Gudmestad, "Slave Resistance, Coffles, and the Debates over Slavery in the Nation's Capital," in *The Chattel Principle: Internal Slave Trades in the Americas*, ed. Walter Johnson (New Haven: Yale University Press, 2004), 72–90; William T. Laprade, "The Domestic Slave Trade in the District of Columbia," *Journal of Negro History* 11, no. 1 (January 1926): 17–34; Mary Beth Corrigan, "Imaginary Cruelties: A History of the Slave Trade in Washington, D.C.," *Washington History* 13, no. 2 (Fall–Winter 2001–2002): 4–27; Ridgeway, "A Peculiar Business," 25–27; Yagyu, "Slave Traders and Planters in the Expanding South," 131–132; A. Glenn Crothers, "The 1846 Retrocession of Alexandria: Protecting Slavery and the Slave Trade in the District of Columbia," in *In the Shadow of Freedom: The Politics of Slavery in the National Capital*, ed. Paul Finkelman and Donald R. Kennon (Athens: Ohio University Press, 2011), 159.

26. *AGDA*, February 3, 1818 ("enclosed," "accommodate"), November 13, 1817 ("likely"), March 18, 1817; *AG*, September 8, 1873, January 5, 1816; Miller, *Artisans and Merchants of Alexandria, Virginia*, 1:272; Williams v. Franklin (1830), Docket 8719, Louisiana First Judicial Court, Louisiana Division, City Archives and Special Collections, NOPL.

27. *AGDA*, February 23, 1822 (quotations), April 27, 1818, September 13, 1820, February 21, 1821; Miller, *Artisans and Merchants of Alexandria, Virginia*, 1:272.

28. Alexandria *Gazette and Advertiser*, November 25, 1824 ("to the country"), June 19 and 21, 1823; *APG*, February 11, 1825 ("either singly"); *GUE*, October 14, 1826, 36 ("the most noted"); *BACDA*, March 11, 1825; Reel of Insolvent Debtors, Arlington County 1820–1830, LOV.

29. *APG*, May 7, 1828 (quotation), June 5, 1826.

30. Williams v. Franklin; *APG*, February 25, 1829, November 28, 1832; Schermerhorn, *Business of Slavery*, 143; Ridgeway, "A Peculiar Business," 45–48.

31. *UST*, May 16, 1828.

32. Williams v. Franklin.

33. Affidavit of Charles A. L. Lewis, John Perkins v. R. C. Ballard and Samuel Alsop, 1829, box 57, file 7, ACCR-HNF; "Natchez Harbor Master Register of Negroes Imported for Sale, 1827–1833," 39–42, 62–64, 120–123 (document in private collection, copies made available to the author by Dale Tomich); Deyle, *Carry Me Back*, 254–255.

34. Advertising text for the *Louisiana Advertiser*, folder 338, RCBP; "Auction Sales of Slaves, 1827–1830," Adams County Records, Series G, vol. 170, microfilm reel 5439, MDAH; Concordia Parish Conveyance Book E, 406, 407, 413, 414, Concordia Parish Courthouse, Vidalia, Louisiana.

35. *APG*, September 1, 1828; Fredericksburg *Herald*, April 15, 1829.

36. William Hayden, *Narrative of William Hayden, Containing a Faithful Account of His Travels for a Number of Years, Whilst a Slave, in the South* (Cincinnati, 1846), 118–129 (quotation on 128); Fredericksburg *Herald*, May 16, 1829; Pen Bogert, "Sold for My Account: The Early Slave Trade Between Kentucky and the Lower Mississippi Valley," *Ohio Valley History* 2, no. 1 (Spring 2002): 11; "Auction Sales of Slaves, 1827–1830," MDAH; "Natchez Harbor Master Register of Negroes Imported for Sale," 64–65.

37. Hayden, *Narrative of William Hayden*, 128–133.

38. Hayden, *Narrative of William Hayden*, 132; Manifest of the Brig *United States*, October 2, 1828, reel 5, SM-NARA.

39. Mason, "Sketches," 2:102–103 (quotation on 103); Charles Augustus Murray, *Travels in North America During the Years 1834, 1835, and 1836* (London, 1839), 2:189; Benjamin Henry Latrobe, *The Journal of Latrobe, Being the Notes and Sketches of an Architect, Naturalist, and Traveler in the United States from 1796 to 1820* (New York: D. Appleton, 1905), 161; Arthur Singleton, Esq. [Henry C. Knight], *Letters from the South and West* (Boston, 1824), 130; Ingraham, *South-West, by a Yankee*, 1:90. Also see Richard Campanella, *Lincoln in New Orleans: The 1828–1831 Flatboat Voyages and Their Place in History* (Lafayette: University of Louisiana at Lafayette Press, 2010), 120–122, 299–301.

40. *Aggregate Amount of Each Description of Persons Within the United States of America; and the Territories Thereof, Agreeable to Actual Enumeration Made According to Law, in the Year 1810* (Washington, DC, 1811), 82; *Abstract of the Returns of the Fifth Census*, 32; William Darby and Theodore Dwight Jr., *Gazetteer of the United States of America* (Hartford, 1833), 349; Lawrence N. Powell, *The Accidental City: Improvising New Orleans* (Cambridge, MA: Harvard University Press, 2012), 346–351; Rashauna Johnson, *Slavery's Metropolis: Unfree Labor in New Orleans During the Age of Revolutions* (Cambridge: Cambridge University Press, 2016), 87–100; Campanella, *Lincoln in New Orleans*, 301–303, 310–312.

41. Darby and Dwight, *Gazetteer*, 349; Campanella, *Lincoln in New Orleans*, 292–294, 324–338; Walter Johnson, *River of Dark Dreams: Slavery and Empire in the Cotton Kingdom* (Cambridge, MA: Harvard University Press, 2013), 79–83; Scott P. Marler, *The Merchants' Capital: New Orleans and the Political Economy of the Nineteenth-Century South* (New York: Cambridge University Press, 2013), 15–52; Linda K. Salvucci and Richard J. Salvucci, "The Lizardi Brothers: A Mexican Family Business and the Expansion of New Orleans, 1825–1846," *JSH* 82, no. 4 (November 2016): 759–788; James E. Winston, "Notes on the Economic History of New Orleans, 1803–1836," *Mississippi Valley Historical Review* 11, no. 2 (September 1924): 201–205, 215–216; Basil Hall, *Travels in North America, in the Years 1827 and 1828* (Philadelphia, 1829), 2:280–287; S. A. Ferrall, *A Ramble of Six Thousand Miles Through the United States of America* (London, 1832), 189–191; Ingraham, *South-West, by a Yankee*, 1:104–106; J. S. Buckingham, *The Slave States of America* (London, 1842), 1:325–327; Murray, *Travels in North America*, 2:185.

42. Darby and Dwight, *Gazetteer*, 349; Winston, "Notes," 206; Johnson, *River of Dark Dreams*, 80–81; Campanella, *Lincoln in New Orleans*, 291–292; Gray, *History of Agriculture*, 2:896–898, 1026; Schermerhorn, *Business of Slavery*, 95–123.

43. New Orleans *Mercantile Advertiser*, January 21, 1830, in *African Repository* 5, no. 12 (February 1830): 381; *Acts Passed at the Second Session of the Seventh Legislature of the State of Louisiana* (New Orleans, 1826), 114–118; *Acts Passed at the Second Session of the Eighth Legislature of the State of Louisiana* (New Orleans, 1828), 22; Lacy Ford, *Deliver Us from Evil: The Slavery Question in the Old South* (New York: Oxford University Press, 2009), 451; Joe Gray Taylor, "Negro Slavery in Louisiana" (PhD diss., Louisiana State University, 1952), 52–53; Winfield Hazlitt Collins, *The Domestic Slave Trade of the Southern States* (New York: Broadway Publishing Company, 1904), 126–127; Herman Freudenberger and Jonathan B. Pritchett, "The Domestic United States Slave Trade: New Evidence," *Journal of Interdisciplinary History* 21, no. 3 (Winter 1991): 459; Laurence J. Kotlikoff, "The Structure of Slave Prices in New Orleans, 1804 to 1862," *Economic Inquiry* 17, no. 4 (October 1979): 497; Gudmestad, *Troublesome Commerce*, 102–103.

44. Frances Trollope, *Domestic Manners of the Americans* (London, 1832), 1:2–3; Manifest of the Brig *United States*, October 2, 1828, reel 5, SM-NARA; New Orleans *Argus*, October 23, 1828. Also see J. E. Alexander, *Transatlantic Sketches*,

Comprising Visits to the Most Interesting Scenes in North and South America, and the West Indies (London, 1833), 2:3–8; Estwick Evans, *A Pedestrious Tour of Four Thousand Miles, Through the Western States and Territories, During the Winter and Spring of 1818* (Concord, NH, 1819), 248–249; Mason, "Sketches," 1:106.

45. Manifest of the Brig *United States*, October 2, 1828, reel 5, SM-NARA; New Orleans *Argus*, October 23, 1828; Louisiana *Courier*, October 22, 1828; *United States Statutes at Large,* Ninth Congress, 2nd sess., 426–430.

46. Manifest of the Brig *United States*, October 2, 1828, reel 5, SM-NARA; *Register of All Officers and Agents, Civil, Military, and Naval, in the Service of the United States, on the Thirtieth September 1835* (Washington, DC, 1835), 56–57.

47. Manifest of the Brig *United States*, October 2, 1828, reel 5, SM-NARA; Follett, *Sugar Masters*, 51–66; Michael Tadman, "The Demographic Cost of Sugar: Debates on Societies and Natural Increase in the Americas," *American Historical Review* 105, no. 5 (December 2000): 1534–1575; Damian Alan Pargas, *Slavery and Forced Migration in the Antebellum South* (New York: Cambridge University Press, 2015), 43–44; Jonathan B. Pritchett, "The Interregional Slave Trade and the Selection of Slaves for the New Orleans Market," *Journal of Interdisciplinary History* 28, no. 1 (Summer 1997): 57–85.

48. Manifest of the Brig *United States*, October 2, 1828, reel 5, SM-NARA. On "soul value," see Berry, *Price for Their Pound of Flesh*, esp. 6, 58–90.

49. Andrews, *Slavery and the Domestic Slave-Trade*, 140. These sorts of preparations were standard practice in the slave trade. See L. A. Chamerovzow, ed., *Slave Life in Georgia: A Narrative of the Life, Sufferings, and Escape of John Brown, a Fugitive Slave* (London, 1855), 111–118; Pargas, *Slavery and Forced Migration*, 48; Walter Johnson, *Soul by Soul: Life Inside the Antebellum Slave Market* (Cambridge, MA: Harvard University Press, 1999), 117–134; Saidiya V. Hartman, *Scenes of Subjection: Terror, Slavery, and Self-Making in Nineteenth-Century America* (New York: Oxford University Press, 1997), 36–42; Tadman, *Speculators and Slaves*, 97–102; Gudmestad, *Troublesome Commerce*, 95–97; Mauric D. McInnis, *Slaves Waiting for Sale: Abolitionist Art and the American Slave Trade* (Chicago: University of Chicago Press, 2011), 125–130, 136–138, 161–163.

50. Winston, "Notes," 223; Samuel Wilson, "Maspero's Exchange: Its Predecessors and Successors," *Louisiana History* 30, no. 2 (Spring 1989): 191–220; Richard Campanella, "On the Structural Basis of Social Memory: Cityscapes of the New Orleans Slave Trade, Part I," *Preservation in Print*, March 2013, 16–17; Alexander, *Transatlantic Sketches*, 2:16–17.

51. Herbert A. Kellar, "A Journey Through the South in 1836: Diary of James D. Davidson," *JSH* 1, no. 3 (August 1935): 358; Wilson, "Maspero's Exchange"; Campanella, *Lincoln in New Orleans*, 112–117, 168–174, 318–319; Baptist, *Half*, 83–109; Ingraham, *South-West, by a Yankee*, 1:93–94, 113–115.

52. Kellar, "Journey Through the South," 358; Campanella, *Lincoln in New Orleans*, 319.

53. Edgar Grima, "The Notarial System in New Orleans," *Louisiana Historical Quarterly* 10 (January 1927): 76–81; "The Civil Law Notary," Clerk of Civil District Court for the Parish of Orleans (website), http://www.orleanscivilclerk.com /civil.htm; John Adems Paxton, *New-Orleans Directory and Register* (New Orleans, 1827, 1830); S. E. Percy and Co., *The New-Orleans Directory* (New Orleans, 1832).

54. Paxton, *New-Orleans Directory and Register* (1830); New Orleans *Argus*, November 6, 1828; Felix DeArmas, vol. 17 (September–October 1828), Acts 1023 and 1024, October 29, 1828, NONA.

55. Felix DeArmas, vol. 17 (September–October 1828), Acts 1023 and 1024, October 29, 1828, NONA; New Orleans *Argus*, May 17, 1828; Judith Kelleher Schafer, *Slavery, the Civil Law, and the Supreme Court of Louisiana* (Baton Rouge: Louisiana State University Press, 1994), 127–148; Judith Kelleher Schafer, "'Guaranteed Against the Vices and Maladies Prescribed by Law': Consumer Protection, the Law of Slave Sales, and the Supreme Court in Antebellum Louisiana," *American Journal of Legal History* 31, no. 4 (October 1987): 306–321; Ariela J. Gross, *Double Character: Slavery and Mastery in the Antebellum Southern Courtroom* (Princeton: Princeton University Press, 2000), 33–34; Gudmestad, *Troublesome Commerce*, 97–98; Johnson, *Soul by Soul*, 12–14, 183–187, 207–213. For a consideration of warranties offered by slave traders outside Louisiana, see Jenny B. Wahl, "The Jurisprudence of American Slave Sales," *JEH* 56, no. 1 (March 1996): 143–169.

56. Felix DeArmas, vol. 17 (September–October 1828), Acts 1023 and 1024, October 29, 1828, NONA; Paxton, *New-Orleans Directory and Register* (1827, 1830).

57. Compiled from database created by the author. Original data appears in notarial books of Joseph Arnaud, William Boswell, Louis Thimelet Caire, Felix DeArmas, John Duncan, Hugh Gordon, Charles Janin, and Carlile Pollack, NONA; and in Williams v. Franklin (1830), Docket 8719, Louisiana First Judicial Court, Louisiana Division, City Archives and Special Collections, NOPL. Franklin probably made a few other transactions in 1828, but the records of notaries Greenbury Stringer and William Lewis have not survived from that year. Notarial acts might be written in English or in French, depending on the customer's preference. Most of Franklin's clients had their transactions recorded in English.

58. Carlile Pollack, vol. 23 (January–December 1828), Act 736, November 29, 1828, and vol. 24 (January–December 1828), Act 742, December 27, 1828, Felix DeArmas, vol. 18 (November–December 1828), Acts 1059, 1102, and 1128, November 4, 20, and 24, 1828, John Duncan, vol. 3 (January–December 1828), Act 186, November 25, 1828, Louis Thimelet Caire, vol. 5A (October–November 1828), Act 540, November 6, 1828, NONA; Paxton, *New-Orleans Directory and Register* (1827, 1830); Stephenson, *Isaac Franklin*, 86–89.

59. William Boswell, vol. 6 (April 30–December 30, 1828), Acts 1058 and 1166, November 14 and 18, 1828, NONA; Paxton, *New-Orleans Directory and Register* (1830).

60. Special mortgages, also known as hypothecated mortgages, worked much like mortgages most modern home buyers agree to, in which the buyer holds title to property that can be seized by the creditor in case of default. On the practice of mortgaging enslaved people, see Bonnie Martin, "Neighbor-to-Neighbor Capitalism: Local Credit Networks and the Mortgaging of Slaves," in *Slavery's Capitalism: A New History of American Economic Development*, ed. Sven Beckert and Seth Rockman (Philadelphia: University of Pennsylvania Press, 2016), 107–121; Bonnie Martin, "Slavery's Invisible Engine: Mortgaging Human Property," *JSH* 76, no. 4 (November 2010): 817–866; Richard Holcombe Kilbourne Jr., *Debt, Investment, Slaves: Credit Relations in East Feliciana Parish, Louisiana, 1825–1885* (Tuscaloosa: University of Alabama Press, 1995), 49–76; Peter Depuydt, "The Mortgaging of Souls: Sugar, Slaves, and Speculation," *Louisiana History* 54, no. 4 (Fall 2013): 448–464.

61. Tadman, *Speculators and Slaves*, 204–208; Deyle, *Carry Me Back*, 121–122; Freudenberger and Pritchett, "Domestic United States Slave Trade," 475–476; Robert Evans Jr., "Some Economic Aspects of the Domestic Slave Trade, 1830–1860," *Southern Economic Journal* 27, no. 4 (April 1961): 329–337; Gudmestad, *Troublesome Commerce*, 11–12.

62. In addition to purchasing 132 acres of land from his father in 1815, Franklin had bought another 150 acres of land nearby in 1823. See Sumner County Tax Lists, 1824, Sumner County Will Book 2, 91–93, Sumner County Deed Book 10, 413–414, Book 12, 213, 224, TSLA.

63. Spotsylvania County Deed Books BB, 495–496, EE, 50, Spotsylvania Personal Property Tax Books, 1830, 1831, LOV. Ballard sold his share of Coventry to Alsop in December 1832.

64. Richmond *Enquirer*, December 25, 1829; George McGehee v. Ballard and Alsop, 1830, box 2, file 39, ACCR-HNF; "Natchez Harbor Master Register of Negroes Imported for Sale," 39.

65. George McGehee v. Ballard and Alsop, John Perkins v. R. C. Ballard and Samuel Alsop, 1829, box 57, file 7, Ballard and Alsop v. John Nevitt, 1829, box 60, file 30, Isaac Franklin v. Richard King, 1830, box 4, file 26, ACCR-HNF; *Louisiana Planter and Sugar Manufacturer* 44, no. 12 (March 19, 1910): 185.

66. *DNI*, December 15, 1828; *L'Abeille*, January 12, 1829; *NOPC*, February 28, 1829; Stephenson, *Isaac Franklin*, 35; Lynchburg *Virginian*, October 9, 1828; *APG*, January 14, 1829; *UST*, January 22, 1829; *NYPC*, February 4, 1829; *Ship Registers and Enrollments of New Orleans, Louisiana: Volume 2, 1821–1830*, (Baton Rouge: Louisiana State University Press, 1941), 30; Manifest of the Brig *Comet*, January 26, 1829, reel 6, SM-NARA.

67. In November 1828, James Rawlings Franklin brought three enslaved people by steamboat from Natchez to New Orleans. By the summer of 1829, he was back in Alexandria, but he returned to New Orleans that October and was almost certainly living in the lower South for most of the year by 1830, as

Eli Montgomery no longer appears as Isaac Franklin's agent on the 1831 Adams County tax rolls. See New Orleans *Louisiana Courier*, November 21, 1828; Natchez *Statesman and Gazette*, January 31, 1829; Janin v. Franklin, Docket 2355, Eastern District, July 1832, Supreme Court of Louisiana, SC-UNO; Auditor of Public Accounts, Adams County Tax Rolls, 1828–1831, record group 29, MDAH; *SIF*, 293.

68. Compiled from database created by the author. Original data appears in notarial books of Joseph Arnaud, William Boswell, Louis Thimelet Caire, William Christy, Felix DeArmas, Octave DeArmas, Hugh Gordon, Charles Janin, Carlile Pollack, and Theodore Seghers, NONA, and William Y. Lewis, Conveyance Book 3, 665, LRD-NOLA. Also see William Christy, vol. 3 (January–October 1829), Act 401, January 8, 1829 (quotation), William Boswell, vol. 8 (January–December 1829), Act 53, January 19, 1829, Felix DeArmas, vol. 19 (January 1829), Act 55, January 15, 1829, vol. 21 (March 1829), Acts 319 and 434, March 4 and 28, 1829, NONA.

69. Felix DeArmas, vol. 19 (January 1829), Acts 52 and 56, January 15, 1829; Follett, *Sugar Masters*, 78–79; Tadman, "Demographic Cost of Sugar."

70. Follett, *Sugar Masters*, 10–13; Tadman, *Speculators and Slaves*, 70–71; Kotlikoff, "Structure of Slave Prices," 503. Herman Freudenberger and Jonathan Pritchett dispute that slave sale seasonality in New Orleans bore any special relationship to crop production or that there was a noticeable temporal pattern to cash or credit sales. In the late 1820s, however, Franklin and Armfield's credit sales came disproportionately in November and December, and then again in May as the selling season came to its close. See Freudenberger and Pritchett, "Domestic United States Slave Trade," 464–466.

71. *APG*, June 22, 1827.

72. *The Friend*, March 7 (first quotation) and 14 (remaining quotations), 1829; *GUE*, June 10, 1826, 322; New York *Commercial Advertiser*, April 19, 1828; Deyle, *Carry Me Back*, 195–203.

73. *The Friend*, March 14, 1829; William J. Anderson, *Life and Narrative of William J. Anderson, Twenty-Four Years a Slave* (Chicago, 1857), 15. Trader indictments in Natchez can be found in box 48, files 2, 4–13, and box 51, files 64–69, 71–76, ACCR-HNF. The certificate law in Mississippi dated to the territorial era. See Ford, *Deliver Us from Evil*, 295–296; Collins, *Domestic Slave Trade*, 128–130; Charles Sackett Sydnor, *Slavery in Mississippi* (New York: D. Appleton-Century, 1933), 161–172.

74. *The Ariel*, September 14, 1827 ("We have heard"); Natchez *Southern Galaxy*, June 11, 1829 ("to prevent," "for any person"); BSMN, 1825–1828, July 15, 1826; Thom Rosenblum, "Forks of the Road Slave Market, Analysis of Historical Occupancy" (unpublished draft, July 2005), 11–15.

75. New Orleans *Louisiana Courier*, January 13, 1829, quoted in Fredericksburg *Herald*, February 18, 1829; Richard Campanella, "On the Structural Basis

of Social Memory: Cityscapes of the New Orleans Slave Trade, Part II," *Preservation in Print*, April 2013, 18. The only comparable influx of enslaved people to New Orleans had come in 1809, when refugees who had left Saint-Domingue for Cuba during the Haitian Revolution were then forced out of that place and headed to Louisiana. Of roughly ten thousand people who landed in New Orleans from Cuba, the more than three thousand who were enslaved doubled the city's enslaved population. See Paul F. Lachance, "The 1809 Immigration of Saint-Domingue Refugees to New Orleans: Reception, Integration, and Impact," *Louisiana History* 29, no. 2 (Spring 1988): 109–141.

76. *Acts Passed at the First Session of the Ninth Legislature of the State of Louisiana* (New Orleans, 1829), January 31, 1829, 38–50.

77. "Messages from the Mayor of New Orleans to the Conseil de Ville," AB506, 1822–1831, vol. 13, 38–39, May 17, 1828, translation from the French original, NOPL; *A General Digest of the Ordinances and Resolutions of the Corporation of New-Orleans* (New Orleans, 1831), 147. Although keeping the slave trade out of the French Quarter was the consistent and overarching goal, the city council struggled to find the precise geographic limits it wanted to impose, and it passed three resolutions in the space of six weeks clarifying the locations where traders could legally keep and display slaves for sale.

78. *APG*, April 22, 1829.

79. Felix DeArmas, vol. 25 (November–December 1829), Act 1210, December 15, 1829, NONA; Paxton, *New-Orleans Directory and Register* (1827, 1830); Schafer, *Slavery, the Civil Law, and the Supreme Court*, 165–168; Taylor, "Negro Slavery in Louisiana," 54–55.

80. Adolphe Mazureau, vol. 2 (January–May 1831), Act 152, April 22, 1831, NONA; Paxton, *New-Orleans Directory and Register* (1830). A map of the property can be found in the 1822 city plan drawn by Joseph Pilie, NONA.

81. *DNI*, February 7, 1829; Gudmestad, *Troublesome Commerce*, 169–172.

82. *APG*, April 22, 1829.

83. *GUE*, January 22, 1830, 155; JMS to DB, November 17, 1829, folder 1, DBP-UTK; Gudmestad, *Troublesome Commerce*, 31. Sales figures compiled from database created by the author. Original data appears in notarial books of Joseph Arnaud, William Boswell, Louis Thimelet Caire, William Christy, Felix DeArmas, Octave DeArmas, Hugh Gordon, Charles Janin, Hugues Pedesclaux, Carlile Pollack, and Theodore Seghers, NONA, and in Conveyance Books 3, 5, and 6, LRD-NOLA. Assuming Franklin and Armfield's sales figures were similar in Natchez to what they were in New Orleans, net profits for 1829 were about 21 percent.

84. Compiled from database created by the author. Original data appears in William Boswell, vols. 7 and 8 (January–December 1829), Louis Thimelet Caire, vol. 8A (November–December 1829), and Felix DeArmas, vol. 25 (November–December 1829), NONA.

85. *APG*, December 11, 1829; *UST*, December 25, 1829; Deyle, *Carry Me Back*, 315n9; Schermerhorn, *Business of Slavery*, 137; Freudenberger and Pritchett, "Domestic United States Slave Trade," 472–475; Stephenson, *Isaac Franklin*, 36; Yagyu, "Slave Traders and Planters in the Expanding South," 145; Sublette and Sublette, *American Slave Coast*, 478; Ridgeway, "A Peculiar Business," 57–58; Donald Mitchell Sweig, "Reassessing the Human Dimension of the Interstate Slave Trade," *Prologue*, Spring 1980, 8n9. Walking enslaved people overland cost about fifteen dollars per captive. While Franklin and Armfield chartered or used the *United States* several times between 1828 and 1830, no other evidence supports some scholarly claims that the company owned the brig.

86. *APG*, October 8, 1828 (quotation), December 11, 1829; Philadelphia *Price Current and Commercial Advertiser*, January 27, 1830; New York *Evening Post*, March 2, 1830; Schermerhorn, *Business of Slavery*, 136–137; Deyle, *Carry Me Back*, 102–103; Manifest of the Ship *Jefferson*, October 20, 1828, reel 5, SM-NARA; *NOPC*, November 15, 1828. Armfield had chartered an entire vessel at least once before, advertising in October 1828 that he would book "freight or passage" on the *Jefferson*. But he does not seem to have offered another charter in the ensuing fourteen months. The *Jefferson* was an enormous ship weighing more than four hundred tons. Armfield's shipment of 158 enslaved people surely did not fill it, and his advertisement suggests some desperation, offering to book passengers "at a very reduced price." He may have waited to be certain he could manage the complexities of a charter before attempting it again.

87. *APG*, December 18 (quotations), March 30, and April 9, 1830; New York *Evening Post*, March 2, 1830; Schermerhorn, *Business of Slavery*, 137.

88. On slaver crews, mostly in the transatlantic slave trade, see Marcus Rediker, *The Slave Ship: A Human History* (New York: Viking, 2007), esp. 222–262; Emma Christopher, *Slave Ship Sailors and Their Captive Cargo, 1730–1807* (New York: Cambridge University Press, 2006); Sowande M. Mustakeem, *Slavery at Sea: Terror, Sex, and Sickness in the Middle Passage* (Urbana: University of Illinois Press, 2016); Gregory E. O'Malley, *Final Passages: The Intercolonial Slave Trade of British America, 1619–1807* (Chapel Hill: University of North Carolina Press, 2014), 75–80. On Black watermen in the United States, see Thomas C. Buchanan, *Black Life on the Mississippi: Slaves, Free Blacks, and the Western Steamboat World* (Chapel Hill: University of North Carolina Press, 2004); Calvin Schermerhorn, *Money over Mastery, Family over Freedom: Slavery in the Antebellum Upper South* (Baltimore: Johns Hopkins University Press, 2011), 63–98; David C. Cecelski, *The Waterman's Song: Slavery and Freedom in Maritime North Carolina* (Chapel Hill: University of North Carolina Press, 2001).

89. Eric Robert Taylor, *If We Must Die: Shipboard Insurrections in the Era of the Atlantic Slave Trade* (Baton Rouge: Louisiana State University Press, 2006), esp. 144–163; Jennie Williams, "*Trouble the Water*: The Baltimore to New Orleans Coastwise Slave Trade, 1820–1860," *Slavery and Abolition* 41, no. 2 (June

2020): 284–288; Manifest of the Brig *United States*, October 2, 1828, reel 5, SM-NARA.

90. New York *Commercial Advertiser*, December 30, 1829.

91. New Orleans *Louisiana Courier*, quoted in New York *Commercial Advertiser*, December 30, 1829; JMS to DB, January 3, 1830, folder 1, DBP-UTK; Ingraham, *South-West, by a Yankee*, 2:234.

92. Notarial records indicate that these men "sold" Isaac Franklin slaves sent by Armfield, usually within a day or two of a vessel's arrival. These transactions were shell sales designed to demonstrate Franklin's legal ownership. In addition to Swann, Davis, and Coote, men who escorted slaves at sea for Franklin and Armfield included John Brown Johnson, Frederick James Dudley, and Stephen Foxwell. Nothing is known about Johnson and Dudley other than that they were from Maryland and Virginia, respectively. Foxwell was a Marylander who was sometimes a crewman on slavers. See *DNI*, December 2, 1830; Janin v. Franklin, Coote v. Cotton, Docket 2410, Eastern District, December 1832, Supreme Court of Louisiana, SC-UNO; Deyle, *Carry Me Back*, 126; William Boswell, vol. 12 (January–December 1830), Acts 60 and 94, January 26 and February 11, 1830, Carlile Pollack, vol. 28 (January 1829–January 1831), Acts 134 and 142, November 15 and December 16, 1830, vol. 32 (January–December 1830), Act 171, March 29, 1830, vol. 33 (January–December 1830), Act 272, April 27, 1830, and vol. 37 (1831), Act 97, February 14, 1831, NONA; Manifest of the Ship *Shenandoah*, December 24, 1829, Manifest of the Brig *United States*, October 19, 1830, reel 6, SM-NARA; New York *Evening Post*, March 2, 1830.

93. Conveyance Book 8, 85–86, November 16, 1830, LRD-NOLA; Manifest of the Brig *United States*, October 19, 1830, reel 6, SM-NARA.

94. Robey soon moved his tavern to his more infamous location, on Seventh Street. See *DNI*, August 25, 1829 (quotation), and November 9, 1830; William Boswell, vol. 7 (January–December 1829), Act 166, May 8, 1829, and vol. 8 (January–December 1829), Acts 515, 524, and 529, May 12 and 15, 1829, NONA; *APG*, October 31, 1829; *NOPC*, November 21, 1829; Bancroft, *Slave-Trading in the Old South*, 54.

95. Articles of Agreement between Jourdan M. Saunders and David Burford, October 27, 1827, folder 1, DB-UTK; 1860 Federal Population Census, Free Schedule, Virginia, Fauquier County, 95, microfilm reel 1344, M653, NARA; Bradley Johnson and Wife v. Admr. of Jourdan Saunders, 1908-048, Fauquier Co. [Va] Chancery Causes 1759–1919, LOV; Samuel A'Court Ashe, *Biographical History of North Carolina from Colonial Times to the Present* (Greensboro, NC: Charles L. Van Noppen, 1906), 3:386–393; *History of Tennessee, from the Earliest Time to the Present* (Nashville, 1887), 821–834; Smith County Will Book 1, 2–4, TSLA; Fourth Census of the United States, Tennessee, Smith County, 39, microfilm reel 125, M33, NARA; Schermerhorn, *Business of Slavery*, 10–32; *Smith County Historical and Genealogical Society Quarterly Newsletter* 9, no. 1 (Winter 1997): 17–19.

96. Articles of Agreement between Jourdan M. Saunders and David Burford, October 27, 1827, folder 1, Account Book of J. M. Saunders and Co., folder 4, DB-UTK; *History of Tennessee*, 821–834; Joseph Martin, *A New and Comprehensive Gazetteer of Virginia, and the District of Columbia* (Charlottesville, VA, 1835), 171–175; *Abstract of the Returns of the Fifth Census*, 17.

97. Account Book of J. M. Saunders and Co., folder 4, JMS to DB, October 29, 1829, folder 1, DB-UTK.

98. JMS to DB, January 31, 1830, folder 1, DBP-UTK; Manifest of the Brig *United States*, October 30, 1829, reel 6, SM-NARA; William Christy, vol. 4A (November 1829–December 1830), Act 6, November 2, 1829, NONA. Smaller traders often boarded at the compounds of larger traders or brokers and rented space there for enslaved people they looked to sell. See Deyle, *Carry Me Back*, 116.

99. JMS to DB, February 13, 1830, folder 1, DBP-UTK.

100. JMS to DB, May 21, 1830, folder 1, DBP-UTK.

101. Account Book of J. M. Saunders and Co., folder 4, DB-UTK.

102. Jourdan Saunders's older brother, Lafayette Saunders, bought and sold property in Gallatin, Tennessee, in the late 1810s and early 1820s and may have met Isaac Franklin or some of his relatives even before Jourdan Saunders did. See Sumner County Deed Book 8, 442–445, and Book 9, 351–353, TSLA.

103. JMS to DB, February 13, 1830, folder 1, DBP-UTK; William Boswell, vol. 9 (January 15–March 1, 1830), Act 130, February 15, 1830, vol. 12 (January–December 1830), Act 27, January 9, 1830, NONA.

104. JMS to DB, December 8, 1830, JA to JMS, December 6, 1830, folder 1, DBP-UTK.

105. Bancroft, *Slave-Trading in the Old South*, 64–65 (quotations); IF to RB, February 28, 1831, folder 1, JRF to RB, January 18, 1832, folder 4, "Franklin Ballard & Co. of New Orleans in Account with R. C. Ballard & Co. of Richmond Va.," folder 341, RCBP; JA to JMS, November 1831, folder 2, DBP-UTK; *BPMA*, May 5, 1820; Frederick (MD) *Republican Gazette and General Advertiser*, August 23, 1823; "Natchez Harbor Master Register of Negroes Imported for Sale," 10–12; Manifest of the Brig *United States*, April 28, 1828, reel 5, SM-NARA; Max Grivno, *Gleanings of Freedom: Free and Slave Labor Along the Mason-Dixon Line, 1790–1860* (Urbana: University of Illinois Press, 2011), 132. Precisely when Franklin and Armfield linked themselves to Kephart and Ballard is unknown, but it is unlikely that Jourdan Saunders was the only extension Franklin and Armfield made for the fall of 1830. While Saunders was recruited first, Kephart probably started working with Franklin and Armfield at around the same time. Ballard may have as well.

106. "An Agreement Between Franklin & Armfield and Ballard & Alsop," March 15, 1831, folder 421, RCBP.

CHAPTER FOUR: CURRENCIES, 1830–1833

1. "Invoice of Thirty Five Negroes Shiped on the Brig Tribune 19 of March 1832," folder 417, JA to RB, March 26, 1832, folder 5, RCBP; Manifest of the Brig *Tribune*, March 14, 1832, reel 7, SM-NARA. Calvin Schermerhorn traces Martha Sweart's story in *The Business of Slavery and the Rise of American Capitalism, 1815–1860* (New Haven: Yale University Press, 2015), 140–142, 159, 162–163.

2. "Purchase Book, 1832–1834," folder 420, RCBP; Manifest of the Brig *Tribune*, March 14, 1832, reel 7, SM-NARA; JRF and IF to RCBC, April 29, 1832, folder 6, RCBP; *NYPC*, April 21, 1832; Joseph Holt Ingraham, *The South-West, by a Yankee* (New York, 1835), 2:234–236; Edward E. Baptist, *The Half Has Never Been Told: Slavery and the Making of American Capitalism* (New York: Basic Books, 2014), 240–244; Edward E. Baptist, "'Cuffy,' 'Fancy Maids,' and 'One-Eyed Men': Rape, Commodification, and the Domestic Slave Trade in the United States," in *The Chattel Principle: Internal Slave Trades in the Americas*, ed. Walter Johnson (New Haven: Yale University Press, 2004), 165–202; Walter Johnson, *Soul by Soul: Life Inside the Antebellum Slave Market* (Cambridge, MA: Harvard University Press, 2000), 113–115; Adrienne Davis, "'Don't Let Nobody Bother Yo' Principle': The Sexual Economy of American Slavery," in *Sister Circle: Black Women and Work*, ed. Sharon Harley and the Black Women and Work Collective (New Brunswick, NJ: Rutgers University Press, 2002), 103–127; Sharony Green, *Remember Me to Miss Louisa: Hidden Black-White Intimacies in Antebellum America* (Dekalb, IL: Northern Illinois University Press, 2015), 17–21; Ned Sublette and Constance Sublette, *The American Slave Coast: A History of the Slave-Breeding Industry* (Chicago: Lawrence Hill Books, 2016), 484–487; Sharony Green, "'Mr. Ballard, I am compelled to write again': Beyond Bedrooms and Brothels, a Fancy Girl Speaks," *Black Women, Gender & Families* 5, no. 1 (Spring 2011): 17–40; Calvin Schermerhorn, *Money over Mastery, Family over Freedom: Slavery in the Antebellum Upper South* (Baltimore: Johns Hopkins University Press, 2011), 110–111; Tomoko Yagyu, "Slave Traders and Planters in the Expanding South: Entrepreneurial Strategies, Business Networks, and Western Migration in the Atlantic World, 1787–1859" (PhD diss., University of North Carolina–Chapel Hill, 2006), 108–109. Also see Alexandra Jolyn Finley, "Blood Money: Sex, Family, and Finance in the Antebellum Slave Trade" (PhD diss., College of William and Mary, 2017); Tiye A. Gordon, "The Fancy Trade and the Commodification of Rape in the Sexual Economy of 19th Century U.S. Slavery" (MA thesis, University of South Carolina, 2015); Emily Clark, *The Strange History of the American Quadroon: Free Women of Color in the Revolutionary Atlantic World* (Chapel Hill: University of North Carolina Press, 2013), 162–187; Emily Alyssa Owens, "Fantasies of Consent: Black Women's Sexual Labor in 19th Century New Orleans" (PhD diss., Harvard University, 2015).

3. "List of Negroes Shiped on Brig Tribune at Alexandria D.C. 2 Novr. 1832," "Invoice of 38 Negroes Shiped on the Brig Tribune at Norfolk 28 of January 1833," folder 417, "List of Purchases for the Year 1832," folder 420, RCBP; Johnson, *Soul by Soul*, 114; Finley, "Blood Money," 253.

4. William Boswell, vol. 9 (January 15–March 1, 1830), Act 167, February 24, 1830, vol. 11 (April–December 1830), Act 683, December 7, 1830, Carlile Pollack, vol. 30 (January–March 1830), Act 118, February 19, 1830, NONA; Manifest of the Brig *Comet*, November 21, 1829, Manifest of the Brig *United States*, October 30, 1829, Manifest of the Ship *Shenandoah*, December 24, 1829, reel 6, SM-NARA; John Adems Paxton, *New-Orleans Directory and Register* (New Orleans, 1830); Yagyu, "Slave Traders and Planters in the Expanding South," 260.

5. William Boswell, vol. 15 (March 30–December 1831), Act 475, May 13, 1831, Felix DeArmas, vol. 31 (January–March 1831), Act 35, January 25, 1831, NONA; Paxton, *New-Orleans Directory and Register* (1830).

6. *Narrative of the Life and Adventures of Henry Bibb, An American Slave* (New York, 1849), 98 ("the basest purposes"); L. A. Chamerovzow, ed., *Slave Life in Georgia: A Narrative of the Life, Sufferings, and Escape of John Brown, a Fugitive Slave* (London, 1855), 18–19, 112 ("the slave-pen"), 116–117. Also see *A Narrative of the Adventures and Escape of Moses Roper, from American Slavery* (London, 1837), 59; William J. Anderson, *Life and Narrative of William J. Anderson, Twenty-Four Years a Slave* (Chicago, 1857), 12; E. S. Abdy, *Journal of a Residence and Tour in the United States of North America, from April, 1833, to October, 1834* (London, 1835), 2:100; E. A. Andrews, *Slavery and the Domestic Slave-Trade in the United States* (Boston, 1836), 166.

7. IF to RB, January 9, 1832, folder 4, JRF to RCBC, March 27, 1832, folder 5, RCBP. Also see Baptist, "'Cuffy,' 'Fancy Maids,' and 'One-Eyed Men,'" 179–181.

8. JRF to RCBC, March 27, 1832, folder 5, RCBP.

9. JRF to RCBC, May 13, 1832, folder 6, IF to RCBC, January 29, 1833, folder 10, RCBP; Manifest of the Brig *Tribune*, November 12, 1831, reel 6, SM-NARA; Schermerhorn, *Business of Slavery*, 141–142.

10. IF to RB, November 1, 1833, folder 12, "Names and Cost of Negroes, 1833," folder 420, "Franklin Ballard and Co. in Account with I. and J. R. Franklin," folder 421, RCBP; Schermerhorn, *Business of Slavery*, 150.

11. IF to RB, January 11, 1834, folder 13, RCBP.

12. JRF to RB, March 7, 1834, folder 13, RCBP; *SIF*, 272, 277, 282. James Franklin's handwriting is unclear. The word "compliant" might be "corpulent," a reference to Sweart's pregnancy. Either way, Franklin alluded to the sexual abuse carried out by him and his partners.

13. JRF to RB, April 16, 1834, folder 14, RCBP; Baptist, "'Cuffy,' 'Fancy Maids,' and 'One-Eyed Men,'" 197n40; Sublette and Sublette, *American Slave Coast*, 486. In May 1858, Rice Ballard sold a forty-two-year-old "mulatto" named Martha in New Orleans for $800 to William Thomas J. Goodman. The notarial

act suggests Ballard sold Martha on behalf of her actual enslaver, and Martha was a common name, so the fact that the woman's described skin color and age match those of Martha Sweart may be coincidence. Nevertheless, she was the only person Ballard had sold in New Orleans in nearly thirty years, and her sale raises the possibility that Ballard may have known exactly where Martha Sweart was and that he had kept track of her for decades. See Antoine Abat, Conveyance Book 78, 45, LRD-NOLA.

14. The literature on the relationships among race, sex, slavery, domination, capitalism, and antebellum white masculinity is large and varied, but the single best introduction to their consideration arguably still remains Drew Gilpin Faust, *James Henry Hammond and the Old South: A Design for Mastery* (Baton Rouge: Louisiana State University Press, 1985).

15. Schermerhorn, *Business of Slavery*, 124–168. On the slave trade and credit networks generally, see Calvin Schermerhorn, "Slave Trading in a Republic of Credit: Financial Architecture of the US Slave Market, 1815–1840," *Slavery and Abolition* 36, no. 4 (2015): 586–602.

16. Compiled from database created by the author. Original data appears in notarial books of William Boswell, Louis Thimelet Caire, William Christy, Felix DeArmas, Octave DeArmas, Charles Janin, Felix Pedesclaux, Hughes Pedesclaux, Carlile Pollack, and Theodore Seghers, NONA; Greenbury R. Stringer, Conveyance Book 5, 76, 77, 362, and 600, and William Y. Lewis, Conveyance Book 8, 83 and 116–117, LRD-NOLA.

17. Franklin and Armfield's impact in the market was arguably even larger than 18 percent. In 1830, notaries registered 364 enslaved people delivered to Isaac Franklin by company agents as "sales," which was technically true. But the people Franklin then sent to Natchez were recorded as having been sold in New Orleans when in fact they never left company custody, and the people Franklin then sold to customers in New Orleans appear to have been sold in the city twice. Subtracting "sales" to Franklin by company agents from the total number of people traders sold in the city leaves around 1,900 people, making the 424 sold by Franklin a bit more than 22 percent of the total. Alternatively, reckoning the 364 people delivered to Franklin as actual sales alongside the 424 he sold would mean Franklin and Armfield played a role in a bit more than a third of all transactions involving slave traders that year. Herman Freudenberger and Jonathan Pritchett contend that in New Orleans in 1830, no individual trader sold more than 115 people, that the four largest traders cumulatively sold just 15.9 percent of all imported slaves, and that the 185 individuals and companies who recorded sales demonstrated "that the market was highly competitive." It may have been, but Franklin and Armfield sold several hundred people more than Freudenberger and Pritchett account for. See Carlile Pollack, vol. 28 (January 1829–January 1831), Act 133, November 15, 1830, Act 134, November 18, 1830, Act 142, December 16, 1830, vol. 32 (January–December 1830), Act 171, March 29, 1830, vol.

33 (January–December 1830), Act 272, April 27, 1830, William Boswell, vol. 12 (January–December 1830), Act 60, January 26, 1830, Act 94, February 11, 1830, NONA; Herman Freudenberger and Jonathan B. Pritchett, "The Domestic United States Slave Trade: New Evidence," *Journal of Interdisciplinary History* 21, no. 3 (Winter 1991): 450n7, 462–463; Richard Campanella, "On the Structural Basis of Social Memory: Cityscapes of the New Orleans Slave Trade, Part II," *Preservation in Print*, April 2013, 18.

18. Lewis Cecil Gray, *History of Agriculture in the Southern United States to 1860* (Washington, DC: Carnegie Institution of Washington, 1933), 2:1027; Stuart Bruchey, *Cotton and the Growth of the American Economy: 1790–1860* (New York: Harcourt, Brace, and World, 1967), 29–30; Steven Deyle, *Carry Me Back: The Domestic Slave Trade in American Life* (New York: Oxford University Press, 2005), 58; Michael Tadman, *Speculators and Slaves: Masters, Traders, and Slaves in the Old South* (Madison: University of Wisconsin Press, 1989), 204; Freudenberger and Pritchett, "Domestic United States Slave Trade," 457, 476; Baptist, *Half*, 174.

19. JRF to JMS, January 13, 1831, folder 2, DBP-UTK. As was true in the transatlantic slave trade, anyone of any age, appearance, or body type might get swept into the domestic trade. See Sowande M. Mustakeem, *Slavery at Sea: Terror, Sex, and Sickness in the Middle Passage* (Urbana: University of Illinois Press, 2016), 36–54.

20. *APG*, December 20, 1830, January 10 ("all well") and February 10, 1831; Carlile Pollack, vol. 37 (1831), Act 93, February 14, 1831, vol. 36 (January 18–December 1831), Act 262, May 4, 1831 ("unabated violence," "reefs and breakers"), NONA; Wendell Holmes Stephenson, *Isaac Franklin, Slave Trader and Planter of the Old South* (Baton Rouge: Louisiana State University Press, 1938), 40–41; Manifest of the Cargo of Slaves on Board the Brig *Comet*, Long Papers, bundle 133, part 2, T 1/3556, the National Archives, Kew, London, UK.

21. Carlile Pollack, vol. 37 (1831), Act 93, February 14, 1831 ("relating to"), NONA; *APG*, February 26, 1831 ("been released"). Also see Charleston *City Gazette*, February 28, 1831; *The Liberator*, April 9, 1831; *GUE*, April 1831, 193.

22. Edward B. Rugemer, "Robert Monroe Harrison, British Abolition, Southern Anglophobia, and Texas Annexation," *Slavery and Abolition* 28, no. 2 (August 2007): 169–191; Matthew Karp, *This Vast Southern Empire: Slaveholders at the Helm of American Foreign Policy* (Cambridge, MA: Harvard University Press, 2016), 17–18; Don E. Fehrenbacher, *The Slaveholding Republic: An Account of the United States Government's Relations to Slavery* (New York: Oxford University Press, 2002), 104–107; Stephenson, *Isaac Franklin*, 41–42n20; *APG*, September 29 and October 7, 1831; IF to JMS, January 13, 1831, folder 2, DBP-UTK.

23. IF to RB, February 28, 1831, folder 1, RCBP.

24. IF to RB, February 28, 1831, folder 1, RCBP; *APG*, December 18, 1830, January 20, 1831; Stephenson, *Isaac Franklin*, 35n6; William Boswell, vol. 14

(January 3–March 25, 1831), Act 144, February 3, 1831, Carlile Pollack, vol. 36 (January 18–December 1831), Act 162, February 3, 1831, NONA.

25. Carrying marine insurance on cargoes of enslaved people was a practice dating to the era of the transatlantic trade. As the antebellum period progressed, American slaveholders also increasingly took out life insurance policies on individual enslaved people. Within weeks of Louisiana lifting the certificate requirement for slave sales, John Armfield changed his usual advertisement in District of Columbia papers to indicate that he would be buying with "no certificates required." See *Acts Passed at the First Session of the Tenth Legislature of the State of Louisiana* (New Orleans, 1831), March 24, 1831, 78; Carlile Pollack, vol. 36 (January 18–December 1831), Acts 263B and 264B, May 4, 1831, NONA; JRF to JMS, May 18, 1831, folder 2, DBP-UTK; Yagyu, "Slave Traders and Planters in the Expanding South," 107–108; Deyle, *Carry Me Back*, 129–130; Jonathan Levy, *Freaks of Fortune: The Emerging World of Capitalism and Risk in America* (Cambridge, MA: Harvard University Press, 2012), 21–31; Anita Rupprecht, "'Inherent Vice': Marine Insurance, Slave Ship Rebellion, and the Law," *Race and Class* 57, no. 3 (January–March 2016): 31–44; Michael Lobban, "Slavery, Insurance, and the Law," *Journal of Legal History* 28, no. 3 (2007): 319–328; Karen Ryder, "'To Realize Money Facilities': Slave Life Insurance, the Slave Trade, and Credit in the Old South," in *New Directions in Slavery Studies: Commodification, Community, and Comparison*, ed. Jeff Forret and Christine Sears (Baton Rouge: Louisiana State University Press, 2015), 53–71; Sharon Ann Murphy, *Investing in Life: Insurance in Antebellum America* (Baltimore: Johns Hopkins University Press, 2013), 184–206; *APG*, April 19, 1831.

26. Staples took the *Tribune* on an initial voyage to Haiti in the late spring, bringing a load of coffee back to New York for city merchants. See Adolphe Mazureau, vol. 2 (January–May 1831), Act 152, April 22, 1831, NONA; *NYPC*, April 6, April 23, July 9, and September 3, 1831; Philadelphia *Inquirer*, July 8, 1831; *APG*, September 5, 1831.

27. In these ways and others, domestic slavers were important to the developing infrastructure of American capitalism, playing roles analogous to those of transatlantic slavers in the broader evolution of early Atlantic world capitalism. See Marcus Rediker, *The Slave Ship: A Human History* (New York: Viking, 2007); JA to RB, October 23, 1833, IF to RB, August 26, 1833, folder 11, RCBP; Schermerhorn, *Business of Slavery*, 138–140; Deyle, *Carry Me Back*, 100–102.

28. *Ship Registers and Enrollments of New Orleans, Louisiana: Volume 3, 1831–1840* (Baton Rouge: Louisiana State University Press, 1942), 211; Manifest of the Brig *Tribune*, March 14, 1832, reel 7, SM-NARA; *APG*, November 3, 1831; Schermerhorn, *Business of Slavery*, 138–139, 147; Jennie Williams, "*Trouble the Water*: The Baltimore to New Orleans Coastwise Slave Trade, 1820–1860," *Slavery and Abolition* 41, no. 2 (June 2020): 279–282.

29. *RI*, February 8, 1834. More generally, the man observed that most domestic slavers were brigs with carrying capacities between 160 and 200 tons and that "they usually carry about one slave to a ton." Calvin Schermerhorn argues that Franklin and Armfield sometimes packed people on their vessels even more tightly than transatlantic slavers did, while Jennie Williams notes the challenges in making such calculations on domestic slavers and suggests only that space allotted to captives was often similar to that on transatlantic voyages. See Williams, *"Trouble the Water,"* 278–284; Schermerhorn, *Business of Slavery*, 137.

30. *APG*, November 3, 1831; "An Agreement Between Franklin & Armfield and Ballard & Alsop," March 15, 1831, folder 421, RCBP.

31. "An Agreement Between Franklin & Armfield and Ballard & Alsop."

32. Joseph Martin, *A New and Comprehensive Gazetteer of Virginia, and the District of Columbia* (Charlottesville, VA, 1835), 188–195; Gregg D. Kimball, *American City, Southern Place: A Cultural History of Antebellum Richmond* (Athens: University of Georgia Press, 2000), 3–36; Mary Tyler McGraw and Gregg D. Kimball, *In Bondage and Freedom: Antebellum Black Life in Richmond, Virginia* (Richmond, VA: Valentine Museum, 1988); James Sidbury, *Ploughshares into Swords: Race, Rebellion, and Identity in Gabriel's Virginia, 1730–1810* (Cambridge: Cambridge University Press, 1997), 151–183; Midori Takagi, *"Rearing Wolves to Our Own Destruction": Slavery in Richmond, Virginia, 1782–1865* (Charlottesville: University Press of Virginia, 1999), 9–36; Yagyu, "Slave Traders and Planters in the Expanding South," 111–121.

33. On the Richmond slave trade, see Frederic Bancroft, *Slave-Trading in the Old South* (Baltimore: J. H. Furst, 1931), 94–119; Deyle, *Carry Me Back*, 115–118; Kimball, *American City, Southern Place*, 38–39, 73–80, 111–112, 156–158; Maurie D. McInnis, *Slaves Waiting for Sale: Abolitionist Art and the American Slave Trade* (Chicago: University of Chicago Press, 2011), 55–84; Tadman, *Speculators and Slaves*, 57–64; Jack Trammell, *The Richmond Slave Trade: The Economic Backbone of the Old Dominion* (Charleston, SC: History Press, 2012); Hank Trent, *The Secret Life of Bacon Tait, a White Slave Trader Married to a Free Woman of Color* (Baton Rouge: Louisiana State University Press, 2017), 34–35, 45–46, 57–59, 63–74; Finley, "Blood Money," 45–50; Yagyu, "Slave Traders and Planters in the Expanding South," 121–128.

34. *Narrative of Henry Watson, a Fugitive Slave* (Boston, 1850), 9; "R. C. Ballard and Co. Expense Book, 1831–1835," folder 425, RCBP; Trent, *Secret Life of Bacon Tait*, 35, 65–68.

35. "Negro Board Book," folder 418, "R. C. Ballard and Co. Expense Book, 1831–1835," folder 425, RCBC to FBC, April 5, 1832, folder 6, RCBP.

36. Promissory notes, March–April 1832, folder 340, tickets "Due at the Bank of Virginia," October–December 1833, folder 341, orders to Cashier of the Bank of Virginia, August–October 1834, folder 343, RCBP; *The American Almanac and Repository of Useful Knowledge for the Year 1831* (Boston, 1830), 221.

37. When a bank bought commercial paper from a client, it was effectively a kind of conditional loan, with the discount pegged to an interest rate and the client still liable for the amount of the bill of exchange should the bank be unable to collect from the person or entity on which the bill was to be drawn. See Schermerhorn, *Business of Slavery*, 128–129; Yagyu, "Slave Traders and Planters in the Expanding South," 101–102; Deyle, *Carry Me Back*, 129; Sharon Ann Murphy, *Other People's Money: How Banking Worked in the Early American Republic* (Baltimore: Johns Hopkins University Press, 2017), 42–49, 58–59; Stephen Campbell, *The Bank War and the Partisan Press: Newspapers, Financial Institutions, and the Post Office in Jacksonian America* (Lawrence: University Press of Kansas, 2019), 146–147.

38. Correspondence among IF, JRF, and RCBC, May 30–June 3, 1831, folder 1, RCBP (quotations from IF to RCBC, May 30, 1831); Philadelphia *Price Current and Commercial Advertiser*, August 25, 1830, January 12, 1831; New York *Evening Post*, July 2, 1829, May 17, 1831; Paxton, *New-Orleans Directory and Register* (1830); Felix DeArmas vol. 25 (November–December 1829), Act 1254, December 30, 1829, vol. 34 (October–December 1831), Acts 724 and 803, November 1 and December 17, 1831, NONA; Schermerhorn, *Business of Slavery*, 128–129.

39. Hugues Pedesclaux, vol. 2 (July–December 1830), Act 812, November 2, 1830, NONA; Linda K. Salvucci and Richard J. Salvucci, "The Lizardi Brothers: A Mexican Family Business and the Expansion of New Orleans, 1825–1846," *JSH* 82, no. 4 (November 2016): 759–788; Murphy, *Other People's Money*, 74–75.

40. Compiled from database created by the author. Original data appears in notarial books of William Boswell, Louis Thimelet Caire, William Christy, Joseph Cuvillier, Felix DeArmas, Octave DeArmas, Louis Feraud, Charles Janin, Adolphe Mazureau, Hughes Pedesclaux, Carlile Pollack, and Theodore Seghers, NONA; and in Greenbury R. Stringer, Conveyance Book 5, 362, 600, Conveyance Book 7, 165–166, 416, William Y. Lewis, Conveyance Book 8, 83, 116–117, 475, 510, 530, LRD-NOLA.

41. IF to RCBC, May 30, 1831, folder 1, RCBP; IF to JMS, January 13, 1831, folder 2, DBP-UTK. Also see Gray, *History of Agriculture*, 2:1027; Bruchey, *Cotton and the Growth of the American Economy*, 29–30.

42. JRF to JMS, May 18, 1831, folder 2, DBP-UTK.

43. JRF to JMS, May 18, 1831, folder 2, JMS to DB, September 22, 1831, folder 3, DBP-UTK.

44. JA to RB, July 23, 1831, JRF to RCBC, August 15, 1831, folder 2, RCBP.

45. Stephenson, *Isaac Franklin*, 16, 95n2; *SIF*, 285; Sumner County Deed Book 12, 364–365, TSLA; Fifth Census of the United States, Tennessee, Sumner County, 134, microfilm reel 181, M19, NARA; IF to RB, August 26, 1833, folder 11, RCBP.

46. Smith Franklin v. Zebulon Cantrel (1837), file 2543, Sumner County Loose Records, Lawsuits, TSLA (quotations); "Franklin Ballard & Co. of New Orleans in Account with R. C. Ballard & Co. of Richmond Va.," folder 341, RCBP.

47. Baptist, *Half*, 206–211; Stephenson, *Isaac Franklin*, 72–76; Lacy K. Ford, *Deliver Us from Evil: The Slavery Question in the Old South* (New York: Oxford University Press, 2009), 297–298, 338–375, 449–465; Robert H. Gudmestad, *A Troublesome Commerce: The Transformation of the Interstate Slave Trade* (Baton Rouge: Louisiana State University Press, 2003), 102–107; Judith Kelleher Schafer, "The Immediate Impact of Nat Turner's Insurrection on New Orleans," *Louisiana History* 21, no. 4 (Autumn 1980): 361–376; Patrick H. Breen, *The Land Shall Be Deluged in Blood: A New History of the Nat Turner Revolt* (New York: Oxford University Press, 2016); David F. Allmendinger Jr., *Nat Turner and the Rising in Southampton County* (Baltimore: Johns Hopkins University Press, 2014); Alison Goodyear Freehling, *Drift Toward Dissolution: The Virginia Slavery Debate of 1831–1832* (Baton Rouge: Louisiana State University Press, 1982).

48. Stephenson, *Isaac Franklin*, 72; Baptist, *Half*, 207; Schafer, "Immediate Impact," 369–370; *APG*, September 29, 1831; *NYPC*, October 22, 1831; *L'Abeille*, November 7, 1831; "New Orleans (La.) Office of the Mayor, Lists of Slaves Imported for Sale in the City of New Orleans, 1831," microfilm #906709, AA253, NOPL; Manifest of the Schooner *Lafayette*, October 15, 1831, Manifest of the Schooner *Industry*, October 28, 1831, reel 6, SM-NARA.

49. "New Orleans (La.) Office of the Mayor, Lists of Slaves Imported for Sale in the City of New Orleans, 1831"; Manifest of the Schooner *Lafayette*, October 15, 1831, reel 6, SM-NARA.

50. Baltimore *Republican*, October 11, 1831; Charles Varle, *A Complete View of Baltimore* (Baltimore, 1833), 80.

51. "New Orleans (La.) Office of the Mayor, Lists of Slaves Imported for Sale in the City of New Orleans, 1831"; Manifest of the Schooner *Lafayette*, October 15, 1831, reel 6, SM-NARA; "Franklin Ballard & Co. of New Orleans in Account with R. C. Ballard & Co. of Richmond Va.," folder 341, "Purchase Book, 1832–1834," folder 420, receipt from Andrew Grimm, May 4, 1831, folder 339, receipts from Nathaniel White, February 17 and September 14, 1832, folder 340, "Office of Disct & Deposit Freds. Bk of Va. In a/c with R.C. Ballard & Co.," folder 416, RCBP.

52. *A General Digest of the Ordinances and Resolutions of the Corporation of New-Orleans* (New Orleans, 1831), 409–411 ("conspiracy or insurrection" on 409); IF to RCBC, October 26, 1831 ("fool us," "a prohibitory," "being passed"), folder 2, and November 10 and December 10, 1831, folder 3, "Franklin Ballard & Co. of New Orleans in Account with R. C. Ballard & Co. of Richmond Va.," folder 341, "Third Shipment List of Names & Prices of Sixty Nine Negroes Shiped on Scooner Industry," folder 417, RCBP; Schermerhorn, *Business of Slavery*, 128–129, 132; Schafer, "Immediate Impact," 364–365; Petition #732, "Letters, Petitions, and Reports to the New Orleans Conseil de Ville, 1804–1835," AB320, microfilm reel #90-156, NOPL.

53. *Acts Passed at the Extra Session of the First Session of the Tenth Legislature of the State of Louisiana* (New Orleans, 1831), 4–11 (quotation on 4). The law also provided a six-day grace period for traders to import enslaved people already headed to New Orleans along the Mississippi River. Pursuant to his musings from earlier in the year, Isaac Franklin actually did become a legal resident of Louisiana in response to new restrictions on the slave trade, but legislators had foreseen that traders would try to exploit such a loophole and so required would-be traders to have had five years of residency to import slaves legally, meaning the maneuver brought Franklin no immediate advantage. See Gudmestad, *Troublesome Commerce*, 104; Stephenson, *Isaac Franklin*, 74–76; Ford, *Deliver Us from Evil*, 452; Schafer, "Immediate Impact," 365–368; Joe Gray Taylor, "Negro Slavery in Louisiana" (PhD diss., Louisiana State University, 1952), 56–58; *SIF*, 330–331, 338.

54. JA to JMS, undated, received November 18, 1831, folder 2, DBP-UTK (quotation); William Boswell, vol. 16 (January–December 1831), Acts 489 and 492, November 19, 1831, NONA.

55. JA to JMS, December 11, 1831, folder 2, DBP-UTK; *Acts Passed at the Extra Session of the First Session of the Tenth Legislature*, 8; Manifest of the Brig *Tribune*, December 3, 1831, reel 6, SM-NARA; *BPMA*, November 2, 1831; *APG*, November 3, 8, 14, December 19, 1831; Natchez *Statesman and Gazette*, December 7, 1831.

56. JA to JMS, undated, received November 18, 1831, folder 2, DBP-UTK; JRF to RCBC, December 14, 1831, folder 3, IF to RB, January 9, 1832, folder 4, RCBP.

57. JA to JMS, undated, received November 18, 1831, folder 2, DBP-UTK; *Acts Passed at the Extra Session of the First Session of the Tenth Legislature*, 4. A torn note in Rice Ballard's papers from July 1835 refers to "rent due for Smoky Row," a street in the Pinch-Gut district that became the Memphis equivalent of Natchez Under-the-Hill. But the slave market in Memphis, like the city itself, was minimally developed in the 1830s, and Franklin and Armfield company dealings there early in the decade were probably about document fraud more than sales. See folder 344, RCBP.

58. JA to JMS, undated, received November 18, 1831, folder 2, DBP-UTK.

59. *RI*, February 8, 1834 ("ever led," "all in his power"); Rachel Brent v. John Armfield, October 1835 ("beat"), Arlington County Freedom Suits, 1823–1858, LOV. Brent had been enslaved by Ariss Buckner in Loudoun County, Virginia, but in 1827 Buckner brought her into Washington City and she lived there continuously for more than five years while Buckner remained a Virginia resident, facts that by law entitled her to freedom. Also see Negro Henry v. John Armfield, October 1832, Arlington County Freedom Suits, 1823–1858, LOV; Rezin Ogleton v. Isaac Franklin, box 30, entry 6, Chloe Ann Johnson v. Isaac Franklin and John Armfield, box 506, entry 6, folder 127, Elizabeth Smith v. James Birch

and John Armfield, box 528, entry 6, folder 261, United States Circuit Court (District of Columbia,) RG21, NARA, available at William G. Thomas III, Kaci Nash, Laura Weakly, Karin Dalziel, and Jessica Dussault, *O Say Can You See: Early Washington, D.C., Law & Family*, http://earlywashingtondc.org/. For an instance of Armfield asking authorities to intervene when someone tried selling him an obviously free person, see *GUE*, January 1831, 160.

60. Refunded sales, canceled sales, and exchanges compiled from database created by the author. Original data appears in notarial books of William Boswell, Louis Thimelet Caire, William Christy, Octave DeArmas, Charles Janin, Felix Pedesclaux, Hugues Pedesclaux, and Carlile Pollack, NONA, and William Y. Lewis, Conveyance Book 8, 530, LRD-NOLA. For lawsuits, see Henry Conner v. Isaac Franklin, 1832, box 10, file 40, ACCR-HNF; Frederick Williams v. Isaac Franklin (1830), Docket 8719, Robert Lewis v. Isaac Franklin (1831), Docket 9126, and Joseph T. Janin v. Isaac Franklin (1831), Docket 9345, Louisiana First Judicial District Court, Louisiana Division, City Archives and Special Collections, NOPL; Janin v. Franklin, Docket 2355, Eastern District, July 1832, Supreme Court of Louisiana, SC-UNO. Of the lawsuits filed against Franklin, one was dismissed on a technicality, the court decided that the evidence in another was inconclusive, and the other two appear to have been settled out of court.

61. Deyle, *Carry Me Back*, 124–125; Baptist, "'Cuffy,' 'Fancy Maids,' and 'One-Eyed Men,'" 170–171. For references to the slave trade as "the game," or to "robbers" or "pirates," see JRF to RCBC, January 18, 1832, folder 4, IF and JRF to RCBC, June 8, 1832, folder 7, IF to RCBC, December 8, 1832, folder 8, JA to RB, December 21, 1832, folder 9, JRF to RCBC, March 24, 1833, folder 10, IF to RCBC, June 11, 1833, folder 11, JRF to RB, February 2, 1834, folder 13, IF to RB, April 9 and May 22, 1834, folder 14, RCBP.

62. Rieffel v. Franklin, case #6225, Orleans Parish Court, Suit Records, 1831–1832, VCP290, NOPL; John Adems Paxton, *New-Orleans Directory and Register* (New Orleans, 1827); S. E. Percy and Co., *The New-Orleans Directory* (New Orleans, 1832).

63. Compiled from database created by the author. Original data appears in notarial books of William Boswell, Louis Thimelet Caire, William Christy, Felix DeArmas, Octave DeArmas, Louis Feraud, Charles Janin, Adolphe Mazureau, Hughes Pedesclaux, Carlile Pollack, and Theodore Seghers, NONA; and Greenbury R. Stringer, Conveyance Book 9, 93, 103, 109, 159, William Y. Lewis, Conveyance Book 9, 129, 131, 152, LRD-NOLA. Isaac Franklin told Rice Ballard that he sold 270 people in the thirty days after the import ban passed, but he was including 30 people sold in two days before the ban passed on November 19. See IF to RB, January 9, 1832, folder 4, RCBP.

64. JA to JMS, December 11, 1831, folder 2, DBP-UTK.

65. JRF to RCBC, December 14, 1831, folder 3, RCBP.

66. IF to RB, January 9, 1832, folder 4, RCBP.

67. IF to RB, January 9, 1832, folder 4, RCBP. Also see Schermerhorn, *Business of Slavery*, 132–133.

68. *SIF*, 293; JA to JMS, undated, received November 18, 1831, folder 2, DBP-UTK; JRF to RCBC, October 30, 1831, folder 2, IF to RCBC, undated, received February 1832, folder 5, RCBP.

69. William Boswell, vol. 16 (January–December 1831), Act 585, December 21, 1831, NONA.

70. *SIF*, 275, 279, 284 ("finest embellished"), 289, 295–296, 299 ("improvements," "decidedly superior"), 302; Sumner County Deed Book 13, 53–55, 81–82, 101–102, "Fairview, Historic American Buildings Survey, District of Tennessee" (1936), TSLA; Stephenson, *Isaac Franklin*, 95–96; Margaret Lindsley Warden, *The Saga of Fairvue, 1832–1977* (Nashville, 1977), 6–7.

71. *SIF*, 275, 277, 279–280, 284–286, 289, 291–292, 295–296, 299, 302–303; Stephenson, *Isaac Franklin*, 96–97; Warden, *Saga of Fairvue*, 6.

72. *SIF*, 275 ("warmed"), 277, 279–280, 284–286 ("finest and most costly" on 284), 289, 291–292, 295–296, 299, 302–303 ("hardly a boat" on 302); "Fairview, Historic American Buildings Survey," 1–8, "National Register of Historic Places Inventory—Nomination Form" (1975), TSLA; Warden, *Saga of Fairvue*, 6–7; Stephenson, *Isaac Franklin*, 96–97.

73. *SIF*, 282.

74. JRF to RCBC, January 18, 1832, JA to RB, January 26, 1832, folder 4, RCBP; *Acts Passed at the Third Session of the Tenth Legislature of the State of Louisiana* (New Orleans, 1832), 140–145.

75. Natchez *Southern Galaxy*, January 28, 1830 ("in a back yard"); Natchez *Statesman and Gazette*, November 30, 1831 ("Franklin & Armfield," "The Tribune").

76. BSMN, 1832–1836, March 6, 13 ("stigma," "in all probability"), 27, April 10 ("some negroes," "found two," "quite sick," "enactment"), 17, 24, May 1, 8, 15, 1832; Natchez *Southern Galaxy*, January 28, 1830; Manifest of the Brig *Ajax*, February 13, 1832, Manifest of the Schooner *Lafayette*, February 13, 1832, Manifest of the Brig *Tribune*, March 14, 1832, reel 7, SM-NARA; JA to RB, January 26, 1832, folder 4, IF and JRF to RCBC, April 29, 1832, folder 6, RCBP; Reports of the Committee on Propositions and Grievances, Natchez Board of Selectmen, n.d., reel A320, GAL; Schermerhorn, *Business of Slavery*, 122; Thom Rosenblum, "Forks of the Road Slave Market, Analysis of Historical Occupancy" (unpublished draft, July 2005), 15–19.

77. JMS to DB, September 22, 1831, folder 3, DBP-UTK.

78. JA to RB, March 26, 1832, folder 5, RCBP; Schermerhorn, *Business of Slavery*, 140; William Calderhead, "The Role of the Professional Slave Trader in a Slave Economy: Austin Woolfolk, A Case Study," *Civil War History* 23, no. 3 (September 1977): 200.

79. Baltimore County Court Land Records, AI-218 (1832), 496–497, Maryland State Archives, Annapolis, Maryland (quotations); Baltimore *Republican*, May 4, 1832; Easton *Star*, December 3, 1833; Varle, *Complete View of Baltimore*, 52.

80. Baltimore *Republican*, May 4, 1832. Busk also dealt in real estate and personal property more broadly, but he stressed that his office was "in a central part of the city, which has many facilities in the way of disposing of *good slaves.*" By the fall of 1832, he was focusing mostly on the slave trade and was effectively the downtown buyer for James Purvis. See Easton *Star*, July 13, 1830; Ralph Clayton, *Cash for Blood: The Baltimore to New Orleans Domestic Slave Trade* (Westminster, MD: Heritage Books, 2007), 16–21; Brian P. Luskey, "Special Marts: Intelligence Offices, Labor Commodification, and Emancipation in Nineteenth-Century America," *Journal of the Civil War Era* 3, no. 3 (September 2013): 360–391.

81. Baltimore *Republican*, October 6, 1832; Easton *Star*, May 29, 1832; *Eastern Shore Whig and People's Advocate*, May 29, 1832; Cambridge *Chronicle*, September 15, 1832.

82. Baltimore *Republican*, October 6, 1832; Calderhead, "Role of the Professional Slave Trader," 200–201; Clayton, *Cash for Blood*, 53–54; Schermerhorn, *Business of Slavery*, 143.

83. "Purchase Book, 1832–1834," folder 420, "Ballard and Co. Ledger, 1831–1834," folder 463, receipt from Andrew Grimm, May 4, 1831, folder 339, receipts from Nathaniel White, February 17 and September 14, 1832, folder 340, "Office of Disct & Deposit Freds. Bk of Va. In a/c with R.C. Ballard & Co.," folder 416, RCBP; Schermerhorn, *Business of Slavery*, 144; Finley, "Blood Money," 42–43; *A Genealogy of the Blakey Family and Descendants*, compiled and edited by Lue Adams Kress (Caldwell, ID, 1942), 54; Richmond *Enquirer*, July 11, 1826.

84. "Ballard and Co. Ledger, 1831–1834," folder 463, "Purchase Book, 1832–1834," folder 420, RCBP. Andrew Grimm was salaried, receiving $250 in 1831 and $350 in 1832, but Ballard's other agents appear to have worked on commission, with travel and other expenses reimbursed. See "R. C. Ballard and Co. Expense Book, 1831–1835," folder 425, folder 430, RCBP.

85. "R. C. Ballard and Co. Expense Book, 1831–1835," folder 425 (first two quotations), "Account with Franklin Ballard & Co. N.O.," folder 421 (third quotation), "Ballard and Co. Ledger, 1831–1834," folder 463, RCBP; Jan Richard Heier, "Accounting for the Business of Suffering: A Study of the Antebellum Richmond, Virginia, Slave Trade," *ABACUS: A Journal of Accounting, Finance and Business Studies* 46, no. 1 (2010): 60–83.

86. *APG*, January 15, 1833, October 1, 1832.

87. JRF to RCBC, March 4, 1832, folder 5, RCBP; Manifest of the Brig *Ajax*, February 13, 1832, reel 7, SM-NARA; Baltimore *Republican*, March 16, 1832; *APG*, February 21, 1832; Baptist, "'Cuffy,' 'Fancy Maids,' and 'One-Eyed Men,'" 175.

88. JRF to RCBC, March 27, 1832, folder 5, IF and JRF to RCBC, April 29, 1832, JRF to RCBC, May 13, 1832, folder 6, RCBP.

89. IF to RCBC, June 8, 1832, folder 7, RCBP.

90. IF to RCBC, May 19, 1832 (quotations), folder 6, IF and JRF to RCBC, June 7, 1832, folder 7, RCBP.

91. JMS to DB, July 4, 1832, folder 2, DBP-UTK ("all the negroes"); *NYPC*, May 19 ("bear's oil"), 26, 1832; Philadelphia *American Daily Advertiser*, September 17, 1832 ("wines &c."); Charleston *Courier*, May 14 and August 15, 1832; New York *Commercial Advertiser*, June 1 and September 3, 1832; Baltimore *Gazette*, September 17, 1832; *APG*, October 29, 1832.

92. IF and JRF to RCBC, January 26, 1832, JRF to RCBC, January 28, 1832, folder 4, IF and JRF to RCBC, February 10, 1832, folder 5, IF and JRF to RCBC, April 24, April 29, May 24, 1832, IF to RCBC, May 19, 1832, folder 6, IF and JRF to RCBC, June 7, 1832, folder 7, "Ballard and Co. Ledger, 1831–1834," folder 463, RCBP.

93. IF to RCBC, May 19, 1832, folder 6, RCBP. Also see IF to RCBC, June 8, 1832, folder 7, RCBP.

94. IF to RCBC, June 8, 1832, folder 7, RCBP.

95. Charles E. Rosenberg, *The Cholera Years: The United States in 1832, 1849, and 1866* (Chicago: University of Chicago Press, 1987; originally published 1962), 13–39.

96. Slave trader Paul Pascal told his partner that it was rumored in Natchez that Franklin left Alexandria with 230 people, which is possible but unconfirmable. See JMS to DB, October 30, 1832, folder 2, DBP-UTK; Paul Pascal to Bernard Raux, November 14, 1832, folder 6, Bernard Raux Slave Trade Papers, 1828–1836, bMS Am 790, Houghton Library, Harvard University; "Franklin Ballard & Co. of New Orleans in Account with R. C. Ballard & Co. of Richmond Va.," folder 341, IF to RB, August 15, 1832, folder 7, RCBP.

97. RCBC to FBC, September 7, 1832, folder 7, RCBP.

98. IF to RCBC, August 15, 1832 ("dissatisfaction," "pressed," "You are"), folder 7, October 5, 1832 ("discussion"), folder 8, RCBP.

99. IF to RCBC, August 15, 1832, folder 7, RCBP.

100. IF to RCBC, August 15, 1832 ("Extreamly," "the slaves," "I must"), folder 7, October 5, 1832 ("cautious," "very large") folder 8, RCBP.

101. RCBC to FBC, September 7, 1832, folder 7, RCBP.

102. IF to RCBC, August 15, 1832, RCBC to FBC, September 7, 1832, folder 7, RCBP.

103. Woodville (MS) *Southern Planter*, November 10, 1832 ("the introduction"); Green v. Robinson, 6 Miss. 80 (December 1840), 102 ("artful," "depraved"); JA to RB, December 21, 1832 ("the convention"), folder 9, RCBP. Also see Joshua D. Rothman, "The Contours of Cotton Capitalism: Speculation, Slavery, and Economic Panic in Mississippi, 1832–1841," in *Slavery's Capitalism: A New History of American Economic Development*, ed. Sven Beckert and Seth Rockman (Philadelphia: University of Pennsylvania Press, 2016), 132; Winfield Hazlitt Collins, *The*

Domestic Slave Trade of the Southern States (New York: Broadway Publishing Company, 1904), 130–131; Ford, *Deliver Us from Evil*, 453–458; Rosenblum, "Forks of the Road Slave Market," 19–21.

104. JMS to DB, October 30, 1832, folder 2, DBP-UTK; IF to RCBC, October 5, 1832, folder 8, RCBP.

105. IF to RCBC, December 8, 1832, folder 8, RCBP. Also see "Invoice of Negroes sent out by land August 17th 1832," folder 417, IF to RCBC, October 5, 1832, JRF to RCBC, November 23, 1832, folder 8, RCBP; BSMN, 1832–1836, October 22, 23, 25, 26, 27, 30, and November 6, 1832.

106. JRF to RCBC, November 23, 1832, folder 8, RCBP; Niles *Weekly Register*, November 24, 1832, 202; JMS to DB, December 8, 1832, folder 2, DBP-UTK; *APG*, October 18, November 5, December 11, 1832; Manifest of the Brig *Tribune*, November 2, 1832, reel 7, SM-NARA.

107. Manifest of the Brig *Tribune*, November 2, 1832, reel 7, SM-NARA; JMS to DB, October 30, 1832, folder 2, DBP-UTK; IF to RCBC, December 8, 1832, folder 8, RCBP.

108. RB to IF, December 2, 1832, folder 8, RCBP.

109. IF to RCBC, December 8, 1832, folder 8, RCBP.

110. IF to RCBC, December 8, 1832, folder 8, RCBP; Schermerhorn, *Business of Slavery*, 111–116, 134–135; Ralph W. Hidy, "The Union Bank of Louisiana Loan, 1832: A Case Study in Marketing," *Journal of Political Economy* 47, no. 2 (April 1939): 232–253; Ralph W. Hidy, "The House of Baring and the Second Bank of the United States, 1826–1836," *Pennsylvania Magazine of History and Biography* 68, no. 3 (July 1944): 269–285; Peter E. Austin, *Baring Brothers and the Birth of Modern Finance* (London: Routledge, 2007), 130–131.

111. *NOPC*, September 13, 1828; Charles Janin, vol. 7 (June–December 1831), Acts 284 and 308, November 24 and December 20, 1831, William Boswell, vol. 15 (March 30–December 1831), Act 939, December 19, 1831, NONA; Percy and Co., *New-Orleans Directory*; Schermerhorn, *Business of Slavery*, 109–120, 134–135; Irene D. Neu, "Edmond Jean Forstall and Louisiana Banking," *Explorations in Economic History* 7 (Summer 1970): 383–398; Jessica M. Lepler, *The Many Panics of 1837: People, Politics, and the Creation of a Transatlantic Financial Crisis* (New York: Cambridge University Press, 2013), 8–42; Scott P. Marler, *The Merchants' Capital: New Orleans and the Political Economy of the Nineteenth-Century South* (New York: Cambridge University Press, 2013), 32–35.

112. William J. Roberts to RCBC, December 31, 1832, JA to RB, December 21, 1832, folder 9, RCBP. Also see Richard Booker to RCBC, December 14 and 18, 1832, JA to RB, December 29, 1832, folder 9, "Franklin Ballard & Co. of New Orleans in Account with R. C. Ballard & Co. of Richmond Va.," folder 341, RCBP.

113. IF to RCBC, January 29, 1833, JRF to RCBC, March 6, 1833, folder 10, RCBP; JRF to JMS, January 2, 1833, folder 2, DBP-UTK; Rothman, "Contours

of Cotton Capitalism," 133; Charles Sackett Sydnor, *Slavery in Mississippi* (New York: D. Appleton-Century, 1933), 163–169; Ford, *Deliver Us from Evil*, 455–457.

114. *Acts Passed at the First Session of the Eleventh Legislature of the State of Louisiana* (New Orleans, 1833), 81–82; IF to RCBC, March 24, 1833, folder 10, RCBP; Ingraham, *South-West, by a Yankee*, 1:181.

115. IF to RCBC, February 19, 1833, JRF to RCBC, March 24, 1833, folder 10, "Invoice of 38 Negroes Shiped on the Brig Tribune at Norfolk 28 of January 1833" and "Invoice of 85 Negroes Shiped on the Brig Tribune 21st of March 1833 at Norfolk," folder 417, RCBP; Neil Kagan and Stephen G. Hyslop, eds., *Smithsonian Civil War: Inside the National Collection* (Washington, DC: Smithsonian Books, 2013), 34–35; Stephenson, *Isaac Franklin*, 36; Manifest of the Schooner *Renown*, April 20, 1833, reel 7, SM-NARA; *APG*, January 17, 21, 23, February 2, 15, 28, March 1, 16, 22, April 16, 22, 29, 1833.

116. JRF to RCBC, April 24, 1833, folder 11, RCBP; Rosenberg, *Cholera Years*, 37; *MJNA*, April 19, 26, May 10, 1833; *NCAJFA*, April 26, 1833; BSMN, 1832–1836, February 6, April 17, 24, 1833; *Code of the Ordinances of the City of Natchez* (Natchez, 1854), 151–152.

117. *APG*, April 23, 1833.

CHAPTER FIVE: DISSOLUTIONS, 1833–1837

1. E. A. Andrews, *Slavery and the Domestic Slave-Trade in the United States* (Boston, 1836), 135, iii; James R. Stirn, "Urgent Gradualism: The Case of the American Union for the Relief and Improvement of the Colored Race," *Civil War History* 25, no. 4 (December 1979): 309–328; John R. McKivigan, *The War Against Proslavery Religion: Abolitionism and the Northern Churches, 1830–1865* (Ithaca: Cornell University Press, 1984), 56–73; *Biographical Dictionary of North American Classicists*, ed. Ward W. Briggs Jr. (Westport, CT: Greenwood Press, 1994), 18–19.

2. William Jay, *An Inquiry into the Character and Tendency of the American Colonization, and American Anti-Slavery Societies* (New York, 1837), 157 ("Slave-Factory"); *The Abolitionist*, October 1833, 148 ("principal dealers"); *The Liberator*, February 11, 1832 ("mart for slave-dealers"); *The Emancipator*, May 12, 1836 ("the trade in blood"); *Weekly Advocate*, January 14, 1837 ("Slave Dealers," "gang of thieves"); *Slave Market of America* (New York, 1836). Also see *The Liberator*, May 17, 1834; *Human Rights*, March 1, 1836; *The Philanthropist*, November 11, 1836; *Anti-Slavery Record* 3, no. 11 (November 1837); Andrews, *Slavery and the Domestic Slave-Trade*, 148; Steven Deyle, *Carry Me Back: The Domestic Slave Trade in American Life* (New York: Oxford University Press, 2005), 174–205; Phillip Davis Troutman, "Slave Trade and Sentiment in Antebellum Virginia" (PhD diss., University of Virginia, 2000), 321–399.

3. *RI*, February 8, 1834; E. S. Abdy, *Journal of a Residence and Tour in the United States of North America, from April, 1833, to October, 1834* (London, 1835), 2:179–180; *American Anti-Slavery Almanac for 1836* (Boston, 1835), 26.

4. Andrews, *Slavery and the Domestic Slave-Trade*, 136–143. Joshua Leavitt also noticed the distress of those imprisoned at Duke Street, writing of women carrying young children that "it seemed to me they hugged their little ones very closely, and that a cold perspiration stood on their foreheads, and I thought I saw tears too." See *RI*, February 8, 1834.

5. Andrews, *Slavery and the Domestic Slave-Trade*, 150; New York *Evangelist*, June 27, 1835. Also see *American Anti-Slavery Almanac for 1836*, 26.

6. "The Diary of Michael Shiner Relating to the History of the Washington Navy Yard 1813–1865," 52–54, at The Diary of Michael Shiner, Naval History and Heritage Command (website), www.history.navy.mil/research/library/online -reading-room/title-list-alphabetically/d/diary-of-michael-shiner.html; Loren Schweninger, *Black Property Owners in the South, 1790–1915* (Urbana and Chicago: University of Illinois Press, 1990), 89; Kim Roberts, *A Literary Guide to Washington, D.C.: Walking in the Footsteps of American Writers from Francis Scott Key to Zora Neale Hurston* (Charlottesville: University of Virginia Press, 2018), 17–22.

7. Barre (MA) *Wachusett Star*, April 18, 1848.

8. Andrews, *Slavery and the Domestic Slave-Trade*, 136, 143, 145–147, 149.

9. Addendum dated May 6, 1833, to "An Agreement Between Franklin & Armfield and Ballard & Alsop," March 15, 1831, folder 421, "Ballard and Co. Ledger, 1831–1834," folder 463, RCBP.

10. *APG*, May 7, 1833; *DNI*, May 9, 1833; Washington *Globe*, May 9, 1833.

11. *APG*, May 7, 1833; William Boswell, vol. 5 (January–April 30, 1828), Acts 87, 91, 106, 108, 112, 124, 132, 134, 139, 142, January 21, 26, 31, February 1, 4, 6, 1828, vol. 7 (January–December 1829), Act 334, December 5, 1829, NONA.

12. *APG*, May 30 and August 27, 1833; William Boswell, vol. 7 (January–December 1829), Acts 334 and 346, December 5 and 10, 1829, vol. 12 (January–December 1830), Act 94, February 11, 1830, Louis Thimelet Caire, vol. 12A (October–December 1830), Acts 820 and 830, October 29 and November 4, 1830, Octave DeArmas, vol. 8 (September–December 1830), Acts 391 and 432, November 2 and December 17, 1830, and Hugues Pedesclaux, vol. 2 (July–December 1830), Act 812, November 2, 1830, NONA.

13. *APG*, October 5, 1833. The historical Uncas was also in the news in 1833, because Andrew Jackson dedicated a monument at his Connecticut grave that summer. See City of Richmond Hustings Deeds, Book 32, 92–93, LOV; JA to RB, October 23, 1833, folder 11, RCBP; *Ship Registers and Enrollments of New Orleans, Louisiana: Volume 3, 1831–1840* (Baton Rouge: Louisiana State University Press, 1942), 213; New York *American for the Country*, September 20, 1833; Middletown (CT) *Sentinel and Witness*, July 3, 1833.

14. IF to RB, August 26, 1833, JA to RB, October 23, 1833, folder 11, IF to RCBC, November 5, 1833, folder 12, RCBP; JMS to DB, May 6, 1833, folder 2, DBP-UTK.

15. JRF to RCBC, October 29, 1833, folder 11, RCBP.

16. JRF to RCBC, May 7, 1833, folder 11, RCBP; *NCAJFA*, May 3, 1833; Deyle, *Carry Me Back*, 125, 320n80.

17. IF to RCBC, June 11, 1833, folder 11, RCBP.

18. Robert V. Remini, *Andrew Jackson and the Bank War: A Study in the Growth of Presidential Power* (New York: W. W. Norton, 1967), 109–153; Richard Holcombe Kilbourne Jr., *Slave Agriculture and Financial Markets in Antebellum America: The Bank of the United States in Mississippi, 1831–1853* (London: Pickering and Chatto, 2006), 25–55; Peter Temin, *The Jacksonian Economy* (New York: W. W. Norton, 1969), 59–68; Jessica M. Lepler, *The Many Panics of 1837: People, Politics, and the Creation of a Transatlantic Financial Crisis* (New York: Cambridge University Press, 2013), 20–21; Edward E. Baptist, *The Half Has Never Been Told: Slavery and the Making of American Capitalism* (New York: Basic Books, 2014), 249–254; Calvin Schermerhorn, *The Business of Slavery and the Rise of American Capitalism, 1815–1860* (New Haven: Yale University Press, 2015), 153–154; Scott Reynolds Nelson, *A Nation of Deadbeats: An Uncommon History of America's Financial Disasters* (New York: Alfred A. Knopf, 2012), 111–113; Stephen Campbell, *The Bank War and the Partisan Press: Newspapers, Financial Institutions, and the Post Office in Jacksonian America* (Lawrence: University Press of Kansas, 2019), 93–115.

19. JMS to DB, September 28, October 20, 1833, folder 3, DBP-UTK.

20. IF to RB, November 4, 1833, folder 12, "Franklin Ballard and Co. in Account with I. and J. R. Franklin," "Franklin Ballard and Co. in Account with R. C. Ballard and Co.," folder 421, "Ballard and Co. Ledger, 1831–1834," folder 463, RCBP; *APG*, October 17 and 31, November 21, December 13, 1833; New York *Commercial Advertiser*, November 22, 1833; Manifest of the Brig *Tribune*, October 16, 1833, reel 7, SM-NARA.

21. JRF and IF to RCBC, October 29, 1833, JRF to RB, May 7, 1833, folder 11, "Franklin Ballard and Co. of New Orleans in Account with R. C. Ballard and Co. of Richmond Va.," folders 341 and 421, RCBP.

22. *SIF*, 293; "Franklin Ballard and Co. in Account with I. and J. R. Franklin," "R. C. Ballard and Co. in Account with I. and J. R. Franklin," folder 421, RCBP; Franklin et al. v. M. L. Rogers et al., 1834, box 42, file 107, ACCR-HNF.

23. JRF and IF to RCBC, October 29, 1833, folder 11, IF to RB, November 1, 1833, folder 12, RCBP.

24. IF to RCBC, November 7, 1833, folder 12, JRF and IF to RCBC, October 29, 1833, folder 11, RCBP.

25. IF to RCBC, November 7, 1833, JRF to RB, December 13, November 14, December 2, December 19, 1833, folder 12, RCBP.

26. IF to RB, December 25, 1833, folder 12, RCBP.

27. IF to RB, December 25 and November 5, 1833, folder 12, RCBP.

28. IF to RB, December 25, 1833, folder 12, "Franklin Ballard and Co. in Account with R. C. Ballard and Co.," folder 421, RCBP; *APG*, November 23, 1833.

29. William Boswell, vol. 22 (May 21–December 1833), Act 1365, December 6, 1833, Michel DeArmas, vol. 20A (July–December 1821), Act 464, December 31, 1821, NONA.

30. Roulhac Toledano, Sally Kittredge Evans, and Mary Louise Christovich, *New Orleans Architecture, Volume IV: The Creole Faubourgs* (New Orleans: Pelican Publishing, 1974), 12–13; Michel DeArmas, vol. 20A (July–December 1821), Act 464, December 31, 1821, NONA; Jay Dearborn Edwards, *J. B. Soubrian Grocery Store, Downriver Side of Esplanade Street*, 1857–1860, HNOC.

31. Samuel Woolfolk had his own office on Moreau Street, near the Canonage property, until at least 1835, and contrary to the conclusions of some historians, there is no evidence that he ever worked directly for Franklin and Armfield. See John Adems Paxton, *New-Orleans Directory and Register* (New Orleans, 1830); S. E. Percy and Co., *The New-Orleans Directory* (New Orleans, 1832); William Boswell, vol. 22 (May 21–December 1833), Act 1364, December 6, 1833, NONA; Wendell Holmes Stephenson, *Isaac Franklin, Slave Trader and Planter of the Old South* (Baton Rouge: Louisiana State University Press, 1938), 70; Schermerhorn, *Business of Slavery*, 156; *Michel's New Orleans Annual and Commercial Register, Containing the Names, Professions and Residences of All the Heads of Families, and Persons in Business of the City and Suburbs, for 1834* (New Orleans, 1833).

32. *Acts Passed at the Second Session of the Eleventh Legislature of the State of Louisiana* (New Orleans, 1834), 6–7; IF to RB, January 11, 1834, folder 13, RCBP; Nelson, *Nation of Deadbeats*, 113.

33. IF to RB, January 11, 1834, folder 13, RCBP.

34. IF to RB, January 11, 1834, folder 13, "Franklin Ballard and Co. in Account with R. C. Ballard and Co.," folder 421, RCBP.

35. JRF to RB, February 2, 1834, folder 13, RCBP; Abdy, *Journal of a Residence and Tour*, 2:179; "Franklin Ballard and Co. in Account with R. C. Ballard and Co.," folder 421, RCBP; JMS to DB, February 8, 1834, folder 3, DBP-UTK; Manifest of the Brig *Uncas*, March 17, 1834, Manifest of the Brig *Tribune*, April 8, 1834, reel 7, SM-NARA; *AG*, February 14, March 19, April 17, May 29, 1834.

36. Louis Feraud, vol. 11 (January–May 1834), Act 1621, February 19, 1834, NONA; Manifest of the Brig *Tribune*, April 8, 1834, reel 7, SM-NARA; Percy and Co., *New-Orleans Directory*. Sales figures compiled from database created by the author. Original data appears in notarial books of William Boswell, Louis Thimelet Caire, Felix DeArmas, Louis Feraud, Felix Grima, Gustave LeGardeur Sr., Adolphe Mazureau, Branch Miller, Carlile Pollack, and Theodore Seghers, NONA.

37. IF to RCBC, February 6, 1834, folder 13, RCBP; Felix Grima, vol. 1 (December 1833–May 1834), Act 132, May 6, 1834, NONA.

38. JRF to RB, February 2, 1834 ("take long paper," "receive one dollar"), IF to RCBC, March 18, 1834 ("could get Lotts," "never Justifyable"), folder 13, RCBP.

39. JRF to RB, February 2, 1834 ("the damd small pox," "come from"), IF to RCBC, March 18, 1834 ("There is very little"), folder 13, RCBP.

40. IF to RB, March 30, 1834, folder 13, RCBP.

41. IF to RB, March 10, 1834, folder 13, RCBP.

42. IF to RB, March 10 ("in the name of God," "at all hazards") and 30 ("untill"), 1834, IF to RCBC, March 18, 1834 ("every thing," "confidence Lost"), folder 13, IF to RB, April 17, 1834 (letter misdated 1835) ("pay your debts"), folder 17, RCBP. Also see JRF to RB, March 7, 1834, folder 13, RCBP.

43. JRF to RB, April 16, 1834, folder 14, RCBP.

44. Baptist, *Half*, 254–256; Nelson, *Nation of Deadbeats*, 115–117; Remini, *Andrew Jackson and the Bank War*, 166–173; Kilbourne, *Slave Agriculture and Financial Markets*, 25–55; Temin, *The Jacksonian Economy*, 68–88; Schermerhorn, *Business of Slavery*, 119–120; Joshua D. Rothman, *Flush Times and Fever Dreams: A Story of Capitalism and Slavery in the Age of Jackson* (Athens: University of Georgia Press, 2012), 7–8; Sharon Ann Murphy, *Other People's Money: How Banking Worked in the Early American Republic* (Baltimore: Johns Hopkins University Press, 2017), 94–95, 99–101.

45. IF to RCBC, May 13, 1834, folder 14, RCBP.

46. IF to RCBC, May 13, 1834, folder 14, RCBP; JMS to DB, August 28, 1834, folder 3, DBP-UTK; Adams County Deed Book V, 238–240, ACC.

47. IF to RCBC, May 13, 1834, folder 14, IF to RB, September 27, 1834, folder 15, RCBP; Stephenson, *Isaac Franklin*, 16; Charlene M. Boyer Lewis, *Ladies and Gentlemen on Display: Planter Society at the Virginia Springs, 1790–1860* (Charlottesville: University Press of Virginia, 2001).

48. Nashville *National Banner and Daily Advertiser*, June 24, 1834; JMS to DB, August 28, 1834, folder 3, DBP-UTK; Administrator's Account of the Estate of James R. Franklin, in Estate of James Franklin Jr., file 1043, and Estate of Smith Franklin (1838), file 717, Sumner County Loose Records, Estates, TSLA.

49. Baltimore County Court Land Records, TK-238 (1834), 262–264, TK-254 (1835), 446–448, TK-255 (1835), 124–126, Maryland State Archives, Annapolis, Maryland.

50. Fairfax County Deed Book A3, 506, LOV; Jessie Biele and Michael K. Bohn, *Mount Vernon Revisited* (Charleston, SC: Arcadia Publishing, 2014), 60.

51. City of Richmond Hustings Deeds, Book 33, 134–136, LOV.

52. Richmond *Whig*, August 16, 1834; *SIF*, 293; James Blakey to RB, June 15, July 23, 25, 30, August 6, 1834, folder 15, Accounts of R. C. Ballard and Co., 1834–1842, folder 431, RCBP; City of Richmond Hustings Deeds, Book 33, 195–196, LOV. After selling the jail, Ballard stayed for several months at the

Eagle Hotel in Richmond, finally leaving along with an enslaved "boy" for Natchez in late October.

53. IF to RB, September 27, 1834, folder 15, RCBP.

54. IF to RB, September 27, 1834, folder 15, RCBP; George W. Featherstonhaugh, *Excursion Through the Slave States* (London, 1844), 1:119–120, 168.

55. Featherstonhaugh's description of the coffle and his encounters with John Armfield appear in *Excursion*, 1:119–122, 152–155, and 160–171. They are also considered in Edward Ball, "Retracing Slavery's Trail of Tears," *Smithsonian Magazine*, November 2015, www.smithsonianmag.com/history/slavery-trail-of -tears-180956968/; Isabel Howell, "John Armfield, Slave-Trader," *THQ* 2, no. 1 (March 1943): 13–16; Frederic Bancroft, *Slave-Trading in the Old South* (Baltimore: J. H. Furst, 1931), 284–285; Stephenson, *Isaac Franklin*, 45–50. A Baltimore slave trader's colleague was almost certainly referring to the same coffle Featherstonhaugh saw when he reported seeing a procession of "about three hundred" in the summer of 1834 "who were all sent over land by one house." See Andrews, *Slavery and the Domestic Slave-Trade*, 78.

56. Featherstonhaugh rendered the vernacular speech of both Armfield and Walker as he heard and remembered it, attempting to convey authenticity and accuracy in a fashion that, while clearly loaded with race and class biases, was common among nineteenth-century authors.

57. The date of Walker's death is unknown, but it probably occurred in 1836 or 1837. See Testimony of Ebenezer Ward, Leah Ingle, and Salathiel Swaim, Deposition of John Armfield, and undated decree, Hanner v. Winburn, North Carolina Supreme Court case 6574 (42 NC 142, December 1850), SANC.

58. IF to RB, September 27, 1834, RW to RB, September 19, 1834, folder 15, RW to RB, October 8, 1834, folder 16, RCBP.

59. *AG*, March 5 and October 21, 1834; RW to RB, September 19, 24, 1834, folder 15, and October 6, 8, 1834, folder 16, RCBP; Manifest of the Brig *Uncas*, October 20, 1834, Miscellaneous Manuscripts Collection, Mss042, Literary Manuscripts Collection, University of Minnesota Libraries, Minneapolis, Minnesota.

60. *AG*, August 30, 1834 (quotations), January 22, 31, March 2, 1835; Manifest of the Brig *Uncas*, October 20, 1834; Manifest of the Brig *Tribune*, November 20, 1834, Argosy Collection, MSS38-461, oversized tray 33, UVA; Manifests of the Brig *Uncas*, December 20, 1834, February 5 and March 26, 1835, Manifests of the Brig *Tribune*, February 26 and May 7, 1835, reel 7, SM-NARA.

61. *AG*, July 28, 1834; Manifests of the Brig *Orion*, November 1, 1834, February 18, 1835, Manifest of the Brig *Virginia*, March 21, 1835, reel 7, SM-NARA.

62. William Boswell, vol. 31 (January–February 1835), Act 164, February 9, 1835, vol. 32 (March 1835), Act 341, March 18, 1835, vol. 33 (April 1835), Act 493, April 17, 1835, NONA.

63. Richard Campanella, "On the Structural Basis of Social Memory: City-scapes of the New Orleans Slave Trade, Part II," *Preservation in Print*, April 2013, 18; Baptist, *Half*, 174; William Boswell, vol. 31 (January–February 1835), Act 164, February 9, 1835, NONA; *A Digest of the Ordinances, Resolutions, By-Laws, and Regulations of the Corporation of New-Orleans, and a Collection of the Laws of the Legislature Relative to the Said City* (New Orleans, 1836), 139.

64. Adams County Deed Books W, 142–143, FF, 268–270, ACC; Jim Barnett and H. Clark Burkett, "The Forks of the Road Slave Market at Natchez," *Journal of Mississippi History* 63, no. 3 (Fall 2001): 168–171.

65. Testimony of Dr. Samuel Hogg, John P. Smith v. Jesse Meek and Richard Johnson 1838 (first quotation), box 64, folder 64, ACCR-HNF; Bancroft, *Slave-Trading in the Old South*, 301n24 (second quotation); Adams County Deed Book W, 428–429, ACC; *NCJ*, January 1, 14, 1836; Thom Rosenblum, "Forks of the Road Slave Market, Analysis of Historical Occupancy" (unpublished draft, July 2005), 63–77.

66. Joseph Holt Ingraham, *The South-West, by a Yankee* (New York: 1835), 2:192. Ingraham's visit to the Forks of the Road is also described in Bancroft, *Slave-Trading in the Old South*, 301–304; Stephenson, *Isaac Franklin*, 50–61; Barnett and Burkett, "Forks of the Road Slave Market," 172–176.

67. Ingraham, *South-West, by a Yankee*, 2:193, 197. Rice Ballard's purchases of dozens of "fur hats," "suits of cord[uroy]," and "Full suits of casinets" for the enslaved sold by Franklin and Armfield in the fall of 1834 appear in "Messrs. Rice C. Ballard & Co. To Franklin Armfield & Co.," folder 343, RCBP.

68. Ingraham, *South-West, by a Yankee*, 2:193–198 (quotations on 194, 195); Walter Johnson, *Soul by Soul: Life Inside the Antebellum Slave Market* (Cambridge, MA: Harvard University Press, 1999), 117–134.

69. Ingraham, *South-West, by a Yankee*, 2:245 (quotations in this paragraph and the two preceding it); *AG*, November 20, 1834.

70. *Sumner County, Tennessee, Cemetery Records*, compiled by Margaret Cummings Snider and Joan Hollis Yorgason (Owensboro, KY: McDowell Publications, 1981), 4-4.

71. Estate of John Franklin, file 357, Sumner County Loose Records, Estates, Sumner County Tax Lists, 1824, TSLA; *Early Middle Tennessee Marriages* (Nashville: Byron Sistler and Assoc., 1988), 2:190.

72. *AG*, August 2, 1834; Testimony of Elizabeth Fields, Absalom Jerel, Henry Yates, and James Ross, Hanner v. Winburn, North Carolina Supreme Court case 6574 (42 NC 142, December 1850), SANC.

73. JA to JMS, December 25, 1834, January 5, 1835, folder 3, DBP-UTK. The company may have still sometimes put money out with former agents, as Robert Windsor told John Armfield in the summer of 1835 about dealings with John Ware and William Hooper, but agent names never appeared in Armfield's advertising again. See Alexandria City Deeds, Books V-2, 257–259, 260–262,

298–301, G-3, 328–331, LOV; Alexandria City Land and Personal Property Tax Assessments, 1833–1842, RG27, microfilm reel 7, APLSC; RW to JA, August 21, 1835, folder 17, RCBP.

74. JMS to DB, February 28, March 15, April 14, July 20, 1835, Sales Account of Jourdan M. Saunders in account with James F. Purvis and Company, April 29, 1835, folder 3, DBP-UTK; *NOPC*, September 13, 1828; William Boswell, vol. 33 (April 1835), Act 542, April 24, 1835, NONA; W. K. King, "Harry R. W. Hill," *Lives of American Merchants*, ed. Freeman Hunt (New York, 1857), 2:501–514; Stephenson, *Isaac Franklin*, 92–93, 200; *SIF*, 345.

75. IF to RB, May 22, 1835 (letter misdated 1834), folder 14, RCBP; *SIF*, 345.

76. West Feliciana Parish Conveyance Book F, 28–32, NOPL; Stephenson, *Isaac Franklin*, 100–101, 126–130.

77. West Feliciana Parish Conveyance Book F, 263–264, NOPL; Stephenson, *Isaac Franklin*, 100–101, 131–133; *SIF*, 471–474; *Biographical and Historical Memoirs of Mississippi* (Chicago, 1891), 2:522–523; Dunbar Rowland, *Encyclopedia of Mississippi History* (Madison, WI: Selwyn A. Brant, 1907), 2:578; D. Clayton James, *Antebellum Natchez* (Baton Rouge: Louisiana State University Press, 1968), 20, 148, 150.

78. *SIF*, 357–359 (quotations on 358); William Boswell, vol. 15 (March 30–December 1831), Act 680, November 17, 1831, NONA.

79. *SIF*, 387; West Feliciana Parish Conveyance Book F, 367–374, NOPL. Records of Francis Routh's West Feliciana Parish land purchases and the mortgages he took on them can be found in parish conveyance records and in AFP, box 1, folders 36–39, 42, 54, box 2, folders 6–15, 17.

80. West Feliciana Parish Conveyance Book F, 31, 263, NOPL. Franklin had so little desire to deal with the property that he gave Routh total control in exchange for an annual payment of $20,000, but Routh was so inept a manager that he never paid it. See John Wall and Robert Norwood v. Isaac Franklin and Francis Routh, 1838, box 20, file 31, ACCR-HNF.

81. "An Agreement Between Isaac Franklin, John Armfield, & RC Ballard, Made and Entered into July 1835," oversized documents, OP-4850, RCBP.

82. *AG*, July 14, April 4, 1835; Adams County Deed Book W, 142–143, ACC; *NCJ*, January 1, 1836; IF to RB, October 14, 1836, folder 18, RCBP.

83. *Ship Registers and Enrollments of New Orleans, Volume 3, 1831–1840*, 106; *AG*, January 10, 1839.

84. Deposition of John H. Kerr, Wall and Norwood v. Franklin and Routh; *AG*, October 14, 1835; Alexandria City Deeds, Book X-2, 37–40, LOV; Louis Thimelet Caire, vol. 50A (April 1836), Act 344, April 23, 1836, NONA; *SIF*, 288.

85. *NCJ*, January 26, 1836; City of Richmond Hustings Deeds, Book 36, 167–168, LOV; Bill from Baher and Little to "Rice Ballard for Magnolia," February 28, 1836, folder 345, RCBP.

86. *AG*, July 14, 1835.

87. Manifest of the Brig *Uncas*, December 6, 1835, Manifest of the Brig *Isaac Franklin*, January 22, 1836, reel 7, SM-NARA. Remaining data compiled from surviving manifests of the *Tribune*, the *Uncas*, and the *Isaac Franklin*, September 1835–November 1836, reel 7, SM-NARA.

88. Donald Mitchell Sweig, "Northern Virginia Slavery: A Statistical and Demographic Investigation" (PhD diss., College of William and Mary, 1982), 219–225; Donald Mitchell Sweig, "Reassessing the Human Dimension of the Interstate Slave Trade," *Prologue*, Spring 1980, 14–16; Robert M. Gudmestad, *A Troublesome Commerce: The Transformation of the Interstate Slave Trade* (Baton Rouge: Louisiana State University Press, 2003), 160–161.

89. *AG*, January 1, 1836; Manifest of the *Isaac Franklin*, January 22, 1836, reel 7, SM-NARA. The Snowden auction was not the first auction at the Duke Street headquarters, nor was it the first time Armfield purchased enslaved people in bulk from estates. See *DNI*, August 11, 1835; Andrews, *Slavery and the Domestic Slave-Trade*, 139; *RI*, February 8, 1834.

90. *APG*, November 19, 1831.

91. Isaac Franklin also received forty-four enslaved people from the schooner *Hunter* in November 1835, but they were probably sent to West Feliciana Parish. Data compiled from surviving manifests of the *Tribune*, the *Uncas*, and the *Isaac Franklin*, September 1835–November 1836, reel 7, SM-NARA. Also see *NOCB*, February 9, 1836; *AG*, March 7, April 23, 1836; New York *Commercial Advertiser*, March 24, 1836; Manifest of the Schooner *Hunter*, October 17, 1835, reel 7, SM-NARA.

92. *NOCB*, October 29, 1835, April 15, 1836; *AG*, July 15, 1836; *NYPC*, May 14, 1836; New York *Commercial Advertiser*, June 6, 29, July 2, 1836; Boston *Columbian Centinel*, May 25, 1836; *BACDA*, June 27, 1836.

93. Manifest of the Brig *Tribune*, September 24, 1836, Manifest of the Brig *Isaac Franklin*, October 3, 1836, reel 7, SM-NARA; *NOCB*, October 26, 1836.

94. Manifest of the Brig *Isaac Franklin*, November 15, 1836, reel 7, SM-NARA; *The Liberator*, December 24, 1836; Manifest of the Brig *Uncas*, October 15, 1836, reel 7, SM-NARA; *AG*, November 1, 1836.

95. *DNI*, November 7, 1836.

96. *AG*, March 14, February 17, 1837.

97. IF to RB, October 14, 1836, BT to RB, August 2, 25, September 12, 23, 1836, folder 18, RCBP; Alexandria City Land and Personal Property Tax Assessments, 1837, RG27, microfilm reel 7, APLSC; Alexandria City Deeds, Book G-3, 328–331, LOV.

98. IF to RB, October 14, 1836, folder 18, RCBP.

99. Malcolm J. Rohrbough, *The Land Office Business: The Settlement and Administration of American Public Lands, 1789–1837* (New York: Oxford University Press, 1968), 221–249; Rothman, *Flush Times and Fever Dreams*, 3–8; Baptist, *Half*, 268–272; Lewis Cecil Gray, *History of Agriculture in the Southern United*

States to 1860 (Washington, DC: Carnegie Institution of Washington, 1933), 2:1026–1027; Stuart Bruchey, *Cotton and the Growth of the American Economy: 1790–1860* (New York: Harcourt, Brace, and World, 1967), 16–21, 29–30; Douglass C. North, *The Economic Growth of the United States, 1790–1860* (Englewood Cliffs, NJ: Prentice-Hall, 1961), 257.

100. *New York Observer and Chronicle*, February 22, 1840; Baptist, *Half*, 174; Ulrich B. Phillips, *American Negro Slavery* (Baton Rouge: Louisiana State University Press, 1966; originally published 1918), chart opposite 370; Herman Freudenberger and Jonathan B. Pritchett, "The Domestic United States Slave Trade: New Evidence," *Journal of Interdisciplinary History* 21, no. 3 (Winter 1991): 457; Laurence J. Kotlikoff, "The Structure of Slave Prices in New Orleans, 1804 to 1862," *Economic Inquiry* 17, no. 4 (October 1979): 498.

101. *New York Observer and Chronicle*, February 22, 1840.

102. Lepler, *Many Panics of 1837*; Murphy, *Other People's Money*, 99–102; Baptist, *Half*, 272–280; Rothman, *Flush Times and Fever Dreams*, 292–298; Alasdair Roberts, *America's First Great Depression: Economic Crisis and Political Disorder After the Panic of 1837* (Ithaca: Cornell University Press, 2012), 13–84; Nelson, *Nation of Deadbeats*, 95–148.

103. IF to RB, letter dated the twentieth of an unnamed month, 1837, folder 19, RCBP; *Christian Secretary*, May 20, 1837.

CHAPTER SIX: REPUTATIONS, 1837–1846

1. Incidents from the life of Madison Henderson described in this section can be found in *Trials and Confessions of Madison Henderson, Alias Blanchard, Alfred Amos Warrick, James W. Seward, and Charles Brown, Murderers of Jesse Baker and Jacob Weaver, as Given by Themselves* (St. Louis, 1841), 13–21. Also see Thomas C. Buchanan, *Black Life on the Mississippi: Slaves, Free Blacks, and the Western Steamboat World* (Chapel Hill: University of North Carolina Press, 2004), 123–147; Timothy F. Reilly, "Slave Stealing in the Early Domestic Trade as Revealed by a Loyal Manservant," *Louisiana History* 55, no. 1 (Winter 2014): 5–39; S. Charles Bolton, *Fugitivism: Escaping Slavery in the Lower Mississippi Valley, 1820–1860* (Fayetteville: University of Arkansas Press, 2019), 165–173; Walter Johnson, *The Broken Heart of America: St. Louis and the Violent History of the United States* (New York: Basic Books, 2020), 93–99.

2. "Purchase Book, 1832–1834," folder 420, RCBP; *MFT* in Baltimore *Sun*, January 4, 1842; *APG*, October 31, November 6, 1833.

3. *Trials and Confessions of Madison Henderson*, 20–36; Buchanan, *Black Life on the Mississippi*, 123–147; *MFT* in Baltimore *Sun*, January 4, 1842.

4. *MFT* in Baltimore *Sun*, January 4, 1842; Buchanan, *Black Life on the Mississippi*, 128. Also see James Blakey to RB, September 25, 1841, JA to RB, October 8, 1841, folder 43, RCBP.

5. *MFT* in Baltimore *Sun*, January 4, 1842.

6. Memphis *Avalanche*, August 19, 1858. The *Avalanche* published a reprint of "The Mammoth Humbug," an 1840 account of a scam perpetrated on Mississippi planters by a North Carolinian named Joseph Seawell "Shocco" Jones. The original story did not include the line about Franklin, Armfield, and Ballard, suggesting that someone who still recalled the debts Natchez slaveholders owed them added that detail. On Shocco Jones, see Edwin A. Miles, "Joseph Seawell Jones of Shocco—Historian and Humbug," *North Carolina History Review* 34, no. 4 (October 1957): 483–506.

7. Michael Tadman, "The Reputation of the Slave Trader in Southern History and the Social Memory of the South," *American Nineteenth Century History* 8, no. 3 (September 2007): 247–271; Steven Deyle, "Rethinking the Slave Trade: Slave Traders and the Market Revolution in the South," in *The Old South's Modern Worlds: Slavery, Region, and Nation in the Age of Progress*, ed. L. Diane Barnes, Brian Schoen, and Frank Towers (New York: Oxford University Press, 2011), 104–119; Steven Deyle, *Carry Me Back: The Domestic Slave Trade in American Life* (New York: Oxford University Press, 2005), 206–244; Robert Gudmestad, *A Troublesome Commerce: The Transformation of the Interstate Slave Trade* (Baton Rouge: Louisiana State University Press, 2003), 62–168.

8. E. S. Abdy, *Journal of a Residence and Tour in the United States of North America, from April, 1833, to October, 1834* (London, 1835), 2:210; Joseph Holt Ingraham, *The South-West, by a Yankee* (New York: 1835), 2:245.

9. Michael Tadman, *Speculators and Slaves: Masters, Traders, and Slaves in the Old South* (Madison: University of Wisconsin Press, 1989), 12; Jonathan B. Pritchett, "Quantitative Estimates of the United States Interregional Slave Trade, 1820–1860," *JEH* 61, no. 2 (June 2001): 474; Calvin Schermerhorn, "Slave Trading in a Republic of Credit: Financial Architecture of the US Slave Market, 1815–1840," *Slavery and Abolition* 36, no. 4 (2015): 597–598; Deyle, *Carry Me Back*, 56; Richard Campanella, "On the Structural Basis of Social Memory: Cityscapes of the New Orleans Slave Trade, Part II," *Preservation in Print*, April 2013, 18; Edward E. Baptist, *The Half Has Never Been Told: Slavery and the Making of American Capitalism* (New York: Basic Books, 2014), 174; Laurence J. Kotlikoff, "The Structure of Slave Prices in New Orleans, 1804 to 1862," *Economic Inquiry* 17, no. 4 (October 1979): 498; Herman Freudenberger and Jonathan B. Pritchett, "The Domestic United States Slave Trade: New Evidence," *Journal of Interdisciplinary History* 21, no. 3 (Winter 1991): 457.

10. Tadman, *Speculators and Slaves*, 12; Deyle, *Carry Me Back*, 57–58; Lewis Cecil Gray, *History of Agriculture in the Southern United States to 1860* (Washington, DC: Carnegie Institution of Washington, 1933), 2:1027; Stuart Bruchey, *Cotton and the Growth of the American Economy: 1790–1860* (New York: Harcourt, Brace, and World, 1967), 30.

11. Robert Gudmestad suggests that white southerners felt sincere discomfort about the slave trade and that large traders like John Armfield tried to ease

their anxiety by presenting themselves as gentlemanly businessmen, concealing the trade's violence, and claiming they avoided separating enslaved families. Michael Tadman, by contrast, argues "that slave owners did not find it necessary to wrestle with their consciences over the trade." Even conceding that some white southerners were genuinely torn about the slave trade and said they abjured associating with slave traders, their unease had little impact in practice. See Gudmestad, *Troublesome Commerce*, 148–168; Tadman, "Reputation of the Slave Trader," 248. Also see Frederic Bancroft, *Slave-Trading in the Old South* (Baltimore: J. H. Hurst, 1931), 365–381; Tadman, *Speculators and Slaves*, 179–210.

12. Theodore Dwight Weld, *American Slavery As It Is: Testimony of a Thousand Witnesses* (New York, 1839), 173; *Slavery and the Internal Slave Trade in the United States of North America* (London, 1841), 67, 68.

13. Weld, *American Slavery As It Is*, 173, 174; *Slavery and the Internal Slave Trade*, 67, 68.

14. Ingraham, *South-West, by a Yankee*, 2:245.

15. IF to RB, letter dated the twentieth of an unnamed month, 1837, folder 19, Summers and Watt to Armfield Ballard and Co., January 2, 1838, John Pease to RB, January 20, 1838, folder 20, Thomas Boudar to RB, February 8, 20, 1838, folder 21, Thomas Boudar to RB, March 1, 1838, Moses Groves to Ballard and Franklin, March 5, 1838, folder 22, IF to RB, April 7, 1838, J. P. Parker to RB, April 19, 1838, folder 23, RCBP.

16. Lawsuits in Adams County, most of which were filed on behalf of Ballard Franklin and Company, can be found in boxes 37, 38, 45, 46, 47, 49, 59, ACCR-HNF.

17. Adams County Deed Books Y, 495–496, Z, 36–38, 551–552, 579–582, CC, 486–487, DD, 442–443, ACC; Madison Parish Conveyance Book A, 415, Madison Parish Courthouse, Tallulah, Louisiana; Concordia Parish Conveyance Books G, 658, H, 183, J–K, 534, Concordia Parish Courthouse, Vidalia, Louisiana; *MFT*, December 28, 1844.

18. Warren Offutt to RB, September 19, 1840, folder 35, N. and J. Dick and Company to Ballard Franklin and Company, March 17, 1838, folder 22, James Blakey to RB, February 20, 1840, folder 31, July 23, 1840, folder 35, April 2, 1841, folder 40, September 25, 1841, folder 43, January 29, 1842, folder 45, Joseph Alsop to RB, December 20, 1841, folder 44, RCBP; Ballard Franklin and Company v. Benjamin Eaton, 1837, box 37, file 63, Ballard Franklin and Company v. Silas Lillard, 1837, box 37, file 93, ACCR-HNF; Adams County Deed Books Z, 320–323, BB, 504–505, CC, 647–649, DD, 620–622, ACC; Concordia Parish Conveyance Book I, 197, Concordia Parish Courthouse, Vidalia, Louisiana; *SIF*, 452–454.

19. Adams County Deed Books BB, 504–505, CC, 647–649, DD, 620–622, ACC; Concordia Parish Conveyance Books I, 197, L, 155, Concordia Parish Courthouse, Vidalia, Louisiana; Thomas Edwards, Curator, v. R. C. Ballard (1859),

in *Reports and Cases Argued and Determined in the Supreme Court of Louisiana* (New Orleans 1860), 14:362; JA to RB, October 28, 1842, folder 56, RCBP.

20. Samuel B. Read to RW, April 6, 1841, folder 40, RCBP; Appointment of Agency to Rice Ballard, 1839, folder 406, Joseph Alsop to RB, January 30, 1838, folder 20, March 16, 1840, folder 32, RCBP; Adams County Tax Rolls, 1838–1839, RG 29, Auditor of Public Accounts, MDAH; Natchez *Courier*, January 24, 1839; New York *Evening Post*, March 28, 1842, May 25, 1843; Eva Coe Peden, *Bible and Family Records of Barren County, Kentucky, and Surrounding Areas*, (Glasgow, KY: E. C. Peden, 1977), 1:145–146; Tomoko Yagyu, "Slave Traders and Planters in the Expanding South: Entrepreneurial Strategies, Business Networks, and Western Migration in the Atlantic World, 1787–1859" (PhD diss., University of North Carolina–Chapel Hill, 2006), 256–257.

21. In 1837, Armfield also became executor for the estate of Martha's brother Henry. See IF to RB, March 5, 1838, Eli Odum to JA, March 22, 1838, folder 22, JA to RB, April 11, 1838, folder 23, RCBP; *AG*, May 2, 1837, May 9, 1838; Bills of Sale, Sumner County, 1837–1841, 257–258, Sumner County Will Book 2, 222–223, Sumner County Deed Book 16, 578–579, Estate of Smith Franklin (1838), file 717, Sumner County Loose Records, Estates, Jane C. Franklin v. John F. Cage et al. (1848), file 4188, A. H. Wood et al. v. John W. Franklin et al. (1876), file 10769, Sumner County Loose Records, Lawsuits, TSLA; Guilford County Inventory and List of Sales, Vol. X-10 (1835–1842), 234–235, Guilford County Deed Book 24, 480, Hanner v. Winburn, North Carolina Supreme Court case 6574 (42 NC 142, December 1850), SANC.

22. James Purvis to GK, December 4, 1837, GK-NJHS.

23. IF to RB, January 6, 1838, folder 20, February 5, 1838, folder 21, March 5, 1838, folder 22, RCBP.

24. IF to RB, March 5, 1838, folder 22, RCBP.

25. Francis Routh to RB, November 6, 1837, folder 19, IF to RB, January 6, 1838, folder 20, March 5, 1838, folder 22, RCBP; Wendell Holmes Stephenson, *Isaac Franklin, Slave Trader and Planter of the Old South* (Baton Rouge: Louisiana State University Press, 1938), 102, 136–137, 141–145; West Feliciana Parish Conveyance Book F, 367–369, NOPL; Baptist, *Half*, 127, 129; Alan L. Olmstead and Paul W. Rhode, "Biological Innovation and Productivity Growth in the Antebellum Cotton Economy," *JEH* 68, no. 4 (2008): 1123–1171.

26. Stephenson, *Isaac Franklin*, 102, 134–146; West Feliciana Parish Conveyance Book F, 355–356, 367–374, NOPL.

27. IF to RB, March 5, 1838, folder 22, RCBP.

28. *AG*, March 14, April 25, 1837, October 23, 1847; *DNI*, February 18, March 14, 1837; Washington *Globe*, March 18, 1837; BT to GK, May 28, 1839, RW to GK, July 26, 1839, GK-NJHS; Alexandria City Deeds, Book H-3, 328–333, LOV.

29. *The Liberator*, April 20, 1838.

30. *The Liberator*, April 20, 1838; Cincinnati *Gazette*, in *GUE*, October 1837, 80.

31. *AG*, September 17, 1838, January 10, 1839, August 11, 1842; *DNI*, September 15, 1838, January 10, 1839; *BACDA*, September 1, 1838; Annapolis *Maryland Gazette*, August 27, 1835. Relationships among Kephart and his associates can be traced through letters, bills, and receipts in GK-NJHS and seen on manifests of the *Isaac Franklin*. Also see Michael A. Ridgeway, "A Peculiar Business: Slave Trading in Alexandria, Virginia, 1825–1861" (MA thesis, Georgetown University, 1976), 103–117; Lisa A. Kraus, "Archaeology of the Bruin Slave Jail" (PhD diss., University of Texas–Austin, 2009), 49–50; Janice G. Artemel, Elizabeth A. Crowell, and Jeff Parker, *The Alexandria Slave Pen: The Archaeology of Urban Captivity* (Washington, DC: Engineering Science, 1987), 35–38; Hank Trent, *The Secret Life of Bacon Tait, a White Slave Trader Married to a Free Woman of Color* (Baton Rouge: Louisiana State University Press, 2017), 60–61, 93–94, 109–110; Bancroft, *Slave-Trading in the Old South*, 51n16, 64–65, 92n11; GK to JA, March 16, 1838, folder 22, RCBP.

32. Joseph Sturge, *A Visit to the United States in 1841* (London, 1842); 77–78; Ridgeway, "A Peculiar Business," 116–117; BT to RB, January 9, 14, 16, 19, 31, 1838, folder 20, Thomas Boudar to RB, February 8, 20, 1838, folder 21, Thomas Boudar to RB, March 1, 1838, GK to JA, March 16, 1838, folder 22, BT to RB, May 1, 1838, folder 24, James Purvis to RB, October 7, 1838, BT to RB, November 25, 1838, folder 25, Thomas Boudar to RB, December 19, 1840, folder 38, RCBP; BT to GK, August 4, 1839, GK-NJHS.

33. Planters' Bank of Natchez to RB, December 29, 1841, folder 44, William Grayson to JA, April 13, 1838, folder 23, William Gwin to Ernest and Ballard as Trustees of the Planters' Bank, March 2, 1842, folder 47, RCBP; Adams County Deed Book DD, 231–232, ACC. Also see Ballard's lists of repossessed bank properties in folders 348 and 413, RCBP.

34. H. D. Mandeville to RB, March 1, 1841, folder 39, RCBP. Ballard also superintended several plantations for the bank, which sometimes preferred to keep their operations ongoing rather than dismantle and sell them.

35. Abdy, *Journal of a Residence and Tour*, 2:180; Sturge, *Visit to the United States*, 85; *AG*, November 14, 1845; Alexandria City Deeds, Books X-2, 495–496, Z-2, 152–154, A-3, 32–34, B-3, 268–269, C-3, 27–29 and 325–328, LOV; Ruth Lincoln Kaye, "The First Fifty Two Years of St. Paul's Episcopal Church, Alexandria, Virginia, 1809–1861," 1–6, 12, APLSC; Isabel Howell, "John Armfield, Slave-Trader," *THQ* 2, no. 1 (March 1943): 18–19. Family stories have it that Martha Armfield followed her husband into Episcopalianism, but even though John Armfield later had extensive involvement with the Episcopal Church and its officials, I have found no substantive evidence of his conversion.

36. *Spirit of the Times*, April 7, 1838, 60; Katherine C. Mooney, *Race Horse Men: How Slavery and Freedom Were Made at the Racetrack* (Cambridge, MA:

Harvard University Press, 2014), 18–88; D. Clayton James, *Antebellum Natchez* (Baton Rouge: Louisiana State University Press, 1968), 254–255; Edwin Adams Davis and William Ransom Hogan, *The Barber of Natchez* (Baton Rouge: Louisiana State University Press, 1973), 202–213; BT to RB, May 25, 1841, folder 41, RCBP.

37. Sixth Census of the United States, Tennessee, Sumner County, 398, microfilm reel 534, M704, NARA; *SIF*, 360; Walter T. Durham, *Old Sumner: A History of Sumner County, Tennessee, from 1805 to 1861* (Gallatin, TN: Sumner County Public Library Board, 1972), 284–285.

38. BT to RB, undated from the first six months of 1839, folder 30, RCBP.

39. Rodney G. Williams, "Seed of the Fancy Maid," in *Slavery's Descendants: Shared Legacies of Race and Reconciliation*, ed. Dionne Ford and Jill Strauss (New Brunswick, NJ: Rutgers University Press, 2019), 54–62.

40. "Purchase Book, 1832–1834," folder 420, RCBP.

41. "Ballard and Co. Ledger, 1831–1834," folder 463, RCBP.

42. *Trials and Confessions of Madison Henderson*, 17; Jesse Cage to William Cotton, August 27, 1839, folder 28, RCBP. On the historical archive and the interpretive challenges it presents for recovering the subjectivity of enslaved women, see Marisa J. Fuentes, *Dispossessed Lives: Enslaved Women, Violence, and the Archive* (Philadelphia: University of Pennsylvania Press, 2016).

43. "Purchase Book, 1832–1834," folder 420, RCBP. Ballard also made a small mark next to the name of a man named Preston, for whom he paid $425, about average for what he spent on young adult men in 1832. Ballard kept Preston in Richmond for some time and made small purchases suggesting he may have used him as a personal servant. See "R. C. Ballard and Co. Expense Book, 1831–1835," folder 425, RCBP. Sharony Green discusses Ballard's relationship with Arvenia White and Susan Johnson in "'Mr. Ballard, I am compelled to write again': Beyond Bedrooms and Brothels, a Fancy Girl Speaks," *Black Women, Gender and Families* 5, no. 1 (Spring 2011): 17–40, and *Remember Me to Miss Louisa: Hidden Black White Intimacies in Antebellum America* (DeKalb, IL: Northern Illinois University Press, 2015), 44–58.

44. "Purchase Book, 1832–1834," folder 420, "R. C. Ballard and Co. Expense Book, 1831–1835," folder 425, Arvenia White to RB, December 30, 1838, folder 25, RCBP; Green, *Remember Me*, 49.

45. IF to RB, January 11, 1834, folder 13, RCBP; Green, *Remember Me*, 45.

46. Arvenia White to RB, September 18, 1838, folder 24, RCBP.

47. Other slave traders in relationships that crossed the color line include but are not limited to Silas Omohundro, Hector Davis, Robert Lumpkin, Bacon Tait, Jourdan Saunders, Henry De Ende, John Hagan, and Theophilus Freeman. See Green, *Remember Me*; Alexandra Jolyn Finley, "'Cash to Corinna': Domestic Labor and Sexual Economy in the 'Fancy Trade,'" *Journal of American History* 104, no. 2 (September 2017): 410–430; Alexandra Jolyn Finley, "Blood Money:

Sex, Family, and Finance in the Antebellum Slave Trade" (PhD diss., College of William and Mary, 2017); Calvin Schermerhorn, *Money over Mastery, Family over Freedom: Slavery in the Antebellum Upper South* (Baltimore: Johns Hopkins University Press, 2011), 110–119; Joshua D. Rothman, "The Life of Jourdan Saunders, Slave Trader" (presented to the Washington Early American Seminar Series, University of Maryland, March 2016), 44; Trent, *Secret Life of Bacon Tait*, 45–63, 117–126, 148–164. For a consideration of the range of experiences for enslaved women and girls forced into sustained relationships with white men, see Brenda E. Stevenson, "What's Love Got to Do with It? Concubinage and Enslaved Women and Girls in the Antebellum South," *Journal of African American History* 98, no. 1 (Winter 2013): 99–125.

48. Manifest of the Brig *Isaac Franklin*, October 6, 1835, reel 7, SM-NARA.

49. *Gallatin Union and Sumner Advertiser*, July 12, 1839; Stephenson, *Isaac Franklin*, 18–20; W. W. Clayton, *History of Davidson County, Tennessee, with Illustrations and Biographical Sketches of Its Prominent Men and Pioneers* (Philadelphia, 1880), 107, 451; Brenda Jackson-Abernathy, "Adelicia Acklen: Beyond the 'Belmont' Legend and Lore," *THQ* 76, no. 1 (Spring 2017): 4–5; Albert W. Wardin Jr., *Belmont Mansion: The Home of Joseph and Adelicia Acklen* (Nashville: Belmont Mansion Association, 2012), 2–3, 5; *SIF*, 341; Eleanor Graham, "Belmont: Nashville Home of Adelicia Acklen," *THQ* 30, no. 4 (Winter 1971): 347–348; John W. Kiser, "Scion of Belmont, Part I," *THQ* 38, no. 1 (Spring 1979): 39; *NRB*, December 11, 1867.

50. Wardin, *Belmont Mansion*, 3–4; Graham, "Belmont," 348–349; Jackson-Abernathy, "Adelicia Acklen," 7–8; Kiser, "Scion of Belmont, Part I," 39–40; Margaret Lindsley Warden, *The Saga of Fairvue, 1832–1977* (Nashville: Warden, 1977), 5–6; *SIF*, 282.

51. Clayton, *History of Davidson County*, 451; Graham, "Belmont," 347; Wardin, *Belmont Mansion*, 1, 3; Jackson-Abernathy, "Adelicia Acklen," 5; Erica Joy Rumbley, "Ornamental Music and Southern Belles at the Nashville Female Academy, 1816–1861," *American Music* 33, no. 2 (Summer 2015): 219–250.

52. Graham, "Belmont," 347–348; Wardin, *Belmont Mansion*, 2–3.

53. Most accounts of the Franklin-Hayes marriage claim it was a strategic exchange of wealth for social respectability, which might be more persuasive were Hayes not already wealthy and were there evidence that Franklin's slave trading ever cost him respectability. See Stephenson, *Isaac Franklin*, 20; Warden, *Saga of Fairvue*, 7; Wardin, *Belmont Mansion*, 5; Gudmestad, *Troublesome Commerce*, 203. On white women and slaveholding, see Stephanie Jones-Rogers, *They Were Her Property: White Women As Slave Owners in the American South* (New Haven: Yale University Press, 2019).

54. Jesse Cage to William Cotton, August 27, 1839, BT to RB, August 4, 1839, folder 28, RCBP; *SIF*, 280, 282, 285, 287, 292, 341, 347; RW to GK, July 26, 1839, BT to GK, August 4, 1839, GK-NJHS.

55. W. A. Ronald to RB, April 23, 1839, folder 26, Samuel Alsop to RB, September 20, 1838, folder 24, RCBP. Also see Sam Wakefield to RB, August 16, 1836, BT to RB, September 12, 1836, folder 18, BT to RB, January 31, 1838, folder 20, C. Mills to RB, April 9, 1838, folder 23, Joseph Alsop to RB, November 22, 1838, BT to RB, November 25, 1838, folder 25, Glover and Brenham to RB, December 28, 1839, folder 29, W. R. Glover to RB, February 20, 1840, folder 31, RCBP.

56. Glover and Brenham to RB, January 10, 1840, W. R. Glover to RB, February 21, 1840, folder 31, Jesse Cage to RB, December 6, 1839, folder 29, W. R. Glover to RB, March 3 and 24, 1840, folder 32, RCBP; *Memoirs of Henry Tillinghast Ireys: Papers of the Washington County Historical Society, 1910–1915*, ed. William D. McCain and Charlotte Capers (Jackson: Mississippi Department of Archives and History and Mississippi Historical Society, 1954), 49–54, 335–337.

57. Frances Bruster to RB, May 14, 1838, folder 24, RCBP; Green, *Remember Me*, 1–11, 33–61.

58. Arvenia White to RB, October 25, 1838, folder 25, September 18, 1838, folder 24, February 2, 1840, folder 31, Joseph Alsop to RB, August 11, 1839, BT to RB, August 16, 1839, folder 28, RCBP.

59. Arvenia White to RB, December 30 ("to of got," "how I shall," "to let me"), October 25 ("friend," "my love"), 1838, folder 25, RCBP.

60. Arvenia White to RB, February 2, 1840, folder 31, RCBP.

61. *Memoirs of Henry Tillinghast Ireys*, 49, 54, 335–336, 341 (quotations on 336); *AG*, April 29, 1840; 1850 Federal Population Census, Free Schedule, Kentucky, District 1, City of Louisville, 8, microfilm reel 206, M432, NARA; *Washington Republican and Natchez Intelligencer*, July 3, 1816; *Mississippi State Gazette*, January 8, 1820, February 2, 1822, January 1, 1823; *NCJ*, April 22, 1836; W. R. Glover to RB, February 4, 1840, folder 31, RCBP; Adams County Deed Book V, 33, ACC.

62. IF to RB, January 7, 1840, folder 31, RCBP.

63. Jackson *Mississippian*, April 21, May 19, 1837; Joshua D. Rothman, "The Contours of Cotton Capitalism: Speculation, Slavery, and Economic Panic in Mississippi, 1832–1841," in *Slavery's Capitalism: A New History of American Economic Development*, ed. Sven Beckert and Seth Rockman (Philadelphia: University of Pennsylvania Press, 2016), 139; Charles Sackett Sydnor, *Slavery in Mississippi* (New York: D. Appleton-Century, 1933), 166–169.

64. Jackson *Mississippian*, May 19, 1837; *MFT*, in *BACDA*, December 21, 1839.

65. *MFT*, in *BACDA*, December 21, 1839 ("decision must"); William Terry to RB, April 8, 1840 ("or else"), folder 33, RCBP; Testimony of Samuel Boyd, Testimony of Alexander Montgomery, Clay v. Ballard, Docket 5234, Eastern District, June 1844, Supreme Court of Louisiana, SC-UNO.

66. BT to RB, January 3, 1840, folder 31, RCBP; Groves v. Slaughter, 40 US 449 (1841); Trent, *Secret Life of Bacon Tait*, 104–107; David L. Lightner, "The

Supreme Court and the Interstate Slave Trade: A Study in Evasion, Anarchy, and Extremism," *Journal of Supreme Court History* 29, no. 3 (November 2004): 236–238; Charles Warren, *The Supreme Court in United States History* (Boston: Little, Brown, and Company, 1923), 2:341–343.

67. Testimony of Alexander Montgomery (quotations), Robert Slaughter and RB to Henry Clay, January 9, 1841, Clay v. Ballard; BT to RB, January 16, 1838, folder 20, W. R. Glover to RB, October 29, 1840, folder 36, RCBP.

68. Groves v. Slaughter, 452, 477. Webster was probably paid by slave traders too. See Testimony of Samuel Boyd, Clay v. Ballard.

69. Groves v. Slaughter, 502, 503; Lightner, "Supreme Court and the Interstate Slave Trade," 240–242; Warren, *Supreme Court*, 2:344–345. Also see Paul Finkelman, *An Imperfect Union: Slavery, Federalism, and Comity* (Chapel Hill: University of North Carolina Press, 1981), 266–271; Earl M. Maltz, *Slavery and the Supreme Court, 1825–1861* (Lawrence: University Press of Kansas, 2009), 68–82; Gudmestad, *Troublesome Commerce*, 193–200; Baptist, *Half*, 288–289; Rothman, "Contours of Cotton Capitalism," 140–142.

70. BT to RB, May 9, 6, 1841, folder 41, September 1, 1840, folder 35, October 14, 1840, folder 36, RCBP; Testimony of Samuel Boyd, Clay v. Ballard.

71. Dupuy, Tate, and Nalle to RB, February 6 ("general panic"), 12 ("want of confidence"), 1842, folder 46, RCBP; Testimony of John Armfield ("a large amount"), Statement of John R. Grymes ("settle[d]"), Clay v. Ballard; Dupuy, Tate, and Nalle to RB, January 26, 1842, folder 45, February 15, 1842, folder 46, A. G. Nalle to RB, May 6, 1842, folder 49, June 3, 1842, folder 51, JA to RB, April 24, 1841, folder 40, Henry Clay to RB, June 23, July 6, 1841, folder 42, RCBP; Testimony of George Yerger, Testimony of Samuel Boyd, Clay v. Ballard.

72. Adams County Deed Book DD, 108–109; Testimony of John Armfield, Clay v. Ballard.

73. Martha Armfield to Louise Ballard, October 8, 1841, folder 43, Ann Julaner Read to RB, May 14, 1839, folder 27, RCBP; BJA; 1850 Federal Population Census, Free Schedule, Kentucky, District 1, City of Louisville, 8.

74. Deposition of John M. Pelton, October 11, 1841, folder 21, Quitman and McMurran to John M. Pelton, December 28, 1841, folder 22, series 1.1, box 2, QP. Also see Ariela J. Gross, *Double Character: Slavery and Mastery in the Antebellum Southern Courtroom* (Princeton: Princeton University Press, 2000), 57–61; Robert E. May, *John A. Quitman, Old South Crusader* (Baton Rouge: Louisiana State University Press, 1985), 111–112.

75. Deposition of John M. Pelton; May, *John A. Quitman*.

76. Deposition of John M. Pelton; Henry Turner to RB, July 31, 1840, folder 35, RCBP.

77. Deposition of John M. Pelton; Testimony of John Armfield, Clay v. Ballard; Subpoenas for Henry Turner, March 29, 1841, folder 20, series 1.1, box 2,

QP. Fielding Turner died in 1841, and his brother assumed responsibility for their partnership debts.

78. Testimony of John Quitman, Clay v. Ballard; Henry Turner to John Quitman, June 26, 1842, folder 25, Terms of Compromise, November 1, 1842, folder 29, Calculations Lists and Schedule of Payments, folder 33, series 1.1, box 3, QP.

79. BT to RB, August 14, 1842, folder 53, RCBP.

80. Henry Turner to John Quitman, June 26, 1842, folder 25, series 1.1, box 3, QP.

81. Henry Turner to John Quitman, June 26, 1842, folder 25, series 1.1, box 3, QP; JA to RB, October 28, 1842, folder 54, RCBP.

82. JA to RB, October 28, 1842, folder 54, RCBP.

83. Jefferson County Deed Book 58, 197–198, Jefferson County Tax Assessment Books, 1843–1847, KDLA; M. D. Robards to RB, February 11, 1845, folder 84, RCBP.

84. Leonard B. Chapman, *Monograph on the Southgate Family of Scarborough, Maine* (Portland, ME: Hubbard W. Bryant, 1907), 28; Dunbar Rowland, *Encyclopedia of Mississippi History* (Madison, WI: Selwyn A. Brant, 1907), 2:280; Testimony of Samuel Boyd, Clay v. Ballard.

85. Ballard's papers contain a Magnolia plantation journal for the years 1838–1840. Titled "McNeales Book," it was probably passed to Ballard and Boyd when they bought the property in December 1842. See Warren County Deed Book S, 49–52, MDAH; Magnolia Plantation Journal, folder 429, Agreement Between Rice Ballard and Samuel Boyd, December 31, 1842, folder 407, Purchases Made at Magnolia Estate Sale, 1842, folder 356, RCBP; William Boswell, vol. 15 (March 30–December 1831), Acts 373 and 496, April 9 and May 21, 1831, NONA.

86. *Narrative of Henry Watson, a Fugitive Slave* (Boston, 1850), 12–21 (quotations on 14, 20, 15); Warren County Personal Property Tax Rolls, 1845, MDAH; Magnolia Journal, 1843–1846, folder 438, RCBP.

87. Warren County Property Deeds, Books U, 200–201, W, 402–403, 545, Claiborne County Property Deeds, Books Y, 31–32, BB, 335, EE, 230–231, MDAH; City of Richmond Hustings Deeds, Book 47, 627–628, Book 50, 45–49, LOV; James Young to RB, February 18, 1845, folder 84, RCBP. Young sold the jail a few months later to slave trader Benjamin F. Cochran.

88. Martha Armfield to Adelicia Franklin, September 6, 1844, box 2, folder 22, AFP; *Life of George Henry* (Providence, RI, 1894), 40; Howell, "John Armfield, Slave-Trader," 11.

89. *Life of George Henry*, 17, 40; Gallatin *Examiner*, March 4, 1905; Estate of Smith Franklin (1838), file 717, Sumner County Loose Records, Estates, TSLA.

90. *AG*, November 14, 1845, October 22, 1836; Sixth Census of the United States, District of Columbia, 241, microfilm reel 35. Martha Armfield's Bible is

held by Kenneth Thomson Jr. of Gallatin, Tennessee, who was kind enough to show it to the author.

91. Martha Armfield to Adelicia Franklin, September 6, 1844, box 2, folder 22, AFP. The dispute between the Armfields may have involved someone they enslaved or employed, as Martha noted that John promised that "my <u>evil genius</u> Wash is to be left behind." Her letter provides no additional detail.

92. *AG*, June 20, 1844.

93. *SIF*, 275 (quotation), 279, 282, 286, 291–292, 301–302, 704, 706; "Fairview, Historic American Buildings Survey, District of Tennessee" (1936), 1, 3–5, TSLA; Warden, *Saga of Fairvue*, 6–8; "The Tennessee Stables," *Spirit of the Times*, July 31, 1841; "Alphabetical List of American Winning Horses in 1845," *Spirit of the Times*, April 4, 1846; *NRB*, July 17, 1844; *Louisiana Morning Courier*, October 16, 1845; BJA.

94. *SIF*, 705–708.

95. *SIF*, 39–50, 83, 348–352, 493, 502–543. Franklin also acquired land across the Mississippi River in Point Coupee Parish.

96. Countless newspaper and magazine articles attribute the name "Angola" to the origin of the people enslaved there. See, for example, Krissah Thompson, "From a Slave House to a Prison Cell: The History of Angola Plantation," *Washington Post*, September 21, 2016, www.washingtonpost.com/entertainment /museums/from-a-slave-house-to-a-prison-cell-the-history-of-angola-plantation /2016/09/21/7712eeac-63ee-11e6-96c0-37533479f3f5_story.html; Thomas Beller, "Angola Prison and the Shadow of Slavery," *New Yorker*, August 19, 2015, www.newyorker.com/culture/photo-booth/angola-prison-louisiana-photos. The plantation was also sometimes described in the nineteenth century as "Angora," a misreading of handwritten renderings of the name.

97. *SIF*, 23, 285, 300–301, 363–378, 470, 518, 524, 528, 535, 536, 782, 786–789, 860–861, 867–868, 886–887; Stephenson, *Isaac Franklin*, 213–221, 243–262, 297–300.

98. *SIF*, 51, 293 ("ill-will"), 347, 366 ("Thieves' Harbor"), 369–370, 440–447, 751, 754, 756, 766, 858, 862–863; Stephenson, *Isaac Franklin*, 111, 230–242.

99. The city council passed additional regulations pertaining to the trade in 1843 and 1845, and it levied a tax on slave-trading facilities in 1856. See *Digest of the Ordinances and Resolutions of the Second Municipality; and of the General Council of the City of New Orleans, applicable thereto* (New Orleans, 1848), 84–85 (quotation on 84); *NODP*, January 2, 1843; *SIF*, 280, 282, 371; Richard Campanella, "The St. Louis and the St. Charles: New Orleans' Legacy of Showcase Exchange Hotels," *Preservation in Print*, April 2015, 16–17; Deyle, *Carry Me Back*, 154; Maurie D. McInnis, *Slaves Waiting for Sale: Abolitionist Art and the American Slave Trade* (Chicago: University of Chicago Press, 2011), 156–168; L. A. Chamerovzow, ed., *Slave Life in Georgia: A Narrative of the Life, Sufferings, and Escape of John Brown,*

a Fugitive Slave (London, 1855), 108–118; W. H. Coleman, *Historical Sketch Book and Guide to New Orleans and Environs* (New York, 1885), 72–73.

100. *SIF*, 290 ("elegance and quality"), 338, 342 ("comfort or amusement"), 359, 361, 363, 364 ("fine residence"), 367–368, 370–371, 372, 373.

101. *SIF*, 275 ("sell his Louisiana property"), 285 ("wind up"), 293, 347 ("proud of").

102. *SIF*, 294; BJA.

103. *SIF*, 280, 282, 292, 296, 338, 342, 345, 361, 369, 371, 438–439, 654–657, 778; BJA; Martha Armfield to Adelicia Franklin, January 8, 1845, box 2, folder 22, AFP; *MFT*, November 6, 1845.

104. *SIF*, 338, 364 ("something very handsome," "private tutors"), 438–439 ("trouble" on 438); JA to RW, October 30, 1845, Papers of Robert N. Windsor, mss2867, UVA; Adams County Deed Book FF, 268–271, ACC; Alexandria City Deeds, Book G-3, 328–331, LOV; JA to RB, December 26, 1845, folder 94, January 25, 1846, folder 95, RCBP.

105. *SIF*, 482; *NRB*, August 20, 1845.

106. *SIF*, 338, 482 (quotations), 739–741.

107. *SIF*, 428–429, 482, 750, 755, 763, 765–767, 778, 784–785. Franklin's body was later moved to Nashville's Mount Olivet cemetery, where it is still entombed.

CHAPTER SEVEN: LEGACIES, 1846–1871

1. *SIF*, 91–92, 429–430 ("excessive hard work" on 429), 502–536, 557–567, 699–709; *MFT*, October 21, 1846 ("estimated considerably below," "fortune exceeding").

2. *MFT*, October 21, 1846 ("slenderly provided," "in the usual way," "activity and intelligence," "momentous expedition[s]," "laid the foundation," "by the acquisition," and "by gaining"), December 30, 1846 ("Tennessee pioneers," "became entitled," "on his father's farm," and "perilous adventure"); *SIF*, 429–430, 566, 707.

3. *AG*, October 2, 1846 ("munificent bequest"); *SIF*, 486–500 ("necessary" on 490, "academy or seminary," "substantial and good," "poor children," "educated and supported" on 498); Wendell Holmes Stephenson, *Isaac Franklin, Slave Trader and Planter of the Old South* (Baton Rouge: Louisiana State University Press, 1938), 116–118.

4. *MFT*, October 21, 1846 ("the vast importance," "money-getting," "truly glorious," and "snatched from"), December 30, 1846 ("of the far-famed," "embalmed," "nobler ends," "grand object," "for the benefit," and "resplendent as a sun beam"). These articles were reprinted in part or in full in papers across the country.

5. New York *Tribune*, in Pennsylvania *Freeman*, January 28, 1847. Robert Gudmestad argues that Franklin's obituary writers avoided referring to his work

in the slave trade so as not to associate his memory with something so publicly suspect. But Michael Tadman observes that slaveholder obituaries rarely discussed slaveholding, and that rather than indicating any particular stigma, Franklin's obituary was part of a larger pattern of white southerners euphemizing both slaveholding and slavery. See Robert Gudmestad, *A Troublesome Commerce: The Transformation of the Interstate Slave Trade* (Baton Rouge: Louisiana State University Press, 2003), 1–3; Michael Tadman, "The Reputation of the Slave Trader in Southern History and the Social Memory of the South," *American Nineteenth Century History* 8, no. 3 (September 2007): 253–254.

6. *SIF*, 470 ("expressed his intention," "especially in reference"), 410 ("accept or execute," "viewing it"), 416, 673; Nashville *Union*, October 27, November 17, December 1, 1847; Nashville *Banner*, November 29, 1847; Sumner County Deed Book 22, 33–36, TSLA; Gudmestad, *Troublesome Commerce*, 203–204.

7. Michael Tadman, *Speculators and Slaves: Masters, Traders, and Slaves in the Old South* (Madison: University of Wisconsin Press, 1989), 12.

8. Randolph B. Campbell, *An Empire for Slavery: The Peculiar Institution in Texas, 1821–1865* (Baton Rouge: Louisiana State University Press, 1989); Andrew J. Torget, *Seeds of Empire: Cotton, Slavery, and the Transformation of the Texas Borderlands, 1800–1850* (Chapel Hill: University of North Carolina Press, 2015); Calvin Schermerhorn, *The Business of Slavery and the Rise of American Capitalism, 1815–1860* (New Haven: Yale University Press, 2015), 204–239; *Compendium of the Enumeration of the Inhabitants and Statistics of the United States* (Washington, DC, 1841), 94; *Population of the United States in 1860* (Washington, DC, 1864), 17; Edward E. Baptist, *The Half Has Never Been Told: Slavery and the Making of American Capitalism* (New York: Basic Books, 2014), 343–396; Walter Johnson, *River of Dark Dreams: Slavery and Empire in the Cotton Kingdom* (Cambridge, MA: Harvard University Press, 2013), 303–420; Matthew Karp, *This Vast Southern Empire: Slaveholders at the Helm of American Foreign Policy* (Cambridge, MA: Harvard University Press, 2016).

9. Lewis Cecil Gray, *History of Agriculture in the Southern United States to 1860* (Washington, DC: Carnegie Institution of Washington, 1933), 2:1027; Stuart Bruchey, *Cotton and the Growth of the American Economy: 1790–1860* (New York: Harcourt, Brace, and World, 1967), 17; Douglass C. North, *The Economic Growth of the United States, 1790–1860* (Englewood Cliffs, NJ: Prentice-Hall, 1961), 257; Baptist, *Half*, 174, 269–270; Schermerhorn, *Business of Slavery*, 234–235; Steven Deyle, *Carry Me Back: The Domestic Slave Trade in American Life* (New York: Oxford University Press, 2005), 57–59, 70–72; Tadman, *Speculators and Slaves*, 204–209; Laurence J. Kotlikoff, "The Structure of Slave Prices in New Orleans, 1804 to 1862," *Economic Inquiry* 17, no. 4 (October 1979): 498; Herman Freudenberger and Jonathan B. Pritchett, "The Domestic United States Slave Trade: New Evidence," *Journal of Interdisciplinary History* 21, no. 3 (Winter

1991): 457; Frederic Bancroft, *Slave-Trading in the Old South* (Baltimore: J. H. Furst, 1931), 339–364.

10. Calvin Schermerhorn, *Money over Mastery, Family over Freedom: Slavery in the Antebellum Upper South* (Baltimore: Johns Hopkins University Press, 2011), 165–166, 168–169, 174–177; Maurie D. McInnis, *Slaves Waiting for Sale: Abolitionist Art and the American Slave Trade* (Chicago: University of Chicago Press, 2011), 147; Deyle, *Carry Me Back*, 111–112; Tadman, *Speculators and Slaves*, 77–79. For an argument that railroad construction itself boosted slave prices, see Mark A. Yanochik, Mark Thornton, and Bradley T. Ewing, "Railroad Construction and Antebellum Slave Prices," *Social Science Quarterly* 84, no. 3 (September 2003): 723–737.

11. Schermerhorn, *Money over Mastery*, 177–180; Baptist, *Half*, 358–359; Deyle, *Carry Me Back*, 112, 130–131.

12. Janice G. Artemel, Elizabeth A. Crowell, and Jeff Parker, *The Alexandria Slave Pen: The Archaeology of Urban Captivity* (Washington, DC: Engineering Science, 1987), 35–41; Michael A. Ridgeway, "A Peculiar Business: Slave Trading in Alexandria, Virginia, 1825–1861" (MA thesis, Georgetown University, 1976), 104–150; Jim Barnett and H. Clark Burkett, "The Forks of the Road Slave Market at Natchez," *Journal of Mississippi History* 63, no. 3 (Fall 2001): 168–187; Thom Rosenblum, "Forks of the Road Slave Market, Analysis of Historical Occupancy" (unpublished draft, July 2005); Bancroft, *Slave-Trading in the Old South*, 305–309, 312–338; Jan Richard Heier, "Accounting for the Business of Suffering: A Study of the Antebellum Richmond, Virginia, Slave Trade," *ABACUS* 46, no. 1 (2010): 60–83; McInnis, *Slaves Waiting for Sale*, 72, 158; Maurie D. McInnis, "Mapping the Slave Trade in Richmond and New Orleans," *Buildings and Landscapes* 20, no. 2 (Fall 2013): 102–125.

13. Deyle, *Carry Me Back*, 112; Schermerhorn, *Business of Slavery*, 169–203.

14. *SIF*, 410 ("accumulated"), 547–549 ("almost inconsolable" on 547–548); Stephenson, *Isaac Franklin*, 116; BJA.

15. *SIF*, 549.

16. Isaac Franklin had also named his brother William as executor, but he never qualified to serve. *SIF*, 132, 339, 411, 413 ("much improved"), 419, 483–484, 498; JA to RB, May 4, 1846 ("You may imagin," "As soon as"), folder 101, RCBP; Sumner County Deed Book 21, 224–226, TSLA; John L. T. Sneed, *Reports of Cases Argued and Determined in the Supreme Court of Tennessee During the Years 1854–5* (Nashville, 1856), 2:328.

17. *SIF*, 339, 389–396, 550–552; Hilary Breton Cenas, vol. 37 (March–June 1847), Act 45, March 8, 1847, NONA; West Feliciana Parish Conveyance Book I, 343–347, NOPL; *MFT*, December 30, 1846.

18. *SIF*, 397–403 (quotation on 400), 418; Hilary Breton Cenas, vol. 38 (July 1847–March 1848), Act 437, February 1, 1848, NONA; West Feliciana Parish

Conveyance Book I, 443–448, NOPL; Sumner County Deed Book 21, 180–182, Davidson County Deed Book 9, 563, TSLA; Isabel Howel, "John Armfield, Slave-Trader," *THQ* 2, no. 1 (March 1943): 22; Stephenson, *Isaac Franklin*, 118–119.

19. William Henley v. L. W. Crump, John Armfield, O. B. Hayes, and others (1850), file 6936 (all quotations but "Surrounded"), Testimony of William Murray, A. H. Wood et al. v. John W. Franklin et al. (1876), file 10769, Sumner County Loose Records, Lawsuits, TSLA; *SIF*, 51, 343, 420, 495 ("Surrounded"), 707; JA to RB, December 4, 1847, folder 121, RCBP.

20. *SIF*, 136–253, 363–367, 376, 491, 493–495 (quotations on 493), 723–910; Stephenson, *Isaac Franklin*, 106–110.

21. Testimony of William Murray ("of first rate quality," "indulged them," "in the light"), Samuel Bugg, W. S. Munday, Response of W. C. Dismukes ("especial objects"), Response of John W. Franklin, A. H. Wood et al. v. John W. Franklin et al.; *Cohen's New Orleans and Lafayette Directory* (New Orleans, 1849–1854); Winborne v. Gorrell et al., North Carolina Supreme Court case 3781 (38 NC 117, December 1843), SANC; Sumner County Deed Book 20, 106, Book 21, 258–259; Howell, "John Armfield, Slave-Trader," 24–25.

22. Jane Franklin formally became John Armfield's ward in 1846, and Armfield continued to support her financially even after 1850, when she became the ward of her cousin John Sanderson. See John Gordon et al. v. Josiah Franklin et al. (1848), file 4031, Jane C. Franklin v. John F. Cage et al. (1848), file 4188, Sumner County Loose Records, Lawsuits, Sumner County Deed Book 21, 231, 234, 239–240, 282, 283, 343–345, 482–483, Book 22, 10–11, 383–385, Book 23, 99–100, Sumner County Bills of Sale, 1854–1860, 34–35, TSLA; *"Love's Young Dream": The Letters of Dr. Edward Noel Franklin to Miss Nannie Hillman, 1871*, ed. Terry L. Martin (Gallatin, TN: Silver Goblet Press, 2018), 8–10; Howell, "John Armfield, Slave-Trader," 25, 28; 1850 Federal Population Census, Free Schedule, Tennessee, Sumner County, 249, microfilm reel 897, M432, NARA.

23. *SIF*, 14–61.

24. *NRB*, December 11, 1867; Eleanor Graham, "Belmont: Nashville Home of Adelicia Acklen," *THQ* 30, no. 4 (Winter 1971): 350, 355; John W. Kiser, "Scion of Belmont, Part I," *THQ* 38, no. 1 (Spring 1979): 40; Albert W. Wardin Jr., *Belmont Mansion: The Home of Joseph and Adelicia Acklen* (Nashville: Belmont Mansion Association, 2012), 6; Brenda Jackson-Abernathy, "Adelicia Acklen: Beyond the 'Belmont' Legend and Lore," *THQ* 76, no. 1 (Spring 2017): 14–15; W. W. Clayton, *History of Davidson County, Tennessee, with Illustrations and Biographical Sketches of Its Prominent Men and Pioneers* (Philadelphia, 1880), 451; James M. Volo and Dorothy Denneen Volo, *The Antebellum Period* (Westport, CT: Greenwood Press, 2004), 35–37.

25. *SIF*, 450–452; Graham, "Belmont," 355; Wardin, *Belmont Mansion*, 6–7; Jackson-Abernathy, "Adelicia Acklen," 15–16.

26. *SIF*, 79–102 (quotation on 82).

27. *SIF*, 417 ("intended"), 130 ("a very large quantity," "his own family"), 79–90.

28. *SIF*, 81.

29. *SIF*, 94–95.

30. *SIF*, 81.

31. New Orleans *Weekly Delta*, June 16, 1851 (quotations); *NRB*, June 21, 1851; Howell, "John Armfield, Slave-Trader," 22.

32. *Reports of Cases Argued and Determined in the Supreme Court of Louisiana* (New Orleans, 1854), 7:395–440 ("comforts," "permanent domicil" on 410, "to a class of tenures" on 412, "set aside," "real estate" on 417).

33. Institute trustees thought they might pay for the school with Franklin's land in Texas, but that plan failed as well. See Sneed, *Reports*, 2:306–359 (quotation on 344); William Franklin v. Descendants of Isaac Franklin, RG 170, box 383, Supreme Court Trial Case Files, TSLA; Howell, "John Armfield, Slave-Trader," 23–24; *NRB*, March 3, 1855; JA to RB, February 13, 1855, folder 226, RCBP; *Texas State Gazette*, March 10, 1855.

34. JA to RB, January 21, 1853 (quotations), January 24, 1853, folder 185, January 14, 1853, folder 184, RCBP; Howell, "John Armfield, Slave-Trader," 26.

35. On Ballard's career after his work with Franklin and Armfield, see Tomoko Yagyu, "Slave Traders and Planters in the Expanding South: Entrepreneurial Strategies, Business Networks, and Western Migration in the Atlantic World, 1787–1859" (PhD diss., University of North Carolina–Chapel Hill, 2006), 209–353; Kathryn Susan Boodry, "The Common Thread: Slavery, Cotton and Atlantic Finance from the Louisiana Purchase to Reconstruction" (PhD diss., Harvard University, 2013), 112–146; Baptist, *Half*, 358–363; William Kauffman Scarborough, *Masters of the Big House: Elite Slaveholders of the Mid-Nineteenth-Century South* (Baton Rouge: Louisiana State University Press, 2003), 133–134, 146, 176, 185, 197, 213–216.

36. SB to RB, May 27, 1848 ("a fair bargain"), folder 127, John L. White to RB, February 19, 1853 ("liable to seizure"), folder 187, William G. Hewes to RB, November 27, 1852 ("well suited"), folder 8, F. A. Freeland to RB, January 8, 1856 ("do better"), folder 238, John Thorn to RB ("conclude"), October 22, 1850, folder 158, RCBP.

37. By 1856, Ballard and Boyd also owned some "wild lands adjoining Karnac and a lot under the hill at Natchez," the latter of which was probably warehouse property purchased in 1842. Other properties owned by Ballard, Boyd, or both included Forest Hill Plantation and Pine Mount, in Adams County, Mississippi; Elk Plantation and Laurel Plantation, in Warren County, Mississippi; and Wagram, in Chicot County, Arkansas. For several years, Ballard also owned land in Tensas Parish, Louisiana. At the outbreak of the Civil War, Ballard and Boyd's partnership owned only Elcho, Lapine, Outpost, and Karnac. Samuel Boyd still owned Forest Hill, and Ballard owned Wagram, which seems never to have been

a partnership property. Magnolia was sold to Oliver Prince in 1857, only to revert back to the estates of Ballard and Boyd after the Civil War when Prince could not pay the mortgage. See Warren County Deed Books X, 63–64, Y, 561–562, AA, 132–134, GG, 263–265, MDAH; East Carroll Parish Conveyance Books G, 279–280, H, 49–50, 379–380, East Carroll Parish Courthouse, Lake Providence, Louisiana; Madison Parish Notarial Record Book F, 73–74, 117–120, 280, Madison Parish Courthouse, Tallulah, Louisiana; Adams County Will Book 3, 315–319, Adams County Deed Book EE, 623–624, ACC; Concordia Parish Conveyance Books L, 151, M, 16, 304, Concordia Parish Courthouse, Vidalia, Louisiana; Chicot County Deed Books H, 464–465, K, 150, M, 619–620, Arkansas State Archives, Little Rock, Arkansas; CMR to RB, January 3, 1854, folder 205, RCBP.

38. *Southern Cultivator* 10, no. 8 (August 1852): 227 (all quotations except "show[ed]" and "see for themselves"); Wardin, *Belmont Mansion*, 7–8; Adelicia Acklen to Corinne Hayes Lawrence, February 22, 1858 ("show[ed]," "see for themselves"), Lawrence Family Papers, 1780–1944, box 1, folder 4, TSLA.

39. Petition of Samuel S. Boyd, November 8, 1860, Warren County Probate Packet 2019, Estate of Rice C. Ballard, MDAH; *MFT*, December 27, 1848.

40. Ballard also enslaved forty people in Arkansas and four people in Louisville. See 1860 Federal Population Census, Slave Schedule, Mississippi, Claiborne County, 438–439, microfilm reel 596, Mississippi, Warren County, 90–91, microfilm reel 603, Louisiana, Carroll Parish, 44–45, microfilm reel 427, Louisiana, Madison Parish, 13–15, microfilm reel 429, Arkansas, Chicot County, 23, microfilm reel 53, Kentucky, Jefferson County, 6, microfilm reel 403, all in M653, NARA.

41. Jacob Westbrook to RB, February 19, 1848, folder 123 ("worms," "the clap"), February 21, 1853, folder 187 ("Tiphoid"), September 18, 1853, folder 198 ("Good Deal"), SB to RB, September 9, 1844, folder 76 ("lock-jaw"), September 2, 1850, folder 157 ("two negroes," "if you chance"), J. H. Cox to RB, June 19, 1846, folder 104 ("bloody flux"), J. Nalley to RB, February 19, 1853, folder 187 ("hooping caugh"), H. Shaw to RB, September 21, 1853, folder 198 ("chills"), RCBP. Also see Ben Parks to RB, May 7, 1852, folder 176, RCBP.

42. W. H. Dixon to RB, August 17, 1844, folder 76, H. Shaw to RB, November 13, 1853, folder 200, RCBP. Also see SB to RB, September 1, 1844, folder 77, RCBP.

43. Picking records at Magnolia, which are the most complete, suggest that the enslaved picked nearly four pounds of cotton for every pound suitable for shipment, which comports with anecdotal evidence from other plantations and slave labor camps. See Accounts of Sales for 1852 and 1855, folders 384 and 397, "Cotton Plantation Record and Account Book," 1855, folder 452, RCBP; Baptist, *Half*, 359; Scarborough, *Masters of the Big House*, 133–134; Yagyu, "Slave Traders and Planters in the Expanding South," 289n57, 317–318; Gray, *History of Agricul-*

ture, 2:674; Ulrich Bonnell Phillips, *Life and Labor in the Old South* (Boston: Little, Brown, and Company, 1929), 278–279.

44. *MFT*, April 26, 1848.

45. RB to Albert Sidney Johnston, April 17, 1844, in Maria Angela Diaz, "Rising Tide of Empire: Gulf Coast Culture and Society During the Era of Expansion, 1845–1860" (PhD diss., University of Florida, 2013), 52. Ballard's politics were defined mostly by conservative business principles, an aggressive proslavery stance, and hostility to abolitionism. He seems to have remained a Whig fairly consistently until the party dissolved in the early 1850s, and he then may have had an affiliation with the nativist American Party to which some former Whigs gravitated. See SB to RB, April 4, 14, 1850, folder 150, April 24, 1850, folder 151, "Know-Nothing Resolutions the Counsel at Louisville Would Not Entertain," folder 413, RCBP; Warren County Probate Packet 2019, Estate of Rice C. Ballard, MDAH; Baptist, *Half*, 354–358; Tom Chaffin, *Fatal Glory: Narciso López and the First Clandestine U.S. War Against Cuba* (Charlottesville: University Press of Virginia, 1996); Johnson, *River of Dark Dreams*, 330–365; Charles H. Brown, *Agents of Manifest Destiny: The Lives and Times of the Filibusters* (Chapel Hill: University of North Carolina Press, 1980), 39–88.

46. Promissory note, January 23, 1841, folder 354, RB to J. M. Morrison, January 15, 1843, folder 58, William D. Nutt to JA, April 4, 1846, JA to RB, April 12, 1846, folder 99, October 10, 1847, folder 119, W. A. Ellis to RB, May 11, 1852, folder 176, RCBP; Warren County Probate Packet 2019, Estate of Rice C. Ballard, MDAH; Answer of Rice Ballard, F. C. Brengman v. James F. Johnston, Jefferson County Chancery Court, case 4195, October 1843, KDLA; *Gabriel Collins' Louisville and New Albany Directory and Annual Advertiser for 1848* (Louisville, 1848); *The Louisville Directory and Annual Business Advertiser for 1855–6* (Louisville, 1855); *A Collection of the State and Municipal Laws, in Force, and Applicable to the City of Louisville* (Louisville, 1857), 6; Louisville *Daily Democrat*, July 17, 1851; Jefferson County Deed Book 80, 194–195, Book 87, 594–595, KDLA.

47. *NODP*, February 10, 1841; CMR to RB, February 19, 1853, folder 187, December 14, 1853, folder 202, November 1, 1849, folder 144, August 6, 1853, folder 196, January 10, 1853, folder 184, RCBP; Yagyu, "Slave Traders and Planters in the Expanding South," 333–346.

48. Baton Rouge *Daily Comet*, December 16, 1853; *NODP*, November 15, 1846, June 14, 1849, November 8, 1851; CMR to RB, December 23, 27, 1852, folder 9, October 29, 1849, folder 143, November 1, 1849, folder 144, March 11, 1850, folder 148, January 7, 30, 1851, folder 164, March 22, 29, 1852, folder 174, June 1, 4, 1852, folder 178, February 19, 1853, folder 187, March 19, 1853, folder 188, April 2, 1853, folder 189, August 6, 1853, folder 196, GK to JA, March 16, 1838, folder 22, CMR to RB, November 19, 1849, Samuel D. Tompkins to RB, November 20, 1849,

folder 144, S. R. Chenoweth to RB, February 7, 1850, Samuel D. Tompkins to RB, February 18, 1847, folder 147, Samuel D. Tompkins to RB, March 12, 1850, folder 148, Thomas Hundley to CMR, June 14, 1850, folder 154, RCBP. Other traders in Rutherford's network included Stephen Chenoweth, Samuel Tompkins, Thomas Hundley, J. M. Martin, Samuel B. Conrey, and D. M. Matthews.

49. SB to RB, December 22, 1852, folder 183 (quotations), January 1, 1853, folder 184, RCBP.

50. CMR to RB, February 27, 1853, folder 187 ("for I know"), March 12 and 19, 1853, folder 188, April 2, 1853, folder 189, April 19, 1853, folder 190 ("special instructions"), RCBP. Also see Yagyu, "Slave Traders and Planters in the Expanding South," 343–344; Baptist, *Half,* 361–363; Scarborough, *Masters of the Big House,* 215–216; Sharony Green, *Remember Me to Miss Louisa: Hidden Black-White Intimacies in Antebellum America* (DeKalb, IL: Northern Illinois University Press, 2015), 25–26.

51. Virginia Boyd to RB, May 6, 1853, folder 191, RCBP.

52. CMR to RB, August 8, 1853, folder 196, RCBP. A recent biography of physician Edward Mazique tells the family story that Mazique's cousin, James Boyd, was the son of Samuel and Virginia Boyd, and that Samuel Boyd kept him behind at Arlington. See Florence Ridlon, *A Black Physician's Struggle for Civil Rights: Edward C. Mazique, M.D.* (Albuquerque: University of New Mexico Press, 2005), 33–34.

53. Ballard also bought Louisville property at the corner of Floyd and Gray Streets, and he acquired land outside the city in partnership with a man named J. C. Hull, but it is not clear how he used these properties. See JA to RB, October 19, 1847, folder 119, LB to RB, November 18, 1847, folder 120, December 5, 11, 1847, folder 121, December 20, 1849, folder 145, Ella Ballard to RB, November 6, 1850, folder 159, November 8, 1852, folder 180, folders 351–355, RCBP; Jefferson County Deed Book 68, 399–401, Book 70, 389–391, Book 76, 465, Book 80, 67–68, Book 88, 94–95, Book 90, 414–415, 534–535, Jefferson County Tax Assessment Books, 1849–1860, KDLA; *Hurd and Burrows' Louisville City Directory for 1858–9* (Louisville, 1858).

54. LB to RB, November 18, 1847, folder 120 ("pretty much tied down"), December 5, 1847, folder 112 (remaining quotations), S. Theobold to RB, April 2, 1842, folder 48, unsigned letter to RB, May 15, 1847, folder 111, RCBP. Also see Green, *Remember Me,* 33–44.

55. LB to RB, February 11, 1848, folder 123 ("a great deal of pleasure," "new life," "take care & double care," "if it was only for a few weeks"), December 11, 1846, folder 121 ("the kick of a mule"), April 22, 1850, folder 151 ("how lonely," "how much pleasure," "they talk of their Papa"), December 20, 1849, folder 145 ("were growing quite fast," "they have your expression"), C. A. Moore to RB, April 12, 1849, folder 139 ("very low spirits"), RCBP.

56. LB to RB, November 8, 1852, folder 200 (quotation), February 18, 1850, folder 147, November 18, 1847, folder 120, December 20, 1848, folder 145, December 30, 1852, folder 183, January 15, 1853, folder 185, March 2, 1853, folder 188, RCBP.

57. W. A. Ellis to RB, May 18, 1852, folder 177, RCBP; Agatha Marshall Logan to Appoline Alexander Blair, April 1, 1856, in Margaret A. Caldwell, ed., *A Web of Family: Letters from a Kentucky Family, 1816–1865* (Cambridge, MA: n.p., 1975), 169. William Ellis was Louisa Ballard's half brother, a child of her mother's by a marriage prior to her marriage to James Berthe. Agatha Logan observed in her letter that Rice Ballard was "a horribly degraded Negro trader," though she was not so much suggesting that his profession made his wife a pariah as thinking it might account for Louisa's misery. See LB to RB, November 29, 1852, folder 179, January 15, 1853, folder 185, RCBP; Green, *Remember Me*, 149n4.

58. W. A. Ellis to RB, March 1, 1857, folder 254, RCBP.

59. Ella Ballard to RB, March 1, 1857, folder 254, RCBP.

60. Baltimore *Sun*, June 9, 1841, *Christian Reflector*, October 11, 1843. Abandoning the slave trade did not mean Purvis turned entirely against slavery. In 1850, he still enslaved a twenty-six-year-old woman and her two children in his Baltimore household. See *BACDA*, February 11, 1846, April 29, 1853; Baltimore *Sun*, June 29, 1843, March 28, 1844, January 23, 1847, February 12, 1849, February 21 and December 24, 1855, January 14, 1857, July 24, 1860, April 13, 1865, April 27, 1869; Frederick *Examiner*, March 22, 1865; Baltimore *Saturday Visiter*, October 26, 1844; 1850 Federal Population Census, Slave Schedule, Maryland, Baltimore County, 571, microfilm reel 300, M432, NARA.

61. Hank Trent, *The Secret Life of Bacon Tait, a White Slave Trader Married to a Free Woman of Color* (Baton Rouge: Louisiana State University Press, 2017), 127–129, 165–166; *AG*, March 4, 1843, April 28, 1851, March 5, 1852, July 17, 1857, January 17, 1859; Cincinnati *Star in the West*, February 9, 1856; 1860 Federal Population Census, Free Schedule, Virginia, Loudoun County, 24, microfilm reel 1359, M653, NARA; Alexandria City Deeds, Book T-3, 353–354, LOV.

62. Schermerhorn, *Business of Slavery*, 66–67; 1850 Federal Population Census, Slave Schedule, Georgia, Muscogee County, 10–11, microfilm reel 93, Virginia, Fauquier County, 23, microfilm reel 986, M432, NARA; 1860 Federal Population Census, Free Schedule, Virginia, Fauquier County, 95, microfilm reel 1344, M653, NARA; Fauquier County Deed Book 50, 404, Fauquier County Will Book 35, 33–35, LOV.

63. Richmond *Daily Dispatch*, July 15, 1854. Rice Ballard and Samuel Boyd loaned Rutherford money for his stake in the National Hotel and held a partial mortgage on it, though debt problems forced Rutherford and his partners to sell the hotel in 1856. See Richmond *Enquirer*, January 28, 1843, May 24, 1847, April 7, 1848; Richmond *Whig*, April 11, 1848, July 18, 1854; Louisville *Daily Courier*,

January 6, 1855; Louisville *Daily Democrat,* July 15, 1856; Thomas Eades v. Calvin M. Rutherford, P. R. Johnson, J. M. Martin, A. O. Robards, and Lewis C. Robards, Jefferson County Chancery Court, case 11611, February 1856, KDLA.

64. Louisville *Daily Democrat,* November 17, 20 ("by all"), December 4, 13, 1855, February 5, 1856 ("of all kinds"); McInnis, *Slaves Waiting for Sale,* 55–83.

65. *AG,* August 23, 1851. Armfield did continue to spend portions of the winter in New Orleans for many years. See *NOCB,* September 5, 1851; 1860 Federal Population Census, Free Schedule, Tennessee, Grundy County, 67, microfilm reel 1252, M653, NARA; E. S. Abdy, *Journal of a Residence and Tour in the United States of North America, from April, 1833, to October, 1834* (London, 1835), 2:180; Testimony of W. S. Munday, A. H. Wood et al. v. John W. Franklin et al.; 1850 Federal Population Census, Slave Schedule, Tennessee, Sumner County, 326, microfilm reel 907, M432, NARA; Isabel Howell, "John Armfield of Beersheba Springs," *THQ* 3, no. 1 (March 1944): 64; Louisiana vol. 10, 445, R. G. Dun & Co. credit report volumes, Baker Library, Harvard Business School.

66. Nalle Cox and Co. to RB, January 7, 1854, folder 206, RCBP. The Fairvue auction was in the fall of 1855, but Nathan Bracken supposedly claimed he drove Armfield for his first visit to Beersheba Springs, suggesting that Armfield enslaved him even before the auction. Martha Armfield did also enslave other women as her personal servants, among them a woman named Matilda Franklin who had been enslaved by her father and who continued to work as Martha Armfield's servant after the Civil War. So did Henrietta and Nathan Bracken's daughter Harriet. See Auction Notice, October 22, 1855, box 2, folder 30, AFP; Howell, "John Armfield, Slave-Trader," 28–29; Nashville *Daily American,* March 3, 1878; *"Love's Young Dream,"* 33.

67. Clopper Almon, ed., *Beersheba Springs, A History, Volume I: General History, the Hotel-Assembly, and Shops* (Beersheba Springs, TN: Beersheba Springs Historical Society, 2010), 5–15; Howell, "John Armfield of Beersheba Springs," 47–50; James L. Nicholson, *Grundy County* (Memphis: Memphis State University Press, 1982), 13–14; Grundy County Deed Book A, 217–219, 225, TSLA.

68. *NRB,* April 4, 1855. Rental tenures were supposed to be for twenty years, at which point the land and the cottage on it would revert to Armfield, but in some cases, Armfield sold the property outright to residents who had paid to build the cottage. Armfield sold Hard Times in the fall of 1855. See Howell, "John Armfield of Beersheba Springs," 50–54, 57–59; Almon, *Beersheba Springs,* 1:15–17, 30; Grundy County Deed Book A, 225–230, 262–264, 306–307, 311–312, 323–324, 369–370, Sumner County Deed Book 23, 251–252, TSLA.

69. *NODP,* April 29, 1857; Memphis *Daily Eagle and Enquirer,* September 5, 1857; *NRB,* July 2, 1858; Almon, *Beersheba Springs,* 1:31; Clopper Almon, ed., *Beersheba Springs, A History, Volume III: Classics* (Beersheba Springs, TN: Beersheba Springs Historical Society, 2011), 24–26.

70. Memphis *Daily Eagle and Enquirer*, September 5, 1857; Howell, "John Armfield of Beersheba Springs," 53–54, 57–59; Grundy County Deed Books A, 394–396, C, 1–7, 12–18, 110–112, 259–260, 272–282, TSLA.

71. Leonidas Polk to Stephen Elliott, August 20, 1856, box 9, Polk Family Papers, MSS090, USS. A recent biography of Polk suggests he and Armfield probably met in New Orleans in the late 1840s or early 1850s, but their friendship may have dated to Polk's years at Alexandria's Virginia Theological Seminary in the late 1820s. See Almon, *Beersheba Springs*, 1:17; Almon, *Beersheba Springs*, 3:24, 26; *NODP*, April 29, 1857; Howell, "John Armfield, Slave-Trader," 18–19, 26–27; Grundy County Deed Book C, 275–277; Glenn Robins, *The Bishop of the Old South: The Ministry and Civil War Legacy of Leonidas Polk* (Macon, GA: Mercer University Press, 2006), 87–95, 135–136; Huston Horn, *Leonidas Polk, Warrior Bishop of the Confederacy* (Lawrence: University Press of Kansas, 2019), 97–121; Joseph H. Parks, *General Leonidas Polk C.S.A.: The Fighting Bishop* (Baton Rouge: Louisiana State University Press, 1962), 98–116; James Otey to JA, February 13, March 26, 1857, James Otey to John H. French, March 26, 1857, box 2, James Hervey Otey Papers, MSS088, USS.

72. Leonidas Polk and Stephen Elliott, "The University of the South," *DeBow's Review*, May 1, 1859, 538–541 (quotations on 539, 540); Moultrie Guerry, "Leonidas Polk and the University of the South," *Historical Magazine of the Protestant Episcopal Church* 7, no. 4 (December 1938): 379–382; George R. Fairbanks, *History of the University of the South at Sewanee, Tennessee* (Jacksonville, FL: H. and W. B. Drew, 1905), 11–21; F. Schaller, "The University of the South," *Southern Magazine*, March 1, 1873, 330–332.

73. James Otey to JA, February 13, 1857, box 2, James Hervey Otey Papers; Polk and Elliott, "University of the South," 541–542; "Southern Episcopal University," *DeBow's Review*, November 1, 1857, 557–558; *Church Journal*, July 21, 1858; Fairbanks, *History*, 22–32; Herschel Gower, "Beersheba Springs and L. Virginia French: The Novelist as Historian," *THQ* 42, no. 2 (Summer 1983): 133.

74. "Subscriptions and Gifts Folder," box 2, George Fairbanks Papers, USS; James Otey to JA, May 11, 1857, box 2, James Hervey Otey Papers; Polk and Elliott, "University of the South," 546; *Church Journal*, August 4, 1858; Guerry, "Leonidas Polk and the University of the South," 382–383; Fairbanks, *History*, 29–33.

75. Fairbanks, *History*, 34–36 ("for beginning operations" on 35); JA to RB, August 29, 1859 (remaining quotations), folder 313, RCBP; Howell, "John Armfield of Beersheba Springs," 58–59; Almon, *Beersheba Springs*, 1:18.

76. Ella Ballard to RB, April 2, 1859, W. H. Johnson to RB, April 7, 1859, folder 305, SB to RB, July 13, 1859, CMR to RB, July 15, 1859, folder 310, SB to RB, August 18, 1859, folder 312, C. A. Moore to RB, April 2, 5, 1860, folder 328, RCBP.

77. W. H. Johnson to RB, March 5, 1859 ("You must not," "Suppose you do not," "your health and comfort"), folder 303, April 23, 1859, folder 306, SB to RB, June 20 ("bother your head"), 30 ("I am very uneasy," "You have been," "bundle up"), 1859, folder 309, RCBP; *New-Orleans Price-Current, Commercial Intelligencer and Merchants' Transcript*, June 18, 1859.

78. Ann Ballard to RB, November 8, 1859, folder 318, Ella Ballard to RB, January 9, 1860, folder 322, RCBP; Passport application #18512, Passport Applications, 1795–1905, National Archives mf reel 89 (June 4–25, 1860), accessed at ancestry.com. At least one portrait of Ballard was commissioned, in 1848, to hang in the Natchez Catholic Orphan Asylum. Executed by portraitist Joseph Henry Bush, the painting has gone missing, but it was displayed for a time at the Mansion House Hotel. See W. Cox and Co. to RB, March 17, 20, 1860, folder 327, Walter Cox to RB, April 13, 1860, SB to RB, April 22, 1860, folder 329, RCBP; *MFT*, December 21, 1848.

79. Testimony of J. W. Knight, Warren County Probate Packet 2019, Estate of Rice C. Ballard, MDAH; Louisville *Daily Democrat*, September 2, 1860; New York *Commercial Advertiser*, May 23, 1860.

80. New Albany *Daily Ledger*, September 1, 1860; 1860 Federal Population Census, Free Schedule, Louisiana, Madison Parish, 283, microfilm reel 413, Kentucky, Ward 3, City of Louisville, 124, microfilm reel 375, M653, NARA; Kentucky vol. 25, 246, R. G. Dun & Co. credit report volumes, Baker Library, Harvard Business School; Warren County Will Book A, 277–280, MDAH.

81. *AG*, May 9, 1844 (quotations), May 4 and December 13, 1841; Baltimore *Sun*, May 15, 1840; New York *Evening Post*, April 26 and 27, 1841; New York *Commercial Advertiser*, May 1, 1841; New York *Shipping and Commercial List*, May 12, 1841, May 11, 1844; Bridgetown (NJ) *Chronicle*, December 16, 1843; *NODP*, May 1, 1844, January 19, 1845; *NOCB*, October 11, November 16, 1844; *British and Foreign Anti-Slavery Reporter* 6, June 25, 1845, 122; A. G. Nalle to RB, May 12, 1841, folder 41, RCBP.

82. George Kephart's other partners included Horatio Harbin, B. O. Sheckell, and W. R. Millan. Early in 1860, John Cook sold his share in the property to Charles Price. See A. Glenn Crothers, "The 1846 Retrocession of Alexandria: Protecting Slavery and the Slave Trade in the District of Columbia," in *In the Shadow of Freedom: The Politics of Slavery in the National Capital*, ed. Paul Finkelman and Donald R. Kennon (Athens: Ohio University Press, 2011), 141–168; *AG*, October 23, 1847, May 3, 1851, July 7, 1857, December 14, 1860; Alexandria City Deeds, Books T-3, 353–354, U-3, 198–199, LOV; *Reports of the Committees of the Senate of the United States*, Forty-First Congress, 2nd sess., vol. 265, report 104, Committee on Claims, April 14, 1870.

83. Moncure Conway, *Testimonies Concerning Slavery* (London, 1864), 21–22 ("letters and papers," "chained"); Washington *National Republican*, May 28, 1861 ("he must have a musket"); *Reports of the Committees of the Senate of the United*

States, Forty-First Congress, 2nd sess., vol. 265, report 104, Committee on Claims, April 14, 1870; Artemel, Crowell, and Parker, *Alexandria Slave Pen*, 41–47; Ridgeway, "A Peculiar Business," 150–153; "Diaries of Julia Wilbur, March 1860 to July 1866," 219, 230, 258, 261, 276, 283, 284, 311–312, 660, www.alexandriava.gov /uploadedFiles/historic/info/civilwar/JuliaWilburDiary1860to1866.pdf.

84. Bancroft, *Slave-Trading in the Old South*, 304–309 (quotation on 304); Reminiscence of Felix Eugene Houston Hadsell (typescript), 1905, HNF; Rosenblum, "Forks of the Road Slave Market," 55–62; Charles Sackett Sydnor, *Slavery in Mississippi* (New York: D. Appleton-Century, 1933), 169–170; Barnett and Burkett, "Forks of the Road," 184–186; New York *Times*, September 6, 1863; Milwaukee *Daily Sentinel*, February 17, 1864.

85. Milwaukee *Daily Sentinel*, February 17, 1864.

86. Nashville *Daily Union and American*, May 5, 1861. The Fifth Regiment of Tennessee Volunteers later became the Thirty-Fifth Tennessee Infantry. See Howell, "John Armfield of Beersheba Springs," 60; *Confederate Veteran* 9, no. 2 (February 1901): 63; Testimony of A. H. Wood, Wood et al. v. Franklin et al., TSLA; "Copy of a Fragment of a Diary Kept by John Armfield Franklin," courtesy of Terry L. Martin.

87. B. S. Cagle v. Dr. John Franklin and others (1874), Supreme Court of Tennessee, Middle Division, Grundy County, range 20, section D, shelf 4, box 8, TSLA (quotations); Wood et al. v. Franklin et al.; Howell, "John Armfield of Beersheba Springs," 60; Isabel Howell, "John Armfield of Beersheba Springs, Part II," *THQ* 3, no. 2 (June 1944): 156.

88. Cagle v. Franklin, TSLA.

89. French kept a diary of her Civil War experiences and later wrote a novel based on them. Entitled *Darlingtonia*, it was serialized in the Detroit *Free Press* in 1879. Gower, "Beersheba Springs and L. Virginia French," 115–116, 120–122 (quotations on 121); Howell, "John Armfield of Beersheba Springs, Part II," 156; Detroit *Free Press*, April 27–August 24, 1879.

90. Gower, "Beersheba Springs and L. Virginia French," 129–131 ("a continuous stream," "hurrying" on 129, "well armed" on 130, "not let" on 131); Cagle v. Franklin, TSLA ("infested," "man of large cash capital"); Howell, "John Armfield of Beersheba Springs," 61–62.

91. Gower, "Beersheba Springs and L. Virginia French," 131–135 (quotations on 131, 132); Herschel Gower, ed., "The Beersheba Diary of L. Virginia French Part I, Summer and Fall, 1863," *East Tennessee Historical Society's Publications* 52–53 (1980–1981): 93–94.

92. Gower, "Beersheba Diary of L. Virginia French Part I," 94–95.

93. Howell, "John Armfield of Beersheba Springs," 62n50.

94. Cagle v. Franklin, TSLA. Isabel Howell's estimate that Armfield had between $120,000 and $250,000 after the war is impossible to reconcile with Armfield's obvious financial difficulties. See 1870 Federal Population Census,

Tennessee, Grundy County, 5, microfilm reel 1532, M593, NARA; Howell, "John Armfield of Beersheba Springs," 63–64.

95. "Copy of a Fragment of a Diary Kept by John Armfield Franklin"; 1870 Federal Population Census, Tennessee, Grundy County, 5.

96. Will of John Armfield, A. H. Wood et al. v. John W. Franklin et al.; Howell, "John Armfield of Beersheba Springs, Part II," 157–158, 163–164; Grundy County Deed Book E, 382–395, TSLA; *NODP*, June 18, 1870; Nashville *Union and American*, September 24, 1871.

97. Nashville *Union and American*, September 24, 1871; *"Love's Young Dream,"* 22, 28, 20.

98. Nashville *Tennessean*, October 13, 1871; Nashville *Union and American*, September 24, 1871.

99. Nashville *Union and American*, September 24, 1871.

100. Howell, "John Armfield of Beersheba Springs, Part II," 166.

101. Armfield had $30,000 in Bank of Louisiana notes and a little more than $1,200 in Confederate notes on deposit, but military officials had sold the banknotes for sixty cents on the dollar, bringing a return of $18,000. See *Congressional Record*, Forty-Eighth Congress, 1st sess., 1020–1023; *Reports of Committees of the Senate of the United States*, Forty-Eighth Congress, 1st sess., 1883–84 vol. 1, no. 41; Baltimore *Sun*, January 10, 1885.

EPILOGUE: THE LEDGER AND THE CHAIN

1. *National Anti-Slavery Standard*, March 12, 1864; Ira V. Brown, "Miller McKim and Pennsylvania Abolitionism," *Pennsylvania History* 30, no. 1 (January 1963): 56–72. Also see *The Independent*, March 24, 1864.

2. Louisa Ballard also filed claims for mules, horses, cattle, and farm equipment taken during the war, but those claims were denied. See Rice C. Ballard Papers, NTC; Petition of Jesse Woodward, 1874, Warren County Probate Packet 2019, Estate of Rice C. Ballard, MDAH; *Consolidated Index of Claims Reported by the Commissioners of Claims to the House of Representatives from 1871 to 1880* (Washington, DC, 1892), 17.

3. Albert W. Wardin Jr., *Belmont Mansion: The Home of Joseph and Adelicia Acklen* (Nashville: Belmont Mansion Association, 2012), 8–22 (quotations on 12, 17); Eleanor Graham, "Belmont: Nashville Home of Adelicia Acklen," *THQ* 30, no. 4 (Winter 1971): 355–361; Brenda Jackson-Abernathy, "Adelicia Acklen: Beyond the 'Belmont' Legend and Lore," *THQ* 76, no. 1 (Spring 2017): 17, 20–29; BJA; 1860 Federal Population Census, Free Schedule, Tennessee, Davidson County, 45, microfilm reel 1246, Slave Schedule, Louisiana, West Feliciana Parish, 105–113, microfilm reel 428, Slave Schedule, Tennessee, Davidson County, 26, microfilm reel 1281, all in M653, NARA.

4. Graham, "Belmont," 361.

5. Samuel Boyd died in 1867, and Bowmar sold Magnolia on behalf of Ballard's and Boyd's heirs in 1869. See Adams County Will Book 3, 315–319, ACC; Warren County Deed Books GG, 263–265, HH, 159–160, KK, 149–151, Claiborne County Deed Books II, 341–344, 352–359, JJ, 17–19, 611–635, LL, 45, MDAH; Madison Parish Notarial Record Book K, 211–212, Madison Parish Courthouse, Tallulah, Louisiana; East Carroll Parish Conveyance Book S, 419–421, East Carroll Parish Courthouse, Lake Providence, Louisiana.

6. Harold D. Woodman, *New South—New Law: The Legal Foundations of Credit and Labor Relations in the Postbellum Agricultural South* (Baton Rouge: Louisiana State University Press, 1995); Edward Royce, *The Origins of Southern Sharecropping* (Philadelphia: Temple University Press, 1993); Roger L. Ransom and Richard Sutch, *One Kind of Freedom: The Economic Consequences of Emancipation* (Cambridge: Cambridge University Press, 1977).

7. Mark T. Carleton, *Politics and Punishment: The History of the Louisiana State Penal System* (Baton Rouge: Louisiana State University Press, 1971), 3–84 (quotation on 20); Graham, "Belmont," 363–364; Wardin, *Belmont Mansion*, 26, 31; Jackson-Abernathy, "Adelicia Acklen," 35.

8. Carleton, *Politics and Punishment*, 20–39; Douglas A. Blackmon, *Slavery by Another Name: The Re-Enslavement of Black Americans from the Civil War to World War Two* (New York: Anchor Books, 2008). Also see David M. Oshinsky, *Worse Than Slavery: Parchman Farm and the Ordeal of Jim Crow Justice* (New York: Free Press, 1996); Matthew J. Mancini, *One Dies, Get Another: Convict Leasing in the American South, 1866–1928* (Columbia: University of South Carolina Press, 1996); Alex Lichtenstein, *Twice the Work of Free Labor: The Political Economy of Convict Labor in the New South* (New York: Verso, 1996); Talitha L. LeFlouria, *Chained in Silence: Black Women and Convict Labor in the New South* (Chapel Hill: University of North Carolina Press, 2015).

9. Kriston McIntosh, Emily Moss, Ryan Nunn, and Jay Shambaugh, "Examining the Black-White Wealth Gap," February 27, 2020, Brookings, www.brookings.edu/blog/up-front/2020/02/27/examining-the-black-white-wealth-gap/; "Fact Sheet: Trends in U.S. Corrections," The Sentencing Project, www.sentencingproject.org/wp-content/uploads/2016/01/Trends-in-US-Corrections.pdf; "The Population of Poverty USA," Poverty USA, www.povertyusa.org/facts.

10. Fairvue Plantation Homeowners' Association (website), http://fairvueplantationhoa.org/; Spring Haven Mansion (website), https://springhavenevents.com/; Beersheba Springs Assembly (website), www.beershebaassembly.com/; Wardin, *Belmont Mansion*, 33–34.

11. "History of Angola," Angola Museum at the Louisiana State Penitentiary, www.angolamuseum.org/history.

12. Patricia Sullivan, "Alexandria Plans to Buy Freedom House, Former Slave Pen Now Home to a Museum," *Washington Post*, January 6, 2020, www .washingtonpost.com/local/virginia-politics/alexandria-plans-to-buy-freedom -house-former-slave-pen-now-home-to-a-museum/2020/01/06/304a8aac-2c13 -11ea-bcb3-ac6482c4a92f_story.html; Robert Gudmestad, *A Troublesome Commerce: The Transformation of the Interstate Slave Trade* (Baton Rouge: Louisiana State University Press, 2003), 206–207.

13. The work of Ser Seshsh Ab Heter–C. M. Boxley, documented at his website, ForksYaRoads, https://forksyaroads.com/, has been especially significant to preservation efforts at the Forks of the Road, which has recently come under the auspices of the National Park Service.

INDEX

Abdy, Edward, 204, 221, 264
abolitionists. *See* antislavery activists
Acklen, Adelicia. *See* Franklin, Adelicia
Acklen, Corinna, 359
Acklen, Joseph A. S., 322, 324, 328, 344
    in West Feliciana Parish
      (Louisiana), 359–360
Acklen, Laura, 359
Adams, George, 128
Ajax (brig), 188
Alabama, 175, 322
    Creeks in, 53–54
    enslaved people in, 58, 104–105
Alexander Brown and Company, 151
Alexandria (Virginia), 5, 97–98, 119,
      143, 147, 172, 203, 215, 218, 229,
      236, 237, 247, 274, 300, 306
    antislavery activists in, 48–49, 131,
      135, 204
    Armfield, John, in, 83, 98–101, 106,
      107, 110, 115, 129, 136–137,
      138–141, 145, 149, 156, 157, 159,
      162, 166, 175, 179, 188, 190, 202,
      204, 206, 211, 221–222, 228, 237,
      246, 248, 249–252, 256, 260, 276,
      284, 293, 301, 326
    Ballard, Rice, in, 84, 85, 113
    banks in, 98, 108, 243
    in Civil War, 349
    Franklin, Isaac, in, 12, 14, 61, 62,
      107, 170, 284
    Franklin, Smith, in, 70, 83, 86
    Franklin and Armfield in, 98–101,
      101 (photo), 107–108, 110,
      111–112, 136–137, 156, 186, 188,
      190, 204, 205 (photo), 209, 210,
      211 (photo), 215, 243, 316, 348
      (photo), 359 (photo)
    growth of, 108
    Mechanics' Bank of, 98, 243
    as part of the District of Columbia,
      108, 131, 137
    retrocession of, 348
    slavery and the slave trade in, 45, 83,
      86, 95, 108–111, 165, 186, 273,
      315, 364

Alexandria (Virginia) (*continued*)
  taverns in, 45, 70, 83, 109–110
  tobacco in, 108
  See also Duke Street (Alexandria)
Alford, John, 109
Allen, Dorcas, 274
Alsop, Benjamin, 43
Alsop, Dorothea, 44
Alsop, Joseph, 44, 85, 112, 269
Alsop, Lucy, 43
Alsop, Samuel, Jr., 42–44, 84, 85, 112,
    113, 127, 164, 173, 184, 187, 191,
    228–229, 285, 331
  Henderson, Madison, and, 257,
    260
  See also Ballard and Alsop
Alsop, Samuel, Sr., 42
Ambler, Mary Ann, 150–151
American Anti-Slavery Society, 203,
    204, 205 (photo)
American Union for the Relief and
    Improvement of the Colored
    Race, 203
Anderson, William, 132
Andrews, Ethan Allen, 203
Angola (Louisiana), 303, 304, 328,
    360, 364
antislavery activists (abolitionists), 5,
    31, 89, 93 (photo), 94, 105, 276,
    314, 348
  in Alexandria, 131–132, 135
  Coffin, Levi, as, 32
  Franklin and Armfield and,
    131–132, 176, 203–209
  Kephart, George, and, 273–274
  Lundy, Benjamin, as, 94–95
  Sturge, Joseph, as, 103
  Weld, Theodore Dwight, as,
    266–267
Ariel (brig), 201
Armfield, Elizabeth "Betsy" (Swaim),
    29, 33, 71

Armfield, Isaac, 28
Armfield, Jane Field, 29
Armfield, John, 25–26, 50, 59–60,
    79, 88, 127, 170, 185, 195, 200,
    207–208, 215, 292, 331,
    355 (photo), 357, 362
  advertisements placed by, 83, 98,
    110, 111, 120, 129, 134, 136, 163,
    188, 202, 210, 211 (photo), 213,
    221–222, 237–238, 247, 249
  and antislavery activists, 204, 206,
    208–209
  argument with Ballard, Rice,
    296–298, 319, 326
  in Alexandria, 83, 84, 98–101, 106,
    107, 110, 111, 115, 129, 136–137,
    138–141, 145, 149, 156, 157, 159,
    162, 166, 175, 179, 188, 190, 202,
    204, 206, 211, 221–222, 228, 237,
    246, 248, 249–252, 256, 260, 276,
    284, 293, 301, 326
  Armfield, Nathan, and, 76–78, 79,
    270
  Ballard, Rice, and Franklin, Isaac,
    and, 1, 3, 4–8, 85, 96–96, 102,
    105, 147–148, 153, 155–157,
    166–167, 171–172, 184, 192,
    198–199, 209, 212, 229, 238,
    246–247, 253–256, 263–264,
    267–268, 293–294, 349, 364
  bastardy case of, 74–75
  Beersheba Springs of, 339–345, 341
    (photo), 350, 351–354
  in Civil War, 350–354
  death of, 354–356
  debt collection by, 293, 320, 326
  enters the slave trade business,
    76–78, 82–83
  as executor for estate of Franklin,
    Isaac, 318–322, 325–326
  financial fortune of, 339, 351, 353,
    356

Franklin, Adelicia, and, 318–320,
    323–324, 325, 344
Franklin, Isaac, and, 75–76, 98,
    106–108, 110, 118, 122, 142, 180,
    298, 301, 306–308
Franklin, Smith, and, 83–84, 242
illnesses of, 234, 236–237, 242, 351,
    354
in Guilford County (North
    Carolina), 29–34, 71, 76
Legg, Eli, and, 110
marriage of, 241–243, 300–301, 351
Meek, Jr., Joseph, and, 85–86, 107
moves from Alexandria to
    Tennessee, 300, 301
in Natchez, 85–87, 349–350
in New Orleans, 82, 86, 107, 321,
    339–340
political affiliation of, 233, 235,
    342–343, 350–351
portrait of, 242 (photo)
public reputation of, 275–276, 277,
    301, 342, 350, 354–356
Quakerism and, 33
scheme to avoid slave import laws,
    174–176, 178, 179, 183
sexual assault/exploitation of
    enslaved women and, 176, 278
as shipper of enslaved people, 1, 115,
    118, 119, 129, 136, 138–140, 141,
    147, 149, 156, 159, 160, 166, 172,
    188, 197, 201, 211, 215, 221, 222,
    247, 249–252, 253, 256, 260–261,
    281
with slave coffle, 229–236, 230
    (photo), 278, 340
supports nieces and nephews, 270,
    300, 321, 339
Surry County (North Carolina),
    store of, 71–74
and University of the South,
    343–344

Walker (enslaved) and, 76–78, 79,
    82–83, 233–235
will of, 351, 354
works as cotton broker, 321, 339
youth of, 29, 31, 32–34
See also Franklin and Armfield
Armfield, John (great-grandfather), 26
Armfield, Martha (Franklin), 241–243,
    248, 276, 284, 293, 300–301,
    321, 340, 351, 352–353, 354, 355
    (photo), 356, 358, 360
Armfield, Mary "Polly" (Dickey,
    Hanner), 29, 33, 71, 75, 243, 270,
    321, 354
Armfield, Nathan, 29–30, 33, 76–78,
    79
death of, 270
Armfield, Solomon, 77
Armfield, William, 27–29
Armfield, William A., 77
Armfield Franklin and Company, 246
auctions. See slave auctions

Bache McEvers, 168
Bachelor's Bend (Mississippi), 285
Bahamas, 159
Balize (Louisiana), 118, 119, 133, 197,
    215, 249
Ball, Charles, 47–48
Ballard, Ann (daughter), 333, 334, 335
Ballard, Ann Graham Heslop (mother),
    37, 38
Ballard, Benjamin, Jr., 36, 38, 39, 41–43
Ballard, Benjamin, Sr., 38–39
Ballard, Bland, 38
Ballard, Charlotte, 333, 334
Ballard, Ella, 293, 298, 334, 335, 336,
    345
Ballard, Emily (Read), 39, 270
Ballard, James, Jr., 248, 249, 269
Ballard, Louisa (Berthe), 287–288, 293,
    298, 333–336, 345, 347, 358, 360

Ballard, Rice Carter, 2, 3, 86, 95–96,
102, 113–114, 160, 169, 175,
179, 216, 225, 229, 236, 237, 270,
272–273, 278, 284, 339, 344–345,
358, 360
absence from family, 333–336, 345
agents of, 149, 187, 210, 230, 260,
338
arguments with Franklin, Isaac,
192–195, 223–224
argument with Armfield, John,
296–297, 319, 326
in Alexandria, 84–85, 113
Alsop, Samuel, Jr., and, 42–43, 44,
84–85, 112–113, 127, 163, 173,
228–229, 285
Armfield, John, and Franklin, Isaac,
and, 1, 3, 4–8, 16, 60, 85, 105,
153, 155, 157, 171–172, 184,
190–192, 197–199, 209–212,
238, 246–248, 252, 253–256,
263–264, 267–269, 273, 275–276,
289, 290–291, 292–294, 298, 312,
315–317, 349, 362–364
banking connections of, 167–168,
173, 179–180, 199 (photo), 200,
223, 226, 275–276, 331
birth of, 34, 36
Boyd, Samuel, and, 298–299,
326–333, 346–347
children of, 279–280, 293, 333–334,
335
death of, 346–347
debt collection by, 268–270,
289–293, 294–297
enters the slave trade business, 84–85
European trip of, 346
fortune of, 346, 347
Hayden, William, and, 113–114
investments in cotton operations by,
248–249, 269, 299–300, 326–327,
328–330
investment in slave trading
operation of Rutherford, Calvin,
by, 331–332
jail of, 151–152, 166, 171, 187, 206,
211, 228, 229, 248, 257, 259, 260,
299, 365
joins Franklin and Armfield,
147–148, 163–165
in Kentucky, 285, 287, 298, 331,
345, 346
lineage of, 36–40, 43
marriage of, 287–288, 298, 334–336
in Natchez, 85, 87, 112, 128, 228,
247, 248–249, 269, 271, 276–277,
288, 328
physical description of, 346
political affiliation of, 291
purchases and sales of enslaved
people by, 8, 112, 128, 150–151,
173, 187–188, 191, 196, 215, 218,
260, 278–279, 294
R. C. Ballard and Company of, 165,
193, 194, 210, 215–216
relationship with Johnson, Susan,
and White, Arvenia, 279–281,
285–288, 333
relationship with Tait, Bacon, 253,
275, 277, 290, 292, 295–296
reputation of, 275–277, 346
in Richmond, 149, 151–152, 153,
165, 166–167, 170, 173, 187–188,
190, 206, 211, 228–229, 238, 248,
275, 299, 316, 365
sexual assault/exploitation of
enslaved women and, 149–155,
278–281, 332–333
slavery on landholdings of, 327,
328–330
in Spotsylvania County (Virginia),
83–84, 113–114, 127, 228, 285
Turner, Henry, and, 294–297
youth of, 34, 41–42, 43

See also Ballard and Alsop; Ballard
  Franklin and Company; Franklin
  and Armfield; Franklin Ballard
  and Company
Ballard and Alsop, 112–114, 127
  banks and, 166–167
  Franklin and Armfield agreement
    with, 163–165
Ballard Franklin and Company, 246,
  249, 253, 272, 281, 293, 294–295,
  320, 326, 330, 339
Baltimore, 12, 14, 48, 83, 107, 165, 247,
  258, 260, 280, 315
  Franklin, Isaac, in, 61
  Franklin and Armfield in, 172,
    185–187
  Purvis, James Franklin, in, 172,
    185–187, 192, 210, 227–228, 337
  slave trade in, 11, 45, 85, 88–96, 108,
    172, 185–186, 274
  taverns in, 45, 88, 89, 90–91
  Woolfolk, Austin, in, 88–96, 107
Bank of Louisiana, 151, 200, 356
Bank of the Mississippi, 66, 189
Bank of the United States, 10
Bank of Virginia, 167, 200, 270
banks, 46, 57, 105, 168, 191, 209, 214,
  225–226, 254–256, 331, 349, 353
  in Alexandria, 98, 108, 243
  Ballard and Alsop and, 167
  Franklin and Armfield and, 167–169,
    179–180, 191–193, 199–200, 224,
    270
  in Mississippi, 66, 189, 292, 302
  in Natchez, 66, 179, 256, 275–276
  in New Orleans, 116, 126, 151,
    199–200, 224, 351, 356
  in Virginia, 223, 226
  See also specific banks
Baring Brothers, 199
Barnes, Elizabeth, 19
Barney, John, 45

Baron, Noel Auguste, 126
Bass, John M., 342
Bean's Station (Tennessee), 234, 236
Bebee, Charles, 125
Beersheba Springs (Tennessee),
  339–345, 341 (photo), 350,
  351–354, 355–356, 363
Bell, Henry, 115, 118, 119
Bell, Maria, 281
Bell, Philip A., 204
Bell Tavern (Alexandria), 109
Bell Tavern (Richmond), 166
Bellevue (plantation), 245, 271, 305,
  306, 308
Belmont mansion, 359, 363
Benevolent Society for Ameliorating
  and Improving the Condition of
  the People of Color (Alexandria),
  131
Berthe, Louisa Cabois. *See* Ballard,
  Louisa
Biddle, Nicholas, 214, 226
bills of exchange, 6, 10–13, 167–168,
  173, 191–192, 255
Birch, James, 274
Birch, William H., 348
Bissell, Benjamin, 140
Blackmon, Douglas, 362
Bladrer, Stephen, 125
Blakey, James, 187, 257, 260, 269,
  338, 339
Blanchard, Samuel G., 260, 261, 262
Blanton, William W., 287
Blantonia (plantation), 287
Blount, William, 22
Blunt, Cecelia, 320
Booker, Richard, 200, 202, 209, 238,
  244
Boswell, William, 125, 180
Boudar, Thomas, 253, 274, 275, 320
Bouny, Pierre Godefroy, 124
Boush, Nathaniel, 237, 247

Boush, Samuel, 247

Bowmar, Joseph H. D., 360

Bowser, William, 94

Boyd, Errol, 360–361

Boyd, Samuel Stillman, 298–299,
    326–333, 345–347, 360

Boyd, Virginia, 332–333

Bracken, Henrietta, 339–340, 354

Bracken, Nathan, 339–340, 354

Bracken, Sallie, 354

Brent, Rachel, 176

Brice, Nicholas, 95

brigs, 161 (photo)
    Ajax, 188
    Ariel, 201
    Comet, 129, 159, 160, 161
    Mark, 82–83
    Temperance, 92
    United States, 115, 116, 118–122,
        124, 138, 140, 141, 144
    See also Isaac Franklin; Tribune; Uncas

Brockman, Asa, 257, 260, 262

Brooks, Noris, 360–361

Brooks, Thomas, 128

Brown, Caroline, 153

Brown, Charles, 262 (photo)

Brown, John, 152

Brown, William Wells, 78–79, 82

Brown and Ives, 10

Bruin, Joseph, 274

Bruster, Frances, 286

Buck, Anthony, 41

Buckner and Hunt, 128

Burford, David, 143, 144–145, 146,
    184, 197, 215, 227

Bush, Walter, 138

Busk, John, 186

Butler, Cynthiann, 67

Butler, Samuel W., 67–68

Cage, Jesse, 284–285

Cagle, Benjamin, 351, 353, 354

Cannon, Newton, 53–54

Canonage, John Francis, 219, 220

Carroll, Phillis, 151

Carter, Frances, 37

Carter, John, 37, 38

Carter, Robert "King," 37

Carter, Thomas, 37

Chabert, Leon, 87, 220

Chapman, C. T., 119

Charleston, 35, 91–92, 251

Chauveau, Louis, 135

Chauveau, Louisa, 135

Cheatham, Adelicia. *See* Franklin,
    Adelicia

Cherokee, 17

Chesapeake, 4, 25, 34, 36, 40, 59, 62,
    80, 83, 86, 98, 102–103, 112, 142,
    148, 156, 209, 217, 240, 246, 320
    Franklin, Isaac, in, 44, 70, 260
    Franklin and Armfield in, 137, 167,
        172, 176, 179, 185, 190, 199–200,
        213, 221, 226, 237, 253, 270, 315
    Woolfolk, Austin, in, 88–96, 185
    See also Alexandria, Baltimore,
        Richmond

Chickasaw, 10, 104

Choctaw, 10, 104

cholera, 1–3, 192, 196–199, 201–202,
    213–214, 217, 223, 227, 239,
    329, 365

Cincinnati, 207, 285–286, 287, 298,
    304

Civil War, 358, 359–360
    Alexandria in, 348 (photo), 349
    Armfield, John, in, 350–354
    Fairvue in, 357–358
    freedpeople after, 360–361
    Natchez in, 349–350

Clack, James, 307, 320

Clay, Henry, 260, 263, 291, 292

Coffee, John, 54, 55, 56

coffee houses, 122

Coffin, Levi, 31–34
coffles, 12, 31–32, 44, 49 (photo),
    50–51, 78, 86, 100, 142–143, 171,
    192, 196–197, 204, 205 (photo),
    229–237, 230 (photo), 253, 266,
    278, 300, 314
Colomb, Christopher, 126
Comet (brig), 129, 159, 160, 161
Commercial Bank of Manchester
    (Mississippi), 302, 331
convict leasing, 361–362
Cook, John, 348
Cooper, James Fenimore, 211
Cooper, Washington, 283 (photo), 284,
    302 (photo), 305–306
Coote, Thomas, 141
Cosby, Elizabeth, 150–151
Cosby, Samuel, 228
cotton, 3, 4–5, 10, 21, 25, 30, 46, 60, 83,
    168, 226, 240, 244, 251, 264, 268,
    269, 288, 292, 294, 298, 303, 339,
    360, 362
  from holdings of Ballard, Rice, and
    Boyd, Samuel, 299, 326, 328,
    329–330, 345, 358
  from holdings of Franklin, Isaac,
    244, 271, 272, 304, 320
  merchant houses and, 5
  in Natchez, 64, 65
  in New Orleans, 117, 122, 339
  price declines for, 169, 212, 216–217,
    220, 255–256, 265
  price increases for, 59, 92, 157, 179,
    226, 254
  price stabilization of, 313–314
  production increases of, 57, 254
  relationship of slavery and the slave
    trade to, 4, 46, 57–59, 64, 86,
    104–105, 130, 152, 157, 169, 190,
    220, 245, 250, 254–255, 265, 285,
    313, 314
Cotton, William, 284–285

Courcelle, Myrtille, 125
Cox, Walter, 346
Creeks, 53–56
Crutchfield, Edward, 331
Cuba, 330–331
Cumberland, 11, 17–19, 340
  Fairvue and, 181, 182
  Native Americans in, 18
  slavery and enslaved people in, 21–24
Curtis, Rice, III, 37

Dahlgren, Charles, 342
Davenport, Isaac, 228
David, Victor, 151
Davidson County (Tennessee), 18, 19,
    21, 23
Davis, George, 141, 320
Davis, Samuel, 320
Dawson, Henry, 129
de Logny, Edouard Robin, 151
DeArmas, Felix, 124, 125, 130
DeArmas, Octave, 130
"defective" slaves, 66–67, 124, 176–177,
    295
Denny, James, 184
Dew, Thomas, 103–104
Dick, James, 244
Dick, Nathaniel, 244
Dickey, Jane, 243
Dickey, Polly. *See* Armfield, Mary "Polly"
Dickey, William, 71, 73, 75, 77, 243
Dicks, Booker, and Company, 244
Diggs, James, 119
discounts on bills and currency, 13,
    167, 168, 179, 187, 188, 191, 194,
    214, 224, 268, 275, 292
District of Columbia, 108, 111, 137,
    142, 167, 172, 173, 204, 205
    (photo), 210, 221, 258, 309
  slave trade in, 131, 135, 348
  See also Alexandria (Virginia),
    Georgetown, Washington City

Dixon, W. H., 329

domestic slave trade

in Alexandria (Virginia), 108–111, 203–209

ban on, in the District of Columbia, 348

cities as nodes of, 14, 45, 61

coastal shipping for, 91–92, 138, 139 (photo), 161 (photo), 162

competition in, 3, 69, 89, 107, 144, 162, 172, 176, 177, 188, 190, 200–201, 216, 220, 226

cruelty and suffering endemic to, 2, 5, 15, 50, 59, 65, 78–79, 92, 120, 121–122, 123, 136, 152–155

enslaved resistance to, 23–24, 81, 105, 108–109, 112, 140–141

evolution of, 7, 23, 40, 46, 58–59, 89–92, 102–105, 106–107, 140, 141–142, 157–158, 165–166, 186, 209, 254–256, 265, 312–317

global implications of, 168

federal protection of, 4, 14, 25, 119

in frontier Tennessee, 22

impact of economic panics on, 91–92, 212, 255–256, 263–265, 275

impact of, on enslaved people, 7–8, 22, 47–48, 78–79, 91, 113–114, 120–121, 150–155, 196, 205–208, 250–251, 253–254, 332–333, 350

in Natchez, 64–66, 132–133, 183–184, 213–214, 239–241, 316, 349–350

meaning of, for traders, 87, 155, 177, 236, 267, 303, 317

memory of, 364–365

in New Orleans, 118, 122–123, 133, 156, 178, 216, 220–221, 238, 316

newspapers and, 61, 89–90

professionalization of, 59, 60–61, 62–63, 67, 68, 89, 102, 141–142

profits from, 126, 157

public officials facilitating, 95, 101–102, 105, 131–132, 135–136, 291–292

Quakers and, 31

in Richmond, 165–166, 315, 316, 339

scope of, 3–4

Supreme Court and, 290–292

railroads in, 314–315

seasonality of, 92, 143, 170–171, 212–213

significance for capitalism and American development, 6–7, 58, 105, 126, 157, 168, 255–256, 263, 314–315, 349, 362–363

in Spotsylvania County (Virginia), 36, 40–41, 44, 113

state laws regarding, 49–50, 95, 118, 124, 132, 133–134, 136, 156, 160–161, 173–174, 175, 195, 288–289, 349

taverns as centers of, 43–44, 45, 83, 106, 165

telegraph in, 315

white opposition to, 48–49, 93, 105, 131–132, 184, 195, 204, 205 (photo), 231–234, 261, 349, 358

See also specific individuals, companies, locations, and topics

Dorsey, Judy, 250

double-entry bookkeeping, 187–188

Douglass, Frederick, 90, 91

Drinker, George, 204

Dufilho, Joseph, 125

Duke Street (Alexandria), 97–98, 107, 110, 219, 348 (photo), 349, 364

as site of Franklin and Armfield headquarters, 98–101, 105, 111, 115, 141, 146, 170, 203–209, 205 (photo) 210, 221, 228, 243, 249, 250, 276, 300, 314, 316, 358

Kephart, George, and, 252, 253, 273, 274–275, 306, 337, 348
Dunbar, William, 64
Dunmore's War, 17
Duralde, Martin, 124

Eagle Tavern (Alexandria), 109
Eastern Shore (Maryland), 16, 90, 91, 107, 186, 210
Eaton, Benjamin, 239, 269
Edgar, John T., 282
Elcho (plantation), 327, 329, 358
Elliott (slave trader), 24
Ellis, William, 335, 336
"empire of liberty," 20
enslaved people
    chances of being taken into the slave trade for, 7
    deaths of, from disease, 1–3, 196–197, 201–202, 213, 214, 223–224, 329
    exchanged for horses, 84
    experiences in the slave trade of, 15, 31–32, 47–48, 50, 78–82, 91, 92, 99–100, 112, 115, 119–122, 134, 136, 149–150, 151–154, 163, 166, 204–208, 229–231, 234–235, 240, 257–261, 278–280, 332–333
    family separations of, 5, 15, 22, 47–48, 78–79, 80, 91, 113–114, 121, 136, 205, 207–209, 250, 274, 300, 333
    imagined as goods, 188–189
    labor of, 20, 21, 30, 46, 57–58, 98, 126, 130, 134, 168, 171, 181, 223, 248–249, 271, 275, 281, 294, 298, 304, 314, 321, 327–328, 329–330, 334, 340, 341, 356
    liberated, 82, 113–114, 159, 176, 206–207, 280, 349, 353, 354, 358

as lottery prizes, 22
    population growth of, 3–4, 20, 23, 30, 40, 58, 64, 104–105, 195, 312–313
    resistance of, 23–24, 48, 62, 78–79, 81, 94, 108–109, 140–141, 147, 171, 206–207, 235, 261, 274, 304, 329, 352–353
    skills of, 123, 144, 150, 187, 278
    used as financial assets, 6, 21–22, 57, 59, 73, 87, 103–104, 105, 126, 157, 168, 178–179, 221, 226, 255, 268, 272, 295, 310, 314, 362–363
    See also specific individuals and topics
Evans, Estwick, 65
Excursion Through the Slave States (Featherstonhaugh), 230 (photo)

Fairvue (plantation), 181–183, 182 (photo), 184, 213, 229, 248, 270, 277, 279, 282, 284, 301–302, 304, 305, 306, 308, 321, 325, 327, 357, 358
    coffles at, 196, 236
    cotton from, 244
    as golf community, 363
    mausoleum at, 310, 320
    prospective academy at, 311, 319, 325
    slave auction at, 340
family separations, of enslaved people, 5, 15, 22, 41, 47–48, 79, 80, 113, 136, 205, 207–209, 360
family units, of enslaved people, 22, 41, 250, 251
"fancies," 150–155, 277
Farley, George, 109
Farmers' Bank of Virginia, 167
Farragut, David, 349
Faubourg Marigny, 116, 117 (photo), 130, 135, 144, 219 (photo), 316
Fearon, Henry Bradshaw, 65

Featherstonhaugh, George, 229–236, 230 (photo), 239, 278

Field, Jane. *See* Armfield, Jane Field

Field, Jeremiah, 29

Field, Mary, 29

flatboats, 4, 9–10, 12–13, 12 (photo), 65, 80, 81, 115, 116, 244, 310

Fleming, William, 188

Fletcher, Calvin, 286–287

Flint, Timothy, 14

foreclosures, 73, 265, 268, 272

Forks of the Road (Natchez), 3, 213, 217, 239–241, 247, 253, 294, 306, 307 (photo), 316, 349–350, 365

Forstall, Edmond Jean, 199–200

Fort Mims (Alabama), 53

Foster, Easter, 277

Foucher, Antoine, Jr., 177

Fowler, William, 45

Franklin, Adelicia (daughter), 302, 317, 319

Franklin, Adelicia (Hayes, Acklen, Cheatham), 282–285, 293, 301, 302, 305, 306, 308, 310, 317–319, 318 (photo), 322–325, 328, 344, 357, 359–360, 361, 363

Franklin, Adelle, 321

Franklin, Ann, 19

Franklin, Edward Noel, 321, 354

Franklin, Elizabeth, 19, 242

Franklin, Emma, 306, 317–318, 319, 359

Franklin, Henry, 243

Franklin, Isaac
   in Alexandria, 61, 62, 107–108, 109
   Armfield, John, and Ballard, Rice, 1, 3, 4–8, 16, 60, 85, 105, 147–148, 153, 155, 157, 171–172, 184, 190–192, 197–199, 209–212, 238, 246–248, 252, 253–256,
      263–264, 267–269, 273, 275–276, 289, 290–291, 292–294, 298, 312, 315–317, 349, 362–364
   Armfield, John, and, 5, 75–76, 83, 98, 106–108, 110, 115, 142, 236, 298, 306–308, 318–319
   Ballard, Rice, and, 192–195, 223–224, 247, 280, 296–297
   banking connections of, 3, 70, 156–157, 179, 191, 199–200, 209–210, 224
   birth of, 19
   children of, 279, 284–285, 293, 306, 317–318, 319, 359
   company responsibilities of, 106, 164–165
   death of, 307–308
   exchanges or returns of enslaved people negotiated by, 176–177
   financial problems of, 178–180, 190–192, 193–194, 216–217, 221, 224–225, 256, 288
   fortune of, 240–241, 309–310, 311–312
   Henderson, Madison, on, 257–263
   investments of, 302–303, 331
   Isaac and James R. Franklin and Company and, 215–216
   marriage of, 282–285
   moodiness of, 160–161, 174, 197, 213–214, 217–218, 256, 271, 288
   in Natchez, 1–3, 25, 47, 61, 63, 64–71, 85, 86, 106, 136, 189–190, 196–197, 213–214, 218, 229, 239–241
   in New Orleans, 13, 115–116, 118–127, 129–130, 133, 135, 137, 144–146, 164, 167–169, 172, 174–180, 188, 197, 199–200, 217–225, 219 (photo), 222–223,

222 (photo), 237–238, 244, 254,
    259–260, 288, 305, 306, 316
obituaries of, 14, 309–311
Panic of 1837 and, 270–273
physical health of, 180, 218, 271, 307
political affiliation of, 69, 191, 214,
    306
portrait of, 283–284, 283 (photo),
    302 (photo), 305–306
recruitment of agents by, 144–147
reputation of, 240–241, 262–263,
    277, 310–312
retirement of, 180–181, 184, 212,
    215–216, 226–227, 243–244, 246,
    248
Routh, Francis, and, 244–246, 248,
    271–272, 303, 304
sales of enslaved people by, 7, 47,
    68, 124–126, 130, 133, 137, 151,
    168–169, 174, 178, 217, 222–223,
    238, 254, 299
schemes to avoid legal restrictions
    crafted by, 174–176, 177–178, 183
sexual assault/exploitation of
    enslaved women and, 151–155,
    156–157, 183, 278–279, 280,
    284–285
in Sumner County (Tennessee),
    19–21, 60–61, 127, 170, 180–183,
    183 (photo), 229, 277, 301–302
talents in managing capital flows,
    155–156, 167–168, 173
vacations of, 227, 340
in War of 1812, 53–56
in Washington City, 61–62
will of, 310–312, 319, 320
will of, contestation of, 323–325
Woolfolk, Austin, and, 95–96
works with relatives in the slave trade,
    11–14, 15, 24, 44–46, 62, 67–70,
    107–108, 111–112, 129, 142

youth of, 19–21
See also Fairvue (plantation);
    Franklin and Armfield; West
    Feliciana Parish (Louisiana)
Franklin, James, Jr., 9–13, 17, 25,
    46–47, 60, 62, 107, 310, 312
Franklin, James, Sr., 16–19, 21, 67,
    127
Franklin, James Rawlings, 111, 144,
    146, 170–171, 175, 183, 192, 196,
    198, 221, 222, 225, 257
death of, 227–229, 237, 238, 241,
    242, 277
Isaac and James R. Franklin and
    Company and, 215–216
in Natchez, 184, 188–189, 196–197,
    201–202, 213, 215, 217, 223
in New Orleans, 158–159, 174,
    177–179, 180, 227, 254
promotion of, 129, 142
sexual assault/exploitation of
    enslaved women and, 150,
    152–153, 154–155, 189
Franklin, Jane, 19, 321
Franklin, John, 11, 12, 17, 25, 44–45,
    60, 111, 241, 242
Franklin, John Armfield, 321, 351,
    353
Franklin, John W., 300, 321, 356
Franklin, Julius Caesar, 306
Franklin, Margaret. See Purvis,
    Margaret
Franklin, Martha. See Armfield,
    Martha
Franklin, Mary Lauderdale, 17, 19
Franklin, Sarah, 19
Franklin, Smith, 69–70, 83, 86, 107,
    111, 242, 270, 300
Franklin, Victoria, 293, 302, 317, 319
Franklin, William, 19, 67–69, 310, 312,
    319, 323, 357–358

Franklin and Armfield
  advertisements for, 98, 110, 111,
    129, 132, 134, 136, 188, 210,
    237–238, 249
  agents and personnel of, 111, 129,
    139–140, 141–148, 158, 173, 175,
    187, 210, 211 (photo), 215–216,
    243, 273–275, 337, 338–339
  in Alexandria, 98–101, 101 (photo),
    107, 110, 136, 156–157, 186, 188,
    190, 203–209, 210, 211 (photo),
    215, 243, 348 (photo)
  antislavery activists and, 132,
    203–209, 252
  Ballard and Alsop and, 163–165
  Ballard, Rice, becomes partner in,
    163–165
  in Baltimore, 172, 185–186,
    227–228
  cash and credit arrangements of,
    130–131, 155–158, 166–169, 173,
    178–180, 185, 189–195, 199–200,
    212, 216–217, 220–221, 223–225,
    226, 263–264
  coffles sent over land by, 192,
    196–197, 229, 236, 253–254,
    278–279
  competitors outdone by, 111–112,
    178, 185, 186, 188, 200–201, 269
  company culture of cruelty in,
    149–155, 189, 277–278
  company reputation of, 176–177,
    209, 267, 273–276
  debts to, 263–264, 267–270,
    294–295
  dissolution of, 292–293
  expansion of, 136–137, 141–148,
    155–158, 171–172, 185–187, 188,
    210–211, 216, 247
  financial problems of, 189–195,
    214–225

  founding of, 5, 106, 118
  fraudulent business schemes by,
    175–178, 183, 206–207
  geographic reach of, 129, 137,
    145–146, 166, 172–173, 210
  Groves v. Slaughter and, 290–292
  insurance policies taken on the
    enslaved by, 161
  institutional legacies of, 362–365
  legacy of, 315–317
  in Natchez, 156, 183–185, 188–190,
    196–197, 200–202, 213–214, 223,
    226, 239–241, 247, 254, 263–264
  in New Orleans, 125–126, 130,
    137, 142, 144, 156, 158–159, 161,
    167–170, 172, 174–180, 188–189,
    197, 215, 217–225, 219 (photo),
    222–223, 222 (photo), 226,
    237–238, 254
  Panic of 1837 and, 263–264,
    267–277
  partnership agreements, terms of,
    106, 163–165, 184, 198–199, 209,
    246–247
  power of, 5, 110, 316–317, 362
  profits of, 126–127, 137, 156, 157,
    168–169, 178, 215, 224, 226
  purchase of *Isaac Franklin* by,
    247–248
  purchase of *Tribune* by, 161–163
  purchase of *Uncas* by, 211–212
  reconfiguration of after death of
    Franklin, James R., 227–229
  responses to slave trading
    regulations by, 134–135, 137,
    174–176, 183, 195, 200–201, 202
  retirement of Franklin, Isaac, from,
    246–248
  in Richmond, 165–166, 187, 210
  sales of enslaved women as "fancies"
    by, 150–155

shipping innovations of, 138–142, 162–163

"Slave-Factory" of, 203–204, 273, 314

total slave sales by, 253–254

Virginia headquarters of, 98–101, 101 (photo), 203–209, 205 (photo), 243, 252, 253, 348 (photo), 359 (photo)

winding down operations of, 209, 238–239, 243–244, 246–256

withdrawal from New Orleans, 238

See also Armfield, John; Ballard, Rice Carter; Franklin, Isaac; specific topics

Franklin Ballard and Company, 164, 166, 215–216, 246

Franklin Hotel
in Natchez, 65–66, 96, 112
in Richmond, 338

Fredericksburg (Virginia), 34–36, 38, 39–41, 42, 113, 165, 187, 191, 200, 210, 257, 299

free Black people, 116, 286
as purchasers of enslaved people, 125
kidnapping of, 104, 132
on sailing vessels, 139

Freeburger, Henry, 45

Freedom House, 364

Freeman, Theophilus, 237, 239, 269, 337

French, Lucy Virginia, 351–352

Gaddis, Delphia, 188

Gaddy, William, 166

Gaiennié, François, 125

Gallatin (Tennessee), 22, 60, 180, 321, 357, 363

Gallatin and Nashville Turnpike Company, 302

Gant, Susan, 151

Garrett, Josiah, 342

Garrison, William Lloyd, 137

Gathright, Martha, 188

Gee, Lucas, 308

Genius of Universal Emancipation, 93 (photo), 94, 110, 137

Gentry, James, 45

George Kephart and Company, 210, 211 (photo)

Georgetown, 61, 108, 142, 172, 243

"Georgia man," 50

Gholson, James, 103

Gholson, Samuel, 289–290

Gibson, James, 360–361

Gilpin, Henry, 291

Golden, Phillis, 188

Goldin, Richard, 73

Goldin, William, 73

Good Hope (sloop), 92

Goodale, Nathan, 126

Goodwin, William, 229

Grady, Sidnum, 274

Grant, Stephen, 158

Graves, I. S., 84, 85

Great Britain, abolition in, 159–160

Great Wagon Road, 26

Greeley, Horace, 311

Grimes, Agnes, 222

Grimm, Andrew, 187, 210, 211 (photo)
with slave coffle, 229–236, 230 (photo)

Groves v. Slaughter, 290–292, 295

Grundy, Felix, 53

Guilford County (North Carolina), 28–29, 71, 72, 75
slavery and enslaved people in, 30–34, 76–78

Hagan, John, 237

Hagan, Watson, 187

Hall, Moses, 125

Hanner, Albert, 350–351
Hanner, John, 351
Hanner, Polly. *See* Armfield, Mary
    "Polly"
Hanner, William, 75, 82, 83, 270, 321
Hard Times (plantation), 321, 339,
    363
Harding, Giles, 45
Harding, Thomas, 342
Hart, Jacob, 82–83
Haxall, R. B., 228
Hayden, William, 80–82, 113–114,
    128
Hayes, Adelicia. *See* Franklin, Adelicia
Hayes, Corinne, 318 (photo)
Hayes, Laura, 306, 318 (photo)
Hayes, Henry, 318 (photo)
Hayes, Oliver Bliss, 282, 308, 317, 318
    (photo), 320, 321, 325
Hayes, Richard Hightower, 283
Hayes, Sarah Hightower, 282,
    318 (photo)
Heermann, Lewis, 219, 220
Henderson, John, 66
Henderson, Madison, 257–263,
    262 (photo), 279
Henderson, Thomas, 87
Henry, George, 300
Henry, Patrick, 36
Hercules (towboat), 118
Hermann, Samuel, 167–168
Heslop, Ann. *See* Ballard, Ann
    Graham Heslop
Heslop, Ann Carter, 37, 43
Heslop, William, 37, 38, 43
Hewlett, John, 122–123
Hewlett's Exchange (New Orleans),
    122–124, 220–221
Hickman v. Rose, 289–290, 295
Hicks, Thomas, 43
Hill, H. R. W., 244, 262–263

Hobson, Matthew, 109
Hodgkin, John, 45
Holston settlement, 17, 18
Hooper, William, 210, 211 (photo)
Hulet, Charles, 61
Hunt, John, 322
Hunter, Mary Jane, 320
Hutchins, John, 66–67

Indian Queen Tavern (Alexandria), 45,
    70, 109–110
Industrial Revolution, 58
Industry (schooner), 172, 173
Ingraham, Joseph Holt, 239–241, 264,
    267
Isaac and James R. Franklin and
    Company, 215–216
Isaac Franklin (brig), 249, 250,
    251–252, 253, 256, 273, 281
    largest shipment on, 252
    purchased by Franklin and
        Armfield, 247–248
    sinking of, 347
    sold to Kephart, George, 252
Isaac Franklin Institute, 312, 319, 323,
    324, 325, 330
Ish, William, 119

J. & D. Long, 66
J. M. Saunders and Company, 143–
    147, 210, 211 (photo)
Jackson, Abraham, 250
Jackson, Armstead, 125
Jackson, Andrew, 19, 69, 181, 232,
    235, 263
    dispossession of Native Americans
        and, 57, 104
    Second Bank of the United States
        and, 191, 209, 214
    War of 1812 and, 54–56, 66, 128
Jackson, Armstead, 125

Jackson, Lucinda, 278–279, 284–285
Jackson, Suckey, 250
Jackson Association, 69
Jacobs, Samuel, 213
jail(s), 24, 45, 62, 79, 83, 85, 90, 91,
        95, 102, 111, 122, 131–132, 136,
        190, 212, 227, 249, 259, 261,
        337, 348
    in Richmond, 166, 253, 274, 316,
        337
    fugitives from slavery in, 45, 62, 95,
        128
    of Ballard, Rice Carter, 151–152,
        166, 171, 187, 206, 211, 228, 229,
        248, 257, 259, 260, 275, 280, 285,
        286, 299, 365
    of Williams, William H., 252
    of Woolfolk, Austin, 89, 93
James, Samuel L., 361–362
James Ballard and Company, 248, 269
James F. Purvis and Company, 210,
        211 (photo)
James Monroe (schooner), 138, 141
Jay, William, 203–204
Jefferson, Thomas, 20, 36
Johnson, Susan, 279–281, 285–287,
        288, 333
Johnson, Spencer, 278
Johnson, William H., 345
Jones, Thomas M., 210, 211 (photo),
        274, 337–338
Jones, Walter, 291
Jordan, Nelly, 277

Karnac (plantation), 299, 326, 327,
        329, 332, 358, 360–361
Kenner, Minor, 342
Kenner and Henderson, 13
Kephart, George, 172, 175, 210, 320,
        337
    antislavery activists and, 273–274

becomes agent for Franklin and
        Armfield, 147
    Duke Street (Alexandria) and,
        252–253, 273–275, 306, 337, 348
    Isaac Franklin (brig) and, 252–253,
        273
Keyauwee, 26–27
kidnapping, of free Blacks, 48, 49
        (photo), 94, 128, 132, 206–207
Killarney (plantation), 245, 304
King, Amus, 187
Knight, Amos, 188
Knight, Henry, 12

Lafayette (schooner), 129, 138, 140,
        160, 172, 188, 201
Lafayette, Marquis de, 233, 234
Lapice, Peter, 128
Lapine (plantation), 327, 329, 358,
        360
Last of the Mohicans (Cooper, James
        Fenimore), 211
Lauderdale, James, 16
Lauderdale, Mary. *See* Franklin, Mary
        Lauderdale
Le Carpentier, Joseph, 123
Legendre, George, 151
Legg, Elias P., 83, 84, 109–111, 119
Letha (enslaved), 352 353
Lewis, James, 222
The Liberator, 252
Lillard, Silas, 248, 269, 297
Lilly, Eli, 45, 88
Lizardi, Miguel, 168
Lizardi y Hermanos, 168
Loango (plantation), 303
Lobdell, John, 308, 319, 323
Lochlomond (plantation), 245, 304
Logan, Agatha Marshall, 335–336
Logan, Caleb, 335
López, Narciso, 331

Louisiana, 10, 13, 125, 127, 145, 171,
    238, 268, 269, 274, 301, 318,
    324–325, 327, 342, 361, 363
  banks in, 199–200
  cotton in, 104, 168
  notaries in, 123–124, 125, 130, 180
  slave trading regulations in, 118,
    124, 133–134, 136, 137, 141,
    159–161, 173–176, 177–178, 183,
    184, 185, 193, 201, 216, 218, 220
  slavery and the slave trade in, 25,
    46, 58, 80, 91, 104, 112, 123, 124,
    126, 130, 136, 143, 211, 223, 254,
    294, 303, 313, 338
  sugar in, 104, 117, 168, 223
  See also New Orleans; West
    Feliciana Parish
Louisiana Board of Public Works, 223
Louisiana State Insurance Company,
    161
Louisiana Sugar Refinery Company,
    199–200
Louisiana State Bank, 151
Lowe, Solomon, 90
Loyalists, 28, 29
Lundy, Benjamin, 93 (photo), 94–95,
    110, 137
Lynch, Charles, 288–289

Madison, James, 98
Magnolia (plantation), 248–249, 299,
    326, 327, 328, 329, 358
Mairot, Jean Claude, 125
malaria, 10
Marigny, Bernard, 130
Marigny, Gustave, 130
Mark (brig), 82–83
Market House (Natchez), 66
Maryland, 16, 26, 36, 108, 135, 147, 268
  slavery and the slave trade in, 4, 11,
    22, 47–48, 62, 69-70, 95, 102-103,

    110, 120, 137, 157, 172, 185, 186,
      203, 313
  tobacco economy in, 4
  See also Baltimore; Eastern Shore
Mason, Abraham John, 103
Mason, George, VI, 228
Mason-Dixon Line, 4, 94
Maspero, Pierre, 122
Mayo, Joseph, 228
McCandless, George, 142
McCargo, Thomas, 332
McCaulock, Thomas, 78
McCoy, Isaac, 123
McGehee, George, 128
McKim, James Miller, 273–274,
    357–358
McNeil, Joseph, 10
McNeill, Alexander, 248–249, 299
measles, 149, 162, 184–185, 335
Mechanics' Bank of Alexandria, 98, 243
Meek, Joseph, Jr., 85–86, 107, 210
Mercer, Charles Fenton, 103
merchant houses, 5
  in Natchez, 66, 224–225
  in New Orleans, 151, 224–225
  in New York, 173
Merchants' Bank of New York, 199,
    200, 226
Merle, Anna, 125
Merle, John Ami, 125
Millaudon, Laurent, 128
Miner, Charles, 131–132, 135–136
Mississippi, 10, 13, 15, 63, 64, 128,
    143, 175, 196, 245, 254, 268, 285,
    299, 342
  banks in, 66, 105, 189, 292, 302
  cotton in, 104–105
  slave trading regulations in, 132, 135,
    195, 200–201, 288–292, 295, 349
  slavery and the slave trade in, 58, 64,
    80, 104, 254, 255, 313

See also Forks of the Road; Magnolia; Natchez
Mississippi Free Trader, 262–263
Mississippi Marine and Fire Insurance Company of New Orleans, 161
Monroe, James, 35, 61
James Monroe (schooner), 138, 141
Montgomery, Alexander, 298
Montgomery, Eli, 129
Moore, Joseph, 215, 237
Morgan, Oliver, 342
Morris, Richard, 187
mortgages, 98, 226, 245, 255, 272
   to Ballard Franklin and Company, 272
   on slaves, 22, 57, 68, 124, 179, 268, 295
   See also "special mortgages"
Mossy, Toussaint, 123
Mountain View (plantation), 338

N & J Dick and Company, 244
Nashville, 9, 10, 13, 18, 143, 180, 227, 282, 302, 304, 308, 319, 321, 322, 351, 354, 359, 363
   slave trade in, 22
Natchez, 1, 5, 13, 14, 61, 113, 147, 195, 229, 236, 331, 365
   Armfield, John, in, 83, 85–87, 293, 349–350
   Ballard Franklin and Company dissolved in, 292-293
   Ballard, Rice, in, 85, 87, 112, 128, 228, 248, 269, 276–277, 280, 288, 294–297, 328, 330
   banks in, 66, 179, 189, 191, 217, 256, 275, 276
   in Civil War, 349–350
   cholera epidemic in, 1–3, 196–197, 201–202, 213–214
   cotton in, 64
   Forks of the Road at, 3, 213, 217, 239–241, 247, 253, 294, 306, 307 (photo), 316, 349-350, 365
   Franklin, Isaac, in, 1–3, 25, 47, 61, 63, 66–71, 85, 86, 89, 136, 153, 189, 198, 213–214, 218, 220, 239, 240–241, 270, 292
   Franklin, James, Jr., in, 46–47
   Franklin, James R., in, 129, 153, 154, 188–189, 213, 215, 223
   Franklin, William, in, 67–69
   Franklin and Armfield in, 106, 126, 137, 156, 170, 175, 183–184, 189–190, 196–197, 200–202, 213–214, 223, 239–241, 254, 263–264, 268–269
   growth of, 63–64
   merchant houses in, 66, 224–225
   selling Franklin and Armfield compound in, 226
   slave auctions in, 66, 133, 220
   slavery and the slave trade in, 10, 64–66, 78, 96, 132–133, 200, 201, 239–240, 245, 290
   slave trading regulations in, 2, 132–133, 136, 183, 202, 239
   Sweart, Martha, in, 150, 153, 154
   Under-the-Hill district in, 63, 65
   See also Forks of the Road
Natchez (steamboat), 215
Natchez Jockey Club, 276
Native Americans, 17, 22, 53, 310
   in the Cumberland, 18, 19, 20
   expropriation of land from, 57, 105
   expulsion of, 4, 17, 104
   New Garden (North Carolina) and, 26–27
   See also specific tribes
New Garden (North Carolina), 26–27, 31

New Orleans, 5, 9, 10, 14, 47, 96,
    117 (photo), 140–141, 365
  Armfield, John, in, 82, 86, 107, 293,
    306, 308, 321, 339, 353
  banks in, 116, 191, 199–200, 224
  cholera in, 197
  cotton in, 10, 57, 117, 292, 321,
    339, 360
  development of, 115–116
  Faubourg Marigny in, 116,
    117 (photo), 130, 135, 144,
    219 (photo), 316
  Franklin, Isaac, in, 13, 115–116,
    118–119, 120, 121–122, 124–126,
    129–130, 135, 137, 144, 146, 154,
    164, 167–170, 172, 174–180, 188,
    191, 197, 217–221, 222–223, 224,
    237–238, 254, 256, 259–260, 261,
    288, 305, 306, 307
  Franklin, James R., in, 129, 142,
    158, 174, 177, 180, 227, 254
  Franklin and Armfield in, 129–130,
    135, 137, 144, 156, 158–159, 161,
    167–170, 172, 174–180, 215,
    217–221, 219 (photo), 222–223,
    222 (photo), 237–238, 249, 254
  Franklin and Armfield withdraw
    from, 238
  merchant houses in, 13, 116, 128,
    130, 151, 167–168, 224–225, 244,
    256, 331
  slave auctions in, 123, 220
  slave trade in, 10, 78, 91–92, 118,
    122, 123–124, 133, 147, 150–151,
    152, 156, 157, 238, 265, 305, 314,
    316, 331
  slave trading regulations in, 134,
    136, 156, 173, 178, 238, 305
  St. Charles Exchange Hotel in, 305
  sugar in, 117, 126, 220–221, 223
  in War of 1812, 56–57
  See also Balize; Hewlett's Exchange

New York City, 5, 35, 116, 191, 192,
    227, 256, 284, 346
  Comet in, 161–162
  merchant houses in, 168, 173
  Merchants' Bank of, 199, 200, 226
  Tribune in, 163, 190
  Uncas in, 211
  Isaac Franklin in, 251, 347
Newman, Joseph, 77
"Niggerville," 239
Northern Virginia Urban League, 364
Northwest Ordinance, 20
notaries, in Louisiana, 123–124, 125,
    130, 133, 180, 254

O'Ferrall, John, 306, 349–350
Offutt, Warren, 113–114, 269
Omohundro, Silas, 187, 337–338
Otey, James, 342, 344
Outpost (plantation), 327, 329, 358,
    360

Paine, Eleazer, 357
Palfrey, Henry William, 107
Panic of 1819, 72–73, 98, 108
  impact on the slave trade of, 59,
    91–92
Panic of 1837, 256–257, 269–273, 292,
    314, 338
  Franklin and Armfield in, 263–264,
    267–269, 270, 271, 293, 298
  impact on the slave trade of, 265
Panola (plantation), 303
Parker, Davy, 187
Parker, William, 47
Parkinson, John, 272
Parks, Benjamin, 187
Paru (steamboat), 271
Patapsco River, 45, 89, 186
Patin, Louise, 125, 130
Patterson, Charles, 73
Patterson, William, 73–74

Paulding, James Kirke, 15
Peyton, John, 9–13
Peyton, Robert, 13
Phaner, Rachel Ann, 197
Phenix Bank of New York, 191
Phillips, Charles, 342
Phillips, Thomas, 80–82, 113
Pilot Knob (Tennessee), 19, 21
"plantation," as terminology, 327–328, 361
Planters' Bank of Mississippi, 179, 189
Planters' Bank of Natchez, 275, 276
Polecat Creek (North Carolina), 29
Polk, Leonidas, 342–343
A Portrait of Slavery in the United States, 49 (photo)
Potomac River, 12, 34, 45, 51, 62, 97, 108, 111, 115, 184, 187, 203, 207, 235, 365
See also Alexandria (Virginia)
Price, Charles, 348, 349
Prieur, Denis, 134
Profit, Moses, 188
promissory notes, 47, 98, 107, 224, 246
as payments for slaves, 107, 112, 124, 126, 151, 179, 290, 294
Providence, 10–11, 13, 251
Prudhomme, Lestang, 151
purchasing agents, of slave traders, 62–63, 68, 69, 70, 91, 111, 129, 137, 142–148, 149, 156–157, 158, 164, 173, 187, 210, 211 (photo), 215–216, 221, 229, 230, 243, 254, 260, 278, 316
Purdy, James H., 358
Purvis, Allen, 61
Purvis, Isaac Franklin, 274, 337
Purvis, James Franklin, 142, 175, 210, 215, 275, 332
becomes agent for Franklin and Armfield, 111

in Baltimore, 172, 185–187, 192, 227–228, 274
leaves the slave trade, 337, 338
with coffle, 229–231, 230 (photo), 235
Purvis, Margaret (Franklin), 19, 61, 111

Quakers (Society of Friends), 26–27, 28, 33, 72, 94, 300
slavery and, 30–32
Quitman, John, 294, 296, 298
Quitman, Eliza (Turner), 294

R. C. Ballard and Company, 165, 193, 194, 210, 211 (photo), 215–216
railroads, 4, 275, 314–315, 362
Randolph, Thomas Jefferson, 103
Rape. See sexual assault/exploitation, of enslaved women
Rappahannock River, 34–35, 37, 38, 113
Read, Emily. See Ballard, Emily
Read, William Freeman, 270
rebellions. See slave rebellions
redhibition, 124, 176
Regulator movement (North Carolina), 27–28, 72
Renown (schooner), 201
Revolutionary War, 17, 18, 28, 36, 37
Richmond, 5, 40, 42, 62, 82, 190, 192, 238, 258, 338
Ballard, Rice, in, 149, 151–152, 165–167, 170–171, 173, 187–188, 206, 210–211, 228–229, 238, 248, 257, 259, 275, 280, 299, 316, 365
railroads in, 315
slave trade in, 165–166, 228, 253, 274, 299, 331–332, 339
Rieffel, Auguste, 177–178
Riley, Armstead, 125
Robbins, William, 45
Roberts, William J., 200

Robey, Washington, 142

Rocketts Landing (Richmond), 165

Rogers (slave trader), 24

Roman, André, 125–126, 173, 220

Roman, Jacques Etienne, 125

Roman, Zenon, 125

Rost, Pierre Adolphe, 325

Routh, Francis, 245–246, 248, 270,
    271–272, 303, 304, 305

Routh, Job, 245

Routh, John, 245, 269

runaway slaves, 32, 48, 62, 329
    captured and sold by slave traders,
        147, 258–259
    sold at auction, 45, 95

Russom, Isaac, 77

Rutherford, Calvin M., 331–332, 333,
    338

Samuel Moss and Son, 168

Sanderson, John, 270

Sarah Jane (schooner), 159

Saunders, Jourdan Michaux, 142–147,
    158, 169, 170, 173, 175, 178, 179,
    184, 196, 197, 210, 215, 227, 243,
    264, 338
    becomes agent for Franklin and
        Armfield, 144–147

Saura, 26–27

Schultz, Christian, 63

Second Bank of the United States, 57,
    70, 105, 167, 179, 189, 191, 209,
    214, 226

sexual assault/exploitation, of enslaved
    women, 5, 78, 150–155, 176, 278,
    279–280, 281, 332

sharecropping, 360–361

"shavers," 224

Shaw, H., 329

Shawnee, 17

Shenandoah (ship), 141

Shenandoah Valley, 16, 26, 146, 229

Shiner, Michael, 207

Shiner, Phillis, 207

shipping, coastwise, of enslaved people,
    1, 23, 82–83, 139 (photo), 142,
    145, 155, 161 (photo), 204, 205
    (photo), 253–254, 257, 262, 273,
    274–275, 315, 316
    Armfield, John, and, 115, 119, 129,
        136, 138–140, 141, 147, 149–150,
        156, 159, 161–163, 172–173, 176,
        184, 197, 211–212, 215, 221, 222,
        237, 247–248, 249–252, 260–261,
        281, 326
    Ballard, Rice, and, 150, 153, 154,
        173, 184, 187, 188, 198, 201, 215,
        223, 237
    customs and other legal regulations
        regarding, 119–120, 174–175
    Woolfolk, Austin, and, 91–93, 94,
        186
    See also names of individual vessels

Shockoe Bottom (Richmond), 165

Sinners, Elijah, 45, 172

Slatter, Hope Hull, 274

Slaughter, Robert, 290–292

slave auctions, 45, 47, 90, 91, 102, 250,
    268, 272, 338–339
    at Fairvue, 340
    in Louisiana, 134, 173
    in Nashville, 22
    in Natchez, 64, 65–66, 133
    in New Orleans, 122, 123, 220,
        305
    in Richmond, 166
    See also runaway slaves

"slave breeding," 103–104, 266,
    403–404n16

"slave country," 21

Slave Market of America, 204,
    205 (photo)

slave prices, 92, 260, 278, 279, 315
    correlation to cotton prices, 59, 92,
        157, 169, 179, 216–217, 226,
        254–255, 265, 313–314
    for "fancies," 150–151, 278, 279
    impact of economic panics on, 59,
        91, 265
    in Natchez, 189, 190, 198, 215, 216,
        217, 223, 240
    in New Orleans, 92, 151, 157, 158,
        169, 178, 220, 221, 223, 238, 265,
        314
slave rebellions and revolts, 24, 94,
    140–141
    See also Turner, Nat
slave trade. See domestic slave trade;
    transatlantic slave trade
slave traders, 6, 87, 118, 196,
    212–213, 255
    agents of, 91, 141
    in Alexandria, 45, 86, 109
    in Baltimore, 45
    backgrounds of, 50
    competition among, 144
    evolution of business models of,
        46, 59, 92, 102, 138, 142, 162,
        314–315
    fear and resistance by the enslaved
        toward, 112, 120, 350
    financial practices of, 40–41, 126,
        190, 316
    fracturing of enslaved families by,
        120–121, 264, 350
    as "Georgia men," 50
    in Natchez, 2, 67, 68, 86–87,
        132–133, 183, 184, 213, 216, 239,
        241, 264, 316
    in New Orleans, 122–123, 133, 134,
        156, 178, 216, 238, 316
    newspaper advertisements by,
        89–90, 210
    numbers of enslaved people moved
        and sold by, 4, 23, 58–59, 104,
        133, 156, 265, 313
    partnership models of, 106, 163
    as "pirates," 177, 178, 190, 201
    post-retirement lives of, 337–339
    profits of, 59, 157
    relationships of, with Black women,
        281
    relationships of, with public officials,
        95, 132
    reputations of, 131–132, 195, 241,
        263–267
    in Richmond, 165–166, 316
    as "robbers," 164, 177, 200,
    stereotypes of, 6–7
    as "soul-drivers," 78as speculators,
        59, 78, 231, 266
    use of enslaved valets by, 78–82,
        258
    use of jails and prisons by, 83, 166
    use of physical and sexual violence
        by, 15, 47–48, 112, 152, 155, 350
    use of taverns for business by, 43–44,
        45, 83, 89, 106, 109, 165–166
    white attitudes toward, 2, 48–49,
        94, 184, 208–209, 261, 263–267,
        311–312, 349
    See also specific individuals, companies,
        and topics
"Slave-Factory," of Franklin and
    Armfield, 203–204, 273, 314
slavery
    antislavery activists and, 31–32, 94,
        357–358
    cotton production and, 57–58, 64,
        104–105
    expansion of, in nineteenth century,
        3–4, 20, 57–58, 104–105, 313
    federal sanction of, 20, 25, 64
    in frontier Tennessee, 20–21

slavery (*continued*)
　in Guilford County (North
　　Carolina), 30
　in Mississippi Territory, 64
　Native American dispossession and,
　　57–58, 104
　Quakers and, 30–31
　relationship of, to American
　　capitalist development, 4, 5, 6,
　　57–58, 105, 362–363
　significance of slave trading and
　　slave traders to, 4, 6
　in Spotsylvania County (Virginia),
　　36
　sugar production and, 104
　in Surry County (North Carolina), 72
　University of the South, and defense
　　of, 342–343
　white southerners imagining empire
　　of, 313, 330–331
　See also specific individuals and topics
slaves. *See* enslaved people
smallpox, 223–224, 227
Smith, John Witherspoon, 125
Smith, William, 215, 247, 252
Snowden, Thomas, 250
Society for the Relief of Destitute
　　Orphan Boys (New Orleans), 130
Society of Friends. *See* Quakers
Southwest Ordinance, 20
Southwest Territory, 20
Sparraw, Allice, 153
"special mortgages," 126
Spencer, Sarah, 187
Spotsylvania County (Virginia), 34–40
　Ballard, Rice, in, 36–44, 83–84, 113,
　　127
　slavery and enslaved people in, 36,
　　40–41, 43–44, 85
　See also Fredericksburg (Virginia)
Spring Bank, 228, 243, 248

St. John de Crèvecoeur, J. Hector, 27
Stannard, John, 40–41
Staples, Isaac, 129, 159, 161–162, 163,
　　172, 190, 215
Station Camp Creek (Tennessee), 18,
　　19, 60, 127, 170, 181, 182
steamboats, 4, 57, 58, 65, 112, 116,
　　203, 217, 235, 260, 286, 308, 329
　Natchez, 215
　Paru, 271
　Tennessee, 308
　used by slave traders to transport
　　captives, 4, 78, 95, 136, 149, 152,
　　154, 166, 175, 208, 257
steam-powered sugar mill, 4
Steele, David, 46–47
Stirling, James L., 324
Story, Benjamin, 151, 200
Stuart, Charlotte, 222–223
Sturge, Joseph, 103
sugar, 25, 36, 72, 122, 226, 294, 304,
　　362
　in Louisiana, 117, 125, 126, 130,
　　143, 168, 223
　merchant houses and, 5
　in New Orleans, 117
　production increases of, 104, 117
　relationship of slavery and the slave
　　trade to, 4, 46, 92, 104, 120, 130,
　　169, 190, 220–221
Sumner County (Tennessee), 9, 11, 19,
　　20, 22, 61, 68–69, 171, 301, 311,
　　321, 325, 351
　land purchases by Franklin, Isaac, in,
　　60, 127, 170, 180–181, 277
　slavery and enslaved people in, 21, 23
　See also Fairvue (plantation);
　　Gallatin (Tennessee)
Surry County (North Carolina)
　Armfield, John, in, 71–75, 270
　slavery and enslaved people in, 72

Swaim, Elizabeth "Betsy" (Armfield), 29, 33, 71, 78
Swaim, Moses, 71
Swaim, Salathiel, 78
Swann, William, 141
Sweart, Martha, 149–150, 151–152, 153–155, 158, 162, 184, 278, 281

Tait, Bacon, 166, 253, 274, 275, 277, 278, 290, 292, 295–296, 337
Taliaferro, Margaret Chew, 43
Taliaferro, Mary "Polly," 74–75
Taliaferro, Zacarias, 43
Talladega (Alabama), 54–55
Tallushatchee (Alabama), 54
Taney, Roger, 290
taverns, 15, 27, 34, 36, 42, 59, 65, 72, 85, 102, 234, 256, 340
    in Alexandria, 45, 70, 83, 84, 109–110
    in Baltimore, 45, 88, 89, 90
    in Georgetown, 142
    in Richmond, 165, 166
    as sites of the slave trade, 43–44, 45, 61, 62, 70, 83, 84, 87, 88, 90–91, 106, 109–110, 111, 113–114, 122, 129, 141, 142, 166, 339
    in Washington City, 61, 142
Taylor, William B. G., 119
telegraph, 315
Temperance (brig), 92
Templeman, Henry, 229
Tennison, Joshua, 61
"term slaves," 94
Terrell, Archibald, 10, 11, 13
Terrell, Timothy, 10, 11, 13
Texas, 303, 309, 313, 322, 330, 332
"Thieves Harbor" (Angola), 304
Third National Bank of Nashville, 353
Thomas, James, 250
Thomas, Mason, 320

Thomas, Matilda, 250
Thompson, Smith, 291
Tichenor, Gabriel, 66
Tiernan and Alexander, 66
Tilman, Dave, 222
tobacco, 16, 21, 30, 35, 36, 47, 63, 64, 72, 82, 97, 165, 168, 251
    declining Chesapeake economy of, 4, 25, 39, 90, 108, 143
Torrey, Jesse, 49 (photo), 50–51
transatlantic slave trade, 3–4, 10, 23, 30, 37, 46, 92, 131, 140, 163, 303, 347
    ban on, 3, 25, 46, 93
Tribune (brig), 149–150, 152, 166, 172, 174–175, 184, 190, 197, 201, 206–207, 211–212, 215, 218, 220, 221, 222, 237, 247, 248, 249, 251, 253
    as an illegal slaver, 347
    decommissioning of, 347
    purchased by Franklin and Armfield, 161–163
    sold to Williams, William H., 252
Turner, Fielding, 294
Turner, Henry, 294–297, 299, 319, 330
Turner, Nat, 171–172, 173, 183–184

Uncas (brig), 212, 215, 221, 237, 247, 249, 251, 252, 253, 260–261, 262
    as an illegal slaver, 347
    purchased by Franklin and Armfield, 211
    sinking of, 347
    sold to Williams, William H., 252
Underground Railroad, 32
Under-the-Hill (Natchez), 63, 65
Union Bank of Louisiana, 199–200, 199 (photo), 209
Unitarian Universalist Society, 228
United States (brig), 115, 116, 118–122, 124, 138, 140, 141, 144

University of the South (Sewanee),
    343–344, 363

Valentine, Mann, 228
Vascocu, Helene, 223
valets, enslaved, 78–82, 113, 233–234,
    258–260
Virginia, 1, 11, 16–17, 36–37, 40, 75,
    84, 107, 112, 120, 127, 128, 176,
    183, 232, 284, 337
  banks in, 167, 200, 223, 226, 270
  Fauquier County in, 143
  secession of, 349
  slavery and the slave trade in, 4,
    24, 36, 40, 44, 62, 70, 77, 80, 90,
    96, 103–104, 110, 129, 132, 137,
    143, 145–146, 149, 157, 166,
    171, 172–173, 187, 203, 253,
    274, 313
  tobacco economy in, 4, 35
Virginia (continued)
  See also Alexandria; Fredericksburg;
    Richmond; Spotsylvania County
Virginia Statute for Religious
    Freedom, 36
Vitant, Jacques, 223

Walker (enslaved), 76–78, 79, 82–83,
    233–235
Walker, Absalom, 188
Walker, Matthew, 45
Walker, Robert, 291
Walker, William, 78–79
War of 1812, 49–50, 49 (photo), 53,
    56–57, 61, 64, 71, 108, 122, 128
  economic boom after, 59
  Franklin, Isaac, in, 53–56
  military action against Creeks in,
    53–56
  Woolfolk, Austin, in, 88
  Young, Robert, in, 98

Ware, John, 210, 211 (photo)
Washington, Abraham, 360–361
Washington, Augustine, 35
Washington, George, 35, 207
Washington, Jane, 207
Washington, Levenia, 197
Washington City, 40, 90, 108, 137,
    172, 187, 203, 207, 260, 274, 290
  Franklin, Isaac, in, 45, 61, 260
  slavery and the slave trade in,
    50–51, 111, 129, 142, 252, 273,
    274, 300
Waters, John, 342
Watson, Henry, 166, 299
Watts, Amy, 150
Webster, Daniel, 291
Weeks, David, 13–14
Weems, John, 135–136
Weld, Theodore Dwight, 266–267
West Feliciana Parish (Louisiana),
    293, 310, 328, 359–360
  holdings of Franklin, Isaac, in,
    244–246, 248, 270, 272–273, 277,
    303–305, 306–308, 309, 325
  Louisiana State Penitentiary in,
    363–364
West Feliciana Railroad, 275
Wheeler, Mary, 151
White, Arvenia, 279–281, 285–288,
    333
White, Lewis, 180
White, Nathaniel, 187
Wilderness Road, 229
Wilkins, Catherine, 298
Wilkins and Linton, 119
Williams, Joseph, 342
Williams, William H., 252, 337–338
Williamson, Lewis, 187
Willis, L. B., 119
Windsor, Robert, 86, 207, 208, 273,
    337–338

as clerk for Armfield, John, 204–206, 236, 237, 253

Woolfolk, Austin, 88–96, 137, 220, 338
Franklin and Armfield as competitors with, 107, 172, 185, 186

Woolfolk, John, 88, 91, 95, 220, 261, 338

Woolfolk, Joseph B., 90–91

Woolfolk, Richard T., 91

Woolfolk, Samuel M., 91, 220

Wright, Richard, 73–74

Young, James, 113–114, 299

Young, Robert, 97–98, 219

Joshua D. Rothman is professor of history and chair of the department of history at the University of Alabama. He is the author of two prize-winning books, *Flush Times and Fever Dreams* and *Notorious in the Neighborhood*. He lives in Birmingham and Tuscaloosa, Alabama.